CAPITAL ON THE KENTUCKY

THIS PUBLICATION WAS MADE POSSIBLE
THROUGH THE COOPERATION OF THE FARMERS BANK
& CAPITAL TRUST COMPANY OF FRANKFORT,
KENTUCKY.

CAPITAL ON THE KENTUCKY

*A Two Hundred Year History
of Frankfort & Franklin County*

CARL E. KRAMER

WILLIAM B. SCOTT, JR.
Photography Editor

HISTORIC FRANKFORT, INC.

Endpapers: from postcards printed c. 1907 in Germany for the Souvenir Post Card Co. in New York *(Jouett Shettinger)*.

Half title: photograph of Old Capitol *(Kentucky Historical Society)*.

Frontispiece: early aerial photograph of Capitol before construction of the Annex (photograph by Bowman Park Aero, Co., *Kentucky Historical Society)*.

Copyright (c) 1986 by Historic Frankfort, Inc.

Library of Congress Catalog Card Number: 85-80829

Typeset in Galliard by Graphic Composition, Inc.

Printed by Thomson-Shore, Inc.

Design by Jonathan Greene

Contents

Preface vii
Acknowledgments viii
1. *Prelude to Settlement* 3
2. *The Settlement of Frankfort* 19
3. *Statehood & Capital* 34
4. *Building Up, Reaching Out* 71
5. *Transition & Turmoil* 117
6. *The Agony of War* 154
7. *The Violent Years* 173
8. *Expansion & Turbulence* 213
9. *A New Century Dawns* 257
10. *The Capital in the New Era* 295
11. *A Generation of Crisis* 321
12. *The Urban Explosion* 351
13. *A Heritage Rediscovered* 381
Photographic Credits 399
Index 402

[Color Photographs Follow Page 182]

Preface

ALTHOUGH TWO HUNDRED YEARS have now passed since James Wilkinson first settled Frankfort, no comprehensive history had ever been written to chronicle Frankfort's two centuries of progress or its rich and colorful past.

Now, in the year of Frankfort's Bicentennial, we of Historic Frankfort, Inc. are very proud to be publishing such a chronicle. Here for the first time is an illustrated scholarly record of our community's history—its trials and tribulations, its successes and failures. It is a record of events, but also of people. It is an account of who we are, where we came from, and what we've become.

This publication of this book would, of course, not have been possible without the generous support of those many people who contributed information and photographs to be used in the book. Neither would the publication of this book been possible without the generous support of the Farmers Bank and Capital Trust Company of Frankfort.

To our parents and grandparents, thank you for the proud heritage that you have left us. To our children and grandchildren, prosper and grow, but preserve for your children the good that we leave behind.

JOHN GRAY
President,
Historic Frankfort, Inc.

Acknowledgments

FRANKFORT IS ONE of the nation's oldest and smallest state capitals. For two centuries the executive decisions, legislative debates, administrative rule making, partisan bickering, and other political maneuvers which are a normal part of life in any capital have given this Bluegrass city an influence over the lives of all Kentuckians which is totally out of proportion with its size. As interesting and important as they are, however, the affairs of state often obscure the fact that Frankfort and Franklin County have a life and history of their own.

Like other Americans in countless other cities and towns, local residents have carried on the routine activities of commerce and industry, farming and banking, work and worship, and education and culture. They have built stores and churches, constructed steamboats and streets, and organized companies and schools. Spearheading these efforts were prominent citizens who were little known outside the city, but whose devotion to their community's well-being made Frankfort a solid, stable city which was able to defeat periodic efforts to remove the capital to some other city.

The purpose of this book is to tell the story of Frankfort and Franklin County as it has developed beyond the glittering dome and marbled columns of the capitol. The book's approach is developmental. I have attempted to examine as thoroughly as time and space would allow the economic, social, technological, political, geographical, and cultural forces which have shaped the community's growth over the past two hundred years. It is my sincere hope that *Capital on the Kentucky* will become an important and useful addition to the literature of Kentucky history as well as an appropriate and cherished vehicle for commemorating Frankfort's bicentennial.

While my name appears on the title page as the author, I am acutely aware that this book could not have been completed without the assistance of many individuals and organizations. It would be impossible to name all of the present and former Frankfort residents who responded to spontaneous telephone inquiries and offered useful documents which were not available in archival sources. I am grateful nevertheless for their help. I am especially indebted to the staffs of several local and state research facilities and public offices. Among those who provided continuing assistance were Linda C. Anderson and Doris

Manley, Kentucky Historical Society; Edna Milliken, Lynn Lady, and Shannon Wilson, Kentucky Department of Libraries and Archives; Ann Hoover, Frankfort City Clerk; Rosanna O'Nan and Blanche Shy, Franklin County Clerk's office; Pat Badgett, executive director, Frankfort-Franklin County Chamber of Commerce; and Randy Shipp, Frankfort Main Street director. Albert E. Dix, publisher of the *State Journal,* gave me access to the paper's microfilm files, and the city room staff were unfailingly courteous in their assistance, despite frequent deadline pressures. Also helpful were the staffs of the Paul Sawyier Public Library, the Kentucky State University Library, the Louisville Free Public Library, and The Filson Club Library.

This book could not have been completed without the commitment of its sponsor, Historic Frankfort, Inc. President John Gray, who oversaw the project, gave me virtually complete scholarly freedom in preparation of the manuscript. Nash Cox, Dr. Richard Taylor, and Tona Barkley reviewed the text and saved me from embarrassing errors. Larry Moore provided valuable research assistance on the history of Frankfort's streetcar companies. Alice B. Blanton made me welcome at "The Beeches" for days at a time during the book's research phase. Bob Polsgrove, a long-time friend, served as my chief confidant throughout the project, provided valuable research files from the Kentucky Heritage Council, and insisted that I explore lines of inquiry which I might otherwise have overlooked. The book is considerably better as a result.

Several talented individuals played critical roles in putting this volume into its present form. Dr. David Burg meticulously edited the entire manuscript. William Scott scoured not only Frankfort and Franklin County but many of the nation's leading photographic archives and museums to obtain the scores of pictures which illustrate the book. Designer Jonathan Greene overcame horrendous scheduling problems to bring the volume to completion. Thomas Appleton provided invaluable editorial work at the eleventh hour. I would also like to acknowledge the assistance of my mother, Mrs. Jane A. Pitman; my step-father, Mr. Joe A. Pitman; and Mary E. Kagin in the preparation of the index.

Finally, if this book gives undue attention to the contribution of the Kagin family in Frankfort's history, it is neither intentional nor coincidental. For more than three years my life has been enriched by the love and support of Mary Elizabeth Kagin, granddaughter of merchant Carl Kagin and daughter of the late Rev. Edwin F. Kagin, Sr. Her mother, Mrs. Mary Rob Kagin, supplied numerous oral history recollections and family photographs and persuaded other friends to lend rare pictures for use in the book. Mary gave me access to voluminous family correspondence and records, proofread all galleys, and remained a constant source of encouragement. Responsibility for any remaining errors of fact or interpretation is mine alone.

CARL E. KRAMER

The approximately 350 photographs used in this book were selected from over 2000 available from public and private collections. Many of these came from the extensive collection of the Kentucky Historical Society, which has been a very active collector of Frankfort views. It is the repository of the negative collections of several local photographers including: Carl Wolff, Harry Gretter, J. Forrest Cusick and Anna Cusick.

During our search for the book's illustrations, numerous members of Historic Frankfort and other members of the community assisted in the project. Historic Frankfort members of particular help in locating local collections were Alice Blanton, John Gray and Robert Polsgrove. Persons owning those collections for which we all should be indebted include: Mr. and Mrs. V. O. Barnard, Mrs. N. M. Berry, Mr. John Booe, Mr. Wilena Cinnamond, Mrs. Pat Cockerill, Mrs. Carolyn Crittenden, Mrs. Louis Cox, Mrs. George Gilpin, Mrs. Agnes T. Gordon, Mr. E. H. Taylor Hay, Mr. Charles Hinds, Mrs. Dorthy Hudson, Mrs. Alice Hume, Mr. Harold Jeffers, Dr. Amanda Lange, Mr. Noble McDougal, Mrs. Viola Parker, Ms. Pinky Richardson, Mr. Winston Rogers, Mrs. Nash Cox Shayon, Mr. Jouett Sheetinger, Mr. Frank Sower, Dr. and Mrs. John Stewart, Mr. Ed Strohmeier, Mr. William Gerrard Talbot of Paris and Mrs. Bosworth Todd. William Coffey, of Paul Sawyier Galleries, was of great assistance in locating original Sawyiers for consideration.

Ms. Mary E. Winter, Photographic Archivist for the Kentucky Historical Society, was of invaluable assistance in sorting through photos belonging to the Historical Society and went out of her way to make this book a priority for several months. Elizabeth Perkins, Museum Curator; Charles Pittinger, Registrar; and Nathan Prichard, Staff Photographer for the Historical Society also made major contributions to the project.

Copying most of the photos, other than those of the Kentucky Historical Society, was done by Photo Duplication Services at the University of Kentucky under the direction of John Mitchell. Robert Van Outer made photographic duplications of views which were printed by William E. Justus. Jody Maggard and Joyce Moore of that office helped greatly in coordinating the photography. Local photographer, Tom Atkins, worked with our color photographs and other photo problems.

A special thanks to my parents and family for their support during this project. Finally, for her particularly loyal help and assistance on this project, my sincere thanks goes to Holly Schaper.

WILLIAM B. SCOTT, JR.

CAPITAL ON THE KENTUCKY

I

Prelude to Settlement

FROM ITS HEADWATERS near Whitesburg in southeastern Kentucky, the Kentucky River winds its way nearly 420 miles before emptying into the Ohio River at Carrollton. Formed some 65 million years ago, the course of this majestic stream has been challenged again and again by alternating geological cycles of uplift and erosion and by competing streams seeking a more suitable channel. During its journey, the Kentucky tumbles through the steep, timbered hillsides of the Cumberland Mountains; the low, rounded ridges of the Bluegrass plain; the box canyon cliffs at Boonesboro; and the broad valley and low hills near Carrollton.

About sixty river miles above its junction with the Ohio, the Kentucky carves a sweeping double curve through a thick bed of limestone deposited more than 450 million years ago by a tropical sea. At this point, the river is about one hundred yards wide in its natural state. Situated on either side and rising several feet above the river is a broad, alluvial plain. Located near the geographic center of Franklin County, this plain is the original site of Frankfort. The surrounding topography is rich in its variety. Lying to the south and extending finger-like into the north central part of the county are the bottom lands and gently rolling slopes of the Kentucky River and Elkhorn Creek basins. The eastern and northwestern sections of the county are characterized by the moderately steep slopes of the Bluegrass uplands. The steepest terrain consists of the timbered ridges which line the Kentucky north of Frankfort and Benson Creek to the west of the city.

The first human visitors to the region were members of the Paleo-Indian culture, a group of nomadic hunters who appeared about 15,000 years ago. Paleo-Indian bands wandered the Bluegrass region for about 5,000 years, hunting elk, deer, beaver, and bison as well as such now extinct species as the mammoth, mastodon, giant peccary, and giant ground sloth. No doubt some nomads established temporary settlements in the area, but the absence of any evidence of burial grounds suggests that the Paleo-Indians established few, if any, permanent settlements in the Bluegrass.

Beginning about 8,000 B.C., the Paleo-Indians evolved into a new culture, the Archaic. Although still basically nomadic, the Archaic peoples tended to move in a seasonal pattern, exploiting varying food sources at different times of the year. Instead of establishing permanent houses and settlements, they camped in rock shelters and open sites near streams. Remains of their camps, discovered throughout Kentucky, suggest that Archaic bands were rather sizable and that their society was characterized by a fairly complex division of labor.

The Archaic culture was succeeded about 1,000 B.C. by the Woodland, which continued to occupy parts of Kentucky until about 900 A.D. As with the earlier societies, hunting and fishing were major economic activities among the Woodland peoples. But they also introduced major technological advances, using pottery in food preparation and cultivating squash, marsh elder, sunflowers, and an early form of maize. Sketchy remains unearthed in rock shelters and caves in central Kentucky suggest that the Woodland peoples occupied small, round houses constructed of poles criss-crossed to form a framework for a bark covering.

The Woodland culture was followed in Kentucky by the Mississippian, which appeared about 1,000 A.D. and flourished for about 650 years. This society originated in the lower Mississippi River valley and moved northward, spreading out along the Ohio, Tennessee, and Cumberland rivers. Far more advanced than previous cultures, the Mississippian peoples developed highly stable communities, often characterized by plazas, temples, and burial mounds. Their rectangular homes were constructed of wattle and daub and set upon log foundations. They were covered with thatched roofs and protected by wall trenches.

The Mississippians also demonstrated considerable economic and social sophistication. Advanced agriculture in the form of intensive cultivation of maize, beans, and squash replaced hunting as the primary means of subsistence. Artifacts unearthed in Mississippian villages testify not only to a high degree of centralized authority and social stratification, but also to the possibility of specialized crafts production.

A contemporary of the Mississippian society in Kentucky was the Fort Ancient culture. Forerunners of the Shawnee, the Fort Ancients were heavily influenced by the Mississippians. Their economy was primarily agricultural, with hunting and fishing used to supplement the food supply. Trade with other tribes was limited, but the discovery in village remains of European trade goods and artifacts from other cultures suggests some degree of contact among tribes.

Fort Ancient villages were located near streams and usually were smaller than those of the Mississippian culture. Villages sometimes were bounded by palisades, and houses were both round and rectangular. But construction materials and styles otherwise resembled those used by the Mississippians. Similarly, the religious and ceremonial practices of the Fort Ancients, as indicated by their temple mounds and burial sites, bore a striking resemblance to those of the Mississippian society.

By the beginning of the seventeenth century, the descendants of the prehistoric Mississippian and Fort Ancient cultures had completed their transition into such linguistic or tribal groups as the Iroquois, Shawnee, Miami, Potawatomi, and Cherokee. As European exploration and settlement of North America progressed, relations among these tribes were thrown into turmoil. The primary cause of disruption was the introduction of European trade goods, including guns, through tribal middlemen on the Atlantic Coast and in the Appalachian Mountains. By pitting tribes against each other, English, French, and Dutch traders could extend their economic influence without excessive commitments of men or money.

The intertribal warfare that resulted from such economic rivalry severely altered Indian settlement patterns, especially in Kentucky. By the end of the seventeenth century, the combined effects of Iroquois aggression and diseases introduced by Europeans had virtually depopulated Kentucky. The Shawnee nation, once the region's most powerful inhabitants, was now broken into two geographically separate groups, one located in the lower Cumberland River valley and the Illinois country and another centered in the South Carolina frontier. Kentucky soon became known as the "Dark and Bloody Ground," a neutral but deadly hunting territory used freely by the Shawnees, Iroquois, and Cherokees.

Indian hunting parties traveled Kentucky over a series of trails beaten out over hundreds of years by migrating herds of buffalo, elk, and deer. One of the most important of these traces, known to the Indians as *Alanant-o-Wamiowee*, began at Drennon's Lick in Henry County, followed the west side of the Kentucky River into Franklin County, crossed the river near Frankfort, and extended into the Inner Bluegrass country of Scott and Woodford counties.

Throughout the early eighteenth century, the tribes fought among themselves for control of the hunting grounds along the Buffalo Trace. But this situation was about to change. As mid-century approached, the English colonists on the frontier were growing restless. In the back country of Pennsylvania, Virginia, and the Carolinas, settlers began to complain about land shortages, loss of soil fertility, overpopulation, a diminishing game supply, and the increasing boldness of hostile Indians. The situation nurtured a surging expansionist impulse which had perhaps its strongest expression among the settlers on the Virginia frontier.

The primary focus of this expansionist sentiment was Kentucky, that verdant finger of virgin forest and lush meadowland just the other side of the Appalachian Mountains. Stimulating the restless mood of the Virginians was a growing image of Kentucky as a western paradise, an unclaimed Garden of Eden rich with rolling, grassy plains; deep, fertile soil; soaring trees; and a plentiful game supply. As one historian has observed, "The image of Kentucky that emerged into American consciousness in the latter colonial period was, in fact, the myth of America itself: a place of boundless land, perfect opportunity, stirring adventure—in short the perpetual frontier."

But Kentucky's edenic image and land hunger among backwoods settlers were only partly responsible for expansionist pressures. Of equal, if not greater, importance were the speculative ambitions of many of Virginia's leading politicians and planters. Efforts to explore and survey Kentucky began in 1750 when the Loyal Company sent Dr. Thomas Walker, a prominent Albemarle County physician and surveyor, to chart an 80,000 acre claim in eastern Kentucky. In April, Walker led his party through Cave Gap, which he renamed for the Duke of Cumberland. After two months of explorations which ranged as far north as the Levisa Fork of the Big Sandy River, Walker's party returned to Virginia, carrying significant information about the geography and potential riches of the Cumberland Mountain wilderness.

No sooner had Walker returned to Virginia than the Loyal Company's chief rival, the powerful Ohio Company, despatched its own agent to lay out a 200,000 acre tract in the Ohio Valley. In the fall of 1750, a North Carolina backwoodsman named Christopher Gist set out on a journey which was intended to take him as far as the Falls of the Ohio. Traveling with a servant and a pack horse, Gist made his way across what is now southern Ohio and visited several Shawnee towns before crossing to the south bank of the Ohio at the mouth of the Scioto. But in mid-March, after reaching the mouth of the Kentucky River, Gist was warned by friendly Shawnees that Indians allied with the French were encamped at the falls and that to continue his journey would be foolhardy.

Rather than tempt fate recklessly, Gist suspended his mission and turned for his home in the Yadkin Valley. He followed *Alanant-o-Wamiowee* to Drennon's Lick and ascended Drennon's Creek into what is now eastern Shelby County. There he crossed Bullskin and Gist's branches of Brashear's Creek, and then followed the Big Benson River valley to the "little Cuttaway [Kentucky] River," where he arrived on March 19, 1751. According to Gist's journal, the party "were obliged to go up . . .[the river] about 1 m[ile] to an island which was the shaolest place We coud find to cross at. We then continued our course in all about 30 m[iles] through level rich land which was broken and indifferent." Thus was Christopher Gist the first white English explorer to make a documented visit to the area that soon would become Frankfort and Franklin County.

The next white man to venture into the area was John Finley, the first of the many "long hunters" who would help open Kentucky to settlement. In 1752 the noted frontiersman paddled a canoe down the Ohio River on a hunting expedition. After spending some time, with very little success, at the Falls of the Ohio, he traveled back upstream and then overland to Big Bone Lick, located near the Ohio midway between the Kentucky and Licking rivers. There he met a band of Shawnees who invited him to join them at their village in central Kentucky. Enticed by their promise of good fur trading, Finley joined the Shawnees on their journey up the Kentucky River into the Indian Old Fields on Lullbegrud Creek in Estill County. On a broad piece of bottom land adjacent to the Indian village, Finley constructed a small log cabin surrounded by a rude stockade and spent most of the next two years hunting and trading with the Indians.

Finley's Kentucky sojourn was interrupted in 1754 by the outbreak of the French and Indian War. The following year he served, along with Dr. Walker and Gist, as a scout for General Edward Braddock's disastrous march against the French at Fort Duquesne. During this mission he met and formed a close friendship with a young North Carolina farmer and teamster named Daniel Boone.

Although the war halted exploration in Kentucky for nearly a decade, the peace between England and France did not unleash a new wave of exploration. The Treaty of Paris in 1763 effectively eliminated the French threat, but their Indian allies remained hostile to any English encroachment. Likewise, King George III, certain that a flood of settlement would ignite an expensive Indian war, issued the Proclamation of 1763, which temporarily prohibited permanent settlement in the territory across the mountains.

A major source of resentment among land hungry colonists and speculators with western land claims, the proclamation nevertheless restrained settlement for five years. But this barrier collapsed in October 1768, when the Iroquois Confederation agreed to the Treaty of Fort Stanwix. This document opened to settlement new lands in New York, western Pennsylvania, and western Virginia, including the area south of the Ohio between the Great Kanawha and Tennessee rivers. The practical effect of the treaty was to deprive the Shawnees, Delawares, and Cherokees of their hunting rights in Kentucky, even though they were not parties to the treaty.

Not surprisingly, the Shawnees refused to recognize the right of the distant Iroquois to sign away a hunting ground upon which the former had depended for generations. In an effort to prevent conflict, the British government tried without success to prohibit settlement across the Great Kanawha River. The Treaty of Fort Stanwix, which pumped new life into land companies that had been moribund for years, triggered a major surge of settlement across the mountains.

One of the first to make the trek was John Finley. With him this time was his wartime compatriot, Daniel Boone. Finley, Boone, and four companions set out from Boone's Yadkin Valley home on a lengthy hunting expedition in early May 1769. Several weeks later, after following the Wilderness Road across the Holston, Clinch, and Powell river valleys, the party passed through the Cumberland Gap into Kentucky. By June 7 they had reached the Red River, near the site where Finley had established his headquarters some seventeen years earlier. The hunt was extremely successful until late December, when Shawnees stole most of the hunters' pelts and killed one member of the

Daniel Boone (1735–1820) painted by Chester Harding. Harding's portraits are considered the most accurate of Boone as they are the only views based on actual sittings. The artist traced the aged pioneer through the wilds of Missouri. Boone is said to have had difficulty in understanding why Harding wanted to portray him.

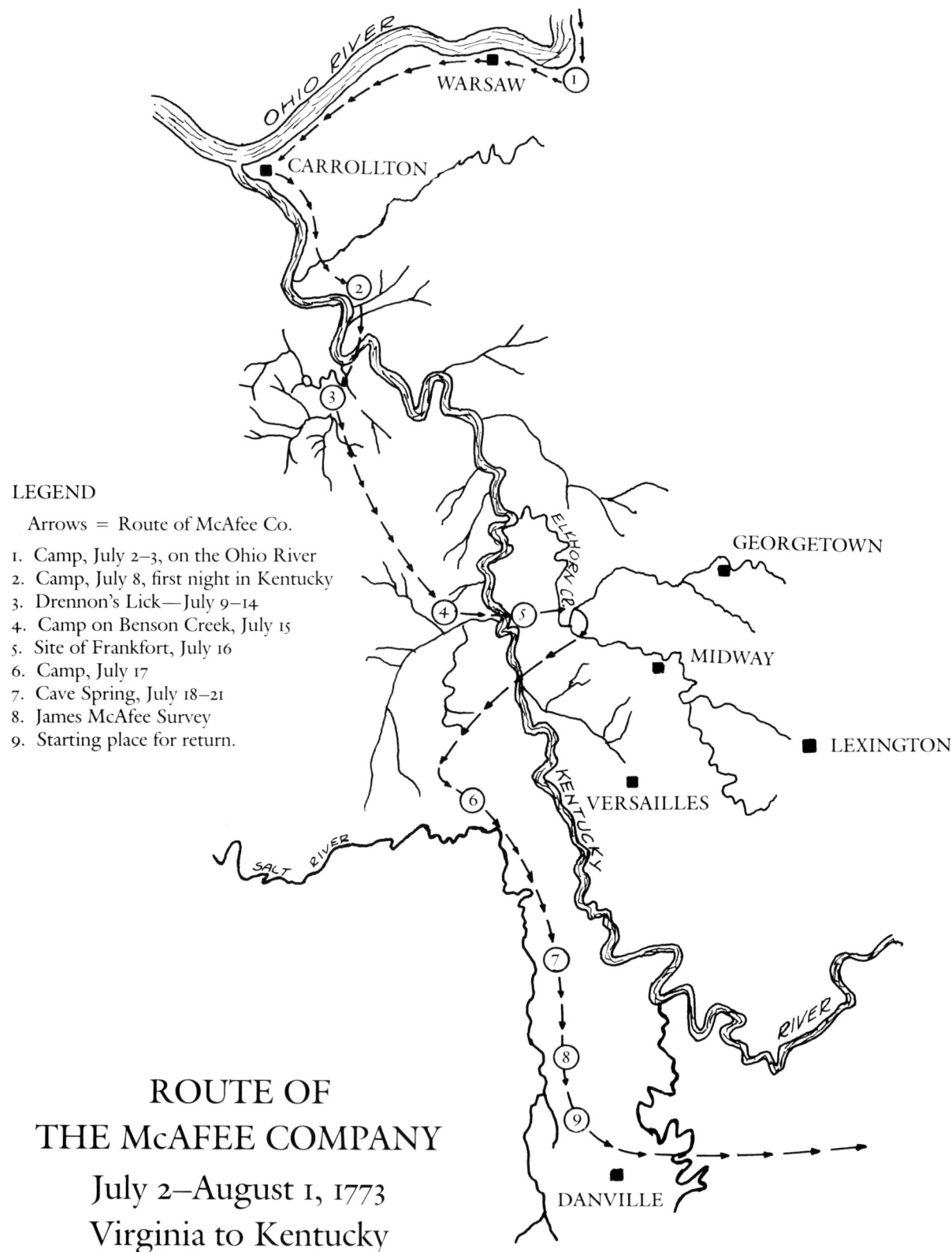

party, John Stewart, who also was Boone's brother-in-law. Despite this setback, the party continued to probe the Kentucky and Ohio River valleys. During the first half of 1770 Boone explored the Ohio River as far as the falls. Returning that summer to his base camp in southern Clark County, Boone followed the old Buffalo Trace, which brought him to the Kentucky River crossing where the village of Leestown soon would be founded.

An anecdote reported by geologist-historian Willard Rouse Jillson suggests that Boone's arrival at the Kentucky River was anything but uneventful. As Boone's son Nathan told the story years later, it appears that when the fabled woodsman reached the river, he spied an Indian fishing intently from an overhanging tree. Apparently suspecting that the Indian was part of the band which had killed Stewart and stolen the party's pelts, Boone decided to settle the score immediately. According to the younger Boone's recollection, his father would say simply, "While I was looking at him, he tumbled into the river, and I saw no more of him." Nathan added, "It was understood from the way that he spoke of it, that he shot and killed the Indian; yet he seemed not to care about alluding particularly to it."

Boone, Finley, and others like them made numerous unrecorded visits to Frankfort and other nearby townsites in the years that followed. But aside from their role as trailblazers, the most important contribution of these intrepid frontiersmen was to fire public imagination about the potential fortunes that could be made across the mountains. As the son of one pioneer speculator recalled decades later, "In those years the fame of the 'Long Hunters' . . . began to circulate that there was a rich and delightful country . . . on the waters of the Ohio." His father and uncles, "all of whom being in the vigor of manhood and full of enterprise and adventure," were stirred by these stories and "longed to see for themselves, as they could not think of being confined to the sterile mountains of Virginia where only small parcels of fertile land could be found at any one place."

One man who recognized this land fever and who was willing and able to exploit it was James Murray, Fourth Earl of Dunmore, who became royal governor of Virginia in 1771. A wily, ambitious, and unscrupulous politician who did not shrink from using his official position to enrich himself, Dunmore aligned himself with some of Virginia's most powerful politicians and land speculators. By promoting their fortunes, he hoped to advance his own. His first step came in 1772, when he reorganized Kentucky and other sections of western Virginia into Fincastle County. To govern the new county, Dunmore appointed some of the area's most influential land owners. The most powerful among them was William Preston, who became county surveyor. Having identified his potential supporters, Dunmore moved to seal their loyalty by issuing them warrants for western lands, ostensibly as a reward for military service during the French and Indian War. Ironically, the awards were provided for by a clause in the same Proclamation of 1763 that had been intended to block settlement beyond the Alleghenies.

In the spring of 1773, several surveying parties set out for Kentucky to turn paper warrants into tangible claims. Among them was a group headed by James McAfee, Jr., and including his brothers, Robert and George; Robert's brother-in-law, James McCoun, Jr.; and a young neighbor, Samuel Adams. Brimming with excitement at "the prospects of making future fortunes, and the honor of being among the first adventurers in the wilderness," the McAfee company left their Botetourt County homes about May 10 and arrived several days later at the Great Kanawha River. After a week's stop to carve out two canoes, they continued their trip down river toward Ohio.

About twenty miles above the Ohio, the McAfee company overtook a surveying party led by Captain Thomas Bullitt, agent for several close friends of Governor Dunmore who held warrants for land in the vicinity of the Falls of the Ohio. Among the members of the Bullitt party were Hancock Taylor, uncle of future president Zachary Taylor, James Douglass, and Isaac Hite. The two companies joined forces and reached the Ohio River on May 29. There they remained for three days, measuring the river and electing Bullitt to command the combined force. Immediately thereafter, Bullitt set out across country to negotiate with the Shawnees at Chilicothe. Meanwhile, the rest of the party continued down river, conducting minor explorations in the vicinity of the Big Sandy and Scioto rivers. After nearly two weeks, they rejoined Bullitt and continued on toward the Kentucky River, where they arrived in early July. On the afternoon of July 7, the Bullitt and McAfee parties bade farewell and resumed their separate missions. McAfee's company, joined by Hancock Taylor, traveled the *Alanant-o-Wamiowee* from Big Bone Lick and Drennon's Lick. On July 16 they crossed the Kentucky River and moved into the high bottom land near the future site of Frankfort.

Robert McAfee was especially impressed with what he saw. "The land on the river seemed to be very full of beech," he wrote in his diary, "with bottom and upland sufficient, with very good water in different places of it." Perhaps believing that he had found the ideal place for his claim, he had Taylor lay out 600 acres in two tracts, one of 200 acres and one of 400 acres. The larger tract, which began at a point on present day Ann Street one block south of Main, included a substantial part of downtown Frankfort.

But the McAfees had not ruled out the possibility that even better land could be found elsewhere in the vicinity. On July 17 they resumed their journey, following the Buffalo Trace into Woodford County and then crossing the Kentucky into Mercer County. Here they found and surveyed tracts that completely fulfilled their desires. Turning his attention immediately to his Mercer County property, Robert McAfee allowed his survey at the bend of the Kentucky to lapse without officially recording it. His initial surveys remained significant, nevertheless. Not only did they mark the first attempt to lay out the site which eventually became Kentucky's capital, but Taylor's survey marks also would guide future surveyors in laying out their own boundary lines.

As events developed, the next surveyor to use Taylor's 1773 survey marks was Taylor himself. The circumstances which brought Taylor back to the bend in the river involved the politics of Governor Dunmore's military warrants. When Bullitt returned from the Falls of the Ohio in September 1773, he presented his party's surveys to Fincastle County surveyor William Preston. But Preston rejected them, claiming they were illegal because neither Bullitt nor any of his associates was one of Preston's deputy surveyors. Forced by Dunmore to record and issue patents for two of the surveys but still insistent on their illegality, Preston sent another surveying expedition to Kentucky, this one commanded by his chief deputy, John Floyd. Among the other members of the thirty-six-man party were Hancock Taylor, James Douglass, and Isaac Hite, all now duly commissioned as deputy surveyors.

Col. John Floyd (1750–1783)

Floyd's company left Point Pleasant in present day West Virginia on April 22, 1774, and arrived at the Falls of the Ohio on May 29. There the party split up, and a crew commanded by Hancock Taylor departed for the Bluegrass. Taylor's party reached the buffalo crossing at the Kentucky River on June 17 and immediately began conducting surveys. The first was for Zachary Taylor, Hancock's brother, who had been a sergeant in a Virginia regiment during the war with France. Unaware that Robert McAfee had abandoned his 1773 survey, Taylor laid out 200 acres for his brother immediately to the east and adjacent to the McAfee claim.

But Taylor did not live to see the settlement of his brother's property. On July 27, 1774, while traveling along the Kentucky River south of Frankfort, his party was ambushed by Indians. One member, James Strother, died immediately. Taylor, mortally wounded, died four days later, after being carried several miles by his surviving companions to Taylor's Fork of Silver Creek, near the present city of Richmond. Buried in an unmarked grave, Taylor's only monument is the creek which bears his name. One of the survivors of the party, Abraham Hepponstall, secured Taylor's survey book, insuring that all of the plats would be officially recorded. In June 1780, Virginia Governor Thomas Jefferson signed Zachary Taylor's grant, making him Frankfort's first landowner.

The years between Hancock Taylor's death and Jefferson's approval of his brother's claim were filled with tension. The bullets that ripped through Strother's and Taylor's bodies were among the early shots fired in Lord Dunmore's War. During the spring and summer of 1774, a succession of clashes between Shawnees and scattered bands of surveyors and settlers had created consternation throughout the Kanawha and Ohio river valleys. After fighting a defensive war for three months, Dunmore decided to take the offensive. On the morning of October 10 a large detachment of Virginia militia under the command of General Andrew Lewis was camped near Point Pleasant, located at the mouth of the Great Kanawha River. Here they were surprised by a large force of Shawnee, Mingo, Delaware, and Ottawa warriors led by the Shawnee chief Cornstalk. After a day of bloody but indecisive battle, Cornstalk quit the field. Deciding that further resistance was futile, he sued for

Gen. George Rogers Clark (1752–1818), engraving based on life sitting recorded by John Wesley Jarvis. Clark, shown in his Revolutionary War uniform, is largely credited with extending the boundary of the western United States to the Mississippi River.

Nicholas Cresswell

peace. Several months of hard negotiating followed, however, and by the time a treaty was signed in the spring of 1775, the English colonies were on the verge of revolt.

The end of Dunmore's War, combined with the outbreak of revolutionary hostilities in April, triggered a new surge of settlement and speculation in Kentucky. Soon new surveying parties were arriving at the buffalo crossing on the bend of the Kentucky River. In mid-May a party led by George Rogers Clark, Nicholas Cresswell, and James Nourse arrived at the mouth of the Kentucky River after a journey down river from Fort Pitt. Traveling in two specially designed canoes, they paddled upriver with the intention of reaching Harrodsburg. On May 24, while camped at Drennon's Lick, they were joined by Captain Michael Cresap. After learning from Cresap that there were no Indians in the area, the party broke up, with Clark and Cresap going their own way and Cresswell, Nourse, and the remainder of the company continuing up the Kentucky.

On May 29 the Cresswell party reached "a great Buffalo crossing, where we intended to kill some meat." The adventurers spent most of the next two weeks hunting, fishing, and exploring widely in Franklin County. In his detailed daily journal, Cresswell recorded graphic descriptions of the region. Again and again he noted the predominance of "Rocks, Cedar Hills and Beech Bottoms." A stretch of upland country, probably in the vicinity of Jett, is described as "the levelest, richest, and finest [the party] ever saw, but badly watered." Commenting on the apparent fertility of another area, he noted, "Land good, weeds as high as a man." And finally, "I believe the land is good in general, through the whole track [sic] with several salt springs as I am told."

Moving over to Elkhorn Creek on June 11, Cresswell and his party encountered a company led by Captain Hancock Lee, a cousin of Hancock Taylor. Lee's company had arrived about June 1 and were beginning what would become an extended survey of several thousand acres for the Ohio Company. The meeting of the two parties proved quite congenial, with Cresswell reporting in his journal that "Capt. Lee . . . treated me very kindly with a dram of Whiskey and some bread, which at this time is a great luxury with me. Captn Lee's brother gave me a Rattlesnake skin about four feet long."

But neither party had much time for palaver. A few days later, Lee's crew traveled to the buffalo crossing at the bend of the Kentucky, where they established Leestown, the first white settlement, after Boonesboro, on the Kentucky River and the first such town on the north side of the river. Lee's selection of this site was no accident. Already familiar with its attributes from descriptions written by his late cousin, he recognized its strategic potential as a jumping off point for explorers and settlers coming into the central Bluegrass by way of the Ohio and Kentucky rivers. The close proximity of an excellent sandy beach; broad, elevated bottom lands; and a gushing limestone spring further enhanced the site's already substantial attractiveness.

It is not known precisely when the first cabins or fortifications were erected

KENTUCKY RIVER (ca. 1805–1812) by GEORGE JACOB BECK (1738/40–1812)

Possibly the earliest landscape done of Kentucky. Beck was trained in London, England, where he exhibited at the Royal Academy from 1790 through 1793 when he came to America. After spending several years in Philadelphia, he relocated in Lexington around 1806 and spent the rest of his life there. The exact location of this painting is unknown, but the chances of Beck's having been inspired by Frankfort's terrain is likely as he was closely associated with General James Wilkinson having decorated Wilkinson's pleasure barge on the Ohio River.

at Leestown, though a block house was constructed sometime during the first year. But the approximate timing of the town's establishment and the founders' aspirations for its growth are documented by no less a personage than George Rogers Clark, who had been employed by Lee as a deputy surveyor. In a letter dated "Lees Town, Kentucke, July 6th 1775," Clark wrote his elder brother, Jonathan, "I embrace the opportunity of Cap'n E[dmund] Taylor to send you this small epistle. . . . A richer and more beautiful country than this I believe has never been seen in America." Confident in the settlement's bright future, he added, "We have laid out a town seventy miles up ye Kentucke [from the Ohio] where I intend to live, and I don't doubt that there will be fifty families living in it by Christmas."

Clark's optimism was premature, to say the least. At the time of his letter to Jonathan, Leestown and its environs had not even been surveyed. In early December, however, Lee finally took measures to secure his claim by laying out a 400 acre survey "upon the North side of Kentuck River, including a large spring, it being the head of the . . .[run] that Empties in at the sand Beech at Lees Town." This tract was one of eighteen private surveys of 400 acres each, totaling 7,200 acres, conducted about the same time by Hancock Lee, his elder brother, Willis, and several other members of their party in the vicinity of the Kentucky and Licking rivers, Benson Creek, and the mouth of Elkhorn Creek.

But it soon became apparent that aspirations and surveys alone were insufficient to insure Leestown's development. While large numbers of pioneers passed through the village on their way to other frontier settlements, few stayed and put down roots. Several forces impeded the town's growth during its early years. Ironically, Leestown's seemingly strategic commercial position seems to have been one of the major factors working against it. As Willard Rouse Jillson observed, the interests of settlers at Leestown were "almost entirely commercial and transitory," whereas the inhabitants of "Harrodsburg and Boonesborough, and, later, those at Louisville and Lexington," were concerned from the beginning with "permanent settlement, land utilization, and home-making."

Another significant problem was the fear of Indian attack. With the outbreak of the revolution, the British exploited Indian resentment against white settlement by instigating and supplying arms and ammunition for raids against scattered frontier settlements. Leestown's position was especially precarious because its transient population made it difficult to mount a strong, continuing defense. The extent of the settlement's vulnerability became apparent in April 1776 when an Indian band suddenly attacked and burned several cabins. The sole victim of the Indians' fury was Willis Lee. The surviving defenders, realizing that Lee's wound was mortal and that their position was indefensible, abandoned the post and fled to Boonesboro. Before leaving, however, they attempted to make the victim as comfortable as possible. Thus, when travelers Daniel Campbell and Robert Edmiston arrived a short time later, they found Lee dead, "a pail of water sitting by his head, his hands lying on his breast, and the blood coming up through his fingers." Additional attacks followed in July, and by 1777 sporadic raids became so troublesome that the residents temporarily abandoned the settlement and relocated to Boonesboro, Harrodsburg, and Lexington.

A potential threat which failed to materialize was Lee's insecure title to his claim to Leestown. Lee's claim was based, of course, on the private survey he had conducted in December 1775 as a deputy surveyor for the Ohio Company. But as westward expansion accelerated and conflicting claims proliferated during the late 1770s, the Virginia Assembly found it necessary to take action to resolve the conflicts. The Virginia Land Law of May 1779 set forth provisions by which the validity of prior grants and claims, including those made under royal authority, would be determined. The legislation also established standards and methods to control the awarding of future claims. The document clearly recognized the rights of chartered land companies, such as the Loyal and Ohio companies. But in the case of surveys executed before 1776, the law required that the surveyor have been commissioned as a surveyor or deputy surveyor for the county in which the survey was made.

Since Hancock Lee and his associates had not been deputized by William Preston, an immediate effect of the land law was to nullify several of their 1775 surveys, including Lee's claim at the buffalo crossing on the Kentucky River. Lee managed to resecure a few hundred acres of the 1775 claims on the Licking River and Elkhorn Creek under the settlement and preemption provisions of the 1779 law. But in the case of his claim at Leestown, Lee's only recourse was to secure the property through a land treasury warrant. He received such a warrant in October 1779, this time for 500 acres adjoining Zachary Taylor's military survey of 1774. The tract finally was surveyed in March 1784, and in July 1786 Governor Patrick Henry signed and sealed the patent officially granting Lee's claim.

Although the Land Law of 1779 forced Hancock Lee to reassert his claim to the Leestown area, it also provided the legal instruments by which numerous speculators and land hungry pioneers established new claims in the same vicinity. By 1790 seven men had platted 3,860 acres of land in the immediate vicinity of Leestown and the original townsite of Frankfort. One of the first beneficiaries of the new law was William Haydon. After exploring widely during 1776, Haydon selected a parcel of upland ground to the east and partially adjacent to Zachary Taylor's property in the vicinity of East Main Street hill. Here he built a cabin and planted a crop of corn. Four years later he appeared before the Kentucky Land Court at Bryant's Station and asserted preemption rights to 1,000 acres "on the Kentucky River situated about two miles above Leestown." The tract was surveyed in January 1783 by John Williams in his capacity as deputy surveyor of Fayette County, Virginia. (Fayette County had been organized in 1780 when the Virginia assembly carved Kentucky County into three new counties—Fayette, Jefferson, and Lincoln.) Governor Benjamin Harrison signed Haydon's grant in June 1784, making him officially the second owner of land situated within the present site of Frankfort.

The third land owner in the area was George Mason, a wealthy Virginia politician, planter, and investor in the Ohio Company. On the basis of a treasury warrant issued in October 1781, Mason claimed a 1,000 acre tract lying south of the bend which stretched from the Kentucky River on the east to Louisville Road on the west and included the lower half of South Frankfort and the state capitol. The tract was surveyed in March 1784 by William McBrayer, assistant surveyor of Lincoln County. Governor Henry signed the claim in September 1785. But the most important claim was yet to come.

While Haydon, Mason, and Lee were putting their claims in order, attorney Humphrey Marshall made the startling discovery that Robert McAfee had allowed his 1773 claim of 400 acres at the bend of the river to lapse. Recognizing the potential value of this unclaimed piece of bottom land, Marshall entered an initial claim for the McAfee tract in May 1784. He based his claim on

Humphrey Marshall (1756–1841), born in Fauquier County, Virginia; Captain in the Virginia cavalry in the Revolutionary War; moved to Kentucky and studied law; delegate to the state constitutional convention; member of the state house of representatives for several years; elected as a Federalist to the United States Senate, and served from March 4, 1795, to March 3, 1801; died near Frankfort, Kentucky, July 1, 1841.

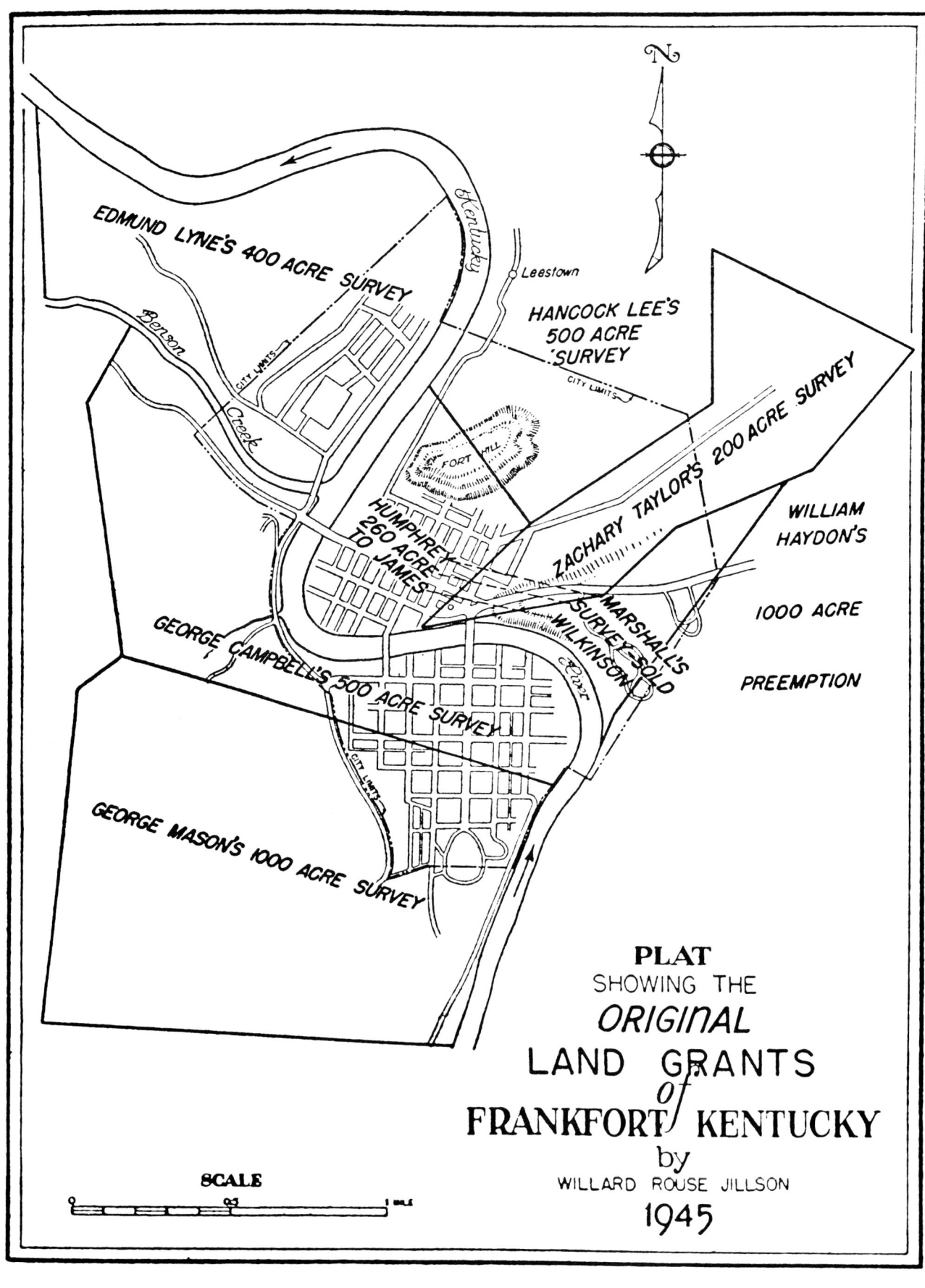

a portion of a Virginia land treasury warrant for about 555 acres which had been purchased two years earlier by one Aaron Darnold and successively assigned to John Bradford and William Marshall, Jr., before coming into Humphrey Marshall's possession. In June 1785, armed with his warrant and a deputy surveyor's commission from Fayette County surveyor Thomas Marshall, Humphrey Marshall and two associates laid out the specific land which he desired. The surveys consisted of two tracts and totaled 260 acres. The largest parcel embraced nearly all of what became the northern portion of the original site of Frankfort. The remaining piece extended in a northeasterly direction from the Kentucky River cliffs, across the Frankfort Cemetery and upper East Main Street into the Thorn Hill bottoms between the nonadjoining portions of Zachary Taylor's and William Haydon's tracts. Governor Henry's signature secured Marshall's claim in August 1786.

Six days after signing Marshall's claim, Governor Henry approved a grant of 400 acres at the mouth of Benson Creek to Edmund Lyne, a member of the Kentucky Land Commission. Lyne's claim, based upon a preemption warrant and located in Jefferson County at the point where the three new counties joined, had been surveyed in December 1784 by J. Hite, a deputy of Jefferson County surveyor William May. The last of the grants composing the original Frankfort site was issued in March 1790 to George Campbell. Beginning at Benson Creek on the west, this 500-acre grant took in the northern half of South Frankfort. Campbell had entered his claim on the basis of a land office treasury warrant issued in March 1782. But he did not have the land surveyed until 1789, accounting for the fact that this important piece of ground remained officially unclaimed for so long.

The land boom of the 1780s was not confined to the townsite of Frankfort. Between 1780 and 1790 at least fifty-one claimants laid out and were granted more than 60,000 acres within present Franklin County. Activity was particularly heavy between 1783 and 1785, the years immediately following the end of the Revolutionary War. Grants ranged in size from 100 acres to 5,000, the latter belonging to John C. Owings, whose claim on Big Benson Creek in Jefferson County was approved in 1784. The following year John Campbell, also an early landowner at Louisville, received an award of 3,920 acres on Benson Creek in Jefferson County. The largest single award in Lincoln County went to John Arnold, who in 1783 received 3,015 acres on Little Benson Creek and the Kentucky River. A grant of about 2,094 acres on Elkhorn Creek to Cyrus McCracken in 1783 was the largest single claim in Fayette County. Other prominent figures who purchased land and settled in the area included John Major, who received 1,000 acres on Elkhorn Creek in 1783; Thomas Paxton, who in the same year took up two tracts of 1,000 acres each on Little Benson Creek and the South Fork of Big Benson Creek; Captain Uriel Mallory, who claimed 2,000 acres on Elkhorn Creek in 1788; and Archibald Hamilton, who obtained 1,000 acres on Benson Creek and the Kentucky River in 1790.

Contributing significantly to the land boom was the gradual alleviation of the Indian menace. This is not to say that the Indians had become less resistant to white expansion. However, as settlement increased between 1773 and 1783, Franklin County gradually was encircled by outlying settlements which formed a relatively strong protective barrier against raids from other parts of Kentucky. These settlements, such as Logan's Fort and Boonesboro, established in 1775, McClelland's Fort near Georgetown and Houston's Station at Paris, both erected in 1776, Squire Boone's Station, built at Shelbyville in 1780, and Arnold's Station in Anderson County and Johnson's Station in Scott County, both planted in 1783, did not provide absolute protection; but the increasingly regular communication among the settlers at the various stations created a network through which the news that Indians were in the vicinity could be transmitted very quickly.

Once in a while, however, the protective network failed, sometimes with fatal consequences. One such occasion occurred in 1780 when William Bryant, Stephen Frank, Nicholas Tomlin, Willson E. Williams, and two other men set out from Lexington and Bryant's Station on a salt boiling expedition to Mann's Lick, located in Jefferson County south of Louisville. Late one night, as the party was camped at a ford on the Kentucky River, they were surprised by a band of Indians. Frank died immediately and Tomlin and Bryant received severe wounds. The others escaped unharmed. The exact location of the attack remains a mystery. Some have suggested Leestown, while others favored Mitchell's Spring in South Frankfort. But from an early date, prevailing opinion favored the ford opposite Devil's Hollow. Very soon after Stephen Frank's death, this short stretch of shallow gravel shoal became a heavily used crossing point for travelers between Lexington and Louisville. As its fame spread, the crossing became known throughout central Kentucky as "Franksford." Thus, Stephen Frank, a simple Jewish pioneer, was on the verge of being commemorated through death in a manner he would never have expected in life.

2

The Settlement of Frankfort

FOR NEARLY SIX YEARS after the death of Stephen Frank eager pioneers continued to pour into central Kentucky across the ford that bore his name. A few stopped at Leestown, but most forged on toward Lexington, Harrodsburg, Danville, and surrounding towns and stations. But one man had the vision to recognize the commercial potential of the bottomland that lay immediately adjacent to Frankfort.

General James Wilkinson arrived in Kentucky in 1784. Only twenty-seven years old at the time, he already had established his reputation as a daring adventurer, brilliant schemer, and efficient administrator. Trained in medicine while still a teenager, he began practicing at age eighteen in a rural area of eastern Maryland. When the American Revolution erupted, Wilkinson rushed to General George Washington's headquarters at Cambridge, Massachusetts. There he became acquainted with such figures as Alexander Hamilton and Aaron Burr. By the fall of 1777, Wilkinson had risen to the rank of lieutenant colonel and held the position of deputy adjutant-general of the forces commanded by Major General Horatio Gates. After defeating the British army of General John Burgoyne at Saratoga, Gates selected Wilkinson, still only twenty years old, to negotiate the surrender terms. His performance was so outstanding that Gates charged him to deliver word of the victory to Congress. The Congressional delegates were so overjoyed with Wilkinson's message that they immediately made him a brigadier general.

During the remainder of his wartime career Wilkinson displayed a remarkable capacity for getting into and out of trouble. Shortly after his promotion, he foolishly became embroiled in the Conway Cabal, a plot by General Thomas Conway and other disgruntled officers to have George Washington replaced by General Gates. When Wilkinson carelessly betrayed the conspiracy to officers friendly to Washington, he shifted blame to Colonel Robert Troup, who was both Gates's top aide and a friend of one of Washington's aides, Colonel Alexander Hamilton. Gates, however, soon learned the truth and publicly chided Wilkinson for his breach of military etiquette in trying to

General James Wilkinson (1757–1825) and Mrs. Ann Biddle Wilkinson, engraved in 1808 by C. B. J. Fe'vrat De St. Memin (1770–1852). "Recalling a physiognotrace, invented by Edme Queneday in 1786, he reconstructed one from memory, drew crayon portraits of sitters in profile, and by means of the antograp reduced them to two inches in diameter. The original drawings were made life-size on red paper now faded to pink, about 16 × 22 inches. To each customer he furnished the original drawing for framing, the engraved plate and twelve impressions for $33. Two proofsets of these engravings were preserved. One is in the Corcoran Art Gallery, and the other is in the Library of Congress." (Edna Talbott Whitley, *Kentucky Ante-Bellum Portraiture*. National Society of Colonial Whitley Dames of America in the Commonwealth of Kentucky, 1956, p. 751.)

cast responsibility for his own indiscretion upon a fellow officer. The embarrassed Wilkinson promptly challenged his superior to a duel, from which both combatants emerged unscathed. With his reputation now severely tarnished, Wilkinson resigned his commission in March 1778.

But Wilkinson was a survivor. After about eighteen months in voluntary civilian exile, he finagled an appointment as clothier general of the Continental Army. In this post he again demonstrated his penchant for mixing efficient performance with questionable ethics. During nearly two years as an apparently effective administrator, he initiated major reforms in the operation of the quartermaster service. But he resigned again in March 1781, just before Cornwallis's surrender at Yorktown, after revelations of "gross irregularities in his accounts."

In 1778, during his brief "retirement," Wilkinson married Ann Biddle, an attractive Philadelphian whose family had close ties with Colonel Aaron Burr. Three years after his resignation as clothier general he and his bride removed to Kentucky, where he built homes in Louisville and in the South Elkhorn country near Lexington. A man of unbounded ambition, Wilkinson wasted little time in putting his many talents to work on the Kentucky frontier. He employed his medical skills freely, dispensing available medicines to the ill and delivering an occasional baby when no midwife was around. As the proprietor of a store in Lexington he frequently traveled the roads around the Bluegrass, peddling goods from bags carried by pack horse.

No doubt one of the most common topics of political conversation in which Wilkinson became engrossed during his rounds involved the problem of trade on the Mississippi. In 1784 the Spanish government announced that in the future the Mississippi River would be closed to American shipping. This action infuriated the growing population of western farmers, who depended upon the Mississippi as an outlet for their livestock and produce. In 1785, in an effort to reopen commerce on the Mississippi, John Jay, the American secretary of foreign affairs, entered into negotiations with Spanish diplomat Don Diego de Gardoqui. The talks dragged on for months as each tried to charm the other while holding firm on fundamental issues. Meanwhile, western blood boiled. As month followed weary month, many Kentuckians began to talk separation—not simply statehood, but formation of an independent political entity which would be free to negotiate and ally with whichever government, United States or Spain, offered the better terms of alliance.

One of those most deeply involved in the western separationist intrigues was James Wilkinson, who saw in Kentucky's independence an opportunity to advance himself both politically and economically. Wilkinson could hardly have been more excited in the spring of 1785 when he learned that title to the vacant McAfee land near Franksford had passed to Humphrey Marshall, his neighbor on South Elkhorn Creek. Recognizing the site's commercial potential as a collecting point for goods intended for export by way of the Ohio and Mississippi rivers, he laid plans to buy it from Marshall. Almost immediately after Governor Patrick Henry signed Marshall's claim in August 1786, Marshall sold the land to Wilkinson. Two months later the Virginia legislature passed a bill which designated "one hundred acres of land in the county of Fayette, the property of James Wilkinson," as the town of Frankfort.

Administration of the new town was placed in the hands of a self-perpetuating board of trustees composed of seven prominent Fayette County citizens—Caleb Wallace, Thomas Marshall, Joseph Crockett, John Fowler, Jr., John Craig, Robert Johnson, and Benjamin Roberts. Most had served with or under Wilkinson during the revolution. The act noted that Wilkinson already had platted the territory into streets and lots, but it authorized the trustees, within six months of the act's passage, to sell at public auction all lots which had not already been sold by Wilkinson. The legislation also required each lot purchaser to build "a dwelling house, sixteen square feet, with a brick or stone chimney, to be finished fit for habitation within two years from the day of sale." Each lot sold was to be transferred to its purchaser in fee simple and the proceeds turned over to Wilkinson. The trustees also had the power to settle disputes over lot boundaries and to establish whatever building regulations they deemed necessary to insure the town's safe, orderly, and efficient growth. If any lot owner failed to build within the time provided, the trustees were empowered to seize the lot, sell it, and apply the money to some useful public purpose.

Even today, when building and planning regulations are all but taken for

"As Surveyor of the Town of Frankfort I hereby certify that the annexed platt contains a copy of the plan of Frankfort as originally laid out and sold by James Wilkinson Esquire who laid out and sold the same. Att:Achilles Sneed"—This copy of Wilkinson's original grid was made for a court case in which Wilkinson's title was challenged. Lot owners are shown on sold lots and first Capitol with jail in rear is shown.

granted in most American communities, such restrictions perhaps appear unusually stringent. But they are not untypical of their time. For a variety of reasons, public officials in the colonial and early national periods tried to promote the carefully planned, compact development of urban communities. In some areas this reflected religious motives and a desire to prevent a few persons from engrossing large tracts of land. Down the coast and along the frontier the adoption of the auction system of land sales often enabled a few persons to acquire large numbers of lots, but other controls remained, motivated by considerations of public safety and a desire to get property on the tax rolls quickly.

In addition to setting standards for physical development and residential construction, the act of incorporation established some economic regulations. Specifically, the act mandated the establishment of a public ferry, which was to be "constantly kept across the Kentucky River, from the lands of . . . James Wilkinson . . . to the opposite shore." The legislation also set rates for the ferry service: "For a man, four pence, and for a horse the same; and for the transportation of tobacco, wheel carriages, cattle and other beasts, the ferry keeper may demand and take the same rates as are allowed by law at other ferries." If the operator charged more than allowed by law, he could be required to forfeit the overcharge to the aggrieved party and to pay a fine of ten shillings for every offense.

The street names that appeared on Frankfort's original gridiron plan clearly reflected the founder's military experiences and honored his wartime friends and acquaintances. The western thoroughfare, expected to be the town's primary residential artery, was named for Wilkinson himself. The next street parallel to Wilkinson was named for his commander-in-chief, General George Washington. The third north-south street honored General Arthur St. Clair, a native of Scotland who became a hero in the battle of Quebec during the French and Indian War and served as one of Washington's most trusted subordinates during the revolution. The easternmost of Frankfort's original north-south streets was Ann Street, named for Wilkinson's beautiful wife, who was said to have been "more popular with the officers and soldiers than was her distinguished husband."

The first east-west cross street, parallel to the river, was dubbed Wapping Street. The name was suggested by John Instone, a visiting Englishman who once had lived on Wapping Street in London. Located near the Thames River, it was considered one of the most beautiful residential streets in the world. The next cross street to the north, now Main, was originally named Montgomery Street in honor of General Richard Montgomery. A former British army officer, Montgomery had resigned his commission and emigrated to America in 1773. When hostilities broke out, he accepted a brigadier general's commission in the Continental Army and died leading the unsuccessful attack against Quebec on December 31, 1775. Laid out immediately to the north was Market Street. Site of the town's first public market and the widest street in old Frankfort, it is known today as Broadway. Clinton Street, the next cross street, honors General George Clinton, a high-ranking staff officer during the revolution, first governor of New York state, and vice-president under both Thomas Jefferson and James Madison. The northernmost of the original cross streets, incorrectly spelled Mero, was named for Don Esteban Rodriguez Miro, the Spanish governor-general of Louisiana, whose headquarters were located in New Orleans.

The fact that the Frankfort trustees named a street for a Spanish official who was helping to keep Kentucky commerce bottled up was hardly coincidental. Indeed, the name Mero Street symbolizes Wilkinson's political and economic objectives for Frankfort and the depth of his involvement in what was becoming known as the "Spanish Conspiracy." During the late summer of 1786 word reached the frontier that Congress had approved John Jay's request that he be allowed to accept a Spanish proposal that the United States agree to a twenty-five year suspension of trade on the Mississippi River in exchange for a commercial treaty which would open other Spanish territory to American trade.

Western reaction to the proposed Jay-Gardoqui deal was so angry that negotiations ceased entirely. Some westerners advocated an alliance with England or Spain, and a few wild-eyed pioneers talked of an armed march against New Orleans. It was against this explosive background that Wilkinson, in June 1787, loaded two flatboats with tobacco, salted hams, and butter collected from Kentucky farmers; took a position in the smaller of the two boats; and headed down the Kentucky River toward the Ohio. His destination was New Orleans. Although he lacked a passport, Wilkinson was certain that his Spanish sympathies would secure him an audience with Governor Miro.

Wilkinson's instincts proved correct. Although arrested upon arrival at New Orleans, he immediately convinced his captors to take him to Miro's headquarters. Assured of Wilkinson's partisanship, the governor enabled him to sell his cargo and extracted an oath of allegiance to Spain. In exchange for the oath, Wilkinson obtained an annual pension of $2,000 and an agreement that trade on the Mississippi would be reopened. As an additional plum, the agreement included a proviso that all trade had to be conducted through Wilkinson personally.

Once back in Kentucky, Wilkinson wasted no time in exploiting his new commercial monopoly in the Spanish trade. He and his agent, Peyton Short, circulated advertisements among central Kentucky farmers urging them to market their produce in New Orleans through Wilkinson's firm. The erstwhile general's access to the New Orleans market quickly made him one of the most popular and powerful men in Kentucky. A few skeptics, including his neighbor Humphrey Marshall, suspected treason, but none could prove it. For most Kentucky farmers, however, accusations mattered not. The Mississippi had been reopened. If Wilkinson benefitted personally, that was just compensation for his daring and courage. As for the eastern-dominated Congress, it had done little to command western confidence or allegiance.

Despite Wilkinson's newly found commercial influence, the town of Frankfort was not growing so quickly as either he or the Virginia assembly had hoped. The reasons for this laggard growth are not entirely clear. No doubt some settlers disdained the crude surroundings of an incipient river town, while others were attracted by the cheap farm land available near outlying settlements and stations. In any case, Wilkinson returned to the Virginia legislature in the fall of 1787, and in November that body gave him a three-year extension to sell his lots. Because a court house fire in 1803 destroyed the

Major Thomas Love served in the Revolutionary War under General Anthony Wayne. After the war he settled permanently in Frankfort where for a number of years he and his wife were proprietors of "The Love House."

WILKINSON'S RESIDENCE

Built about 1784 by Wilkinson at the southwest corner of Wilkinson and Wapping streets. Its proportions far exceeded anything in town at the time, even containing a ferry landing. A few years later, Wilkinson relinquished use of the house to the state for seven years. In November 1793, the second session of the legislature was held here, and its use is credited to the establishment of Frankfort as the permanent capital. After the state's use of the house, it was temporarily occupied by Andrew Holmes. For the next seventy-five or more years the house was a tavern known as "The Love House." It was razed in 1870.

original deeds, it is impossible to discern the precise pattern of sales during the intervening years. From other sketchy evidence, however, it appears that Wilkinson sold most of the more attractive lots to several of his former military comrades.

Despite the time extension for lot sales, Frankfort's growth was anything but spectacular during Kentucky's final years under Virginia authority. Wilkinson himself built the second house in Frankfort, a two-story, double log cabin located at the southwest corner of Wilkinson and Wapping Streets. But when his aristocratic wife Ann, repelled by the rude frontier environment, refused to live in it, Wilkinson sold the house to Andrew Holmes, another pioneer entrepreneur. A short time later Holmes transferred it to Thomas Love, who converted it into a tavern. In the decades to come, Love's Tavern

MAJOR'S STATION
Part of John Major's Station of 1784–1785. Gambrel roof was added during remodeling around the turn of the century after a fire.

Reverend William Hickman, one of Kentucky's earliest "pioneer ministers."

would host such notables as Aaron Burr, Bourbon Prince Louis Philippe of France, the Marquis de Lafayette, Henry Clay, and adventurer Philip Nolan. Wilkinson, though, remained an absentee landlord, conducting his business from Lexington and Louisville.

Wilkinson's decision not to settle in Frankfort did nothing, however, to dampen his enthusiasm for the town's commercial prospects. Like many other urban entrepreneurs, he recognized that a town's growth depended upon the ability of its residents to exploit effectively the agricultural products and natural resources of the surrounding hinterland. Since the mid-1780s settlers had been pouring into the area, clearing farms and building houses near the defensive stations owned by the larger land owners.

In late 1783 John Major, Sr., a Revolutionary War veteran, bought a large tract of land on Dry Run and South Elkhorn Creek from the Reverend Lewis Craig, a pioneer Baptist preacher. Here he built a blockhouse which became known as Major's Station and which for some time served as the only defensive post between William Haydon's Station on the Kentucky River near Frankfort and McClelland's Station at Georgetown. This pioneer neighborhood grew quickly, and within four years it had enough settlers to support an organized church. In late 1787 Major traveled into what is now Jessamine County and persuaded the Rev. William Hickman to relocate to Dry Run. The following January, Major assembled a group of local settlers at his home and there established the Forks of Elkhorn Baptist Church, the first organized congregation in Franklin County. Within two or three years, the settlement also had the county's first school house, probably built of logs, which stood near the intersection of Leestown Road and Versailles Pike.

VALLEY FARM

Stone house built on the banks of South Elkhorn Creek by Joel Scott, keeper of the penitentiary. The Greek Revival portico was added at a later date. Fire destroyed this great house in 1961.

Several more stations and settlements, as well as a few large individual farms, were established during the mid-1780s. James Arnold left Virginia in 1784 and built a double log cabin on his 1000-acre tract on the west side of the Kentucky River opposite the mouth of Glenn's Creek. Later in 1784 or early 1785, Joel Scott, another wealthy Virginian, purchased a tract on the South Elkhorn. Here he built a one and one-half story limestone house, which he later expanded by adding a full two-story, dressed-stone house in the Virginia plantation style. To the northeast of Frankfort a pioneer named Joseph Gore built a log station in the upland area between Elkhorn Creek and the Kentucky River near the point where the Owenton and Peak's Mill roads converge. Shortly thereafter, in Quinn's Bottoms, located about five miles northeast of Frankfort on a low divide between two dry meanders of Elkhorn Creek's main channel, Judge Harry Innes built a heavily fortified double log cabin on a stone foundation.

By the early 1790s many of the residents in these settlements were growing large quantities of tobacco. But they also needed facilities where their crops could be collected and inspected for the market. Wilkinson was more than happy to oblige. In 1791 he returned again to the Virginia legislature and obtained an act allowing the establishment of a tobacco warehouse on his land in Frankfort, which was now part of Woodford County. The legislation required the proprietor—Wilkinson—to build the warehouse and to pay the inspectors an annual salary of twenty-five pounds. The profits, of course, would go to Wilkinson. Again, as in the case of his trip to New Orleans, Wilkinson's efforts to exploit the region's embryonic tobacco industry reflected his entrepreneurial vision.

Wilkinson's efforts at Frankfort were not totally unrivaled, however. Back at Leestown, Hancock Lee was taking measures to offset the general's initiatives. In March 1789, in response to the time extension given Wilkinson to sell his lots, Lee conducted a similar public sale of lots. To increase the attractiveness of the lots to potential purchasers, Lee promised to build a public road through Leestown between Louisville and Lexington. That same month, while the sales were in progress, Leestown was visited by Dr. Jedidiah Morse, the prominent American geographer. Whether or not Morse visited Frankfort is unclear. If he did it is certain he was more favorably impressed by Leestown, because his *American Geography*, published later in 1789, omits any mention of the future capital. On the other hand, he wrote of Leestown: "It is regularly laid out and is flourishing. The banks of the Kentucky river are remarkably high, in some places 300 and 400 feet, composed generally of stupendous perpendicular rock. The consequence is there are few crossing places; the best is at Leestown, which is a circumstance that must contribute much to its increase."

In fact, Dr. Morse's comments were more a reflection of local aspirations based upon natural advantage than an objective assessment of reality. Neither Frankfort nor Leestown had yet developed to the point that its long-term survival was guaranteed. Nor was it clear which town would eventually triumph over the other. As Judge Samuel Wilson observed nearly a century and a half later, "In . . .[1792] it was still an open question whether Frankfort was to become a mere suburb of Leestown or Leestown was to be relegated to the subordinate role of a suburb to Frankfort." With statehood, the resolution of that issue lay in the hands of a five-member commission appointed to recommend a permanent capital for Kentucky.

Meanwhile, the settlers around Frankfort and Leestown had to withstand a final series of Indian forays before the area could be considered free from attack. The Indians had been rather quiescent since the 1780 attack that had cost the life of Stephen Frank, and the process of settlement during the early and middle 1780s had gone virtually unchallenged. But as the end of the decade approached, sporadic attacks resumed.

The first incident occurred some time in 1788. Stephen Arnold, half-brother of James Arnold of Glenn's Creek, and a companion were returning to Arnold's Station after a wild turkey hunt. As they approached the vicinity of the former Blakemore Distillery site near the old Frankfort and Lawrenceburg Road, they suddenly came upon five Indians. Arnold quickly called for his friend to shoot, while at the same time firing his own weapon at the closest attacker.

Arnold's shot killed two Indians who happened to be in the line of fire. But his companion froze and was captured immediately. Unable to fire again, Arnold turned and ran for home, being pursued by two of the remaining Indians, the third having stayed back to guard the captive.

Outnumbered and still three miles from his brother's home, Arnold's situation appeared grim. On a dead run, he tried to reload his rifle and get off another shot. But his ramrod became entangled in a bush and knocked the weapon from his hands. With the pursuers hot on his heels, Arnold had no time to recover it. To make matters worse, recent rains had left the ground soaked, and his moccasins were becoming waterlogged. Finally, in an effort to increase his speed, he took out his hunting knife, and while still running, cut the strings of his moccasins and continued his flight barefooted. Having lightened his load, Arnold successfully outraced his pursuers. When they came within site of Arnold's Station, the Indians gave up the chase, fearing a counterattack from the fort's defenders. A short time later, the Indians released their captive to some other white settlers who returned him to his home.

The next and much more dangerous attack came four years later at Cook's Station. Settled during the fall of 1791, Cook's Station consisted of some half-dozen cabins located in Quinn's Bottom, a crescent-shaped lowland about three miles below the forks and about twelve miles upstream from the Kentucky River. The cabins were occupied by the families of Jesse Cook, his brother Hosea Cook, their brother-in-law Lewis Mastin, Lewis Bledsoe, William Dunn, and a man named Farmer. Nearby was a cabin occupied by several of Judge Harry Innes's Negro slaves and their overseer.

The Cook brothers were conscious of the possibility of Indian attack. But it had been some time since the last raid, and they and their neighbors, lulled into a false sense of security, were becoming careless and failing to recognize signs that another attack might be imminent. Their carelessness proved fatal. On the spring morning of April 28, 1792, Jesse and Hosea Cook were shearing sheep. They had no idea that their cabins were surrounded by a party of some one hundred or more Wyandottes prepared to strike. Suddenly a hail of gunfire and flights of arrows shattered the morning calm up and down Cook's Station. Hosea Cook fell dead at the first volley, and Jesse was mortally wounded. While he struggled to reach the nearest cabin, the wives gathered their two children and a Negro child and hustled them to the same house. As soon as he reached the house, Jesse dropped to the floor dead, leaving the women to defend themselves and the children. They bolted the door and readied themselves for what proved to be a most remarkable stand.

Before the Indians reopened fire their chief, who spoke some English, called upon the women to surrender, promising that they would be well treated. When the widows refused the entreaties, the Indians opened fire with rifles and arrows. When they failed to penetrate the cabin, the tribesmen applied the torch, hitting first the door, then the walls, and finally the roof. Each time, however, the women succeeded in extinguishing the flames. At first they used buckets of water, which had been kept on hand for just such an eventuality. When the water ran out, the resourceful defenders cracked a large quantity of eggs and beat them to a liquid consistency and used them to help extinguish the flames. Before the fire was finally quenched, the heroic women had to resort to Jesse Cook's blood-soaked coat to suffocate the last surviving flames.

Compounding the ladies' problems was the fact that they could not find the bullets necessary to use the muskets their husbands had left behind. Finally, one of the women found a piece of lead, which she split and fashioned into a makeshift bullet. While the Indians were trying to break down the door, she loaded the bullet and some powder into a musket, placed the muzzle through a small crack between the logs, and fired point blank at the chief, who toppled over dead. This so infuriated the Indians that they made repeated efforts to break into the cabin. But against the women's stout resistance, their efforts proved futile, prompting them to withdraw out of fear that the alarm might already have been sounded.

Hosea and Jesse Cook were not the only victims of the raid. Moments after they were attacked another element of the war party fired on Lewis Mastin and a passerby named McArthur. Mastin sustained a knee wound and died from a second shot while trying to escape to his cabin. McArthur, meanwhile, grabbed one of Mastin's small children and they escaped by horseback. Nearby, William Dunn and his two sons, one nine and the other sixteen, escaped into the woods; but there they accidently became separated. The father made a successful getaway, but both sons were captured and tomahawked. Finally, the attackers reached the overseer's cabin. Finding one of the slaves ill, they slew him immediately and kidnapped the other two slaves who happened to be there. Both captives were taken to a Wyandotte village in the Great Lakes country, where one later died. The surviving slave eventually gained freedom from the Indians only to be returned to his master in Kentucky.

The attack against Cook's Station appears to have been the most costly among a coordinated series of attacks at various places along Elkhorn Creek. Among other settlements that sustained attack were Innes's Station, where Ambrose White, the overseer of the slaves kidnapped at Cook's Station, also was taken captive, and Dry Run, where young Gerard Demint was captured en route to a neighboring farm on Elkhorn Creek's main stream. Demint soon escaped and returned to Dry Run, but White was carried along with the slaves to the Wyandottes' northern camp. He was adopted into the tribe and remained a captive for two years before seizing an opportunity to escape and return to Kentucky.

Another victim of the raid was Robert Todd, who stopped at Hamilton's Station that evening during a journey to his home in Lexington. Word of the attacks had reached Frankfort, Hamilton's Station, and other nearby communities by mid-afternoon; and Robert Hamilton, master of the station, cau-

JUDGE HARRY INNES' DOUBLE LOG CABIN

In 1792 one of the bloodiest Indian massacres in the annals of Franklin County occurred in this neighborhood. This house successfully withstood the attack without loss of life. In later years the house was expanded in the rear and covered with clapboard. Long neglected, it burned in the summer of 1961.

tioned Todd that it was dangerous to go on. But Todd dismissed the warning and proceeded toward the Kentucky River at Frankfort. A short time later the people at Hamilton's Station heard a series of shots in the direction of Frankfort. Two of the pioneers, James White and Robert Gullion, followed Todd's tracks to Coleman's Spring near present day Steele Street in South Frankfort. From the signs they could tell that Todd had been shot while he stopped to water his horse. With his wounded rider still in the saddle, the horse had eluded the Indians, however, and continued toward Arnold's Station. About one-half to three-quarters of a mile from the station, though, Todd stopped to examine his wound. But his untethered horse continued on to Arnold's Station, where he was found the next morning. A hurriedly formed party back-tracked the trail and soon found Todd's still warm body lying where he had dismounted.

Whether the attacks at Cook's Station, Innes's Station, and Dry Run were the extent of the Wyandottes' objectives or merely small-scale incidents in a much larger operation that never materialized is not entirely clear. What is notable about the engagements, as one historian has said, is that "all of the fighting seemed to have been done by the women. The men did not strike a blow." While this particular chronicler was writing only about the attack on

Cook's Station and therefore missed Todd's death and the incidents at Innes's Station and Dry Run, he does underscore the often overlooked fact that women as well as men braved the risks and rigors of settlement.

The year 1793 saw at least one attack, as an Indian band pursued a group of hunters to within four or five miles of Frankfort, but there were no casualties. The following year was not so lucky. The first incident occurred in the summer of 1794 when a small party of warriors moved from near the Ohio River, across Indian Creek in Owen County, into Franklin County. Following a path through Indian Gap, they arrived in the bottom lands of Elkhorn Creek below Peak's Mill. There two members of the party split off and attacked the home of a man named Stafford, located at the mouth of Pond Branch. The settler put up a stiff fight, killing one of the attackers and prompting the survivor to rejoin his companions. Meanwhile, several nearby settlers, attracted by the shooting, quickly assembled and tracked the fleeing Indians all the way to the Ohio River before losing the trail. About this same time, another Indian band slipped into the western part of the county and attacked a settlement on Benson Creek near old Conway's Mill about four miles from Frankfort. One man was killed attempting to defend his home.

The last Indian raid in Franklin County occurred in the fall of 1794. James Downey, a settler who lived in the Elkhorn Creek bottoms below Indian Gap, became concerned one evening when his daughter Mary failed to return from a nearby spring where she had gone for drinking water. Investigating for himself, he found her empty bucket and evidence that she had put up a fierce struggle before being overpowered by her captors.

The circumstances of Mary Downey's rescue are particularly romantic. It seems two young men in the neighborhood—one an Englishman and the other an Irishman—had expressed deep love for the young woman but that she had been unable to choose between them. When Mary was kidnapped, her distraught father called upon his fellow settlers for assistance in pursuing her captors. At the same time he promised her hand in marriage to whichever of the two suitors would aid in rescuing and returning her alive. The adventuresome Irishman immediately accepted the challenge, but the Englishman declined the opportunity to risk his life for the woman he professed to love.

Once assembled, Downey and his party set out to find Mary, following a trail left by the fleeing Indians and their struggling captive. After tracking the Indians into the early hours of the morning, the rescuers finally found their quarry sleeping in a camp on the Kentucky River bank opposite the mouth of Six Mile Creek. Stealthily surveying the camp, Downey found his daughter, disheveled but otherwise unharmed, lying sound asleep between two of her captors. Two more guards were asleep nearby, their guns within easy reach. After cautioning them against any errant shot that might injure his daughter, Downey and his cohorts surrounded the sleeping Indians, slew those lying alongside his daughter, and wounded the other two, who promptly escaped across the river into Henry County. With Mary now safe, the rescue party split, with several of the men continuing to track the fugitives until losing the trail. Meanwhile, Downey, Mary, and her Irish lover returned to the Downey home near Indian Gap. The next day Mary Downey and her sweetheart were married in ceremonies that attracted a large crowd of settlers from the lower Elkhorn.

Certainly the celebration that accompanied Mary Downey's rescue and marriage was warranted by the occasion alone. But in a symbolic sense these events have even greater significance. Not only did they mark the last violent confrontation between whites and Indians in Franklin County, but they also followed Kentucky's admission as a state and Frankfort's designation as the capital in 1792 and the organization of Franklin County two years later. The end of hostilities meant that settlers gradually could divert their primary attention away from insuring their physical safety to advancing their communities' social, economic, and political development. For James Wilkinson it meant that his vision for Frankfort was about to be realized, not so much through the business of commerce as through the business of politics.

3

Statehood & Capital

ON FEBRUARY 4, 1791, both houses of Congress passed legislation providing for the admission of Kentucky to the Union. Fourteen months later, a convention convened at Danville to prepare the constitution that would complete the process of statehood. After nearly two months of intense debate, the delegates completed their work, and on June 1, 1792, Kentucky became the fifteenth state. Kentucky's admission also ended one of the fiercest struggles for statehood in American history.

From its beginnings in the early 1780s, Kentucky's battle for statehood reflected grievances felt by western settlers as far back as the late seventeenth century. As pioneers poured across the Appalachian Mountains, both the political and the physical distance between the frontier and the capital of Virginia, first at Williamsburg and then Richmond, increased. The sources of the settlers' discontent were numerous. Land policy was a major source of aggravation. Many persons of modest means resented the fact that large land firms like Richard Henderson's Transylvania Company and the Ohio Company had been allowed to engross thousands of acres of prime land. Not only did settlers dislike the quitrents charged by the speculators, but they also were angered by the fact that late-comers often had to pay higher prices for poor lands than early settlers had had to give for much better tracts. They also were infuriated by rumor mongering speculators who spread the word that existing titles were invalid and that settlers might lose their property without compensation.

Another source of antagonism involved Virginia's alleged failure to provide adequate protection against Indian attack. For state officials, providing such protection was a complicated matter, fraught with problems of distance, high cost, lack of supplies and provisions, and a shortage of manpower. All of these difficulties were compounded by many Kentuckians' stubborn refusal to bear the expense of the protection they demanded. Kentucky frontiersmen, on the other hand, were embittered by the fact that the Virginia government steadfastly blocked their attempts to cross the Ohio and attack the Indians in their own territory, despite the fact that Congress had urged such action.

Administration of justice also was a source of frustration among westerners. Not only did eastern legislators insist upon passing legislation that fell short of meeting the settlers' needs, but the high cost of litigation often made it impossible for pioneers to exercise their right to appeal. All of these problems made communication between frontier and capital difficult and increased the possibility of misunderstanding between well-intentioned parties on both ends of the message. Under such circumstances, petitions for relief proliferated and threats of separation became increasingly strident.

The political process which led to Kentucky statehood began in late 1784 when Colonel Benjamin Logan, angered at Kentucky's seeming inability to protect itself against marauding Indians, called a convention of militia officers. The meeting convened at Danville on December 27 and continued for ten days. The delegates accomplished two immediate objectives. Their short-term purpose was to fashion a plan to protect Kentucky against attack. But their primary work was to draft a petition to the Virginia assembly for permission to join the Confederation as an independent state. In addition, they elected Samuel McDowell and Thomas Todd to the respective positions of president and clerk, posts they held throughout the quest for statehood. Their initial work accomplished, the delegates adjourned, providing for a second convention to be composed of locally elected delegates who would assemble at Danville in May 1785.

Justice Thomas Todd (1765–1826) was born in Virginia and served in the Revolutionary War. He moved to Kentucky in 1786 and lived with Judge Harry Innes, studying law and beginning a successful practice before serving as clerk of the federal court for the district of Kentucky. Later he became clerk for the Court of Appeals. In 1806 Governor Greenup appointed him Chief Justice of Kentucky. This portrait by Matthew Jouett was painted shortly before Todd's death when he was sitting on the bench of the United States Supreme Court as an appointee of President Jefferson.

The second convention met as scheduled and adopted a series of resolutions which, among other things, requested permission for Kentucky to separate from Virginia without a promise to join the Confederation. Their apparent motive for this departure was a growing skepticism over the political health of the Confederation. One of the delegates who most strongly endorsed this independent course was the notorious James Wilkinson, who was quick to exploit prevailing grievances for his own political purposes.

Wilkinson's handiwork was even more apparent at the third convention, which met in August 1785 to complete work begun a few months earlier. One of the more recent pieces of legislation to raise the ire of Kentuckians was a revenue act that proposed to tax all of the state's districts equally, regardless of disparities in population, wealth, or representation. Shrewdly equating the tax act with obnoxious British colonial taxes, Wilkinson wrote, and persuaded the delegates to adopt, a new address to the assembly. The document contained a detailed petition of grievances and concluded with a ringing call for immediate separation. Most of the delegates were so certain their petition would be heard that the convention adjourned without a call for a fourth meeting. They were confident that the next call would be issued by the Virginia General Assembly—for the constitutional convention which would make Kentucky a "free, sovereign, and independent republic."

But the petition was not greeted in Richmond with the same enthusiasm with which it left Danville. Virginia already had yielded control of its territory north of the Ohio to the Confederation government, and most politicians realized that it was only a matter of time before Kentucky's inevitable separation occurred. But even western sympathizers such as Thomas Jefferson, James Madison, and James Monroe admitted serious misgivings and urged caution in providing for independence. Moreover, legislators were becoming increasingly aware that self-serving promoters such as Wilkinson had goals other than making Kentucky a member of the Confederation. These patriotic Virginians did not intend to allow their political offspring to fall into the Spanish orbit.

The upshot was an enabling act, passed January 10, 1786, which provided that Kentucky's separation would not be allowed until legal and political arrangements could be made for the district's admission into the Confederation. Instead of a constitutional convention, the act called for another convention to further discuss the matter of separation.

Although irritated by the lack of a call for a constitutional convention, Kentuckians otherwise seemed to favor the enabling act, and the fourth convention met in September 1786. Unfortunately, its work was severely hindered by George Rogers Clark and Benjamin Logan's foolhardy raid against the Wabash and Shawnee tribes in southwestern Indiana. So many delegates were also militia officers that the convention was unable to muster the necessary quorum. Finally, in January 1787 the convention's remnant dispatched a message to Richmond requesting more time to consider the separation question. The patient legislature complied, passing a second enabling act, which set January 1, 1789, as the date on which Kentucky could join the Union, if the Confederation Congress gave its consent before July 4, 1788.

The year 1787 was critical in Kentucky's drive for statehood. Discontent flared anew early in the year when Governor Edmund Randolph censured Clark and Logan for overstepping their authority in their embarrassingly unsuccessful Indiana raid. Hard on the heels of Randolph's action came the word that the Spanish had withdrawn the right of deposit at New Orleans. As anger over these issues increased, so did differences of opinion as to how the matter of separation from Virginia should be approached. By the time the fifth convention met in September 1787, the delegates increasingly found themselves divided into two factions. The Court Party, led by James Wilkinson, was so named because its other dominant members—John Brown, Benjamin Sebastian, and Harry Innes—were judges on the Kentucky district court. Endorsing an immediate declaration of independence from Virginia, this faction believed that an independent Kentucky could take the action necessary to reopen the Mississippi and thus be in a position to negotiate favorably with the Confederation. The opposition Country Party, spearheaded by Federalists such as Rice Bullock, Humphry Marshall, and Robert Breckinridge, also desired immediate separation, but they wanted it coupled with quick admission to the union of states.

When the meeting convened in Danville on September 17, the most conspicuous absentee was the Court Party's ringleader. Recognizing the volatility of the Mississippi navigation issue, Wilkinson had attempted to strengthen his faction's position by shrewdly timing his New Orleans venture with the opening of the convention. Meanwhile, the delegates successfully petitioned the Virginia assembly to authorize the election of Wilkinson's henchman John Brown to Congress.

Upon arriving in Philadelphia, Brown found the Confederation government in the throes of death, awaiting its replacement by the government which would take office under the new Constitution. Congress finally convened in the spring of 1788, but it was not until July 3, the day before the second enabling act was due to expire, that Brown finally got an opportunity to present Kentucky's petition. Lacking adequate time to consider the memorial, the Confederation Congress referred the document to the new Congress of the United States. Brown left Philadelphia frustrated by the seeming indifference of eastern Congressmen to Kentucky's needs and convinced by Wilkinson's exploits at New Orleans that Kentucky could get a better deal from the Spanish.

The fifth convention marked the Court Party's zenith. When the sixth meeting convened in July 1788, Wilkinson, now on the Spanish payroll, was prepared to lay out his complete separationist scheme. But most of the delegates, hoping to frame a constitution, voted to adjourn when they learned of the indifference of Congress. Meanwhile, Virginia had ratified the new Constitution of the United States, despite heavy opposition from Kentucky. Wilkinson got another chance to unveil his plan when a seventh convention assembled in November 1788. The first delegate to speak, Wilkinson presented a frightening picture of the damage Kentucky had suffered since the closing of the Mississippi and again called for immediate independence. As Wilkinson sat down Brown rose for the purpose of presenting, or so Wilkinson thought, detailed plans for Kentucky to separate from Virginia, form an independent government, and establish commercial and political ties with Spain, which could in the process reopen the Mississippi to western produce. But somewhere along the line Brown had a change of heart. Not only did he expose the deeper conspiratorial nature of the Spanish plot, but he also asserted that Kentucky was now in a position to deal effectively with Congress if the delegates acted in unison. When Brown sat down, Wilkinson's Spanish conspiracy was dead.

A good deal more political wrangling followed before the statehood process could be completed. The failure of the dying Confederation Congress to act necessitated a third enabling act, and the transfer of power to a new Congress required still a fourth. Accompanying each new enabling act was another convention. Finally, the ninth convention met in Danville on July 26, 1790, and accepted the terms of Virginia's fourth enabling act. But the politics of constitution making were almost anticlimactic, given the intrigues of the 1780s. When they completed their work in May 1792, the delegates had fashioned one of the most democratic state constitutions to that point. All free,

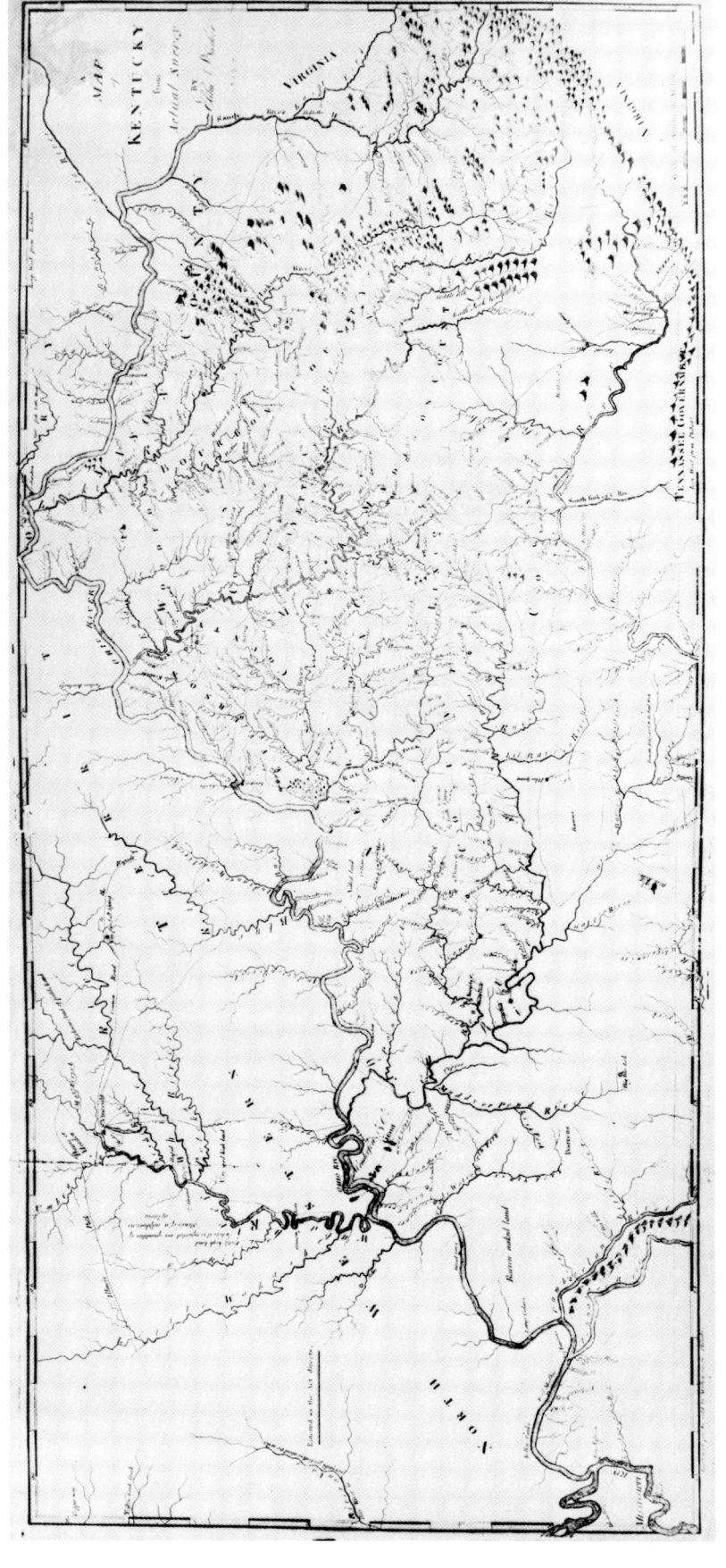

ELIHU BARKER'S MAP OF KENTUCKY (1792)

This first edition of Barker's map is the earliest in general circulation to show the location of Frankfort. Engraved and sold by Matthew Carey of Philadelphia, it is the first map of Kentucky to be based on actual surveys.

white, resident males twenty-one years of age or more were permitted to vote. The bill of rights included twenty-eight sections, which dealt not only with such matters as freedom of religion, press, speech, and assembly, but which also prohibited forfeiture of suicides' estates. The one matter left unsettled was the location of the permanent capital.

The new constitution set forth the process by which the location of the capital was to be chosen. Under Article X the legislature, at its first meeting, was to appoint a board of five commissioners who had the power to select a capital site and accept individual donations of land, money, and materials with which to finance development of the new seat of government. In accordance with the law, the legislature met for the first time in Lexington in June 1792. Shortly thereafter it officially appointed five prominent men recommended by Governor Isaac Shelby to constitute the capital selection commission. Those appointed were Robert Todd, of Fayette County; Thomas Kennedy, of Madison County; Henry Lee, of Mason County; and John Allen and John Edwards, of Bourbon County. In the appointment resolution the legislators also instructed the commissioners to "accept the best proposals that were made in a moneyed point of view, as a bonus for this coveted honor and to enter into contracts pledging the public faith with those parties whose propositions and donations should be accepted by them."

The commissioners held their first meeting in Lexington in early August 1792 and elected Kennedy as chairman. Over the next two or three months the commission reviewed and evaluated at least eight proposals. James Ledgerwood and several associates offered land at Ledgerwood's Bend in what is now Mercer County. Joseph Delaney proposed a site adjoining his ferry operation near the mouth of Craig's Creek in Woodford County, and Abraham Owens presented a proposal from Louisville. The four sites given the most serious consideration, however, were Petersburg, Leestown, Lexington, and Frankfort.

DETAIL OF ELIHU BARKER'S
MAP OF KENTUCKY
SHOWING FRANKFORT

Each town had its own attractive features. Probably the least known of the contending sites, Petersburg in Woodford County had been laid out by General Charles Scott with the explicit hope that it could become the capital. But Scott dropped the town building project after the proposal was rejected and he was recalled to military duty against the Indians in late 1792. Leestown, offered by Hancock Lee, benefitted from its position at the Kentucky River crossing. Similarly, Lexington had heavy support because it was the largest town in the state. In the final analysis, however, the selection rested upon economic considerations. Kentucky was in dire financial straits, cash was at a premium, and the Frankfort proposal was the strongest from an economic standpoint.

Early in 1792, James Wilkinson had sold his tobacco warehouse and remaining lots in Frankfort to Andrew Holmes in exchange for some 300,000 pounds of tobacco. Now one of Frankfort's leading landowners, Holmes offered several town lots, rents on his tobacco warehouse for seven years, and

STATE HOUSE, FRANKFORT, KENTUCKY

John Scoles of the *New York Magazine* recorded the only view known of the first permanent statehouse in 1796. The "brick house exhibited on the right" may have been the jail.

an assortment of building materials including "ten boxes of glass, 10 x 12, 1,500 pounds of nails, 50 pounds of locks and hinges, an equivalent of stone and scantling for building" as an inducement to select Frankfort as the capital. If more space were needed, Holmes promised to lay off an additional fifty acres and share the property with the commissioners. Adding further support was a commitment by eight underwriters—Harry Innes, Nathaniel Sanders, Bennett Pemberton, Benjamin Craig, Jeremiah Craig, William Hayden, Daniel James, and Giles Samuel—to pay the commissioners $3,000 in specie.

Recognizing Holmes's proposal as far superior to its competitors, the commissioners resolved on December 5, 1792, that "Frankfort is the most proper place for the Seat of Government" and that "the proposals of Andrew Holmes, Harry Innes, Esquire, and other subscribers, be accepted and agreed to." The General Assembly approved the commissioners' recommendation three days later, adjourned their meeting at Lexington and, appropriately, called their "next session in the house of Andrew Holmes, at Frankfort on the Kentucky River."

Having resolved the problem of designating a capital town, the legislature turned to the question of the capitol building. Three days before the first session adjourned, the lawmakers empowered the governor to appoint five "Directors of Public Buildings," who would determine which of the lots acquired from Andrew Holmes were most appropriate as the site of the statehouse and related public buildings. The directors also were to superintend planning of the building, employ the workers, and oversee construction.

After considerable deliberation, the directors selected the eight lots bounded by Market, Clinton, Madison, and Lewis streets and designated as "Public Ground" in Holmes's proposal to the commissioners. Construction began in 1793 and proceeded for a time under the watchful eye of the legislature, which met at Andrew Holmes's residence at Wilkinson and Wapping streets in November 1793. Built of rough limestone blocks and topped with a small cupola, the three-story edifice was completed in time for the November 1794 session of the General Assembly. The total cost of the first capitol is not clear. Legislative records indicate that the assembly appropriated about $3,500 toward construction, but these funds were supplemented by an undetermined amount of individual donations.

The first floor of the new statehouse was occupied by several of the state's executive offices—auditor, treasurer, registrar, and public printer. Located on the second floor were the house of representatives, the court of appeals, the general court, and the federal district court. The third floor housed the senate chamber and the secretary of state's office. The new wilderness capitol did not go unnoticed by observant travelers. In July 1795, Lewis Condict, a young Morristown, New Jersey, physician, visited Frankfort while en route to his mother's home at Cox's Creek in the Salt River Valley. In his journal, Dr. Condict described the capitol as "a spacious and superb building, being nearly 100 ft. in length and three stories high and built of stone." The Reverend James Smith, who visited about five months later, observed that "the state house . . . is most worthy of notice. It is an elegant stone building 3 stories high, a steeple on top and a portico on each side."

Frankfort's selection as Kentucky's capital was critical to the town's permanence because it assured the frontier town a unique reason for existence. But this new seat of government hardly became an overnight center of urbanity. The town had no sidewalks until 1800; the unpaved streets remained in a perpetual state of disrepair; and log wagons outnumbered carriages and other wheeled vehicles. Most of the houses were rude log cabins or small frame dwellings.

Nevertheless, Frankfort began to take on characteristics of permanence and even elegance during the closing years of the eighteenth century and the first fifteen years of the nineteenth. In June 1797, sixty-five residents and twenty-four nonresidents owned taxable property in the capital. Three years later, census takers found 628 people clustered at Frankfort, making it the second largest town in the state after Lexington, which had 1,795 residents. Ranking behind Frankfort were Washington, with 570 inhabitants; Paris, with 377; and Louisville, with 359.

When English traveler Fortescue Cuming visited the capital seven years later, he found it in a pronounced state of transition. Viewing the town from the cupola of the statehouse, he counted every house, "the number of which

Governor James Garrard (1749–1822)
Mrs. James Garrard (1751–1832)

In 1799 the Garrards arrived at the new Governor's Palace, as the Mansion was originally referred to, in a carriage drawn by four black horses. The first Christmas dinner, typical of hospitality extended by the first family, included two turkeys, several ducks, fifty pounds of roast beef, bacon, vegetables, other side dishes, and concluded with Mrs. Garrard's homemade peach wine.

St. Leger de Happert painted portraits of the couple; copies were made for each of their children by Chester Harding in 1819.

was exactly ninety, most of them well built with brick, and some with rough but good marble of a dusty cream colour.... The old wooden houses are rapidly disappearing to give place to brick, since about two years ago." By 1810 Frankfort's population had grown to 1,099, an increase of 75 percent over the previous census.

Indicative of the improving situation suggested by Cuming's observations and Frankfort's growing population are several outstanding houses erected between 1796 and the War of 1812. The first and perhaps most palatial was Liberty Hall, built by United States Senator John Brown for his parents in 1796. Located at the southwest corner of Montgomery (now Main) and Wilkinson streets, this house is an outstanding example of the Georgian style. The most striking aspect of the fourteen-room mansion is its frontal bay, which features a classical entry portal topped by a handsome second-story Palladian window, both of which are flanked by twelve-pane sash windows with shutters. The entire unit is crowned by a large dentiled pediment pierced by a lunette. Both the brick and the few nails used in the structure were manufactured on the grounds. All of the wood, including the black walnut used for much of the interior and the cypress used for the roof and cellar window sills, was dried for two years in a large shed located nearby.

The year 1796 also witnessed construction of the first Governor's Mansion at the southwest corner of High and Clinton streets. Built during the administration of Governor James Garrard and frequently referred to as "the Palace," the structure's basic layout and brickwork are Georgian, though Victorian elements were added later in the nineteenth century. Two of the craftsmen who participated in its construction—Thomas Metcalf and Robert P. Letcher—later resided in the house while serving their own terms as Kentucky's chief executive.

Several more elegant homes were erected during the early years of the nineteenth century. The residence of Senator John J. Crittenden, a two-story, red brick structure in a simple colonial form, was constructed at the southwest corner of Montgomery and Washington streets by Charles Sproule about 1800. Standing a block away is the former home of Judge Thomas Todd, who served as associate justice of the United States Supreme Court from 1807 to 1826. Erected about 1812 by William Waller, this story and a half brick house is highlighted by three imposing frontal gables. Back near the Capitol Square, an important Federal survivor is the double house at 406–408 High Street. With its massive chimney, joined by a flat parapet on the party wall, this structure retains its fundamental Federal character despite later Victorian alterations.

But population growth and the construction of elegant Georgian and Federal homes were merely two elements in a process of urban development that began to take hold after Frankfort's designation as capital. The next two decades witnessed important changes in local government, major improvements in transportation, expansion of the community's economic base, the devel-

JOHN J. CRITTENDEN HOUSE (401 West Main Street)

Built about 1800, probably by Dr. Joseph Scott. Crittenden occupied the house from 1819 through 1863. The house was owned briefly by Aaron Burr prior to its acquisition by the Crittendens.

opment of major public services, and the emergence of rudimentary forms of cultural and social life. Meanwhile, Frankfort became embroiled in one of the most controversial political and diplomatic intrigues in American history and a local "secession" crisis which divided the town for more than fifty years.

One of the major problems facing Frankfort after becoming the state capital was its virtually nonexistent local government. When the General Assembly met in 1793, it received petitions from Frankfort residents complaining that the original trustees had not met or acted for some time. Realizing that the seat of government could not operate effectively without adequate local government, the legislators amended the incorporation act and created a new five-member, self-perpetuating board of trustees. They appointed John Logan, Thomas Todd, Daniel Weisiger, James Roberts, and Isaac E. Gano to the new board. Among other things, the new trustees had the authority to establish building regulations, supervise clearing and cleaning of streets, and employ a surveyor to lay out a plat of the town and have it recorded by the county clerk.

Frankfort operated under this board for less than a decade. By 1802, it was clear that the town had outgrown the capacity of the existing board to deal adequately with its problems. Furthermore, it was apparent that the continued existence of a self-perpetuating board of trustees was inconsistent with the increasingly democratic political ideology that was abroad in Kentucky. In

LOT MAP OF FRANKFORT, KENTUCKY (1802)
One of the earliest recorded layouts, showing both sides of the river. Redrawn by Bayless Hardin in 1936.

December 1802 the assembly again amended Frankfort's incorporation act to replace the self-perpetuating board with a seven-member elected body. The act required the new trustees to be freeholders and residents of Frankfort. The legislation also considerably expanded the body's powers. To implement its supervisory authority over street maintenance, the board was authorized to call out taxpayers and other titheables "for the purpose of working on the streets and roads leading from several landing places on the Kentucky River, and for removing nuisances, under the superintendance of a surveyor . . . to be appointed by the board." In giving the trustees the power to compel citizens to do public work—or pay for substitute labor—the legislature invoked a tradition of demanding civic responsibility that dated back to early colonial times.

In addition, the trustees won the authority to assess both individuals and property for taxation, to formulate procedures for collecting taxes, and to establish an appeals process for persons who believed their property had been unfairly valued. The act also set penalties for certain infractions of law, such as racing a horse in the streets, shooting at a target within the town limits, and allowing hogs to run free. Noting finally that the original plat still had not been recorded and that the town's boundaries already had been expanded, the act again empowered the trustees to have an official plat drawn and recorded.

Apparently the provisions for compelling public labor on work projects were unpopular, for in December 1805 the assembly again amended the law in a way which, in effect, made the provision optional. The trustees were empowered to levy a special tax of up to $300 on each citizen or titheable "for the purpose of repairing the streets, and the like." Such payments exonerated the individual from public work. However, the law also allowed a person subject to the levy to discharge the obligation in the form of labor if he so desired. Stiff penalties could be assessed, however, if the individual did not appear when summoned for work. To make sure that all taxes were collected promptly, the trustees also were empowered to hire and compensate a tax collector.

Frankfort's charter continued unamended for six more years. But as the town's population and boundaries expanded, the trustees needed greater authority to keep up with the changes. Thus the General Assembly substantially revised and expanded the incorporation act in early 1812. The new legislation required the trustees to meet monthly. They were empowered to erect, repair, and supervise a public market house. Their power to levy and collect taxes was broadened to permit a poll tax on free, white males over twenty-one and a special levy on showpeople. Additionally, the trustees were authorized to pave sidewalks and to apportion the costs to adjoining proprietors, to establish a night watch for the maintenance of public order, and to disburse monies and publish a statement of receipts and expenditures.

Nor were changes in local government limited to the town of Frankfort. By the time Kentucky was admitted to the Union, its three original counties had been expanded to nine—Fayette, Jefferson, Lincoln, Nelson, Bourbon, Mercer, Madison, Mason, and Woodford. In 1792, during the first two legislative sessions that followed statehood, seven more counties were created—Washington, Scott, Shelby, Logan, Clark, Hardin, and Green. As the result of this rapid creation of new counties, Frankfort and the surrounding territory were divided among Woodford, Mercer, and Shelby counties. In 1794, in an effort to rectify this situation, the General Assembly carved away adjoining portions of these three counties and created Franklin County. The new entity remained in its original form only four years. In 1798 a section was cut away to create Gallatin County, and additional pieces were taken away to form Owen County in 1819 and Anderson County in 1827.

The first Franklin County Court, appointed by Governor Isaac Shelby, consisted of justices of the peace John Logan, Bennett Pemberton, Anthony Crockett, Baker Ewing, Richard Apperson, William Ware, Thomas Lillard, and John Arnold. The court appointed Willis Atwell Lee, nephew of Hancock Lee, as the first county clerk, while Governor Shelby commissioned John Smith as the first county sheriff and appointed Turner Richardson coroner. Charles M. Bird was the first county attorney. The first district court convened in February 1796, with Buckner Thurston and James G. Hunter serving as judges.

Willis Atwell Lee (1775–1824). Born in Culpepper Co., Virginia, he was raised and educated by his uncle Hancock Lee. He came to Kentucky in 1793 to take a position in Thomas Todd's law office. At the time of his death he was clerk of the county and general courts as well as clerk of the Senate of Kentucky.

The statehouse doubled as the Franklin County Courthouse until September 1806, when a new courthouse was opened at the southeast corner of the Capitol Square. According to Fortescue Cuming, it was "a plain brick building" with a piazza of five arches" that opened "on the hall for the county courts." Located on the same floor were the clerks' offices. "The jury rooms are on the second floor, and on the third is a masonic lodge."

One of the major consequences of the strengthening of local government was to improve the community's capacity to develop public facilities and services necessary to support population growth and economic expansion. It must be understood, however, that the provision of such services was not always a direct function of local government. Because small frontier communities usually lacked the legal power and financial resources to provide such improvements on their own, they had to rely on a combination of public and private resources. Local government leaders, who were frequently persons of substantial means, often used their political prowess to obtain state legislation which enabled them to mobilize private resources to fulfill public purposes. Local civic and economic leaders favored the mixture of public authority and private resources in projects of a developmental nature because such enterprises, if successful, promised to improve the community's economic environment while spreading the risk in case of a project's failure.

One area where the strengthening of local government was of critical importance was transportation. To a capital whose very reason for existence required regular visits by persons from out of town, an adequate transportation system was essential. By 1805, therefore, the Frankfort trustees had taken advantage of their power to compel public labor and had platted and opened High, Hill, and Holmes Streets, which joined the original townsite to the east of Ann Street. Ten years later, the trustees obtained permission from the General Assembly to extend Catfish Alley between Broadway and Clinton streets and rename it Madison Street and to open Buffaloe Alley between Clinton Street and the courthouse and rename it Lewis Street.

County government likewise took pains to improve the roads under its jurisdiction. Even before the creation of Franklin County, Fayette and Woodford officials had attempted to make the area more accessible by improving the old buffalo roads and pioneer trails. As early as 1780, for example, Leestown Road was opened between Leestown and Lexington. Another early road led through the valley of Big Benson Creek to Louisville. Later the road was shifted from Benson Valley and rerouted up the hill above Devil's Hollow through Bridgeport, Graefenburg, and Shelbyville to Louisville.

In 1797, under general legislation pertaining to public roads, the Franklin County Court obtained the power to open, alter, and maintain roads "within the county for the convenience of travelling to their county courthouse, or to any public ware-house, landing, ferry, mill, lead or iron-works, or seat of government." The legislation authorized the court to appoint three or more persons to serve as road viewers, who were to inspect the proposed route and report their findings to the justices. Once a route had been approved and land owners properly compensated, the court could appoint a surveyor to oversee construction and maintenance of the road.

Like the Frankfort trustees, the justices could compel "all male labouring persons of the age of sixteen years or more," except masters of two or more slaves over sixteen, "to work on some public road." The year after the law's passage, the court instructed James Arnold to lay out a road from the mouth of Glenn's Creek to Frankfort. The road entered the capital over the present Louisville & Nashville Railroad right-of-way, passing just to the west of and below the tunnel. Between 1798 and 1800 roads were laid off and constructed in virtually every direction from Frankfort, and most were joined laterally by public crossroads.

But in a county like Franklin, ribboned as it is with a winding river and numerous creeks, a road system was terribly incomplete without means of crossing the streams. Thus the flurry of road building that occurred during the late 1790s and early 1800s was accompanied by the construction of bridges and the expansion of ferry services. The most difficult task was to bridge the Kentucky River at Frankfort, where the stream's great width and limestone cliffs made any bridge building effort a monumental engineering feat. In December 1799, Christopher Greenup, Daniel Weisiger, and William Trigg incorporated the Frankfort Bridge Company. Their purpose was to erect a span from the south end of Ann Steet to the south side of the river.

In 1805, the initial effort having failed, the General Assembly repealed the company's charter and authorized John Pope to attempt a similar project at the same location. To help pay for the bridge, the legislature empowered Pope to fix a toll for passage. But that did not provide construction capital. During the same session, the assembly gave Thomas Tunstall the right to erect a bridge across the Kentucky between the west end of Montgomery Street and his property on the other side of the river. The provisions of Tunstall's charter were virtually identical to those in Pope's.

Apparently some construction did occur under one of the charters, although precisely which one is not clear. When Fortescue Cuming visited in 1807, he observed that "the erection of a permanent wooden bridge over the Kentucky has been lately commenced, which will be about one hundred and forty yards long from bank to bank, the surface of which is about fifty feet above low water mark." Meanwhile, passage across the river was by means of a pontoon bridge, described by Cuming as "a bridge of boats . . . about sixty-five yards between the abutments."

Again, however, the effort proved futile, and in January 1810 the legislature incorporated a new Frankfort Bridge Company, this time authorizing Thomas V. Loofburrow and William Trigg to construct a bridge across the river at St. Clair Street. The incorporators were permitted to raise up to $20,000 through the sale of stock at $100 per share. The law specified that the "bridge shall not contain more than one pier in the channel of the river, and which pier shall

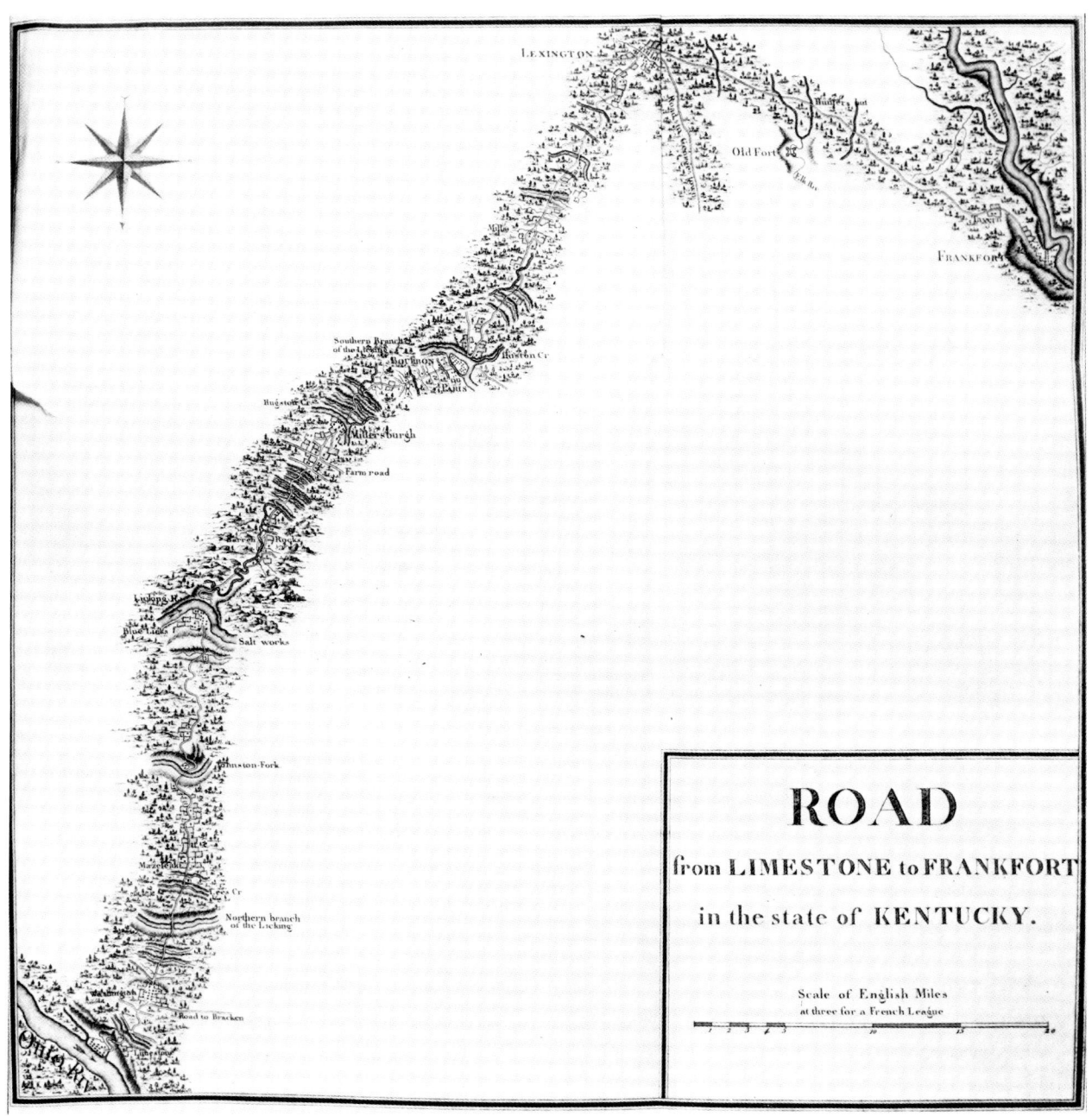

ROAD FROM LIMESTONE (MAYSVILLE) TO FRANKFORT IN THE STATE OF KENTUCKY

This very detailed map of 1796 was drawn by General Collot, a spy for the French. Frankfort's prominence is stressed by orienting the map with north towards the bottom of the page. The main objective of the map was to promote Frankfort's accessibility by land as well as by water.

not be less than sixty feet high from its foundation." If the bridge were not completed within two years, the company would forfeit all rights granted by the legislation.

This time, however, the builders succeeded, though not without delay. In January 1812, with development lagging, the legislature extended the company's construction deadline to 1816. The extension made possible the completion of the first permanent bridge across the Kentucky at Frankfort. A chain bridge built at a cost of $25,000, the entire structure was 700 feet long, including approaches and a 335-foot main span. The bridge had one center pier sixty-five feet high and a width of eighteen feet. The chains which held the bridge were forged at Pittsburgh; fashioned of one and one-half inch square iron bar, they weighed about six tons apiece. The primary obstacle to construction was quicksand, which made it difficult to secure a foundation for the south abutment. Working day and night, construction crews attempted to pump out the quicksand, but water rushed back in as quickly as it could be emptied. In view of the construction problems, the completion of this first bridge was a remarkable accomplishment quite apart from its importance as a transportation link.

While the Frankfort Bridge proved to be the most troublesome such project in the county, it was not the only one to encounter difficulties. In 1798 the county court authorized Nathaniel Sanders and Charles Patterson to erect bridges across the branches of Elkhorn Creek near the Forks. The contractors agreed to keep the spans in good repair for seven years. But well before their obligations expired, the bridges had fallen into such serious disrepair that the court filed suit to enforce the contract. Both bridges were completely rebuilt in 1807, the South Fork span by Benjamin Head and the North Fork span by Hezekiah Keeton. Head and Keeton's work lasted a mere four years, with both spans being rebuilt in 1811.

Completion of these and other spans in the county constituted an important step in integrating Franklin County's early road system. But at several points on the Kentucky River ferry lines continued to play a major role in the transportation network. In December 1794 the legislature recognized the pivotal role of Wilkinson's Ferry by requiring it to provide free transportation to all citizens residing on the south side of the river on county court days, during meetings of the court of quarter sessions, on election day, and on the militia's general muster days. Four years later, the East Frankfort Ferry was established to provide access to the Reverend Elijah Craig's ropewalk, located a mile upstream from Frankfort near the old Cochran Distillery site. The most important ferry operation outside Frankfort, and certainly one of the longest lived, was the Glenn's Creek Ferry in southern Franklin County. Established by John Green at the mouth of Glenn's Creek in 1814, this enterprise later came under the ownership of James Arnold, who operated it as Arnold's Ferry. The line eventually passed to his son-in-law John Cardwell, who operated it as Cardwell's Ferry, a name retained by Cardwell's daughter, Mary E. Johnson, who continued to conduct the ferry into the twentieth century.

Perhaps the most challenging transportation problem facing Franklin Countians, and indeed the leaders of several nearby counties, was improving navigation on the Kentucky River. General Wilkinson's voyage to New Orleans had dramatized the river's commercial potential. But knowledgeable observers realized that the stream was almost totally unnavigable above Frankfort, while an assortment of snags, sandbars, rock shoals, submerged islands, and changing currents often made passage difficult between Frankfort and the Ohio River.

At Frankfort the major obstacle was Fish Trap Island, a large drift pile about nine hundred yards long which split the river's main channel just below the mouth of Benson Creek. During low water, the channel dropped to about fifteen inches on either side of the island. Before the beginning of white settlement, Indians captured large numbers of fish by setting V-shaped fish traps in the channel. White settlers quickly copied the technique.

Serious discussions aimed at improving the Kentucky's navigability began as early as 1799. On November 28 the Frankfort *Palladium* carried a lengthy article in which it was estimated that for an expenditure of $95,000 the river could be made navigable in all seasons for vessels drawing no more than fifteen inches. Two years later, the General Assembly enacted legislation to create the Kentucky River Company, which was empowered "to examine and clear out all obstructions in the Kentucky river, from the mouth of the South fork to the mouth of [the] . . . river." To fund its operations, the company was authorized to sell up to $10,000 worth of stock at $50.00 a share, and to collect tolls from boats using the river. The commissioners appointed to sell the stock were a formidable group, including future Governor Christopher Greenup, Bennett Pemberton, and Thomas Todd from Franklin County. Nevertheless, the company accomplished very little, and nearly three more decades passed before a new, comprehensive program of river improvements was attempted.

Later efforts initiated locally were hardly more successful. In 1803 the assembly passed new legislation authorizing Martin Hawkins to clean the river's western channel at Fish Trap Island and to maintain a navigable channel at a width of thirty feet. To accomplish this, he built a dam across the upper end of the eastern channel, which directed water into the western channel. As compensation for his services, Hawkins was allowed to build a saw and grist mill on the eastern side of the island.

Designed to withstand the high water that covered it at flood stage, Hawkins's mill proved quite successful. Similarly, boats moving downstream had no difficulty navigating the western channel of his works. But for vessels coming upstream it was another matter. Unable to overcome the channel's swift current under normal means, vessels had to be towed through the chute by means of a line attached to a capstan on the bow at one end and a tree at the other. However, this process proved quite arduous, the current sometimes being so strong that the tree would be uprooted. After nearly a decade the legislature concluded that Hawkins's works had become as big a barrier to navigation as Fish Trap Island itself. In January 1813 the assembly repealed the 1803 act and ordered Hawkins to remove his dam within nine months.

One of the most difficult problems of growing cities everywhere has been the provision of a safe, clean, plentiful supply of water. Whether for drinking and sanitary purposes, economic and health needs, or as fire protection, an adequate water supply is absolutely necessary for any urban community. Frankfort was the first town in Kentucky to confront this problem systematically.

As early as 1774 travelers in the Frankfort area discovered Cedar Cove Spring, an excellent source of clear, clean water in the vicinity of Thorn Hill. In 1804 Richard Throckmorton began laying a water line from Cedar Cove Spring, along Brown's Bottom into Frankfort, a distance of about three miles. During 1805, however, Throckmorton exhausted the local resources available to him, even though essential aspects of the project remained uncompleted. Recognizing the importance of Throckmorton's effort, the General Assembly passed legislation in December 1805 to create the Frankfort Water Company. The act named Senator John Brown, William Trigg, and Achilles Sneed as incorporators and authorized them to conduct a sale of stock to raise the construction capital for the system.

Section of cedar pipe used to bring water to the city from Cove Spring.

Their efforts resulted in the completion of the works in accordance with Throckmorton's design. Under this plan a strong rock wall about twenty-five or thirty feet high was constructed across the ravine into which the spring flowed. The effect was to create a large reservoir. The distribution system consisted of a network of wooden tubes constructed from cedar logs cut from trees taken off nearby hillsides. The logs were bored with a one and one-half inch auger and then fastened end-to-end with wooden pins. The entire system functioned so successfully that it remained in operation until 1886, when it was replaced by a more modern works.

The creation of the first water system certainly did not revolutionize Frankfort's fire fighting capacity, but it did create a ready supply of water with which to fight a blaze. The major limitation upon the community's ability to combat fire during these years was not a shortage of water but inadequate organization and personnel. On December 15, 1806, the county clerk recorded a subscription list signed by forty-six persons forming a fire company in Frankfort. The day after Christmas the legislature passed a bill authorizing Governor Greenup to pay up to $700 to a Philadelphia company for a fire engine for the new department. The expenditure of state money for an ostensibly local purpose was justified as a means of protecting public property in the capital. Apparently, however, Greenup failed to follow through on his responsibility, for in 1809 the assembly enacted another bill authorizing and requiring the Frankfort trustees to buy the engine with the funds previously set aside. Whether the engine ever was acquired is not clear. However, the retrospective observation by a late nineteenth century mayor that "prior to

March 29, 1819, the Fire Department consisted of a few individuals who with axes, buckets, etc., repaired to every fire and did what they could to save and prevent the destruction of property adjacent to the property on fire" strongly suggests that the department was limited to the most rudimentary apparatus available.

Another problem related to public safety in urban communities is crime and violence. This was particularly the case in fledgling towns where a "rough and ready" frontier mentality prompted people to take the law into their own hands and to avenge personal slights by extralegal means. This tendency was reinforced by forms of institutional violence, such as slavery.

Frankfort certainly was not immune to such problems. Early court records reveal that numerous felonies were committed before 1800, a period in which most convicted felons were hanged. One of the earliest victims of the gallows was Catherine London, a spinster charged with murder. Tried and convicted on April 3, 1798, she was sentenced to death. On May 10, 1798, about six weeks after her conviction, Catherine London dropped through the trap door of a gallows built near the county jail in Frankfort. A year later a laborer named Augustine Adams met a similar fate after being convicted for horse stealing. Three months later Henry Fields was convicted and sentenced to die for the brutal murder of his wife Sallie. Some astute legal maneuvering by his young attorney, Henry Clay, gained Fields an additional month of life, but the convicted murderer met his death on September 19, 1799. Fields was the last person to be indicted for murder or manslaughter in Franklin County until 1814.

While the law generally ordained the death penalty for felons, there were exceptions. The primary source of exception was the old English concept of "benefit of clergy." As originally conceived, the principle only exempted clergymen from the criminal process before a secular judge. In later years, however, the privilege was extended in some cases to lay people as a means of mitigating the harshness of the law. But laymen were placed on a lower plane than clergy, being subjected to a slight punishment and denied use of the benefit a second time. To prevent a repeat performance, any layman claiming benefit of clergy was branded on the hand with a hot iron. In many cases the identification itself became the punishment. So it was with Hugh Johnson and James Mills, both of whom claimed benefit of clergy after being convicted of felonies in 1798 and 1799 respectively.

Although the punishment inflicted upon felons was a source of drama in the closing years of the eighteenth century, the most frequent penalties were those meted out for minor offenses. Most offenders, therefore, were branded on the hand or sentenced to the pillory, stocks, whipping post, or dunking stool, or some combination thereof. Through the infliction of public humiliation or physical pain, officials sought to prevent repeat offenses while using the embarrassment of the offender to reinforce the majesty of the law.

Imprisonment for crime was a rare occurrence, the jail being used primarily to hold persons accused of crimes and awaiting judgment. As the nineteenth

FIRST KENTUCKY PENITENTIARY (Completed 1799)

century approached, however, Kentucky came under the influence of a widespread reform movement in criminal justice. The primary complaint against the existing system arose from an observation that juries frequently refused to convict clearly guilty offenders rather than submit them to punishments that were out of line with their crimes. Except in the severest cases, the reformers argued, the appropriate solution to crime was not execution, humiliation, or physical brutality but incarceration—denial of personal freedom for a period reasonably proportionate to the gravity of the crime.

Local officials had even more reason to seek alternative means of punishment. Because Frankfort was the capital, the Franklin County jailer often found himself charged with the custody of an unusually large number of accused offenders from other counties who were awaiting trials or hearings in state courts. In 1797 the legislature approved the payment of an additional allowance for these state prisoners, but this did not entirely relieve Franklin County government of the extra costs of these inmates.

Reformist ideology and economic necessity converged in 1798 when the General Assembly passed a bill providing for the acquisition of one acre of ground for a state penitentiary and appropriated $500 for its construction. The act designated Judge Harry Innes, Alexander Scott Bullitt, Caleb Wallace, John Coburn, and former Governor Isaac Shelby as commissioners to select a location for the prison. Innes resolved his colleagues' problems by donating an acre of ground at the intersection of High and Holmes streets.

Construction began in early 1799 and was completed in June 1800. The contractor was Colonel Richard Taylor. The original structure was erected of stone and consisted of a medium-sized two-story block with iron-barred windows and doors. The entire building and grounds were surrounded by a one-story wall in the form of a rectangle. A structure this substantial hardly could have been built on the $500 originally provided by the legislature. Before its completion the assembly found it necessary to appropriate an additional

Richard Taylor (1777–1835)

$8,600 for the project. The facility opened in September 1800 after being approved by a board of inspectors made up of James Blair, Richard Apperson, Nathaniel Richardson, Thomas Love, William Payne, and Daniel Weisiger.

The new penitentiary's first occupant was John Turner, a Madison County laborer sentenced to two years of confinement for horse stealing. The prisoner was placed in the custody of John Hunter, who served as the institution's keeper from 1799 to 1806. Following him were Samuel Taylor and John Glover, who served successive terms up to 1815, when Andrew Miller took over.

If Frankfort's designation as the state capital made politics and government one of the town's chief businesses, public improvements, such as roads, bridges, a water system, and even the penitentiary, improved the overall business climate, whether public or private. And Franklin Countians certainly found many ways to make a living. Outside the town limits of Frankfort agriculture was the mainstay of the county's economic base. On small farms and large estates local farmers raised livestock and cultivated hemp, tobacco, and corn.

But even Frankfort's skilled craftsmen and the professional, financial, commercial, and industrial businesses which developed during these years depended heavily upon the county's agrarian base. Farmers retained Frankfort attorneys to handle their legal matters, had their crops processed by local manufacturers, and sent the finished goods to market through area warehouses.

Franklin County is well suited for agriculture. Much of its soil is very fertile, formed by a rotting limestone rock that serves as a fertilizer, continuously replenishing its productive power as nutritive elements are removed by cultivation. From the beginning local farmers have planted a variety of crops. Cereal grains, including wheats, rye, oats, and barley, were raised in abundance. Similarly, various kinds of fruit were cultivated as early as 1790. Some farmers even saw a future in the wine industry. As a result, several vineyards had been planted by 1800. The county's primary crops, however, were hemp, tobacco, and corn. Along with other grains, they also undergirded local industrial operations.

Hemp cultivation is one of Kentucky's oldest industries. For more than a century it also was one of the most important. As early settlers moved into the Bluegrass, they discovered that the soil was especially suited to the cultivation of the plant's glossy, oval seed. Credit for producing the commonwealth's first hemp is given to Archibald McNeill, who raised a crop on his farm near Danville in 1775. Because of a shortage of seed, hemp cultivation spread rather slowly. By 1790, however, the plant was being grown, broken, and dew retted on farms throughout the Bluegrass. As the nineteenth century dawned, hemp already had become Kentucky's great staple crop, supplying cordage and bagging manufacturers not only in Kentucky but in New Orleans and on the East Coast. Demand was especially strong in the South where the expanding Cotton Kingdom developed a huge appetite for baling cord and bagging material.

Fayette County was the center of Kentucky's hemp industry. But surrounding counties like Franklin quickly assumed strong secondary positions. By the mid-1790s farmers were raising patches of hemp throughout the county. As demand increased so did prices, and in April 1798 hemp sold at Frankfort brought twenty-six shillings per hundredweight. The man who offered this price was the Rev. Elijah Craig, who had just opened a ropewalk on the north bank of the Kentucky River about a mile above Frankfort. In 1809 Major Peyton Short advertised for sale a tract about five miles from town that included a flour mill, a distillery, and "an extensive rope walk." Three years later, Samuel R. Brown reported in his *Western Gazetteer* that several ropewalks were doing business in Frankfort.

While hemp was the major component of Franklin County's agrarian economy during the early years of statehood, tobacco was coming on strong. Like hemp, it found the Bluegrass soil very congenial, but for totally different reasons. Where hemp placed a minimum of strain upon the soil, tobacco tended to exhaust it. However, area farmers soon discovered that by allowing tired ground to lie fallow for a few years, its fertility would be restored by the unique recuperative powers of the rotting limestone that undergirded the soil.

Along with hemp and flour milling, therefore, tobacco cultivation provided a major source of the produce that supported Franklin County's growing warehousing business. In 1798, following in the footsteps of James Wilkinson, the county court appointed Stephen Arnold and William Payne as a committee to find a location for and supervise construction of a large warehouse for the storage of local farm products. Situated on the river bank near the foot of the Louisville Road Hill, the completed storehouse had a capacity of 400 hogsheads of tobacco, 500 barrels of flour, and large quantities of hemp.

As farms became more productive, the demand for storage space increased. In April 1811 the court gave Robert McKee a license to erect a warehouse at the mouth of Benson Creek for the reception of hemp, tobacco, and flour. Two months later, Colonel Richard Taylor received permission to build a public warehouse for the same purpose on the Kentucky River at the mouth of Leestown branch. To exploit the growing production in the southern part of the county, John Green built a warehouse for tobacco, flour, and hemp at the mouth of Glenn's Creek in 1814. No doubt a sizeable portion of the goods coming to Green's warehouse had been produced at the nearby Glenn's Creek grist mill built by John Parker a year earlier.

Another major crop and the basis of one of Franklin County's earliest industries was corn. Part of the local corn crop, of course, went to feed people and livestock. But with a lack of good roads, Franklin Countians, like many other westerners, faced a problem in getting the surplus corn to market. This surplus took on a very real economic value, however, when converted to whiskey. By the end of the eighteenth century Franklin County had become a major center for producing the state's own unique form of the product—Kentucky Bourbon.

The origins of Kentucky Bourbon long since have been obscured in a fog of conflicting fact, fiction, and folklore. Some students favor the claims for Evan Williams, the Jefferson County distiller and politician who in 1783 was criticized for serving a poor quality beverage to his fellow Louisville trustees. Others have pointed to Daniel Stewart, an Irish immigrant who is said to have operated a still at his Fayette County home near Lexington as early as 1789. Perhaps the most popular tradition assigns credit for the invention of Bourbon to the Rev. Elijah Craig, the Scott County ropewalk operator, distiller, and Baptist preacher who supposedly discovered that aging in charred kegs gives Bourbon its mellow aroma and reduces its sharpness. Whatever the truth may be, it is certain that numerous Franklin Countians quickly learned how to turn their surplus corn into a liquid asset.

Ironically, the best indicator of the magnitude of Franklin County's distilling industry is the record of court action against accused evaders of the federal excise tax on whiskey. In 1791, at the request of Secretary of the Treasury Alexander Hamilton, Congress slapped an excise tax upon distilled spirits. The measure had the legitimate purpose of generating national revenue, but it also worked a hardship upon western farmers for whom distilling was the only practical way to make a profit on their surplus corn. The tax itself was onerous enough, but in an area where hard money was scarce, its impact was compounded by the fact that the law demanded payment in specie and required distillers to purchase a federal license to operate their stills.

As news of the loathsome tax spread, anger flared in western Pennsylvania, the Blue Ridge Mountains, and the Kentucky Bluegrass region. Politicians openly branded the measure as unconstitutional. When armed rebellion threatened in Pennsylvania, President George Washington called out the militia to quash talk of further resistance. The most common form of resistance was noncompliance. In Franklin and surrounding counties many distillers simply refused to pay the tax.

Colonel Thomas Marshall and Thomas Carneal, the key federal revenue officers in Kentucky, moved slowly but deliberately in their efforts to collect the tax, trying all the while to work out an accommodation with the recalcitrant distillers. But their efforts to enforce the law continued unabated. Against this pressure, some resisters inevitably gave in, paid their taxes, and bought the necessary distiller's license. Many continued to resist, however, and it was not until 1798 that federal officials finally worked out an arrangement with Federal District Judge Harry Innes to bring the matter to a conclusion. Under the agreement, prosecutors brought indictments against several prominent violators. Innes, whose political sympathies lay with the resisters, assessed token penalties and gave the resisters from thirty to ninety days to pay the fines.

Records of the proceedings indicate that 177 pioneer distillers were hauled

Judge Harry Innes (1752–1816). Innes came to Kentucky from Virginia in 1785. He became the major spokesman of Kentucky's need for protection from hostile Indians. Active in the fight for statehood, he was appointed United States District Judge for Kentucky in 1789 by President Washington, a position he held until his death. This portrait by Matthew Jouett is one of two painted from memory after the Judge's death.

into court. Franklin and Mason counties tied for fourth place behind Scott, Bourbon, and Fayette in the number of violators brought to justice. Fourteen paid fines in both Franklin and Mason counties, along with thirty-one in Scott County, twenty-three in Bourbon, and sixteen in Fayette. Woodford County was sixth with thirteen. Over half of all the Bluegrass region's illicit distillers operated in these six counties, with the remaining cases scattered among fifteen other counties. Among Franklin County's most prominent "moonshiners" was Thomas Tunstall, Judge Innes's own court clerk. Completing the irony of the story is the fact that records of the distillers who paid their taxes and license fees before suffering court action were destroyed by the 1937 flood, making it impossible to determine the total scope of Franklin County's early distilling industry.

While agriculture and related commercial and industrial enterprises formed the core of Franklin County's economy, Frankfort quickly spawned numerous small businesses, many operated by individual craftsmen. In 1801 a hatter named George Baltzel advertised that he had moved his shop to a new location "next door to the Market-House," and expressed "most grateful thanks to his friends and the public in general, for their past favors" and his "hopes by strict adherence to business to merit a continuance of their patronage." A short time later, one of Baltzel's competitors, James McClear, announced that he had "commenced the Hatting Business, in the house lately occupied by Mr. Adam Caldwell" and hoped to "merit a share of the public patronage by the most unremitting Industry and attention to the orders of his customers."

In the spring of 1802 tailor Lewis Moore informed local residents that he had opened a shop at the corner of High Street and Broadway "where he continues to carry on his business as usual, and will be thankful for a continuance of public favor." Moore's business must have been fairly strong because he advertised for an apprentice, "a lad of good disposition and character," to join him in the shop. Some businesses necessary to urban life were not welcome within the town limits. So in March 1803 tanner William Porter advertised that he had opened a tanyard about one mile from Frankfort and promised payment in cash "for green or dry hides." Perhaps reflecting the local shortage of currency, he also pledged to "tan on shares."

Other entrepreneurs established a variety of shops and businesses in the market house and at numerous other locations. In 1793 two businessmen named Samuel and Lafon announced the opening of an "elegant livery stable." Six years later John Mullanphy requested public patronage of his new store, which offered a wide assortment of dry goods, teas, and books. Mullanphy took special pride in the quality and variety of his book selection, whose subjects included law, physics, history, and divinity, with titles by Coke, Adam Smith, Gibbons, Burke, and Volney.

Among the early professionals in Frankfort was Isaac E. Gano, who advertised in 1798 that he had just returned from Philadelphia with "a large and general assortment of fresh and genuine medicine." Gano offered his goods

Mrs. Harry Innes (1760–1851). Ann Harris Shiell, a widow, became the second wife of Judge Harry Innes in 1792. Their only child, Maria Knox Innes, became John J. Crittenden's second wife. Mrs. Innes was known as a highly intelligent woman and lived among her many friends in Frankfort after the Judge's death.

Hon. Isham Talbot (1773–1837). Born in Virginia, Talbot came to Kentucky as a child. Later he practiced law for a time in Frankfort. He served in the State Senate from 1812 to 1815 and in the United States Senate from 1815 to 1819 and from 1820 to 1825.

Martin D. Hardin (1780–1823). Born in Pennsylvania, he established himself in Frankfort as a highly respected lawyer. After fighting in the War of 1812, he served in the Kentucky legislature, in the United States Senate, and was appointed Secretary of State by Governor Isaac Shelby in 1812. He spent the last years of his life practicing law in Frankfort. The date of this portrait is thought to be between 1818 and 1820.

"cheap for cash" to the individual purchaser and promised "a generous allowance . . . to physicians purchasing a quantity." In addition to selling medicines, he also appears to have carried on his own medical practice.

As a state capital Frankfort attracted a particularly large number of attorneys. The local bar already had a goodly membership by 1800, including such prominent figures as Isham Talbott, Felix Grundy, Thomas Todd, James Blair, William H. Hunter, and James Brown. Among the leading attorneys from other counties who frequently appeared in the local courts were Henry Clay, Richard M. Johnson, Robert Breckinridge, and Humphrey Marshall. Ten years later the local bar had added such lawyers as Martin D. Hardin, John J. Marshall, William Littell, John Rowan, and Robert B. McAfee.

Frankfort's status as capital also led to its becoming an early banking center. In 1806 the General Assembly chartered the Bank of Kentucky and authorized the subscription of up to $1 million in capital stock. Headquartered in Frankfort, the institution provided local farmers and merchants in this cash-starved community with a much needed source of capital, despite the fact that stock sales were spread rather evenly throughout the state. Because of several overtly political features of the bank's charter, it was a major source of controversy well into the 1820s. Nevertheless, the Bank of Kentucky virtually monopolized banking activity not only in Frankfort but in the Commonwealth as a whole until the War of 1812, when the legislature created branches in several other towns around the state. This broke Frankfort's monopoly, but it hardly quieted charges from opponents that the Bank of Kentucky tended to favor established borrowers, mainly well-to-do merchants and farmers, in evaluating its loan applications.

Despite its limited size, early Frankfort's status as a political, economic, and financial headquarters caused it to attract an unusually urbane population. Many of the lawyers, planters, bankers, and politicians who formed Franklin County's leadership corps were the sons and daughters of landed Virginia aristocrats, and they demanded the finer things of life, even on the frontier. Consequently, Frankfort also became a vigorous social, cultural, and intellectual center, not only for the elite but for the average citizen as well.

For many people the church was the primary locus of community life. The Baptists, who already had organized the Forks of Elkhorn Church in 1788, continued their organizing activity, forming four new congregations—South Benson, North Fork, Bethel Church, and Union Church—between 1800 and 1810. Close behind were the Presbyterians, who formed the Upper Benson Church in 1795 and the Lower Benson Church in 1806. Instrumental in organizing both congregations was the Rev. Samuel Shannon, a Princeton graduate who served both churches until 1812, when he resigned to become an army chaplain during the War of 1812.

While these congregations served the spiritual needs of outlying residents, Frankfort remained unchurched. In 1810 Mrs. Margareta Brown, wife of Senator John Brown, and Mrs. Elizabeth Love, wife of Major Thomas Love, organized the first Sunday school west of the Allegheny Mountains. Classes met in the garden of Liberty Hall when weather permitted and in the drawing room during inclement weather. But Mrs. Brown and Mrs. Love's classes primarily served the needs of children. Adults, unfortunately, had no place for formal worship.

The constitutional doctrine of separation of church and state not withstanding, the General Assembly moved to rectify the problem in 1812 when it authorized the Frankfort trustees to erect a public house of worship at such location on the public square that "the Governor should deem least incommodious to the buildings of the commonwealth." To raise money the legislators appointed Judge Harry Innes, former Governor Christopher Greenup, Senator Brown, Daniel Weisiger, George Madison, Martin D. Hardin, and Thomas V. Loofburrow as managers of a lottery.

The law also provided that the church "be open and free for any sect or denomination who shall perform divine services therein in a regular and orderly manner." Predictably, many preachers condemned the existence of a church built with "money so unrighteously obtained," but this did not keep them from using it. Baptists and Presbyterians shared the facility for several years without serious competition. Bitter conflict developed, however, when the Methodists requested to use it in the early twenties. The antagonism continued until 1825, when the structure burned to the ground while serving as a temporary chamber for the House of Representatives.

Mrs. Martin D. Hardin (Elizabeth Logan) (1784–1861)

While the earliest churches were organized outside Frankfort, literary endeavors were distinctively town-centered. Frankfort's first newspaper was the *Kentucky Journal*, a short-lived weekly sheet which began publication in November 1795 under the editorship of Benjamin J. Bradford, a cousin of John Bradford, who edited the *Kentucky Gazette* in Lexington. Few copies of this early paper are extant, and the date of its demise is unknown. Three years later, however, a new paper called the *Palladium, a Literary and Political Repository*, made its appearance. Its editors and publishers were William Hunter and William H. Beaumont. The latter resigned from the partnership in 1799, but the paper remained under Hunter's direction until 1809, when he sold it to Robert Johnson and George W. Pleasants. Pleasants died in 1812, but Johnson continued to publish the journal until 1814, when he was joined by Joseph Buchanan. The two men published the paper as the *Kentucky Palladium* until 1816, when they sold out to G. E. and J. B. Russell. The Russells suspended its publication almost immediately when they merged with Amos Kendall, publisher of the influential *Argus of Western America*.

Margaretta Brown (1772–1838)

The Palladium faced no less than five competing publications during its lifetime. The *Kentucky Telegraphe* was published briefly during 1799. James M. Bradford, son of Lexington's John Bradford and cousin of Benjamin Bradford, edited the weekly *Guardian of Freedom* for his father between 1798 and 1805. The following year Joseph M. Street and John Wood began publishing the *Western World*. Wood resigned as editor a short time after publication began, but not before exposing himself to several libel actions as a result of his vitriolic editorials on the so-called Burr Conspiracy. Publisher Street sold the *Western World* to Henry Gore and Trolius Barnes in 1809, and it ceased publication in June 1810. Shortly thereafter, Humphrey Marshall initiated the *American Republic*, the first official organ of the Federalist party in Kentucky. His paper remained in print until 1812. Its demise left the *Argus of Western America* as the *Palladium*'s only competitor. Organized by William Gerard in 1806, the *Argus* later passed to Moses G. Bledsoe and Elijah C. Berry. They held it until 1816 before selling out to Kendall, who soon made the *Argus* one of the nation's leading exponents of Andrew Jackson's political fortunes and Kendall one of America's most powerful editor-politicians.

Newspapers were not early Frankfort's only literary endeavors. Several books related to Kentucky government, politics, and history appeared between 1799 and 1812. The first publication, entitled *The Constitution or Form of Government for the State of Kentucky*, came off the press of Hunter and Beaumont in 1799. Six years later, Achilles Sneed issued *Decisions of the Court of Appeals of the State of Kentucky, 1801–1805*. Because of widespread land litigation, the volume was grabbed off the shelves quickly, making it Frankfort's first "best seller." Two of Kentucky's most important early political works were produced by William Littell, a Frankfort attorney. His *Political Transactions in and Concerning Kentucky* appeared in 1806. Over the decade from 1809 to 1819, Littell turned out his five-volume masterwork, *The Statute Law of Kentucky*. Both works were published by William Hunter.

Unquestionably the most controversial publication of the time was Joseph Hamilton Daviess' 1807 tract *View of the President's Conduct*, a vitriolic recounting of the charges against former Vice-President Aaron Burr by the prosecutor who had failed to convince a local grand jury that Burr was involved in a treasonous conspiracy to set himself up as emperor of a separate American empire in the West. Finally, the year 1812 witnessed publication of Humphrey Marshall's *The History of Kentucky*, intended as the first of two volumes. Friends and foes alike recognized this intensely partisan book as a defense of the author's Federalist political views.

As with religion, organized education first made its appearance outside Frankfort, with the establishment of the Dry Run school about 1790. In Frankfort proper the well-to-do depended upon private tutors to educate their children until about 1800 and for years thereafter upon private schools. But for many people such institutions were inadequate or too expensive. Their needs were better met by quasi-public seminaries or academies whose construction was financed by the proceeds of land grants but which charged the students some tuition. The assembly passed legislation authorizing such grants in 1798. Two years later it passed a bill incorporating the Kentucky Seminary in Frankfort and authorizing its trustees to lay out and sell 6,000 acres of unclaimed land in Franklin County to support the institution. Among the distinguished trustees appointed to direct the school's affairs were Thomas

Aaron Burr

Todd, George Madison, Isaac Gano, Daniel Weisiger, William Trigg, and Joseph H. Daviess. The seminary building, a two-story brick structure, was erected on the Capitol Square facing Lewis Street. The headmaster for many years was Kean O'Hara, father of the famed poet Theodore O'Hara.

A further effort to enhance local intellectual life was the establishment in 1812 of the Frankfort Library Company. Created by the General Assembly, this corporation was authorized to sell stock in a local library corporation and to use the proceeds to build and operate a library. Opened in April 1814, the facility operated from the front room of the Kentucky Seminary. According to a notice in the *Palladium*, the librarian held regular hours from 10 a. m. to 1 p. m. each Saturday. Potential patrons were required to pay a subscription of one dollar or an equivalent donation in books.

Churches, schools, newspapers, books, and libraries played an essential role in giving the early frontier some semblance of urbanity. But they were not, in the final analysis, the quintessential social and cultural expressions in a frontier community. That honor, in Frankfort and elsewhere in pioneer America, belonged to the inns and taverns. At their basic level these businesses provided food, drink, and frequently entertainment for local citizens, as well as overnight lodging for travelers. But even more importantly, they were sources of information. In a time and place where many people did not read and those who did often found up-to-date reading material scarce, the public spaces of the inns and taverns provided an opportunity to obtain and pass on the latest news, exchange gossip, and debate political issues. In a capital town like Frankfort enterprises such as Love's Tavern; Daniel Weisiger's Tavern, at the northeast corner of Montgomery and Ann Streets; or J. J. Marshall's Mansion House at Montgomery and St. Clair streets provided short-term homes for legislators and others in town on political business.

Competition for the patron's dollar was fierce. Some twenty-nine residents of Frankfort and Franklin County held an "ordinary license" between 1795 and 1811. This document was required for anyone to maintain a hotel, tavern, inn, or other public place where liquor was served. Given the intensity of the competition, tavern operators resorted to frequent newspaper advertising which detailed and lauded their services. Richard Price, for example, operated The Friendly Inn, located "at The Sign of the Buck" at the corner of Ann and Montgomery streets. Admitting that "it is usual to puff, in advertisements of this kind," he assured readers "that it will be the steady, constant, and uniform industry of the keeper of this Inn, to merit the patronage and custom of his fellow-citizens." To further entice potential customers, he offered "a large and convenient STABLE, well supplied with everything necessary, and a good and attentive Hostler, his BAR shall be well supplied with every necessary liquor, foreign and domestic." Further, he pledged "to keep his TABLE as well furnished as any in the place" and added that "MEMBERS OF THE LEGISLATURE, and others can be well accommodated with BOARDING."

But apart from their roles as communications and economic agencies, inns and taverns served the social function of bringing together all segments of society on a common ground for entertainment and conviviality. As Willard Rouse Jillson once observed, "Here, in an elemental society, where hunters in deerskin coats and breeches and coonskin caps met, mingled, and bartered . . . with cultured gentlemen from the eastern tidewater towns and plantations dressed in broadcloth and silk tops, tavern jollity afforded the principal amusement of life." In such "stoutly built, well chinked structures," he added, "before great open fireplaces of stone, where logs piled high . . . blazed highly throughout the night, there foregathered the best spirits of the old town." With an ample supply of good food and drink, "including a deal of handmade corn whiskey," the patrons "passed the long cold winter nights in a pleasant round-about of story, jest, and rollicking song."

No doubt one of the more controversial subjects debated by visitors at Frankfort's taverns, especially those which catered to the political trade, was one of the less attractive elements of local society—the institution of slavery. Slavery had come to Kentucky with the earliest settlers. Bondsmen felled trees, built cabins, cleared farms, and helped fight Indians, often alongside their owners. The precise date the first slaves arrived has not been ascertained, but a 1777 census of Harrodsburg listed 19 of the 198 settlers as slaves. When Kentucky's first census was taken in 1790, some 11,830 of the district's inhabitants were in bondage. At that time Kentucky stood seventh among the states and territories in the number of slaves compared to thirteenth in size of the white population.

The peculiar institution also was a serious issue in Kentucky's struggle for statehood. When the Constitutional Convention met at Danville in 1792, Presbyterian minister David Rice urged the delegates to "resolve unconditionally to put an end to slavery in Kentucky." But the efforts of Rice and the minority who shared his views were unsuccessful. Emancipationists failed again to achieve their objectives at the Second Constitutional Convention in Frankfort in 1799. With radical and gradual emancipationists divided over tactics, pro-slavery elements carried the day, with opponents of slavery succeeding only in securing a revision which assured slaves "the privilege of an impartial trial by a petit jury" in legal actions against them. Otherwise, the most stringent restrictions imposed upon slavery came in legislation passed in 1794, which prohibited the commercial importation of slaves into Kentucky from any foreign country. Nothing in the law, however, prevented slaveholders from importing slaves from other states for their own use.

The concerns of Frankfort and Franklin County residents paralleled those of other Kentuckians. From an early date local farmers employed slaves in breaking hemp and cultivating tobacco; slaves were employed in ropewalks and warehouses; and bondsmen served as cooks, maids, coachmen, and gardeners, among other positions, in the homes of wealthy farmers and townsfolk alike. Suggesting the extent of Franklin County's dependence upon slave labor, the 1795 tax lists indicate 706 adult blacks in bondage. Slave children,

JOHN D. RICHARDSON RESIDENCE

Built by Richardson in about 1790 near Collins Lane on a 200-acre farm. An example of a two-story dogtrot log house covered by clapboard.

who represented a capital investment in the future, were not even listed. Fifteen years later, when Frankfort had a total population of 1,011, over 37 percent, or 412 individuals, were listed as slaves.

Indicative of the distribution of slave ownership in Frankfort during the early years, eighty-nine families, or 56.7 percent of Frankfort's 157 households, were listed as owning slaves in the 1810 census. While this suggests fairly widespread slave ownership, a mere ten families owned 174, or 42.7 percent of the town's bondsmen. The largest single slaveholder was John Instone, James Wilkinson's friend from London, who owned 33 slaves. Close behind were William Trigg, attorney and politician, with 29, and tavern keeper Daniel Weisiger, with 20. The remainder of the top slaveholding group owned from 10 to 19 slaves. An additional nine households owned from 6 to 9 slaves, or 58 persons, amounting to 14.1 percent of the total. The remaining 180 slaves, or 43.2 percent of the total, were spread among seventy households who held between 1 and 5 persons. The largest group consisted of thirty-six families who owned one or two bondsmen. These figures suggest that while slave ownership was a fairly widespread phenomenon in early Frankfort, the slaveholding elite was rather small. In future years the distribution of slave ownership would become increasingly narrow and the local slave population concentrated in the hands of fewer and fewer people.

As the slave population increased, the trustees faced the problem of controlling the movement and behavior of servile labor in an urban setting. In 1812 the General Assembly expanded the trustees' powers to police the behavior of all blacks, whether slave or free. Those who appeared to be riotous, disorderly, or without visible means of support could be arrested, jailed, and hired

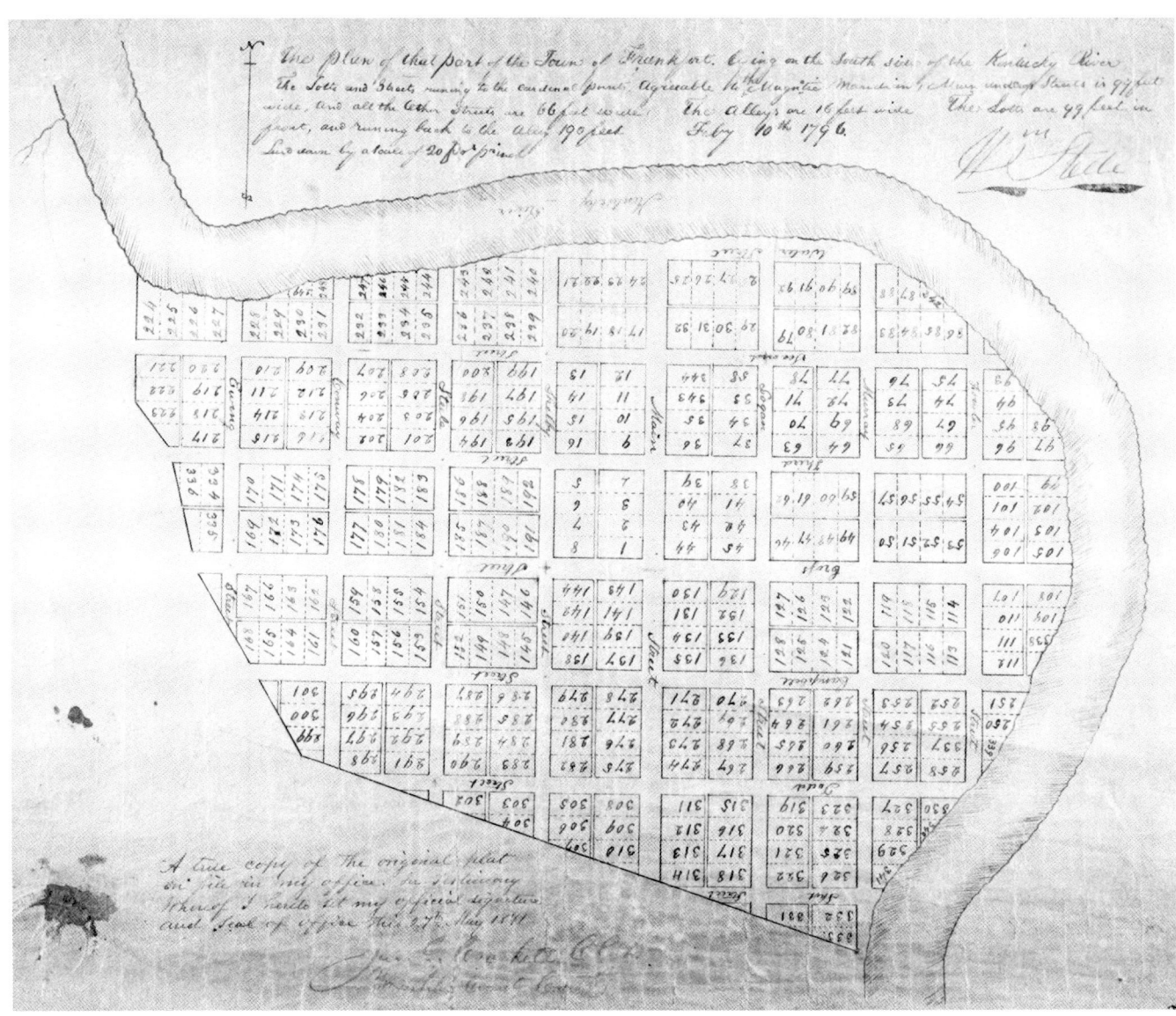

PLAN OF SOUTH FRANKFORT (Feb. 10, 1796)

One of the earliest known layouts of South Frankfort, by local surveyor William Steele. It shows Steele Street, which was named for the surveyor.

out to the highest bidder for up to a month to prevent them from becoming a burden on the town. A slave found off the premises of his or her master after dark without a pass could be punished with ten lashes at the whipping post. To keep them from competing with white tradesmen and from developing the freedom of movement that might result from a degree of independence, slaves were prohibited from working for themselves or hiring out for wages. Any black so charged could be convicted and hired out for up to ten days to the highest bidder, with money so received going to the town coffers. As methods of controlling the black population became even more stringent, the discipline of slaves became another issue in the debate between proslavery and antislavery forces.

While slavery and its future most certainly raised passions among local residents, it was not the only subject of debate. Numerous issues of local, national, and international importance had their way of affecting the lives and raising the ire of local citizens. One local matter, related to Frankfort's physical expansion and population, involved the control of South Frankfort. Although early settlement concentrated on the north side of the Kentucky River, a handful of pioneers were living on the south side by 1794, when the legislature provided them with free passage on Wilkinson's Ferry on election day and similar occasions. It is safe to say, however, that the ferry did not lose much money under this act. South Frankfort was described at the time as a "hilly hollow" eroded by deep ravines, subject to flooding, and dotted with sinkholes. Compared with the flat plain of North Frankfort, these were hardly conditions to encourage settlement. Indeed, only four houses were recorded south of the river in 1805.

But town officials recognized that future growth on the south side was inevitable. When the new plat of Frankfort was finally recorded in 1805, it showed South Frankfort subdivided into 340 lots laid out on a gridiron of eight north-south streets—Ewing, Conway, Steele, Shelby, Main (now Capitol Avenue), Logan, Murray, and Fowler—crossed by six east-west streets—Water (First), Second, Third, Cross (Fourth), Campbell, and Todd. This plat obviously represented a plan for development, not a depiction of what already existed. Those "streets" that were open were little more than dusty lanes, and most were nothing more than lines on the surveyor's map.

Yet the very naming of the South Frankfort streets represented the emergence of a sense of local identity. Unlike North Frankfort, many of South Frankfort's street names commemorated local figures. Shelby Street honored Governor Isaac Shelby; Logan Street probably celebrated General Benjamin Logan; Ewing Street undoubtedly was named for Baker Ewing, first registrar of the Lincoln County land office and an early local businessman; Murray Street honored Attorney General William Murray; Steele Street commemorated William Steele, a state legislator and surveyor who laid out the 1805 plat of Frankfort; and Todd Street was named for Justice Thomas Todd, who also had a home in South Frankfort for several years before relocating to his better known residence at the corner of Washington and Wapping streets.

JOHN HANNA HOUSE

Built for Hanna in 1817–1818. City Hall on Second Street now occupies this site.

Another early resident of South Frankfort was Edward Spillsbee Coleman, a native of Orange County, Virginia, who in 1806 settled on a tract bounded by Steele, Campbell, Conway, and Todd streets. Purchased somewhat earlier by Coleman's father, the tract's chief feature was an abundant spring, first known as Brown's Spring, which Coleman renamed for himself. Nearby he built a tanyard, drawing water from the spring on the same piping principle used in Frankfort's Cedar Cove water works. Sometime later Coleman built a house at 307 West Campbell Street. As settlement increased he was joined by John H. Hanna, who arrived about 1807 and erected a home at 306 West Second Street. A lawyer and federal court clerk, Hanna later became involved in several stage coach lines and was a founder and first president of Farmers Bank of Kentucky.

During the early years South Frankfort apparently was treated as part of Frankfort. But in 1812 it "seceded" from the town and was recognized by the General Assembly as a separate town with its own board of trustees. At the same time the assembly broadened the powers of Frankfort's trustees; it specifically forbade that body from exercising "any power or authority over either persons or property, within South Frankfort." The following year the legislature empowered South Frankfort's trustees to impose poll taxes on free male inhabitants over twenty-one and to assess real and personal property for tax purposes. However, the trustees were prohibited from taxing any warehouse within the town. North and South Frankfort remained totally separate towns until 1850, when they were consolidated under the same municipal government. Certain property and financial matters were not resolved until 1880, however.

One of the hottest controversies ever to engulf Frankfort involved the so-called Burr Conspiracy. During 1805 and 1806, Frankfort hosted intermittent visits by Aaron Burr, who had come west after killing Alexander Hamilton in a duel shortly before the end of his term as vice president of the United States. In Frankfort the former vice president was occasionally observed having back room meetings with various other visitors and politicians at the Love House and other taverns. But few paid much attention until mid-October 1806 when *The Western World* openly accused Burr of treason. The essence of the charge was that Burr and several other conspirators planned to seize part of Mexico from Spain, separate the western lands from the Union, and then forge both areas into a new empire with Burr at its head.

These hysterical charges had many advocates, including President Thomas Jefferson, whose hatred for his ex-vice president was deep and abiding. In Kentucky, one of the staunchest believers was Joseph Hamilton Daviess, the United States attorney, who, ironically, was a Federalist and brother-in-law of Chief Justice John Marshall, for whom Jefferson also shared an intense dislike. Convinced that Burr was involved with General James Wilkinson in a treasonous conspiracy, Daviess asked Federal District Judge Harry Innes for a warrant for Burr's arrest. Not sharing the prosecutor's certainty, Innes refused the warrant but did convene a grand jury to investigate the charges. With attorney Henry Clay at his side, Burr answered the charges to the satisfaction of the jury, which declined to indict him.

But the charges refused to die. Burr was arrested in the Mississippi Territory, escaped custody, and was arrested for the second time in Alabama in 1807. Taken to Richmond, he stood trial for high treason before a federal court conducted by Chief Justice Marshall. The charge, which grew out of the Frankfort episode, was that Burr had committed treason by making war against the United States. But Burr was saved by the Constitution, which requires two witnesses to the same overt act in order to prove treason. When the government was unable to prove that an overt act of treason had even been committed, the jury found Burr innocent, stating that the charge was "not proved."

Although officially acquitted, Burr's reputation had been so damaged by the trials and widespread public belief in his guilt that he exiled himself to Europe. Until recently scholarly opinion has tended to support the belief in his guilt. But new research has demolished this position. It is clear that Burr indeed had conspired with Wilkinson and others to create a rebellion and set up a separate empire in territory to be seized from Spain. But there is no evidence that he intended to separate the western lands from the Union. Moreover, the single most damaging piece of evidence against him, ostensibly a letter to Wilkinson in his own hand outlining final plans for the campaign, recently has been demonstrated to have been written not by Burr but by Senator Jonathan Dayton, a party to Burr's real conspiracy.

To the extent that betrayal did occur, it was committed by Wilkinson, who having been promoted to commander-in-chief of American forces, decided that further participation in the scheme would damage his career. To remove himself from harm, Wilkinson falsified a copy of Dayton's letter and sent it to Jefferson with a claim that it had been written by Burr. The government prosecutors seized upon the letter as a damning piece of evidence. While some who knew the parties recognized that the letter was not Burr's writing, it was Chief Justice Marshall's statement that it contained not a word to suggest treasonable activity that carried the day. Burr unquestionably fell victim to his own conspiratorial bent, but as Wilkinson's early career demonstrates, the former vice president's undoing came at the hands of an even more cunning conspirator.

Undoubtedly the most controversial international issue to confront Franklin Countians during this period—indeed, for generations—was the War of 1812 and the ensuing massacre of River Raisin. The Kentucky frontier had been a hotbed of anti-British sentiment during the months immediately preceding the outbreak of hostilities, one of the chief War Hawks being Congressman Henry Clay of Lexington. When war came Franklin Countians responded in disproportionate numbers to the call for troops, eventually raising two full companies. The first, mustered into service in August 1812, was a rifle company commanded by Captain Paschal Hickman, Franklin County jailer and son of the Rev. William Hickman, pastor of the Forks of Elkhorn Baptist Church. The other officers were Lieutenant Peter Dudley and Ensign Peter G. Voorhies. With the noncommissioned officers and privates, the company totalled eighty-six men.

Five months later the troops were part of a larger force of Kentuckians, under the command of General James Winchester, based on the Maumee River in northern Ohio. About January 10, 1813, Winchester received word from some of the inhabitants that the British had placed a sizable quantity of food supplies at Frenchtown (now Monroe, Michigan), located on the River Raisin just below Detroit. After a brief war council, Winchester dispatched about 660 men under Colonel William Lewis and Colonel John Allen to capture the supplies. In this they were successful. But Colonel Henry Procter, British commander in the vicinity, realized that Winchester had spread his forces too thinly and decided to seize the advantage. On January 22 his troops overwhelmed the Americans at Frenchtown. Over one hundred Kentuckians

Colonel John Allen (1772–1813). Born in Rockbridge Co., Virginia, Allen came to Kentucky in 1780. Brave and competent, he was a well-known officer in the wars with the Indians. He was master of Hiram Lodge No. 4 from 1806 to 1809 and Grand Master of Kentucky from 1808 to 1811. He was killed at River Raisin during the War of 1812.

died and an additional five hundred were captured. Many of those who died were hacked to pieces by Indians under Procter's command.

After the battle ended Procter recrossed the Detroit River, taking with him prisoners who were able to march. Left behind, in the care of American doctors, were a goodly number of wounded prisoners, including many members of Hickman's Company. Following Procter's departure, the Indians began looting Frenchtown. Finding a quantity of whiskey, they became drunk, went on a rampage, and tomahawked and scalped somewhere between thirty and one hundred prisoners. The severely wounded Captain Hickman, whose legs already had been amputated, had his head bashed in and his body thrown into a burning house. Between battle casualties and the massacre only a handful of the Franklin Countians survived.

One who did was Lieutenant Dudley, who escaped and returned to Frankfort to raise another company of soldiers. Hearing Dudley's story of the River Raisin massacre, men flocked to arms. Within minutes after his drive began over one hundred men had joined his line. When he marched out to join General William Henry Harrison, newly promoted Captain Dudley commanded a company that numbered 122 men.

The aftermath of River Raisin did not end with Dudley's successful recruiting drive. Kentuckians got their military revenge in October 1813 at the battle of the Thames, where the Shawnee Chief Tecumseh lost his life. To sweeten the victory, a large number of British prisoners were transferred to Frankfort and confined at the state penitentiary. As prisoners of war the English deeply resented being held in a civilian prison. But neither local citizens nor state officials expressed much sympathy with an army which had left so many of their own friends and relatives exposed to the barbarities that followed the River Raisin. The prisoners eventually were exchanged, but in the meantime they endured the scorn of the local populace.

Colonel Peter Dudley (1787–1869). This view of the War of 1812 veteran was taken in 1859 when he served as instructor at the Kentucky Military War Institute.

To make matters worse, the bodies of the American dead had been left unburied after the massacre, exposing them to the attacks of dogs and hogs, as well as the elements. A few months later Governor Isaac Shelby, now in his second term, sent an expedition to recover the bodies of the dead. Sixty-five skeletons were found and buried. In 1818 they were removed and reinterred in the cemetery at Monroe, Michigan. The bones were exhumed and reburied again in Detroit before being returned to Kentucky and reburied in Frankfort in 1834. Tragically, however, no record of the burial site was preserved, and to this day its location remains unknown.

Consonant with the tone of tragedy that must have pervaded Frankfort and Franklin County during this period was the destruction of the first capitol. Fire swept through the building on November 25, 1813, while citizens were still savoring the victory at the battle of the Thames. Again, Frankfort was forced to make its best bid to remain the seat of government. In January 1814 the General Assembly passed legislation designating John Brown, Daniel Weisiger, Richard Taylor, William Hunter, and Jeptha Dudley as commissioners to oversee site selection, fund raising, and construction for the new capitol. While all were Frankfort residents, they received explicit instructions not to guarantee that the new capitol would be erected in their town. However, local citizens again came through, pledging more than $19,600 for the new statehouse, a figure far in excess of the $550 raised in Woodford County, which ranked second in contributions to the building fund. Such an overwhelming response guaranteed that Frankfort would remain the state capital, and construction of the new capitol proceeded on schedule as the end of the war signaled the passing of an era.

4

Building Up, Reaching Out

JUST AS THE destruction of the first capitol marked the close of Frankfort and Franklin County's formative period, the completion of the second statehouse in 1816 ushered in a new era of growth and expansion. Erected on the same site as its predecessor, the new capitol was a two-story brick structure with a half-story attic. It had an imposing pediment supported by four columns. The entire structure was topped by a tall cupola, which housed a bell forged in Philadelphia. The first floor was devoted to court and committee rooms. The chambers of the state senate and house of representatives occupied the second floor. Other state offices were located in detached brick buildings situated on either side of the capitol. The treasurer's and auditor's offices were located on the west side of the capitol, while the secretary of state's quarters and the land office were located on the east side. The entire project cost approximately $40,000.

Like the first statehouse, its successor was the subject of favorable remark by informed travelers. William Faux, an English farmer who visited America in 1819, commented on Frankfort's "good state, or parliament house." Visiting the same year, Adlard Welby, an English aristocrat who generally disliked anything American, referred to the structure as "a fine object." Two years later George W. Ogden, a Quaker merchant from Massachusetts, was impressed by the "large and elegant . . . statehouse" in Frankfort.

The new capitol was not the only feature which drew the favor of these travelers. Found equally impressive were Frankfort's natural setting, other physical improvements, and its hospitable community. "This pleasant town stands in a fine valley, roomy enough to contain it, but little to spare," observed William Faux. "Nature has fortified and shut it in with inaccessible rocks and hills all around, but the rocks are neither rough nor broken." As for the quality of life, he commented that Frankfort "displays more taste and cleanliness than Lexington city . . . and has the best inn or tavern which I have yet seen in the state. Here is all the accommodation that I need."

Nor did Welby find any reason to speak ill of Kentucky's capital. "The

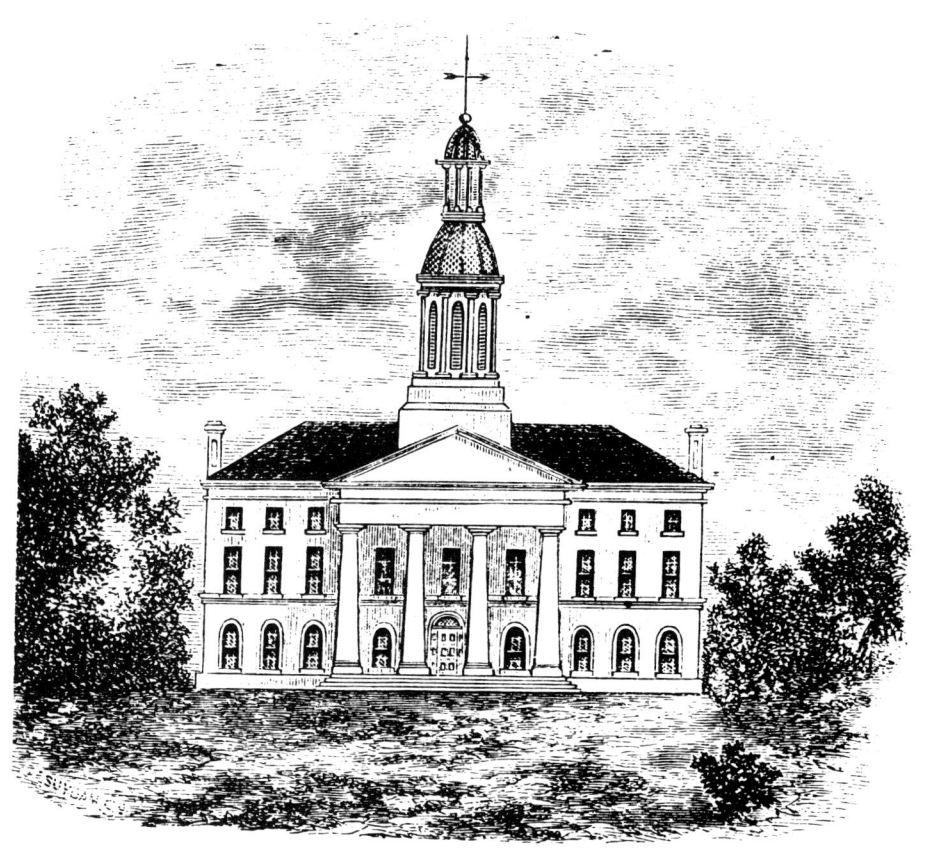

SECOND STATE HOUSE (Built 1814–16)

approach, as well as the country immediately around this capital of Kentucky, is beautiful," he wrote. "Some of the private houses [are] very well built of brick (the general material here) and very handsomely fitted up within." Welby found the Franklin County Courthouse "a very neat building" and spoke in glowing terms of the "excellent tavern and hotel for families lately established by Colonel [Richard] Taylor." Not only did its physical appearance merit favorable comparison with similar houses in London, but "our meals were served with every comfort and polite attention from his lady." Except for Frankfort's limited trade area, he found its "whole effect . . . a far preferable residence to Lexington."

Ogden was equally impressed with Frankfort's physical characteristics, but he also expressed confidence in the town's economic prospects. "Frankfort is a very flourishing town, regularly laid out, containing a number of handsome buildings, both of brick and wood, and is a place of some commercial importance," he observed. But the future seemed to lie in some of the area's infant manufacturing concerns, "which bid fair to become of importance to the state."

These views of Frankfort and its prospects do not appear to have been overstated. While Frankfort did not grow at the same rate as Louisville during

BROWN-SWIGERT HOUSE (300 Washington Street)

Originally a four-room house facing Main, built by Dr. Preston W. Brown in 1815. In the mid-1840's, Jacob Swigert added a one-room deep facade on Washington Street, re-orienting the entrance of the house. An attic story was also added at the time. William Bailey owned the house when this photo was taken in 1922.

the first half of the nineteenth century, it certainly became the thriving core of a growing hinterland community. Between 1810 and 1840, Frankfort's population nearly doubled, growing from 1,099 to 1,917 inhabitants. Growth outside the town was more erratic as portions of Franklin County were carved away to create Owen County in 1819, Anderson County in 1827, and Gallatin County in 1838. Despite these episodic losses, the county's population grew from 8,013 in 1810 to 9,400 in 1840, an increase of 17.6 percent.

Frankfort's growth continued to be clustered within the boundaries platted in 1805. As Welby and Ogden suggested, many of the better houses built between 1815 and 1840 were constructed of brick. One of the more popular neighborhoods consisted of the blocks along Wapping, Wilkinson, Washington, and Montgomery (Main), streets between St. Clair Street and the Kentucky River. This neighborhood has been known since the early twentieth century as the "Corner in Celebrities," because of the some forty distinguished men who have lived there since the late eighteenth century. At least a half dozen outstanding brick homes in the Federal, Greek Revival, and early Italianate styles were constructed in this area between 1815 and 1840.

One of the first was the residence of William Waller. Located at 314 West Main Street and built about 1815, this Federal style house was later the home of Governor William Owsley. About the same time Dr. Preston Brown, brother of Senator John Brown, built a four-room dwelling near the northeast corner of Washington and Montgomery streets. Between 1843 and 1845, Jacob Swigert constructed major additions to the house, which later served as the home of Colonel Edmund H. Taylor, Jr., one of Frankfort's leading distillers.

Governor Robert P. Letcher (1788–1861). After studying law with Humphrey Marshall, Letcher served in the War of 1812. He served in the state legislature at different times from 1813 until 1840, and as governor from 1840 until 1844. Taken by Mullen of Lexington, this may be the earliest photograph of a Kentucky governor.

Governor George Madison (1763–1816) Serving one of the shortest terms, Madison was governor from June 1, 1816 until his death on October 14, 1816.

About 1820 musician and cabinetmaker John Goodman built a home at the southeast corner of Washington and Montgomery streets. Here he conducted a popular music school and built a piano for the daughter of James Garrard, who had served as governor between 1796 and 1800.

The year 1835 saw construction of two more outstanding houses in the neighborhood. The more important was the Orlando Brown house, located near the northwest corner of Wilkinson and Wapping streets and built for the second son of Senator John Brown. The two-story, red brick, Greek Revival structure is one of several in Frankfort designed by the distinguished Kentucky architect Gideon Shryock. While Brown's home was under construction work proceeded on the office of Jacob Swigert, clerk of the Kentucky Court of Appeals. Situated at 308 Washington Street, this two-room structure was enlarged three decades later and became the home of fishing reel manufacturer John Milam. A block and a half to the south, at the northwest corner of Washington and Wapping streets, is the home of Robert P. Letcher, who served as speaker of the United States House of Representatives before being elected Governor of Kentucky in 1840. Several years passed, however, before Letcher had an opportunity to enjoy the house to its fullest, for it was completed about the time his gubernatorial term began.

The Statehouse neighborhood also remained popular. Among those living in the vicinity when the period began were George Madison and Solomon P. Sharp, two of Frankfort's more prominent politicians. Madison, who lived near the northwest corner of Broadway and Madison Street (Catfish Alley), served briefly as governor in 1816 before dying in office. His next door neighbor was Colonel Sharp, whose assassination in 1825 climaxed one of the most heated political controversies in Kentucky history.

Across the Capitol Square, at the corner of Ann and Clinton streets, is the home of Achilles Sneed, a prominent early businessman and politician. Originally designed in the Federal style and constructed about 1820, the brick structure featured a fanlight-topped entrance which was altered and enlarged later in the century. Located across the street from Capitol Square, at 419 Lewis Street, is the three-story, brick Federal home built about 1835 by the Taylor brothers. Standing just over a block away at the corner of Ann and Mero streets is the three-story Greek Revival house built between 1835 and 1840 by Alfred Z. Boyer. It later became the home of Samuel I. M. Major, editor and publisher of the *Kentucky Yeoman* and one of Frankfort's most influential nineteenth century journalists.

Accompanying the growth of the original town of Frankfort was the expansion of adjoining communities such as South Frankfort, Leestown, and Bellepoint. South Frankfort grew slowly during the first half of the century, but completion of the bridge across the Kentucky River in 1816 did stimulate growth somewhat. By 1824 the town had twenty houses and about 120 residents. Six years later the population had grown to 170 persons. Still, development was sluggish enough that local citizens occasionally blocked off little-

Mrs. Alexander Humphreys (Mary Brown, 1763–1836). Born in Virginia, Mary met and wedded Dr. Alexander Humphreys. After his death in 1810, she brought her seven children to Kentucky, settling near Frankfort, where her brother Senator John Brown lived at Liberty Hall. A vivacious woman, Mrs. Humphreys at seventy-three led the Assembly Ball at Frankfort in a black taffeta gown and lace bonnet similar to the attire shown in the portrait by Matthew Jouett.

used portions of the streets and alleys. At one point the trustees ordered John Hanna to reopen the alley near his home at Second and Conway. On other occasions they required Daniel Epperson to remove obstacles from the alley between Shelby and Steele streets and cited Philip Swigert and Lucas Brodhead for running a fence across Main Street.

Once in a while the trustees got into the street closing business, selling unused portions of streets to private citizens. Judge Thomas Todd once paid $100 for "so much of Main Street as lies between Todd's street and the Town limits." Benjamin Hensley, a Frankfort trustee, bought portions of Water Street between Main and Shelby and between Shelby and Steele for twenty-five dollars. In 1834, Mrs. Mary Humphries gave fifty dollars for the west end of Second Street, and in 1837 Sanford Goins got all of Conway Street south of Campbell for the bargain price of three dollars.

Although South Frankfort grew slowly, it was not without its share of the capital's elite. Larkin Samuel lived in a blue, brick home at the corner of Second and Logan streets. According to tradition, he once faced John Hanna in a contest for local office. Balloting was by voice vote, and when all ballots had been cast except those of the candidates, the result was a tie. As frequently happened in such situations, Hanna politely voted for his opponent, whereupon Samuel complimented Hanna as "a gentleman of good judgment" and promptly announced that he would vote the same way, thus winning by two votes. Among the other prominent residents of South Frankfort during this period were Professor Burwell B. Sayre, who lived on Shelby Street; politician

John H. Hanna. Born in Pennsylvania, Hanna spent much of his life in Frankfort. He was a clerk of the United States Circuit and District Courts for over 30 years. A businessman and landowner, he was the first president of Farmers Bank. On December 19, 1831, along with J. Dudley and J.J. Marshall, he gave to the county the land on which the Court House was built. In 1850, he built, furnished, and gave to the congregation the Episcopal Church of the Ascension.

S.I.M. Major House (519 Ann Street). Built for Alfred Z. Boyer in 1844. In 1852, after Boyer's death, the house was sold to S.I.M. Major, Sr. His son, S.I.M. Major, Jr., inherited the house. During his ownership it became a noted gathering place of Frankfort's principal literary and political figures.

William Starling
Portrait is by Matthew Jouett.

S.I.M. Major, who was elected a trustee in 1827; and Charles Scott Bibb, the attorney who represented Jereboam Beauchamp against charges involving the assassination of Solomon P. Sharp.

The most prominent resident of South Frankfort was Charles S. Morehead, a Nelson County native who was elected Kentucky attorney general in 1832. The following year he erected a handsome residence with Federal and Greek Revival elements at 217 Shelby Street. In 1834, Morehead was elected to the South Frankfort board of trustees, and in 1855 he was elected governor of Kentucky.

Settlement at Bellepoint began during the mid-1770s, when Richard Benson, who came to Kentucky with James Harrod, located on the Kentucky River at the mouth of Benson Creek. The area which became Bellepoint was part of the 400-acre tract granted to Edmund Lyne by Governor Patrick Henry in 1786. The land was still thickly forested in 1805 when Governor Christopher Greenup established a ferry, which passed from the west end of Broadway, across the Kentucky River, to a point below the mouth of Benson Creek.

One of the earliest homes in the area was erected about 1799 or 1800 by William Starling. Circuit Judge Samuel Todd purchased the home in 1835, and tradition holds that his second wife, Monarcha Fenwick Todd, entertained President-elect William Henry Harrison with an elegant dinner after his election in 1840. According to the story, Harrison once had unsuccessfully courted the young Miss Fenwick, and on their parting he gave her a ring set with seven garnets and pledged that when he became president of the United States he would grant any request she might make. Dinner at the Todd house for Harrison and his party was her means of redeeming the promise.

Another distinguished Bellepoint family—indeed, the one who gave the neighborhood its name—were the Blairs. James Blair came to Kentucky from Virginia in the late eighteenth century, and by 1800 he was one of Frankfort's leading attorneys. In 1810 he was elected Franklin County attorney, and he later served as attorney general of Kentucky. Meanwhile, Blair purchased a sizable tract of land near the mouth of Benson Creek. Because the land came to a point where the Kentucky River and Benson Creek joined, the site became known as Bellepoint. It was here that Blair's son, Francis Preston Blair, Sr., built the substantial log house which became his summer home. The younger Blair quickly dubbed his home Bellepoint.

A political journalist with a gift for invective, Francis P. Blair was associated with Amos Kendall in publication of the *Argus of Western America*. When Kendall moved to Washington to join President Andrew Jackson's administration, Blair became editor of the *Argus*. But he did not hold the post very long. By mid-1830 Jackson had become disenchanted with the Washington political newspapers which for some time had represented his viewpoint. Because these papers were not under his control Jackson determined to establish a journal which would be responsible to his operatives. When it came time to hire an editor, Kendall recommended his former associate. In the autumn of

GLEN WILLIS

As it appeared in the 1890's. The porch, greenhouse, and two-story wing, all additions to the original house, have since been removed.

1830, Blair rented out his home on Benson Creek, moved to the nation's capital, and became editor of the *Washington Globe*. For the remainder of Jackson's administration Blair served mightily as a "blaring trumpet" for Old Hickory's principles.

With Frankfort's triumph over Leestown in the capital selection contest, the latter community quickly slipped behind its rival in the struggle for primacy in Franklin County. Nevertheless, several prominent citizens continued to express their confidence in the community's future. In 1783, Captain Hancock Lee had given his nephew, Willis Atwell Lee, an acre of ground on Leestown Pike near the Kentucky River, about a mile north of Frankfort. Here Willis Lee built a two-story, double log house which served as his residence for more than thirty years. During this period he became a prominent public official, serving as clerk of the state senate and the county, circuit, and general courts. In 1815 Lee replaced his original home with a one and a half-story brick residence which he named "Glen Willis." He occupied the home until his death in 1824. At that point the house passed to Humphrey Marshall, the tempestuous politician and historian, who resided there until his passing in 1841. During the 1850s, Glen Willis was expanded to three stories and altered in style with the addition of numerous Italianate details.

Another who demonstrated his faith in Leestown was Harrison Blanton, founder of a construction materials business which remained in family ownership for more than 150 years. In 1818 Blanton built the first phase of a Federal

Harrison Blanton. Prominent local contractor during the first half of the nineteenth century. Among his projects are the Morehead House on Shelby and the Orlando Brown House. He also supplied the stone for the Old State House.

STEDMANTOWN

This view, painted during the late nineteenth century, is the earliest known of the community.

style, brick home which stands near Dailey Avenue. Known as "The Beeches," a name which reflected the grove of old beech trees which surrounded the house, its most prominent feature is a beautiful front entranceway topped by a delicate fanlight and framed on both sides by four-paned sidelights.

While the heaviest concentration of population growth occurred in Frankfort and its immediate vicinity, most of Franklin County's increase was scattered among smaller country settlements. One of the major communities in the southeastern section of the county was Forks of Elkhorn, which continued to attract new residents because of the extreme fertility of the soil. In 1822, a short distance to the south, Thomas Jett purchased a farm near the Woodford County line and gave his family name to the community of Jett. To the immediate northwest of Forks of Elkhorn lay Stedmantown, which grew up around the paper mill owned during the early 1820s by editor Amos Kendall and purchased later by Ebenezer H. Stedman. Some distance to the northeast, near the Scott County line, the village of Switzer began to develop in the vicinity of North Fork Baptist Church and Elk Hill, the estate of Charles and Elizabeth Patterson. The village was named for John Switzer, a local storekeeper, whose family moved into the area very early in the nineteenth century.

A key growth center in the northeastern part of the county was Peak's Mill. Located on Elkhorn Creek, the community grew up around Gouldman, Saunders & Bryant's Mill, established in 1819 by Thomas H. Gouldman. He died in 1825, but the mill remained in the hands of his widow and her second husband until 1838, when they sold it to John J. Peak. A Virginia native, Peak operated the mill until his own death in 1853.

Bridgeport, situated on South Benson Creek, was an important village in the southwestern section of the county. At first centered near Abraham Bai-

Ebenezer H. Stedman

ley's tavern, on the main road between Frankfort and Louisville, the focus of development shifted during the 1820s to the intersection of Frankfort and Shelbyville Turnpike and South Benson Road. In 1826 a former Marylander named Frederick Robb arrived in the neighborhood, purchased a tavern, and began speculating in land. During the mid-1830s he sold tavern sites near the intersection to Morris Fox, John Jenkins, and Shelah Bailey, Abraham Bailey's son. Meanwhile, the community had become known as Bridgeport because of two nearby covered bridges which spanned Armstrong's Branch and South Benson Creek. The name achieved a degree of official standing with the establishment of a post office in 1837. The village was incorporated eleven years later with John Jenkins, Frederick Robb, and H. Edwards as the first trustees.

Along with these villages came the construction of several handsome country homes by some of Franklin County's more affluent landholders. During the early years of the century, possibly between 1810 and 1815, Clement Bell, who served as a justice of the peace from 1809 to 1816 and later as county sheriff, built a home known as Bellsgrove on the North Elkhorn upland near Forks of Elkhorn. In 1821, James Major built the two-story brick farmhouse known as Arrowhead. Located off the old Versailles Pike near Jett, the property may have served later as a tavern. Not far to the south of Arrowhead is Wheatland, a brick home built about 1825 as the home of Walker Vaughn.

The substantial population growth experienced by Frankfort and Franklin County between 1815 and 1840 contributed in turn to several political, economic, technological, social, and cultural developments necessary to support a growing community. The presence and power of government at local, county, and state levels increased substantially. The county experienced strong economic growth despite the ravages of nationwide financial upheaval and economically motivated political controversy and violence. Major internal improvements, which resulted in part from technological innovations, contributed to advances in transportation and communication. The growing pains which occurred as more and more people settled in close proximity necessitated better public services. Finally, social, cultural, and intellectual institutions not only proliferated, but many flourished and became more sophisticated as a growing population provided a broader base of support.

The significance of Frankfort's role as state capital was dramatized anew on November 4, 1824, when fire again gutted the capitol. A local newspaper described the destructive impact of the blaze two days later: "On Thursday morning, at half past seven, . . .[a] small blaze was seen issuing forth from near the summit of the building shooting up above the bell vane, and fast extending itself around the cupola. In a few moments the cupola was wrapped in flames, the roof and sides as yet untouched. For a moment this splendid edifice stood to compare great things to small, like a vast lighted lamp—the blazing cupola shooting its vivid flame high in the air. In the meantime, the devouring element was rapidly spreading among the combustible materials of the attic story and beneath the roof, through which it burst in a hundred

SUBSCRIPTION

FOR REBUILDING THE CAPITOL

IN THE TOWN OF FRANKFORT.

WHEREAS, by an act passed at the last session of the General Assembly, the sum of three thousand dollars is appropriated to the Trustees of Frankfort, for the purpose of commencing the rebuilding the Capitol; and the Trustees feeling a deep interest, in common with the citizens of Franklin and the adjoining counties, in having the Capitol rebuilt as soon as practicable, have, in pursuance of the wishes of the citizens of this place, as expressed at a public meeting, ordered subscription papers to be printed and circulated to afford all persons an opportunity of subscribing who may feel interested in effecting so desirable an object: Therefore,

We, the subscribers, do hereby bind ourselves, our heirs, executors and administrators, to pay to the Trustees of the Town of Frankfort, or their successors, the several sums of money annexed to our respective names, at the several periods hereinafter mentioned, viz: *One third* of the sum subscribed, to be paid on the first day of March next; *one third* on the first day of July, and the remaining *third* on the first day of November.

FRANKFORT, JANUARY 3d, 1826.

places. Within a half-hour the roof timbers began to collapse, and in less than two hours the entire structure had been reduced to a pile of smoking rubble."

The destruction of the second capital forced the state senate to establish temporary quarters in the Kentucky Seminary east of the capitol site and the house of representatives to take refuge in the public house of worship on the west side. The house had occupied its temporary chambers a mere thirteen months when another fire destroyed the church and forced the body to move to the Methodist Church located on nearby Ann Street. In January 1827, more than two years after the destruction of the second capitol, the General Assembly enacted legislation to rebuild the statehouse. Again, some of Frankfort's most prominent citizens, including former Senator John Brown, Daniel Weisiger, Captain Peter Dudley, Senator John J. Crittenden, state legislator John Harvie, Evan Evans, and James Shannon, were appointed commissioners and empowered to contract on behalf of the state for the construction of the new capitol.

Unlike the two previous boards of capitol commissioners, this one made no pretense of looking outside Frankfort for a site. The two years since the loss of the Statehouse had been a period of stagnation in the community, and the commissioners were determined that any uncertainty over Frankfort's status be resolved immediately. Armed with a cash appropriation of $15,000 plus $5,000 in articles from the penitentiary, the board quickly solicited plans for rebuilding the capitol, offering a $150 premium for the plan which was finally accepted. In mid-February they adopted plans and estimates submitted by a twenty-four-year-old architect named Gideon Shryock. Their decision proved remarkably significant for the future of public architecture in the Commonwealth.

Born in Lexington on November 15, 1802, Shryock had only recently completed a period of study in architecture and engineering under William Strick-

Gideon Shryock (1802–1880). Portrait by Matthew Jouett about 1827, when Shryock was supervising construction of the Old State House.

land, a leading Philadelphia architect. Because of his inexperience the young designer had given little thought to seeking the capitol commission. But some of his friends, who realized that even an unsuccessful but well-considered submission would bring his name before the public, persuaded him to enter the contest. His winning design marked the beginning of a career which would make Shryock the Father of Greek Revival architecture in Kentucky and one of the leading exponents of the style in the United States. Among his other major Kentucky works were the Jefferson County Courthouse and Morrison College in Lexington, plus several other commissions in Frankfort.

His plans approved, Shryock moved to Frankfort in the spring of 1827 and began work on the new Statehouse almost immediately. The edifice was constructed primarily of "Kentucky Marble," a type of limestone quarried by Humphrey Evans and Jack Holbert and supplied by Harrison Blanton. Joel Scott, keeper of the penitentiary, aided significantly in the construction work by inventing a steampowered sawmill to cut the rough stone. Although occupied by the General Assembly in December 1829, the new capitol was not completed until 1830—after three years of construction and a cost of $85,000.

Designed in the Greek Ionic order, the structure features a marble pediment supported by six columns, each one four feet in diameter and thirty-three feet high. It was originally covered by a copper roof and is topped by an imposing cupola. The cupola sits on a twenty-five foot square pedestal, which rises two feet above the apex of the pediment. The cupola itself consists of a circular lantern, which measures twenty-two feet in diameter and twenty feet in height, topped by a hemispherical dome. The entire structure, including the portico, is 132 feet long and 70 feet wide. The aesthetic success of the new capitol brought Shryock almost instantaneous fame, and more than 150 years later it remains a masterpiece of Greek Revival architecture.

The third capitol was not the only new building constructed on the Public Square during this period. For some years the state had stored arms and ammunition in a small gun house located on the square. In 1834 the legislature passed a bill authorizing the demolition of this structure and the construction of an arsenal at the northeast corner of the square. Appointed to oversee the project were Colonel James Davidson, Thomas S. Page, and Edmund H. Taylor. The new arsenal was completed quickly at a cost of $2,000. Some of the surviving materials from the old gun house were used in the new building.

Unfortunately, the new arsenal was not fire proof. Recognizing the danger posed by this situation, the General Assembly at its 1835 session enacted legislation to solve the problem. But the action came too late. About three o'clock on the morning of March 12, 1836, before corrective measures could be taken, some of the powder exploded, and the arsenal soon became engulfed in flames. "The coldness of the night, the unusual hour, and the rapid march of the fire," according to a newspaper account, "all combined to prevent anything like a successful attempt to subdue the flames. In a short time nothing remained but a heap of rubbish." One of the few items to survive was a brass

THIRD (PERMANENT) STATE HOUSE

Only through the urging of friends did the 25-year-old architect Gideon Shryock submit this plan for the new statehouse. Shryock could hardly have realized the building's significance at the time as the first Greek Revival style capitol in the United States.

cannon which had been captured by American forces at the battle of Saratoga, returned to the British when American General William Hull surrendered Detroit in 1812, and retaken by General William Henry Harrison at the battle of the Thames in October 1813.

The new capitol and arsenal were not the only facilities that occupied the attention of state government during the period. In 1815 John Glover was succeeded as keeper of the penitentiary by Anderson Miller, who in turn yielded the position to William Starling, a Frankfort merchant, in 1816. Starling remained in the post until 1819, when he turned it over to General William Hardin. Under Hardin's supervision, work opportunities for convicts were considerably expanded, and the facilities were enlarged to provide the space necessary for these new activities.

In 1822, for example, Hardin obtained authorization to build a smoke house inside the penitentiary, enabling the facility to participate in Franklin County's growing meat packing industry. In March 1823 James I. Miles, an agent for the prison, announced in the *Argus* that the penitentiary store had been moved into a three-story brick house on Montgomery Street. Here the public could purchase a wide variety of goods manufactured by the convicts. Among the many articles for sale were farm implements, tools, iron rods and hooks, drawing and log chains, kitchen and fireplace utensils, bridles and other leather goods, furniture, bits and screws, and a host of other items. The same year the original building was enlarged and enclosed by a stone wall twenty-six feet high.

Despite these apparent improvements, the General Assembly had reason to question the competence of Hardin's management. The January 1824 report of a joint committee appointed to study penitentiary operations spoke favorably of the quality of both the materials and workmanship that went into the recent physical improvements. But it found the workshops in bad repair and too cold for winter use, suggested that the convict work force was not employed in the most profitable manner, complained that many of the articles on sale at the prison store were overpriced, and expressed concern over the shortage of cells for solitary confinement. Reflecting the prevailing corrections theory of their time, the legislators were certain that convicted criminals required solitary confinement so that they could contemplate and meditate on the enormity of their crimes. The shortage of individual cells necessitated placing convicts together, undermining "the reform of the culprit."

After months of further study, the legislature solicited proposals from private contractors desiring to manage the penitentiary. The assembly received numerous responses, but the most impressive came from Joel Scott, a Scott County millwright who operated a successful cloth manufacturing business. The General Assembly was so taken with Scott's program that in January 1825 it elected him keeper and invited him to implement his ideas.

Scott wasted little time putting his program into effect. During his first year he made physical repairs designed to reduce escapes, conducted a general

Joel Scott (1781–1860). Scott was the seventh keeper of the Kentucky Penitentiary from 1825 to 1834. Under his guidance, convict labor was used in enterprises such as furniture making and quarrying. Scott invented a saw consisting of 16 parallel blades to swiftly cut stone for the third statehouse.

FRANKLIN COUNTY COURT HOUSE

In June, 1832, a plan submitted by Gideon Shryock was adopted for the new Court House. Completed in 1835, the new structure cost $12,500. The building appears as it did before its remodeling in 1909.

clean-up of buildings and yards, and dramatically improved the quality of clothing and food. He also broadened the range of manufacturing activity available to convicts and reduced the prices of articles at the penitentiary store. For nine years, through a combination of firm discipline, sound program management, and humane treatment, Scott made the institution a source of profit to the state and an object of pride to the public. The house of representatives resolved at the time of Scott's retirement in January 1834, "Mr. Scott . . . had the satisfaction of knowing that while under his care [the penitentiary] . . . had been completely revolutionized—changed from a den of filth and corruption to the dignity of respectability."

Scott turned over management of the penitentiary to Thomas S. Theobald in 1834. Also a resident of Scott County, Theobald had been a merchant, soldier, postmaster, and United States customs official before coming to Frankfort as keeper of the penitentiary. Sharing much of Scott's philosophy, he continued to operate along the same lines as his predecessor. Theobald's primary accomplishment involved physical expansions that Scott desired but had been unable to achieve. During 1835 and 1836 the workshops and other buildings and grounds were enlarged. Meanwhile, in 1835 the legislature provided the money necessary to expand solitary confinement. Although materials shortages delayed construction, the expansion was completed in 1837, along with the castle-like twin towers that housed the keeper's office and which became the institution's front entrance. Said to have been a replica of Warwick Towers in England, this imposing edifice symbolized Kentucky's penal system—for good or ill—for more than a century.

Penitentiary Towers

The problem of expanding or rebuilding government buildings in Frankfort was not limited to the state. By 1815 the original Franklin County jail had become overburdened, and county officials determined that it should be replaced. Appointed to supervise the project were John J. Marshall and Richard Taylor, who already had built the penitentiary. Using $2,500 appropriated by the county court, they erected a new jail near the corner of Lewis and Clinton streets. Five years later the court authorized $3,000 for the construction of a brick wall, twelve feet high, around the jail and its grounds and for a jailer's home at the rear of the institution. Whether as a result of excessive strain on the facilities or inadequate capacity, the entire jail had to be rebuilt and the jailer's house repaired in 1822.

By the early 1830s county officials were running out of space in which to administer the affairs of the growing county. In June 1832 the court engaged Gideon Shryock to develop plans for a new courthouse. Appointed to supervise the enterprise were Henry Wingate, James Shannon, and Charles S. Morehead. Again employing the Greek Revival style, Shryock designed an elevated, two-story, limestone structure highlighted in front by four stone columns. The first floor was devoted to the court room and offices of the justices of the peace and the sheriff, while jury rooms occupied the second floor. Although in use by 1835, the building was not paid for until 1840, reflecting perhaps the financial hard times which followed the panic of 1837.

While state and county governments expended much of their time and revenue on physical facilities, the town officials devoted most of their energies and resources to more substantive matters. Indeed, Frankfort remained without a town hall throughout the first half of the century, and the board of trustees rotated its meetings among sites such as the county courthouse and Kentucky Seminary. As for business, the trustees spent most of their time dealing with housekeeping and police duties, such as paving streets and sidewalks, laying gutters, maintaining the fire company's apparatus, sinking wells and maintaining pumps, collecting taxes and paying bills, removing nuisances, regulating the market house, and policing the behavior of slaves.

Such matters continued to dominate the trustees' agenda until at least February 1835, when passage of a new incorporation act substantially altered the structure and expanded the powers of town government. Under the new act the board of trustees remained a seven-member body, but the president was elected independently of the other six trustees and took on minor judicial powers. The new body also obtained the power to lay off the town into wards and to assign "an equal proportion of trustees" to each ward according to population. In addition, the structure of government was widened by the creation of the offices of town clerk, assessor, treasurer, marshal, and market master.

Besides preserving and expanding the trustees' existing powers, the legislation broadened their authority by permitting them to operate and receive real estate for a public school; to purchase a cemetery; to erect and supervise a work house for vagrants and rioters; to tax and regulate taverns, stores, entertainers, and auctioneers; to license wagons, carts, and other vehicles; and to regulate traffic. Two months after passage of the new incorporation act, the trustees passed a comprehensive ordinance which codified all new and existing ordinances for the health, safety, and general operation of the town. In addition to subjects mentioned above, the new code contained a section which prohibited kite flying "in, or over any of the streets, or public grounds." A free person who violated the ordinance was subject to a fine of two dollars, while a slave who did the same risked ten lashes.

The new town structure did not remain in full force very long. In February 1837 the assembly passed new legislation which abolished the independent position of chairman of the board of trustees. Under the amendment, the board reverted to its former situation, with the chairman being elected from among the members by the body itself. In addition, the chairman lost his judicial powers, which were transferred to the newly created position of police court judge, who was to be appointed by the governor and who would hold a life-time appointment.

However mundane its powers might have been, the board of trustees continually attracted to its ranks members of Frankfort's political, economic, and social elite. Among the distinguished citizens who served on the board between 1818 and 1840 were journalists Francis P. Blair, Sr., Amos Kendall, and

Francis Preston Blair (1791–1876). In 1845, prominent American artist Thomas Sully portrayed Blair while he was editor of "The Globe" in Washington, D.C. This engraving of the portrait was made by John Sartain in the same year.

William Hunter, jail commissioner Allen F. McCurdy, businessmen Achilles Sneed and Philip Swigert, South Frankfort land owner Benjamin Hensley, educator Mann Butler, tavern keeper Daniel Weisiger, Colonel James Davidson, and civic leaders Thomas V. Loofburrow and Henry Wingate. These men and others like them moved easily in the highest state and national financial and political circles. That they devoted so much time to the undramatic affairs of local government is not so much a unique local phenomenon as it is a tribute to the continuing sense of responsibility among local elites to the well-being of their own communities during the first half of the nineteenth century.

Amos Kendall

The citizens of South Frankfort likewise witnessed the expansion of local government. In January 1817 the General Assembly passed legislation for the annual election of a five-member board of trustees, all of whose members were to be residents of the town. As in Frankfort proper, the South Frankfort trustees were empowered to maintain and repair streets, impose and collect taxes, regulate and tax shows and other entertainments, and appoint a town clerk to oversee the day-to-day operation of town affairs. Twelve years later the assembly authorized the trustees to elect a treasurer, who would administer the town's financial matters. Two days after passing this legislation, the assembly created a new constableship in Franklin County and required the new officeholder to reside in South Frankfort.

South Frankfort's municipal government remained essentially unchanged for nearly a decade thereafter. But in February 1838 the powers of the trustees were expanded again, specifically permitting them to receive donations of private property for streets and alleys, to remove and abate nuisances, to organize and operate fire companies, and to appoint a town marshal along with the clerk and treasurer. Copying the legislation passed for Frankfort a year earlier, the assembly also provided for the appointment by the governor of a police court judge in South Frankfort. Like his counterpart north of the river, the new judicial officer would have jurisdiction over minor criminal and civil matters and the power to issue warrants for breach of the peace and violations of town bylaws.

As in Frankfort, local government in South Frankfort attracted the town's leading citizens, including a goodly number who later served comparable positions in Frankfort. Among South Frankfort's more prominent trustees were Evan Evans, who was appointed a capitol commissioner in 1827; Samuel South, who served several years as a state legislator and as state treasurer; the Rev. Eli Smith, first pastor of First Presbyterian Church in Frankfort; Samuel I. M. Major, a local civic leader; the Rev. Samuel M. Noel, a prominent lawyer and minister; and George W. Gwin, who later served as mayor of Frankfort. In addition, Henry Wingate, a long-time Frankfort trustee, became clerk of the South Frankfort board of trustees in 1820.

Supporting the expansion of government between 1815 and 1840 was the growth and diversification of the local economic base. Agriculture remained

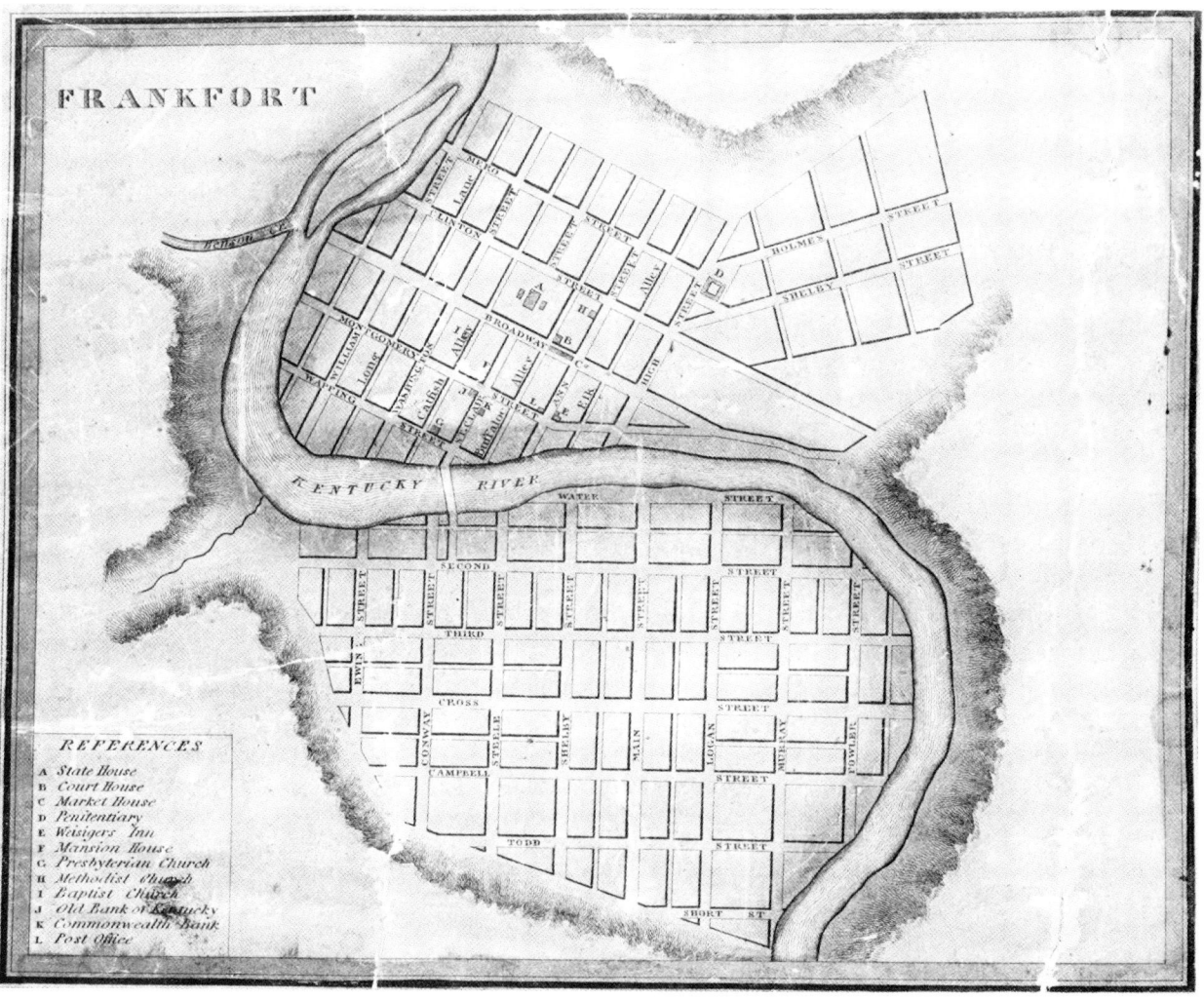

FROM MUNSELL'S 1834
MAP OF KENTUCKY

a mainstay of Franklin County's economy, with hemp, tobacco, and cereal grains continuing to provide a major portion of the agricultural income.

Hemp was a particularly important commodity, as production in Franklin and eight neighboring counties constituted two-thirds of Kentucky's entire crop by 1840. The growth of the hemp economy was directly related to the westward expansion of Southern cotton production. As the Cotton Kingdom spread, it required larger quantities of rope and bagging materials used in picking and shipping the product. Because of the relative simplicity of hemp cultivation, farmers in the hemp counties found that with a comparatively small number of slaves they could realize a steady, substantial return on their investment.

Tobacco, while remaining an important crop in Franklin County, proved much riskier and less profitable than hemp. Much more so than hemp, it was subject to cycles of fluctuating prices and profits. During the 1830s and 1840s, in an effort to put their land to more lucrative use, many Bluegrass farmers turned to livestock as their primary source of income. As early as 1816, Henry

Clay imported two pairs of Hereford cattle into Kentucky and set them to grazing on the luxurious Bluegrass at Ashland, his Fayette County farm. By the late 1820s, livestock and hemp ranked as Kentucky's leading exports, and Franklin County was a major center for the production of both.

While its extensive grazing areas were significant in the growth of Kentucky's livestock industry, two other factors were important as well. First, the feeding of cattle and hogs provided an alternative use to distilling for the region's corn crop, relieving growers of the federal excise tax which they had to pay when converting their corn to whiskey. Second, Louisville's emergence as a major Western livestock market, symbolized by the establishment of Bourbon Stock Yards in 1834, provided Franklin County farmers with a dependable outlet for their livestock.

The receipt and shipment of Franklin County's agricultural goods continued to be a major component of local commerce. Thus, in November 1817 inspectors at the Frankfort Warehouse reported that the facility had received 389 hogsheads and shipped 306 hogsheads of tobacco during the previous season. The following year, exports of all commodities from three warehouses in Frankfort and Leestown had a total value of $324,164, while the value of imports coming into the two communities totalled $312,630. Major exports included flour, processed beef and pork, tobacco, lard, bagging, rope, bacon, candles, and soap. Leading imports were salt, iron, beer, sugar, fish, and earthenware.

As important as it was, however, warehousing was not an easy business, as Samuel Lewis's experience with the Frankfort Warehouse suggests. The nationwide depression that followed the panic of 1819 cut deeply into Lewis's business. In the fall of 1821 he reassured potential shippers that his establishment was "now in complete order for receiving produce, and is admitted by all persons to be one of the most convenient and extensive Ware Houses in the Western Country." But recovery brought new problems. "An erroneous opinion has gone out," he noted, that obstructions in the Kentucky River posed "great danger in shipping from the Frankfort Ware-House to the Leestown Ware-House." In an attempt to ease their minds, he reassured shippers that "no boat has ever been injured passing from my Ware-House to Leestown," but that the boatmen in his employ had the highest experience of any available. A year later Lewis advertised that he had moved to the warehouse to provide closer management and offered extremely advantageous rates, including "no commission for shipments . . . to and from Louisville." But these efforts proved futile. In early 1824, Lewis signed a deed of trust authorizing Harrison Blanton to sell the warehouse to pay off a debt Lewis owed to the Bank of Kentucky.

One of the most important developments in local commerce between 1815 and 1840 was the emergence of a rudimentary central business district in Frankfort. Wholesale and retail activity was concentrated initially in the market house, which stood in the middle of Broadway between Ann and Lewis

FRANKFORT, KY

streets. But as time progressed, activity gradually expanded along St. Clair to Montgomery between Washington and Ann streets.

In the absence of any but the sketchiest records, it is almost impossible to describe day-to-day business operations at the market house. By May 1819, however, the volume of business and accompanying problems had reached such a magnitude that the trustees found it necessary to impose extensive regulations for the market. Much of the ordinance dealt with basic matters such as operating hours, quality of goods, and the duties of the market clerk. Among other things, the clerk was obliged to settle disputes between sellers and buyers, insure the accuracy and honesty of weights and measures, oversee the physical arrangement of the market, and direct the movement of traffic within and around the premises. The legislation also prohibited speculation, by forbidding the purchase of any article at a given price and its resale at a higher price on the same day.

After the General Assembly's passage of the incorporation act of 1835, the trustees issued an even more extensive set of market regulations. While the basic provisions of the 1819 ordinance remained in force, the scope of the trustees' authority, exercised through the newly created position of market master, was broadened considerably. The new ordinance provided for regular maintenance of market facilities, prohibited competitive sales within Frankfort during market hours except in the market house, strengthened account-

J. J. MARSHALL'S MANSION HOUSE

Built in the shape of a letter L, extending along Main & St. Clair streets with office and lobby at the corner. The first floor consisted mainly of two-room apartments, with an entrance to the street from the front room of each apartment. The rear room of each apartment opened onto a wide gallery that extended around the inside of the building.

ing procedures, and prohibited retail sales of alcoholic beverages in the market house.

Although the market house remained a major center of trade, merchants began at an early point to establish businesses at locations other than Broadway. In 1819, S. A. Van Duerson operated a bakery on Lewis Street between Broadway and Montgomery. Along Montgomery Street itself one could patronize grocery stores operated by Alexander Boggs and Strother J. Hawkins, a confectionary owned by F. & J. Reynolds, jewelry stores owned by Warham P. Loomis and Samuel Phelps and by Wooldridge and Moss. The same year William Hunter opened an auction and commission business on Montgomery Street. The firm specialized in books, watches, jewelry, dry goods, and "fancy articles."

The expansion of the central business district continued into the 1820s. In November 1820, a Doctor Washington advertised the availability of nearly a hundred "Fresh Medicines" at his apothecary shop on Montgomery Street. The following year merchant Charles Miles offered for sale a wide range of clothing and other cloth goods from New York and Philadelphia. In 1822 Amos Kendall and Gervas Russell offered a wide assortment of literature at their Frankfort Book Store. During the 1830s several new businesses opened along St. Clair Street. One of them was Keenon and Robertson's Book and Stationery Store, opened in 1834 near the capitol. The new establishment carried "a great variety of Standard works of the latest and last editions in History, Belles Lettres, Poetry, Laws, Medicine and Divinity," as well as popular novels, school books, Bibles, stationery, and business supplies.

Inns and taverns continued as well to constitute a major segment of downtown business. As the nineteenth century matured, J. J. Marshall's Mansion House, erected during the first decade of the century at the corner of Montgomery and St. Clair streets, superseded Love's and Weisiger's taverns as the town's leading hostelry. About 1818 this large, three-story, brick structure came under the ownership of Colonel Richard Taylor, who promoted it as "one of the largest establishments in the Western Country, . . . fitted for comfortable accommodations on the most extensive scale."

By the mid-1830s, however, the place had begun to show the effects of age and required extensive repairs. In November 1835, William Owsley, Edmund H. Taylor, Mason Brown, Charles S. Morehead, Harrison Blanton, Orlando Brown, John Hanna, and some eighteen other prominent Frankfort businessmen formed a joint stock company to purchase and repair the Mansion House. The new company committed to sell stock amounting to $12,500 to cover the purchase price and an additional $5,000 in stock to repair and refurbish the hotel. Partially because of the success of their efforts, the life of the Mansion House was extended for more than fifty years.

While the Mansion House purposefully sought the most elegant clientele, other establishments catered to more specialized markets. Mrs. Hannah Price's boarding house on Montgomery Street, for example, sought the patronage of young, single women who had come to Frankfort to attend one of the local female seminaries or music schools. A short distance away, at what is now 101 West Main Street, John Hampton operated a popular river tavern. Built about 1815, this finely crafted stone structure appears to have served as a tavern until 1840, when it was expanded and converted into a residential dwelling. Still another type of establishment was the Franklin Exchange, owned and operated by F. D. Pettit. Located on St. Clair Street and opened in 1835, his house sought the patronage of "gentlemen" who liked good food and drink. To satisfy his customers' tastes, Pettit offered "the best Foreign and Domestic liquors the town afford [sic]" and promised "strict attention . . . to the cookery, so as to render it equal, if not superior to any done in the west."

Providing lodging for travelers also was an important business along the main roads outside Frankfort. One of the most popular of Franklin County's many country inns was William Owen's Tavern, located in Benson Valley on the old Boone's Trace, which extended in one direction to Louisville and in the other to New Castle and Madison, Indiana. Originally constructed about 1820 as a home for William Owen, Jr. and his family, the large, two-story structure was built of poplar logs. Across the front stretched a high veranda. But the place served its intended purpose only a short time. In 1821 Owen appeared before the Franklin County Court seeking a tavern operator's license.

Once having opened, Owen had little if any latitude in the prices he charged, because "tavern rates" were fixed by the county court. On the basis of rates in effect at the time, a single traveler on horseback could obtain a night's lodging, eat three meals, and stable and feed his horse for the princely sum of $1.25. Liquor was extra, with prices ranging from 12½ cents for a half-pint of whiskey to $2.00 a quart for Madeira and other imported wines. Owen presided over his establishment until his death in 1837. It passed to his daughter, Emily, and her husband Leroy Wooldridge, who conducted the business until 1865.

One of the most important developments in the local economy was the diversification of manufacturing activity. Such well-established activities as hemp processing, whiskey distilling, and grist milling continued to thrive mostly on a small scale. By 1840, however, local factories were turning out such products as glass, brushes, boxes, monuments, linsey and jeans cloth, pork, lumber, cabinets, barrels and kegs, wagons, steamboats, and a wide array of tools, farm implements, and other iron products.

The diversification of Frankfort's manufacturing base began at a fairly early date. In 1819 John West opened a coach and harness factory on Lewis Street. In mid-1825 John P. Cammack announced that he had moved his rather extensive cabinet and furniture shop from South Frankfort to a location at Montgomery and Ann streets.

Mill at Stedmantown

Industrial operations proliferated during the 1830s. By 1831 Thomas McGrain had established the Frankfort Tin Ware Manufactory. Located on Montgomery Street opposite Weisiger's Tavern, the shop produced kitchen goods ranging from brass kettles to cooking stoves and boasted prices competitive with those anywhere else in the United States. McGrain got some competition in 1836 when John D. McGee and John C. Melcher opened their sheet iron manufacturing business. Situated on St. Clair two doors north of Montgomery, the establishment also manufactured stoves and numerous tinware products. Meanwhile, in 1834 brothers Ebenezer H. and Samuel Stedman had purchased Amos Kendall's Franklin Paper Mill on Elkhorn Creek. Within a short time, the Stedman brothers were producing almost every conceivable type of paper and shipping it all over the country.

The year 1839 witnessed incorporation of the Franklin Mining and Smelting Company. But perhaps the most famous business start of the year was the partnership founded by Jonathan B. and Ben F. Meek to manufacture fishing reels. Originally watch and jewelry makers, the Meeks began making reels for themselves and their friends during the mid-1830s. As word of the quality of their workmanship spread, potential customers came to them for custom reels. In 1839 the brothers abandoned watchmaking and began making reels full time. They later were joined by B. C. Milam, himself a former watchmaker, who eventually gained control of the firm. First located at 222 West Main Street, the business subsequently won prizes at such events as the Chicago World's Columbian Exposition of 1893 and the International Exposition at Paris in 1900.

The Milam fishing reel.

One of the critical problems that confronted farmers, merchants, and manufacturers during the period was Kentucky's chaotic banking system. When the War of 1812 ended, the United States was already in the midst of a major economic boom. Triggered by wartime demand, the expansion continued after the war, nourished by easy credit from the newly created Second Bank of the United States. Along with the boom came skyrocketing inflation, rampant land speculation, and ballooning debt. By 1817 the boom had nearly exhausted the credit capacity of the Bank of Kentucky and its branches. The demand for new credit to sustain the boom intensified a campaign to permit the establishment of independent banks. The 1817–1818 session of the General Assembly finally yielded to expansionist pressures and passed a bill which permitted the chartering of forty-six independent banks with a total capital of $9 million. Among the new institutions was the Frankfort Bank, chartered in January 1818 with a capital stock of $500,000. The directors of the new bank, located on the north side of the Kentucky River between Ann and St. Clair streets, were John H. Hanna, Henry Crittenden, Samuel Lewis, William Hunter, and George Adams.

The new Frankfort Bank had little opportunity, however, to make a major impact on the local financial scene. Two months after passage of the independent banking legislation, the collapse of the financial empire of James Prentiss, a leading Lexington manufacturer and insurance financier, punctured Kentucky's economic balloon. As capital began to dry up, the Louisville and Lexington branches of the Bank of the United States started calling in their loans. With similar deflationary tendencies developing in other states, the economy went into a tailspin. By 1819 Kentucky was engulfed in the nation's first great depression. The Bank of Kentucky was forced to curtail its loans severely, and most of the independent banks collapsed.

As the crisis deepened, a new conflict emerged between relief advocates, who sought inflationary legislation that would enable debtors to repay their obligations with cheap money, and anti-relief forces, who opposed any measures that would undermine creditor interests and relieve debtors of paying their just debts. The relief campaign got underway in June 1819 when a citizens' meeting in Frankfort drafted a series of resolutions which blamed the panic on the banks and their inflationary loans and note issues. The Frankfort Resolutions called upon the banks to alleviate suffering by suspending specie payment and by issuing moderate amounts of paper money. They also urged the legislature to allow the banks to remain in operation while suspending specie payment. In short, the relief advocates were demanding as medicine for the crisis the same inflationary practices which they blamed for the crisis!

When the legislature met in December 1819, the relief forces were in command. They quickly enacted legislation to suspend collection of unpaid debts for sixty days, to allow debtors to delay payment of obligations for one year if the creditor would accept Bank of Kentucky notes—two years if he would not—and to cancel the charters of all the independent banks created in 1818. The relief forces gained further momentum with the narrow victory of their gubernatorial candidate, General John Adair, in August 1820. The next session brought a new round of relief legislation. The keystone of the program was the new Bank of the Commonwealth, a state-owned and operated institution which was authorized to print unsecured paper money which debtors could use to pay their debts. Creditors who refused the paper were barred from pressing their claims for two years. When the legislation passed in December 1820, Adair signed it immediately, an act which reflected the triumph of political judgment over economic wisdom.

Over the next few years, the struggle between the proponents and opponents of relief continued on two levels. Economically, the fight pitted the Bank of Kentucky and its deflationary policy against the Bank of the Commonwealth and its inflationary policy. Ironically, the leader of the Bank of the Commonwealth during this period was John J. Crittenden, a conservative protegé of Henry Clay, who was elected president by the legislature as a means of increasing the bank's public acceptance. At the political level the conflict continued not only in the legislature, but in the courts and at the ballot box.

The court struggle began when opponents challenged the relief measures in Clark County Circuit Court. Judge James Clark held the laws unconstitutional, and the Kentucky Court of Appeals upheld Judge Clark's decision in 1823, declaring the laws an unconstitutional breech of contract. Thrown off track, the relief faction first attempted to remove the "aristocratic" justices from office but were unable to obtain the necessary two-thirds vote in the legislature. Having failed once, the Relief Party turned to an electoral solution. In the state elections in 1824 they won a landslide victory for Joseph Desha as governor and overwhelming majorities in both houses of the assembly.

In December 1824 the offending justices—John Boyle, William Owsley, and Benjamin Miles—were summoned to answer questions from the General Assembly. Lecturing their inquisitors that "no country was ever legislated out of debt," the judges so enraged the legislators that on Christmas Eve the assembly passed and Governor Desha quickly signed legislation which abolished the "Old Court" and established a new one. But relief opponents and the ousted judges refused to recognize the law, and for more than a year attorneys appealed cases to both courts, depending upon which one they favored. In the midst of this confusion, supporters of the Old Court mounted a strong campaign to recapture the legislature in 1825. Although successful in controlling the house, the Old Court party failed to retake the Senate, and the confusion continued for another year. By the 1826 elections, the public had had enough, and the Old Court advocates captured both houses of the legislature. A short time later, the body dissolved the New Court and restored the Old, along with payment of back salaries.

One event which undoubtedly fed public disgust with the situation was a tragic incident which occurred in Frankfort. Throughout the conflict, Franklin County was dominated by the relief or New Court faction. When it came time for the 1825 legislative races, both factions attempted to recruit the can-

Governor William Owsley
(Fourteenth Governor)

Col. Solomon P. Sharp. Sharp served in the state legislature, the U.S. Congress, and as Kentucky's attorney general. He resigned the latter position to run against John J. Crittenden as Representative of Franklin County in 1825. President Madison remarked that he "was the ablest man of his age who represented the West."

didates who would attract the maximum favor at the polls. The relief party chose as its standard bearer for the house of representatives Col. Solomon P. Sharp, the popular incumbent attorney general, who previously had served two terms each in the Kentucky legislature and the United States House of Representatives. In an effort to match Sharp's popularity, the Old Court party nominated John J. Crittenden, recently president of the Bank of the Commonwealth. After a vicious contest riddled with voting fraud, Sharp defeated Crittenden by sixty-nine votes. But Sharp did not live to take his seat.

On Sunday evening, November 5, 1825, after leaving a legislative strategy session at Weisiger's Tavern, Sharp answered a call at the door of his Madison Street home. As Sharp came to the door, he confronted a masked assailant who plunged a dagger into his chest, about two inches below the breast bone, killing him instantly. Suspicion rested at first upon Patrick H. Darby and John U. Waring, two Crittenden partisans who had conducted a smear campaign against Sharp. Waring wrote two letters threatening Sharp's life and both men charged in hand bills that he had fathered an illegitimate child by Miss Ann Cook of Simpson County. But it soon became apparent that both Darby and Waring had airtight alibis, and a few days later officials arrested Jereboam O. Beauchamp, a young Glasgow attorney. Beauchamp also was the husband of Ann Cook.

The son of a Simpson County farmer, Beauchamp had lived only a short distance from Miss Cook's farm. Becoming infatuated with the young woman, he proposed marriage. After resisting for a time, she finally consented, but only on the condition that the suitor kill Colonel Sharp, who she said had exposed her to public ridicule. Beauchamp set out as early as 1821 to murder Sharp, but he failed in his mission. Beauchamp and Miss Cook finally married in June 1824, but the groom had not forgotten his promise. Apparently deciding to strike while Sharp's fame was at its peak, Beauchamp traveled to Frankfort on November 5, 1825. After taking a room at the home of penitentiary keeper Joel Scott, he lay in wait for and slew his intended victim.

Tried and found guilty of murder, Beauchamp was hanged on July 7, 1826. But the hangman was almost too late. On the morning of his execution, Beauchamp's wife visited him in his cell in Frankfort. With her she carried a concealed knife. About ten o'clock in the morning she made a request of the guard which necessitated his leaving the cell block momentarily. When the guard returned, Ann Cook Beauchamp announced, "we have killed ourselves." In a scene that would do credit to Puccini or Verdi, the couple had inflicted upon themselves mortal wounds in a mutual suicide pact. By the time the bleeding murderer reached the gallows he was so weak that he had to be supported by two other men while the noose was placed around his neck. The trap door fell at approximately 12:30 P.M. About the same time, Ann Beauchamp breathed her last.

Whether the motives that led to Sharp's assassination were entirely personal or a mixture of personal and political probably never will be settled. What is

Bank of Kentucky, Frankfort Branch (212 St. Clair)

clear, ironically, is that the financial circumstances which originally had precipitated the Old Court-New Court fight and the Sharp-Crittenden race had been largely resolved. By late 1822 the extreme depreciation of the currency had begun to replace relief measures as the primary public concern. In November the legislature repealed the charter of the Bank of Kentucky, and in 1823 the assembly began dismantling the relief program. During the same year the Bank of the Commonwealth gradually began withdrawing its paper from circulation and burning it. By 1832 only $300,000 of the $3 million issued by the bank remained in circulation. Meanwhile, the institution had suspended all banking activities, and by 1830 the Louisville and Lexington branches of the Bank of the United States were the only active banks in Kentucky.

The financial and political crisis that followed the panic of 1819 left Kentuckians chastened but without adequate sources of currency and credit. Finally, in 1834 the legislature issued a new charter for the Bank of Kentucky. Based in Louisville and opened in January 1835, the new bank had a thirty-year charter and authorization to subscribe $5 million in capital stock. Later the same year the Frankfort Branch of the Bank of Kentucky opened its doors. Located on St. Clair Street next door to the courthouse, its first board of directors consisted of Charles S. Morehead, Edward P. Johnson, Jacob Swigert, Leander J. Sharp (brother of Solomon P. Sharp), John L. Blaine, Ezra Richmond, Addison S. Parker, Thomas Theobald, and Churchill Samuel. Morehead was president, and Col. Edmund H. Taylor served as cashier. Like

Edmund Haynes Taylor (1799–1873). The son of Richard Taylor, he moved with his family to Frankfort in 1811. In 1818 he was made Keeper of the State House and Public Square, a post he held until 1821. The next year he was made Quartermaster General of Kentucky. Taylor sided with the Union during the Civil War.

other Kentucky institutions, the Branch Bank reeled under the effects of the panic of 1837, which was triggered in part by President Andrew Jackson's war against the Second Bank of the United States. But this time the legislature resisted the radical relief measures of the 1820s and the new branch survived the crisis in reasonably good order.

Another important factor in Franklin County's growth between 1815 and 1840 was a series of major internal improvements and technological innovations which significantly improved the movement of goods and people and which linked the area more tightly with other communities and markets. Throughout this period, municipal and county officials exhibited a continuing concern for such longstanding problems as paving streets and sidewalks and building and maintaining bridges. But the three primary developments were the construction of a turnpike network which improved the flow of overland traffic; the perfection of the steamboat as the key mode of river commerce, combined with navigation improvements on the Kentucky River; and the advent of the railroad, a transportation innovation which was faster than the turnpike and stagecoach and more flexible than the waterbound steamboat. Sometimes these innovations were initiated outside Frankfort, frequently by entrepreneurs in Louisville and Lexington. But civic leaders in Franklin County became deeply involved when their community's best interests were at stake.

The need for an expanded road system reflected the fact that once isolated, self-sufficient towns and villages were gradually becoming part of an expanding regional economy in which each community had to look beyond its own borders for a substantial portion of its goods, services, and markets. Consequently, the subject of roads became an increasingly prevalent topic of debate, with the problem of financing being the most heated issue. One solution was to build public roads financed from tax revenues. Several roads of this type were constructed, including a few which originated in Frankfort. As early as 1822 the General Assembly authorized the building of a state road from the capital to Bowling Green. Between 1830 and 1834 the legislators provided for similar roads which linked Frankfort with Owenton; New Castle and the Ohio River town of King's Ferry; and Williamsburg, in Grant County.

But many community leaders, especially legislators who had to face the voters annually, realized that the taxpayers would never consent to the enormous tax burden which would be required to build a complete, publicly financed road system. The most practical alternative, therefore, was private capital. The primary mechanism was the private turnpike company, which received a state charter that authorized it to raise capital through the sale of stock and to build and operate a road between two specified terminal points. The investors would be rewarded through the payment of dividends from the revenues collected at the tollgate.

The turnpike movement in Kentucky began in 1817 with the chartering of the Lexington and Louisville and the Maysville and Lexington turnpike road companies. The panic of 1819 intervened before anything could be accomplished, and the two companies lapsed. But the recovery brought a renewed interest in turnpike development and several new companies were chartered during the late 1820s. Of particular significance was the Lexington and Frankfort Turnpike or Railroad Company.

Chartered in February 1828 and headquartered in Frankfort, the company was authorized to sell up to $100,000 in capital stock. Commissioners appointed to conduct stock sales in Frankfort were Charles P. Bacon, John J. Marshall, Peter Dudley, John H. Hanna, Samuel Wallace, John Harvie, and Richard Taylor. The charter detailed the company's powers and the responsibilities of its officers, outlined construction specifications, established toll rates, detailed procedures for acquiring rights of way, established rules of the road, and set penalties against those who attempted to evade tolls.

During 1830 the legislature issued charters for the construction of turnpikes between Frankfort and Georgetown and between Frankfort and Lexington by way of Versailles. Unlike the charter for the Lexington and Frankfort, whose standards adhered to but did not specify it by name, the two new documents required that the Georgetown and Versailles turnpikes be constructed on the "McAdams plan," a method developed by Scottish engineer John Loudon MacAdam in which broken stone, which usually did not exceed six ounces, was spread on the road according to anticipated wear, to a depth of nine or ten inches near the edges and increasing to about thirteen inches at the center. Otherwise, both new roads were to operate in basic accord with the provisions of the Lexington and Frankfort charter.

Unfortunately, none of these roads was able to subscribe the stock necessary to begin construction. Charters for new Frankfort and Lexington and Georgetown and Frankfort turnpike companies were issued in 1831, but to no immediate avail. For all the discussion of recruiting private money for road building, it was soon apparent that such investments were beyond the means of all but a very few citizens of Kentucky's Bluegrass communities, including Frankfort.

By 1834 it was clear that a combination of private and public resources would be required to finance turnpikes. This was accomplished by creating county boards of internal improvements which supervised the construction of specific turnpikes. In some cases, the project was carried out by an independent company; in others, the improvements board exercised the powers of the company. To improve stock sales, county courts were allowed to purchase stock in the turnpike project, provided that the citizens voted to levy a property tax with which to purchase the stock. Dividends from the stock owned by the county were to be returned to the local treasury to reduce the levy. In addition, the technique provided that once each county involved in the stock subscription had sold a specified number of shares, the governor could purchase an equivalent number of shares for the commonwealth. Opportunities for public support were broadened again in 1835 as county courts were empowered to purchase stock in some otherwise entirely private enterprises, such as the Frankfort, Lexington, and Versailles Turnpike Road Company, without the supervision of a board of internal improvements and in the absence of a stock purchase by the state.

These new means of financing turnpikes were not immediately successful in all cases. The boards of internal improvements established in 1834 to build a turnpike between Frankfort and Crab Orchard were still having problems selling their stock four years later. Nor did all of the other projects involving the town of Frankfort move as quickly as their sponsors hoped. But the fact remains that by 1840, Frankfort was integrated into a turnpike network which connected it either directly or indirectly with Lexington, Louisville, Shelbyville, Georgetown, Versailles, Paris, New Castle, Bedford, Ghent, Owenton, and New Liberty as well as other nearby towns.

This new transportation network resulted in a substantial increase in the speed and reduction in cost of overland commerce, improved patronage for inn and tavern operators, and intensified competition for local stage coach companies, such as Edward P. Johnson & Co., owned by Edward P. Johnson, Philip Swigert, John H. Hanna, and Jacob Swigert, and Johnson, Weisiger & Co., operated by Johnson and Daniel Weisiger. Given their vested interest, it is hardly surprising that Johnson, Hanna, Philip Swigert, and Jacob Swigert found the time to serve on several occasions as stock subscription commissioners, turnpike company directors, and internal improvements board members.

The turnpikes played a critical role in stimulating commerce and moving goods and people within the state. But for residents of Frankfort and Franklin County, the Kentucky River, with its access to the Ohio and Mississippi river systems, remained the primary channel to more distant markets. During the first decade of the century, shippers continued to depend upon primitive flatboats and keelboats to carry their goods. River trade got a major stimulus in October 1811 when the steamboat *New Orleans* landed at Louisville on its maiden voyage from Pittsburgh to Natchez. It took a few years to adapt a craft which had been built for the deep rivers of the East to the shallower, shifting channels of the western waters, but within a short time the steamboat had opened a colorful new era of commerce on the Kentucky River.

The steamboat era at Frankfort began about 1817. The first vessel to navigate the Kentucky River was the *Sylph*, commanded by Captain John Armstrong and owned by the firm of Samuel and Jamison. It was followed quickly by *The Kentucky*, operated by the firm of Hanson and Boswell, which carried cargo between Louisville and Frankfort. The third steamer to operate in the Frankfort trade was the *Governor Shelby*, a 120-ton vessel built in Louisville in 1817. Indicative of the rapid technological advances in the steamboat industry, the fourth steamboat in Frankfort was *The Napoleon*, a 322-ton vessel commanded by Captain Henry Miller Shreve, of Louisville, one of the leading steamboat designers and engineers on the western rivers.

Falls City II, one of the last of the Kentucky River packets to compete with railroads for freight and passengers is shown here under steam on the Kentucky River. It ran between Louisville and Valley View from 1898 to 1908. One of the larger boats to play the river, she could carry "90 hogsheads of tobacco down in the hold, with some 125–140 around the decks."

As the steamboat's advantages became more apparent, Frankfort became the hub for freight and passenger traffic between Louisville and central Kentucky. Among the vessels which made regularly scheduled stops at the Frankfort wharf were *The Exchange*, a 200-ton boat built at Louisville and owned by David Ward; the *Saint Louis*, a 220-ton craft constructed at Shippingport, immediately below Louisville, in 1818; and *The Rifleman*, a 250-ton craft built the following year at Louisville. During the 1830s several new vessels joined the flourishing Kentucky River trade. One of the best known was *The Argo*, commanded by Captain John Armstrong. Built in Louisville specifically for the Kentucky River trade, it plied the river between 1832 and 1840. Joining it two years later was the *Plough Boy*, a light draft, upper cabin steamboat whose master was Captain J. C. Harris. *The Eagle* joined the Louisville-Frankfort trade in 1837, followed in 1839 by the *John Armstrong* and *The Frankfort*, both of which were designed for the Kentucky River traffic.

Although steamboat arrivals and departures at Frankfort became a routine matter by the early 1820s, commerce on the Kentucky was never without risk. Like other western rivers, the Kentucky was fraught with obstacles, such as hidden snags, sand bars, and shifting channels which could go undetected by even the wariest captain and crew. One of the most unusual episodes on the Kentucky occurred when *The Charleston*, one of the more famous vessels in the Kentucky trade, ran aground on Fish Trap Island near the foot of Mero Street during a period of summer low water. The boat tipped over on its side and remained in that position until the rising water in the fall lifted it from the gravel and returned it to an upright position.

Accidents such as this fed a growing demand for canalization and other improvements that would regularize the river's depth and increase the safety of navigation. In 1828 and 1829 Lieutenants William Turnbull and Napoleon B. Buford, topographical engineers for the War Department, surveyed the river from Carrollton to Boonesboro. They recommended to Congress that an experimental wing dam be constructed near Frankfort at a cost of $10,704. But President Andrew Jackson, who opposed federal funding for state internal improvements, vetoed the project. Lacking federal support, the state decided to move ahead on its own. In 1835 the Kentucky River was resurveyed by state engineer R. Philip Baker and former Lieutenant Buford, now a civilian engineer. They recommended construction of seventeen locks and dams to create a six-foot slack water depth between Carrollton and Beattyville.

The state could not consider such a visionary scheme, but it did complete five locks and dams between Carrollton and Oregon, a few miles above Frankfort. Lock and Dam No. 4, located just below Leestown, were completed and the lock opened for navigation in February 1840. The lock walls were 200 feet long and thirty feet high. They were constructed of locally quarried gray limestone at a cost of $120,000. Tolls paid by shippers underwrote the operating costs, but the state recovered only a small portion of the project's construction costs. But the system did achieve its purpose of stimulating economic development in the Kentucky River Valley and the Bluegrass region by making it easier for farmers and other producers in the interior to move their goods to market.

Of the internal improvements initiated during this period, the one with the greatest long-term impact was the railroad. It was also the major instance in which Frankfort's future was affected by the struggle between Louisville and Lexington for political and economic supremacy in Kentucky. Paradoxically, railroad advocates in Frankfort came to Lexington's rescue before the enterprise was completed.

In 1820 Lexington was still the largest town in the commonwealth. But the coming of the steamboat, followed by the depression of 1819, severely undermined the Bluegrass town's economy, and by the mid-1820s the Falls City had emerged as the state's premier urban community. In the hope of reestablishing their city's commercial leadership, several of Lexington's leading citizens, spearheaded by General Leslie Combs, proposed in late 1829 that a railroad be built to link the Bluegrass city with the Ohio River.

After several months of controversy over the designation of the Ohio River terminus—an honor sought by Louisville—the General Assembly issued a charter in January 1830 which empowered the new Lexington & Ohio Railroad Company to construct a line from Lexington to one or more points on the Ohio River. Two months later the company directors hired Professor Shaler Mathews of Transylvania University to do preliminary surveys of a route to Louisville through Frankfort and Shelbyville. Upon resuming his academic duties, Mathews was succeeded by two engineers named Kneas and McIlvaine. They completed their right-of-way surveys in the spring of 1831.

Lexington & Ohio Railroad Co. Depot. Thought to be the first depot west of the Alleghenies, it was built during the early 1830's. Situated on the east hill above Frankfort, the station was used until the construction of the tunnel in the 1850's. This photo was taken about 1900, shortly before the depot was torn down.

The results were more favorable than anyone had anticipated. The most troublesome problem was a 200-foot inclined plane at Fankfort, but it was not insurmountable. Construction began at Lexington on October 22, 1831, marked by formal rail-laying ceremonies presided over by General Combs. Despite some problems with weather, the first six miles were in operation by March 1833. Ten months later the first section had been completed between Lexington and the top of the East Main Street hill at Frankfort. The railroad's arrival at the capital was celebrated in an appropriately grand style. Unfortunately, financial difficulties and route designation problems at the Louisville terminus caused the road to be stalled at Frankfort for several years. Things moved so slowly, in fact, that the section between Lexington and Frankfort was reincorporated as the Lexington and Frankfort Railroad Company.

At first the new line operated under equine power. But in 1835 the horses were replaced by a locomotive purchased in the East. Despite several accidents and consequent complaints about management, the railroad continued to gain public patronage. When accidents occurred, the company initiated physical improvements to eliminate the causes. Near the end of the decade the Lexington & Ohio Company contracted for construction of a railroad bridge across the Kentucky River. When the company's precarious financial condition threatened the project, the city of Louisville issued $30,000 in bonds and the Bank of Louisville sold an additional $10,000 worth to help finance the span, but to no avail. By the end of the decade, however, the company had spent $511,385 to build and operate the railroad between Lexington and Frankfort and an additional $411,653 on the unfinished portion between the capital and Louisville. Several more years would elapse before the company's problems were resolved and the road was completed.

But supporters of the project retained their faith in rail transportation. Indicative of the farsightedness of some of Frankfort's leaders, Philip Swigert and John Hanna, partners in the stagecoach firm of Edward P. Johnson & Co., pulled out in 1838. Under the name of Swigert and Company, they leased the completed section of the road for four years. Over the life of the agreement, Swigert and Hanna initiated extensive improvements and repairs, while their rent payments provided a new source of capital for the ailing company. The events of the coming decades would justify their faith.

As Frankfort's population grew during the early decades of the nineteenth century, so did the magnitude and complexity of its urban problems. More people living in close proximity increased opportunities for crime and violence. Rapid but erratic economic growth meant wealth for some but poverty for others. Ignorance about the causes of disease left the community open to periodic epidemics. And rapid but often unsound construction combined with an increasingly inadequate water system and fire fighting capability made Frankfort vulnerable to occasionally serious fires. It is not surprising, therefore, that local officials spent a good deal of their time and the town's limited financial resources in dealing with basic problems of public health and safety.

One of Frankfort's most critical problems by the mid-1830s was the inadequacy of its water system. During the first decade of the century Frankfort had become the first town in the Commonwealth to establish its own waterworks. But as growth continued, the single pipeline from Cedar Cove Spring proved less and less capable of meeting the community's water needs. Increasingly, residents and businesses depended upon wells sunk at various locations throughout the town. These were supplemented by cisterns dug in the streets to be used in case of fire. Still, the wells and cisterns did not provide a water supply adequate to the town's combined public and private water requirements.

Finding this situation intolerable, local leaders approached the General Assembly seeking authority to expand the capacity of the water works. The assembly responded by empowering Edmund H. Taylor, Sr., Philip Swigert, Thomas S. Page, Mason Brown, and John J. Vest to conduct a lottery to raise up to $100,000, which was to be divided equally between construction on the water works and establishment of a new public school. Completed in 1839 at a cost of about $38,000, the project appears to have been essentially an enlargement of that executed by Richard Throckmorton more than thirty years earlier. The supervisor was John Moore, whose work drew a resolution from the board of trustees praising his "integrity and moral worth" and offering the "individual thanks . . . and the acknowledgments of the citizens" for the "faithful, skillful and workmanlike manner" in which he conducted construction of the water works.

For a capital town whose statehouse had burned twice during the lifetime of many residents, the expansion of the public water system was one more advancement in the fire fighting capability of a department which already had seen many changes during the past twenty years. Although Frankfort had a rudimentary fire company as early as 1806, thirteen more years elapsed before a formally organized, tax supported department began to develop. In February 1819 the General Assembly enacted legislation which abolished the old Frankfort Fire Company and authorized the board of trustees to organize "such company or companies for extinguishing fire in said town, as they may deem necessary and sufficient for that purpose." The legislation also empowered the board to furnish from its own revenues "such engine or engines, and other machines and implements . . . as are proper . . . for extinguishing fire, or for preventing its progress." In addition, the board obtained authority to enforce fire prevention measures throughout the town, such as the imposition of fines against property owners for failure to maintain a specified number of fire buckets on their premises.

The following month, the trustees passed an ordinance which designated every male housekeeper as a member of a new fire company. The ordinance also authorized the appointment of eight prominent citizens as engineers who, according to their rank, would take command at any fire alarm and conduct regular drills. Each engineer was required to attend company drills, and anyone who failed to attend, except for illness or absence from town, was subject to a three dollar fine. If any company failed to return the fire engine to its house after use, the engineer and all members of the company so negligent could be fined one dollar each. The engineer in command at any fire also had the power to require the assistance of any citizen, and anyone who refused to help was liable for a similar fine. The first engineers appointed under the ordinance were Jeptha Dudley, William J. Phillips, Allen F. McCurdy, Amos Stout, John Woods, Moses C. Bledsoe, Peter Dudley, and Benjamin Hickman.

The ordinance also implemented the act's fire prevention clause, requiring every housekeeper to maintain one two-gallon leather bucket for up to three fireplaces. Anyone having four or more fireplaces was required to have one bucket for each two fireplaces. Owners of rental property were to supply a corresponding number of buckets for their tenants. Any property owner who failed to supply the proper number of buckets was subject to a fine of one dollar per month for each bucket he was deficient. The buckets also served an important public fire fighting role, as every fire fighter was required to bring his buckets when he reported to a drill or fire. If he forgot his buckets, he faced a two dollar fine.

The fire company continued under this structure until 1834, when state legislation provided for the establishment of a new company consisting of at least twenty but not more than seventy-five local citizens. The company was to elect a captain, two lieutenants, a treasurer, and a clerk who could appoint other officers as necessary and adopt regulations for the company's efficient management. Members were subject to disciplinary rules similar to those of the old organization, with the officers empowered to assess fines for infractions.

With the fines serving as a source of revenue, the company was authorized for the first time to compensate its officers. Any remaining money could be used to build a fire house, repair and maintain an engine, and purchase other apparatus. The law also exempted fire company members from militia duty during peacetime and provided for the expulsion by vote of the company of any member "for bad character, reprehensible neglect of duty, or refusal and failure to pay the fines assessed against him."

While day-to-day command of the company lay in the hands of its officers, ultimate authority for its equipment remained with the trustees. With this quasi-public form of organization, the Frankfort Fire Company closely resembled other fire fighting organizations of its time, including those of Louisville and Lexington.

One of the weakest public services of nineteenth century American cities was police protection. Many communities lacked any paid police agency whatsoever, and in those that did have one the officers generally were untrained, poorly paid, and too few in number to be effective against the episodes of vandalism, mob violence, and other disturbances that shattered the public peace. Southern cities in particular demonstrated a major concern for unlawful assemblies by slaves and free blacks. Frankfort was no exception.

For more than a decade after the War of 1812, Frankfort's chief law enforcement officer was a town sergeant, who took his instructions directly from the board of trustees. He was to enforce a wide range of ordinances, many of which had little to do with preserving public order. At various times the board charged the sergeant to ascertain public opinion regarding sidewalks, to warn store keepers against selling liquor to slaves, to have nuisances removed from the streets, and to notify property owners who allowed stagnant water to stand on their premises that they were subject to a fine. In numerous instances, he was instructed to jail slaves for loitering or illegally hiring themselves out for wages.

The local police authority apparently remained in the hands of the town sergeant until 1831 when Massie Franklin was appointed captain of patrol. Four years later, under the new incorporation act, a town marshal replaced the captain of patrol as Frankfort's chief law enforcement officer. The ordinances which followed set out the marshal's duties in detail. With the support of his deputies, he was to patrol the town daily and to "be vigilant in detecting retailers of spirits without license [and] keepers of disorderly houses"; to "arrest all persons . . . engaged in the commission of any riot, rout, unlawful

"From the Hills of Benson Creek" c.1830. Drawn by Samuel M. Lee and engraved by C. G. Childs. Rare view from interesting perspective. Domed structure directly above pioneers appears to be the Capitol.

assembly, or breech of the peace"; and generally to enforce all other ordinances involving everything from tax collection to removal of nuisances. He also had the power to call out a posse to "assist him in the execution of the duties of his office."

The town marshal was reinforced at night by a watchman, who was appointed annually by the board of trustees. The watchman's primary functions were to attend to prisoners at night and to report suspected breaches of ordinances to the chairman of the board of trustees. There was little else that could be done, given the lack of street lighting. Consequently, would-be lawbreakers were free to roam the town at will. Several decades would pass before the situation changed appreciably.

There were some urban problems which the community simply did not have the necessary resources to confront. At a time when the line between poverty and criminality was only narrowly perceived, the General Assembly empowered the trustees, in the 1835 incorporation act, to erect a workhouse in which to confine misdemeanants, vagrants, beggars, rioters, and others perceived to be a threat to the peace. But for good or ill the town simply could not finance such a facility.

Frankfort was also subject to periodic epidemics. In late June 1833 residents faced the arrival of the dreaded Asiatic cholera, which had been moving westward from India since 1826. The pestilence struck terror in larger cities such as Louisville and Lexington and caused a large number of deaths in both cities. Frankfort was not hit quite so hard, but the epidemic left its mark. During its three-week visitation cholera killed ten persons in North Frankfort and seven in South Frankfort. The effects were much more severe out in the country, however, where the death toll brought the total for the county to approximately 150.

However significant the number of deaths might have been, the psychological impact was traumatic. As Captain Sanford Goins recalled the epidemic more than fifty years later, it was "one of the greatest calamities that ever befell Frankfort.... All business closed and a pall and gloom hung over the whole town. People died by the scores and our little city was almost depopulated." If Frankfort was depopulated, it was more because of people fleeing in fear than because of death. But Goins can be forgiven for perhaps overdramatizing the impact, as he, his father, and his brother volunteered to dig graves, a task which kept them "busy for days digging and digging the last narrow resting [place] for our friends and citizens." Fortunately, he added, "we passed through this to bloom out even brighter than before." Unfortunately, once life returned to normal, the town did little if anything to prevent another such outbreak.

Problems such as fire, crime, and epidemic certainly demonstrate the dark side of town life in the first half of the nineteenth century. But as broadcloth replaced buckskin on the streets of Frankfort, the tenor of social, cultural, and intellectual life became increasingly sophisticated. The capital's elite entertained with a flair reminiscent of Richmond and Baltimore; churches and schools multiplied; and literary and cultural societies took on a degree of permanence.

Occasional visits by national and international dignitaries provided an ideal opportunity for lavish entertainment. One of the first such affairs came in 1817 when President James Monroe stopped in the capital while on a western tour. Accompanying him were two military officers who themselves later became president—General Andrew Jackson and Captain Zachary Taylor. During their visit the president and his party were treated to the hospitality of Senator and Mrs. John Brown at Liberty Hall.

The premier social event of the era occurred on May 14, 1825, when the Marquis de Lafayette visited Frankfort during his tour of the United States. The guest of Governor Joseph Desha, the French hero of the American Revolution and his entourage came to Frankfort by way of Louisville. A large parade greeted Lafayette and his party on the edge of town and escorted them downtown. After a round of welcoming speeches, he attended a tea at Liberty Hall. That evening he was the guest of honor at a sumptuous dinner and ball at Weisiger's Tavern. Among those who greeted the Frenchman was Colonel Anthony Crockett, one of Frankfort's elder statesmen, who as a young Virginia officer had carried Lafayette from the battlefield after he had been severely wounded at the battle of Brandywine.

It was also during this period that Frankfort began to take on a vigorous church life. Until 1825 local religious activity centered upon the public meeting house. It was there in 1816 that a group of Presbyterians under the leadership

Captain Daniel Weisiger (1763–1829). A Virginian, he was a captain in the United States Army until he had to retire because of ill health. In 1793 he was a commissioner on the committee to build a road to Cincinnati; in 1799 he was elected the first master of Hiram Lodge No. 4. He operated Weisiger tavern until his death.

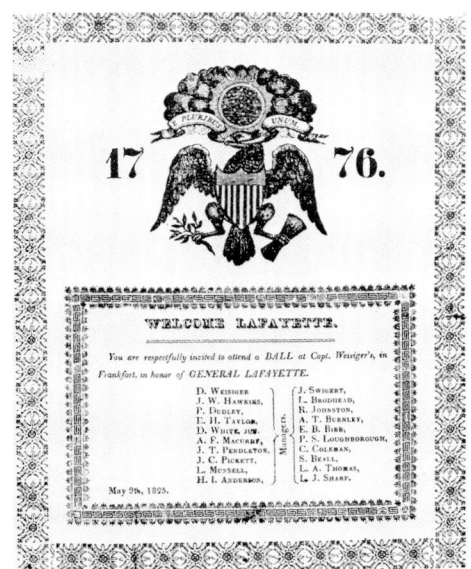

Original 1825 Invitation

of Thomas Paxton, a former ruling elder at the Upper Benson Church, formed the First Presbyterian Church of Frankfort. The first permanent pastor was the Rev. Eli Smith, who arrived in 1817 and remained for about a decade. It was under his leadership that in 1824 the congregation moved out of the meeting house into a newly erected brick structure located on the north side of Wapping Street between Washington and St. Clair. In 1825 the membership roll contained fifty-nine names, of whom forty-five were women, making for a distinctly female congregation.

The year 1816 also witnessed the formation of First Baptist Church, which was organized by thirteen former members of the Forks of Elkhorn Church who had been dismissed for that missionary purpose. The new congregation joined the Presbyterians at the meeting house, using it every fourth Sunday and meeting at members' homes on intervening Sundays. The first sermon was delivered by the Rev. Silas M. Noel, the preacher-attorney who was both a founder of Georgetown College and an associate circuit court judge. Noel declined an offer to be the first pastor, and the pulpit was filled by the Rev. Henry Toler. But Noel eventually accepted a call and served the congregation from 1823 to 1825. About the time his pastorate ended, the old house of worship burned, and the Baptists relocated to a new building at 314 Lewis Street. The first pastor to serve in this edifice for an appreciable length of time was the Rev. Porter Clay, brother of Henry Clay, who served until 1829.

The first Methodist meeting in Frankfort was held by Bishop Francis Asbury on October 17, 1810. Other preachers visited periodically over the next dozen years, but the first congregation was not organized until October 1822. Apparently established under the guidance of the Methodist Church at Lexington, the new congregation had an initial membership of sixty-eight persons, including thirty-one blacks, many of whom were slaves of white church members. The first pastor was the Rev. William Holman, who conducted

First Presbyterian Church. Constructed on Wapping Street in 1823–24 of brick in Flemish bond, it had separate doors for men and women. Considered the denominational meeting house in Frankfort, it was used by the Presbyterians until 1849. Used thereafter by Frankfort's Roman Catholic congregation, this structure was replaced by the Church of the Good Shepherd in the 1850's.

services at the meeting house for a year or so. In April 1823 Benjamin Hickman gave the congregation a fifty-foot lot which fronted on Ann Street. Here the congregation erected a small frame building, where they remained until 1849, when it was replaced by a brick structure.

Another Protestant congregation organized during the period was First Christian Church. The organizing force of this congregation was the Rev. Philip S. Fall, a British immigrant who had arrived in Franklin County in 1819 to teach in a school for young women near Forks of Elkhorn. Quickly joining the local church, he soon felt a call to the ministry and was ordained in 1820. The following year, he accepted a co-pastorate at First Baptist Church in Frankfort. There he remained until July 1822 when he accepted the pastorate of a small congregation in Louisville.

While in Louisville Fall adopted the antidenominational views of Alexander Campbell and persuaded his congregation to reorganize themselves as the First Christian Church. After several years in Louisville and Nashville, Fall returned to Frankfort to organize the Female Eclectic Institute. Meanwhile, the Forks of Elkhorn Church split over the Campbellite doctrines. In 1832 Fall joined John T. Johnson to establish a Campbellite congregation in Frankfort. Beginning with seven members, the congregation met in private homes for the next decade. By 1840 the congregation had gained enough adherents to support a church edifice. At that point they acquired a lot on the west side of Ann Street between Montgomery and Broadway. Two years later the flock moved into its new building, which was completed at a cost of $4,531.

In addition to these congregations, both the Episcopalians and the Roman Catholics were actively involved in organizing churches as the 1830s came to an end. In 1835, Bishop Benjamin B. Smith organized a congregation of eight Episcopalian communicants. The following year a $1,000 gift from a donor in New York enabled Smith to buy a lot on Washington Street to serve as a church site. Likewise, Catholics held regular services in Frankfort during the 1820s and 1830s, frequently meeting in the home of Mrs. Ellen Barstow, one of the parishioners. In 1835 the congregation began meeting at a "chapel-office" located near the site of the present railroad tunnel. Two years later Bishop Benedict Flaget of Bardstown purchased a building on High Street and placed it in trust for the congregation. Throughout this period, however, Frankfort's Catholics were under the supervision of the priests at the Church of St. Pius, located at White Sulphur in Scott County. As the new decade began, it would still be nine years before local Catholics gained their own parish with their own priest.

The leading school in Frankfort during the first quarter of the century was Kentucky Seminary. For most of the second decade the headmaster was Kean O'Hara, an Irish-born educator who became a virtual legend among the youth of Frankfort's leading families. When O'Hara left in 1821 to establish his own school, he turned his position over to Mann Butler, who became one of Kentucky's premier educators and founder of the Louisville public school

John T. Johnson. A follower of the Rev. Alexander Campbell, Johnson helped establish a Campbellite Congregation in Frankfort in 1832, now known as the First Christian Church.

Tunnel House.
Located at the southeast corner of High and Broadway, this house served as the Catholic church between 1835 and 1849.

system. Kentucky Seminary accepted male and female students alike and offered them a classical curriculum that was heavy on mathematics, history, English, French, Latin, and Greek. To assure that the school and its pupils performed according to expectations, the trustees were invited to observe and report to the public on the students' performances at examinations. After attending examinations in the fall of 1821, a panel that included George M. Bibb, Orlando Brown, and Mason Brown reported that "all the classes in History, Mathematics and the Languages, acquitted themselves in a manner highly creditable to the instructor." They added that "the female pupils . . . gave an additional proof that the talents of both sexes are equal."

The seminary remained in operation until November 1824, when it was forced to vacate its quarters to accommodate the state senate after the destruction of the capitol. Despite its high reputation, however, the seminary was already drawing competition and private schools proliferated after the institution closed. One of the earliest competitors was Kean O'Hara's Select Seminary, which promised "an extensive and solid Academical Education" and assured parents that "every rank of . . . pupils will be faithfully attended to." Reinforcing O'Hara's claims was the testimony of visitors who monitored examinations conducted in July 1821. "We can assure the patrons of this institution that we have not witnessed a better general progress, according to age and other circumstances, than we have seen in the pupils of Select Seminary," the visitors reported. Among the notables who signed the report were Governor John Adair, Senator John J. Crittenden, and Orlando and Mason Brown.

Several academies were established for girls. Such schools usually combined classical subjects with those calculated to enhance the pupils' feminine graces. In August 1821 the Reverend Mr. Field announced the opening of his Female

Academy at the home of Mrs. Mary Rennick. Offering courses such as reading, writing, English grammar, astronomy, natural philosophy, logic, "and if necessary, the classical Languages," he also promised "a faithful attention to the young ladies, not only to aid their advancement in learning but to lead them to an agreeable and interesting behavior."

During the early 1830s, William D. Young, head of the Franklin Female Seminary, placed an even greater stress on young women's intellectual development. Asserting that "the course of female education is generally too superficial and that too great a proportion of time is devoted to the ornamental branches," he placed heavy stress on the "exact sciences." Thus by the time a young woman reached his third class, she was prepared to study astronomy, chemistry, and, at the option of her parents, geometry, algebra, trigonometry, and surveying. "Ornamental branches" such as music were available if demanded, but received distinctly less attention than the sciences.

Other schools, such as Leo Tymann's Public Seminary and H. W. Carter's Seminary, continued to offer a basic classical education to youths of both sexes. Whatever the number, curriculum, or quality of these schools, however, one fact remained: they all were private institutions which charged tuition. With the continuing absence of a free, tax supported school system, a large number of youth in Frankfort lacked the opportunity to attend any kind of school. Movement in the direction of such a system gathered momentum during the mid-1830s. The incorporation act of 1835 empowered the town to establish and support a public school. Two years later the legislature endorsed the concept of a common school system for the state as a whole. And in 1838 the bill which provided for the expansion of the Cedar Cove Spring water works also provided money for "the use and benefit of a city school" in Frankfort. While a substantial amount of money was raised, it was not until after the Civil War that the idea of a public school system became a reality in Kentucky's capital.

Along with churches and schools came a variety of literary and intellectual activities. In 1822 the legislature enacted a bill to create a new public library, which replaced the apparently defunct Frankfort Library Company. While its core collection was a "magnificent Law Library" intended to serve the capital's many lawyers, it also offered a good assortment of books for the general reader. The year 1834 saw formation of the Frankfort Lyceum, the local branch of a popular literary and cultural movement that swept the country during the 1830s. Four years later, some of the capital's leading citizens incorporated the Kentucky Historical Society. The organization did not last very long, but it represented many Kentuckians' early concern for preserving their state's heritage and established the precedent for the organization's reincorporation forty-two years later.

Politics continued to be a primary subject of intellectual inquiry in Frankfort during the era, and the basic source of political intelligence was the newspapers. Since the founding of the republic most American newspapers had

Albert G. Hodges (1802–1881). Moved from Lexington to Frankfort in 1826 and formed a partnership with James G. Dana in publication of the *Commentator*. In 1838 he began publication of the *Commonwealth*. Later he was elected Public Printer, a position he held for a quarter of a century.

served the interests of a particular political party, candidate, or philosophy. As party strife in Kentucky became more pronounced, this became increasingly the case in Frankfort. Thus, the *Argus of Western America*, established in 1806, became vehemently Jacksonian under the direction of Amos Kendall, Gervas E. Russell, and Francis P. Blair during the 1820s. Representing the emerging Whig party was the *Commonwealth*, formed in 1833 by state printer Albert G. Hodges and edited by Orlando Brown. Hodges earlier had been associated with the *Commentator*, established in 1817 by Moses O. Bledsoe.

Several papers sprang up to defend specific issues and then died when the matter had been resolved. One such issue was the court fight of the 1820s. A weekly called the *Harbinger*, established in 1823 by Humphrey Marshall and edited by lawyer Patrick H. Darby, affirmed the position of the Old Court party. The following year Darby reorganized the paper as the *Constitutional Advocate* and Marshall and Jacob H. Holman established the *Spirit of '76*, both of which upheld the Old Court. Defending the New Court party was *The Patriot*, a short-lived journal established in 1826 by William Tanner.

These papers and others like them played a significant role in educating citizens and stimulating public debate over state, national, and international issues. Their advertisements also provided useful economic information. But like other political newspapers of their time, they were woefully short on local news, particularly on controversial issues whose agitation in the press might have divided the supporters of the same state and national candidates.

One of the issues most likely to be omitted from local newspapers was slavery, especially expressions of antislavery sentiment. The peculiar institution was a frequent subject of debate in religious convocations, especially among Presbyterians and Baptists, and within the columns of antislavery journals such as the *Abolition Intelligencer and Missionary Messenger*, published in neighboring Shelbyville during the early 1820s, and the *Philanthropist*, established in 1835 by the Kentucky-born planter-turned-abolitionist James G. Birney. While debates over slavery were notably absent from the local press, however, the institution remained a pervasive presence in local social, economic, and political life.

Patrick Henry Darby. Born in Ireland, Darby settled in Frankfort where he became a prominent member of the bar. Matthew Jouett agreed to paint this portrait without any formal sittings with his subject.

Statistical data on slavery in Frankfort and Franklin County are hard to come by, but those figures that do exist indicate that slaves were a very substantial part of the local populace. In 1810, 402 of Frankfort's 1,099 residents, or 36.6 percent of its population, were listed as slaves. Ten years later, 643 or 39.7 percent of the town's 1,619 inhabitants were so designated. Percentages for the county as a whole were not quite so pronounced, but are significant nevertheless. In 1840 some 30.2 percent or 2,846 of the county's 9,420 residents were slaves.

While the greatest single concentration of slaves was in Frankfort, the vast majority lived on the farms scattered throughout the county. A goodly number lived on larger farms with specialized labor forces. For example, at Bellsgrove, Clement Bell's estate near Forks of Elkhorn, male field hands tilled the crops, tended the lifestock, and gathered the harvest in the fall. Male house servants, viewed by the master as "more intelligent and trustworthy," took care of the master's personal needs, traveled with him on business, and carried out other positions of responsibility on the farm. Slave women, under the supervision of the mistress, served as house maids, seamstresses, nurses, cooks, and handmaids. Some large farms were highly self-sufficient, with slave craftsmen manufacturing everything from barrels and furniture to dresses and gloves.

Some county slaves worked on tobacco farms, but more were engaged in hemp cultivation, a task which, along with its simplicity, was so dirty and laborious that hemp was widely referred to by Kentuckians as a "nigger crop." Indeed, the work was so unpleasant that owners reserved it almost exclusively for slave men. Unlike their cotton-growing counterparts in the Deep South, Kentucky hemp farmers usually found women totally unfit for cultivating hemp. As one local farmer commented in 1839, "none but our strong, able negro men can handle it to advantage."

Slave men were in heavy demand for the manufacture as well as the cultivation of hemp. Most of the ropewalks and bagging factories in and around Frankfort used industrial slaves almost exclusively, because white men would not submit to such onerous labor. As early as 1817, Zadoc Cramer, author of *The Navigator*, pointed out that William Hunter and John Instone employed "about 25 hands, blackmen and boys" in their "extensive bagging factory" in Frankfort. Four years later Charles Miles advertised his desire "to purchase six likely Negro Boys, from fourteen to twenty-one years of age for the express and only purpose to put into a Ropewalk, and for which he will engage to pay a fair price in CASH." Miles expressed a preference for those with experience in spinning hemp and promised to pay accordingly. Notably, Miles's notice appeared in December, a time when farmers frequently had field hands with little to do, but who still had to be fed, clothed, and housed. By selling off or hiring out some of his hands during the winter, the farmer could cut his overhead.

Franklin County slaveholders generally thought of themselves as benevolent masters who had the best interests of "their people" at heart. Slavery was certainly a paternalistic institution in which most owners employed a minimum of physical force and saw to their slaves' basic needs, if only to protect their heavy capital investment. But hard experience had taught them that bondsmen resented their condition and would exploit any opportunity to escape or otherwise improve their situation. Slave discipline thus became a major concern, especially in Frankfort, where town conditions made it easier for slaves to escape the constant scrutiny of their masters.

The demand for stringent discipline translated into state laws and local ordinances which, apart from the limitations inherent in chattel slavery, further restricted the bondsmen's freedom. Ordinances prohibited the sale of liquor to or its purchase by slaves without permission of the owner; forbade the sale of goods in the public market by slaves without the owner's permission; and prohibited loitering and otherwise limited freedom of movement. Punishments ranged from ten to thirty-nine lashes across the bare back. In those cases where slaves committed acts which also were unlawful for free persons, the latter might pay a small fine while the slave received lashes. The bondsman escaped public punishment only if his master paid the fine or otherwise compensated the town for its expense in the case.

Despite the limitations on their freedom, slaves in Franklin County managed to develop a semblance of community life over which they had some control. On the larger farms the primary center of community was the slave quarters, where from dusk to dawn family values could be nurtured; cultural traditions could be passed from one generation to the next; parents could train and discipline their children according to their own lights; and husband and wife could share love and companionship while providing the mutual support necessary to survive the indignities of their condition. The quarters also were a center for community celebrations, such as weddings and holidays, or special occasions such as corn shuckings, which brought together blacks from miles around to celebrate the end of the harvest.

In town the church became the focal point of community life among slaves and free blacks alike. During the first quarter of the century, both races attended worship together, with slaves accompanying the families of their masters. Once inside, segregation prevailed. During the early 1830s, however, white Baptists decided it would be preferable if blacks worshipped on their own. After consultation between black and white leaders within the congregation, John Ward, a free black property owner, donated a lot at Clinton and High streets for the construction of a building for a new black church. For more than a decade, while struggling to raise the money to erect a building, the congregation met in private homes. In 1838 they called their first pastor, the Rev. Henderson Williams, a powerful preacher who served into the early 1840's.

The year after the Reverend Williams arrived, black Methodists established the congregation which became St. John African Methodist Episcopal Church. They immediately created a small edifice on a lot facing Lewis Street, which was donated by a Mrs. Triplett, a white woman who had two servants, Benjamin Dunmore and Benjamin Hunley, who were members of the congregation. The first pastor, the Rev. George Harlan, arrived in 1840. Together First Baptist Church and St. John A.M.E. Church formed the nucleus of a community which nurtured its members through the closing years of slavery, the anxieties of the Civil War, and the uncertainties of emancipation.

The emergence of churches and other institutions in Franklin County's black community mirrored a similar if more elaborate process in Frankfort and Franklin County as a whole between 1815 and 1840. During this period, the capital not only witnessed rapid physical, economic, and institutional growth, but its fortunes also became increasingly intertwined with those of distant towns and cities as transportation and other technological advances made all parts of the state more and more interdependent. During the next two decades, the process of local integration accelerated as Frankfort made the transition from town to city and North and South Frankfort became one. But political unification was accompanied by increasing turmoil on the issue of slavery, and by 1860 Frankfort may have been the most divided capital in the country outside Washington.

5

Transition & Turmoil

THE TWO DECADES which preceded the Civil War marked one of the most turbulent periods in American history. The combined effects of industrialization, urbanization, and immigration shattered long established social and economic patterns and radically transformed the daily lives of millions of Americans. Technological innovations such as the steamboat, railroad, and telegraph broke barriers of time and distance and, combined with the spirit of Manifest Destiny, accelerated the westward movement of the population and contributed to a growing pattern of economic specialization by region. Unfortunately, this specialization aggravated long-standing sectional tensions over slavery and brought the United States to the abyss of Civil War.

The period was likewise one of change for Frankfort and Franklin County. It was a time of significant population growth, in which the descendants of native stock were joined by immigrants from Ireland and Germany. While its growing population became increasingly heterogeneous, the capital made the transition from town to city, and the towns on both sides of the Kentucky River came under the authority of a single municipal government. Simultaneously, local entrepreneurs caught the industrial spirit and invested a growing portion of their capital in manufacturing and related industrial enterprises. Significantly enhancing Frankfort's economic potential was the completion of a transportation network which linked road, river, and rail to vastly improve local access to distant markets.

Although the 1840s and 1850s were a time of political and economic progress, the local community was not able to escape the national tensions of the day. Scores of young men answered the call for troops during the Mexican War, and some did not return alive. As the debate over slavery in the territories intensified after the Mexican War, a few politicians tried to defuse the issue by refocusing American anxieties upon the growing immigrant populace. Like Louisville and several northern cities, Frankfort experienced its share of violence as nativist propaganda became increasingly vitriolic. Anti-foreign sentiments peaked on election day in 1857 but subsided soon thereafter as events such as the Dred Scott Decision, the Bleeding Kansas, and the Lincoln-Douglas Debates once again pushed slavery into the forefront of American politics.

One of the fundamental realities of growth in Frankfort and Franklin County during the antebellum period was a major increase in population. With its boundaries now fairly well established, Franklin County's population increased from 9,420 in 1840 to 12,462 in 1850, an increase of 32.3 perent. The growth rate declined sharply during the following decade, and in 1860 the county's population was just 12,694, a mere 2 percent increase over the previous census. Nevertheless, the county experienced an overall population increase of 34.8 percent during the two decades.

Frankfort's growth was considerably more pronounced than the county's as a whole, but again, most of the increase occurred during the 1840s. In 1840 Frankfort's population stood at 1,917. Ten years later it had reached 3,308, a 72.6 percent increase. The city gained a mere 394 new inhabitants during the next decade, placing the 1860 population at 3,702. Compared with 1840, this is a 93.1 percent increase. What is particularly notable is that the city's absolute population growth during the fifties was nearly twice that for the county as a whole, suggesting the probability of a substantial migration from the country to the city.

Throughout the period blacks, both free and slave, remained a substantial segment of the local populace. But as the county grew the black population began to decline relative to the total. In 1840 some 3,080, or 32.7 percent, of Franklin County's inhabitants were black. Ten years later the absolute figure had grown to 3,722, but it accounted for only 29.9 percent of the total. The black population increased slightly, both absolutely and proportionately, during the 1850s, reaching 3,834 persons and 30.2 percent of the total in 1860. In short, while the black population as a proportion of the total rose slightly during the 1850s, it did not return to the level of 1840.

Blacks constituted a somewhat larger portion of Frankfort's population, growing from 1,229 in 1850 to 1,282 in 1860. However, they declined from 37.2 percent of the city's population in 1850 to 34.6 percent a decade later. The reasons for this decline are not clear, but the experience of larger Southern cities, including Louisville, suggests that the relative decline could have resulted from increasing demand and higher prices for slaves in the Deep South.

Like many other American cities, Frankfort's population was affected significantly by foreign immigration, especially from Ireland and Germany. The Irish began arriving during the early 1840s, bringing to the capital such names as McDonald, Noonan, and Griffin. But the greatest influx started in 1847 as survivors of the potato famine poured into the United States. Several of these nearly destitute sons and daughters of Erin made their way to Frankfort, some to work on the railroad and others to take up farming. Among the more prominent Irish names added to the local population as a result of the migration were Meagher, Sullivan, and Haly. The year 1847 also marked the begin-

Four Generations of Weitzels (l. to r. William L. Weitzel, Walter C. Weitzel, Sr., Walter C. Weitzel, Jr., and Louis Weitzel)

ning of the German influence, as immigrants such as Louis Weitzel and Valentine Berberich fled the prospect of compulsory military service in their native land. Over the next few years they were joined by such families as the Lutkemeiers, Sowers, and Walbaums. By 1860 Franklin County's population included 588 immigrants.

As Frankfort's population increased, prominent citizens continued to erect fashionable houses in the Corner in Celebrities and Statehouse neighborhoods. About 1840 attorney Landon A. Thomas built a large, two-story, brick Federal house at 312 Washington Street. Five years later, state Representative John Bibb, of Logan County, built Gray Gables, a Gothic style house at 411 Wapping Street. It was here that Bibb, an amateur horticulturalist, developed the lettuce that bears his name. Another noteworthy dwelling is the townhouse at 212 Washington, built by businessman George Macklin about 1850. During the middle of the decade Major Thomas Carneal erected a Greek Revival home at 405 Wapping Street. When the Civil War erupted, local Southern sympathizers used the house as headquarters for the Confederate Military Board.

The Statehouse neighborhood also continued to see its share of attractive new dwellings. The year 1844 witnessed the construction of a Greek Revival house at 518 Ann Street for Mrs. Mary Train Runyon, who later operated the Greenwood Seminary next door at Ann and Mero streets. The school accepted both young men and young women, but the Runyon house also served as a dormitory for women from outside Frankfort. Another Greek Revival home in the neighborhood is the John Haly home, built at 410–412 Ann Street by the Irish-born contractor. Constructed about 1860, the Haly house was perhaps the last Greek Revival house built in the neighborhood.

By the mid-1850s, nearly all of the Corner in Celebrities neighborhood and most of the Statehouse area south of Mero Street were substantially developed. But a great deal of open space remained in South Frankfort to accommodate Frankfort's growing populataion. Indeed, when the city was remapped in 1854, fewer than 100 of South Frankfort's 333 lots had been developed. The earliest construction had been scattered along Second Street between Main and Conway streets and along Shelby and Steele streets between Second and Third. Development in this area continued during the 1840s and early 1850s, but a considerable amount of construction occurred in the area south of Cross (Fourth) Street and west of Main. By 1854 more than thirty houses had been erected in the area, being scattered as far south as Todd Street.

One of the major consequences of Frankfort's growth during the 1840s was a change in its legal status. On February 21, 1849, the General Assembly passed legislation which made Frankfort a city. The immediate effects of the change were more symbolic than real. While the board of trustees became the board of councilmen and its chairman was designated mayor, their powers and duties changed very little. The first mayor under the new structure was Philip

Valentine & Sophie Berberich

George B. Macklin

Philip Swigert (1798–1871). A prominent civic and masonic leader, Swigert also imported and bred cattle.

Swigert, one of the city's leading entrepreneurs, who served eight consecutive one-year terms. Succeeding him in 1857 was George W. Gwin, a long-time councilman, who also had served as deputy clerk of the Kentucky Court of Appeals and as master commissioner of the Franklin Circuit Court. Gwin served through the Civil War, retiring at the end of 1865. Like the mayor and board of councilmen, the city's chief appointed officials, such as the police judge, marshal, and clerk, continued to exercise the same powers as they had under the town form of government.

Perhaps the most serious real change foreshadowed in the legislation was a section which enabled the city to annex "the new frame dwelling house lately purchased by William T. Herndon from George W. Robinson, situated on the South Side of the Kentucky River." Although the law specifically exempted any other property under the authority of South Frankfort from Frankfort's jurisdiction, it did suggest that South Frankfort was vulnerable. The bridging of the Kentucky River had ended the town's isolation from the north side, and new turnpikes and a railroad offered access to the outside. Most commerce and industry, major sources of tax revenues, were located in North Frankfort, as were most churches, schools, and social institutions. By 1850 leaders of both communities had concluded that it was in their mutual interest to merge.

On March 1, 1850, the General Assembly repealed all laws relating to South Frankfort and annexed the town to Frankfort. The old town was designated a ward, and a few weeks later, the voters of South Frankfort trooped to the polls to elect a councilman to represent them on the Frankfort Board of Councilmen.

Compared with today the cost of operating this newly merged city government was incredibly low. In 1851 the total value of Frankfort's real and personal property was about $1.2 million. The city's potential income, including real and personal property taxes, capitation taxes, license fees, and utilities usage fees amounted to the huge sum of $12,639.91. According to the year-end report of city treasurer William M. Todd, the city collected total revenues of $12,357.97 and paid out $12,269.62, leaving a balance of $88.35. The largest single budget item was interest on the city's bonded indebtedness. Salaries accounted for $1,143 and the water works for about $2,150. Combined expenditures for the night watch, fire department, and market house were less than $350.

As these figures suggest, municipal government was hardly a major enterprise in Kentucky's capital city. Nevertheless, the transition from town to city and the annexation of South Frankfort ushered in a new era of urban maturity. Several more years would pass before the city's governmental structure could be expanded to cope effectively with all the problems and complexities of urban life. But the change in the community's legal status does appear to have symbolized a new sense of optimism which pervaded the city during the pre-Civil War years.

"EARLY HEMPBRAKE AND FACTORY"

Painted in watercolor by S.I.M. Major in the 1850's, this appears to be the hemp factory located at the end of Holmes St. This view shows breaking the hemp for its use in rope production.

Nowhere else was this sense of possibility stronger than among the economic leadership. And the economic growth statistics for the period appear to have justified the optimism. In the agricultural sector a few commodities lost ground or remained stable, but the vast majority experienced major production gains. Thus, tobacco production dropped from 113,300 pounds in 1840 to 37,125 pounds in 1850, as farmers turned their soil to more lucrative uses. Corn production, for example, increased from 268,550 bushels to 549,723 bushels, and hemp and flax production grew from 148 tons to 273 tons over the same period. In cereal grains, wheat production dropped from 45,401 bushels in 1840 to 25,335 in 1850, and rye fell from 12,295 to 2,985 bushels during the same decade. On the other hand, production of oats soared from 57,495 bushels in 1840 to 98,742 bushels in 1850. Potato production nearly tripled, moving from 10,081 bushels to 28,045 bushels during the period. Hay production increased slightly, growing from 1,126 tons to 1,415 tons between 1840 and 1850.

A somewhat similar pattern appeared in the livestock industry. The number of cattle grazing on Franklin County farms declined slightly, from 5,790 head in 1840 to 5,493 head ten years later. However, sheep production increased at a similar rate, from 8,262 head to 8,685 head during the same decade. But these slight changes in cattle and sheep production were overshadowed by figures for swine production, which soared from 15,310 head in 1840 to 25,421 in 1850.

The value of all livestock raised in Franklin County in 1850 was $305,838, while the income realized for slaughter livestock was $69,869. A goodly portion of local swine were slaughtered in local packing houses, but a substantial number of cattle, sheep, and hogs were driven overland via the Louisville and Frankfort Turnpike to slaughterhouses in Louisville.

While agriculture continued to flourish outside the city, local commerce became increasingly concentrated in Frankfort's expanding central business district. The public market house remained a major center of trade, serving particularly as a farmer's market for fresh meat, eggs, meal, dairy products, and produce. Until the early 1850s, the market house remained in the middle of Broadway between Ann and Lewis streets. But the extension of the railroad down the center of Broadway necessitated the removal of the market house to the south side of Broadway between Ann and the alley which extended from Broadway to Main between Ann and High streets. Completed by 1854, the new market was gutted the following year by a fire which also destroyed a nearby coach factory. Quickly rebuilt by carpenters Hiram and George Berry, the new market building was a one-story structure consisting of a roof which rested on brick pillars and sides of three-inch oak planks spaced about one and a half inches apart so that air had free passage through the building. This structure remained an important trade center until 1884.

As commerce expanded, however, the position of the market house declined steadily relative to activity in the central business district as a whole. As early as 1840, the federal census counted twenty-three retail dry goods businesses with a total capital investment of $110,350 in Franklin County. A few were scattered among outlying settlements such as Bridgeport, Peak's Mill, Switzer, and Forks of Elkhorn, but the majority were located in Frankfort. By the mid-1850s, St. Clair and Main streets formed the main intersection of a commercial district bounded by Broadway on the north, Catfish Alley on the west, Wapping Street and the Kentucky River on the south, and High Street on the east.

The range of goods and services available in downtown Frankfort by the mid-1850s was considerable. Richard Knott's store at No. 2 Swigert's Row (about 314 St. Clair) advertised both "CHEAP AND FASHION GOODS," including a "large room devoted exclusively to CARPETS AND QUEENSWARE." Knott's next door neighbor at No. 1 Swigert's Row was W. M. Todd, whose line of goods ranged from wallpaper and fire screens to men's and boy's hats and shoes for the entire family. Several grocery stores depended heavily upon the river to bring in goods from distant markets. Gray & George's store at the northeast corner of Main and Lewis streets offered "Paint and Whitewash Brushes, FAMILY GROCERIES, Liquors, Havana Segars and Foreign and American Sweetmeats." Specializing in heavier goods, Steele & Taylor advertised New Orleans sugar, bar iron, bags of Rio coffee, molasses, nails, and whiskey.

While most downtown businesses were conducted by native white men,

THE CAPITAL HOTEL
(Photograph c. 1900)

several were operated by women, blacks, and immigrants. In 1850, Mrs. Mary Lewis advertised her "New Millinery Establishment," located on Main Street opposite the Mansion House Hotel. Competing with Mrs. Lewis were Mrs. Fannie A. Lyon and Mrs. Margaret Herrensmith, a German woman who operated a millinery shop on the south side of Main Street near Lewis. Among early black businessmen were Edmund Head, who operated a fruit stand; and John Ward, a grocer, who also was instrumental in organizing the black First Baptist Church. Both Head and Ward were doing business as early as 1842. During the early 1850s two black men named Trumbo and Marrs operated a grocery store at the corner of Ann and Broadway. Henry Trumbo was murdered one evening as he emerged from the east end of the railroad tunnel while on his way home from work. Perhaps the most popular immigrant businessman in the city was James "Paddy" Burns, who conducted a grocery store and smoke house on the north side of Main Street near Ann.

The most lavish commercial structure erected in Frankfort during the middle years was the Capital Hotel. As the midpoint of the century approached, several of Frankfort's leading businessmen and politicians concluded that the state capital needed a new hotel. There recently had been some agitation in other quarters about moving the capital to another city, and local civic leaders felt it necessary to take tangible measures to quell such talk. One means was to provide first-class accommodations for legislators and others coming to the city on business. Spearheading the effort was a building committee composed of Mayor Swigert, John H. Hanna, Edmund H. Taylor, Jacob Swigert, Albert G. Hodges, and James Harlan. The logical name for the new house, given its location and purpose, was the Capital Hotel.

John B. Temple was born in Logan County and studied law at Transylvania University. He was appointed State Auditor in the late 1840s. He became Farmers Bank's first cashier in 1850, a post he held for seventeen years.

Farmers Bank & John Haly's Office. This, the earliest view of the Farmers Bank, appeared in an 1859 state gazetteer. Its builder, John Haly, had the office to the right of the bank.

Located at the northeast corner of Main and Ann streets, on the site of the old Weisiger Tavern, the new hostelry was designed by the distinguished architect Isaiah Rogers and his young associate Henry Whitestone, who would himself soon become Louisville's leading architect. Construction began in 1852 and the cornerstone was laid in April 1853. The contractor was John Haly. Covering a full half-block, the main portion of the structure measured 200 by 250 feet. The exterior walls were finished with Kentucky River limestone. Including its elevated basement, the hotel rose to three stories. The front was dominated by a massive classical portico supported by six columns and topped by a sleek pediment. The roof was highlighted by a large cupola. Upon completion in December 1854 the place could accommodate from 200 to 250 overnight guests. Entertainment facilities included a dining room and a ballroom, each measuring forty feet by seventy feet. The total cost was $100,000.

One of the most important events affecting the city's long-term commercial growth during the middle of the nineteenth century was the planning of the modern banking system. Since 1835 the primary source of credit was the Frankfort Branch of the Bank of Kentucky. This institution was governed by a local board, but it was responsible to its headquarters in Louisville. As midcentury approached, local business leaders became increasingly desirous of a bank which was headquartered in Frankfort and governed by a board sensitive to local business needs and economic conditions. But it was a long struggle. Louisville had emerged as the primary center of economic power in the commonwealth during recent years, and its leadership opposed any legislation on behalf of other communities which tended to erode that power.

In February 1850, after several years of legislative maneuvering, the General Assembly enacted a bill to create Farmers Bank of Kentucky. Headquartered in Frankfort and authorized to subscribe up to $2.3 million in capital stock, Farmers Bank was positioned to play a formidable role in the economic affairs of central Kentucky. Reinforcing its position and contributing to its successful emergence from the legislature was its authority to establish branches in Covington, Princeton, Henderson, Bardstown, Maysville, Mount Sterling, and Somerset.

The organizing officers and board of directors of Farmers Bank included some of Frankfort's most distinguished citizens. Elected president was John H. Hanna, prominent lawyer, industrialist, and philanthropist, who served until 1859. Hanna's chief confidant and successor as president was Mayor Philip Swigert, who as president *pro tem* presided over the bank's affairs when Hanna was out of town. The other directors were the Rev. James M. Lancaster, pastor of the Roman Catholic Church of the Good Shepherd and a man of considerable personal wealth; James Harlan, secretary of state under Governor Robert P. Letcher; the Rev. Stuart Robinson, pastor of First Presbyterian Church; Richard M. Knott, Sr., a leading merchant; and Randolph Bailey, a prominent Woodford County farmer and brother-in-law of Senator

John J. Crittenden. Among the bank's administrative officers were two former state auditors—John B. Temple, who served as cashier, and Thomas S. Page, first clerk.

Farmers Bank opened in quarters near the southeast corner of Main and Lewis streets. By 1854, however, the institution needed more space, and in August it purchased from Philip Swigert and Captain Isaac Wilson a lot located directly across Main Street from the original site. Constructed of Kentucky River limestone, the bank was erected under the supervision of John Haly, the Irish immigrant who was fast becoming the city's leading builder. The bank moved into its new offices in 1855 and remained there for more than a century.

Interspersed among the various commercial and financial enterprises located in downtown Frankfort were a growing number of professional offices. By 1850, for example, the Frankfort bar listed twenty-six members, many of whom had offices on Washington and St. Clair streets in the vicinity of the courthouse. Several were also prominent state and local politicians. Among them were a former governor, Robert Letcher, and a future governor, Charles S. Morehead; former, current, and future state legislators, James Harlan, Landon A. Thomas, James Monroe, Thomas N. Lindsey, Lysander Hord, John M. Hewitt, and Andrew Monroe; and Mayor Philip Swigert. Patrick U. Major was elected Franklin County attorney in 1854. John C. Herndon was elected Franklin County judge after adoption of the Constitution of 1850. Austin P. Cox served on the board of trustees during the early 1840s. And Mason Brown, son of Senator John Brown, served on numerous local boards and commissions.

Judge Mason Brown (1799–1867). Brown graduated from Yale and studied law briefly with John J. Crittenden and at Transylvania. Recognized as one of the great lawyers of Kentucky, he served as Commonwealth Attorney, Circuit Judge, and Secretary of State under Gov. Charles S. Morehead. He was U.S. District Attorney for several years prior to his death.

Several physicians likewise had established their practices in Frankfort by mid-century. Certainly the most famous was Dr. Luke Pryor Blackburn, who served as governor of Kentucky during the early 1880s. Associated with him in his practice was Dr. Churchill J. Blackburn. Among their colleagues were Dr. Alexander M. Blanton, Dr. W. T. Price, Dr. E. H. Watson, and Dr. O. S. Willson. No doubt some of these physicians participated in the first organizational meeting of the Kentucky Medical Society, held in Frankfort in 1841. This meeting came to naught. But when Kentucky doctors met in Frankfort a second time ten years later, they laid the foundation for a permanent, effective medical organization.

Downtown Frankfort suffered the greatest calamity in its history on April 29, 1854, when fire destroyed most of the block bounded by Broadway, St. Clair, Main, and Lewis streets and part of the block immediately to the east. The fire erupted about 10:30 P.M. in the large grocery and confectionary store owned by the firm of George and Todd at the southwest corner of Main and Lewis. Within a short time, the blaze gutted the store, spread to several adjoining business houses, and jumped across Lewis Street, where it destroyed a vacant building at the southeast corner of Main and Lewis. Heroic action by the fire company as well as quick thinking by some property owners and bystanders, who pulled down a few small frame buildings in the fire's path, gradually brought the conflagration under control.

The immediate economic losses were staggering. Initial estimates placed property damage at between $200,000 and $250,000, and a substantial part of the losses was uninsured. Twenty-four buildings were destroyed, along with inventories, records, and business and residential furnishings. Fortunately, many of the business owners rebuilt immediately, and some property owners sold or rented their land to new operators who in turn built larger and more handsome buildings than those destroyed by the fire. By 1860 the burned over area had been completely rebuilt and was the center of a still thriving commercial district.

One area of Franklin County's economy which was not seriously injured by the fire was manufacturing. Although a couple of the shops damaged in the fire were of an industrial nature, most other downtown industry came through unscathed. Consequently, the local manufacturing sector continued on an upward course of growth, which had been under way since before 1840. At that time Franklin County had something over two dozen active factories involving a total capital investment of $119,080. Two decades later the number of plants had risen to fifty-one and capital stock invested in manufacturing had increased to nearly $343,000. These factories employed nearly 350 persons who earned over $88,000 in wages and produced goods valued in excess of $794,000.

Franklin County's industrial economy already had begun to show considerable diversification by 1840, and this trend continued over the next two decades. Traditional industries such as bagging, distilling, and flour milling remained strong, but newer enterprises challenged them for dominance. During the mid-1840s, Philip and Jacob Swigert built a highly lucrative pork slaughtering and packing business. The following decade A. W. Macklin & Company moved in to offer competition, killing in excess of 10,000 hogs annually between 1853 and 1856. By 1860 pork packing had emerged as the county's largest single industry, with a total capital investment of $168,000 and annual production valued at $168,500.

A. W. Macklin (1799–1863)

Another major growth area was cotton and woollen manufacturing. In 1852 the General Assembly granted a charter to the Frankfort Woollen Company. Founded by John H. Hanna, Philip and Jacob Swigert, and several other local businessmen, the firm was authorized to issue up to $100,000 in capital stock. It did not come close to the authorized issue; nevertheless, it and three other woollen companies, with a total investment of only $13,000, were turning out goods valued at $83,000 by 1860. Two years after organization of the Frankfort Woollen Company, Hanna, the Swigert brothers, and a couple of their associates in the enterprise joined James M. Todd and Orlando Brown to form the Frankfort Cotton Company. Located on the bend in the Kentucky River near the intersection of Wilkinson and Wapping streets, this firm also had authorization to subscribe up to $100,000 in capital stock. By the end of the decade it was producing $35,000 worth of goods on a capital investment of $19,000.

Two more industries which accounted for a substantial part of the county's manufacturing growth were printing and lumber milling. By 1860, nine local saw mills, with a capital investment of $16,000, were turning out lumber worth more than $62,000, while a sizable printing company was doing an annual business of $61,500. But the breadth of the local industrial base was as important as the size of the individual firms. And on the eve of the Civil War local manufacturers also were producing boots and shoes, baked goods, clothing, barrels, cabinets and furniture, marble and stone work, saddlery, and tin, copper, and iron ware.

Crutcher & Starks

A critical force in Franklin County's antebellum economic growth was the expansion of the local transportation system. Along with innovations in communications, improvements in surface transportation, bridges, steamboat technology, and railroad connections further enhanced the county's access to outside markets and suppliers.

The emphasis in surface transportation after 1840 was placed upon filling gaps in the road network. Some new roads were intended to provide access to communities within the county; others improved connections to more distant points. In 1843 the General Assembly chartered the Frankfort and Lee's Branch Turnpike Road Company and authorized it to construct a turnpike from Frankfort to the bridge across Lee's Branch, near the mouth of the Kentucky River about two miles south of the capital. The following year the legislature provided for construction of a state road from Frankfort to Lebanon, in Marion County, by way of Lawrenceburg, in Anderson County, and Williamsburg and Springfield, in Washington County. In 1847, after that effort failed, the legislature incorporated the Frankfort and Lawrenceburg Turnpike Road Company and authorized Franklin County government to purchase stock in the new company. In 1850 the assembly granted a charter to the Franklin and Clifton Turnpike Road Company and authorized it to subscribe up to $50,000 in stock for the purpose of building a road between the capital and a point near the town of Clifton, situated on the Kentucky River in neighboring Woodford County.

The expansion of the road network also helped to speed up and improve scheduling of stagecoach traffic. By 1851 scheduled runs were being conducted daily between Frankfort and Louisville. For a fare of two dollars, a traveler could leave the capital at eight o'clock in the morning and arrive in the Falls City at five o'clock in the evening. A daily round trip run was available between Frankfort and Georgetown, with the stage leaving the capital early in the morning and arriving back in town about two o'clock in the afternoon. Stage runs also were conducted daily to Lexington and Harrodsburg and three times a week to Madison, Indiana.

Helping to fill the gaps in the road network was the construction of several

BRIDGE AT SWITZER

Taken ca. 1906, this interesting view shows the bridge during repairs, revealing the intricate truss work. This bridge type is known as a "Howe Truss."

new bridges. In 1849 a new bridge was built across Benson Creek near its junction with the Kentucky River. About a year later, a long covered bridge was erected across the North Fork of Elkhorn Creek at Switzer. Of critical importance to Frankfort was the rebuilding of the St. Clair Street Bridge. During the early 1830s the bridge, which had been completed in 1816, began to deteriorate. In July 1834, while the span was undergoing extensive repairs, its entire middle section collapsed, requiring the entire bridge to be rebuilt. Work on the new bridge was completed in mid-December 1835, but the day after Christmas, just eight days after it reopened, the entire span fell into the river, carrying with it two wagons, their drivers, and their teams along with six or seven pedestrians. Remarkably, only two people died in the plunge, but Frankfort was again without a bridge, leaving ferries as the only means of traffic across the Kentucky.

Efforts to rebuild the span began in January 1841 when the General Assembly amended the charter of the financially strapped Frankfort Bridge Company to enable it to build a new bridge that was "permanent, safe and useful." The project moved slowly, however, and it took a $6,000 stock sub-

ST. CLAIR STREET BRIDGE
This early view of the bridge shows the span from North Frankfort to South Frankfort.
The trusswork of the interior and Gothic walkway entrances can be seen in this view.

scription by county government in 1844 to get the project moving. In exchange, local citizens obtained free usage of the span while residents from outside the county had to pay a toll. The completed span, which opened in 1847, was a double-roadway, wood-covered bridge supported by three piers. The covered bridge operated as a toll bridge until the early 1870s, when the city of Frankfort purchased it and removed the charges.

The two decades before the Civil War were the heyday of steamboat commerce in Frankfort and Franklin County. With the railroad still struggling toward completion between the capital and the Falls City, the Kentucky River remained a primary trade channel, as steamers carried millions of dollars worth of hemp bagging, rope, tobacco, wheat, flour, corn, meat—and slaves—from central Kentucky to points in the Deep South.

By the early 1840s steamboat traffic was carefully scheduled to provide dependable service for both passengers and cargo. The most sophisticated operation was conducted by Philip Swigert and William R. McKee, who had become Swigert's partner in the lease of the Lexington and Frankfort Railroad in 1843. Combining the railroad and several steamboats, the two businessmen established the Lexington and Louisville Transportation Line. By early 1844 their company was advertising regularly scheduled railroad and steamboat service between Louisville, Frankfort, and Lexington.

Swigert and McKee's line included some of the most famous vessels and masters anywhere on the western rivers. The captain of the *Tom Metcalf*, named after former Governor Thomas Metcalf, was John A. Holton, who had prowled the Ohio and Mississippi valleys for more than twenty years. The *Bob Letcher*, named for incumbent Governor Robert P. Letcher, was commanded

William R. McKee

by Captain Harry Innes Todd. Grandson of Judge Harry Innes and stepson of Senator John J. Crittenden, Todd claimed a lineage that could be matched by few others in his profession. A gentleman in the finest Bluegrass tradition, Todd was particularly known for the quality of his ship's table. His personal relationships with the farmer-patrons on his route were so cordial that he held frequent dinners for visitors just to use up the gifts of farm produce which his friends regularly bestowed upon him.

Steamboat operators took extra pains to serve the most temperamental of their passengers—the state legislators who swarmed into Frankfort for three months each year. In 1841 a special line was organized which carried lawmakers from Bowling Green by way of the Green and Barren rivers to the Ohio and then up the Kentucky to the capital. During their days aboard these floating smoke-filled rooms, legislators had ample opportunity to weave their often Machiavellian plots to carve up the state's pork barrel to suit their own political needs.

New vessels joined the Kentucky River trade on a regular basis. *Blue Wing I*, the first of three ships to bear the name, was launched in 1845. Commanded by Captain Todd, it made a regularly scheduled, twice weekly run between Louisville and Frankfort. Also launched in 1845 was the *W.R. McKee*, which was followed in 1846 by the *Isaac Shelby*, *The Fashion*, and *The Kentucky*. They were joined in 1847 by the *Sea Gull*, a sister ship of the *Blue Wing*. Among the boats which entered the trade during the 1850s were *The Planet*, *Little Ben Franklin*, *Blue Wing II*, *Blue Wing III*, *Dove I*, and the *City of Frankfort*. These vessels not only conducted regular trade with Lexington and Louisville and nearby communities such as Madison and Cincinnati, but they also took occasional excursions to Pittsburgh, New Orleans, and St. Paul.

Although the steamboat dominated local commerce during the antebellum era, the days of its supremacy were numbered. But this was hardly apparent in 1840. With the Lexington and Ohio Railroad stalled at Frankfort for lack of capital and the completed portion between Lexington and Frankfort leased to a private company, the railroad's future appeared anything but optimistic. Indeed, the situation continued to deteriorate. Short on cash and unable to sell its bonds in eastern financial markets, the L & O failed to pay the interest on its state-guaranteed bonds. Finally, in 1841 the General Assembly authorized the state to sell the entire property, including the Lexington and Frankfort, at public auction. In accordance with the legislation, the state auditor conducted the sale in January 1842, and the state purchased the road for just over $178,500.

After making some improvements in the Lexington and Frankfort, the state signed a new lease with Swigert and McKee. The agreement, signed in March 1843, extended their control of the railroad for seven years. The leaseholders faced a daily struggle to keep the road in operation, and at one point it had a reputation as the worst built railroad in the nation. Again, the source of the problem was money. The revenues provided by daily shipments of livestock

ORIGINAL BROADWAY RAILROAD DEPOT
Following the completion of the railroad tunnel a new railroad station was built on Broadway in the early 1850's.

and coal, plus about one thousand passengers, were sufficient to meet the line's regular operating expenses and to pay for some repairs, but hardly enough to carry on the extensive rebuilding which was necessary for the railroad's long-term profitability.

But the line's fortunes began to change in 1848 when the heirs of the recently-deceased William McKee requested release from their partnership in the railroad lease. The state granted the request and assumed McKee's place in the lease agreement. Meanwhile, the city of Lexington had turned its eyes southward in search of new markets. Convinced that completion of the road between Lexington and Louisville was essential, the city council voted in May 1848 to levy a property tax in favor of the Lexington and Frankfort Railroad. With the state again holding a partnership interest in the road, efforts to complete it were redoubled. One of the first orders of business was to eliminate the inclined plane at Frankfort. This was to be accomplished by diverting the track from its existing bed, beginning about four miles outside the city. The new route entailed construction of a tunnel 600 yards in length under the Main Street hill, which would direct the track into downtown Frankfort by way of Broadway. Construction began in late 1848 or early 1849 and was completed in January 1850.

While the Lexington interests were rejuvenating the Lexington and Frankfort, new movements were afoot to complete the line between the capital and the Falls City. Convinced that the Lexington and Ohio Railroad Company had lost its capacity to complete the project, the legislature chartered the Louisville and Frankfort Railroad Company in March 1847 and authorized it to complete the road between St. Clair Street and the Ohio River at Louis-

RAILROAD BRIDGE

With a center span of 261 feet this bridge is a rare example of a Fink truss bridge. Albert Fink, who designed the bridge, was chief engineer of the Baltimore & Ohio Railroad.

ville. After an extensive resurvey of the route, construction of the roadbed and track began in March 1849. Six months later, the new company encountered its own financial difficulties, but the city of Louisville intervened with a $20,000 bond issue, followed in early 1850 by an additional $1.9 million in loans to assist in construction financing. With $1 million of the money dependent upon speedy completion, construction moved quickly. On June 1, 1851, the railroad was completed to LaGrange, and a year later it was completed to Frankfort, a total distance of sixty-seven miles.

The capital of Kentucky now was connected by rail with the Commonwealth's two largest cities, and both lines conducted a flourishing business. But several more years passed before the unified system envisioned by the original incorporators of the Lexington and Ohio was realized. In the first place, the system remained incomplete for lack of a bridge across the Kentucky River. In June 1851 a contract was let for the construction of a wire suspension bridge between the foot of Broadway and the neck of land near the mouth of Benson Creek. The project was finished and the two roads were joined in the summer of 1852. Unfortunately, there was reason to believe that the new span might not hold a locomotive heavier than six tons. This prevented the operation of through trains and temporarily stymied movement toward merging the two lines.

Nevertheless, both companies operated profitably from the start, and by mid-decade a movement toward consolidation began to develop. In March 1856 the General Assembly authorized the directors of the Lexington and Frankfort and the Louisville and Frankfort to enter into leases for joint operation of the two companies. The shareholders of both firms ratified such an agreement in November, and joint operations began in January 1857. Thirteen months later, the lawmakers passed an act of consolidation which created the Lexington, Frankfort and Louisville Railroad and provided for its operation by a joint board of six members.

FIRST GAS WORKS

Designed by John Jeffery, one of the most progressive engineers in the United States. His brother and partner, Alexander, supervised construction of the Frankfort works. At the time they constructed the Frankfort plant, 1851–1853, they had built over 20 plants in seven states and Cuba.

Eventually absorbed into the Louisville and Nashville Railroad, the Lexington, Frankfort and Louisville never fulfilled the vision of the promoters of the Lexington and Ohio, who dreamed of a direct rail connection between the Bluegrass and the Cotton Kingdom. But the LF&L did provide a vital early link in a railroad network which ultimately connected the Bluegrass with the rich markets of the Northeast, the Deep South, and the East Coast. For Kentucky River cities like Frankfort it often served as a flexible alternative to the water bound commerce conducted by the steamboat. In combination with the steamboat and the turnpike, the railroad opened trading opportunities which might have been difficult for any single mode of transportation. Finally, the very completion of the LF&L was a tribute to the vision of leaders such as Philip Swigert and John H. Hanna, who stepped in to rescue the project during its darkest hours, when promoters in the wealthier communities of Lexington and Louisville proved unable to untie the complicated financial and political tangles which impeded progress between 1835 and 1845.

The expansion of steamboat traffic and the completion of the Lexington, Frankfort and Louisville Railroad also represented major technological advances. But technological improvements were not limited to transportation. In February 1848 the first telegraph service was inaugurated between Frankfort and Louisville with a transmission announcing the death of former President John Quincy Adams. The telegraph not only speeded personal and business communication between cities, but it later helped to improve the safety of rail and river transportation by making it possible to notify conductors and captains of unexpected obstructions and changing weather conditions.

One technological innovation proved a mixed blessing. Until the late 1840s the streets of Frankfort were illuminated after dark only by the light of the heavens. But in 1848 an artificial gas plant was constructed at the northwest corner of the Capitol Square, and lamps were installed around the capitol and much of the surrounding business and residential area. The plant's dedication on July 3, 1848, was an occasion of celebration and speechmaking. When the lamplighters ignited the lamps that evening, the light cast a brilliance on the capitol the likes of which had never before been seen in Frankfort. But such beauty came at an objectionable cost, as escaping gas and coal tar gave off a stench so severe that legislators and citizens alike demanded an end to the problem.

The oppressiveness of the odor was reflected in the report of a legislative committee presented in March 1851. The document suggested that "the propinquity of certain 'gas works' to this Capitol neither add to the beauty of the prospect nor to the comfort of the legislature," but that they produced "the most villainous compound of foul scents, that the human olfactories are ever subject to." The committee concluded that the gas works were "a nuisance" in their existing location and recommended that "either the gas works or the capitol be changed to some other part of Frankfort." Within a short time, the gas plant was relocated to a site near the southwest corner of Washington and Mero streets.

Not all of the new amenities that appeared in Frankfort during the period involved technological innovations. Indeed, one of the most important improvements to the local landscape was associated with the fundamental reality of life—the inevitability of death. During Frankfort's early years, most burials took place in small family cemeteries, many of which were located outside the city. As the community grew, an increasing number of interments occurred in a burial ground on the back side of Fort Hill, which then bordered Frankfort on the north. By the early 1840s, the Fort Hill burial grounds were filling up, creating a need for a new cemetery. Adding to the pressure was a desire among many of the capital's public-spirited citizens for a place where the commonwealth's more illustrious dead could be buried. They accomplished their objective with remarkable speed as well as pleasant aesthetic results.

In February 1844 the General Assembly issued a charter for the Frankfort Cemetery Company, organized by Edmund H. Taylor, Albert G. Hodges, Henry Wingate, Mason Brown, Jacob Swigert, Austin P. Cox, Philip Swigert, Orlando Brown, and M. R. Stealey. The charter authorized the company to purchase up to sixty acres of land for use as a cemetery. It also provided that "any portion of the grounds and buildings not sold for burial lots could be used for horticultural purposes" so long as such use did not detract from "the reverence and respect due the Cemetery of the dead." A short time later the company purchased a thirty-two acre section of Hunter's Garden, a picturesque site located on a promontory high atop the East Main Street hill, overlooking the Kentucky River. To assure that the site's greatest potential might be realized, the directors hired Scottish landscape designer Robert Carmichael to lay out the grounds. A short time later he was appointed the cemetery's first superintendent.

The first burial of a Kentucky hero preceded the original public sale of lots. Since his death and burial in Missouri in 1820, Kentuckians had dreamed of returning the remains of Daniel Boone and his wife Rebecca to the Commonwealth for reinterment. After establishment of the Frankfort Cemetery Company, representatives of the legislature negotiated permission from Missouri officials and Boone's descendants to exhume and transfer the remains to

Daniel Boone Monument. Stone for the monument came from Boonesboro, and the base is Georgia granite. Relic hunters so severely damaged the panels of the monument they had to be duplicated in 1906.

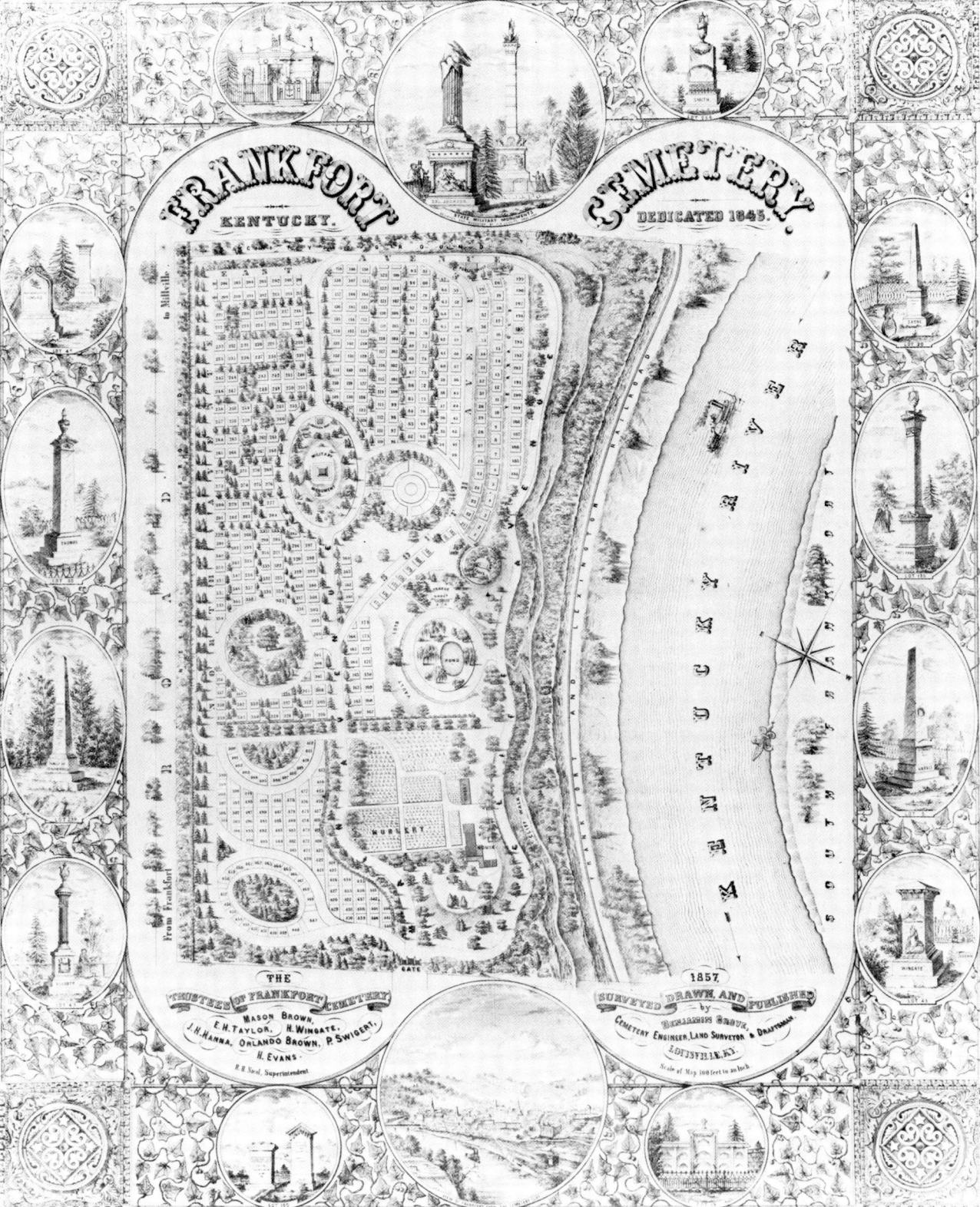

Kentucky. The honor of this responsibility fell to a committee composed of Thomas L. Crittenden, Philip Swigert, and Colonel William Boone, Daniel Boone's nephew. The committee returned to Frankfort on July 23, 1845. The bodies of Daniel and Rebecca Boone lay in state in the capitol while plans were made for their funeral.

Conducted on September 13, 1845, the funeral was a state occasion of the highest order. The arrangements committee was chaired by Governor Robert P. Letcher and included over two dozen of the capital's most prominent citizens. Special guests represented almost every county in Kentucky as well as several Southern and Western states. All local businesses closed for the day, and large crowds assembled along a procession route which began on Wapping Street, followed Washington to Main, and proceeded up the hill to the cemetery. The funeral cortege comprised twenty-one units, including local, state, and national government officials, fraternal and religious organizations, and eight military units from Lexington, Versailles, Danville, and Frankfort. Missing from the commemoration, however, was a marker. This omission was rectified in 1860, when the state legislature appropriated funds for a handsome monument. Carved from Italian marble, the monument was erected by John Haly in 1862.

Although other burials had been conducted in the meantime, books were opened for the sale of cemetery lots in 1846. The following year the legislature authorized the company to dedicate and transfer to the state a section of the burial ground for the interment of illustrious Kentuckians. Burials could be made in this section only by action of the legislature. During the years that followed, the Frankfort Cemetery became the final resting place for former Vice President Richard M. Johnson, fourteen governors, ten United States senators, and five chief justices of the Court of Appeals, as well as a host of generals, artists, politicians, military heroes, and other distinguished Kentuckians.

In 1848 the General Assembly appropriated funds for the construction of a monument "to those who have fallen in defense of the country." Commissioned to design the monument was Robert E. Launitz, a skilled New York sculptor. The shaft was carved from Carrarra marble, with initial work performed by Italian craftsmen according to models prepared by Launitz. The partially completed blocks were then shipped to the United States and delivered to Frankfort, without injury, by riverboat. Launitz then completed the detail work and supervised the assembly of the shaft. The completed monument, which measures sixty-five feet in height, rests on a twenty-foot square base of Connecticut granite and is topped by a statue of Victory which was executed by Launitz. Completed in 1850, the monument initially honored Kentuckians killed in the Mexican War. But it was eventually inscribed with the names of victims of the Civil War and the Indian wars, and it remains today a tribute to Kentuckians who have fallen in all the nation's wars.

Erected a short distance down the hill from the cemetery was a major public

Col. Richard Mentor Johnson (1781–1850) monument. In 1851, the state Legislature contracted with Robert E. Launitz of New York to execute this monument to Johnson. Costing $900, it is made of Italian marble with a granite base. The shaft is ten feet tall and the base is four feet square. It is located at the northernmost end of the Military mound.

improvement of a different sort. In 1850 the General Assembly appropriated $8,000 to build a new state arsenal to replace the one which had burned fourteen years earlier. Appointed to supervise construction were Ambrose W. Dudley, Philip Swigert, and Edmund H. Taylor. Colonel Taylor, cashier of the Branch Bank of Kentucky, had been one of the commissioners for the construction of the 1835 arsenal. The legislation for the new facility stipulated that it be built within a half-mile of the capitol and that the governor approve the site. But as the commissioners began to evaluate potential locations, they soon realized that an appropriate site was not available within the half-mile limit. Returning to the legislature, they secured a repeal of the original site clause and obtained permission to choose a suitable location within Frankfort or its immediate vicinity.

With this change, the commission selected a piece of land at the head of Main Street near its junction with Broadway and the Georgetown and Versailles Turnpike. Contracted to build the arsenal was C. N. Cook, who executed a two-story, red-brick, Gothic Revival structure which resembles a late medieval castle. Completed late in 1850, the arsenal housed the arms and equipment of the Kentucky State Guard and its successor units for more than a century.

Ironically, the sense of institutional permanence and architectural dignity embodied in a structure devoted to the exigencies of war was most nearly paralleled during mid-century in Frankfort's churches. Between 1842 and 1852, five downtown congregations built new edifices, four of which remain today. In 1842, First Christian Church dedicated its new building at 316 Ann Street. Reflecting a practice not uncommon for the time, the sanctuary was divided into two vestibules, one for men and the other for women, each with its own front door. The segregation of the sexes during worship continued until 1853. The Rev. Philip Fall held forth as pastor of the congregation until October 1858, when he was succeeded in the pulpit by the Rev. William Thomas Moore.

In the meantime First Presbyterian Church, under the dynamic pastoral leadership of the Rev. Joseph J. Bullock and the Rev. Stuart Robinson, had begun to outgrow its existing structure at the northwest corner of St. Clair and Wapping streets. In 1848 the congregation hired Jacob Beaverson, a Louisville architect, to design and erect a new structure at 416 Main Street. The members moved into their new, modified Gothic Revival structure the following March. Still unfinished at the time of the move, the building was completed a short time later at a total cost of $14,000. Not long after the move, the congregation welcomed General Zachary Taylor, a Kentucky hero of the Mexican War, who was on his way to Washington, D. C., to take the oath of office as president of the United States.

When the Presbyterians abandoned their site at St. Clair and Wapping, they created an opportunity for Frankfort's burgeoning Roman Catholic congregation. Swelled by the influx of Irish and German immigrants, the parish was

Military Monument. Imported from the quarry of C. Fabricotti Carrara, the marble for this monument was considered the purest and richest ever brought to America. Shipped to Frankfort from New Orleans by way of the Mississippi, some of the blocks weighed as much as five tons; the entire structure weighed one hundred fifty tons. The Statue of Victory, which crowns the sixty-five-foot monument, was placed in position in June, 1849.

FRANKFORT CHURCHES

First Presbyterian Church (410 W. Main). This view, made in 1932, shows the church in basically its original condition. Note the gothic house on the left.

Above & below: Episcopal Church (315 Washington)

Good Shepherd Sanctuary, Wapping St. Original interior of church. This photo was taken in Feb., 1918.

not only straining the capacity of the chapel on High Street but reaching a size which justified a full-time pastor.

In 1848 the Rev. James Madison Lancaster arrived in the capital to become pastor of the newly organized Church of the Good Shepherd. Father Lancaster brought with him a distinguished career as a college president as well as high levels of personal energy and financial acumen. Upon his arrival, the priest threw himself into the work of parish building. In April 1849 he purchased the old Presbyterian Church property for $5,000. There the congregation held mass for about a year. But the structure proved inadequate in both size and arrangement for the most effective conduct of worship. In 1850, therefore, Father Lancaster and his flock initiated construction of a new edifice. Services continued in the old building while the walls went up around it. Supervised by John Haly, a member of the congregation, construction of the rich, Gothic Revival structure was performed largely by the men of the church. When the new building was almost complete, the old church was torn down and removed, and the new sanctuary was finished. Before the year was out the congregation of Good Shepherd were worshipping in their beautiful new church.

Within two years of the completion of the Church of the Good Shepherd, the local Episcopal congregation was completing its new building. In 1842 the congregation had replaced the wooden structure built by Bishop Benjamin B. Smith with a larger edifice. At that point the congregation chose the name Church of the Ascencion in honor of the New York church whose financial support had been so critical during the formative years. But within a decade, under the vigorous guidance of the Rev. John N. Norton, membership had exceeded capacity to the point that a new church building was needed. Thus, in 1852, Frankfort banker and industrialist John H. Hanna donated the money necessary to design and build a new church. Upon its completion, the Gothic Revival edifice was the subject of admiring comment. "This church in style and finish, reflects the greatest credit upon all concerned in its erection," noted the *Frankfort Commonwealth*. "A more perfect piece of workmanship is not to be found in the Union. . . . It will, in all likelihood, stand for ages, an ornament to our town, and a fitting monument of enlarged and open-hearted benevolence."

The last of the new churches built in downtown Frankfort during the antebellum period was First Methodist Church. From 1823 to 1849 local Methodists worshipped in a small frame chapel on Ann Street. This structure was replaced by a somewhat larger brick building which stood until 1854 when it was gutted by fire. At this point the congregation took the opportunity to move the church's location and purchased a lot on the east side of Washington between Wapping and Main. Drawing heavily upon the financial generosity of Jacob Swigert, Sr., the congregation erected a new Gothic Revival church, which opened in late 1854.

In the area of education the primary theme during the antebellum years was

Rev. Stuart Robinson (1814–1882). Robinson's pastorate lasted from 1847 through 1854.

Rev. Philip Slater Fall

Mrs. Mary Train Runyon

Burwell B. Sayre

not the construction of imposing buildings but the evolution of new institutional forms. As the 1840s began, private academies such as the Rev. Philip S. Fall's Female Eclectic Institute, Mrs. Mary Train Runyon's Greenwood Female Seminary, and Burwell B. Sayre's Institute for Boys in Frankfort continued to be the primary avenues of education for local youth. Of these and other private schools that operated in Franklin County during the antebellum decades, Sayre's was unquestionably the most famous.

A native of Virginia, Sayre moved to Frankfort about 1835 and taught for some years at an institution called the Kentucky Academy, created from the merger of two schools operated by the Rev. William Purviance and L. B. Nash. After gaining a reputation as one of the school's most effective teachers, Sayre opened his own academy. Between 1842 and 1848 his school was located in a building at the corner of Main and St. Clair streets. Sayre's institution changed location a few more times over the next two decades, but his reputation as a teacher attracted pupils from far and wide. Both loved and feared, he demanded thorough mastery of English, Latin, Greek, and mathematics as well as the other subjects which constituted his classical curriculum. The consequences of Professor Sayre's rigorous teaching methods were most apparent in his students' achievements. At one time, for example, seven of his students served in the United States Senate simultaneously.

The most important innovation in private education was the establishment of the Kentucky Military Institute. The seeds of KMI were sown in 1843 when Colonel Robert T. P. Allen and his wife visited Franklin Springs, a popular health resort located on the old Lawrenceburg Pike about six miles outside Frankfort. Impressed by the beauty of the springs, Colonel Allen decided that it would be an excellent location for a military school. He purchased the property two years later and established what was known at first as Kentucky Institute. In 1847 the General Assembly granted a charter to the Kentucky Military Institute, empowering the governor to appoint nine persons who, along with the state adjutant general, would constitute a board of visitors. As the institute's governing body, the visitors had the responsibility to appoint the superintendent.

Although no one was surprised by Colonel Allen's appointment, it might have seemed ironic to some of his instructors back at West Point. As a sixteen-year-old cadet at the Military Academy, Allen had conspired with some other students to rid the campus of an old building which long since had become a nuisance. Late one evening the youthful pranksters set the building on fire and burned it to the ground. An inquiry followed immediately, and Cadet Allen was the only culprit who had the courage to admit his part in the episode. But when ordered to identify his fellow conspirators, he balked. Recognizing that Allen would hold firm, academy officials charged him with insubordination and expelled him from the school.

Allen was not ready, however, to end his military career so early. As was his right, he appealed the academy's decision to another military figure, President

KENTUCKY MILITARY INSTITUTE

The principal building in the center was erected in 1838, but burned in 1855. It may have been altered by the head of the school, Col. Edwin W. Morgan, who had an interest in architecture. The buildings to the left are from the original spa, used by KMI as dormitories.

Andrew Jackson. Impressed by Allen's steadfast refusal to betray his friends, the president ordered his reinstatement. Upon graduation in 1834 he served as a captain in the Seminole War and later, after his promotion to colonel, he supervised military engineering activities on Lake Michigan. Meanwhile, he had married Julia Bond, President Jackson's niece, whom he had met while appealing his expulsion at the White House. After his retirement from the Army, Allen served for three years as a mathematics instructor at Transylvania University in Lexington before organizing KMI.

Under Colonel Allen's leadership, KMI became a mecca for Southern lads who desired a military career, and many of the colonel's students went on to gain commissions during the Civil War, especially in the Confederate Army. After the war, several KMI graduates rose to political prominence in the South, among them one United States senator and several congressmen. Colonel Allen operated the school until just before the Civil War, when declining health forced him to transfer control to his son, Colonel Robert D. Allen.

While private institutions continued to educate the sons and daughters of Franklin County's more affluent citizens, the struggle to establish a permanent system of free public schools continued with only limited success. The lack of legal authority and financial resources was not the primary problem. In 1837

The renowned curative powers of the water of Franklin Springs made it a well-known resort of the 1840's. Managed by Dr. Joseph G. Roberts, the lodgings could accommodate 200 to 300 guests.

W. E. Fay in his KMI uniform. An Ohioan, Fay was one of the few KMI cadets who fought for the Union.

the state legislature had adopted a measure for the establishment of county common schools. The following year the same lottery measure that raised money for the expansion of the Cedar Cove Spring water works also provided revenue for a local public school.

The success of the lottery seemed to suggest a reasonably strong sentiment for a public school system. In October 1840, after lengthy public discussion, local voters adopted the Frankfort common school system and approved a school tax of forty-five cents on every hundred dollars of assessed valuation. Elected trustees to oversee the system were five of Frankfort's leading citizens—Jacob Swigert, Thomas B. Stevenson, Thomas S. Theobald, Austin P. Cox, and Henry Wingate. More than a year later, in November 1841, classes opened at three separate locations. A branch for males, located in a brick building next to Keenon's Bindery at 317 St. Clair Street, was directed by Samuel Harris and a Mr. Cutler, the latter a graduate of Brown University. Heading the girls' branch was Mrs. Mary Helen Price, daughter of Kean O'Hara, who taught a class in her home at the southeast corner of Broadway and Lewis streets. Assisting Mrs. Price was Miss Elizabeth Mills, who conducted a class in her mother's home.

The first session lasted for ten months. The curriculum in the female branch included reading, writing, arithmetic, geography, grammar, and some Latin. As originally planned, the curriculum for the males was quite similar. But Mr. Cutler's departure early in the session limited the course of instruction to the "common English branches." Instructional expenses for the first year amounted to $2,290, including salaries, rent, and fuel. Expenses for furniture, stoves, repairs, printing, and other materials brought the total to $2,723. Unfortunately, a substantial degree of tax resistance limited local revenues to $1,468. Tuition payments for children from outside Franklin County accounted for an additional $200. But the added student load so overtaxed the system's capacity that the trustees recommended that any future session not accept pupils from outside the district.

Despite overcrowded classes and a severe budget deficit, the trustees remained committed "to the broad doctrine, that provisions should be made for the education of the entire youth of the community at the public expense, and with the least delay." They based this commitment upon "the belief that the physical, moral and intellectual habits which will be created by the general adoption of a system of Common Schools, will prevent much of the poverty, vice and crime which now abound."

Certain that the long-term social benefits of public education fully justified the "small pittance [of] support" required through taxation, the trustees urged the voters to continue the system for a second year and pledged to eliminate some of the errors which they had made the first session. The electorate did reelect the trustees in November 1842, but it is not clear if a second session ever began. It is apparent that the public school system folded at some point. A brief effort to rejuvenate it surfaced in the summer of 1855 under the leadership of banker John B. Temple, Dr. William C. Sneed, and Judge George W. Craddock. But the effort apparently failed to muster the necessary public support, and it was not until after the Civil War that a permanent public school system took root in the capital.

Newspapers continued to be the primary form of literary endeavor during the antebellum years, and politics remained their major source of copy. The chief continuing political organs were the *Commonwealth*, which represented the Whig position, and the *Kentucky Yeoman*, which succeeded the *Argus of Western America* as the Democratic voice. Although the *Commonwealth* remained under the ownership of its founder, Albert G. Hodges, its editorship changed several times during the antebellum period. As the 1840s dawned, Orlando Brown held the editor's chair. His successors over the next two decades included Thomas B. Stevenson, John W. Finnell, W. L. Callendar, Thomas M. Green, and J. H. Johnson.

The *Yeoman* was founded in 1840 by James R. Adams and Edgar W. Robinson. But the paper's founders were quickly obscured by their successors, who made the *Yeoman* one of the Commonwealth's leading journals for more than four decades. Succeeding Adams and Robinson as both editor and publisher in 1841 was William Tanner, who had weathered the bank relief war fifteen years earlier. He was joined in 1843 by Theodore O'Hara, son of educator Kean O'Hara and later one of Kentucky's leading poets. Following Tanner and O'Hara in 1850 were S. McChesney and W. W. Stapp. They were succeeded two years later by Samuel I. M. Major, who edited the paper through the remainder of the antebellum period and the Civil War years. More than any other single figure, Major was responsible for establishing the *Yeoman* as a formidable voice of the Democracy in Kentucky.

While the *Commonwealth* and the *Yeoman* served as the ongoing vehicles of partisan debate, they were supplemented from time to time by numerous short-term journals, especially during national elections. For a year beginning in April 1840, Orlando Brown edited the *Campaign*, a weekly devoted to the interests of William Henry Harrison and John Tyler. For a brief period during 1843, Theodore O'Hara and William Tanner produced the *Tocsin*, a sheet which promoted the presidential aspirations of Kentucky's favorite son, Colonel Richard M. Johnson. It also contained "news, poetry and incidents of the Day." The following year, O'Hara joined H. C. Pope in editing the *Kentucky Democratic Rally*, presumably to defend the Democratic platform and candidates in the 1844 election. Representing the views of Henry Clay and William Owsley, Whig candidates for president and governor, was the *Campaign of 1844*, edited by Thomas B. Stevenson. A similar publication was the *Campaign for 1859* published by Albert G. Hodges and edited by Thomas M. Green.

Green also was a principal in one of the most celebrated nonevents in Frankfort's journalistic history. Throughout the nineteenth century journalism was a highly personal as well as political affair. Many great editors were

Col. Theodore O'Hara (1820–1867) by William Besser, 1908. O'Hara is best known for his poem "The Bivouac of the Dead" which he wrote for the ceremony honoring soldiers who fell at Buena Vista. He was brevetted Major for his gallantry in the Mexican War. During the Civil War, he fought for the Confederacy under Gen. Albert Sidney Johnson. He was at one time editor of the *Frankfort Yeoman*.

Invitation to the 1859 Assembly Ball. The Kentucky Legislature first asked the local Man's Club to organize the ball in 1852. Today it is the second oldest German Cotillion in the United States.

masters of invective and personal insult. At a time when the victims of insult occasionally chose to defend their reputations on the field of honor, the editor's chair could be a very dangerous place. In 1857 Green was editor of the *Commonwealth* and Samuel I. M. Major was his counterpart at the *Yeoman*. As the political atmosphere grew increasingly heated over issues such as slavery in the territories and nativism, so did the level of invective exchanged between local editors. Finally, the controversy became so bitter that on May 30 Green sent Major a letter asking "what place outside the State a note from me will reach you?"

Major responded that he would be in Jeffersonville, Indiana, on June 1. On that date Thomas Buford presented Major with Green's challenge. Major chose John O. Bullock as his second, and he and Buford planned the confrontation. As the representative of the recipient of the challenge, Bullock set the match for June 11 in western Virginia near the mouth of the Big Sandy River. Weapons chosen were Kentucky rifles at ninety yards. Informed of the terms, however, Green balked. When further negotiations proved fruitless, Green withdrew the challenge, and the duel was never fought. Green thus escaped with his skin intact, but with his honor tarnished, as even his seconds were chagrined by his refusal to adhere to traditional duelling terms.

If the danger of personal violence represented the dark side of political life in the capital, then the Assembly Ball Club symbolized its lighter side. The task of entertaining legislators was one in which Frankfort residents had delighted since 1793. But in 1852, Edmund H. Taylor, Sr., cashier of the Branch Bank of Kentucky, decided that a more organized approach to this responsibility was necessary. He thus recruited the assistance of John H. Hanna and Philip Swigert, his competitors at Farmers Bank, and together they and several other leading citizens formed the Assembly Ball Club. Their sole purpose was to throw a lavish annual dinner-dance in honor of the General Assembly.

Organization of the Assembly Ball Club coincided with the completion of the Capital Hotel in 1853. For more than a half-century the hotel ballroom was the site of an elegant masked ball for the legislators and their ladies, as well as for the civic elite of Frankfort and Franklin County. Those attending the festivities were treated to expensive favors and dinners. When the dues of the members failed to cover the event's expenses, which was frequently the case, Taylor made up the difference from his own pocket. The Assembly Ball was suspended temporarily in 1859 when the Capital Hotel changed ownership. But it resumed in 1864, and it remained under Taylor's leadership until 1876. Without question, the Assembly Ball was the most important occasion on Frankfort's social calendar during the 1850s.

Whether it involved organizing an Assembly Ball, establishing a school system, running a railroad, directing a bank, or governing the city, Frankfort was blessed throughout the antebellum period with a core of leadership which was committed to the community's growth and progress. To men such as John H. Hanna, Philip and Jacob Swigert, Orlando and Mason Brown, Ambrose W. Dudley, Thomas B. Stevenson, and Samuel I. M. Major the responsibilities of leadership were not simply a matter of economic self-interest, but an obligation of their station which the public expected them to perform without complaint. But the progress of the 1840s and 1850s did not isolate Frankfort from the turmoils which engulfed the rest of the nation. As the abortive duel between Major and Green illustrates, the tensions of national politics often invaded state capitals as well.

The first such event to capture the imagination of local residents was the Mexican War, which erupted in the spring of 1846 after a long diplomatic struggle between the United States and Mexico over the boundary between Texas and Mexico. The prospect of war had been a much debated issue in Congress, and the question of a declaration of war was discussed with considerable heat. But once the shooting began, young men throughout the country, and especially in the South, flocked to the colors.

Franklin County furnished two companies of troops. One unit was Company C, 1st Kentucky Mounted Volunteer Regiment, commanded by Captain Benjamin C. Milam, the jeweler and fishing reel maker. The other officers of the forty-four member company were First Lieutenant James H. McKee and Second Lieutenant Richard D. Harlan. The second unit was Company B, which was mustered into the 2nd Kentucky Foot Volunteer Regiment. Composed of fifty-eight men, its commander was Captain Frank Chambers. His chief subordinates were First Lieutenant James Monroe and Second Lieutenants Henry C. Long, William D. Robertson, and Samuel P. Barbee. Once mustered into service, both companies marched off to join General Zachary Taylor, commander of the United States Army in northern Mexico.

It did not take long for the Franklin County soldiers to get their first taste of war. On January 22, 1847, eleven members of Milam's company were captured during an encounter with the Mexicans near the town of Encarnacion. A month later Mexican troops commanded by General Santa Anna, the scourge of the Alamo, attacked Taylor's army near Buena Vista Ranch. Although most of Taylor's command enjoyed a strong defensive position, his

Capt. Benjamin Cave Milam. Renowned fishing reel manufacturer, Benjamin Milam commanded a calvary unit in the Mexican War, Company C, 1st Kentucky Mounted Volunteer Regiment.

left flank was severely exposed. On February 23, after a brief and inconclusive skirmish the night before, Santa Anna hit Taylor's left wing full force. The Americans fell back and, in the process, created a potentially disastrous opening through which the Mexican troops could slip behind and overrun Taylor's remaining forces. At this critical point, the general appeared on the battle scene with reinforcements. The fresh troops joined the fight immediately, forcing the Mexicans back with devastating fire. Later in the day, Taylor tried to capture the initiative, but three regiments were cut to pieces in the attack. Taking advantage of the American failure, Santa Anna counterattacked, this time attempting to overwhelm the United States troops with sheer numbers. But Taylor massed his artillery and unleashed a withering barrage against the advancing Mexican forces.

By day's end each side had suffered heavy casualties, but neither had lost much ground. From a purely tactical standpoint, the battle was a draw. But a new day was coming. By morning Taylor would receive enough reinforcements to give him troop strength roughly equivalent to Santa Anna's. The Mexican commander, meanwhile, concluded that his battered army had only a minimal chance for success against Taylor's growing force. He therefore decided to retreat during the night and claim victory on the basis of the guns, flags, and other material captured early in the battle. When Taylor's troops awakened in the morning to find that Santa Anna had moved out, general and private alike hailed a victory.

Brevet Major Philip Norbourne Barbour. One of the first veterans buried in the Military mound in the Frankfort Cemetery, Barbour was brevetted for valor in the Florida War and brevetted Major for gallantry in the Mexican War. He died at the head of his command storming Monterey on September 21, 1846.

But the shouts of victory did not conceal the fact that the battle of Buena Vista had been a hard day for the Kentuckians in Taylor's army. Among the more noted dead were Colonel William R. McKee and Lieutenant Colonel Henry Clay, Jr., son of Senator Henry Clay. Three members of Milam's company and four members of Chambers' company also perished, along with at least another dozen Kentuckians. One outgrowth of the battle was two public, military funeral ceremonies at the new Frankfort Cemetery in honor of the fallen Kentuckians. On July 27, 1847, a crowd estimated at between 15,000 and 30,000 turned out to honor Colonel McKee, Lieutenant Colonel Clay, and fourteen other Kentuckians who had died in battle. Thirty units marched in the funeral procession, including sixteen military companies from surrounding communities. Senator Clay and former Vice President Richard M. Johnson attended, and the young Lexington attorney John C. Breckinridge was the speaker for the occasion.

In the meantime the Frankfort trustees and the Franklin County Court appropriated $200 each to bring the bodies of Franklin County's dead back home for burial. Major Benjamin C. Milam returned to Mexico to secure the remains of his men and those of Captain Chambers who had fallen at Buena Vista. With that task accomplished, Milam arranged for the bodies to be returned to Frankfort by Ruben A. Hawkins. Milam traveled ahead and, along with Chambers and other dignitaries, received the bodies at the wharf when they arrived at the capital. On September 16 the remains of the seven men who died at Buena Vista, plus four soldiers who perished in other engagements, were reinterred with military honors in the state section of the Frankfort Cemetery. Some 3,000 people from Franklin and surrounding counties attended the funeral ceremonies.

The signing of the Treaty of Guadalupe Hidalgo in February 1848 ended the military conflict between the United States and Mexico. But it ushered in a new era in the debate over the future of slavery, as both North and South sought to dictate the terms under which the lands acquired from Mexico would be organized into territories. During the 1850s, as debate intensified over such specific issues as the Compromise of 1850, the Kansas-Nebraska Act, and the Bleeding Kansas affair, some conservative Whigs tried to defuse the controversy over slavery in the territories by refocusing public attention on other subjects. The greatest threat to American republican values, they argued, was the growing political and economic power of foreign immigrants, especially Roman Catholics.

During the early and mid-1850s nativists expressed themselves in the formation of secret societies such as the Order of the Star Spangled Banner. They soon began nominating candidates for office, electing several congressmen as well as a considerable number of state and local officials. In many instances elections were marred by violence directed against immigrants and Catholics who tried to vote. When questioned about their involvement in nativist activities, members responded, "I know nothing"—thus their informal designation as the Know-Nothing party. By 1855 the Know-Nothings had begun to coalesce behind the banner of the American party, and in 1856 they offered ex-President Millard Fillmore as their presidential candidate. The 1856 election was the political high-water mark of Know-Nothingism, particularly in the North. But in many border state communities, where Whigs found satisfaction with neither the Democratic nor the new Republican parties, nativist sentiments lingered. Such was the case in Franklin County.

Having elected Charles S. Morehead to the governor's office in 1855, the Know-Nothings attempted to expand their grip in 1857. Leading the agitation for the American party in Franklin County was Thomas M. Green, editor of the *Commonwealth*. With the county evenly divided between Democrats and Know-Nothings, the campaign became increasingly bitter as election day approached. On election day, August 3, hard feelings erupted into violence as nativist mobs tried to block Irish and German voters from exercising their franchise. The Irish appear to have been the primary targets of nativist wrath. When an Irishman approached the polls, someone would shout, "move him," and immediately the hapless immigrant would be showered with rocks, sticks, brick-bats, and bottles. As L. Frank Johnson observed, "It was almost worth an Irishman's life for him to undertake to vote without someone, native born, with him."

The first violent confrontation occurred when an Irishman named Griffin arrived at the courthouse to vote. About forty feet from the polls, Griffin was

FOR SALE,
A LARGE AND SPLENDID FARM,
And Extensive and Various Personal Property.

Scotland Broadside. Originally known as "Locust Hill," Scotland was offered for sale by Robert W. Scott in 1871.

MY HEALTH REQUIRING ME TO SPEND my remaining winters in Florida, I must discontinue Farming and Stock-raising, and I therefore desire to sell the farm on which I have long resided, known as "LOCUST HILL," situated on the Eastern border of Franklin county, Ky., and partly in Woodford, in an upland rolling country of great salubrity of climate and fertility of soil, and not surpassed, all things considered, if, indeed, it is equaled, by any other in the State.

ROADS.

The Louisville and Lexington Railroad, and the State road from Frankfort to Lexington, pass through it, under the same lines of fence—affording a commanding front view of the principal dwelling-house and adjacent grounds. The Frankfort and Versailles Turnpike is on the western boundary; Ducker Depot is within a mile and a half, and thus easy access is had, from all directions, it being five miles from Frankfort, nineteen from Lexington, and seventy from Louisville.

SOCIETY

Is excellent; and religious, educational, and social conveniences abundant and varied.

GENERAL FEATURES.

The farm contains over *seven hundred and eighty acres*, all under a high state of cultivation, subdivided into twenty fields and pastures, with numerous small lots for stock of all kinds, with four woodlands located on different parts of the farm; all securely and appropriately inclosed by rail, post-and-rail, hedge, and paling fencing, in good condition, made in the best manner, and of the best materials.

THE SOIL,

Originally fertile and covered by dense forests and canebrakes, and underlaid by stratified limestone convenient for fencing, is still kept in a high state of fertility by various enriching processes, thereby producing, in proper rotation, remunerating crops of hemp, corn, wheat, barley, tobacco, and oats, alternating with luxuriant crops of red and white clover, timothy and orchard grass, and, not least, the blue-grass, which is the gold and glory of Kentucky.

THE WOODLANDS,

Of ash, walnut, cherry, oak, hickory, and sugar maple, are well cleaned and set in blue-grass, and not encumbered with weeds or bushes, and afford abundant supplies of fuel and of valuable timber, not only for agricultural, but also for mechanical purposes. Beautiful and valuable groves and rows of black locust have been fostered and planted in various parts of the farm, and the supply of this valuable material is largely beyond the requirements of the farm, and would find ready sale. Several long lines of red cedar have been planted as screens to the fields, orchards, and stock lots, and are in luxuriant growth.

WATER FOR THE FARM

Is supplied by two large and permanent rivulets, numerous perennial springs and their branches, and by small stock ponds, thereby affording water in almost every lot, field, and pasture; while a large cistern and a deep well afford a household supply, and two larger ponds afford fish and bathing in summer, and ice and skating in winter.

THE BUILDINGS

Consist of the family mansion, of brick [herewith illustrated], and of adjacent buildings adequate to accommodate from fifty to one hundred persons; besides three other comfortable dwellings on other parts of the farm, one of which is of brick, with five rooms, another of frame, with six rooms, and the other of logs, &c., with three rooms—all in good repair, and supplied with appropriate out-buildings, making a division of the farm easy and convenient, if at any time it should be desirable, into four separate tracts, each of which would contain appropriate and comfortable dwellings and other improvements.

THE MANSION HOUSE

Was built by me in 1845–'47; all the work of brick, cut stone, and wood, being of the best material, and executed in permanent and tasteful style. It contains twenty rooms, including basement and attic, all neatly and appropriately finished, and fire-proof as far as practicable, and warmed by a furnace, each room having fire-place and grate also. The dwelling fronts to the northeast, having a commanding elevation, and overlooking a grass lawn of eight acres, and a fish pond of two and a quarter acres, under hedge and post-and-rail fences, with the railroad and State road at the foot of the lawn, affording a fine view of passing trains, vehicles, &c.

THE SPACIOUS YARD

Is fully planted with deciduous and evergreen native and exotic trees and shrubs, interspersed with numerous and choice fruit trees of various kinds.

THE GARDEN,

Of over two acres, is inclosed by a paling fence; is of the best soil, and under high cultivation; and is abundantly stocked with trees, vines, bushes, and plants and flowers, conducing to the greatest profit, comfort, and beauty.

THE ORCHARD

Contains over six acres, securely inclosed, and with a cedar hedge on the northwest side of it; is of fertile soil, and is fully planted with a choice collection of apple, pear, peach, and cherry trees, all in bearing; and the location of it, and of the adjacent garden and yard, being high, and with a favorable exposure, the fruit rarely fails, and is abundant now.

THE OBSERVATORY

On the top of the house overlooks a large portion of the farm, and commands a cultivated landscape of uncommon beauty and loveliness.

This property is not only well suited in all respects for a large farmer and stock-raiser, but also presents strong inducements as a location for a religious community, a literary or charitable institution, or for a body of immigrants.

A DIVISION OF THE FARM

Can be easily effected, and I will sell separately that part of it which lies on the north side of the railroad, containing over two hundred and sixty-eight acres, all of which is first-rate land, with lasting water, superabundant timber, with two comfortable tenements, one of brick and the other of logs, with appropriate out-buildings, all yielding valuable and heavy crops of all kinds.

POSSESSION

Can be delivered in time to sow small grain, and completely in October or November next.

THE PAYMENTS

Will be made easy, with one half cash on receiving possession, and the payment of interest on the deferred payments.

Purchasers are invited to inspect the premises in person, or apply by mail for full description.

SALE OF STOCK & PERSONAL PROPERTY.

I will also sell, at *public auction*, on Tuesday, the fifth of September next, fifteen or twenty head of THOROUGH-BRED Durham Cows and their calves, the thorough-bred bull DUKE of MAPLETON, 7863, and four young Bulls, all having Herd-book Pedigrees, and being of best milking stock;

Also, about one hundred head of my "IMPROVED KENTUCKY" SHEEP, males and females;

Also, about one hundred head of CASHMERE OR ANGORA GOATS, male and female, full blood, thorough-bred and grade, and all with wool long enough to be shorn;

Also, about one hundred head of FATTENING HOGS, and sows and pigs of best practical farm breed;

Also, thirty or forty head of MARES and HORSES, of all ages, and good for farm, and draft, and saddle;

Also, fifty to one hundred acres of Corn in the shock or field, and Hay and Oats in the stack;

Also, Farm Machinery and Implements of all kinds, and Blacksmiths' and Carpenters' Tools, &c.

Full particulars will be given in handbill form, which will be sent to applicants by mail.

TERMS—Cash for all sums under one hundred dollars; and approved negotiable notes at four months for all sums over that amount.

ROBERT W. SCOTT.

NEAR FRANKFORT, KY., JUNE 27, 1871.

accosted by a mob which began assaulting him. When the victim's brother came along and drew a gun in an effort to assist him, a rioter hit the brother on the head and seriously injured him. Only the intervention of Lewis E. Harvie and several other native Democrats, who beat back the mob, saved the Griffin brothers from further injury and possible death. Later in the afternoon, United States District Judge Thomas B. Monroe accompanied another Irishman to the polls. Again, when the Irishman started to vote, the cry rang out, "move him," and the mob closed in. This time Monroe whipped out a large knife, denounced the Americans as bullies, and dared the mob to make any further advances. The Irishman voted! A German who attempted to vote that afternoon was not so fortunate. As he neared the polls and the shout of "move him" went up, the immigrant decided to put personal safety before his right to vote—but not quickly enough for the mob. Some rioter struck him on the head with a rock and the man nearly died.

As it turned out, the election of 1857 sounded the death knell of Know-Nothingism in Kentucky. The Democrats overwhelmed the Americans at the polls and closed a brief but turbulent episode of intolerance and bigotry in Franklin County's public life. But the American party's fall from grace did not necessarily mean a change in attitude among its adherents. In explaining his party's defeat, Thomas M. Green was certain they were the victims of a conspiracy. "The fact is," he charged, "that in this race we have had the whole power of the patronage of the Federal Government, the Roman Catholics, the Dutch and Irish, and the whole gang of those mercenary wretches who fight for those who are able to pay best, and as might have been expected, we have been defeated by them."

Public disgust with nativist bigotry and violence doubtless was an important factor in the demise of the American party. But more significant was the simple reality that the slavery issue had not gone away. As the state capital, Frankfort long had been a major center of agitation over the slavery question, with articulate spokesmen defending both sides of every aspect of the question. The debate grew even more intense as the Civil War approached.

Because Kentucky was a slave state, the advocates of the peculiar institution automatically held the upper hand in arguments on the matter. Their position was further undergirded by a web of law and custom which protected the rights of slaveholders in the control and use of their human property. If slavery was to be eliminated from the Bluegrass state and from its capital, its opponents would have to develop arguments powerful enough to overcome the day-to-day reality that thousands of Kentucky farmers had a substantial investment in slaves and that they depended upon chattel labor for their economic survival. Certainly the militant abolitionism of Northerners such as William Lloyd Garrison and Wendell Phillips would not be politically acceptable in Kentucky, even among large numbers who opposed slavery.

During the first quarter of the nineteenth century, Kentucky possessed a small but vocal abolitionist element which consisted largely of clergy and

Robert Wilmot Scott (1808–1886). Although both an attorney and keeper of the penitentiary, Robert Scott is best known for his advances in livestock breeding, being the first to introduce Cashmere and Angora sheep to the area. He also owned numerous prize Thoroughbred Durham Cows.

committed lay persons from the Baptist, Presbyterian, and Methodist churches. The primary institutional channel for their efforts was the Kentucky Abolition Society, founded in 1808. By the mid-1820s, however, it was clear that antislavery forces lacked the political muscle to obtain complete abolition. In 1827 the Kentucky Abolition Society ceased to exist. Abolitionism flared again during the 1830s when James G. Birney, a former Alabama planter, returned to his native state, freed his slaves, and organized the Kentucky Anti-Slavery Society in 1835. The same year he began publication of the *Philanthropist*, an abolitionist sheet published at Danville. But Birney's views triggered so much public indignation that he fled to Cincinnati in 1836 to protect his own personal safety.

As it became increasingly clear that a full-scale moral and political assault upon slavery was both politically untenable and dangerous to one's health, opponents began looking for new strategies. For many Kentuckians, as well as moderates in other states, one logical strategy seemed to be a program of gradual, compensated emancipation combined with the colonization of freed slaves in Africa. In an effort to advance this scheme many of the state's emancipationists formed the Kentucky Colonization Society in 1829. For more than two decades the society worked closely with its parent organization, the American Colonization Society, to collect the money necessary to transport freed blacks to Liberia.

The gradualist position drew support from many quarters. Among those joining the ranks were a number of slaveholders, many of whom had moral qualms about slavery but whose position as slaveholders caused them to shun the militant abolitionism of Garrison and Birney. Perhaps the most notable of such persons was Henry Clay. A slaveholder and one of the founders of the American Colonization Society, Clay spent much of his political career ridiculing the proslavery position while attempting to compromise political differences over the expansion of slavery which threatened to destroy the Union. Another major support base was the Presbyterian church, whose clergy as well as many lay leaders took prominent positions in the colonization movement. In the forefront of the struggle were the Reverend Dr. Robert J. Breckinridge, the fiery pastor of First Presbyterian Church in Lexington; his brother, the Reverend William L. Breckinridge, pastor of First Presbyterian Church in Louisville; the Reverend Stuart Robinson, pastor of First Presbyterian Church in Frankfort; and the Reverend A. M. Cowan, the American Colonization Society's agent in Kentucky. The movement also drew considerable support from local business and civic leaders, especially those who leaned toward the Whig position in politics. In Frankfort, for example, emancipationist leadership included such figures as journalists Albert G. Hodges and Orlando Brown, businessman and politician Jacob Swigert, banker John B. Temple, and politicians Thomas S. Page, James Harlan, and James Davidson.

Despite its influential leadership, the gradualist party's victories were limited and often temporary. In 1833, for example, public outrage over the brutal

Rev. Robert Jefferson Breckinridge
(1800–1871)

interstate slave trade resulted in passage—after five years of struggle—of the Non-Importation Act. Also referred to as the Negro Law of 1833, this legislation prohibited the importation of slaves into Kentucky for the purpose of sale. With its heavy penalties for violators, the law severely curtailed the business of slave traders by forcing them to rely on the natural increase of Kentucky slaves for sales to Southern buyers. Proslavery interests fought for sixteen years to have the law repealed. In the meantime, as the demand for slaves increased in the Cotton Belt, many slave owners in Kentucky began raising slaves explicitly for the Southern market, often giving as much attention to the breeding of slaves as they did to breeding their livestock.

The next major confrontation between the antislavery and proslavery forces came in 1849. For the emancipationists it was an unmitigated disaster. In 1847 the Kentucky General Assembly, after years of agitation for constitutional reform, enacted a call for a constitutional convention. After approval by the voters in a second referendum in 1848, the convention was set to convene in late 1849. Emancipationists saw the convention as an opportunity to rid the state of slavery's curse. Their mission took on additional urgency in early 1849 when the legislature repealed the Non-Importation Act.

During its annual meeting at First Presbyterian Church in Frankfort in January 1849, the Kentucky Colonization Society set the stage for the establishment of an emancipationist party in the commonwealth. On April 25, after three months of planning, 150 delegates assembled at an emancipationist convention in Frankfort. Twenty-one of the delegates were ministers, thirteen of whom were Presbyterians.

Most of the delegates favored a program of gradual emancipation and colonization. The primary issue which divided them was tactical. One group favored writing their emancipationist scheme directly into the new constitution. But the majority, led by Robert J. Breckinridge, advocated a more pragmatic approach. Recognizing that emancipation was an emotional and unpopular issue that the constitutional convention might otherwise reject outright, they preferred to write the recently repealed Non-Importation Act into the constitution along with an "open clause" which would allow the assembly to call a convention on the slavery question at any future time. Although William Breckinridge spoke passionately for the former position, his brother's eloquence, with the support of Frankfort's Stuart Robinson and the Reverend John C. Young, president of Centre College, carried the day.

The Frankfort convention was the zenith of the emancipation movement. With the approval of the open clause, the convention closed ranks, and the delegates prepared to lay their position before the voters. Seeking the votes of nonslaveholders who also feared the prospect of competition from large numbers of free blacks, Robert Breckinridge and other emancipationists explained their program as a means not only of eliminating slavery but of turning Kentucky into an exclusive home of free whites. But it was not to be. When Kentuckians went to the polls to elect convention delegates in August

THE TERRACES

Built for Philip Swigert in 1847. With its riverfront terrace, it was undoubtedly one of the most picturesque Greek Revival mansions on the river. Situated next to the Paul Sawyier Library, the house was replaced in the mid-1950's by a parking lot.

1849, they elected an overwhelmingly proslavery convention. When the delegates convened, they not only reinforced the position of slaveholders in the Commonwealth, but in retaliation against the influence of the clergy in the emancipation party, they included a provision barring ministers from public office.

Having failed to get their program written into the new constitution, some of the emancipationists made a last ditch effort to scuttle the document at the polls. Breckinridge played a leading role in the campaign, serving as a columnist for the *Old Guard*, a Frankfort-based paper edited by Thomas F. Marshall and dedicated to the constitution's defeat. But it was to no avail. The new constitution triumphed, and slavery seemed more secure than ever.

To make matters worse, the Kentucky Colonization Society's program of transporting free blacks to Liberia was proving to be nothing more than a futile gesture. In 1851 the organization reported that only 297 Kentucky blacks had gone to Liberia since the organization had been founded two decades before. More than ten thousand free blacks remained in the Commonwealth. Colonization advocates continued their efforts for the remainder of the decade, going so far as to seek state funds to support their transportation scheme.

But it was no use. What white colonizationists viewed as "a matter of benevolence towards a degraded and pitiable portion of our population," blacks recognized as a cynical, one-sided effort to transplant them to a strange, malaria-ridden tropical land from which they were now many generations removed and in which they were no more prepared to settle than the white men who were trying to move them.

For the city of Frankfort and the nation as a whole the year 1860 marked the end of an era. After attempting for forty years to compromise sectional differences over slavery and its expansion, the United States stood on the brink of a bloody, four-year civil war. For Frankfort and Franklin County, 1860 meant the end of its pioneer period. Between 1786 and 1860, Frankfort grew from a frontier village to a small but thriving city. During this period, local political and civic leadership was transferred from a transplanted colonial and revolutionary elite to an energetic, home-grown business and professional group dedicated to the city's growth and prosperity. Under their leadership, the community developed a strong economy based upon a combination of agriculture, commerce, and manufacturing, as well as politics. Undergirding this growth was the development of a transportation network which combined road, river, and rail to provide access to distant as well as nearby markets. The community also began to take on the trappings of urbanity, developing a variety of social and cultural amenities and a few rudimentary urban services, including a pioneering water system. A great deal remained to be accomplished, especially in areas such as police and fire protection, public health, and public education. But these would have to wait until after the nation had settled the slavery issue.

6

The Agony of War

John C. Breckinridge (1821–1875)

IN THE AUTUMN of 1860, Frankfort was a thriving city which seemed poised to make even greater advances in population growth and economic development than it had recorded over the past three or four decades. These prospects were overshadowed, however, by a deep sense of anxiety, a feeling which citizens of Frankfort and Franklin County shared with people throughout the nation. For more than forty years politicians had been attempting to find a satisfactory compromise to the slavery question, but each compromise seemed to raise more issues than it resolved. As the 1860 presidential election approached, all persuasions seemed determined to decide the matter once and for all. As the capital of a critical border state, Frankfort felt the agony of "the impending crisis" perhaps more deeply than most cities in the nation.

As the nation's voters trooped to the polls on November 6, 1860, they could choose from as many as four presidential candidates, depending upon where they lived. Abraham Lincoln, a Kentucky native and former Illinois congressman, represented the youthful Republican party. An ex-Whig who promised not to disturb slavery where it already existed, Lincoln firmly opposed its further expansion and was viewed throughout the South and by many in his native state as a "Black Republican" and abolitionist. He had extremely limited support in Kentucky, and his name did not appear on the ballot in most Southern states. Representing the Northern faction of the Democratic party was Senator Stephen A. Douglas, Illinois' "Little Giant," who favored settling the slavery issue through a policy of "popular sovereignty"—that is, by allowing the voters of a particular territory to decide for themselves whether it should be free or slave.

While Lincoln's and Douglas's names appeared on the ballot, the chief contestants in Franklin County and the rest of Kentucky were Vice President John Cabell Breckinridge, the Southern Democratic candidate, and John Bell, standard bearer for the Constitutional Union party. Born in Fayette County, Breckinridge had practiced law for a period in Frankfort during the early 1840s. His meteoric political rise began in 1849 with election to the Kentucky

CAPITOL SQUARE

Taken in 1859, this photo is the oldest known of Capitol Square. Unique features of the view are the mid-1840's wings of the old State House and the inscription "that waved Sept 62" which refers to the period when a Confederate flag flew above the Capitol. The objects on the corner appear to be bundles of shingles.

House of Representatives. He was elected two years later to the United States House of Representatives and served two terms before being elected vice president with James Buchanan in 1856. A moderate Unionist rather than a radical secessionist, Breckinridge nevertheless firmly supported the Southern position on the issue of the extension of slavery. Senator John Bell, a conservative Whig from Tennessee, found his support in the border states and Upper South, where a staunch Unionism was combined with a deep respect for the slaveholder's right to the security of his slave property.

When the votes came in, Bell won Kentucky by a margin of approximately 13,200 votes over Breckinridge. The results were reversed by a narrow margin in Franklin County, where Breckinridge polled 907 votes to Bell's 790. Douglas garnered thirty-seven votes while Lincoln received none. The balloting seemed to indicate a clear urban-rural division. Bell ran a very strong race in Frankfort, where he enjoyed the support of Albert G. Hodges' newspaper, the *Commonwealth*. But Breckinridge, with the endorsement of S. I. M. Major's *Kentucky Yeoman*, ran even more strongly in the rural precincts based at Forks of Elkhorn, Peak's Mill, Bridgeport, and Bald Knob. The *Commonwealth*'s charges of election fraud notwithstanding, these results suggest that

John Jordan Crittenden (1787–1863) by Theodore Sydney Moise. Crittenden represented Logan County in the state legislature for six terms from 1811 to 1817 and served as Speaker of the House during his last term. He was then elected to the U.S. Senate. Between 1825 and 1832, he represented Franklin County in the state legislature, and was reelected U.S. Senator in 1835. He served as U.S. Attorney General under Presidents Harrison and Fillmore, and between these posts, he served again in the U.S. Senate and as Governor of Kentucky. "Let all the ends thou aimst at be thy country's, thy God's and truth's," were among Crittenden's last words and the rule of his life.

Sarah O. Lee, first wife of John J. Crittenden, by Matthew Harris Jouett

it was the votes of the farmers whose economic well-being depended upon the maintenance of slavery which made the difference in the election.

But the outcome did not mirror the nation as a whole, where the 180 electoral votes which Lincoln received in the North more than doubled the 72 which Breckinridge, who finished second, won in the South. With Lincoln's election the threat of secession became a reality. On December 20, 1860, delegates assembled in convention in Charleston, South Carolina, unanimously passed an ordinance of secession formally dissolving the legal and constitutional bonds "between South Carolina and the other States under the name of the United States of America." Within two months, Mississippi, Florida, Alabama, Georgia, Louisiana, and Texas had taken similar action, joining South Carolina to form the Confederate States of America.

While the secession movement gained momentum, a few die-hards made one last, desperate effort to resolve the issue by compromise. Numerous proposals were submitted, but the most important bore the name of a distinguished Frankfort resident, United States Senator John Jordan Crittenden. Attempting to take up Henry Clay's mantle as a compromiser, Senator Crittenden introduced a series of resolutions and unamendable amendments to the Constitution which amounted to four basic provisions. The most important was the reestablishment of the Missouri Compromise line and its extension to the Pacific Ocean. This would forever protect slavery below the line and prohibit it above the line. The second provision would forbid Congress to interfere with slavery in the states where it already was legal and prevent it from tampering with the slave trade. The third element required the national government to compensate the owner of any runaway slave whose arrest and recovery was prevented by force. Finally, the compromise prohibited abolition of slavery in the District of Columbia without the consent of the inhabitants of Virginia and Maryland as well as the citizens of the district itself.

As the president of the Senate, Vice President Breckinridge appointed a bipartisan, regionally balanced committee composed of thirteen of the Senate's most distinguished members to study the Crittenden Compromise. After detailed study, the committee rejected the compromise by a vote of seven to six, with the Republicans and Deep South Democrats uniting against the Northern Democrats and border state senators. The point which provoked the unusual unity of the Republicans and Deep South Democrats was their mutual dissatisfaction with the elements dealing with slavery in the territories.

Although Crittenden's proposals died in the Senate, they served as a basis for discussion at a peace conference called by Virginia in an effort to head off further division and prevent a civil war. The conference attracted 150 delegates from twenty-one of the states which remained in the Union. The conference met in Washington, D. C. in February and continued into early March 1861, holding secret sessions chaired by former President John Tyler. The conference adopted a program very similar to the Crittenden Compromise. Again, however, the program failed. Kentucky and other border states approved it, but the seceded states ignored it; and Republicans, with Lincoln's approval, rejected it as a piece of constitutional blackmail which would forever engraft slavery into the Constitution. The Republicans still hoped for peace, but not at Crittenden's price.

The formation of the Confederacy and the failure of compromise placed increasing pressure upon the Upper South and border states to make a decision between Union and secession. In Kentucky the question lay in the hands of Governor Beriah Magoffin and a severely divided General Assembly. Elected in 1859, Magoffin was simultaneously a professed Unionist and Southern Democrat who sympathized with the desire of slaveholders to protect their slave property and who opposed coercive measures against the seceded states. Accused of having been an arch-secessionist, he was in fact an advocate of compromise who had formulated his own plan before endorsing the Crittenden Compromise.

Governor Magoffin presented his views forcefully when the legislature convened in special session on January 17, 1861. At his request, the assembly passed a resolution which condemned the use of force by the national government to coerce the seceded states back into the Union. At the same time, however, the governor resisted pressures from the secessionist faction to call a sovereignty convention. Instead, on February 11 the legislature recessed until March 20, waiting in the meantime to see what the Washington peace conference might accomplish. During the recess secessionists organized a lobbying effort designed to persuade the legislature to call a sovereignty convention when it reconvened. But when the peace conference failed and the legislature reassembled, the secessionist faction lacked the muscle to achieve its objective, and the special session adjourned on April 5 without taking decisive action.

Less than two weeks later the events occurred which seemingly should have forced Kentucky to take a stand. On April 12 South Carolina troops opened fire on Fort Sumter in Charleston Harbor. The next day, after thirty-four hours of shelling, the fort's Kentucky-born commander, Major Robert Anderson, struck his colors. On April 15 Lincoln issued a call for 75,000 ninety-day volunteers to supress the rebellion. When Magoffin received official notice of the call, he replied to Secretary of War Simon Cameron that Kentucky would "furnish no troops for the wicked purpose of subduing her sister Southern States." The governor sent an equivalent response to Confederate Secretary of War Leroy P. Walker when the secretary requested an infantry regiment for service in the Southern Army. However, Magoffin did betray his personal sentiments when he did nothing to stop Confederate recruitment in Kentucky.

While the states of the Upper South responded to Lincoln's call by calling secession conventions, Magoffin reconvened the legislature and recommended an extralegal policy of armed neutrality. The assembly responded with a formal declaration of neutrality. On May 20, 1861, Governor Magoffin implemented the declaration by issuing a proclamation which prohibited the quartering of troops in the Bluegrass state by either of the warring nations.

Rather than a final, definitive policy stance, neutrality turned out to be a

Maria Knox Innes, second wife of John J. Crittenden

Elizabeth Ashley, third wife of John J. Crittenden

Major Robert Anderson (1805–1871)

waiting game. To the Northern government and Kentucky Unionists it entailed the commonwealth's continued participation in all aspects of national life except the war to save the Union. To the Confederacy and its Kentucky sympathizers, neutrality meant the state was one step away from declaring its independence and joining the new Southern nation. In fact, neutrality was a war of nerves in which each side outwardly respected Kentucky's position while waiting for the other side to violate it.

While North and South jockeyed for position, Kentucky Unionists strengthened their power base. In June the governor called a congressional election to elect representatives to a special session of Congress, scheduled to meet on July 4. Unionist candidates triumphed in nine of Kentucky's ten districts. In state legislative elections the following month, Unionists overwhelmed the secessionists, capturing seventy-six seats in the house of representatives and twenty-seven of the thirty-eight seats in the senate. The war of nerves finally broke on September 3, 1861, when Confederate General Leonidas Polk ordered General Gideon Pillow to secure Columbus, Kentucky, a key point on the Mississippi River. Two days later, General Ulysses S. Grant countered Polk by crossing the Ohio River and occupying Paducah. The Unionist legislature promptly branded Polk's move a violation of Kentucky's neutrality and declared the state's loyalty to the Union. The waiting game was over.

Although Kentucky waited for five months after the fall of Fort Sumter to declare its allegiance to the Union, many individual citizens had long since made their decision. During the summer of 1861, Union sympathizers throughout Franklin County held numerous barbecues and similar public events designed to rally support for the national government. On July 27, hundreds of people from Franklin and surrounding counties turned out for a huge barbecue at Julian's Woods on Louisville Road. Large crowds also attended a public reception at the Capital Hotel on September 6 to honor General Robert Anderson, the commander of Fort Sumter.

But such enthusiasm also was symptomatic of a severely divided community. Even before the legislature ended Kentucky's professed neutrality, both the Union and Confederate governments were conducting barely concealed recruiting efforts. Once neutrality ended, these activities were accelerated. In the process, almost every family in the county sent at least one member into military service. In many instances brother was divided from brother and father divided from son as individuals felt compelled to place conscience before family.

One of the most dramatic cases of such division involved the family of Senator John J. Crittenden. Born in Woodford County in 1786, Crittenden established residence in Frankfort in 1819 after representing Logan County for several years in the Kentucky House of Representatives. During his long and distinguished career, he had served as United States senator, governor, and United States attorney general. As the secession movement gathered momentum the aging senator had seized control of the peace leadership and made one last ditch effort to prevent civil war, but his efforts proved fruitless as both sides had reached such a level of moral commitment that compromise had become impossible.

Senator Crittenden had personal as well as political reasons for preventing war, because he was the father of two sons whose career patterns held great potential for placing them on opposite sides if war became a reality. The elder son, George Bibb Crittenden, was born in Russellville in 1812. After graduating from West Point in 1832, he served in the Black Hawk War. He resigned from the service in 1833 and later moved to the Republic of Texas and joined its army. While in the service of his adopted country, he was captured by the Mexicans in 1843. Following his release, he rejoined the United States Army and won the brevet rank of major for gallantry during the Mexican War.

When the conflict ended, Major Crittenden remained in the army and had risen to the rank of lieutenant colonel by 1861. When Texas seceded and joined the Confederacy, he resigned his commission and accepted the position of brigadier general in the Confederate Army. He became a major general before the year was out. But his career in command was shortlived. On January 19, 1862, one of his chief subordinates, General Felix Zollicoffer, disobeyed orders and forced Crittenden to make a premature attack against federal troops under General George H. Thomas at Mill Spring, located on the Cumberland River in southern Kentucky. Because of the unfavorable circumstances of the attack, Crittenden suffered a severe defeat, losing his artillery and supply trains as well as the battle. Shaken by the defeat, he resigned his commission and served the remainder of the war in subordinate posts.

Like his elder brother, Thomas Leonidas Crittenden was born in Russellville, in 1819. Choosing a legal rather than a military career, he was admitted to the bar in 1840, and two years later he was elected Franklin County commonwealth's attorney. Nevertheless, when the Mexican War erupted, he enlisted in the army and rose to the rank of colonel, serving on the staff of General Zachary Taylor and as commanding officer of the Third Kentucky Infantry Regiment. Returning to civilian life when the war ended in 1849, he accepted an appointment by his old commander, President Taylor, as counsel at Liverpool. He returned to Frankfort four years later and followed his father in adhering to the Union when the Civil War broke out.

Major General Thomas Leonidas Crittenden (1819–1893). *Photo by Matthew Brady*

For a brief period Thomas L. Crittenden commanded the state forces which remained loyal to the Union after General Simon B. Buckner led the majority into the Confederate Army. In September 1861 he accepted a commission as brigadier general of volunteers, and he commanded a division at the battle of Shiloh the following spring. Commissioned a major general in July 1862, he was one of General William S. Rosecrans' chief subordinates at the battles of Tullahoma and Chickamauga. The latter campaign, however, was a disaster for Rosecrans, and he attempted to shed some of his own responsibility for the defeat by preferring charges against Crittenden and two other subordi-

William Wirt Adams (1819–1888)
Photo by Matthew Brady

Humphrey Marshall, Jr. (1812–1872)
Photo by Matthew Brady

nates. All three were cleared by a military court, but the fact that the charges had been filed left a cloud over their military careers. Consequently, Crittenden resigned his commission in late 1864.

The Crittenden brothers returned to Frankfort after the war, Thomas to serve for a brief period as state treasurer and George to take the position of state librarian. But whatever reunification occurred was partial and shortlived. Senator John J. Crittenden died at his home in July 1863, while his sons were still at war. Paradoxically, Thomas L. Crittenden, whose primary career had been as an attorney, returned to military service after his brief tenure as state treasurer, having accepted an appointment as a colonel in the regular army. He held the position until his retirement in 1881. In the meantime, his brother had died in 1880 and was buried in Frankfort Cemetery, where his father had been interred seventeen years earlier. The family's final reunification came in October 1893 when Thomas died in Annandale, New York, and was returned to Frankfort for burial with his father and brother in Frankfort Cemetery.

Along with General Thomas L. Crittenden, nearly 440 other Franklin Countians responded to the call of conscience, approximately 190 joining the Confederate Army and about 253 remaining with the Union. The vast majority of Confederate volunteers joined one of four units. The largest Confederate unit from Franklin County was Company C of the Ninth Kentucky Cavalry, commanded by General John Hunt Morgan. Composed of fifty-four men, Company C's officers included Lieutenant A. J. Church and Dr. Ben Duvall, a surgeon. The largest infantry unit was Company K, Fifth Kentucky Infantry Regiment. The officers of this thirty-nine member unit were Captain W. D. Acton and Lieutenants J. T. Gaines, D. S. Crockett, and J. C. Robb. Thirty-four Franklin Countians joined Company E, Fourth Kentucky Infantry. Initially commanded by Major Thomas B. Monroe, its other officers included Captain Ben J. Monroe, Lieutenants George B. Burnley, Isham T. Dudley, and Robert A. Thompson, and Dr. Preston B. Scott, surgeon. The unit saw action at Shiloh, where Major Monroe and Captain Monroe were killed, and at Chickamauga. In addition, twenty-two local men served in Company E, Second Kentucky Infantry, and some nineteen volunteers were scattered among other companies in the Second and Sixth Kentucky Infantry regiments.

Frankfort also was the birthplace of four Confederate generals. William Wirt Adams was born in 1819, received his education at Bardstown, and served in the Texas army in 1839 before establishing a business and political career in Mississippi. When the war broke out, he raised a cavalry regiment and was promoted to brigadier general for gallantry at Vicksburg in 1863. His younger brother, Daniel Weisiger Adams, was born in 1821. After reading law, he established a legal practice in Mississippi before moving to Louisiana. He began his military career as a lieutenant colonel in a Louisiana regiment, which he commanded at Shiloh. Promoted to brigadier general in May 1862, he subsequently commanded a brigade at Perryville, Murfreesboro, and Chickamauga. He was wounded on three different occasions.

Unlike the Adams brothers, Humphrey Marshall, Jr., and Thomas Hart Taylor remained in their native state. Born in 1812, the son of the old Federalist politician and historian, Marshall graduated from West Point in 1832 and resigned his commission the following year to practice law. He served as a colonel in the First Kentucky Cavalry during the Mexican War and was elected to several terms in Congress between 1848 and 1859, his tenure punctuated by a year's term as United States minister to China. A Breckinridge supporter in 1860, he was an advocate of Magoffin's neutrality policy. When neutrality failed, he accepted a brigadier general's commission in the Confederate Army. After serving under General Braxton Bragg during his invasion of Kentucky in the fall of 1862, Marshall resigned his commission and established a law practice in Richmond, Virginia, in 1863. A short time later, he was elected to the Confederate Congress as a representative from Kentucky. After the war, he returned to Kentucky and practiced law in Louisville until his death in 1872. He is buried in the state section of the Frankfort Cemetery.

Thomas H. Taylor was born in 1825 and studied at Centre College. After serving as an officer in the Third Kentucky Infantry during the Mexican War, he became involved in several business ventures. When the Civil War began, he was appointed a captain in the Confederate Army and soon became a lieutenant colonel in the First Kentucky Infantry. Appointed a brigadier general in November 1862, he served under Generals Edmund Kirby Smith in east Tennessee and under John C. Pemberton at Vicksburg. Near the end of the war he was post commander at Mobile, Alabama. Taylor returned to Kentucky after the war and served five years as a deputy federal marshal before becoming Louisville police chief, a post which he held for eleven years. He died in 1901 and is buried in the Frankfort Cemetery.

Thomas Hart Taylor (1825–1901)
Photo by Matthew Brady

Most Union volunteers from Franklin County joined the Third and Ninth Kentucky Cavalry regiments or the Twenty-Second Kentucky Infantry. The largest unit was Company E, Ninth Kentucky Cavalry. The captains of this eighty-man company were Henry J. Sheets and James R. Page, who later received a promotion to major. The lieutenants were Thomas Mahoney, Thomas M. Page, and Richard H. Parrent. Forty-one local men joined Company C, Ninth Kentucky, but it does not appear that any of its officers were from Franklin County. Company B, Third Kentucky Cavalry was composed of thirty-one Franklin Countians. The unit's first captain, Albert G. Bacon, was killed by a sabre thrust from Confederate General Nathan Bedford Forrest during a cavalry skirmish in December. His successor, Captain Robert H. King, rose to the rank of lieutenant colonel. The company's other commissioned officer was Lieutenant John J. Roberts.

The Twenty-second Kentucky Infantry Regiment, drawn heavily from Franklin County, was commanded by Colonel Daniel Weisiger Lindsey, a prominent Frankfort lawyer, who held the post of city attorney when the war began. In November 1863 Lindsey became inspector general of Kentucky, a responsibility which included a state commission as major general and acting command of all state troops serving within the state. One of Lindsey's chief

General Daniel W. Lindsey (1835–1917). During the Civil War, Lindsey was appointed Inspector General of Kentucky and acting commander of all military forces of the state. After the war he was appointed Adjutant General of Kentucky.

subordinates, Lieutenant Colonel George W. Monroe, later was brevetted a brigadier general of volunteers.

The vast majority of Franklin Countians in the Twenty-second Kentucky were in either Company F or Company I. The first commander of Company F was Captain Daniel Garrard, Jr. Upon his death at the battle of Chickasaw Bluffs near Vicksburg, Mississippi, in December 1862, he was succeeded by Captain William W. Bacon. The company's lieutenants were William H. Sneed and Richard F. Frayne. Two members of the company who rose from the ranks were Orlando Brown, Jr., and Joseph W. Roberts. The grandson of Senator John Brown, Orlando Brown, Jr., enlisted as a private and was successively promoted to adjutant, major, and lieutenant colonel. Similarly, Private Roberts rose to the rank of major and was appointed regimental adjutant. Officers of Company I included Captain Frank A. Estop and Captain William K. Gray. In addition, one of their privates, Jacob Swigert, Jr., later attained the rank of captain. Among other Franklin Countians who held commissions above the rank of lieutenant were Lieutenant Colonel John M. Bacon, Major John G. Keenon, and Captain Lewis Finnell.

Kentucky troops opposed each other on many occasions, on many battlefields, throughout the war. But perhaps none of these encounters so dramatized the tragedy of the Civil War as those in which the troops engaged each other on their home soil. The most significant such meeting brought the war not only to Kentucky but directly to the capital itself. In mid-August 1862, Confederate armies commanded by Generals Braxton Bragg and Edmund Kirby Smith moved northward from Chattanooga and Knoxville into Kentucky. The plan was for Kirby Smith to march on Richmond and Lexington and then for the armies to launch a joint attack against Louisville, which controlled northern access into the western theatre of war by both river and rail. When the invasion began, the rebel prospects appeared excellent. Bragg and Kirby Smith had a combined force of approximately 40,000 veteran troops. Louisville and central Kentucky, on the other hand, were defended by General Don Carlos Buell, whose Union army was scattered throughout central Tennessee and northern Alabama. Louisville itself was protected only by a weak home guard and a handful of raw recruits.

In the beginning everything went according to plan for the Confederates. On August 30 Kirby Smith arrived at Richmond, where he routed 7,000 green Indiana recruits under Brigadier General Mahlon D. Manson. Kirby Smith's victory caused a general panic among Unionists in Lexington, Frankfort, and Louisville. Many Lexingtonians abandoned their homes and fled to the Falls City. On September 1 troops under Kirby Smith's command marched into Lexington, where they were greeted by overjoyed Southern sympathizers, who hailed them as conquering heroes.

Kirby Smith wasted no time in following up his advantage. As soon as Lexington was secure, he ordered units to spread out and expand the territory under rebel control. Dispatched to Frankfort was a Louisiana cavalry unit

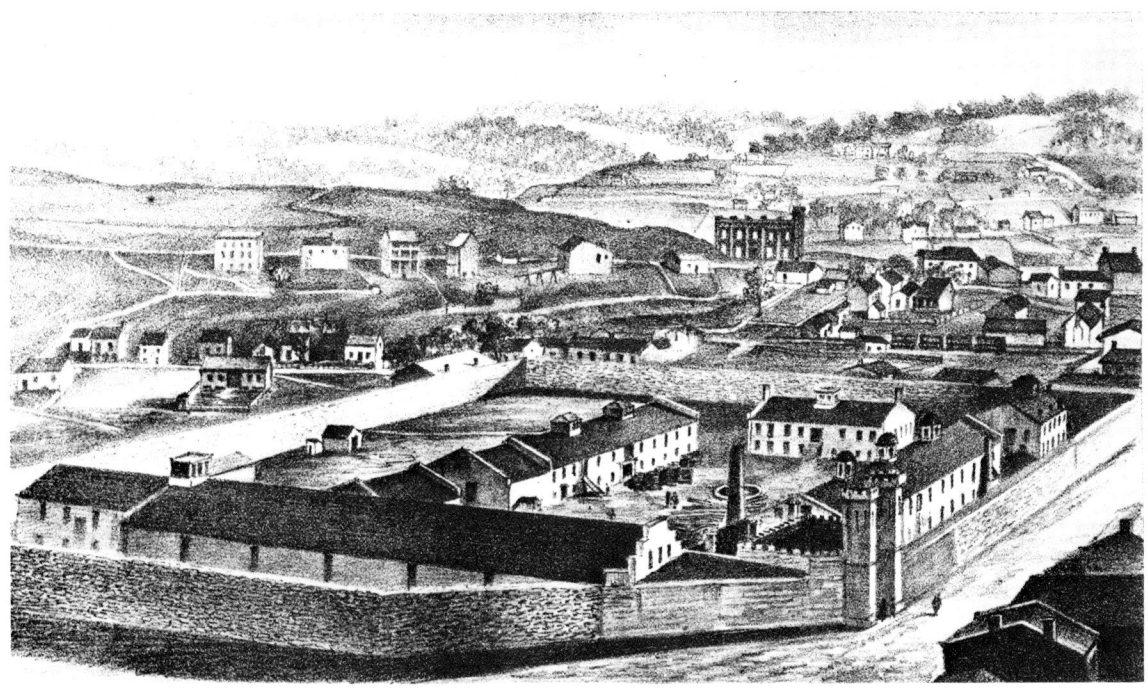

BIRD'S-EYE VIEW OF THE PENITENTIARY FROM BLANTON'S HILL (1860)

commanded by Colonel John S. Scott. While Scott hurried to the capital, Governor James S. Robinson, the General Assembly, and other state officers and prominent Unionists fled to Louisville. Covering their retreat was a cavalry force commanded by Brigadier General James S. Jackson, a former congressman from Hopkinsville. (Robinson had succeeded Magoffin as governor upon the latter's resignation less than three weeks earlier.)

On September 3, Scott's cavalry rode into the capital via the turnpike from Lexington. Stopping at the top of East Main Street hill near the cemetery, he sent word into the city demanding its immediate surrender. The reply that came back was anything but unfriendly. The state government and other Unionists having evacuated, Frankfort was in the hands of Southern sympathizers who were eager to welcome the dashing young cavalry officer and his troops. Thus, with flags and banners whipping briskly in the breeze, Scott and his troopers rode down the hill into the heart of the city, where they were met by a citizens committee headed by Thomas N. Lindsey, a prominent attorney, former state legislator, and father of General Daniel W. Lindsey. After ceremonies of capitulation that were more a welcome than a surrender, Scott dashed to the capitol, along with a throng of well-wishers. There he mounted the flagpole, tore down the Stars and Stripes, and replaced it with the Stars and Bars.

Frankfort remained under Confederate control more than a month. During this interim communications with Louisville and Cincinnati were severed and most business was suspended. Day to day civil affairs were directed by Thomas N. Lindsey, who was appoionted mayor by the Confederate military

Newton Craig, Keeper of the Penitentiary, March, 1844 through 1855. Under Craig's direction, prison labor earned the state a total of $59,725.36. Of that amount $37,899.30 was retained by the state and $21,826.06 by Craig. This might explain why the keeper's job was a very politically lucrative position.

authorities. But Kirby Smith and his subordinates were in command of the situation. From a political standpoint, the capture of Frankfort was an important victory for Kirby Smith. As a practical matter, control of the city also gave him an opportunity to refit a few of his bedraggled, shoeless troops. For local businessmen this was a mixed blessing. Confederate troops had strict orders that no private property was to be destroyed or disturbed. However, they were to pay for anything they took with Confederate currency, which was all but worthless. Numerous businesses lost money through transactions with the Confederates, but the biggest loser was the Frankfort Woollen Company, which had to give up 74,960 yards of Kentucky jeans cloth. The firm had expected to sell the material for as much as $1.50 per yard in the prevailing currency; instead, it got $1.00 per yard in Confederate money.

While Kirby Smith attempted to expand and consolidate his control of the Bluegrass, Bragg moved northward from Chattanooga and into southern Kentucky. With Louisville as his ultimate objective, he marched into Glasgow on September 14. Advance units reached Bowling Green the following day, and on the seventeenth Bragg captured Munfordville and its 4,148-man Union garrison. Bragg was now situated directly across Buell's line of march, apparently blocking the Northern general's rush back to Louisville. At this point the rebel commander committed a major tactical blunder.

Instead of leaving behind a small rear guard to detain Buell and joining Kirby Smith for a full-scale attack upon Louisville, Bragg remained at Munfordville and wasted three days in an unsuccessful attempt to maneuver Buell into an engagement. Finally realizing that this tactic was futile, Bragg headed in a northerly direction. But instead of moving directly against Louisville, which was still exposed and poorly defended, he captured Bardstown, set up headquarters, and sent to Lexington for supplies. This error opened Buell's path and enabled him to march into Louisville and to secure the city's defenses.

Bragg compounded his error by meddling in politics. While still in Bardstown, he boldly declared to the people of Kentucky that the Confederate Army had come to set them free from Yankee bondage and urged them to embrace the Southern cause. He then dashed to Frankfort, where he and Kirby Smith planned to inaugurate Richard J. Hawes, a former Bourbon County judge, as Confederate governor of Kentucky. While the two rebel generals played politics, Buell rebuilt his army and prepared to take the offensive. On October 1 Buell's 55,000 troops moved out of Louisville in three wings. Three days later the Confederates in Frankfort were in the midst of Hawes' inauguration when Union artillery batteries attached to General Joshua Sill's command began shelling the city. Bragg, Kirby Smith, Simon B. Buckner, and several other generals fled the capital immediately, their retreat being covered by Colonel Scott's cavalry.

In their effort to impede the Yankee advance, Scott's troops burned the railroad bridge across the Kentucky River. They were about to burn the covered bridge at St. Clair Street when acting-Mayor Lindsey and other civilians persuaded Scott not to use the torch, noting that the area was in the midst of a severe drought and that the fire would quickly ignite the tinder-dry buildings and perhaps destroy the city. Furthermore, Lindsey pointed out, the drought had left the river so low that Union troops could cross the river easily, with or without the bridge. Lindsey and his colleagues did agree, however, to tear out the floor of the bridge as a means of rendering it impassable. The following morning, dozens of residents gathered at the bridge, ripped up the joists and floor boards, and threw them into the river. As one writer later observed, the prevailing opinion was that "nothing but a squirrel or a cat could cross the bridge in its then condition."

As Lindsey expected, the destruction of the bridge floor did little to impede the Union advance. When the advance elements of Sill's infantry arrived at the Kentucky River the next day, they found an old boat near Devil's Hollow and quickly began ferrying troops across the river. Meanwhile, the Ninth Kentucky Cavalry, commanded by Colonel Richard Taylor Jacob, raced down river, crossed Benson Creek, and then forded the Kentucky near Lock and Dam No. 4. Neither the infantry nor the cavalry met any opposition, and a short time after entering the city the federals pitched their camp on the grounds of the capitol. Later in the day General Sill arrived in Frankfort with the remainder of his command. The following morning, October 7, his engineers rebuilt the St. Clair Street Bridge. That afternoon Sill's troops began pulling out, having received orders to march toward the town of Perryville, located about thirty-five miles south of Frankfort. By the morning of the ninth, all of Sill's troops were gone, having left the capital in the hands of a skeleton force of walking wounded under the command of Lieutenant John J. Roberts, an officer of the Third Kentucky Cavalry, who was home on furlough.

No sooner had Sill's troops left the city than Scott's cavalry reappeared atop East Main Street hill above the arsenal. Recognizing that he could not push back a direct assault with a handful of convalescing wounded, Roberts resorted to deception. He moved his soldiers up the Louisville hill to the site of the Berry Hill estate, and then kept them moving in a pattern which created an appearance that he had more troops than were actually present. In the meantime, he obtained the wheels and axle of a horse cart and placed a couple of stove pipes across the axle to create an illusion of artillery. Roberts' hoax worked for several hours, but when Scott finally realized he had been tricked, he sent a force under a Captain Garriott to attack Roberts' base. Hoping for surprise, Garriott led his men down the East Main Street hill, across the Kentucky River below the dam, and up the river toward Louisville hill. But Roberts apparently had detected the movement and had placed his troops securely behind a stone wall, which enabled them to drive back the Confederates with a hail of fire. After being driven back a second time, the rebels were in the process of a third attack when two cavalry regiments attached to the command of General Ebenezer Dumont arrived on the scene, having been sent to fill the gap left by General Sill's evacuation. Charging down on the Confederates, the Union cavalry headed straight for the St. Clair Street Bridge. Colonel Scott tried valiantly to rally his forces, but to no avail. Finally recognizing that the federal numbers were too great to overcome, Scott led his men back up the hill and out of Frankfort, leaving the city to General Dumont.

While Sill's troops were moving out of Frankfort on October 7, other elements of Buell's army were maneuvering with units of Bragg's rear guard for position around several water holes in the vicinity of Perryville. On the morning of the eighth, Union troops under General Alexander McDowell McCook advanced toward the Chaplin River, apparently unaware that enemy troops were present in large numbers near the stream. From a nearby hill General Philip Sheridan saw the Confederates preparing to attack and tried to signal McCook of the danger. But the message did not get through. At 1:30 P.M. the rebels opened fire. The battle of Perryville raged until nightfall. When the smoke cleared, 510 Confederates and 845 Federals lay dead, and more than 5,500 men on both sides were wounded. In proportion to its brief duration and the number of troops involved, Perryville was one of the bloodiest battles of the war.

Tactically the battle was a Confederate victory. Bragg employed approximately 15,000 men to drive back about 25,000 Union troops. But he knew that Buell had committed only about half of his army and that the Northern commander could be expected to regroup and attack in force the following morning. Bragg therefore ordered a retreat toward Harrodsburg. With their fires burning brightly, the rebels broke camp about midnight and moved out silently. At Harrodsburg, Bragg joined Kirby Smith, who had abandoned Frankfort, and they waited two days for an anticipated attack. When none came, they retreated into east Tennessee.

Because of Bragg's retreat and Buell's failure to follow up his advantage, Perryville was a militarily indecisive struggle. But from a political perspective Perryville was critical in that it ended the Southern dream of winning Kentucky's allegiance to the secessionist cause. As for Frankfort, Union troops continued for a couple more weeks to skirmish with remnants of Bragg's army which had remained in the vicinity of the capital. By November 5, Frankfort was back in Unionist hands, and state government prepared to resume operations at the capitol.

While Perryville was the Confederate high-water mark in Kentucky, the invasion of 1862 was not the capital's final encounter with the rebels. On June 2, 1864, approximately 2,500 Confederate cavalrymen under the command of General John Hunt Morgan slipped into Pike County, eluded federal troops commanded by General Stephen Burbridge, and made their way to Mount Sterling in Wolfe County. On June 8 Morgan arrived at Mount Sterling, where his troops robbed the local bank. Riding on to Lexington, Morgan conducted a hit-and-run raid and then turned toward Cynthiana. In the mean-

General Stephen Burbridge
Photo by Matthew Brady

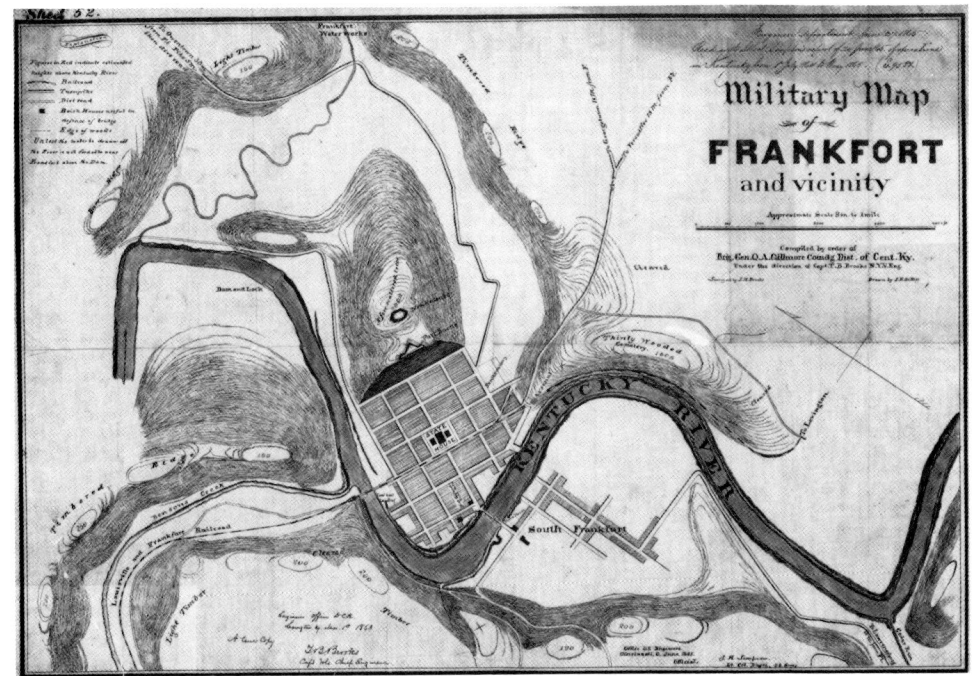

MILITARY MAP OF FRANKFORT & VICINITY (1863)

time, he dispatched a force under Lieutenant Colonel Moses Tandy Pryor to attack Frankfort.

Correctly anticipating that Frankfort was one of Morgan's objectives, Governor Thomas Bramlette moved quickly to defend the city against the expected assault. One of his first actions was to dispatch a message to General Ulysses S. Grant requesting that he release State Inspector General Daniel W. Lindsey from his divisional command and allow him to return to Frankfort to organize the city's defense. Grant yielded to the governor's plea and Lindsey sped to the capital.

With the authority of martial law behind him, Lindsey began immediately to reorganize the Home Guard and to prepare the city for the expected attack. Learning that Colonel George B. Monroe, his former second-in-command with the Twenty-second Kentucky, was home on leave, he directed his ex-subordinate to take active field command of all forces in the Frankfort area. Lindsey also mobilized the militia battalion, which was commanded by Colonel Edward Keenon. Two militia companies under Captains Uberto "Buck" Keenon and A. Jud Graham were assigned to defend the arsenal, and other units were placed at the wooden bridges and ordered to guard key roads into the city. Meanwhile, General Lindsey established his command post at Fort Boone, located atop Fort Hill, which was strengthened with additional artillery redoubts and manned in part by a large number of civilians who rallied to the city's defense.

The expected attack began early in the evening of Friday, June 10, as Colo-

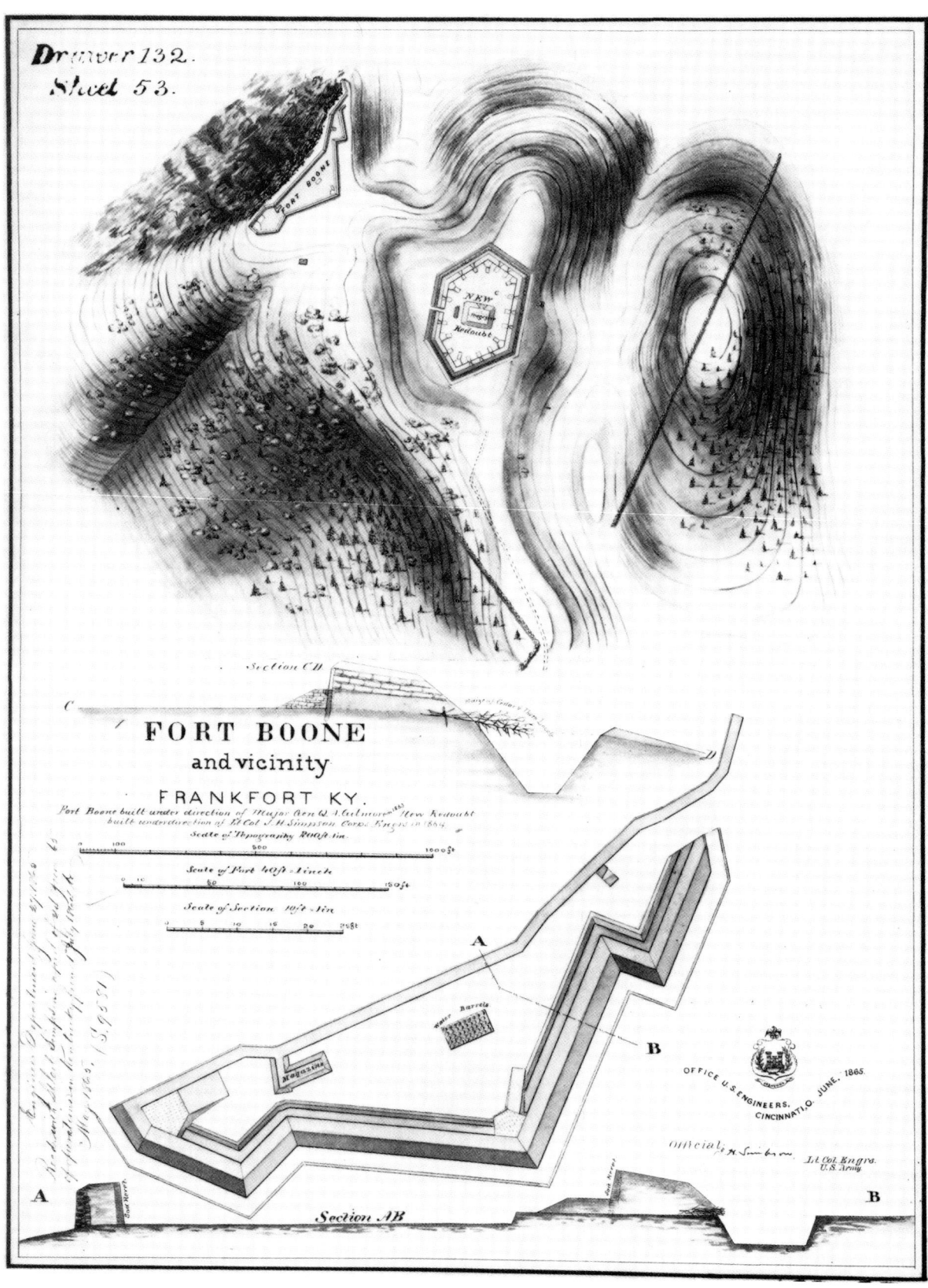

nel Pryor's troops made an unsuccessful assault against Lindsey's force on Fort Hill. Failing to breech the Union defense on the north, Pryor decided to try from the south. During the night between 250 and 300 Confederate soldiers took positions on the hills above South Frankfort. About eight o'clock on Saturday morning Union pickets saw a flag of truce approaching the covered bridge from Louisville Pike. A few moments later guards intercepted the flag bearer, blindfolded him, and took him to Colonel Monroe's headquarters. There the messenger identified himself as Colonel Pryor's adjutant and verbally delivered a demand from the Confederate commander for an immediate, unconditional surrender. Perhaps astonished by such audacity so early in the fight, Monroe scornfully replied that he would not even accept such a request unless it was in writing. After spurning the message, the colonel told the adjutant to tell his commander that he had no intention of surrendering. Ninety minutes later another truce flag appeared. This time the messenger carried a written demand for surrender.

Pryor's message was clear and succinct. "As Commander of the Confederate Forces," he wrote, "I demand the unconditional surrender of your forces, with statement, that all will be treated, as prisoners of war, and private property respected. But, if a useless and stubborn resistance is made, we will not answer for the consequences of an assault." Whether or not Monroe took the surrender demand seriously enough even to consult with Lindsey and the governor is not clear. But his terse reply, "I will not surrender," was unmistakably clear. A short time later, as if to reinforce the point, the defenders opened with a combination of shell, canister, and rifle fire. Several times during the day small Confederate detachments attempted to find and probe weaknesses in the Yankee defenses, but each time they were detected and driven back with a withering hail of fire from Fort Boone and the arsenal. Meanwhile, the Union defense was strengthened by the arrival of reinforcements from the Ninth Pennsylvania Volunteer Cavalry.

As the day wore on, Lindsey and Monroe learned from civilians who arrived in the city by their own means and at their own risk that the shelling was having its desired effect. Neither side suffered serious casualties, but the intense shelling from Fort Hill was making it impossible for the Confederates to mount a serious attack. By the end of the day Colonel Pryor concluded that further efforts to take the city would be futile and broke off the attack. The next day General Burbridge attacked Morgan at Cynthiana and broke the back of the raiders' invasion. In the process he also stopped the last serious military threat to Kentucky's safety during the Civil War.

But Burbridge's victory did not halt war-related violence in Franklin County. Indeed, his own efforts to combat violence eventually made Burbridge the most hated military figure in the Commonwealth. A native of Scott County and a graduate of Kentucky Military Institute, Burbridge had organized the Twenty-sixth Kentucky Infantry Regiment, fought at Shiloh, and commanded a brigade in the Arkansas and Vicksburg campaigns before temporarily succeeding General Jeremiah T. Boyle as commander of the Kentucky military district in February 1864. Burbridge's appointment was especially pleasing to his good friend Governor Thomas Bramlette, and through the governor's intervention, General Grant made Burbridge's appointment permanent in mid-March.

Once in permanent command, Burbridge acted quickly to assist Bramlette in combating such problems as interference with the draft and the publication by some newspapers of information considered detrimental to the war effort. During the first four months of his tenure, Burbridge and the governor got along quite well. By June, however, their friendship began to founder as a result of the general's attempt to deal with the guerrilla problem.

As the Civil War entered its final year, lawlessness became a source of growing concern to both civil and military officials in Kentucky and the other border states. The border states were particularly susceptible to guerrilla marauding because the large numbers of Southern sympathizers offered raiders a degree of protection. Guerrilla activity was primarily of two types. Occasional raids were conducted by detached Southern army units, mostly cavalry, and these usually had at least nominal military purposes. But the vast majority of raiders were bands of brigands and deserters, largely from Confederate units. Often posing as Confederate cavalry, they looted, pillaged, and murdered Union sympathizers, without any military purpose. So dangerous and destructive were these guerrillas that Confederate officials publicly disavowed them and threatened to report them to Union authorities.

Philip Selbert, local jeweler, served in the Civil War as a bugler.

At first there was little opposition to Burbridge's guerrilla policy because his capacity to solve the problem was limited. Kentucky was divided between two military departments, Burbridge's in the Department of the Ohio and Western Kentucky in the Department of the Tennessee. Western Kentucky was infested with guerrillas whose raids spilled into Burbridge's district. With Bramlette's support, Burbridge sought to have Kentucky merged into a single command, but without success. But in the spring Burbridge's superiors, notably General William T. Sherman, began issuing orders which enabled Burbridge to take tougher action against guerrillas and to suppress public dissent by persons who opposed Union civil and military policy. In late July and early August, Burbridge began arresting prominent citizens, supposedly for expressing Southern sympathies. Among those arrested was Joshua T. Bullitt, chief justice of the Court of Appeals. This act brought a public repudiation by Governor Bramlette.

But the action which exposed Burbridge to an avalanche of public hatred was his General Order 59, issued in mid-July, which among other things established an execution-in-reprisal policy. "Whenever an unarmed Union citizen is murdered," the order stated, "four guerillas will be selected from the prisoners in the hands of the military authority, and publicly shot to death in the most convenient place near the scene of the outrage." Burbridge enforced his order enthusiastically. Between July 19, 1864, and January 10, 1865, no fewer than fifty-eight persons were shot in retaliation for the murder of Unionists by guerrillas. While it is probable that most of those executed were in fact guerrillas, it is likewise apparent that several legitimate prisoners of war became the innocent victims of Burbridge's retaliation order.

Like many other counties, Franklin County suffered its share of guerrilla violence, and it eventually felt the heavy hand of Burbridge's retaliation. Guerrilla activity became particularly acute in late August 1864, when marauders ransacked John Stedman's store at Stedmantown, robbed the home of Zachary Lewis, stole a horse from Lawson Noel, and generally terrorized numerous other citizens. Perhaps the most unusual aspect of this series of incidents is that one of the raiders was identified as Hugh Harrod, a Union deserter, and it has been suggested that his cohorts were also Union deserters. On January 24, 1865, another guerrilla band, led by a man named Taylor, pillaged the stores and robbed many citizens at Bridgeport. The next night the same group hit Farmer's store at Farmdale.

The most celebrated incident in Franklin County occurred at Peak's Mill, when a guerrilla troop murdered a Unionist named Robert Graham. On November 2, 1864, General Burbridge ordered the removal of four Confederate prisoners of war—Elijah Horton, of Carter County; Thomas Hunt and John Long, of Mason County; and Thornton Lafferty, of Pendleton County—from Lexington to Frankfort. That afternoon they were taken to a vacant lot at the corner of Todd and Shelby streets in South Frankfort, where they were shot to death in retaliation for Graham's murder. The executions in Frankfort marked the beginning of a three-week reign of terror during which an additional twenty-two suspected guerrillas and prisoners of war were shot.

By late November, Bramlette, other state officials, and even some of the general's military colleagues had begun to lobby for Burbridge's removal. Their position gained strength the following month when Burbridge ordered the arrest and banishment of Lieutenant Governor Richard Taylor Jacob, apparently at the behest of the Reverend Robert J. Breckinridge, for reasons of personal revenge. Nevertheless, precisely because of Breckinridge's influence with Lincoln, the struggle to remove Burbridge was an uphill battle. But on February 7, 1865, Burbridge made the mistake of issuing an order to disband the Kentucky militia. Bramlette immediately protested to Secretary of War Edwin Stanton, who agreed with the governor that the order was an "unwarranted assumption of power" by Burbridge. Breckinridge and his allies pulled every string available in their efforts to save Burbridge, but it was too late. The general had become a political liability which the Lincoln administration could no longer afford. Fifteen days after issuing his militia order Burbridge was replaced by General John M. Palmer.

Placed on leave for thirty days, Burbridge had not yet been reassigned when the Civil War ended in April 1865. By October, still without a command, he had patched up his friendship with Governor Bramlette. But the general's outrages during his year in power were not easily forgotten, and certainly not forgiven, by Kentuckians who believed that he had committed abuses ranging from interference with trade to murder. Such feelings were an ever present reality as citizens throughout the state, including Frankfort and Franklin County, struggled to rebuild their lives and communities after four years of bloodshed and hatred.

7

The Violent Years

THE CIVIL WAR ended on April 9, 1865, with General Robert E. Lee's surrender at Appomattox Court House, Virginia. After four long and bloody years, the shooting had stopped and the rebellion had been crushed. The goal which Unionists had sought was now a reality. Now it was time to heed the words of President Abraham Lincoln and "bind up the nation's wounds."

But Reconstruction proved to be a longer and even more complicated task than putting down the rebellion itself. The war had caused immeasurable economic and human losses, even apart from the 600,000 soldiers who died in battle or from other war-related causes. Across the South, cities, factories, and fields lay in ruins. The plantation economy had been destroyed, a victim not only of shot and shell but of a seriously diminished labor force as freed slaves by the thousands left to pursue freedom on their own terms. Reconstruction entailed unique problems in Kentucky and other border states where issues which had pitted brother against brother and friend against friend could not easily be papered over. Compounding the problem were numerous wartime incidents which aggravated tensions and created an atmosphere of hostility that continued for many years after the war's end.

Within the political realm, tensions were reflected in an unusually high level of factional and partisan strife. Among the Democrats ex-Confederates successfully challenged the conservative Unionists for control of the party machinery and the statehouse. About the only source of unity between the factions was their mutual contempt for the incipient Republican party, which was associated with such "radical" schemes as Negro suffrage. The less politically articulate frequently expressed their hostility through mob violence. But the organized parties did not hesitate to exploit the mob when it served their purposes. It also was a period of intense interpersonal conflict, as individual disputes, sometimes of a political nature, climaxed in the assassination of antagonists.

The sources of hostility and lawlessness were numerous. Former Southern sympathizers harbored resentment against the abuses perpetrated by General

Stephen Burbridge in the enforcement of his antiguerrilla policy. Aggravating the situation was widespread anger with his successor, General John M. Palmer, who used his military power to free slaves without the legal authority to do so. Unionists remained bitter over the violence of guerrillas or "bushwackers" who continued to maraud the countryside after the war was over.

Blacks were a major target of anger as they deserted the farms in droves, before passage of the Thirteenth Amendment, leaving farmers short of the labor necessary to rebuild after the war's disruptions. Compounding the problem was the tendency of many blacks to resort to thievery when freedom alone proved an inadequate basis for subsistence. Whites often retaliated with physical intimidation, whipping, house burnings, and occasional lynchings. Further exacerbating the discord were a variety of old regional, sectional, and personal animosities and the habit of political officials of all persuasions to ignore those violent incidents which served their interests.

Franklin County was in no way immune from the violence. Between 1866 and 1876 the county experienced nearly a dozen major incidents of lynching, mob action, and assassination. Most had strong racial overtones, with blacks charged with some crime frequently becoming the victims of lynch law. Often such extralegal punishments came with the tacit consent, if not direct involvement, of the established community leadership.

One of the first such events occurred on May 7, 1866, when a young black man named Charles, who had been accused of assaulting a seven year old white girl, was spirited from the county jail by a mob and hanged. The extent to which the public approved of the lynching was suggested by attorney-historian L. F. Johnson, who commented forty-six years later that "the hanging was done without any excitement or disorder. A merited punishment was sternly and speedily administered, an example . . . which has been closely followed for half a century and which ought to be a sufficient warning to the negro race . . . that the women and girls of Franklin County must be protected." That a man such as Johnson, who served as a state legislator from 1904 to 1907, should openly endorse such a gross denial of fundamental criminal rights nearly a half-century after the fact is only partially indicative of the depth of racial injustice which pervaded the United States after the Civil War.

A similar but even more celebrated incident occurred about twenty months later. In late January 1868 a black man named Jim Macklin allegedly assaulted a young Irish woman and threw her body down the hill near the railroad tunnel. On the evening of January 30 a mob composed largely of Irishmen broke into the jail and attempted to remove Macklin. In an effort to prevent a lynching, the commonwealth's attorney sought the assistance of the Reverend Lambert Young, pastor of the Church of the Good Shepherd. Father Young rushed immediately to the jail and pleaded with his angry parishoners to cease their barbarous behavior. But it was for naught. The mob dragged Macklin to the site of the crime and hanged him.

Under civil rights statutes in force at the time, the United States District

Court had jurisdiction over the case. Shortly after the lynching United States marshals arrested thirteen men, most of whom were Irish, for their alleged participation in the hanging. The suspects were taken to Louisville, where they were to be examined by a federal grand jury. The attorneys in the case included some of Franklin County's best legal minds. Representing the government was John Mason Brown, grandson of Senator John Brown, while Judge George Washington Craddock, Judge Patrick Major, and D. W. Carpenter represented the defendants. The proceedings were barely underway when Brown moved to dismiss one defendant because of a lack of evidence against him. After the hearings were completed, charges against seven more of the accused were dismissed by the judge.

But the grand jury did not have the opportunity to hear all of the potential evidence against the defendants. One of the prosecution's major witnesses was Father Young, who was asked to identify those persons whom he saw in the mob which took Macklin from the jail. When called to the stand, however, the priest refused to testify. Father Young's decision did not stem from any lack of courage, or disrespect for the law, or sympathy for mob violence. Rather, it was a matter of preserving the trust in his priestly office and preventing its abuse by civil authority which prompted his stance. "It was because of my office that I was requested to seek admission at the jail," he told the jurors, "and it was in my character of priest that I was called to enter its precincts. Under the circumstances, . . . to testify at all on the subject would be to prostitute my office and to bring disgrace upon my priestly character."

Father Young's decision of conscience won him widespread applause and a jail sentence for contempt of court from an irate judge. After three days in the Jefferson County Jail, the priest became ill and was transferred to St. Joseph Infirmary, where he remained for three weeks, still under court jurisdiction. Upon his discharge from the hospital, Father Young was released on $2,000 bail, but the contempt charge was allowed to lapse. Unfortunately, it appears that the same thing happened with the remaining defendants in the Macklin case, who also had been released on bail.

Franklin County likewise suffered its share of Ku Klux Klan violence. At the time of the fall elections in 1870, there were forty-five black voters registered in the Bald Knob precinct. But a concerted campaign of Klan intimidation discouraged all but one of them from voting. For the next twenty-five years, Abe Dotson was the only black voter in the neighborhood. A few months later, on December 6, 1870, the Klan visited the home of Harrison Blanton at Leestown in search of a Negro named Freeman Garrett. When they failed to find their quarry, they vented their anger by shooting two other blacks who lived on the place. Klan violence continued through 1871 and 1873, when the hooded marauders raided the home of John R. Gay and whipped several of his servants. Three suspected Klansmen—John Triplett, John Willson, and Charles McDaniel—were arrested and tried. McDaniel was convicted, but Triplett and Willson were acquitted.

The Klan's outrages drew considerable condemnation from people in Frankfort, but such censure did not prevent racial violence, especially at election time. During city elections in early 1871, a small riot almost erupted into a race war. The trouble began at the courthouse. In short order, William Newman, a Market Street grocer, was killed; Captain W. G. Thompson was wounded in the arm; two black men, James Winter and Winston Coleman, sustained serious wounds; and several other participants, both black and white, were slightly injured. Cooler heads prevailed, however, and a more serious confrontation was avoided.

But the calm was only superficial. The city continued to seethe with racial tension, awaiting a new spark to disrupt the public peace. It was only a matter of months before another incident occurred. In early August a black man named Henry Johnson was accused of raping a German woman named Mrs. Pfeiffer. Arrested and jailed, he was still in confinement on August 7, state election day. The balloting itself proceeded in an atmosphere of relative calm. About four o'clock in the afternoon, however, tensions began to rise as a crowd of drunks, both black and white, gathered in the vicinity of the market house. At first the disturbance consisted mainly of shouting, cursing, and hat waving. As the evening wore on, the crowd grew in numbers and several pistols appeared.

Sensing that a major riot was brewing, a bystander suggested to the police that they arrest the drunks who appeared to be provoking the disturbance. But the gendarmes responded that they could not make any arrests until actual conflict erupted. They did not have long to wait. Shortly after the polls closed, the train from Louisville pulled into the depot, located on the south side of Broadway immediately east of the market house. A passenger standing on the platform of the rear car later noted that he saw a crowd of white men and boys pursuing a group of blacks near the train. Retreating at first, the blacks finally stood their ground and an exchange of rocks and stones followed. Suddenly, a young white man pulled a revolver and aimed it at a Negro. The witness saw the gunman pull the trigger, but the weapon misfired. Seconds later, however, a shot rang out from the white crowd. It was never determined who fired the shot, but it set off a hail of indiscriminate shooting by whites and blacks alike. Moments later, the blacks stampeded, with the whites close behind.

When the crowd dispersed, the extent of the mayhem became clear. Dead were William Gilmore, a white bystander who was a clerk in the state auditor's office, and Silas N. Bishop. Among those wounded were two policemen, Jerry Lee and Richard Leonard, and several blacks, including Henry Washington, who was taken to jail. In an effort to restore peace, Mayor Edmund H. Taylor, Jr., called out the militia. For several hours, troops patrolled the streets and stood guard at the courthouse and jail. As midnight approached, however, the troops began to disperse and return to their homes. Mayor Taylor stated his determination to protect the jailed prisoners and appealed for the militia's assistance. Several militiamen remained for a while to guard the jail. But soon this force began to dwindle as well. Sometime after midnight, the mayor reluctantly dismissed the remaining militia. Learning that the guard had disappeared, the white mob quickly reassembled. They demanded and received the keys to the jail, removed Henry Johnson and Henry Washington from their cells, and took them to South Frankfort, where they hanged both men from a tree near the city school. A short time later, three men—James Alley, Richard Crittenden, and D. Howard Smith, Jr., the son of the state auditor—were arrested and charged in relation to the lynching. All three were tried in the federal court in Louisville, but none was convicted.

While the election day riots, Ku Klux Klan abuses, and similar incidents demonstrate that race was a major factor in the violence which swept over Franklin County, it was not the only source of bloodshed. Several assassinations appear to have had distinctly different roots. Indeed, in a couple of cases, the murders never were solved and the causes never determined. One of the most mysterious incidents involved the assassination of butcher Ben Farmer at his home near Farmdale on the evening of March 5, 1870. At the time Farmer was asleep on a sofa, his head near a window which opened onto a porch. With him were friends Thomas J. Mayhall and William Wright. When a shot rang out, the two men rushed to the door to see who had fired it, but they saw no one. Reentering the room, they attempted to awaken Farmer, only to find him dead from a head wound. Authorities arrested a Negro named Charles Holmes on suspicion of murder, but released him when the evidence against him failed to hold up. Some time later William Hawkins and Charles Polk were arrested for the crime, but only Hawkins was indicted, and he was acquitted by the jury.

Farmer's assassination was still unsolved in April 1876 when Martin V. South, also a butcher, was murdered at the market house in Frankfort. Arrested were Walker Stephens, Robert G. Shields, Hick Kersey, and Thomas H. Holder. Apparently the only suspect indicted, Stephens was held without bail. The grand jury proceedings attracted large crowds, prompting Stephens to seek a change of venue for his trial. The case was transferred to Henry County, where he was acquitted. Thus, Martin South's murder, like Farmer's, remained unsolved. But some observers interpreted the fact that both victims were butchers, along with other circumstances in the assassinations, as evidence that one person committed both killings.

The most dramatic example of interpersonal violence during the postwar period was the assassination of Appellate Court Judge John Milton Elliott by Thomas Buford of Henry County in 1879. Several years earlier, Buford had invested his personal fortune, as well as the entire estate of his sister Mary, in a land deal. In addition to a substantial cash investment, the Bufords executed several notes to finance their purchase. Later the Bufords learned that there was a cloud on the title to the property, which severely jeopardized their investment. Meanwhile, the note holder had sold the obligation to James Guthrie of Shelby County, who sued to foreclose the lien and have the entire tract sold for payment of the debts. Mary Buford responded with a request that the entire transaction be cancelled because of the clouded title.

The Bufords also asked for a change of venue, which moved the case to Fayette County. But things did not go well for them. The Fayette County judge ordered the sale of the land for $12,500, the amount owed by the Bufords. Guthrie promptly bought the land at the bargain price. As a result the Bufords lost $20,000, which they already had paid toward the purchase of the property. The Kentucky Court of Appeals upheld the local judge's ruling, leaving Thomas Buford vengeful and embittered. About one o'clock in the afternoon of March 26, 1879, Judge Elliott encountered Buford on the steps of the side entrance to the Capital Hotel. Buford discharged a double-barreled shotgun loaded with twelve gauge buckshot into the unarmed jurist, killing him instantly.

Because Elliott was so popular in Franklin County, it was necessary to move Buford's trial to Owenton in neighboring Owen County. The trial involved a singular collection of legal talent. Representing the state were Judge O. D. McManama, William C. P. Breckinridge, John Redman, and Jerry Lillard. Leading the defense team was the noted New York attorney Judge George M. Curtis. His local colleagues included W. R. Kinney of Louisville; Phil Thompson of Harrodsburg; Theodore Hallem of Covington; and Evan E. Settle, Judge Thomas Gordon, and Judge J. W. Perry, all of Owen County. The trial began in January 1881, nearly two years after the crime. Buford pled that he was insane, and Judge Curtis won the case with an eloquent closing statement. On the basis of the jury's verdict, the court ordered Buford's confinement in the state asylum for the insane at Anchorage in Jefferson County. Shortly after his commitment, however, Buford escaped and fled to Indiana. When the Hoosier governor refused to extradite him, Buford literally became a free man.

Despite this backdrop of violence, Franklin County's population grew steadily during the immediate postwar years. On the eve of the Civil War the county had claimed 12,694 inhabitants. Ten years later the figure stood at 15,300, an increase of 20.5 percent. The growth rate was an even healthier 22.2 percent during the 1870s, giving the county a total population of 18,699 in 1880.

Particularly interesting are the racial aspects of this growth. Between 1860 and 1870 the white population increased form 8,810 to 10,637, a rate of 20.1 percent. The black population increased at a slightly higher rate of 21.6 percent, from 3,834 to 4,663 during the same period. But growth patterns changed dramatically during the following decade. The white population increased to 13,839 in 1880, a 32.6 percent growth rate over 1870. The black population, however, grew a mere 4.2 percent to 4,860. Representing an increase of fewer than two hundred persons, the latter figure suggests that many freedmen left Franklin County in pursuit of greater opportunity and to avoid anti-black violence. As a result of such movement, population growth by natural increase barely replaced the loss by outmigration.

Frankfort also grew rapidly between 1860 and 1880. During the 1860s the capital's population increased by 45.8 percent, from 3,702 to 5,396 inhabitants. The growth rate slowed somewhat during the following decade. Nevertheless, the city's population stood at 6,958 in 1880, a reasonably healthy 28.9 percent increase. Frankfort's white population grew from 2,420 to 3,061, a rate of 26.5 percent. Ten years later the number had reached 3,759, an increase of 22.8 percent. The heaviest growth occurred in the black population as freed slaves left the farms to seek employment in the city. Between 1860 and 1870 the number of black inhabitants grew from 1,282 to 2,335, a whopping 82.1 percent increase. The movement of blacks to the city slowed considerably during the following decade. Nevertheless, the black population rose from 2,335 in 1870 to 3,199 in 1880, an increase of 37 percent.

The Corner in Celebrities and Statehouse neighborhoods continued to absorb some of Frankfort's population growth, but most of the expansion occurred in fringe areas such as Crawfish Bottom, along East Main Street Hill, and in South Frankfort. Remembered by most Frankfort residents as the "Bottoms" or simply "Craw," Crawfish Bottom was a low-lying tract between Clinton Street and the base of Fort Hill, bounded by Wilkinson Street on the west and St. Clair on the east. Frequently subject to flooding, the area apparently drew its name from the hordes of crayfish which would be left stranded by retreating flood waters. Scattered construction occurred in the area before the Civil War, but for the most part the flooding problem made it unattractive for development.

The end of the war brought an influx of former slaves seeking shelter and employment. As one of the least desirable building sites in the city, Craw also was the cheapest land available. Thus, between 1865 and 1880 dozens of modest frame houses and cottages sprang up along the streets and alleys in the neighborhood. Most were rented to blacks, while others were occupied by poor whites. In numerous cases Craw provided homes for the families of men serving terms in the nearby state penitentiary. A few blocks to the east land was being subdivided, and dwellings were being built along Holmes Street and Georgetown Pike. By 1880, more than two dozen houses had been constructed along stretches of Owentown Pike and Georgetown Pike immediately east of the city limits. The city was beginning to reach beyond its long established legal boundaries.

The neighborhood which experienced the greatest expansion after the Civil War was South Frankfort. During the postwar years, the neighborhood attracted not only a substantial number of downtown merchants, industrial executives, and prominent politicians and government officials, but also large numbers of working class residents. The result was a rich mixture of architectural styles which ranged from modest vernacular cottages to the large Italianate and Queen Anne houses of the well-to-do.

FRANKFORT RESIDENCES OF THE 19TH CENTURY

Edgewood, home of Col. John L. Scott, was located on the Georgetown Turnpike (now East Main).

B. B. Sayre Residence, located in today's Tanglewood Subdivision.

The Meagher Home, located on Second Street (now Rogers Funeral home). This photo was taken in the 1890's prior to the changing of the portico and tower roof at the turn of the century.

The Wells Residence in South Frankfort.

Generally speaking, the wealthier citizens built their homes in the areas between Logan and Conway streets. This area is characterized by large, multi-storied homes set on large lots with deep setbacks. Major concentrations of residential construction betwen 1860 and 1880 occurred south of Third Street along Cross, Conway, Steele, Shelby, Campbell, Todd, and Logan streets. The most popular architectural expressions during this period were the Italianate and Gothic Revival. The residences at 325 Shelby Street and 104 East Todd Street, with their pierced window openings, projecting bays, low-pitched roofs, and wide, overhanging eaves supported by paired brackets are excellent examples of the neighborhood's Italianate architecture. Outstanding groups of Gothic Revival dwellings stand along the 100 block of East Third Street. The house at 113 East Third is especially notable for its elaborate porch, with Gothic details that include all manner of scroll brackets, ornamental pendants, and chamfered columns. Close by, 119 East Third exhibits such motifs as steeply-sloped gables with decorative bargeboards and pendants, pointed arch windows, and projecting bay windows.

While the upper middle class dominated the central core of South Frankfort, the working class predominated in the residential blocks between Logan Street and the Kentucky River. Until 1880 residential development was concentrated along Second, Third, Logan, Murray, and Fowler streets. Second and Third streets were a black enclave, while the remaining streets were populated by whites. Drawn to this section of South Frankfort by job opportunities at the Hermitage Distillery and several nearby sawmills, working families generally occupied a variety of small frame cottages built on small lots. Particularly popular were the T-plan and shotgun styles, which generally were characterized by a standard floor plan but differentiated by a rich variety of exterior ornamentation. Aesthetically, the importance of such vernacular dwellings derives not from their style but from the rhythm and continuity of scale which result from the frequency and regularity of their distribution around the neighborhood.

Perhaps the most unusual residential structures built in South Frankfort after the war were the Frankfort Barracks, located in the 600 blocks of Shelby Street and Woodland Avenue. Intended to house two companies of the Fourth United States Infantry Regiment, stationed in Frankfort during Reconstruction, the six buildings were erected in 1871 on land owned by Alexander Goldsmith Brawner. A local master mason, Brawner designed and constructed the buildings and then leased them to the United States government for $250 per month. The soldiers occupied the barracks in December 1871 and used them until 1876. In addition, the complex included a guardhouse, a bakery, a hospital, stables, and several other wood frame structures. The present capitol grounds served as a parade ground.

The same forces of urbanization that affected Frankfort also spilled over into Bellepoint, the fringe settlement located across the Kentucky at the mouth of Benson Creek. Figures for 1860 are not available, but the village's population jumped from 91 persons in 1870 to 249 in 1880, an increase of 173.6 percent. Residential growth concentrated along Benson Street, which parallels the creek, and Front Street, which follows the river. However, development also was beginning to occur along Wilson, Todd, and Major streets. The primary factor in Bellepoint's growth appears to have been the convergence of river and rail transportation, which made it possible for nearby business owners to move their goods quickly and easily to market, and for through shippers to transfer their products from one mode of transportation to another efficiently.

While Frankfort and its environs absorbed the greatest single portion of the county's population growth, several rural communities also experienced substantial growth. Census information for these smaller districts was not provided until 1870, but the data for 1870 and 1880 are at least partially indicative of country growth patterns. The heaviest growth occurred in the Bald Knob precinct, where the population increased from 1,732 inhabitants in 1870 to 2,236 in 1880, an increase of 29.1 percent. The primary clusters of settlement were Bald Knob, Bailey's Mill, Flag Fork, Joshua, and Polsgrove. But considerable growth also took place along Bald Knob Pike and the Frankfort and Flat Creek Pike.

Another rural growth center was Peak's Mill. The largest rural precinct in the county, its population grew from 1,985 in 1870 to 2,513 in 1880, a rate of 26.6 percent. The greatest concentrations of settlement were in the villages of Peak's Mill and Elmville. But a substantial number of residents also lived along Cedar Creek Pike and Peak's Mill Pike.

In Forks of Elkhorn precinct, where the largest settlements included Forks of Elkhorn, Stedmantown, Switzer, and Woodlake, the population remained unusually stable. Indeed, the number of inhabitants grew by less than a dozen, from 1,375 in 1870 to 1,386 in 1880. The reasons for this are not entirely clear. However, given the fact that in 1870 Forks of Elkhorn had the third largest black population in the county behind Frankfort and the Bridgeport precinct, it is likely that its extreme stability resulted from the migration of a substantial portion of its black population to the city. This outmigration was then offset by natural increase. A similar black outmigration no doubt accounted for the population loss experienced by the Bridgeport precinct, where the number of inhabitants dropped from 1,766 in 1870 to 1,693 a decade later. Since more than 31 percent of the precinct's 1870 population was black, even a modest outmigration could have caused a loss in population, unless replaced by a strong white immigration and an unusually heavy natural increase by the remaining population.

Although the postwar years were a time of significant population growth in Franklin County, such was not the case in the economic realm. Where the antebellum period was broadly characterized by economic expansion and diversification, the Reconstruction era was marked by economic uncertainty and change. The agricultural sector witnessed considerable expansion, as mea-

JOHN BROWN (1757–1837)
Painted 1792
John Trumbull, Artist
(Yale University Art Gallery)

LIBERTY HALL
Built 1797–1803
(William B. Scott, Jr.)

GOVERNOR THOMAS METCALF (1780–1855)
Painted c. 1850 by William S. Shackleford
(Kentucky Historical Society)

Elizabeth Young Love George Washington Love James Young Love Harriet Love Mary Brown Love
(Mother)

THE LOVE FAMILY, Painted c. 1810 by Samuel H. Dearborn *(The Filson Club)*

OLD GOVERNOR'S MANSION
Built 1797–98
(Kentucky Tourism Cabinet)

IV

ORLANDO BROWN (1801–1867)

Painted c. 1850 by Louis Morgan
*(The National Society of Colonial
Dames in America)*

MARY WATTS BROWN

Painted c. 1838 by Moise & Fowler
*(The National Society of Colonial
Dames in America)*

THE ORLANDO BROWN HOUSE

Built 1835–36
Gideon Shryock, Architect
(Kentucky Tourism Cabinet)

VI

OLD STATE HOUSE
Built 1827–30
Gideon Shryock, Architect
(William B. Scott, Jr.)

HOUSE OF REPRESENTATIVES
(Kentucky Tourism Cabinet)

KENTUCKY MILITARY INSTITUTE,
Chartered 1846 — Six Miles from Frankfort, Ky.
Col. R. T. P. ALLEN, Sup't.

VIII

THE CITY OF FRANKFORT - 1854

Hart & Mapother, Publisher
(Mrs. Hugh Hudson)

THE CITY OF FRANKFORT - c. 1860
Watercolor by S.I.M. Major, Jr.
(Winston Rogers)

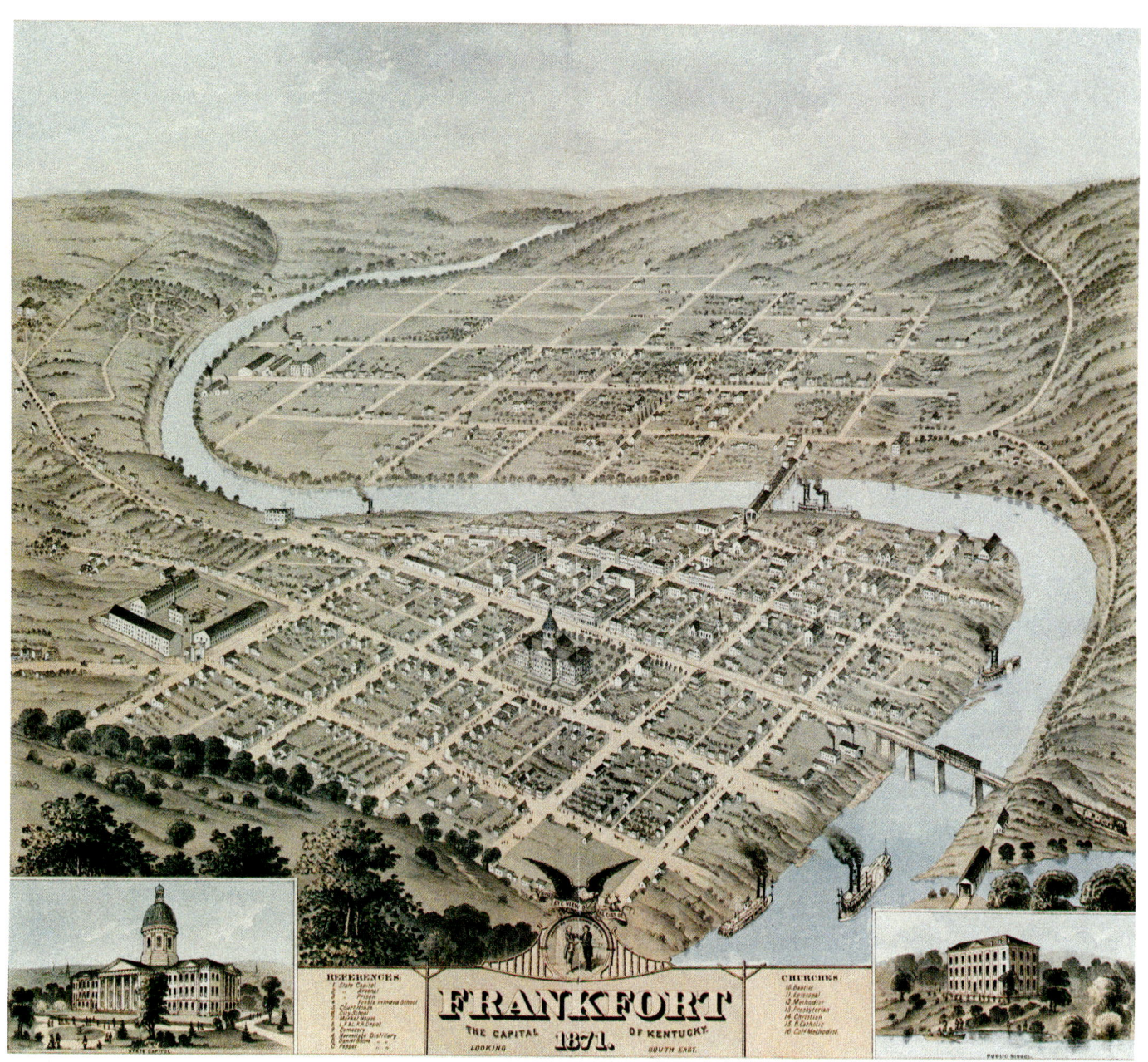

FRANKFORT, THE CAPITAL OF KENTUCKY - 1871

Rugers Map Company, Publisher
(Library of Congress)

XI

TAYLOR DISTILLERY

Painted c. 1890 by Paul Sawyier
(E.H. Taylor Hay)

XII

BIBB BURNLEY HOUSE & VIEW OF WAPPING STREET

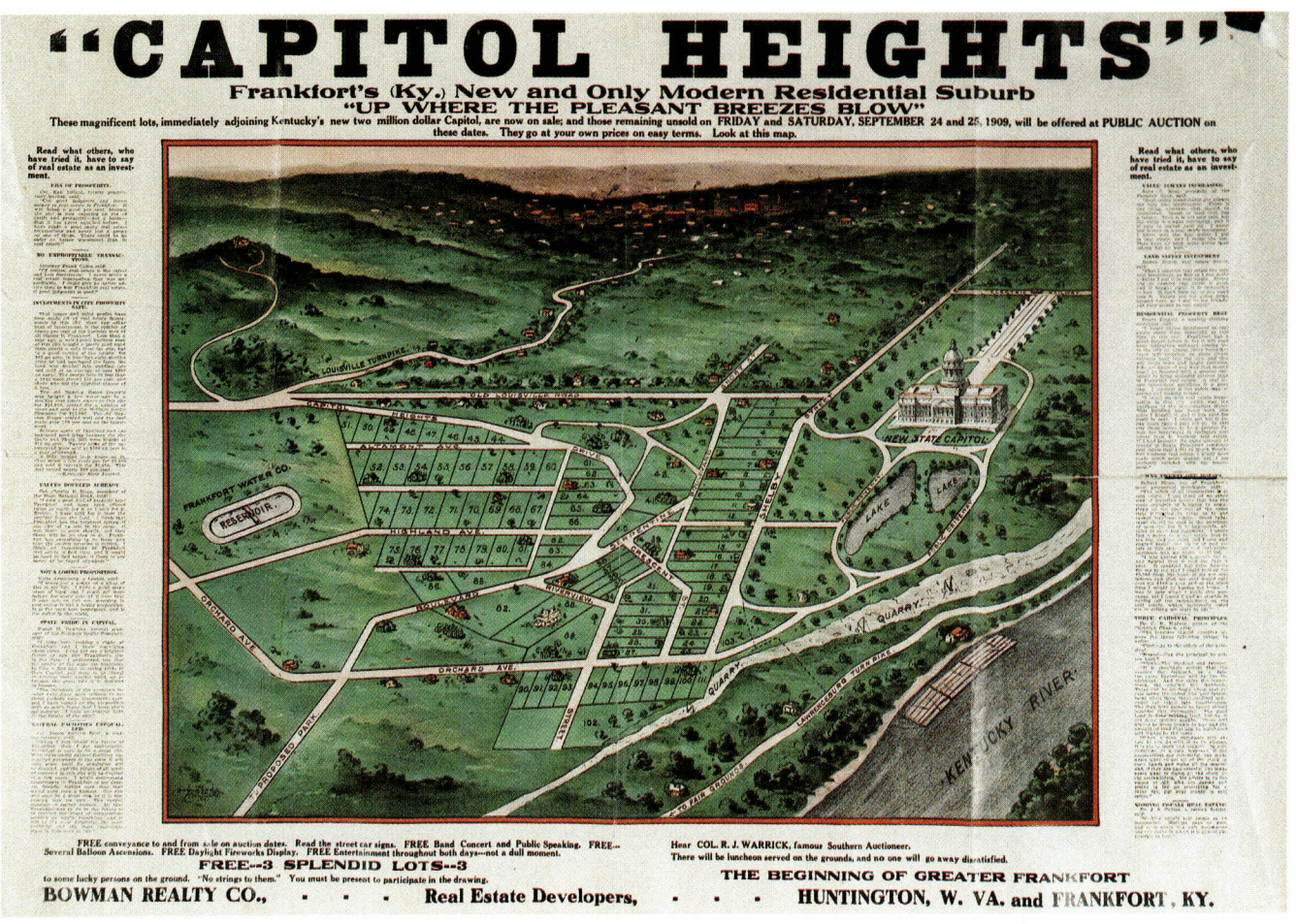

CAPITOL HEIGHTS - 1911

(John Gray)

XIV

KENTUCKY RIVER BEHIND LIBERTY HALL LOOKING TOWARD THE RAILROAD BRIDGE
Artist Unknown
(The National Society of Colonial Dames in America)

MARY HENDRICKS SWIGERT AS LITTLE BO PEEP
Painted c. 1883–1890 by Robert Burns Wilson
(Kentucky Historical Society)

XVI

sured by such indicators as the size and number of farms, acreage under cultivation, and livestock and crop production. On the other hand, the Civil War had so disrupted the farm economy that production figures for some commodities in 1880 had not yet recovered to 1850 levels. The situation appears to have been much steadier in commerce, with considerable new business activity in banking, insurance, and retail enterprise. But Franklin County lost some ground in manufacturing during the 1870s, suffering substantial losses in number of plants, value of production, and the size of the industrial workforce. National conditions doubtless contributed to the instability of the local economy, but important decisions by businessmen and farmers in response to changing markets were even more important.

The Civil War was a terribly disruptive force for Kentucky agriculture. Again and again, farmers suffered major losses as Confederate cavalry raiders and guerrillas destroyed fields, killed livestock, burned buildings, plundered supplies, and commandeered foodstuffs. Although officially loyal, the Commonwealth also suffered from heavy-handed administration by Union military officials who constantly impressed farm goods and paid for them with vouchers that frequently went unpaid. Adding to the disruption, as the war moved to a close, was the steady increase in the numbers of slaves who fled their owners. Soon after the end of the war came emancipation, which radically altered the state's agricultural labor situation. These disruptions were so severe that production levels for 1870 ranked well below those for 1850 in such important categories as dairy and beef cattle, sheep, swine, corn, oats, wool, potatoes, and butter.

In spite of the setback dealt by the depression following the Panic of 1873, the agricultural sector experienced a healthy resurgence between 1870 and 1880. The number of farms in Franklin County nearly doubled, increasing from 664 to 1,296. However, farms remained small, with more than half falling into the range of twenty to ninety-nine acres. The average farm was ninety acres. The vast majority of farms were owner-operated, but sharecropping was becoming increasingly prevalent on farms of ten to fifty acres.

Even more indicative of recovery than the number of farms was improvement in production. Between 1870 and 1880 increases were recorded in all phases of the county's livestock industry. The number of horses grew from 2,651 to 3,628; dairy cattle increased from 1,642 head to 2,419; and beef cattle jumped from 2,146 to 3,248 head during the same period. In 1870 there were 4,170 sheep grazing on Franklin County farms. A decade later, the number had risen to 6,012. Similarly, the number of swine grew from 11,583 in 1870 to 15,023 in 1880. Still, cattle figures in 1880 were barely ahead of those for 1850 and the comparable figures for sheep and swine still lagged far behind.

While all segments of the livestock industry improved during the 1870s, crop production was mixed. In cereal grains, wheat production nearly quadrupled, rising from 28,981 bushels in 1870 to 103,475 bushels in 1880. Barley also experienced healthy growth, soaring from 1,800 bushels to 13,599 in the same period. Corn, the county's largest grain crop, jumped from 423,259 bushels to 543,749 bushels. On the other hand, rye fell from 19,337 to 8,093 bushels and oats plummeted from 53,638 to 31,894 bushels during the decade. Except for oats, however, production in all areas for 1880 had surpassed the 1850 totals.

Other indicators reinforce this somewhat mixed agricultural picture during the 1870s. Wool production was up from 16,366 pounds in 1870 to 31,746 pounds in 1880, while butter production more than doubled, rising from 82,429 pounds to 185,156 pounds during the same interim. These figures mirror the improvement of sheep and dairy cattle production during the decade. The growth of the livestock industry also stimulated the demand for hay, which increased from 1,430 tons in 1870 to 1,876 tons ten years later. On the other hand, production of Irish potatoes fell from 16,366 bushels to 13,815 bushels, and sorghum molasses slipped from 18,452 gallons to 17,318 gallons during the decade.

The single most dramatic change in agriculture after the Civil War was the resurgence of tobacco and its replacement of hemp as the county's major cash crop. During the late 1860s tobacco began to recover from its prewar doldrums, and by 1870 local production stood at 123,250 pounds of leaf. Local hemp production, on the other hand, amounted to 278 tons or 556,000 pounds. But the demand for hemp already had begun to slip, as 1870 production was substantially below that of 1850. During the 1870s, however, the hemp market crashed, and local production plummeted to 72 tons or 144,000 pounds in 1880. Meanwhile, tobacco production increased more than sevenfold, reaching 880,366 pounds in 1880.

Several factors account for this reversal in the relative positions of tobacco and hemp. The most significant factor was the collapse of the Southern hemp market. With the coming of the Civil War, Kentucky's rope and bagging manufacturers no longer were able to sell their goods to Southern cotton planters. In the absence of traditional hempen materials, planters discovered cheaper and more efficient materials and techniques for baling their cotton. The result was a precipitous drop in the long-term demand for hemp. By the end of the war, however, many of the manufacturers who produced the alternative baling materials had been wiped out. This forced planters to return to Kentucky bale rope as a substitute, which triggered a brief recovery in the hemp market. But as Southern manufacturers regained their capacity to produce the new baling materials, planters abandoned hemp products entirely. The result was a gradual decline in hemp demand during the 1870s, which culminated in a precipitous drop in 1879.

A contributing but much less significant factor in the sagging hemp market was the loss of the marine market. Kentucky always had faced problems with selling its hemp for marine purposes because the quality of the fibers compared poorly with imported products such as sisal or manila. By the late 1870s the substitution of wire rigging for rope on sailing vessels wiped out every-

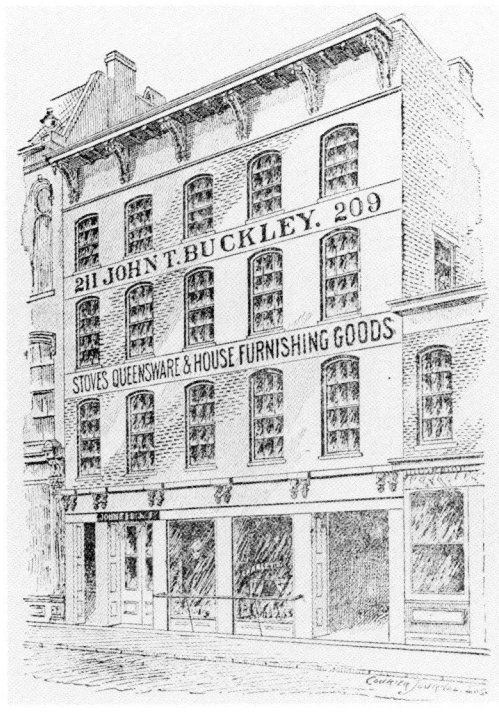

John T. Buckley Building, located at 209–211 St. Clair St (now Marcus Furniture).

thing that remained of the Commonwealth's ever so small marine hemp market. Compounding the loss of the cotton and marine markets was emancipation. More than any other commodity, Kentucky's hemp production depended upon slave labor. With the loss of their slaves and unable to attract sufficient numbers of whites or blacks to cultivate the crop on a wage basis, hemp farmers turned their land to other commodities.

One of the major uses to which they devoted their land was tobacco, specifically, white burley. Until 1870 only dark tobacco was grown and manufactured in Kentucky, and most of that was cultivated in western Kentucky. The production of Franklin and the surrounding Bluegrass counties was minuscule compared to that of such western counties as Daviess, Christian, and Todd. But the porous, alkaline limestone soils of central Kentucky proved ideal for the newly developed strain called white burley, so named for its pale green or greenish white color early in the growing season. Although its origins are rather obscure, one tradition attributes the discovery of white burley to a Brown County, Ohio, farmer who in 1868 discovered that some seeds which he had ordered from the Department of Agriculture produced lighter colored stems and large, light colored leaves. The species soon found its way into Kentucky. A variation of the story holds that some Brown County tenant farmers traveled to the Bracken County farm of George Barkley, found some plants which produced light-colored tobacco, and took them back to Ohio. Whatever its origins, however, white burley revolutionized tobacco cultivation in Kentucky.

At first, manufacturers and users alike objected to white burley because of its bright color. But in late 1872 the Chicago firm of Spaulding & Merrick

EARLY VIEWS OF DOWNTOWN FRANKFORT

Philip Selbert Jewelry Store, located at 333 St. Clair Street. After the death of Philip Selbert, his widow moved the store to the west side of St. Clair.

North side of Main Street looking from Lewis St. to Ann St. The building with the large awning and large half circular windows is the D. C. Crutcher Building. To the left is the Averill Building and to the right the Noonan Building and the portico of the Capital Hotel.

North side of Main Street, looking from Lewis to St. Clair.

Murray's Building, located at 328 St. Clair Street. I. Davis was the building's well known tenant for a number of years.

The Buhr Hotel, shown just after it was remodeled in 1880

used white burley in a brand of smoking tobacco which immediately found favor in the market. Within three years, the central Kentucky leaf had been incorporated into several popular brands of chewing tobacco. As demand increased, so did prices and acreage in production. Making the product even more attractive was the fact that its labor requirements were not nearly as intensive as for hemp. By 1880 Franklin County farmers were producing high-quality white burley at an average yield of between 700 and 800 pounds per acre.

Unlike agriculture, local commerce weathered the Civil War years in reasonably good order and experienced fairly strong growth, despite the ravages of a major fire in downtown Frankfort and the Depression of 1873. Most of the county's commercial expansion occurred in Frankfort, but notable growth also appeared in outlying communities. By 1880 country dwellers supported a considerable number of thriving commercial establishments. In the Benson neighborhood, dry goods merchant L. D. Hulette dealt in notions, queensware, tinware, boots and shoes, and "fancy groceries." A few miles to the south, Bridgeport merchant John Angraves offered his customers "all kinds of fresh meat." Farmdale's leading enterprises included B. Farmer & Son, dealers in dry goods and groceries, and C. M. Jones's horse and mule trading business.

In the southeastern corner of the county, G. C. Hughes operated a successful dry goods store on Frankfort and Georgetown Turnpike at Forks of Elkhorn. G. W. Coharn and J. W. Oliver conducted similar establishments in the vicinity of Woodlake. At Switzer, postmaster J. H. Switzer dealt in dry goods and tobacco products, while miller G. W. Hopkins operated a custom flour, feed, and meal business. Directly to the north, in Peak's Mill precinct, W. S. McCord kept an extensive dry goods and grocery store at Elmville, while E. F. Bacon operated a blacksmith shop at Peak's Mill.

A variety of businesses were located in the Bald Knob district. Dry goods merchant A. A. Bailey kept "a first-class country store" near Bailey's Mill. His chief competitor was James A. Violette, who conducted a law practice and served as postmaster as well as operating a dry goods, grocery, and hardware store. At Polsgrove's Landing, situated about four miles northeast of Bailey's Mill on the Kentucky River, Charles B. LeCompte dealt in drugs and medicines as well as dry goods and groceries, while M. I. Barker operated a tobacco warehouse on the river bank near the mouth of Flat Creek. One of Joshua's leading businessmen was James Sanford, a contractor and builder. Not only did these country businesses handle basic goods and services needed by rural Franklin Countians, but store keepers such as Hulette, Switzer, and Bailey provided outlets for local farm produce. As such, they played a critical role in the county's agrarian economy.

When the Civil War ended, Frankfort had no fewer than forty retail businesses. Establishments dealing in dry goods, groceries, clothing, boots and shoes, books and stationery, and food and drink predominated. Among the

R. K. McClure & Son Shoe Store, located at 212 St. Clair Street, 1898.

Richard Knott McClure

well-rooted businesses of the day were William H. Averill's drug store, located at 206 West Main; George W. Gwin's hardware store on St. Clair Street; Robert K. Jillson's dry goods store; and Louis Weitzel's confectionary on St. Clair Street. Along with at least a dozen other similar establishments, these businesses survived the rigors of economic upheaval as well as the day to day pressures of commerce and flourished into the 1880s.

The fifteen years that followed the war witnessed the creation of at least seventy-five successful retail businesses. The vast majority followed well-tested product lines. But the new enterprises also included two farm implement and seed companies, a flour and feed store, six real estate and insurance firms, and a commercial cleaning establishment. Among the more successful new concerns was R. K. McClure & Sons, a shoe store founded in 1870 by Richard K. McClure and his son William M. McClure. Located at 212 St. Clair Street, the company handled hats, school books, and stationery as well as shoes. The following year, Peter C. Sower left his position as a baker at the Capital Hotel and opened his own bakery and confectionery on Main Street. Sower left the business in 1881, but he ended his retirement in 1890 to open a hardware store with George L. Hannan.

One of Frankfort's oldest continuing businesses is the M. A. Selbert Jewelry Store, established in 1872 and originally located on the east side of St. Clair near Broadway. The store's founder was Philip Selbert, a Bavarian immigrant who learned watchmaking in Cincinnati before moving to Frankfort. Philip Selbert operated the store until his death in 1889, when it came into the possession of his widow, Mary A. Selbert, who gave the business its present name. Although Mrs. Selbert owned the business, her son John managed it for the remainder of the century. A year after Philip Selbert opened his business, on the eve of the depression, D. C. Crutcher moved to the capital from Shelbyville and opened his men's clothing store in a handsome, three-story building at 338 Main Street. Only twenty-three years of age at the time, Crutcher soon gained a reputation as a successful, "wide-awake businessman" who offered goods of the highest quality and demonstrated a "superior judgment in the matter of arranging and displaying . . . goods."

Like Selbert's, Crutcher & Company survived the Depression of 1873 and remained a fixture downtown for more than a century. Many other businesses were not so lucky. The Depression of 1873 was perhaps the worst in the nation's history to that point, and it contributed to the failure of numerous local firms. Business remained at a low ebb for about three years. But as recovery set in and as businessmen began to regain confidence, the number of business starts accelerated. One of the first new enterprises established after the depression was Isadore Davis's dry goods store. Opened in 1877 at 228 St. Clair Street, I. Davis offered a wide range of women's apparel for more than fifty years. Three years later Cornelius E. and Michael Collins opened a saloon and hardware store at 321–323 Broadway. Fourteen years later the brothers dissolved their partnership. Cornelius Collins closed the saloon and expanded the hardware line to include building materials, sewer and flue pipe, blasting powder, and McCormick farm implements. His brother, meanwhile, established a competing hardware store at 237 Main Street.

In addition to retail business, the Civil War and its aftermath saw a significant expansion in the number of individuals and firms offering personal, business, and financial services. The number of professional offices in Frankfort more than doubled, while the range of services expanded to include dentists and photographers as well as physicians and attorneys. Most professionals continued to operate as solo practitioners, but the period also was marked by a growing tendency toward partnerships. In several instances the partners were family members. The law firm of Rodman and Rodman was composed of John Rodman and his son John W. Rodman. General Daniel W. Lindsey and his brother John B. Lindsey were both attorneys and insurance agents. Law partnerships with unrelated members included Hord & Trabue, composed of Lysander Hord and Stephen F. J. Trabue, and Major & Jett, made up of Patrick U. Major and William L. Jett. Another such firm was the medical partnership of Rodman & Duvall, comprised of Doctors William B. Rodman and Benjamin F. Duvall.

Mrs. I. Davis

Frankfort's expanding commerce, coupled with its position as state capital, increased the demand for short-term housing. One of the entrepreneurs who attempted to meet this need was George Buhr. Born in Lorraine, Germany, about 1833, Buhr emigrated to the United States in 1858 and arrived in Frankfort the following year. After serving in the Union Army, he traveled for a few years before returning to Frankfort in 1867. A short time later he opened a billiard room in the Capital Hotel. Before the year was out fire destroyed some buildings on the south side of Main Street near Lewis. From his vantage point at the Capital Hotel, Buhr recognized the need for more transient rooms. He purchased the burned over lot and began constructing a two-story, brick hotel. Completed in October 1869, the establishment included a bar and billiard room on the lower floor and a photographic studio on the second level, along with the lodging rooms. Known as the Buhr Hotel, it was remodeled and enlarged during 1879 and 1880. The eighteen-room addition opened in February 1881.

Mr. I. Davis

Another need created by Franklin County's growing population and economic base was for a variety of financial services. Efforts to meet these needs were not always successful, however. One institution that did prove fruitful was the Deposit Bank of Frankfort. Chartered by the General Assembly in 1863, the bank was required to subscribe a minimum of $25,000 in capital stock before banking operations could begin. Six commissioners were appointed to supervise the subscription—Cornelius Drake, Alexander Julian, Thomas Farmer, John R. Scott, Samuel I. M. Major, and Ambrose W. Dudley. Their task apparently proved rather difficult, because regular banking operations did not commence until 1869. The new bank was located at 307 St. Clair Street. The first president was Philip Swigert, who had retired a year earlier as chief executive of Farmers Bank. Swigert remained in the position until his death on December 31, 1871. His successor was William J. Chinn, a former Franklin County sheriff and a prominent dairy cattle farmer and breeder, who held the position for more than a decade. Working closely with Swigert and Chinn as the first cashier was John Watson.

Two financial enterprises which did not materialize were the Frankfort Fire and Marine Insurance Company and the Frankfort Building and Loan Association. Since the early 1840s several local businessmen had served as agents for insurance companies based in Lexington; Cincinnati; Hartford, Connecticut; and even London, England. These companies mostly handled marine, fire, and life insurance. In 1869 a dozen Frankfort businessmen and politicians, including Captain Harry Innes Todd, Governor John W. Stevenson, druggist William H. Averill, and distillers William A. Gaines, Edmund H. Taylor, Jr., and James Saffell, incorporated the first Frankfort-based insurance company. Under its charter the Frankfort Fire and Marine Insurance Company was authorized to subscribe at least $100,000 and not more than $1 million in capital stock at $25 per share. The company also received full power to insure all types of property against loss or damage by fire, lightning, wind, rain, flood, tornado, and other such disasters, and to write all types of marine and fire insurance for steamboats and other commercial craft and their cargoes. Apparently, however, the organizers proved unable to sell the necessary stock because no evidence can be found in local business publications to indicate that it formally established operations.

A similar fate awaited the Frankfort Building and Loan Association. Precursors of the modern savings and loan associations, building and loans in other communities enabled a growing number of middle and working class citizens to both save and borrow the money necessary to purchase adequate housing. The Frankfort Building and Loan Association was organized by nineteen local citizens, including publisher Samuel I. M. Major, confectioner Lewis Weitzel, merchant Leopold Hermann, photographer John B. Heffner, and fishing reel manufacturer Benjamin F. Meek. Chartered by the General Assembly in March 1872, the association had incorporators empowered to subscribe up to 500,000 shares of stock and to loan its funds at a rate of 10 percent for the purchase and sale of real and personal estate in and near Frankfort. The organizing directors evidently failed, however, to sell sufficient shares for the initiation of operations because no evidence can be found that the association ever made its first loan.

Economic upheaval and inadequate markets were not the only problem faced by local commerce. Another was the constant danger of fire. One of the more spectacular conflagrations of the period occurred on the night of April 2, 1869, when a blaze swept through George B. Macklin's whiskey warehouse on the north bank of the Kentucky River near the St. Clair Street Bridge. At the time the building housed 3,500 barrels of whiskey owned by several eastern parties. As the fire spread it ignited the whiskey, which had begun running

James Saffell, c.1850. Negative by Matthew Brady. Saffell and his partner, John T. Gray, were the second owners of the Capital Hotel. Saffel at one time was a distiller at Cedar Run Distillery on Lawrenceburg Pike at the headwaters of Cedar Run Creek.

ST. CLAIR STREET LOOKING NORTH TOWARDS THE OLD STATE HOUSE.

in a broad stream down the bank and onto the surface of the river. Soon the river itself was engulfed in a bluish flame which extended for some distance in both directions. Besides presenting an unusual visual spectacle, the fire also threatened the bridge. The span in fact caught fire several times, but the flames were quickly extinguished each time, causing little or no structural damage. The warehouse, however, was a total loss, which cost the insurance companies $350,000.

Even more destructive in its impact upon the city's commercial fabric was the blaze which occurred exactly nineteen months later. About one o'clock in the morning on November 2, 1870, fire alarms shattered the slumber of residents along St. Clair Street near Broadway. The blaze began in the house of a Mrs. Stoughton, but it spread quickly to adjoining houses and stores in the northern half of the block bounded by St. Clair, Broadway, Lewis, and Main. As the blaze spread from one building to the next, residents worked frantically to remove furnishings and goods to the sidewalks. At the same time, the fire department pressed every available piece of apparatus into service to check the conflagration. But the tightly packed, tinder-dry buildings, combined with a

Southwest corner of Broadway at St. Clair.

fierce wind, created a situation which overpowered the cooperative efforts of residents and firefighters.

As it approached Lewis Street it appeared that the blaze finally might burn out because of a lack of fuel. Suddenly flames shot from the cupola of First Christian Church, located across the block on Ann Street. The church, too, was soon engulfed in flames, ignited by sparks carried to the roof by the howling wind. Three hours after the fire began, most of the buildings in the northern half of the square bounded by St. Clair, Broadway, Ann, and Main Streets had been reduced to ashes. When the damages were assessed, well over two dozen business and residential structures, along with extensive furnishings and inventories, had been destroyed. The loss was valued at more than $113,000, of which only $66,950 worth was insured. Damage to the Christian Church was placed at $5,000. Also destroyed was the Odd Fellows Hall, located on St. Clair Street. The loss was estimated at $11,500. At least five other concerns suffered losses of $10,000 or more.

On the positive side, this destructive fire triggered a downtown building boom which continued into the early twentieth century. At first, construction was concentrated in the burned out area, which was substantially rebuilt by 1880. But the itch to build soon spilled over into adjoining sections of the central business district, including Main Street and the undamaged blocks of St. Clair and Broadway. The most prevalent artistic expression of the building boom was the Italian Renaissance palace, an aristocratic style which communicated an aura of success. Structurally, most such buildings erected in Frankfort reach from two to four stories in height. They have load-bearing brick walls at the sides and rear, and often share common side walls with neighboring buildings. Their original facades, usually of brick or limestone, were adorned with distinct, often bracketed cornices; tall, multipaned windows with decorative hood moldings; and all manner of pilasters, engaged columns, and rhythmic arches. Especially representative of the Italianate style are the Duvall Building at 221–223 St. Clair Street, the Henry Ringold Building at 334–340 St. Clair Street, 232–238 West Main Street, and the entire remaining south side of the 200 block of West Broadway.

As dominant as it was, the Italianate palace was not the only expression of Frankfort's commercial exuberance during the 1870s. Even more elaborate, and certainly more eccentric, than the surrounding Renaissance mercantile structures was the V. A. Kaltenbrun Building. Erected at 323–331 St. Clair by boot- and shoe-maker Vincent Kaltenbrun, this three-story, five-bay, brick French Second Empire structure is characterized by a linear Mansard roof, pierced on each side of the central bay by two sets of triple windows topped with pediments, and tall, Italianate windows with hood moldings on the second story. Although stylistically different from the typical Renaissance palace, the Kaltenbrun Building is consistent in form, scale, and rhythm with neighboring structures.

While the construction of handsome new mercantile buildings symbolized

Vincent A. Kaltenbrun in his Knights Templar uniform in the 1880's.

the underlying strength of Frankin County's commercial economy, a much different picture appeared in the industrial sector. On a purely statistical level, Franklin County's industrial base appears to have experienced dramatic growth during the 1860s, only to have crashed during the 1870s. Between 1860 and 1870 the number of manufacturing concerns increased from fifty-one to ninety. In the process the number of industrial wage earners more than doubled, growing from 347 to 893, including men, women, and children. Wages soared from $88,087 to $244,284, an increase of 177 percent. Investment in capital stock increased more than threefold, from $342,800 to $1,089,170. And the value of goods produced grew from $794,337 to $1,819,982, a 129.1 percent increase.

The statistical picture for the 1870s was almost as bleak as that for the 1860s was bright. The number of industrial establishments dropped to seventy-nine in 1880, a loss of eleven. The number of industrial workers decreased to 551, and the number of adult males in manufacturing fell by 347. The number of female workers over fifteen years of age dropped from thirty-nine to ten. But the number of children so employed increased from twenty-three to fifty-seven, suggesting that financially strapped employers were doing everything in their power to reduce labor costs. They apparently succeeded, as the amount paid in wages dropped to $175,534, a 28.1 percent decrease. The amount invested in capital stock declined by less than $2,000, but the value of goods produced fell to $1,491,589, an 18 percent decrease.

The reasons for such an apparent reversal are not entirely clear. No doubt the lingering effects of the Depression of 1873 played a part. But recovery long since had set in, justifying an expectation that the economy might at least have returned to its pre-panic level. Another possibility is that the dramatic increase in burley cultivation stimulated a major redirection of capital from manufacturing to agriculture. A third possible explanation, especially affecting the number of manufacturing operations, might be intensified competition and its tendency to eliminate inefficient operations during a time of economic crisis. Any or all of these forces might very well have played a part in the reversal. But upon closer analysis of the figures, an even more fundamental explanation stands out: the collapse of the hemp market wiped out Franklin County's hemp processing industry, accounting for the loss of some 330 jobs, over $375,000 in capital investment, nearly $60,000 in total wages, and approximately $627,000 in annual production.

To the extent that hemp manufacturing remained a factor in the local industrial sector, it involved a primary shift in the market and the construction of a new processing plant. In 1878 nine local investors—George R. McKee, John W. Finnell, Duncan Campbell, Pamelia [sic] Sawyier, John R. Procter, Russell W. McRery, N. J. Sawyier, David J. Spencer, and Dr. Nathaniel S. Shaler—organized and constructed Kentucky River Mills. The new plant, equipped with the most modern machinery, was located adjacent to Lock and Dam No. 4 near Leestown. Where earlier firms had emphasized the produc-

Dr. Nathaniel S. Shaler. Considered one of the leading geologists in the country, Shaler served as State Geologist and Director of the Kentucky Geological Survey for many years.

The Kentucky River Mills. Initially constructed in 1877–78, these buildings burned on October 6, 1883.

tion of bagging materials, the founders of Kentucky River Mills intended to manufacture yarn used in the backing of Brussels carpets. But within a year after initiating operations, company officials recognized that a rapidly increasing use of self-binding reapers in the nation's Wheat Belt, and an accompanying need for binder twine, created an even more lucrative market than carpet backing. Within a short time, the company accounted for one-fourth of the nation's binder twine output. Still, its production was only a small fraction of the county's 1870 bagging production.

Once we look beyond the devastating reversal of the hemp industry, it is clear that other major industries experienced significant growth during the 1870s. Capital investment in cotton manufacturing increased from $31,000 in 1870 to $60,000 in 1880, while employment grew from thirty-three to fifty persons. The number of flour mills doubled, from three to six, while capital investment soared from $26,000 to $88,100, and value of production jumped from $77,620 to $237,579. Among the new flour milling companies was Miles & Son, organized in 1873 by J. E. Miles. From an initial production of 50 barrels per day, the firm's capacity grew to 500 barrels daily by 1898, with customers located throughout the nation.

Lumber milling also was a major growth industry, as the number of plants increased from eight to thirteen and employment grew from 74 to 115 between 1870 and 1880. Wages grew from less than $24,700 to more than $42,300, while capital invested jumped from $60,000 to $152,000. Most importantly, the value of production soared from $113,617 to $279,300. Because of the industry's dependence upon waterborne transportation, the Kentucky River banks became a favored location for milling operations. By 1880 seven mills were located on the river in the immediate vicinity of Frankfort and Bellepoint. Two were located in South Frankfort, one at the foot of Murray Street

J. E. MILES & SONS FLOUR ELEVATOR AND MILL

and a second near the foot of Cross Street. G. R. Rodman and J. L. Sneed's Steam Saw and Planing Mill was situated just north of the railroad bridge between Broadway and Clinton Street. Sneed operated a second mill set on the east bank midway between Lock and Dam No. 4 and the railroad bridge opposite Bellepoint, while the Champion Saw Mill was located on the west bank just north of Benson Creek in Bellepoint. But lumber milling was not confined to the river. F. C. Carr operated a saw and grist mill on Elkhorn Creek at Peak's Mill, while G. W. Parker conducted the Cedar Creek Saw and Flouring Mill at Elmville.

Barrel making also experienced significant growth. There were three cooperages in Franklin County in 1870. Ten years later, the number had fallen to two, but they operated on a scale which far exceeded that of the previous decade. Thus, cooperage employment increased from twenty-one in 1870 to thirty-five in 1880. Investment in capital stock rose from $6,600 to $21,000; the value of materials employed in the industry increased from $9,344 to $36,000; and the value of product increased from $17,578 to $75,000 during the same period. Expansion of the flour milling business no doubt stimulated the demand for barrels. But an even more significant factor, in all probability, was the strong resurgence of whiskey distilling.

The distillation of bourbon whiskey had been a mainstay of Franklin County's economy since pioneer days. Until after the Civil War, however, both the quality and the quantity of the product left much to be desired. As one historian noted, in reference to antebellum distilleries at Glenn's Creek and Leestown, "the structures used were unsuited, the appliances crude, the methods imperfect, and the output raw and unfinished as well as insignificant in quantity." But the postwar years witnessed a revolution in distilling techniques. The leader of this revolution was Colonel Edmund H. Taylor, Jr.

Son of the antebellum banker and civic leader and grandnephew of President Zachary Taylor, the younger Taylor was not only a wizard at distilling

Colonel Edmund H. Taylor, Jr. This photo of Taylor in his business office was taken in the 1880's.

FRANKFORT DISTILLERIES

E. H. Taylor Distillery employees, c.1870

Old Crow Distillery—c.1870
The house on the left is the residence of the distiller.

Old Taylor Distillery—Bottling room of the 1880's.

Old Taylor Distillery—Landscaped gardens prior to building of Medieval Castle which covered buildings in foreground. Probably taken in the early 1880's.

Old Taylor Distillery, c.1887. The photo was taken during the building of the famous medieval castle.

Old Taylor Distillery—Medieval castle and entrance in 1912.

O. F. C. Distillery

technology, but also a genius in the merchandising, financing, and promotion of liquor. Beginning in 1868, Taylor established three modern distilleries in Franklin County. The Old Taylor Distillery, situated on Glenn's Creek near Frankfort, resembled a medieval castle, with heavy stone walls, arch windows, towers and crenelated battlements, a red slate roof, stone bridges, a sundial, and a sunken garden. The carefully landscaped lawn included pergolas and pools. Inside, Taylor substituted modern, sanitary distilling equipment for the unclean, wooden beer still which distilleries had used for decades.

Less romantic but even more advanced technologically were Taylor's Carlisle and O. F. C. (Old Fire Copper) distilleries, which shared common grounds on the Kentucky River at Leestown, about a quarter-mile below Lock and Dam No. 4. At a time when the fermentation rooms of most distilleries still had dirt floors, the O. F. C. and Carlisle fermenting rooms were "constructed of rough limestone, whitewashed to a dazzling brightness" and the floor was "grouted in the best English cement, beveled by side-troughing." The plant's pumps and machinery were described as "the very finest that money can buy," and the O. F. C. distillery was "the only distillery where the product is in contact with copper alone from the time the grain is ground until the finished whiskey is barreled in the splendid oak packages made at the company's cooper shops from selected and seasoned timber." Taylor's third distilling complex was the Hermitage Distillery, located on the Kentucky River between Second and Cross streets in South Frankfort. In addition to the main distillery buildings, the complex included a cooperage and seven warehouses.

Although recognized as a pioneer in modernizing the distilling industry, Taylor was not without competition. His chief rival was W. A. Gaines & Company, whose leading members included William A. Gaines, Hiram Berry,

E. H. Taylor, Jr. Building, located on West Main Street. This photo was taken just after the structure's completion in the early 1870's.

197

George H. Allen, Marshall J. Allen, and Frank S. Birch. Gaines & Company made its mark by adapting Dr. James C. Crow's sour mash process to modern distilling techniques. Crow was a Scottish chemist and physician who arrived in Kentucky in 1823. He later established a distillery on Glenn's Creek, where he commenced making whiskey according to such exacting standards of quality that he obtained only two and a quarter gallons of liquor from a bushel of grain. At that time most distillers squeezed as great a quantity as possible from a bushel. With Crow's death in 1856, his methods almost died with him. But Gaines & Company perpetuated Crow's name and his process in their "Old Crow" brand. Produced at the Old Crow Distillery, located on the Woodford county line near the mouth of Glenn's Creek, Old Crow soon became one of the most popular brands in the world. Old Crow remained Gaines & Company's top seller, but the firm broadened its product line later in the 1870s by purchasing Taylor's Hermitage Distillery.

The success of Taylor's and Gaines's enterprises stimulated further expansion during the 1870s. John Cochran established the Spring Hill Distillery on the Kentucky River opposite the Hermitage Distillery. J. N. Blakemore opened Arnold's Spring Distillery, located on Frankfort and Lawrenceburg Pike near the Anderson County line, where he produced handmade, sour mash, copper distilled whiskies. And James Saffell and his son James M. Saffell operated the Cedar Run Distillery adjacent to their flour mill on Cedar Run Turnpike south of Frankfort. The dimensions of the distilling industry's growth are readily apparent in economic statistics. Overall, the number of establishments declined slightly as new, modern distilleries pushed old ones out of business. But the operational scale of the newer companies more than compensated for the declining number of distilleries. Capital investment in distilling increased from $347,000 in 1870 to $620,000 in 1880. The number of employees increased from 68 to 103, while their wages grew from $24,241 to $42,100 during the same period. The total value of the whiskey produced increased from $410,424 in 1870 to $614,000 in 1880. Distilling remained a major constituent of Franklin County's economic base until the onset of prohibition.

A major contributor to the expansion of Frankin County's economic base was its excellent transportation connections. For the most part, however, commerce after the Civil War depended upon a transportation network which already was in place. During the fifteen years that followed the war, most local transportation projects involved improvements in or extensions of the existing network rather than new technological innovations. In the spring of 1867 the county court appropriated funds for new bridges. One replaced the old Ganey Bridge across Benson Creek, about a mile west of Frankfort, which had been washed out by a flood the previous February. Also replaced was the bridge across Elkhorn Creek on Owenton Road. New spans also were constructed across Benson Creek near its mouth and across Leestown Branch. The following year, the Louisville and Nashville Railroad built a pedestrian

Forks of the Elkhorn Bridge. Located on the Forks-Switzer Road, this wooden truss was eleven feet wide and consisted of two 60-foot spans.

way on the railroad bridge across the Kentucky River. The walkway, combined with the Benson Creek bridge, provided citizens of Bellepoint and the surrounding neighborhood with easy access to Frankfort. In 1870 a second addition was constructed to carry vehicular traffic.

The period also witnessed the completion of several turnpike projects. In March 1867 the General Assembly empowered the Franklin County Court to subscribe stock at a rate of $500 per mile to aid the Cedar Creek Turnpike Road Company in the construction of a road across the northeast corner of the county between Scott and Owen counties. Three years later Bald Knob Turnpike Road was completed between Frankfort and Bald Knob. By the mid-1870s the Frankfort and Flat Creek Turnpike had been completed from Frankfort, along Flat Creek into the northwest section of the county.

While new bridges and roads improved access to nearby country markets, shippers who depended upon water traffic were beginning to face severe problems. During the Civil War, state government was unable to repair and maintain the navigation facilities which had been constructed earlier in the century. As a result, the Kentucky River above Frankfort became increasingly clogged with snags and other obstacles and commerce dwindled, just at a time when shippers were beginning to recover from the debilitating effects of war. In 1865, recognizing that public funding would be in short supply for some time to come, the General Assembly transferred responsibility for river maintenance to the Kentucky River Navigation Company, a public corporation funded through bonds issued by the river counties. But a court decision struck down the arrangement, and navigation continued to deteriorate as state and federal officials searched for new means to finance the needed improvements.

In 1878 Major General Napoleon Bonaparte Buford, who as a young mili-

Knight's Bridge—located on the Peaks Mill Road at its crossing point at the Main Elkhorn. The bridge was built by John Gault in the summer of 1863.

Louisville Turnpike Bridge. Located at the Shelby County Line, the bridge was 14 feet wide with one span of 100 feet and another of 90 feet.

tary engineer had surveyed the river fifty years earlier, presented a bill in the state legislature to raise $1 million to revitalize the navigation system. But the assembly rejected Buford's plan and turned instead to the federal government. After considerable pressure from the Kentucky delegation, Congress appropriated funds for a major rehabilitation project. Navigation between Frankfort and Beattyville was suspended for nearly two years while Army engineers demolished old timber cribs, reconstructed dams, repaired locks, and removed snags from the shipping channel. The reopening of navigation in March 1881 resulted in major savings for shippers. Coal shippers alone saved $66,000 in freight charges during the year after operations resumed. Army engineers evaluating the project reported that "the people tributary to the river seem to have been stimulated to new life by these conditions, as is evident by the generally-improved conditions of the farms and farm houses and the increased acreage under cultivation."

The only major railroad development program of the period never got beyond paper. Throughout the postwar South a core group of politicians, journalists, businessmen, and other civic leaders promoted railroad construction as a stimulus to industrial development. Since public subsidies in the form of county and state stock purchases in turnpike and railroad companies were commonplace before the war, it was but a small step to expand subsidies after the war. Unfortunately the private investment necessary for such projects to succeed did not always match the promoters' enthusiasm, which often led to a project's collapse and to a substantial loss of the public's investment.

Such was the case with the Frankfort, Paris, and Big Sandy Railroad Company. In 1871 a group of promoters in central and eastern Kentucky set out to build a new railroad between Frankfort and the Big Sandy River by way of Georgetown, Paris, and Owingsville. Among the Franklin Countians boosting the project were civic elder statesman Philip Swigert, journalist J. Stoddard Johnston, attorney Daniel W. Lindsey, and distillers Edmund H. Taylor, Jr., and William A. Gaines. Their ultimate purpose was to provide a cheaper and more efficient means for shipping eastern Kentucky coal into a potentially industrialized Bluegrass region. In March they obtained a charter from the state legislature. The company was authorized to subscribe up to $5 million in capital stock. To improve the firm's chances of sellings its securities, both counties and municipalities were authorized to purchase blocks of stock by vote of the people. As in the heyday of turnpike building, any dividends realized on the stock purchases were to be used to retire bonds or reduce taxes employed to purchase the stock. Local citizens proved reluctant, however, to invest in the Frankfort, Paris and Big Sandy. Only Scott County voted a subscription, and its $300,000 investment in July 1871 was insufficient to attract private capital. Without the private money, the company never graded the first foot of roadbed nor drove the first spike.

Although rebuilding and expanding Franklin County's economy was a major item on the agenda of the community's business and civic leadership, the capacity of the state, county, and municipal governments to operate effectively in a time of political and economic stress was a vital concern as well. One of the primary concerns facing Frankfort's leaders was the city's future as the capital. Even before the Civil War, discontent had begun to arise over Frankfort's apparent domination of state politics. Before 1860 approximately 80 percent of all elected state officeholders, regardless of party, had been Frankfort residents and voters before their election. While it was natural for politically astute residents of the capital to gravitate toward state office, this situation aroused considerable feelings of jealousy and bitterness toward the city.

The animosity stemmed in part from urban rivalry, especially on the part of Lexington and Louisville. Early in his career Senator Henry Clay had alienated Frankfortians by his strong campaign to remove the capital to Lexington. Similarly, Louisville publisher George D. Prentice editorialized mightily on behalf of the Falls City. But as the 1850s drew to a close, others joined the chorus seeking removal. A major allegation was that Frankfort was the state's chief source of political corruption. Thus, a Louisville newspaper characterized Frankfort as "the abode of political deviltry in general—in short the most God forsaken town that has escaped the hands of the destroying angel since the days of Sodom and Gomorrah." Frankfort's "political tricksters," the paper added, "have ruled the city with a rod of iron, and applied the lash with an unsparing hand upon all who would not lick the foot that kicked them."

The Civil War pushed the removal issue into the background, but it reemerged after the war. As a practical matter, removal was a difficult proposition because the state Constitution required a two-thirds majority of all members of the legislature to approve a change. Equally if not more difficult would be getting the legislators to agree on a new capital. Nevertheless, Frankfort partisans began agitating for improvements calculated to prevent further loose talk about removal. In February 1868 the *Yeoman* commented that the existing capitol was "falling into dilapidation" and had "gone out of style," in addition to being a firetrap. The upshot of such rhetoric was a decision by the

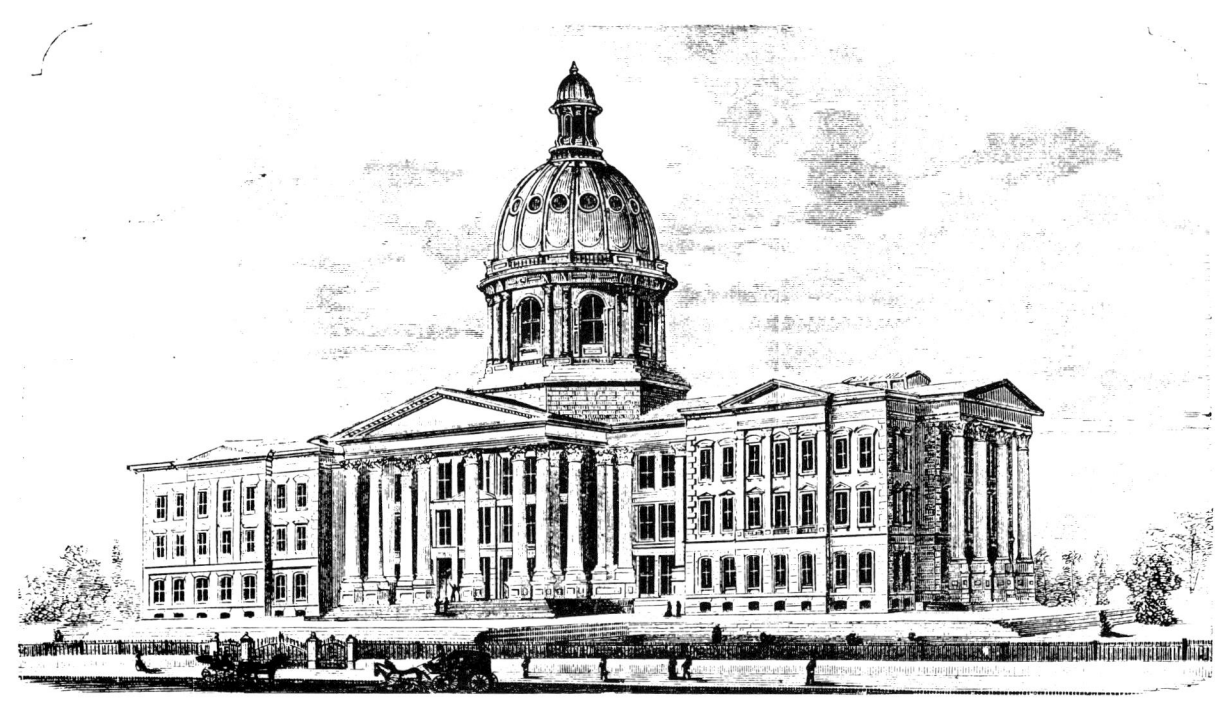

PROPOSED 1869 STATE HOUSE DESIGNED BY BRADSHAW AND VODGES.

General Assembly, in February 1869, to construct new fireproof offices immediately to the east of the capitol.

The commissioners appointed to oversee the project evaluated six designs, several of which incorporated the new offices and the old capitol into a new, expanded capitol building. The most ambitious plan was drawn by the Louisville architectural firm of Charles Stancliffe and John Andrewartha. The commissioners appreciated the majesty of their plan, but its $6 million price tag was prohibitive. The best Stancliffe and Andrewartha got was a resolution of commendation. Chosen instead was a classical design submitted by the competing Louisville firm of H. P. Bradshaw and F. W. Vodges. Like Stancliffe and Andrewartha, Bradshaw and Vodges proposed to combine the old capitol and the new office building into a single structure. Their projected cost for this plan was $750,000. But an alternative plan also provided for construction of the office building alone at a cost of $100,000.

The complete Bradshaw and Vodges plan envisioned an edifice about 316 feet wide, divided into five sections: a central building flanked on either side by intermediate sections and on each end with fireproof office wings. The first floor of the east wing, as specified in the enabling legislation, was to contain the offices of the governor, auditor, and treasurer as well as their chief subordinates. The second floor was reserved for the senate chamber and the attorney general's office. The west wing was designated as the house of representative's chamber and for supporting offices. Construction contracts were let in early June 1869, with Haly, Mahoney & Company of Frankfort serving as the general contractor. Construction began immediately under the direction of John Haly. By late September the gray, Russellville limestone walls were well underway. In 1870, however, a parsimonious legislature cancelled plans for the new capitol; and work on the office building was completed, in a modified form, in 1871 at a cost of $155,000. The new edifice eventually housed the governor and auditor, as originally planned, as well as the secretary of state and other state officials. But the senate chamber remained in the capitol.

City government continued on much the same course it had followed since the early nineteenth century. The mayor's office changed hands somewhat more frequently, but political power remained in the hands of the city's commercial and industrial elite. Banker John B. Temple succeeded merchant George W. Gwin in January 1866 and served only a month before resigning. His successor was A. J. James, who served through 1867. Following James was publisher Samuel I. M. Major, who held the office for four years before relinquishing it to distiller Edmund H. Taylor, Jr., in 1871. Taylor remained in office through 1876 and was reelected in 1877. But he resigned in June, and the city council elected banker William J. Chinn as his replacement. Chinn held the office through 1878 and was succeeded in 1879 by S. I. M. Major, who remained in the post for the rest of the decade.

Capitol Square, as it appeared just after the completion of the east wing of the proposed 1869 Capitol.

In March 1869 the General Assembly enacted a new charter for Frankfort, but its primary effect was to consolidate into a single document several changes in the structure of government which had occurred since passage of the 1839 charter. While some powers were revised or elaborated, the most significant change was a provision for the election of the police judge. Formerly an appointive office, the judge was now to be elected along with the board of councilmen and then commissioned by the governor before taking office. Seven years later, the police judge's election was changed to coincide with the election of the governor and lieutenant governor.

More significant than the Charter of 1869 in their impact on local government operations were the codified ordinances of 1879, which enhanced the city's authority to protect the public health and safety. The chief innovation in the document was the creation of a city health officer. Required by law to be a practicing physician, the health officer was to make a regular, personal inspection of all streets and other public areas and report any health hazards or other nuisances to the city marshal, who was to assure the removal of the offending conditions. The health officer likewise was empowered to check cellars and lots for stagnant water, ensure that privies were kept in a sanitary condition, and provide free vaccinations and medical treatment for indigent citizens. The health ordinance also empowered the mayor, city marshal, and health officer to enforce measures, including quarantine, to prevent the introduction and spread of contagious disease, especially smallpox.

Much of the authority for enforcing public health regulations fell on the city marshal. One of his tasks was to prevent hogs from running at large. The problem of swine in the streets had long posed a dilemma for American city officials. At a time when sanitary and refuse collection technologies were primitive, hogs served as scavengers which cleaned up the garbage thrown into the streets. On the other hand, several hundred pounds of pork moving at top speed posed a serious threat to life and property. In 1878 the General Assembly finally passed legislation authorizing the mayor and city council to prohibit pigs from roaming unattended. The law also approved measures for the impoundment and sale of errant porkers and for fining owners who allowed their swine to run free. The following year, the council took the strongest possible action by outlawing entirely the keeping of swine in the city and by providing a fine of $2 to $10 per day for violations.

The city marshal continued as well to exercise certain law enforcement powers aimed at maintaining public order. For the most part, however, such responsibilities involved serving warrants and processes for the police judge. The day to day responsibilities of preserving the peace lay with the police department. Under the ordinances of 1879 the department consisted of four full-time members—one day watchman and three night watchmen. If unusual circumstances required additional assistance, the mayor had authority to hire extra personnel for up to two days without approval of the council. As to their duties, the ordinance required the police "diligently to endeavor to detect offenders against the laws of the State, or Ordinances or regulations of the city, and, when occasion requires, to arrest and commit them; to see that all disorders or disturbances of the peace are broken up, and that good order and peace be maintained." In cases where the police had reason to believe a crime was about to occur, they were empowered to arrest the suspect and, if his explanations were unsound, to take him before the police judge.

Until 1876 nearly all persons convicted of misdemeanors and minor felonies served their sentence in the Franklin County Jail, which doubled as the city watch house. In 1876, however, the city finally exercised its long-held power to establish a workhouse, where offenders, "common mendicants," and vagrants could be confined at hard labor, and where persons owing fines could work off their debts at a rate of two dollars a day. The facility was erected at the base of Fort Hill near the head of Ann Street. For several weeks after it opened the workhouse often held as many as fifteen to twenty-five inmates per week. But as a common routine developed and the police judge acquired a better understanding of which cases were best suited for the workhouse, the number fell to five or six weekly.

The need for improved health and safety services was just one more indicator of Frankfort's growing size and complexity. Indeed, the social, political, and economic upheavals triggered by the Civil War contributed directly to several major social and cultural advances between 1865 and 1880. Improvements were particularly apparent in the field of education. When the Civil War ended private academies still provided the only source of primary and secondary education for the children of Franklin County. Fifteen years later public education was available to both white and black children, though on a segregated basis with considerable differences in the quantity of the resources available to the education of the races.

As Reconstruction began, private schools such as Mary Train Runyan's Greenwood Seminary, at the southwest corner of Clinton and Mero streets, continued to enjoy the patronage of Frankfort's elite. Nor was private education limited to the children of the city. A few miles to the southwest, Dr. John B. Stout conducted the Bridgeport Lattice School, a combination boarding and day school for girls. Located in the quarters of the former Bridgeport Female Institute, it opened in 1864 and remained in operation until 1875.

The best known private schools established during the postwar years were the Dudley Institute and the Excelsior Collegiate Institute. Organized in 1876 by Mr. and Mrs. T. M. Turner and Episcopal Bishop Thomas U. Dudley, the Dudley Female Institute began operations in the old John H. Hanna house on Second Street in South Frankfort. As enrollment increased the school moved to the Orlando Brown house on Wilkinson Street, and in 1879 became Dudley Institute, a reflection of its new coeducational enrollment. One of the school's early faculty members was the renowned artist Robert Burns Wilson, and its graduates included artist Paul Sawyier. Located at Jett in southeastern Franklin County, the Excelsior Collegiate Institute was organized in 1879 by the Reverend James K. Polk South and his wife Eudora Lindsay South, who served as principal. The school opened its doors in 1880, accepting both male and female students in primary, intermediate, and collegiate departments. The collegiate department offered a complete four-year high school curriculum, which included heavy doses of mathematics, English, history, classics, and religion.

Schools like the Dudley and Excelsior institutes continued for many years to perform an important educational role in Franklin County. But as the nineteenth century drew to a close, they were increasingly overshadowed by a maturing system of public education. The successful emergence of public education began in February 1867 when the General Assembly passed "An Act for the better organization of Public Schools in the City of Frankfort." This legislation authorized the mayor and city council to propose to the voters a tax levy of up to twenty-five cents on one hundred dollars of assessed valuation for the benefit of common schools. If the levy passed, the council was to appoint three citizens as school trustees to serve until the next regularly scheduled city elections.

Shortly after passage of the legislation, the city council ordained and the voters approved the prescribed tax levy. On May 21, 1867, the council approved the appointment of John Mason Brown, John M. Mills, and Denis L. Haly as school trustees. All were elected by the voters in January 1868. The trustees spent most of 1868 constructing a school building and recruiting a teaching staff. They took the sum of $29,800 from the old 1838 public school-water works lottery fund and purchased from Judge George C. Drane a large lot on the north side of Second Street at Ewing Street in South Frankfort.

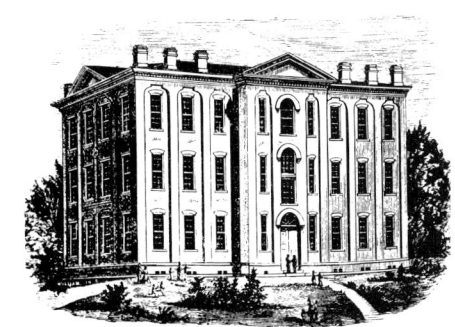

High School Building

There they built a three-story brick building which contained ten classrooms and a chapel. When funds ran short, the trustees submitted to the voters a $25,000 school bond issue, which passed overwhelmingly. To administer the system, they lured one of Louisville's top school officials, Mr. S. P. Browder, who accepted the post of school principal.

The new school opened its doors on October 8, 1868, with an enrollment of 171 white students and six teachers—J. T. Gaines, Nevil P. Whitesides, William W. Symmes, Mrs. Agnes L. Franklin, Miss Sallie E. Coleman, and Miss Fanny V. Cullum. Joining them a short time later were Miss Emma Paddock of Jeffersonville, Indiana, and Miss Mollie F. Johnson of Louisville. The curriculum, copied in large measure from the Louisville school system, included reading, spelling, penmanship, language, geography, mental and written arithmetic, algebra, geometry, American history, natural philosophy, Latin, rhetoric, English grammar, bookkeeping, physiology, and composition. Despite the public support indicated in the approval of the tax levy and bond issue, the system faced some residue of hostility when it opened in the fall. But as the year wore on the school won over many skeptics, and enrollment rose steadily. By the close of the year in June 1869, 453 children were enrolled.

Although the Second Street school admitted only white pupils, the year 1868 also witnessed the beginning of public education for black youth. Under state law, the local school trustees were charged with providing education for both races. "As a matter of justice, and, . . . in accordance with general public sentiment," the school trustees "scrupulously kept separate all money collected from colored taxpayers, and . . . devoted it solely to schools for colored children." At a time, however, when such "justice" rarely implied equality, the limited property owned by blacks hardly generated enough income to develop an educational program for black children equal to that available to white youth at the Second Street school. Nevertheless, the pittance of $155.92 collected from black taxpayers was divided evenly to fund the establishment of two black schools.

Details on these early black schools are sketchy, but the trustees apparently determined that the situation was less than satisfactory. Black citizens certainly agreed. For the 1869 school year school officials decided to concentrate classes at a single site and, at the suggestion of black citizens, placed direct administration in the hands of a black teacher named Henry Marrs and a female assistant. Both persons, the board reported, "were carefully examined and found to be excellently qualified." Under the circumstances, the trustees considered the new arrangement quite salutary. However, these prominent white men expressed deep misgivings about the system's ability to meet the educational needs of the black population. "It must be said for them," the trustees observed, "that the colored people have shown a most laudable thirst for instruction." But the board members shared the concern of some black leaders that too many black youth were deprived of education because they had to work to help support their families. The result was often a total loss of interest

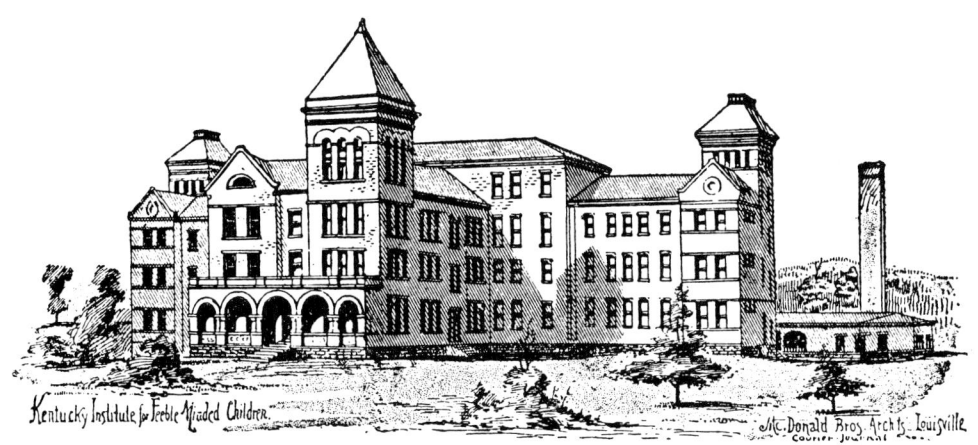

FEEBLE-MINDED INSTITUTE

in education. As a means of overcoming this barrier, the trustees expressed the unusually progressive view that "it would be best . . . if the colored schools could be directly under the management of a responsible Board of Trustees, selected from among the colored people." However advanced this view might have been, the system went relatively unchanged, and blacks did not even get their first school building until 1882.

Somewhat removed from daily public view was another educational facility, the state Institution for the Education and Training of Feeble-Minded Children. Established in 1860, this institution was located on a sixty-acre tract at the southeast corner of the Georgetown and Glenn Creek pikes. Adjoining the school was its 465-acre farm of hill and bottom land. The institute accepted mentally retarded children ages six to eighteen from any part of the state. Instruction was provided without fee for up to ten years. Physical activity in the form of calisthenics also was included in the course of studies "so as to amuse and instruct, and at the same time promote good health among the pupils."

Like the rest of the state's social welfare agencies, the Feeble-Minded Institute was woefully underfinanced. But it does not appear to have been victimized by the brand of pork barrel politics which caused severe fluctuations in the funds appropriated annually to larger institutions such as the Eastern Lunatic Asylum at Lexington and the Western Lunatic Asylum at Hopkinsville. The major blow to the Frankfort institution's funding came from the Depression of 1873. Appropriations jumped from $21,521 in 1872 to $36,937 in 1874. The full impact of the depression hit in 1875 when appropriations plunged to $22,043. But as recovery set in, funding rose gradually to $26,971 in 1880.

Organized religion had become strongly rooted in Franklin County by 1870. According to the national census, approximately 60 percent of the county's residents were members of one of twenty-three local churches. The Baptists recorded the largest number of adherents, with 3,750 members in ten congregations. Ranking second was the Christian Church with 1,500 members

First Baptist Church. Built in 1827 on Lewis Street, this building burned in 1867.

First Christian Church located on Ann Street. Dedicated on August 11, 1872, the structure cost $26,000 to build.

Mrs. Emily Tubman. A sister of Landon A. Thomas, she was raised in Frankfort. Besides giving money to rebuild the First Christian Church, she also endowed a chair at Bethany College and materially assisted the Kentucky University and the Orphan School at Midway.

in five congregations. Census takers also found 1,200 Episcopalians in two churches, 1,000 Methodists in three congregations, 1,100 Presbyterians in two congregations, and 600 Roman Catholics in a single parish. Together these congregations owned property worth $158,000.

Among the more important events in local church life during the postwar years were the destruction and reconstruction of First Baptist and First Christian churches. The old First Baptist Church, erected about 1828 at 314 Lewis Street, was destroyed by fire in 1867. After the fire church officials appointed J. R. Graham, E. Whiteside, and Thomas Rodman to select a new site closer to the center of the city. They picked the lot at 209 St. Clair Street. In 1868 the congregation completed an exuberant Victorian structure which combines Romanesque towers and window arches with a basic Gothic Revival form. Two years later First Christian Church was destroyed by the great downtown fire. The ruins remained for months until Mrs. Emily Tubman, a wealthy Georgian who grew up in the congregation, donated virtually the entire sum necessary to rebuild the church. The new red brick, Classical Revival edifice was completed and dedicated in August 1872.

Another important religious event was the emergence of new black congregations, a phenomenon which reflected the growth of the black population as freedmen moved from farm to city. A contributing factor as well was the division of existing congregations as the result of internal disputes. A disagreement within the black First Baptist Church in 1876 led to the formation of the Independent Baptist Church, now Corinthian Baptist Church. Its first pastor was the Rev. James H. Parrish of Louisville, who served until 1879, when he was succeeded by the Rev. C. C. Stumm. In 1887, during the pastorate of the Rev. R. H. C. Mitchell, the congregation built "a substantial and Commodious brick edifice" on Mero Street between St. Clair and Washington Streets.

Meanwhile, blacks in South Frankfort established Grace Methodist Episcopal Church. Organized as a mission in 1880 under the supervision of the Rev. Mun Walton, presiding elder of the Lexington District, the congregation met in a house on Third Street between Murray and Fowler. The first pastor was the Rev. S. P. Lawson, who remained for three years. The congregation evidently flourished, for when the house burned about 1887, during the pastorate of the Rev. D. E. Skelton, the people rebuilt immediately and paid off the debt in short order.

As with other aspects of life in Franklin County, the Civil War and postwar politics had a direct impact upon the newspaper business. The political triumph of a Southern-oriented Democratic party and the death of Albert G. Hodges' *Commonwealth* in 1872 left Samuel I. M. Major's *Kentucky Yeoman* as the city's most powerful journalistic voice. Strengthening that voice was the presence on the *Yeoman*'s staff of two of Kentucky's most distinguished literary figures, Colonel J. Stoddard Johnston and Major Henry T. Stanton. A journalist and historian with a forceful prose style, Johnston joined the paper as associate editor in 1867 and quickly became its chief editorial writer. A celebrated poet who had been a journalist in Maysville, Stanton joined the Frankfort paper as an associate editor in 1870. Under Johnston and Stanton's influence the *Yeoman* became a popular literary vehicle as well as a powerful Democratic party organ.

The death of the *Commonwealth* left a major gap in local political journalism. Thomas P. Foster, formerly of Vanceburg, attempted to fill the void in 1873 when he established a Republican journal called the *Kentucky State Register*. But Foster's prospects in Frankfort proved even bleaker than his party's, and the paper folded before the year was out. Nor was Foster the only publisher who found it hard to prosper in Frankfort. In 1879, R. K. McClure & Brother established the *Fireside Journal* as an advertising device for their dry goods store. According to the *Yeoman*, this shortlived, illustrated paper contained "some amusing reading matter" and provided "information as to where the best and cheapest boots and shoes can be had."

The following year Ben Deering established the *Capital Gazette*, a semi-weekly Democratic rival to Major's *Yeoman*. Announcing the *Gazette*'s forthcoming appearance, another local paper described Deering's journal as "a paper for all classes, full of local and general news, an advocate of Democratic principle, defending the party against the corruption and evil influences of rings, cliques, combinations, or individuals. It will be independent in all its expressions and views, and neutral in nothing which appertains to the good of society or the welfare and progress of the people." Despite such a glowing description, Deering's *Gazette* failed to catch on, as did its successor, the *Daily Capital Gazette*. In December 1880, after a physical and legal fracas with distiller Hiram Berry, Deering apparently concluded that Frankfort was not ready for his reformist notions, and he moved on to Lexington. Somewhat more successful than either Foster or Deering was M. Stuart Cann, a native of Scranton, Pennsylvania, who established the *Frankfort Daily Dispatch* in 1878. This paper, devoted almost exclusively to items of local interest, lasted until 1882.

The *Yeoman*'s one successful competitor was George A. Lewis's *Frankfort Roundabout*. Claude Buckley founded the journal as the *Weekly Roundabout* in 1877. The following year the thirty-two year old Lewis, who already had some twelve years of experience as a reporter for the *Yeoman* behind him, bought a half-interest in the *Roundabout* and immediately became its editor. Two years later he purchased Buckley's remaining interest and changed the paper's name to the *Frankfort Roundabout*. Having witnessed the failure of Foster and Deering's efforts to compete with the *Yeoman* on a daily basis, Lewis took a different direction. He kept the paper a weekly but enlarged its size and filled the pages with spot news, lively commentary, human interest stories, and literary offerings. Under Lewis's editorship, the *Roundabout* emerged as a popular and indispensable source of information about Kentucky's capital. It remained so until its suspension in 1908.

The *Kentucky Yeoman* Building, 123–125 St. Clair St.

George A. Lewis

J. Stoddard Johnston

Major Henry T. Stanton

While newspapers such as the *Yeoman* and the *Roundabout* became important literary outlets during the postwar years, they in no way dominated the city's cultural and intellectual life. Indeed, J. Stoddard Johnston and Henry Stanton were instrumental in the establishment of the Frankfort Lyceum, which became the city's chief center of literary inquiry during the last quarter of the century. The Lyceum began in 1875 as the Castilian Club. Its first president was Dr. H. A. M. Henderson, a local Methodist minister. Jennie Chinn Morton served as vice president and Stanton as treasurer. Johnston held the office of critic and succeeded Henderson as president about 1880. He remained in the position until 1885. Meanwhile, the club had changed its name to the Frankfort Lyceum in 1877.

The organization had both social and literary objectives, which it pursued through regularly scheduled presentations of prose and poetry, discussions of standard and current books, and performances of musical works. The group met in the homes of its members, and its activities were recorded in the *Chronicle of the Frankfort Lyceum*, a handwritten newsletter. Henry Stanton was the first editor. He was succeeded by Laura C. Ford, Julia W. Rodman, and Jennie C. Morton. Much of the poetry read at the meetings was amateurish, and most of it has been lost forever. But on occasion the Lyceum was treated to the verse of Robert Burns Wilson, the Pennsylvania-born poet and artist who made his home in Frankfort from 1875 until 1901, when he moved to New York.

Although the Lyceum's primary purpose was to broaden the literary horizons of its own adult members, its success inspired a local educator to create a similar organization for young people. In October 1875 Professor J. W. Dodd established the Polymnian Society, a literary organization for youth sixteen years of age or more. Named for the classical muse of eloquence and oratory, the society's objectives were "to promote the acquisition of literary knowledge and to encourage cultivation and improvement in the arts of reading, speaking, and composition." In pursuit of these objectives, young people passed through eight degrees of membership based upon mastery of literature demonstrated by successful completion of examinations on the works of writers such as Shakespeare, Homer, Milton, Spenser, Hume, Bacon, Dryden, Macauley, Byron, Goldsmith, Irving, Carlyle, Scott, Longfellow, Tennyson, Bryant, and Thackeray. Five years after its founding, sixteen diligent young people had completed the Polymnian Society's rigorous membership tests.

While Frankfort's literary life revolved around the newspapers and organizations such as the Lyceum and Polymnian Society, the performing arts centered on Major Hall, popularly known as the Opera House. Until its destruction by fire in December 1867, most of Frankfort's theatrical productions were staged at Metropolitan Hall, a large building at 317 St. Clair Street. The following summer, a community drive raised the money necessary to build a "large and commodious hall and theatre." The site was a lot on the south side of Main Street next to Buhr's Hotel. In the fall of 1869 construction began on

Major Hall. Named for Mayor S. I. M. Major, the structure measured 66 feet along Main Street and extended to a depth of 138 feet. The ground floor provided space for the local post office and Barrett's Bookstore. The second floor concert hall seated 1,500 persons.

Major Hall opened in January 1869 with Skiff and Gaylord's Minstrels as the first attraction. Over the next thirteen years, it offered theatregoers such works as *Uncle Tom's Cabin*, *Rip Van Winkle*, *Ten Nights in a Barroom*, *The Daughter of the Regiment*, and *H. M. S. Pinafore*. Among the famous performers who graced the stage were Louisville's Mary Anderson; the Boston Philharmonic; Blind Tom, the pianist; Buffalo Bill; and Captain A. H. Bogardus, "Champion Wing Shot of the World." Major Hall remained Frankfort's primary theatrical house until November 1882 when it too was destroyed by a devastating fire.

Public support for construction of Major Hall, the triumph of public education, and the emergence of organizations like the Frankfort Lyceum and the Polymnian Society are indicative of Frankfort's growing urbanity following the Civil War. In combination with the county's marked population growth, the economic change and social turbulence wrought by emancipation, and the political triumph of neo-Confederate Democracy, this new sense of cultural sophistication signified the beginning of a new chapter in the life of Frankfort and Franklin County. Symbolic perhaps of this transition was a gradual but nevertheless apparent changing of the guard in local leadership.

Between 1865 and 1880 Franklin Countians mourned the deaths of many stalwart antebellum figures. Judge Mason Brown, prominent jurist and politician, died on January 27, 1867. John A. Holton, a premier steamboat captain, died on June 13, 1869. He was followed three days later by Peter Dudley, hero of the War of 1812. Judge J. M. Hewitt passed away the following November. Thomas N. Lindsey, attorney and Confederate mayor, died on November 22, 1871. Perhaps no death was more symbolic, however, than that of Philip Swigert, antebellum banker, mayor, railroad promoter, manufacturer, and philanthropist, who succumbed on December 31, 1871. Finally, John Cardwell, pioneer ferry boat operator, died on September 17, 1879.

A few younger members of the antebellum leadership, such as Samuel I. M. Major and Captain Harry Innes Todd, remained vigorous for years after the war. But as the 1870s wore on a new generation steadily gained control. By 1880 the community's economic and political fortunes were being shaped by business and professional figures such as distiller Edmund H. Taylor, Jr., General Daniel W. Lindsey, brewer Sigmund Luscher, journalists J. Stoddard Johnston and George A. Lewis, attorney George C. Drane, and dry goods merchant Jerry Brislan.

One of the major accomplishments of this new leadership corps was the final unification of North and South Frankfort into a single corporation. In 1880 a joint committee composed of Daniel W. Lindsey, Benjamin F. Meek, and Green Clay Smith, representing South Frankfort, and W. P. B. Bush, J. W.

Mrs. Jennie Chinn Morton. She was for many years the editor of the Kentucky Historical Society's *Register*. A poet, she wrote "Her Dearest Friend" and many other verses.

Pruett, and W. T. Reading, representing North Frankfort, was appointed to settle the accounts of the two corporations and to determine how their remaining debts should be paid. After considerable discussion, the committee decided it would be in the best interest of both parties to cancel all accounts between them and to make all property belonging to North Frankfort the common property of the city of Frankfort and all debts of both corporations the common liabilities of the city. Both the city council and the General Assembly accepted the agreement, and Kentucky's capital entered the last two decades of the century unified financially and legally. It would take more than unity alone, however, to deal effectively with the challenges of the 1880s and 1890s.

8

Expansion & Turbulence

THE CIVIL WAR had been over for fifteen years when Frankfort's corporate unification came to fruition. But the seeds of discord sown by the war flowered through the remainder of the nineteenth century. In spite of the violence, the resurgence of prosperity during the 1880s contributed not only to substantial population growth and economic expansion, but to numerous technological innovations and cultural advancements which further improved the daily lives of most residents of the capital and its environs.

The Depression of 1893, however, dealt a severe blow to progress. For the first time since it had acquired its permanent boundaries earlier in the century the county lost population. At the same time falling agricultural prices, declining demand for manufactured goods, and soaring unemployment contributed to a climate of economic instability and social tension. When combined with a fabric of partisan strife, political corruption, and interpersonal violence, these conditions created a potentially explosive situation. The climax came on January 30, 1900, with the assassination of William Goebel, the controversial Democratic candidate for governor of Kentucky in 1899.

The rapid population growth and urbanization which became apparent during the 1860s continued unabated into the 1880s. Franklin County's population grew from 18,699 in 1880 to 21,267 in 1890, an increase of 13.7 percent. The growth occurred entirely within the white population, which advanced from 13,839 to 16,508 during the decade. Meanwhile, the black population declined from 4,860 to 4,757 persons, or by 2.1 percent. Growth during the 1880s was most apparent in Frankfort, where well over one-third of the county's new inhabitants resided by 1890. Remarkably, the capital's population increased from 6,958 to 7,892, or by 13.4 percent, despite the fact that the black population dropped from 3,199 to 2,634 persons, a 17.7 percent decrease during the decade.

The picture changed radically during the 1890s, however, as Franklin County suffered the debilitating effects of the worst depression in the nation's history to that point. Largely as a result of a substantial black outmigration,

C. E. Collins Residence, 203 Shelby St.

Judge W. H. Sneed Residence, 110 W. Todd St.

Vernacular Cottages along Kentucky River below Frankfort

Mrs. W. J. Dudley Residence, 309 Washington St.

the county's population dropped to 20,852 in 1900, a decline of .2 percent over the previous enumeration. This loss can be explained in large measure by the loss of more than 400 black residents. Accompanying the decline in the overall county population was a major reduction in the number of persons living outside the Frankfort city limits. Between 1890 and 1900 the number of country dwellers declined from 13,375 to 11,365. The white population in the rural areas declined from 11,252 to 10,333, an 8.2 percent loss, while the number of black inhabitants fell from 2,123 to 1,032, a 51.4 percent drop.

Offsetting the loss of rural population was a substantial increase in Frankfort's citizenry, both white and black. The capital's population grew from 7,892 in 1890 to 9,487 in 1900, an increase of 20.2 percent. Whites accounted for the bulk of the increase, growing by 17.4 percent from 5,256 persons in 1890 to 6,168 in 1900. The proportionate increase in the black population was even greater than that for whites, as the number of Negroes in the city increased by 25.9 percent, from 2,634 in 1890 to 3,316 a decade later.

Within Frankfort and its immediate vicinity, growth between 1880 and 1900 was concentrated in South Frankfort, along Holmes Street and Owenton Pike between the city limits and Thorn Hill, and in Bellepoint. South Frankfort continued to attract the city's well-to-do citizens, such as merchant John Meagher, distillery executive George H. Watson, and journalist George A. Lewis. The most popular residential style among this element was the Queen Anne, a multi-storied Victorian dwelling characterized by an irregular floor plan, elaborate ornamentation, and a variety of surface textures, materials, and colors. Among the Queen Anne's most prominent features are towers with conical roofs, projecting attic gables, tall chimneys, domed turrets, and encircling verandas. Many are decorated with shingles and elaborate timber work. Such houses were constructed throughout the western half of the neighborhood, from Third Street on the north to Todd Street on the south. Especially prominent examples appear along Ewing, Conway, and Shelby streets.

The Holmes Avenue-Owenton Pike corridor and Bellepoint attracted substantial working class populations. By 1900 the dirt streets in both neighborhoods were lined with small vernacular cottages perched on narrow lots

The Mansion House, c.1880. During the period shortly after the Civil War, the St. Clair Street facade of the Mansion House was remodeled.

Frankfort Water Company, Lawrenceburg Road, c.1890

carved out of the hillsides along the Kentucky River below Frankfort. As early as 1889 merchant Llewellyn B. Marshall platted Thorn Hill Park, one of the county's first new suburban subdivisions, bounded roughly by Holmes Street, Dailey Avenue, Fifth Avenue, and Alexander Street. Across the river, Bellepoint experienced a major population boom, growing from 249 residents in 1880 to 457 four years later. Such growth made Bellepoint an inviting target for eventual annexation by Frankfort.

Several mutually reinforcing factors contributed to Frankfort's late-nineteenth century population growth. One of the most obvious was annexation. For the first time since it was originally platted in 1805, Frankfort experienced a major extension of its legal boundaries. In April 1890 the General Assembly enacted legislation which approximately doubled the city's land area. The new territory encompassed Fort Hill, the Holmes Street-Owenton Pike corridor out beyond Meagher Street, and a large expanse east of the city which embraced Frankfort Cemetery, the Feeble-Minded Institute, and also the State Normal School, situated on Georgetown Pike. Four years later, after the state legislature transferred annexation powers to municipal governments, the city council annexed Bellepoint. The action withstood considerable opposition before going into effect on January 1, 1895. However, the annexation not only added more than 450 new residents to the capital's population, but also increased the city's valuation by $125,000.

Further stimulating the city's growth were a series of improvements in public utilities which enhanced the comfort, safety, and health of urban life. In 1876 Alexander Graham Bell revolutionized personal and business communications with the invention of the telephone. Two years later, coal dealer George W. Macklin became the owner of the first telephone in Frankfort when he installed a line between his office at the corner of St. Clair and Wapping streets and his coal yard near the east end of the L & N Railroad bridge. W. A. Gaines & Company owned the city's second telephone, and by 1880 enough residential and business phones were in operation to support a telephone exchange. The following year the East Tennessee Telephone Company initiated the Kentucky Telephone Exchange, with twenty-two subscribers.

The new exchange was located on the ground floor of the Mansion House hotel at Main and St. Clair streets, where it shared offices with the Western Union Telegraph Company. Managing both firms was Charles E. Taylor, who had run the telegraph office for several years. The exchange grew quickly under Taylor's management. In 1882 farmer Hunt Reynolds installed what appears to have been one of the first telephones in Franklin County outside the capital. The same year lines were completed to Versailles, Lexington, and Paris. In 1883 a line was opened between Frankfort and Louisville. With the expansion of intercity operations more and more homes and businesses obtained service. Before the end of the decade, the exchange had outgrown the capacity of the Western Union office, and Taylor transferred operations to 332 St. Clair street. In 1899 the company moved again, this time to 228 West Main.

The East Tennessee Telephone Company, later known as the Cumberland Telephone Company, was not without competition. In 1895 the city granted the American Telephone and Telegraph Company of Kentucky permission to initiate long distance service. During the early twentieth century, the Home Telephone Company began service in the capital. With each company serving its customers through a separate exchange, many businesses found it necessary to subscribe to both systems in order to communicate effectively with their own customers. This confusing situation remained until 1912, when AT&T's subsidiary, the Southern Bell Telephone and Telegraph Company, bought and consolidated the Cumberland and Home systems.

A similar process of expansion and consolidation occurred in local gas lighting and heating services. The city gas works had provided street lighting for the capitol grounds and certain other parts of the city since 1848. In 1866 service was extended to a portion of South Frankfort. By the early 1880s, however, the city had expanded beyond the reach of the existing service, and many of the old mains and lamps had begun to deteriorate. But to expand and rehabilitate the system required capital expenditures which were beyond the city's means.

In May 1882 Mayor Edmund H. Taylor, Jr., and the city council attempted to resolve the problem by selling the gas works and its pipes and lamps to the Southern Gas Company for $40,000. The sale included a franchise agreement which required the company to provide the city and individual customers with the best gas available at a price of $2.00 per one thousand cubic feet and to light the streets at an annual charge of $24 per lamp. The agreement also required the company to upgrade production facilities and to extend mains to unserved areas of the city, including a major portion of South Frankfort. The city agreed in return to use not less than 100 lamps and to abate all local taxes which the firm would have paid on income from local gas services.

The sale of the gas works to an outside company did not set well, however, with many citizens. Numerous public meetings were conducted in which the mayor and council were roundly condemned for signing a contract which, in the opinion of the protesters, ignored the interests of the local populace. Spearheading the opposition was General Daniel W. Lindsey. Under his leadership, several citizens organized the Capital Gas & Electric Light Company and entered into negotiations to purchase the gas works from the Southern Gas Company. In late June, less than a month after the initial sale, the two companies reached an agreement which transferred the works to the local firm on terms similar to those of the earlier contract. Capital Gas & Electric Light continued to provide gas lighting until its purchase in 1912 by the Kentucky Public Service Company.

For the average residential and commercial customer, an even more hopeful development was the application of natural gas and electricity to heating and lighting of homes and businesses. As early as March 1883 the Hughes and Chiles Drug Store at 228 West Main was illuminated with electricity. By the end of the century several more homes and businesses had electric lights. The major producer of electricity appears to have been Capital Gas & Electric Light Company, whose power plant had the capacity to supply 1,000 incandescent and 95 arc lights by 1898. However, the fact that Hughes & Chiles had electricity even before the founding of Capital Gas & Electric suggests that some buildings may have been lighted from small, self-contained generating stations.

Capital Gas & Electric also emerged as the chief producer of natural gas. In so doing, it vanquished two other potential competitors. The Franklin County Natural Gas-Light and Heating Company was organized nearly a year before Capital Gas & Electric by Henry T. Stanton, Daniel Glanton, J. A. Grant, Edward P. Bryan, Hiram Berry, George F. Berry, and Pat McDonald. The company's charter authorized it to sell $25,000 worth of capital stock and to provide gas lighting, heat, and fuel to residential and commercial customers in Frankfort and other nearby towns. But the enterprise failed to raise the necessary capital and may have been out of business even before organization of Capital Gas & Electric.

A similar fate befell the Frankfort Heating Company. Organized in 1886 by Bryan, McDonald, Jerry Brislan, James Andrew Scott, S. I. M. Major, and James F. Witherspoon, the company planned to produce and distribute petroleum, natural gas, and salt water in Frankfort. Its charter authorized $100,000 stock subscription, the proceeds of which could be used to drill wells, build production machinery, and lay pipe through the city streets. However, the company's success depended upon obtaining a franchise from the city to lay its pipes through the streets and other public spaces. Unable to obtain the franchise, the company folded quickly, and Capital Gas & Electric Light Company held a virtual monopoly in the heating and lighting business through the remainder of the century.

Another major improvement was the new water works. By the early 1880s it was apparent that the old Cedar Cove Spring system was no longer capable of providing an adequate water supply to a growing city. It was equally clear, however, that the city lacked the financial resources necessary to erect a new water works. In 1884, after an effort to refurbish the existing reservoir failed, the city council sold the Cedar Cove works to the Frankfort Water Company, a private firm organized in December 1883 by Dennis Long & Company, a Louisville water pipe manufacturer.

In accordance with the sale contract and an accompanying franchise agreement, the water company built a new plant on a hill southwest of the city. The facility consisted of a pumping station and a two-basin reservoir with a capacity of 3.4 million gallons. A fourteen-inch cast-iron main was laid in Steele and Short streets between the reservoir and the river, and mains ranging from six to fourteen inches were installed to distribute water to customers in every section of the city. Completed in 1886, the new water system included 100 fire hydrants, which were placed at regular intervals throughout the city. The hydrants considerably reduced both the danger of fire and local fire insurance rates.

Along with the new, modern water system came a series of usage regulations designed to limit waste and assess charges according to quantity and purpose for which water was used. For the first time, meters were installed to record water usage by large consumers. The company established a detailed rate schedule for private dwellings, beginning at $3.00 annually for a one-room residence and continuing at increments of sixty cents per room up to $9.00 for an eleven-room house. Additional rooms brought a charge of fifty cents each. A variety of other charges included $2.50 a year for each bathtub, $3.00 to $10.00 for each steam heating boiler, $1.25 for a buggy or carriage washed by hand, and $3.00 for a similar vehicle washed by hose. The company promised that rate schedules and other rules would be "strictly and impartially enforced" and that water would be "shut off from any consumer for nonpayment of rents or any other violations of . . .[the] rules." Such regulations and rates may have seemed onerous for a community which had been used to paying flat rates for unmetered, unregulated service, but these measures also assured consumers one of the safest, most dependable, and most efficient water systems in Kentucky.

Closely related to improvements in the water system as a growth stimulant was the construction of a sewer system. Throughout the nineteenth century, Frankfort, like most other communities its size, depended upon privies and ditches for the disposal of human and other waste products. But as the city increased in population and area and as knowledge of the relationship between sanitation and public health became more widespread, community leaders realized that a safer and more sanitary sewerage system was necessary. In May 1886 the General Assembly passed legislation which permitted the city council to float a $10,000, twenty-year bond issue to finance the construction and maintenance of "good and sufficient sewers for the better draining" of Frankfort. A short time later, the council enacted its own ordinance authoriz-

Railroad Bridge. In 1894 the bridge was raised 8 feet, in compliance with an order from the Secretary of War, in order to prevent obstruction to steam boat navigation.

ing the bond issue. The bonds were sold in 1890. By the end of the year construction had been completed on three separate street mains, totaling 3,331 feet. Recognizing that this was only a beginning, the council also adopted a plan for the future construction of sewers throughout the entire city.

Perhaps the most important technological stimulus to Frankfort's expansion was the streetcar. The beginnings of the streetcar business in the capital are obscure. It appears, however, that the first service was a mule car line operated by the Frankfort, Bellepoint, and Leestown Street Railway Company. This company was incorporated in 1886 by Edward P. Bryan, John Starks, Dallas Crutcher, James Andrew Scott, W. L. Collins, and Samuel I. M. Major. The firm's legislative charter permitted it to construct and operate, with consent of the city council, a line which would begin at any point on Main, St. Clair, or Broadway, traverse any of the adjoining city streets, and then extend to Leestown and Bellepoint. The charter also authorized the company to subscribe up to $100,000 in capital stock to finance the venture. Precisely when service commenced and on what routes is not clear, but it did extend as far as T. J. Congleton & Brother's Lumber Yard and Saw Mill near Leestown. The company also operated a car barn between Frankfort and Leestown near Glen Willis.

While the mule-drawn streetcar vastly improved the mobility of residents who could not afford their own carriage or the fare of a hackney coach, it still was a slow and often uncomfortable method of transportation, with open cars which were scorching hot in the summer and chillingly cold in winter. But with the advent of electricity, the mule car also was shortlived. In the spring of 1890 six local businessmen—W. Horace Posey, J. W. Pruett, John T. Buckley, John Meagher, Fayette Hewitt, and Pat McDonald—organized the Capital Railway Company. A short time later they obtained a charter which authorized the firm to construct an electric railway which could carry passengers not only within the Frankfort city limits but to points up to five miles beyond the municipal boundary in any direction. The charter likewise permitted the company to subscribe an initial capitalization of $100,000 and gave it the

Lexington Interurban Car. By the mid-1890's these cars were making numerous trips daily between Lexington, Versailles and Frankfort. This photo was taken on Main Street near Ann St.

right to raise the figure to a half-million dollars if the directors deemed it necessary.

But possession of a charter alone did not guarantee a franchise. It required two years of political maneuvering for the Capital Railway Company to obtain its franchise. On April 26, 1892, the city council finally enacted an ordinance which detailed the terms under which any streetcar franchise holder would have to operate. The specified route provided for access to all parts of the city, including South Frankfort, the East Main Street hill area, and Wilkinson Boulevard to the Leestown vicinity. The fare was set at five cents per trip, and other provisions were intended to maximize safety and convenience and to minimize obstructions to other traffic. Overhead wires had to be placed in such a way "as to protect the traveling public from danger." Cars were prohibited from traveling more than ten miles per hour through the city, and conductors were required to announce the names of approaching streets.

The ordinance provided for a twenty-year franchise, dated from the time of its passage, and required the successful bidder to complete the entire line within three years. Passed by a vote of seven to two, the ordinance was referred to the council's streets committee, which advertised the franchise for bid. Two weeks later, the majority of the committee reported that it had sold the franchise to John Meagher, a director of Capital Railway Company, for $265. Councilman James Darnell, partner in a local livery stable business, opposed the sale, insisting that the price was too low and that the bid had been poorly advertised. But the council adopted the majority report, despite Darnell's objections.

A year later the council amended the franchise to permit the streetcar company to transport both freight and passengers on Wilkinson Street north of

Main Street streetcar lines being laid, c.1893

Frankfort and Suburban Railway Company Streetcar, c.1896

Broadway and on neighboring sections of Mero, High, Holmes, and Clinton streets. The ordinance also allowed the company to transfer freight between the local yards of major intercity trunk lines serving Frankfort and industrial establishments adjoining the streetcar lines. These amendments delayed construction. But work finally commenced in August 1893, and cars began running in early 1894. By 1895 the Capital Railway Company operated over five miles of electrified tracks in the city. But the company was also in severe financial trouble. In 1897, after going into receivership, its franchise was transferred to the Frankfort and Suburban Railway Company. In some respects this transfer was no more than a paper transaction. The president and vice president of the new firm were Patrick McDonald and John T. Buckley, who had held the same positions in the old firm. However, the new company had financial links with a group of Springfield, Ohio investors who provided the infusion of new capital which was necessary to maintain and expand operations.

By the early twentieth century Frankfort's streetcar system included almost nine miles of track and four primary routes. One served South Frankfort, crossing the old St. Clair Street bridge and looping the neighborhood via Second, Shelby, Todd, and Murray streets. Another route followed East Main Street past the Frankfort Cemetery and extended as far as the present Kentucky State University. A third route began on Ann Street and followed Mero, Holmes, Wright, and Wallace into Owenton Pike and up the hill into Thorn Hill. The fourth line proceeded from Ann Street to Leestown by way of Mero and Wilkinson Streets. By significantly increasing the speed of passenger travel, the trolley made it possible for Frankfort residents to separate their homes from their places of work. This in turn further stimulated residential development on the city's fringe.

If annexation and technological improvements account for Frankfort's population growth, they also explain a major portion of the population loss experienced by the rest of Franklin County. Unfortunately, major revisions in magisterial district lines between 1890 and 1900 make it nearly impossible to analyze long-term population shifts. It is clear, however, that the shifts which began in the 1870s continued through the rest of the century. The population of Forks of Elkhorn precinct increased from 1,386 in 1880 to 1,662 in 1890. The Bridgeport precinct's population declined only slightly from 1,693 to 1,652 during the same decade. However, the village of Farmdale boasted 390 residents in 1890.

The Benson, Bald Knob, and Peak's Mill precincts suffered major losses during the 1880s. Benson, the smallest precinct, declined in population from 934 inhabitants in 1880 to 843 in 1890, a 9.7 percent decrease. Bald Knob suffered the most dramatic loss, its population declining from 2,236 to 1,365, a 39 percent drop. The population of Peak's Mill fell by 24.7 percent from 2,513 to 1,893 residents during the decade.

Peak's Mill precinct also was the site of the town of Wigginton. Incorporated by the General Assembly in May 1884, the town centered at George W. Parker's Cedar Creek Saw and Flouring Mill and encompassed all the land for a radius of one half mile in every direction. Included within Wigginton's boundaries was the village of Elmville. Named for a prominent Elmville family, Wigginton's first board of trustees, appointed by the legislature, included Wyatt Parker, Dr. J. A. Estis, George W. Parker, D. J. Gaines, and John T. Spencer. John M. Parker was designated police judge, and S. D. Wigginton was appointed town marshal. The charter empowered the trustees to levy a property tax of up to twenty-five cents on every $100 of taxable property and a poll tax on every male citizen over the age of twenty-one. Wigginton was apparently a shortlived venture, for no references subsequent to its incorporation can be found.

Franklin County's erratic population growth during the last two decades of the nineteenth century paralleled the behavior of the economy. All sectors experienced vigorous growth during the 1880s, as the nation moved from recovery to expansion following the Depression of 1873. The Panic of 1893, however, inflicted severe hardship upon nearly every segment of the local economy. By the late 1890s, many despaired for Franklin County's future. But optimists were certain that the crisis was a transient phenomenon and that Franklin County had only begun to realize its potential. To this end they launched an economic development campaign designed to broaden the county's commercial and industrial base.

On the surface the 1880s were prosperous years for Franklin County farmers. Local agriculture was marked by increased cultivation of land, stable or rising prices, and expanding livestock and crop production. The number of farms rose from 1,296 in 1880 to 1,411 in 1890. Nearly 75 percent of farms in 1890 were cultivated by their owners, and the remainder by tenants or sharecroppers. Total farm acreage grew from 116,629 acres in 1880 to 120,714 in 1890,

PEAKS MILL FARM OF JOHN C. CHURCH (c. 1880)

while the number of improved acres increased from 89,502 to 100,746. Financially, the value of farm land and buildings advanced from less than $2.9 million in 1879 to more than $3.2 million a decade later. The value of livestock owned by local farmers rose from $422,301 to $724,640, and the estimated value of goods produced for sale increased from $605,177 to $793,370 during the decade.

All species of livestock except swine experienced substantial growth during the 1880s. The greatest expansion occurred in the cattle industry, where the total herd increased from 5,741 head in 1880 to 7,651 in 1890. The expansion was particularly notable in beef cattle, which grew from 3,284 to 4,637 head during the decade. At the same time the dairy herd increased from 2,419 to 2,970 head. Even more important than sheer numbers was Franklin County's reputation for quality cattle. In July 1883, for example, dairy farmer William J. Chinn conducted a sale of registered Jersey cattle. The largest event of its kind ever conducted in nineteenth century Kentucky, the sale attracted a huge crowd plus Jersey breeders from nineteen states and Canada. Approximately forty-five animals were sold, bringing more than $36,000 and an average of $812 per head.

The sheep industry grew somewhat more modestly than the cattle business. Between 1880 and 1890 the number of sheep grazing on Franklin County pastures increased from 6,012 to 6,663 head, or about 10.8 percent. Curiously, wool production fell by more than 30 percent, from 31,746 pounds in 1880 to

Thistleton—Home of E. H. Taylor, Jr. Located on the Louisville Road, this was no doubt one of the most splendid Queen Anne-style residences in Franklin County. It was torn down in the 1960's to build a motel and apartment complex.

22,175 pounds ten years later. Since wool production had for years paralleled the size of the herd, this reversal is difficult to explain. One possible explanation is the emergence of the Kentucky spring lamb market. In 1889 some 1,799 of the county's 2,949 spring lambs were sold for slaughter and an additional 211 were killed by dogs or for family consumption on the farm. Although it was not until the early twentieth century that Kentucky emerged as the nation's leading producer of spring lambs, expansion was clearly underway by 1890. This may have reduced the number of sheep available for shearing.

The 1880s also witnessed considerable growth in the equine industry, as the number of horses on local farms increased from 3,628 to 3,982 during the decade. No doubt most of these were draft animals devoted to pulling plows, wagons, and carriages. But a few ranked among the fastest trotters and thoroughbreds in the state. Especially in the fertile Forks of Elkhorn precinct, farmers attempted to cash in on their fellow Kentuckians' appreciation for fine horse flesh. One of the leading horse farms was Woodlake, owned by H. C. McDowell and "devoted exclusively to breeding trotting horses." Also specializing in trotters were McDowell's neighbors, E. W. Ayres, J. H. Bowen, and W. J. and W. H. Lewis. Stephen Black, however, raised thoroughbreds, while A. W. Macklin and Isaac Wingate billed themselves as breeders of "all kinds" of high grade and blooded stock.

The only sector of the livestock industry that experienced an apparent decline in production over the decade was swine. In 1880 local farmers reported 15,023 hogs. A decade later the number had fallen by 2.3 percent to 14,681. This does not mean, however, that pork farmers had fallen on hard times. Indeed, it appears that the Kentucky hog market was particularly strong during 1889 and 1890, with high prices encouraging farmers to deplete their swine inventories. Given the relatively short gestation period for pigs, farmers could afford to sell heavily when demand was strong and to rebuild their herds later.

The most important single development in crop farming was the overwhelming triumph of burley tobacco as Franklin County's chief cash crop. After displacing hemp during the 1870s, burley production soared from 880,366 pounds in 1880 to more than 2.94 million pounds in 1890. In that year farmers planted 3,838 acres in tobacco and realized a yield of nearly 768 pounds per acre. Hemp production, meanwhile, declined from 144,000 pounds to 96,000 pounds during the same period.

The triumph of burley did not come without some redistribution of effort and resources. Franklin County farmers virtually abandoned the cultivation of barley and drastically slashed production of rye and sorghum. The wheat crop fell from 103,475 bushels in 1880 to 84,758 bushels in 1890. On the other hand, corn production grew from 543,749 bushels to 589,070 bushels; oats jumped from 31,894 to 85,507 bushels; Irish potatoes increased from 13,815 to 37,448 bushels; and hay soared from 1,876 tons to 6,997 tons during the decade. Simultaneously, farmers invested substantial resources in orchard crops, which in 1890 resulted in an apple harvest of 39,481 bushels.

As the 1890s began, the county's agrarian economy still displayed a veneer of prosperity. Beneath the surface, however, signs of weakness began to appear. The number of farms under ten acres had almost doubled during the previous decade, and the average size of farms was declining as well. More importantly, sharecropping had increased by nearly 50 percent, suggesting that the position of small farmers was becoming increasingly unstable. These weaknesses became dramatically apparent in 1893, when widespread monetary uncertainty plunged the nation into a major panic. Farmers in central Kentucky, where agriculture was relatively diversified, did not suffer quite so seriously as those in western Kentucky, where dark tobacco overshadowed everything else. Nevertheless, Franklin County agriculturalists experienced their share of low prices, rising debt, increasing tenantry, and declining production.

Because the worst effects of the depression appeared between 1893 and 1898, data from the 1900 census are somewhat misleading as indicators of the depression's real impact. Nevertheless, the figures do suggest some of the catastrophe's long-term consequences. For example, while the number of farms in Franklin County increased from 1,411 to 1,668, or 18.2 percent, between 1890 and 1900, the number of farms under 50 acres increased by 44.2 percent. By the same token, the number of farms between 100 and 500 acres dropped from 432 to 122 and the average size of all farms dropped to 77.4 acres. Further suggesting the predicament of local farmers, sharecropping increased from 16.8 percent of farms in 1890 to 26.4 percent in 1900.

While the depression hurt both crop and livestock producers, its lingering effects were more readily apparent in crop farming. Because of low prices, tobacco production in 1900 was nearly 200,000 pounds below the figure for 1890. Corn production dropped by more than 210,000 bushels, oats by more than 46,000 bushels, Irish potatoes by nearly 24,000 bushels, apples by more than 4,700 bushels, and hay by more than 2,900 tons. Also registering losses were barley, rye, and sorghum. But declining production was not an across-the-board phenomenon. Wheat production soared from 84,758 bushels in 1890 to 131,420 in 1900, surpassing the 1880 figure of 103,475 bushels in the process. Less dramatic was the improvement in hemp production, which increased modestly from 96,000 pounds to just over 105,000 pounds during the last decade of the century.

N. F. Richardson Store—Bridge St. Interior in 1899.

The depression's impact on the livestock industry is more deceptive. Swine production suffered major losses as the number of hogs on local farms dropped from 14,681 head in 1890 to 9,128 in 1900, a decline of 37.8 percent. However, production of cattle and sheep showed substantial improvement, and the equine population increased modestly over the decade. But an increasing stock population can be misleading. In a strong market higher populations might mean that farmers are expanding to meet demand. In a weak market such figures may indicate that farmers are unable to sell their stock, even at low prices. The latter appears to have been the case in 1900 when, in a time of rising stock population, the value of the county's combined herd dropped to $552,227 after reaching $724,640 a decade earlier. Such figures suggest that the county's agrarian economy had a long way to go before returning to the levels of 1880.

As in agriculture, local commerce experienced strong expansion during the 1880s, followed by a pronounced contraction during the depression of the 1890s. In 1883 Frankfort boasted over 100 retail and wholesale businesses, ranging from dry goods and grocery stores to boarding houses and saloons. By 1891 the number had increased to nearly 190. But the depression took a grim toll, and by 1896 at least 50 of these enterprises had failed. Businesses which suffered especially high mortality included boarding houses, agricultural implement dealerships, grocery stores, meat markets, and saloons. More than 50 percent of the city's saloons closed their doors between 1893 and 1896.

George C. Shaw

Dismal though these figures may seem, the fact remains that many of the businesses organized during the 1880s survived the crisis of the nineties. James Heeny established his wholesale and retail grocery business at the corner of Second and Shelby streets in South Frankfort in 1882. By the end of the century he was one of the city's most prosperous merchants and a member of the city council. About the same time Heeny opened his store, Woodford County native George C. Shaw commenced his wholesale and retail flour and feed

Local merchants Weitzel and O'Donnell gave this view of the famous Covered Bridge away as advertising. Prominent local photographer, H. G. Mattern, was responsible for this and many other Frankfort photos of the 1880's and 1890's.

business on Broadway. In 1883 Lewis Mangan and James S. Darnell initiated their livery stable business in a large building at the southeast corner of Main Street and Catfish Alley. By 1898 they were working forty horses and had a "fine equipment of stylish and serviceable turnouts." Both men served terms on the city council.

One of the more prominent immigrant entrepreneurs of the day was Frank Heeny. A native of Ireland, he arrived in the United States in 1881 and moved immediately to Frankfort. After working three years as a clerk for the E. H. Taylor Distillery Company, he established a dry goods business on the south side of Broadway near St. Clair. By the late 1890s he was specializing in silks, dress goods, and pattern novelties, and his store rooms alone took up two complete floors of his building. One of Heeny's chief competitors was the firm of Weitzel and O'Donnell. Organized in 1884 by Charles J. Weitzel and Harry B. O'Donnell, the business began on St. Clair Street. But within a few years it outgrew its original quarters and moved to a handsome building on nearby Main Street.

A leading clothier of the time was the firm of Hudson, Humphries & Cassell, located at the southeast corner of Main and St. Clair streets. Established in 1885 by William P. Hudson, Jr., T. F. Humphries, and John H. Cassell, the firm conducted an extensive merchant tailoring business as well as selling accessories and a variety of off-the-rack apparel. In January 1887 Samuel D. Johnson opened a dry goods store on the south side of Main near St. Clair. By the mid-1890s Sam D. Johnson & Company was noted particularly for its high-quality rugs and carpets and for carrying the finest lines of china and cut glass. In February 1896 Johnson joined forces with Charles E. Hoge and S. French

Hudson, Humphries & Cassell clothing store.

ST. CLAIR STREET LOOKING SOUTH FROM BROADWAY IN 1890.

Hoge to form Johnson & Hoge. With Johnson and Charles Hoge handling merchandising while French Hoge conducted the company's financial and administrative affairs, Johnson & Hoge enjoyed "the patronage of the best trade in Frankfort and the surrounding community."

Frankfort's new enterprises during the 1880s did not consist entirely of dry goods and clothing stores. In 1888, after moving to the city from Williamstown, Kentucky, jeweler William L. Coppersmith opened a store at 227 St. Clair Street. Through a combination of ability and "steady application to business," he built a thriving trade which included "a full line of jewelry, watches, clocks, cut glass, lamps and jewelry bric-a-brac." Entering business the same year as Coppersmith was John R. Todd, who founded a confectionary and restaurant on St. Clair Street near the river. A talented baker and astute entrepreneur, Todd quickly expanded his business to include catering and selling fruits, nuts, cigars, and tobacco. By 1895 his operations had outgrown their quarters and he built a new building on the site of his old one. From this new building Todd served a clientele that reached well beyond the city of Frankfort. A major feature of his business was the shipment of fancy ice confections to the small, outlying communities of Franklin County.

While the Depression of 1893 put the quietus on new development, numerous budding entrepreneurs were waiting for the crisis to pass before plunging into their own enterprises. Among the first to test the post-depression waters were Carl and Edwin Kagin, who came to the United States with their parents, Urban and Elizabeth Burgin Kagin, in 1880. The Kagin brothers may have inherited their business sense from their mother, who operated a successful saloon, restaurant, and boarding house business at the corner of Broadway and Lewis streets. Her boarding house appears to have been one

The Kagin family. From left to right: Edwin, Carl & G. E., with their mother, Elizabeth Burgin Kagin.

of only two out of sixteen such establishments in 1891 that survived the depression. The Kagin brothers commenced their dry goods business at 105–107 St. Clair Street in 1896, when Carl returned to Frankfort after participating briefly in a similar store in Gaston, Kentucky. A few years later Edwin sold his interest in the business to another brother, G. E., and left Frankfort to pursue a distinguished career as a Presbyterian minister, missionary, and religion professor. In the meantime the firm of C. Kagin & Bro., which later moved to 235–239 Main Street, had become noted for its "varied assortment of fancy notions, stamped goods, fancy work, and dry goods." Also in 1896, R. P. Thompson and W. K. Toombs opened their saloon or "sample room" on the south side of Broadway near St. Clair. Within two years their establishment had become one of the most popular in the city, offering "a choice stock of old whiskies, liquors and cigars" and serving as "special agents for J. W. Harper's famous whiskey."

Broadway, looking west from Lewis St. intersection.

The 1880s also were a time of considerable activity in finance and insurance. Three new banks were organized in the county, though only one survived. In 1888 William Lindsay, Edward P. Bryan, John P. Starks, Patrick McDonald, and W. L. Collins organized and obtained a twenty-five year charter for Citizen's Bank of Frankfort. Authorized to subscribe up to $100,000 in capital stock, the institution appears never to have opened for business. Organized a short time later, the Frankfort State Bank began operations on St. Clair Street. Its officers were J. S. McKendrick, president; Edmund H. Taylor, Jr., vice president; and John W. Pruett, cashier. By 1891 the bank advertised a capital stock of $100,000. However, it failed to survive the depression and was out of business by 1896.

The story was much different for State National Bank of Frankfort. Organized and chartered in 1889 with a capital stock of $150,000, its first president was Fayette Hewitt, former adjutant general and three-term state auditor. The vice president was H. P. Mason, son of Claiborn R. Mason, bridge builder for Confederate General Thomas J. (Stonewall) Jackson. Elected cashier was Charles E. Hoge, who succeeded to the presidency upon Hewitt's death. Among other organizers were Kentucky Chief Justice and United States Senator William Lindsay and W. F. Dandridge, who later followed Mason as vice president. State National opened for business in the Hume Building across Main Street from Farmers Bank. Within a decade the bank was firmly established as one of Frankfort's strongest general banking institutions.

Fayette Hewitt

State National Bank's success was largely a testament to the financial sagacity, executive ability, and political connections of General Hewitt. Indeed, the bank was only one of several financial enterprises in which he held a position of leadership. As late as 1896 he was president of the Frankfort Safety Vault and Trust Company, general manager of the Kentucky Investment and Building Company, and a principal in Hensley, Clark & Company, a general insurance agency.

Hewitt and his associates at Hensley, Clark & Company faced considerable

Capitol Theatre and City Hall, Main St., designed by Chicago architect Oscar Cobb in 1883.

Dr. E. E. Hume Building, 327 Main St., when occupied by The State National Bank

competition in their insurance business. By the early 1890s Frankfort had nine insurance agencies, at least six of which apparently survived the depression. Two of the largest agencies were Payne & Berry and Jacob Swigert & Company. Organized in 1881 by George L. Payne and G. F. Berry, the former company represented nineteen American and foreign companies and specialized in fire insurance. Swigert & Company, formed about 1883 and located in the basement of the Capital Hotel, served as agents for about fifteen major firms. It handled surety and accident as well as fire insurance. Other agencies of the period which survived the depression included Charles Exum, J. B. Lindsey, and G. R. Rodman & Company.

One major consequence of Frankfort's commercial expansion during the 1880s was the continuation of the downtown building boom which began during the previous decade. As in the 1870s, the boom was aided by fire. In November 1882 a blaze which began in neighboring Buhr's Hotel gutted the fourteen-year-old, city-owned Major Hall. Because it housed city offices in addition to serving as the center of local theatrical life, city officials wasted no time debating whether or not the structure should be rebuilt; the only question was the site. After considering three different locations, the city council decided to rebuild on the Major Hall lot. Meanwhile, Mayor Edmund H. Taylor, Jr., contacted Chicago architect Oscar Cobb and invited him to prepare drawings for a new opera house and city hall. Cobb's plans were ready for viewing by May 1883, and construction began during the summer, under the direction of contractors John and Denis Haly. Completed in late December, the two-story building featured Italianate hood moldings over the second story windows and was topped by a prominent Victorian Gothic turret. In the years to come such stars as Madame Modjeska, Maurice Barrymore, George Arliss, Marguerite Sylva, the Four Cohans, Julia Marlowe, and Lily Langtry graced its stage.

MAIN STREET, C. 1880, LOOKING EAST FROM ST. CLAIR STREET INTERSECTION. MANSION HOUSE CORNER IS ON THE LEFT.

The Italianate style, which dominated the 1870s and which was prominent in the opera house, continued to dominate through the 1880s. Its influence is apparent in such structures as the W. A. Gaines & Company building, a four-story, red brick structure located at 229 West Main Street and attributed to the Louisville firm of Charles J. Clarke and Arthur Loomis; the Mason-Hoge Building, constructed in 1888 at 245 West Main; and the Duvall Building, erected the following year at 221–223 St. Clair.

New construction was not limited to the Italianate style, however. About 1890 Clarke and Loomis executed the handsome D. C. Crutcher Building at 202–204 West Main. This three-story, red brick Richardsonian Romanesque structure is characterized by two large second-story arches which enclose triple windows. Another Romanesque structure is the Masonic Lodge at 308 Ann Street. Erected of stone and constructed in 1893, it likewise is attributed to Clarke & Loomis. The depression ended Frankfort's late-nineteenth century building boom. However, with the exception of a handful of new buildings erected during the early twentieth century, the construction of the 1870s and 1880s was largely responsible for the central business district's present architectural configuration.

W. A. Gaines Bldg., 229 W. Main St.

The boom and bust cycle which afflicted Franklin County's agricultural and commercial sectors was even more apparent in manufacturing. The number of local industrial establishments increased from 90 to 100 between 1880 and 1890. At the same time the aggregate value of industrial plant and other capital assets increased from about $1.1 million to nearly $3 million, suggesting that much of the community's industrial growth occurred in large-scale manufacturing operations. Rising production also necessitated increased expenditures for materials, the cost of which rose from $980,740 to $1,547,753, an increase of 57.8 percent. However, rising costs were more than offset by the rising value of products sold, which increased by 94.2 percent from $1,819,982 in 1880 to $3,534,858 in 1890.

The industrial prosperity of the 1880s was of great benefit to local workers. In the first place, the number of persons employed in industrial jobs grew from 893 to 1,087, while their aggregate wages soared from $244,284 to $425,339 during the decade. This amounted to a per capita pay increase from about $274 in 1880 to more than $391 in 1890. Most of the growth in employment occurred among blue collar adult males, with the number of wage earners increasing from 484 to 776. At the same time the number of female workers quintupled, from ten to fifty-one, while the number of child laborers dropped from fifty-seven to forty-five. The latter figures suggest that in a time of prosperity factory owners were less tempted to hire children at excessively low wages in order to cut labor costs.

But many of the gains of the 1880s were wiped out by the depression. Indeed, the damage was so great that some observers feared for the city's future. On January 24, 1895, during the depths of the crisis, a local newspaper remarked that local "manufacturing establishments have almost passed out of existence. . . . The lumber mills have diminished, . . . the old cotton and woolen mills have entirely disappeared and today outside the Kentucky River Mills, there is not a manufactory in Frankfort employing as many as one hundred workmen." Noting further that the presence of the penitentiary was a "disadvantage to the city's growth," the paper asked, "Are we advancing in wealth, population and business?" To the editorialist, the answer was clear.

Capitol Theater Portico, looking east on Main St.

The devastating effects of the depression were still apparent in 1900, when the number of industrial concerns dropped to ninety-one and the total value of industrial capital fell below $1.9 million. The value of products, meanwhile, plunged to $2.4 million, but this decrease was not balanced by significant reductions in the cost of materials, which declined only slightly to $1.4 million. Consequently, employers sought to reduce costs by eliminating labor. The wage cuts had mixed results for laborers. On the one hand, only 667 persons held industrial jobs in 1900, a decrease of 38.6 percent over the previous decade. On the other hand, the total wages earned by the remaining employees amounted to $304,823. This represents a per capita wage of $457, or a 16.9 percent increase over the per capita wage a decade earlier.

Throughout the nineteenth century most of Franklin County's industrial activity was centered in Frankfort. In 1900, sixty-six of the county's manufacturing establishments were located within the capital. These firms accounted for approximately 84 percent of the county's industrial capital and produced a similar percentage of its industrial output. Most of the enterprises located outside the city were fairly small. However, several larger plants, such as Saffell's Distillery on Cedar Run Pike near the Kentucky River and the Frankfort Distillery near Forks of Elkhorn, were considerably larger and employed a disproportionate number of rural wage earners.

Despite the economic upheavals of the period, Franklin County did experience some degree of industrial diversification during the last two decades of the century. In 1880 Sigmund Luscher installed an ice making operation at his brewery, located on the east side of Ann Street near the base of Fort Hill. Five years later the city witnessed creation of the Capital Steam Laundry. Under the management of W. L. Williams, it was known by 1898 as "one of the most popular and prosperous [industries] in the community." In 1886 Henry Burckhardt and John Ries established a large sausage manufacturing and packing plant on St. Clair Street. A dozen years later Burckhardt & Ries had built a large trade based on a reputation for making the "finest quality" meats.

Capital Steam Laundry, south end of Ann Street on the west side.

Two years after the meat packers formed their business, George Salender, Louis Weitzel, Peter C. Sower, Joseph Schraff, and William C. Lutkemeier organized a new brewery to compete with Luscher. The same year, S. F. J. Trabue and eight other local businessmen organized the Frankfort Mining, Reducing and Manufacturing Company for the purpose of acquiring lands and mineral rights in Franklin County.

Although the onset of the depression slowed local industrial expansion, a few stalwart entrepreneurs braved the storm. Among them were Lambert Suppinger and his half-brother-in-law Fred J. Sutterlin, who was an elder half-brother of Carl Kagin. In 1895 Suppinger and Sutterlin established the Frankfort Ice Company. Within a short time they were producing 115 tons of ice daily, a fifteen-fold increase over Luscher's production of 1880. Along with their ice business, they conducted a cold storage operation and served as local agents for a Cincinnati brewery. They later expanded into coal sales and the firm became Frankfort Ice and Coal Company. The business continued in Sutterlin family hands until 1967.

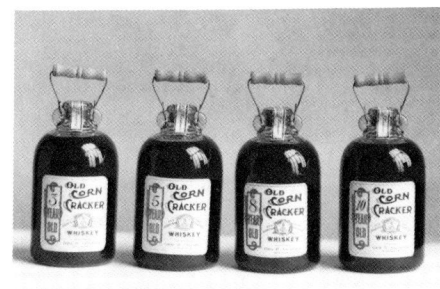

"Old Corn Cracker Whiskey," distributed solely by George B. Salender. Note the 3, 5, 8, and 10 year old labels.

While such new enterprises helped to broaden the county's economic base, expansion was strongest among the community's traditional industries. By 1898 a dozen local distilleries produced 600 barrels daily of "the finest old-fashioned, copper distilled bourbon whiskey." Two large flour mills, the J. E. M. and the Royal, had a daily capacity of 750 barrels and shipped large cargoes to Liverpool, London, and Paris.

Frankfort also was the hub of Kentucky's lumber industry. As the century came to an end, seven saw and planing mills were cutting some 15 million feet of pine, oak, ash, hickory, maple, and poplar logs, which were rafted down the Kentucky River from the eastern Kentucky forests by tough, crude logmen like "Blowy Jim" Bishop and "Bad Jim" Cole. The lumber from Frankfort's mills supplied a local furniture plant and the South's largest chair factory as well as several lumber and building materials companies. In addition, the local industrial sector included Kentucky River Mills and other factories which produced buggies and carriages; granite and marble stonework;

Frankfort Ice Company, located on Second Street

Dr. E. E. Hume

M. P. Gray

brooms, shoes, bricks, ironwork, wire nails; brass and copper articles; soap and glue; packing boxes; and whiskey barrels.

As recovery from the depression set in, pessimism about the future gradually turned to optimism. In the process, many business and civic leaders concluded that the city's economic future should not be left to chance. Thus, in October 1897 some seventy-seven businessmen and government officials formed the Commercial Club of Frankfort. Their intent was to promote and plan for Franklin County's economic and civic resurgence by injecting new vigor into existing enterprises, attracting new businesses, reducing the cost and improving the performance of local government, and polishing the community's image as a good place to live and to conduct business.

The Commercial Club's officers and directors represented a broad range of business and professional fields. Elected president was Dr. E. E. Hume, a physician. The first vice president was E. L. Samuel, cashier of the Branch Bank of Kentucky, while hardware dealer M. P. Gray served as second vice president. E. H. Elliott, bookkeeper at Kentucky River Mills, was chosen secretary, and insurance executive George L. Payne assumed the office of treasurer. His assistant was W. McKee Hardie, a druggist. Among the more prominent directors were jeweler William L. Coppersmith, dry goods merchants Henry Ringold and Richard K. McClure, reel manufacturer Benjamin C. Milam, dentist Vincent A. Kaltenbrun, physician U. V. Williams, and hardware dealer Peter C. Sower.

As a promotional tool, the club published a small booklet which contained its by-laws and a description of Frankfort. The latter section, written by Dr. Williams, outlined the community's advantages in glowing terms. In addition to its existing economic base, Williams pointed to Frankfort's physical advantages, including its situation on a broad plateau "with natural and sanitary drainage," "infinite" room for expansion beyond its corporate limits, and a healthy climate, free from malaria. Closely related were the transportation advantages provided by the "perfect system of locks and dams" on the Kentucky River and the competition offered by the railroads, which assured low freight rates.

Excellent transportation facilities enhanced still a third advantage—Frankfort's convenient access to major natural resources, including timber, coal, and iron ore. Another advantage was the city's public facilities, such as its excellent water system, outstanding electric light and streetcar systems, and well-paved streets. Finally, Williams pointed to several social advantages, including fine private and public schools, flourishing churches, and exciting arts opportunities. In short, the good doctor concluded, Frankfort was an ideal place for "all enterprises, . . . all capital, and . . . all labor seeking profitable investment, remunerative employment or happy homes."

As Williams implied, the 1880s and 1890s saw several major improvements in Franklin County's transportation network. Aside from the electrification of the streetcar, the most important improvement in Frankfort was the new St.

St. Clair Street Bridge, Feb., 1894, looking south. The Hanna House can be seen in the distance. At the time this view was taken, the bridge was only open to foot traffic.

Clair Street Bridge. Progress toward replacing the old covered bridge began in April 1890, when the General Assembly authorized the city council, which owned a two-thirds interest in the span, and the Franklin County Court, which owned the other third, to issue up to $75,000 in bonds to finance construction of a new bridge. The legislation also specified that the bridge be high enough for river commerce to continue unobstructed and that two-way passage be provided for vehicles and pedestrians alike.

It took more than two years for both governments to agree on the terms under which the new bridge would be erected. Finally, in July 1893 city and county officials signed a contract with the King Bridge Company of Cleveland, Ohio, to replace the covered bridge with a modern steel span. Construction began in August 1893 under the local supervision of a committee composed of Pat McDonald, representing Frankfort, and county attorney L. F. Johnson, representing Franklin County. Numerous problems arose during construction, and officials were so dissatisfied with work on the south abutment that they nearly refused to accept ownership of the bridge. At one point during the winter of 1894 construction ground to a halt while the committee and the contractor ironed out their differences. Once the problems were resolved, work resumed and the structure opened to pedestrian traffic in February 1894. Completed at a cost of $65,700, the St. Clair Street Bridge opened to vehicular traffic on March 24, 1894. With its open grate floor, which creates

"Minnesota," docked on north side of river. Second Street School can be seen behind the smoke stacks.

a variety of musical pitches depending upon the degree of weight, speed of traffic, and numerous other factors, the span soon became known as the "Singing Bridge."

With the completion of repairs to Lock and Dam No. 4 in 1881, navigation improvements on the Kentucky River were confined for the remainder of the century to the upper river between Frankfort and Beattyville. However, as a result of the recent repairs, traffic between the Ohio River and the capital experienced a strong resurgence. Shippers returned to the Kentucky as a channel for transporting merchandise, coal, and other products into central Kentucky, while farmers and manufacturers continued to use the river as an outlet to outside markets. In mid-July 1884 annual commerce between Carrollton and Frankfort was valued at $5 million. By 1887 the figure had grown to nearly $10.8 million.

The halcyon days of river traffic were shortlived, however. By 1887 the Louisville & Nashville Railroad and the Cincinnati Southern Railroad were locked in a fierce struggle for control of the Bluegrass burley trade. By cutting once prohibitive rates, both roads hoped to increase their patronage among Kentucky farmers. In so doing, they gradually began to undercut barge and packet rates. The result was a substantial movement of tobacco trade from river barge to rail car. By 1900 the primary commerce on the river was timber, much of it in the form of loose logs, which damaged the locks and dams. This discouraged the expansion of steamboat traffic and spurred the movement of numerous other commodities from river to rail.

Accompanying the rivalry between the Louisville- and Cincinnati-based

Frankfort & Cincinnati Railroad. Typical engine of this line.

Railroad Station at Switzer—small passenger train pulling out of Switzer.

railroads for the central Kentucky tobacco market was a concerted effort by many interior communities to stimulate their own economic growth by developing strategic railroad connections. The coveted prize was a direct connection with one of the major trunk lines. But most communities placed their hopes on local short lines which connected their county seat towns to Louisville, Lexington, or another key rail hub. Since the amount of local private capital available for such ventures was limited, state law permitted municipal and county governments, as with turnpikes a generation earlier, to underwrite construction by purchasing stock in the railroad company. Unfortunately, such financing mechanisms resulted in overbuilding. This forced several roads into receivership and resulted in substantial losses for the communities which bought their stock.

One of the more notable failures was the Kentucky Midland Railroad, which served Frankfort and Franklin County. The origins of the Kentucky Midland go back to the early 1880s, when the General Assembly chartered the Paris, Georgetown, and Big Sandy and the Paris, Georgetown, and Frankfort railroads. Neither company laid a mile of track, and both were defunct by 1887, when the Kentucky Midland took over their charters. The new railroad's own charter authorized it to build a road from Frankfort to Paris and from there to a connection with another line or into the timber and coal country of eastern Kentucky.

With Judge William Lindsay serving as president, the Kentucky Midland went searching for financial assistance from communities along the right-of-way. Assuring local citizens that the "Kentucky Midland . . . will be a revenue and dividend paying road" from the time of its completion, Lindsay and his associates raised $750,000 from towns and counties along the proposed rail line. Both Franklin County and the city of Frankfort were major investors in the project. In July 1887, in an election marked by street parades, brass bands, and other forms of hoopla, county voters approved a $150,000 common stock subscription by a vote of 2,838 to 1,208. However, the lopsided margin is deceiving. City voters approved the measure unanimously, while rural voters in all precincts but Forks of Elkhorn opposed the investment. Not surprisingly, when it came time to establish a specific right-of-way, county officials required the company to route the line as nearly as physically possible to Forks of Elkhorn. Further indicating the capital's support of the railroad, the city approved an additional $100,000 subscription of preferred stock in 1888.

Construction began in 1888, with the $725,000 contract going to the Home Construction Company. This firm was organized and owned by Judge Lindsay and his associates, who expected to pay themselves a handsome profit on the project. Unfortunately for promoters and investors alike, it cost far more than anyone anticipated to complete construction. Shackled with a large bonded mortgage debt, the Kentucky Midland proved unable either to meet its mortgage obligations or to pay dividends to municipal and county common stock holders. In 1894 the company finally went into receivership. Purchased at a foreclosure sale by outside interests, it was reorganized as the Frankfort and Cincinnati Railroad. Four years later the Commercial Club touted the Frankfort & Cincinnati as one of Franklin County's key transportation advantages. For shippers who depended upon good rail connections, the F & C was indeed an asset. But for citizens whose taxes continued to pay for a subscription which never paid a dividend, all railroads were becoming targets of anger and resentment.

While economic growth and upheaval were perhaps the most dramatic attributes of the period, the closing decades of the century also witnessed significant alterations in the structure of city government. At first these changes represented efforts by local citizens to adapt their government to the needs of a growing community. In 1880 the General Assembly authorized a major realignment of the board of city councilmen. The city was reconstituted into three wards and the voters in each ward were allowed to elect three councilmen in biennial elections. South Frankfort constituted the First Ward. The Second Ward consisted of the area north of the Kentucky River and east of St. Clair Street, and the area west of St. Clair comprised the Third Ward. The new nine-member council continued the former practice of electing one of its members as mayor, but the chief executive now served a two-year term.

The next major alteration in the structure of city government came in 1888, when the General Assembly approved an extensive reorganization of the executive branch and several changes in the legislative branch. For the first time, the voters were authorized to elect the mayor independently from the city council. The legislation specified that he could be elected for a single three-year term, and that he be at least thirty years old, an owner of property within the city, and have lived in the city for at least five years. For an annual salary of between $500 and $1,000 the chief executive was to "exercise a general supervision over all the executive and ministerial officers of the city, and see that their official duties be honestly performed." Among other duties, the mayor was designated as "head of the police" and authorized to "command them in the performance of their duty."

Although the mayor no longer functioned simultaneously as a legislator, he

Judge William Lindsay (1835–1909)

Wilkinson St., c.1890, looking north from Wapping St. The Sutterlin House (right) can be seen between the Orlando Brown House and Liberty Hall.

still had to share his power with the council. The legislative body, now headed by its own president, was empowered to submit to the mayor the names of nine local citizens from whom he appointed four to serve with him as a police and fire commission. The commission then appointed police and firemen, oversaw the departments' operations, and set the salaries of the officers. Authority to appoint the chiefs of both departments rested with the mayor, but it required the consent of the commission before he could remove either official.

Because of an unusual set of circumstances, not a single mayor served a full three-year term under the 1888 legislation. In September 1892, in an effort to standardize the governmental structure of Kentucky cities, the legislature passed a bill to divide them into classes according to population. The act classified Frankfort as a third class city, along with Paducah, Owensboro, Henderson, and Bowling Green. The following June the assembly enacted a series of measures to implement the classification law. The act for third class cities necessitated several important changes in all branches of Frankfort's municipal government.

The legislation created a twelve-person common council whose members served two-year terms. Each member was required to live in the ward from which he was elected, but all councilmen were required to be at least twenty-four years old, freeholders in the city, and residents for a minimum of two years before their election. The legislation also included conflict of interest provisions which prohibited any councilman to hold a city contract or franchise and required a member who had a personal stake in any issue before the

Richard Tobin

Judge Ira Julian

council to reveal his interest and to abstain from voting on the question. Finally, the law broadened the scope of the council's authority to include such matters as annexation, utilities franchises, and a variety of licensing matters without case-by-case legislation by the assembly.

As for the executive branch, the legislation extended the mayor's term to four years and prohibited him from succeeding himself. The mayor's duties remained much as they had been under the previous structure. Indeed, to the extent that they changed, his powers were broadened. The chief executive replaced the president of the city council as that body's presiding officer and obtained the power of veto over all ordinances passed by the council. The mayor did have to share some of his power with a new board of public works. This body, with the assistance of the city engineer, had authority over the construction and maintenance of streets, alleys, sidewalks, bridges, sewers, parks, wharves, and virtually all other elements of the city's physical property. The mayor retained full power over the police department, however, including the right to hire and fire officers and to appoint the chief.

A wide range of administrative functions remained in the hands of other elected and appointed officials. Selection of the city attorney, who represented the municipality in all its civil affairs, reverted to the city council after many years as a responsibility of the voters. The city attorney was appointed every two years, as were the clerk, auditor, treasurer, assessor, and collector of taxes. The voters continued to elect the city marshal and the prosecuting attorney. Elected to a four-year term, the marshal still held the powers of a police officer, but his primary duties lay in keeping order in and serving papers for the city police court. The city prosecutor, a new position on the municipal scene, also stood for election every four years. Because his responsibility was to represent the city in all criminal matters, the law required him to be a practicing attorney.

Judicial authority remained in the hands of the police court. The police judge retained exclusive jurisdiction over all offenses against city ordinances and by-laws and shared jurisdiction with county justices of the peace over violations of state law within the confines of the capital. The legislation provided that any offender who could not pay his fines might be committed to the city workhouse and required to work off his obligation through public work at a rate of one dollar per day.

Although the structure of city government changed considerably between 1880 and 1890, the character of leadership and even some of the faces remained much the same. The city's business and professional elite continued to dominate public offices. Edmund H. Taylor, Jr., the distillery magnate, resumed the mayor's chair in 1881 and remained in the post through 1890. Succeeding him briefly were Louis Morgan and Richard Tobin, the latter a prominent city councilman. The first mayor to serve an elected four-year term was Ira Julian, an attorney, who held office from 1894 through 1897. His successor was W. S. Dehoney, an undertaker and former dry goods merchant who earlier served two terms as the elected county coroner after being appointed to fill a vacancy. He also served as a vice president and director of Farmers Bank.

The story was much the same in the judicial branch where two men dominated the police court for half a century. William H. Sneed presided as judge from the early 1880s into the 1890s, when he was succeeded by William C. Herndon, who occupied the bench for more than forty years. While its members' shorter terms resulted in a fairly high turnover rate on the city council, some councilmen recorded fairly long tenure. Livery operator Lewis Mangan occupied a seat as early as 1882 and still held it in 1890. Benjamin C. Milam also held a seat in 1882, lost it in 1884, and regained it by 1890. None of the men holding seats in 1890 were still on the council eight years later. However, as the twentieth century approached, the council still was dominated by businessmen such as James Heeny, George Salender, William C. Lutkemeier, George C. Shaw, James N. Miles, Robert B. Jilson, Jr., W. McKee Hardie, and James S. Darnell, who was Mangan's business partner.

Judge William H. Sneed

The city's growing population, along with the changes in its governmental structure, resulted in some improvements in local services. By 1884, for example, the police department consisted of a chief, H. J. Hyde, and seven patrolmen. Despite the political nature of the job, two of Hyde's officers were still on the force six years later, and only three men—Hyde, B. B. Jeffers, and Mace Williams—wore the chief's badge between 1884 and 1901. Few cities of any size today experience such stable tenure among their police chiefs. Except for sewer and water services, which entailed heavy capital costs, the police and fire departments also accounted for the largest expenditures of city revenues. In 1890, for example, the city spent nearly $6,200 of its $64,326 operating budget for police protection and $5,146 for the fire department. An additional $5,000 went for street building and maintenance, $1,200 to care for paupers, and $1,237 for interest on bonded indebtedness.

Although the challenges of public office continued to attract some of the city's most able business and professional men, their efforts apparently did not please some of their critics. On October 1, 1896, the editor of the *Western Argus*, a Democratic newspaper, described Frankfort as "the worst governed city that ever existed." The immediate source of the problem, he asserted, was that the city council was spending beyond the community's financial means. Complaining that the salaries of some public officials were too high and that some positions were unnecessary, he proclaimed that "the government needs a shaking up from the bottom to the top." Among other things, he recommended that the city marshal's job be abolished and his duties be transferred to the police chief. Adding that the city needed only one treasurer and one attorney, he implied that the positions of collector of taxes and prosecuting attorney should be abolished.

Lewis Mangan

Though Democratic in its views, the *Argus* laid responsibility for the city's financial problems at the doorstep of both parties "because each carried their friends on the pay rolls for political favors." This caused high taxes and poor

U.S. Court House & Post Office, Frankfort. Original plan by the Supervising Architect of the U.S. Treasury Department, James G. Hill. This design is much more elaborate than the actual building.

service, an intolerable situation during hard times. "The taxpayer is never thought of until he is made to pay the limit of taxation," the editor noted. "There is not a business in the city or State that could exist twenty-four hours run as loosely as city government," he added. But the editor's cries apparently fell on deaf ears. No offices were abolished, and the traditional ways of doing political business survived.

For good or ill, the city's position as the county seat and state capital made government a significant presence in nearly every facet of life in Frankfort and Franklin County. Yet, the national government played a particular role in local development. The agent of that role was the post office. By 1880 eight unincorporated villages—Farmdale, Flag Fork, Forks of Elkhorn, Jett, Joshua, Peak's Mill, Polsgrove Landing, and Switzer—had post offices. Frequently located in country stores or other businesses, the local post office helped give these settlements a sense of legal identity which they otherwise could not have attained, short of incorporation. Moreover, as a federal patronage employee, the postmaster was the chief federal official in most communities and a powerful political influence in his own right. As leaders in local rural politics, the postmasters wielded great collective power in county government and politics.

Overshadowed by prominent local and state officials, the postmaster of Frankfort may not have exercised political influence within the city proportionate to that of his rural counterparts. However, his headquarters eventually became a major physical presence in the capital. Until it moved to the Mansion House in 1850, the local post office rarely stayed in one location more than two or three years. Under the direction of postmasters James W. Todd, William A. Gaines, and Dr. James G. Hatchett, the office remained at the Mansion House until 1876, when it moved to Major Hall. There it stayed until 1882, when the hall was destroyed by fire. For the next five years it occupied a building on St. Clair opposite Selbert's.

Meanwhile, the wheels were set in motion to build a permanent post office building for Kentucky's capital. In April 1882 President Chester A. Arthur signed a bill appropriating $100,000 for construction of a Frankfort Post Office and Federal Building. A short time later a committee composed of General Daniel W. Lindsey, former Mayor S. I. M. Major, and Postmaster Hatchett was appointed to select a site for the new structure. After evaluating several locations, they chose a tract near the southwest corner of St. Clair and Wapping streets occupied by Saffell's Valley Mill. Selected as the architect and builder was D. A. Murphy of Danville.

Site clearance began in March 1883 and the cornerstone was laid eleven months later in a ceremony marked by a parade, military bands, political speeches, Masonic rites, and an artillery salute. Construction proceeded on schedule for several months, but the project was mysteriously suspended for about a year before its completion in February 1887. Postmaster G. Russell Rodman and his staff moved into the first floor of the beautiful Romanesque Revival structure on February 28. The federal courts and customs office occupied the second floor. For nearly a century thereafter, the building at St. Clair and Wapping, towering over the Kentucky River, symbolized an influential federal presence not only in Frankfort but in the rest of central Kentucky.

While government at all levels provided a variety of vital public services, many needs could not have been met without the intervention of numerous public-spirited individuals and organizations. This was especially true in the realm of social and health services. Two historic Franklin County institutions symbolize this benevolent spirit—the Stewart Home Training School and King's Daughters Hospital.

In 1893, after sixteen years of service, Dr. John Q. A. Stewart left his position as superintendent of the Kentucky Feeble-Minded Institute to organize his own school for mentally retarded children. Chosen as the site of the new school was the recently abandoned campus of the Kentucky Military Institute near Farmdale. Stewart purchased the KMI facilities and opened his new school on September 1, 1893. Dr. Stewart operated his school according to the "cottage system." Accepting children over the age of five, he divided the students by age and sex into small "families," each of which occupied its own living quarters under the direction of a matron. Acclaimed as a pioneer in education for the mentally handicapped, Dr. Stewart attempted to provide a program of physical activity, academic education, and industrial training individually tailored to the needs of each child.

The Stewart Home remained under the direction of its founder until January 1898. Upon his father's death, Dr. John P. Stewart became the superintendent. Under his leadership and that of his own son Dr. John D. Stewart, the Stewart Home became recognized across the United States as a vital force in the field of special education. That it maintains that reputation nine decades later is a tribute to the vision of Dr. John Q. A. Stewart and to the dedication of his successors, who have captured and passed on that vision.

The effective origins of King's Daughters Hospital date to September 1894. During that month the Rev. B. Fay Mills conducted a highly successful series of evangelistic meetings under a tent pitched at Second and Steele streets. One of those moved by the evangelist's preaching was Mrs. J. H. Stuart. Shortly after the meetings ended, she invited several of her friends to a gathering at her home. On October 1, fourteen young women met and organized the Silent Workers Circle of the King's Daughters and Sons. Brimming with youthful idealism and eager to do God's work, the women sought to identify an unmet need which their efforts might fulfill. Almost immediately they concluded that the community's greatest need was for a hospital. The circle members had no idea how much money they might eventually need or how to raise it, but the task did not daunt them.

By March 1896, after eighteen months of fund-raising efforts, the organization had accumulated only $350. Nevertheless, they formed a committee to "rent a building and open a hospital." The committee's task proved quite difficult. There were many vacant houses in the city, Mrs. Stuart later recalled, "but the neighbors did not want us." Finally, a property on East Main Street which had been owned by grocer Jerry Brislan became available. The circle secured the Brislan house rent free for a year and, with the help of city workmen and a local building materials supplier, converted it into a medical facility. King's Daughters Hospital opened on July 16, 1896. It had two wards with two beds each and a single private room. For the next eight years the Silent Workers Circle put their dues into a building fund. By July 1904 the fund contained the huge sum of $800. With this the women purchased the East Main property and opened a new chapter in the development of King's Daughters Hospital.

The closing decades of the nineteenth century also witnessed continuing growth and expansion in Franklin County's cultural and social life. In the area of public education, opportunities increased for children of all ages, both black and white. As more and more citizens realized the benefits of education, school enrollments soared. When the schools opened in the fall of 1887, officials reported an enrollment of 600 white and 400 black pupils. A decade later the number of white students had doubled, while black enrollment had increased to more than 500 children.

Several forces contributed to climbing enrollments, including the growth of the city's population through annexation. However, other factors involved improvements in the instructional program. In 1887 the trustees created a night school specifically for boys who were employed during the regular

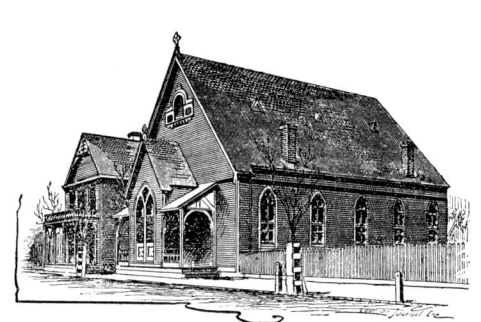

Southern Presbyterian Church, c.1890.

Lebanon Baptist Church, c.1890, Located in Northwest Franklin County and built in 1889. Jack Rodgers and Arbie Pulliam are posing in buggy.

school day. By the late 1890s kindergarten classes had been added for preschool children and manual training programs had been organized for adolescents.

Even more important was the formation of a high school. Ironically, the creation of the high school was partially the result of a disaster. In 1885 Second Street School was destroyed by fire. The new school, completed the following year at a cost of $30,000, provided space for a library and a science laboratory, which were essential for an adequate secondary curriculum. The first high school class, which consisted of seven students, met about 1889. The students completed their three-year program and received their diplomas in 1892. At first the high school curriculum resembled that of the city's private schools. However, commercial classes were added in 1905, and the program was extended to four years in 1909. The present Frankfort High School at the corner of Fourth and Shelby streets was erected in 1925.

A major advance in the education of the city's black children came in 1882 with the construction of Clinton Street School, located at the east end of Clinton Street near the edge of the city. Chosen principal was William H. Mayo, a nineteen-year-old Cincinnati youth who had graduated first in his high school class less than a year earlier. His only professional experience was six months as an assistant bookkeeper for the Sol P. Kineon Coal Elevator Company, of Cincinnati. Despite his youth and inexperience, Mayo proved to be an energetic and resourceful leader. While carrying out his administrative duties he pursued his own education and by 1889 had completed his master's degree. He was a leader in statewide efforts to improve educational opportunities for black youth and twice served as president of the State Teachers' Association of Kentucky. Most importantly, by 1900, under Mayo's leadership, the Clinton Street School's eleven faculty members were providing kindergarten, elementary, and high school education for approximately 500 children, despite the handicaps imposed by racial segregation and inadequate financial support.

One of the major struggles in which Mayo took a leadership role was the effort to establish the State Normal School for Colored Persons. Created by an act of the legislature in 1887, the school's purpose was to prepare teachers for Kentucky's black schools. Although sponsored by the state, the normal school received substantial assistance from the city of Frankfort, including the donation of $1,500 in cash and a large hilltop tract of land between East Main Street and the L & N Railroad tracks, which served as the site of the new campus. At first the school served only as a teacher training institution. But in 1890 it became a federal land grant college, and its curriculum was broadened to encompass agriculture, mechanics, and home economics.

Classes began in what is today named Jackson Hall, a late Gothic Revival structure characterized by crenellated battlements which resemble a medieval castle. The structure was named for John H. Jackson, the school's first president. A Kentuckian and graduate of Berea College, Jackson taught for several

Second Street Public School. Designed by architect M. G. Wilson of Louisville, the cornerstone of this structure was laid in an impressive ceremony on July 17th, 1886. Occupied in March, 1887, the structure cost over $30,000.

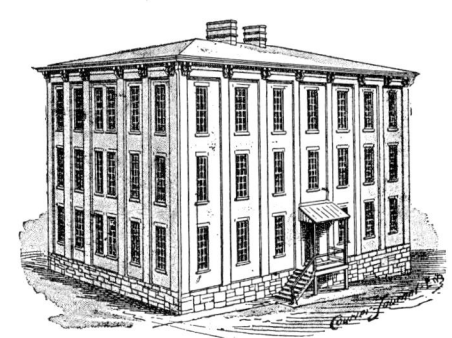

Clinton Street School.

Kentucky State University, formerly the State Normal School for Colored Persons. Jackson Hall (left) and the school's band (right), about 1910.

years in Kansas City, Missouri, before returning to his native state to head the normal school. Jackson's colleagues in the endeavor included Professor Moses A. Davis, a graduate of Hampton Institute, who taught mechanics; Professor W. D. Thomas, an instructor in agriculture, mathematics, and natural sciences; Professor T. Augustus Reid, a Jamaican who served as the principal of several similar colleges before coming to teach English in Frankfort; Miss Mary E. Jackson, a former Maysville High School teacher, who taught in the normal school; and Mrs. Bettie M. Bailey, who taught home economics. By 1898 this predecessor of Kentucky State University had an enrollment of 152 students.

The educational advances of the 1880s and 1890s were not necessarily duplicated in other areas of cultural life. The popularity of the theatre resulted, of course, in the immediate construction of a new Opera House when Major Hall burned in 1882. Likewise, the city's intellectual elite continued their literary pursuits through the Frankfort Lyceum. The only notable innovation, however, appears to have been the Capital City Orchestra, a shortlived ensemble organized during the mid-1890s and directed by W. H. Van Winkle.

Lack of innovation certainly was not a problem in local journalism. As the 1880s dawned, S. I. M. Major's *Kentucky Yeoman*, a tri-weekly, and George A. Lewis's *Roundabout*, a weekly, still dominated the local news scene. Many new editors and publishers entered the business over the next twenty years. Most failed. But in so doing, they often identified unserved news markets and paved the way for others who made permanent changes in the conduct of local journalism.

One of the major developments of the period was the establishment of the city's first "long run" daily paper. Numerous others had tried it, the most recent examples having been M. Stuart Cann, whose *Frankfort Daily Dispatch* ran from 1878 to 1882, and Russell Sneed and John B. Dryden, who cooperated with Cann in the establishment of the *Daily Post Dispatch* in 1880. However, the latter paper folded the following year. Mose O'Conner finally accomplished what Sneed, Cann, and Dryden had failed to achieve when he established the *Evening Journal* in August 1887. Originally a small, four-page sheet, the *Evening Journal* remained in continuous publication for nine years. By the time it suspended publication 1896, Dryden's *Daily Call* had been on the streets for four years. It was still in business in 1900 when John Meloan, L. G. Wallace, and J. N. McDonald established the first *Kentucky State Journal*, a predecessor of the present *State Journal*.

Another major development was a struggle for dominance as the city's chief Democratic organ. In 1885, just a year before his death, the aging and ailing Samuel I. M. Major suspended publication of the *Kentucky Yeoman*. This left a vacuum in the capital's political journalism. Major barely had closed his office doors when the Capital Printing Company on St. Clair Street established the *Capital* and appointed John D. Wood as its editor. The *Capital* operated as a Democratic paper from 1885 to 1892. For a brief time it was published as a daily by Colonel Polk Johnson. In 1892, however, W. S. Forrester, a Republican, purchased the paper, moved its offices to Broadway, and changed its party identification. It remained a Republican paper until it ceased publication in 1897.

Col. E. Polk Johnson

The *Capital*'s conversion to a Republican paper left the field open for Pat McDonald, who had been Major's business manager, to claim his mantle with the *Western Argus*. Named for the *Argus of Western America*, the old Jacksonian paper published by Amos Kendall and Francis P. Blair, Sr., McDonald's *Argus* was established in September 1886 and remained in circulation until February 1902. But McDonald was not without his challengers. In 1887 Clarence Egbert founded the *Frankfort Herald*, a small Democratic weekly published on the second floor of the Odd Fellows Building. It remained in business until September 1888. Seven years later, W. J. Conner established a shortlived weekly called the *Sunday Leader*, and Woodford Longmoor began publication of the *Frankfort Ledger* in December 1896. Neither sheet, however, lasted more than a few months, leaving the *Argus* as the capital's leading Democratic paper until it was superseded in that role by the *Kentucky Journal* in 1901.

The first newspaper aimed specifically at the black population was the *Blue Grass Bugle*. It was established in October 1899 as a weekly by the Bugle Publishing Company, headed by Thomas L. Brooks and Edward W. Lane. William H. Mayo, principal of Clinton Street School, was a member of the board of directors. Under the editorial leadership of Dr. Edward Ellsworth Underwood, the *Bugle* remained in publication until 1918. The subscription was ten cents monthly or one dollar annually.

Franklin County's first rural news publication seems to have been the *Jett's*

Enterprise. L. A. Trumbo established this monthly publication in September 1892. Its editor was Miss Virginia (Jennie) Jett. Consisting of four illustrated pages, the *Enterprise* was essentially a lively "gossip sheet." In addition to local news and personal tidbits from the Jett community, it carried a variety of humorous pieces, editorial comment, some poetry, and serialized stories, along with a few advertisements. It was printed by Trumbo's good friend, George A. Lewis, and remained in circulation until mid-1893.

One of the most important developments in Franklin County's social realm was the flowering of an active organizational life. For a century most Franklin Countians depended upon the church as the center of their social life. A few citizens belonged to fraternal lodges such as the Masons, Odd Fellows, and Knights of Pythias. And during the 1870s the Grange became an important political and social institution for many rural families. But it was not until the 1880s and 1890s that the community began to support a wide array of voluntary organizations over a long period of time.

While secret and benevolent organizations had been a part of local society since the late eighteenth century, they proliferated during the 1880s. By 1891 Franklin County boasted at least six Masonic lodges, including one in Polsgrove Landing and another in Frankfort whose membership was entirely black. Frankfort had two chapters of the Independent Order of Odd Fellows and three lodges associated with the black Grand United Order of Odd Fellows. The Good Samaritans had seven chapters, and the Knights and Ladies of Honor, Knights of Honor, German Benevolent Society, Knights of Pythias, and Royal Temples of Temperance each had at least one chapter. Local Catholic organizations included St. Joseph's Catholic Society and the Catholic Knights of America. In addition to the Masonic lodge and Odd Fellows, there were three other black organizations, including the Knights of Friendship and two chapters of the United Brothers of Friendship.

The organizational spectrum broadened still further during the 1890s with the formation of several groups dedicated to the community's civic and moral betterment. In September 1894 forty women from leading families organized the Frankfort Women's Club. For many years to come the women's club was in the forefront of most of the city's major civic improvements. The following year a group of religious, business, and professional leaders founded the Young Men's Christian Association. Their aim was to improve the physical and spiritual lives of the community's young men, including those moving into the city to seek employment in government and local business. In September 1897, Captain and Mrs. S. Urban initiated the Salvation Army's work in Frankfort. The army's first office was an upstairs room on Main Street. Three years later, the headquarters moved to Wilkinson Street. In 1905 the South Frankfort Presbyterian Church arranged for the army to receive the donation of a building on Clinton Street, where it remained until 1915. One of the Salvation Army's original directors was Fred J. Sutterlin, a prominent businessman and Presbyterian layman, who served on the board for some fifty-five years.

Frankfort Fire Department, c.1886. Left to right: Ed Haley, Phil Goins, Harry Stevens, Gene Phillips; two of the boys are Hugh Smith and Sam Phillips.

Although benevolent societies and community improvement organizations proved to be important continuing vehicles of social and civic activity, Frankfort's centennial celebration in 1886 undoubtedly ranked as the leading community event of the era. Planning for the celebration began in June 1886 with the appointment of a temporary organizing committee. Designated chairman and secretary respectively were Colonel John L. Scott and L. F. Johnson, both local attorneys. When it became apparent that organizing the centennial observance was too large a task for a small group to handle, the committee determined that the planning process should be broadened to include far more people. On August 23 the committee conducted a mass meeting at which eight prominent persons were selected for the purpose of organizing the Frankfort Centennial Association. Five days later the committee recommended that General Daniel W. Lindsey be designated president of the organization and that Judge William H. Sneed, S. C. Sayre, and H. B. Ware be appointed secretaries. The report also suggested seventy-two vice presidents, including several of Frankfort's most prominent businessmen. Heading the list was journalist J. Stoddard Johnston.

More than a month of intense planning followed the adoption of the committee's report, with centennial day set for October 6. A participant in Frankfort's centennial celebration described it as "the greatest day in the history of the city." An estimated 25,000 people crowded into the streets to watch the largest parade ever assembled in the city. Virtually every secret society, religious organization, school club, and state military company participated, and thirty-six local businesses entered floats which advertised their products.

Commemorative ceremonies were conducted on the grounds of the old

Centennial Day Parade, October 6, 1886. The longest parade ever seen in Frankfort, it consisted of virtually every secret and benevolent order, Christian organization, and military faction in the state, and floats representing 36 local businesses.

249

capitol. The speaker's platform stood between the front gates facing the capitol, with seats extending almost to the statehouse itself. The speaker's rostrum was bedecked with evergreen trees, flags, and flowers. Mayor Edmund H. Taylor opened the observance and introduced Judge William Lindsay for the welcoming address. Mrs. Eudora South, Mrs. Jennie C. Morton, and Kentucky poet laureate Henry T. Stanton read poems prepared for the occasion. After a brief speech by politician William C. P. Breckinridge, Frankfort attorney John Mason Brown delivered the main address, entitled "The Political Beginnings of Kentucky." The day was closed with a spectacular fireworks display on the city's riverfront.

While the centennial was a joyful celebration of the capital's heritage, some of the period's major events were better left uncelebrated. The 1880s barely had begun when on May 15, 1880, fire destroyed the Odd Fellows Hall and two neighboring residences in the center of Bridgeport. Thirty months later a fire in downtown Frankfort wiped out not only Buhr's Hotel and Major Hall but took several private offices and residences, as well as the post office, along with it. Dr. James G. Hatchett, the postmaster, managed to save almost everything in the post office, but financial losses amounted to between $70,000 and $80,000. In addition, several citizens were injured while helping the fire department to fight the conflagration. Almost as destructive was the blaze of August 10, 1885, which wiped out Peter C. Sower's property at the corner of Main and St. Clair streets and adjoining buildings belonging to Sol Harris and Edmund H. Taylor, Jr. Total damages were almost $60,000. Fortunately, all the buildings were replaced quickly during the continuing building boom.

The 1890s had their share of fire as well. On October 19, 1894, a spark touched off half a can of blasting powder and severely damaged Tom Pence's saw mill at Bellepoint. The explosion and accompanying fire inflicted serious burns and other injuries on two workmen, Joe Downey and Howard Masters. A few weeks later, on November 12, a fire swept through a state-owned warehouse filled with the inventory of a local chair company. The building, valued at $8,000, and about $16,000 worth of chairs were totally destroyed, but the entire loss was insured.

The largest victim of fire during the decade was the Institute for Feeble-Minded Children, which suffered a series of blazes during 1896 and 1897. The initial fire struck on September 2, 1896, inflicting about $65,000 worth of damage. A second blaze on May 3, 1897, caused an additional $50,000 in damages. Finally, on September 18th, a third fire destroyed several frame structures on the institute grounds which had provided temporary shelter for several of the students following the initial fire. In the wake of the third fire, the children were moved into temporary quarters in Frankfort and on a local farm until the reconstruction of the institute was completed in late 1897.

Far more devastating than any fire was the damage inflicted by the 1883 flood. The Kentucky River began rising in early February as the rain-swollen

BELLEPOINT DURING THE FLOOD OF 1886.

Ohio started backing up into its tributaries. By the eleventh most of the residents in the lower parts of the city had been evacuated, and "Craw" was completely covered. That evening many residents who remained in the city stayed up all night, waiting to see the flood waters wash away the St. Clair Street Bridge. Although the bridge held, their fears were not unfounded. A heavy drift was running and began to accumulate against the piers. Adding to the pile were large pieces of houses which were rushing down the river like so many toy boats and crashing into the center pier. A large, recently completed tobacco barn washed off its foundation and smashed into the piers, sending timbers flying in every direction. This resulted in great damage to the span's sidewalk and tore away large sections of the floor, walls, and roof.

At its height the flood covered more than half the city. The water stood two to three feet deep in the penitentiary yard, and backwaters completely surrounded Fort Hill, leaving it an island. Every road except Versailles Pike leading into the city was covered by two to four feet of water. Traffic across the St. Clair Street Bridge ground to a halt and the drift caused severe damage to the railroad bridge. All houses on the east end of Broadway and High Street were completely surrounded, and more than one hundred dwellings were destroyed when they crashed into the St. Clair Street Bridge. Numerous industries, including the O. F. C., Carlisle, Hermitage, and Saffell distilleries were inundated with two to ten feet of water, and the flood engulfed the gas works, leaving the city in darkness.

The devastation caused by a flood of such magnitude is difficult to measure in financial terms. Even more difficult to assess is the cost in human suffering.

As the waters receded, for example, more than two hundred families in Frankfort and its environs were homeless. More remarkable, perhaps, than the physical and financial damages inflicted by the flood was the resiliency of the human spirit, demonstrated in countless acts of heroism, large and small, as Franklin Countians pitched in to hold back the surging waters; to feed, clothe, and house its victims; and to rebuild the city after the flood.

Giving local citizens even less cause to celebrate was the cloud of corruption and violence which shrouded the community for the rest of the century. In the superheated political atmosphere of late nineteenth century Kentucky, charges of corruption were every politician's stock in trade, and an honest politician was one who when bought, stayed bought. One man who appeared to stand above the fray was a Franklin County native named James William Tate. Born on Elkhorn Creek and schooled in state politics from early childhood, "Honest Dick" Tate developed a demeanor of friendliness, a reputation for generosity, and an image of bedrock integrity. In 1867 Tate won the Democratic nomination for state treasurer. Beating his Republican rival at the polls, he kept the job for the next twenty years.

But the base of "Honest Dick's" popularity was the source of his undoing. From the beginning he made a host of friends by making unauthorized loans from the treasury and by accepting worthless checks from "honest debtors," who repaid his favors by returning him to office every two years. By the mid-1880s the treasury had accumulated some $150,000 in uncollected debts as a result of Tate's generosity. But in early 1888 rumors of Tate's dishonesty began to circulate in the capital. Soon an impetuous freshman legislator introduced a resolution calling for a "sort of general investigation of state affairs, beginning with the treasury." Suddenly, one historian noted, "such a flash of lightning, and peal of thunder as was never before seen or heard came out of a clear sky, and rocked the state as nothing had done since the war."

Events now rolled quickly to a climax. On March 20, 1888, after a brief inquiry, Governor Simon B. Buckner dispatched a message informing the legislature that irregularities in the treasury had been discovered and that "Honest Dick" Tate had been suspended. Within a month the treasurer had been impeached and convicted for high crimes and misdemeanors. In June he was convicted on criminal charges of embezzlement. But Tate had not stayed around to defend himself. Even before the governor's message reached the assembly, Tate fled the state, apparently taking with him a substantial portion of the Commonwealth's hard currency. He was never again seen in Kentucky, and his whereabouts after his flight remain a mystery. The ultimate extent of Tate's larceny was never determined, but estimates range from $175,000 to $247,000. The long-term consequences of Tate's thievery, however, were not so much financial as they were political and constitutional. In 1891, remembering the Tate episode, the delegates to the Constitutional Convention inserted a provision limiting all elected executive officials to a single four-year term. "Thus the restless ghost of Dick Tate lingers on in the corridors at Frankfort,"

James W. Tate

Thomas D. Clark has written, "to remind Kentuckians of the folly of a permanent love affair with a public servant."

Unfortunately, Tate's thievery was just one more incident in a pattern of corruption and violence which had begun during the Civil War and which continued through the end of the century. There were numerous eruptions of interpersonal violence, but others contained racial, political, and economic overtones. On September 10, 1882, Police Chief Jerry Lee was shot to death during a street altercation between two local thugs, Frank Egbert and Stephen Scarce. Nine years later a local jury acquitted former deputy sheriff Ambrose Polsgrove after he killed his brother-in-law, Jerry Williamson, at the crowded corner of St. Clair and Main streets. Anti-Negro violence resurfaced on August 14, 1894, when a black man named Marshall Boston was hanged from the St. Clair Street Bridge and his body riddled with bullets after he allegedly raped a white woman, Mrs. Martin Nolan. An election eve riot on November 1, 1897, cost the lives of three men when Republicans thwarted an attempt by Democrats to round up black voters and incarcerate them in a barn on Georgetown Pike until the city election was over.

The "Corner-Stone" of Frankfort. On October 6th, 1899, members of the Kentucky Historical Society unveiled this monument marking the site of the beginning of Hancock Taylor's survey of June, 1773, at the corner of Main and Ann Streets. Taylor's granddaughter, Mary Jouett Dudley, is shown to the left of, and facing, the monument.

But such incidents pale in comparison to the organized lawlessness of the notorious Tollgate Wars. During the 1880s farmers in central Kentucky began to rebel over what they considered exorbitant rates for carrying their goods to market on often deteriorating turnpikes. The situation worsened during the depression of the 1890s, when agricultural prices plummeted and money to pay the tolls was increasingly dear. At first, opponents of the turnpikes argued that roads were a governmental responsibility and that they should be taken over by county governments and the tolls removed. But the Commonwealth and many counties, owning stock in the turnpike companies, resisted the public demand for free roads.

When their pleas fell on deaf ears, angry farmers resorted to violence. For many months between 1896 and 1898 tollgate keepers and their families found themselves roused from their beds, terrorized by sometimes drunken masked men, and hustled outside to see their homes and their tollgates put to the torch. A few courageous men who attempted to protect their homes and gates were murdered for their efforts.

In Franklin County the tollgate raids peaked in the autumn of 1896. During October raiders burned gates on the Louisville and Lawrenceburg roads. On November 13 they hit the toll house on Owenton Road. By the end of the year, night riders had destroyed virtually every tollgate in the county. Neither the raiders nor their cause won much friendship in Frankfort. George A. Lewis's *Roundabout* characterized the marauders as a "valliant [sic] band of brave and daring knights of the white mask who are traveling about the country at night warring against the defenseless toll gate poles and intimidating the old men and widows" who attended them. The paper also questioned whether the "good citizens" who were burning the tollgates would "pay a cent of toll to keep up the turnpikes of the county if they were made free." Pat Mc-

Donald's *Western Argus* joined the *Roundabout*'s condemnation of the raids, but went further to question not only the economic feasibility but also the legality of any move by the fiscal court to buy out the turnpike companies.

Ultimately, however, the court had little choice. Maintenance of the roads was essential to commerce, and it was clear that public opinion outside the city would not allow the gates to be rebuilt. By 1900 the Franklin County Court had joined neighboring counties in purchasing the stock of local turnpike companies and making them free.

The Tollgate Wars were still fresh in the minds of most Franklin Countians when Kentucky embarked upon the most bizarre political campaign in its history. The 1899 gubernatorial election pitted Attorney General William S. Taylor, who was attempting to succeed fellow Republican William O. Bradley, against two Democrats—William Goebel, a state senator from Covington, and former Governor John Young Brown, a conservative nominated by a rump convention of Democrats angry at Goebel. Part reformer, part boss, and totally ruthless in his quest for power, Goebel had made some influential enemies, most notably the Louisville & Nashville Railroad. Nevertheless, the election might have been an easy Democratic victory had Goebel not alienated so many conservatives, and even some former allies, with the abusive tactics he employed to gain the nomination.

Despite the passions raised by the campaign, election day passed quietly around the Commonwealth. When the ballots came in, Taylor barely had edged out the controversial state senator. But one clause in a recently passed election law, conveniently sponsored by Goebel himself, provided that in the case of a challenge to the outcome of a gubernatorial election, a special board was to be appointed by lot from the legislature to examine the contest results and to report back to the assembly, which had the authority to decide the contest. Since the Democrats held an iron grip on the assembly, the outcome in such a situation was all but certain. Because the 1899 election was so close and evidence of fraud—by both sides—so rampant, Goebel's friends had little difficulty persuading him to file a challenge. A good deal of political and legal maneuvering followed, but by January 30, 1900, a decision by the legislature was near. Meanwhile, armed partisans of each candidate were moving into Frankfort, and some feared a civil war if the General Assembly decided in Goebel's favor.

On the morning of January 30 Goebel and his two body guards—Jack Chinn, of Mercer County, and Eph Lillard, warden of the state penitentiary—met in the lobby of the Capital Hotel and then walked the few blocks to the capitol. The crowd was unusually sparse as the trio walked through the gate and into the capitol grounds. As they neared the fountain in front of the statehouse, a shot rang out from an upper window of the secretary of state's office in the executive office building. Goebel dropped to his knees and then rolled onto his side. When they were sure the shooting had stopped, friends carried the mortally wounded politician back to the hotel.

Capitol Square, February 1900, with guards posted at the gate and militia posted on the grounds. The inaugural stand is the white square to the right of the gate behind the electric pole.

With tensions already at a fever pitch, the shooting created a state of near panic. Within moments rumors of Goebel's death began to circulate. After briefly deferring action, the legislative committee charged with examining the election returns voted along strict party lines that the contest should go to Goebel and his running mate, J. C. W. Beckham. Upon hearing the decision, Taylor, who in the meantime had been sworn in as governor, declared a state of insurrection and ordered the legislature to adjourn and reassemble in London. The Republicans heeded Taylor's demand, but the Democrats defied it. The next day, after soldiers blocked their repeated efforts to assemble in various public halls, the Democrats from both houses met under cover of darkness at the Capital Hotel and declared Goebel the governor of Kentucky. A short time later Chief Justice James H. Hazelrigg gave Goebel and Beckham their oaths of office. The dying Goebel immediately signed an order commanding the troops to disperse. But the soldiers remained where they were, and so did William S. Taylor.

William Goebel died on the evening of February 3, four days after he was shot. Beckham was sworn in immediately as his successor, and the partisan standoff—and the threat of civil war—continued. Forty-eight hours after Goebel's death several of Taylor's chief advisors met with key Democratic officials in an effort to resolve the situation peacefully. The parties agreed that Taylor would step down and be given immunity from prosecution for any involvement in Goebel's assassination. The Democrats agreed that a new, fair election law would be enacted. But Taylor, a weak and vacillating man, rejected the arrangement.

In a final effort to end the dispute, both parties filed suit, with the cases being consolidated by mutual consent for a decision by the highly respected Jefferson Circuit Judge Emmet Field. Judge Field refused to overrule the legislature, and on April 6 the Kentucky Court of Appeals upheld his decision. After the United States Supreme Court affirmed the court of appeals on May 21, Taylor secretly fled the state, traveling to Indianapolis where he practiced law until his death in 1928. With possession of the governor's chair decided, the troops dispersed and the mobs of civilian partisans went home. But bitter memories of the Goebel case were periodically resurrected for more than a decade as those implicated in the assassination alternately came up for trial, appeal, and retrial. But the citizens of Frankfort and Franklin County, bewildered by a generation of economic upheaval, social turmoil, and political strife, eagerly hoped that a new century would bring a brighter, more peaceful future.

9

A New Century Dawns

FOR A COMMUNITY which had suffered through more than three decades of turbulence, the dawn of the twentieth century offered the promise of a new era of social, political, and economic progress. This promise did not go totally unrealized; Frankfort and Franklin County certainly experienced a degree of political and economic change during the first two decades of the twentieth century. After decades of recurrent agitation to remove the capital to another city, the construction of a new statehouse assured that Frankfort would remain the Commonwealth's seat of government for decades to come. At the same time, the advent of the automobile gradually increased the mobility of the populace and opened a variety of new business opportunities for entrepreneurs seeking to sell and service the horseless carriage.

On the other hand, it also became apparent that more than an epochal change in the calendar was necessary to translate the hope of a brighter day into reality. For nearly a decade after the new century began, periodic outbreaks of racial and economic violence continued to disrupt the peace. Similarly, the problem of declining population, which first appeared during the 1890s, continued into the twentieth century, affecting the city of Frankfort as well as the rest of the country. Finally, with the onset of prohibition and the near total loss of its distilling industry, Franklin County experienced severe economic dislocations in agriculture, commerce, and manufacturing.

At first glance, the problem of stagnant population growth appears to have been reversed during the first ten years of the new century. While the growth rates were modest, both city and county gained population during the decade. The population of Franklin County increased from 20,852 in 1900 to 21,135 in 1910. Likewise, Frankfort's population jumped from 9,487 to 10,465 inhabitants, a 10.3 percent increase, during the same period.

But a more detailed analysis of the figures shows that the underlying pattern of stagnation was becoming even broader. The rural sections of the county continued to lose population, even without the transfer of land area to Frankfort through annexation. The Forks of Elkhorn district suffered a net

Goebel Monument at State Cemetery. The monument was unveiled on the tenth anniversary of Goebel's death, with ex-Governor J. C. W. Beckham acting as master of ceremonies. The bronze statue on a marble base was paid for by popular subscription.

First Baptist Church. Located on the northwest corner of High and Clinton Streets, the building was designed by Leo Oberwarth and constructed in 1908.

loss of nearly sixty residents during the first decade of the century, and the Peak's Mill district lost over twenty. The Bald Knob district suffered the greatest loss, however, with its population dropping from 3,242 persons in 1900 to 2,379 a decade later. Indeed, Bald Knob's 26.6 percent loss overwhelmed the gains of the Bridgeport district, where the population grew from 2,185 to 2,431 during the interim.

The continued outmigration of blacks accounts for part of the loss in rural population. But during this particular decade, four times as many whites as blacks left rural Franklin County. Many whites, unable any longer to grub a living from the infertile, rocky hillsides of the Blad Knob and Peak's Mill areas, no doubt moved to Frankfort, where they tried their hand in commerce or industry. But this does not appear to have been the case with blacks. Indeed, Frankfort's overall population increase occurred despite a net loss of 465 Negroes, indicating that the capital's white population was the only group in the entire county to show a major increase during the first decade of the twentieth century.

The county slipped even more deeply into the doldrums during the next decade, as the problem of declining population began to affect the capital as well. After the brief recovery between 1900 and 1910, Franklin County's population dropped sharply to 19,357 in 1920, and the lowest figure since 1880. In the process, Frankfort's population fell to 9,805, a loss of 6.3 percent over the previous census. This time the downward trend was apparent among whites as well as blacks, as the number of white residents fell from 7,614 to 7,559 and the number of black inhabitants fell from 2,851 to 2,246.

Geographically, Frankfort's losses were most pronounced in the Third Ward, which embraced the area north of the river and west of St. Clair Street. Encompassing the city's heaviest concentration of black residents as well as some of its oldest housing stock, the Third Ward lost 574 persons, or 17.3 percent of its total population. Losses were not so severe in the Second Ward, the city's largest, where the population slipped from 4,178 to 4,017, a net decline of 161 persons. Only in the First Ward, South Frankfort, did the city continue to grow. But even there the improvement was modest, with the population climbing from 2,966 in 1910 to 3,041 in 1920, an anemic 2.5 percent increase.

The situation was even more lackluster outside the city. The white population of rural Franklin County dropped from 9,775 inhabitants in 1910 to 8,937 in 1920. At the same time the black population dipped from 895 to 615. All four rural magisterial districts suffered substantial losses. Most heavily affected was Peak's Mill, which lost 625 residents. Bridgeport, which had shown some growth during the previous decade, lost 195 inhabitants, while Bald Knob and Forks of Elkhorn lost 186 and 112 citizens, respectively.

The reasons for Franklin County's erratic growth between 1890 and 1920 are anything but clear. However, there are several plausible explanations, any or all of which may have some validity. Some potential migrants into the county may have been put off by the violence which pervaded the community after the Civil War. But Franklin County was far from unique in this respect. Violence was endemic to Kentucky, the South, and, indeed, the nation. The only real differences were the forms and targets of the violence from one region to another. More clearly apparent was the migration of blacks from the rural South to northern industrial cities in search of better employment opportunities.

Some observers believed that Frankfort was "hampered by the bugaboo of Capitol removal," which throttled business investment, discouraged building, and retarded the flow of people into the community. This may have been the case. But it is clear as well that construction of the new capitol did not appreciably change the situation: Franklin County continued to lose population for a decade after completion of the new statehouse. Finally, it is probable that World War I was a major cause of the population losses between 1910 and 1920. Even before the United States entered the war in 1917, large industrial plants in the Northeast and Midwest began expanding production to fill European war orders. This created thousands of new jobs and opened new opportunities for many Southerners, both black and white, urban and rural.

Whatever the reasons for Franklin County's laggard population growth during this period, one of its consequences was a minimum of new residential development. As the earlier figures suggest, the only neighborhood in the capital to experience even a modest rate of growth throughout the period was South Frankfort. Still the favorite of the city's business and civic elite, the neighborhood continued to witness the construction of stylish upper middle class homes. However, the homes erected between 1900 and 1920 exhibit a distinct architectural departure from the exuberant Victorian styles of the previous generation. Where the Victorian styles abounded in elaborate ornamentation, the new twentieth century homes are notable for their simple lines and lack of adornment.

"Ingleside" on Versailles Road three miles east of Frankfort in about 1908, when the house was "colonialized" by Col. Charles E. Hoge. Oberwarth was responsible for designing the remodeling. The house was torn down in the 1960's.

Especially popular was the Colonial Revival style, often characterized by sloping gambrel roofs and broad gambrel dormers. Another favorite was the arts and crafts style. Particularly evident along the east side of Shelby Street, these blocky structures of brick or frame construction are characterized by hipped and gabled roofs, dormer windows, massive chimneys, and a bare minimum of ornamentation. Numerous homes also were built in the craftsman bungalow style. These single-story houses with broadly pitched, overhanging gables are quite prominent in the 700 and 800 blocks of Shelby Street near the new capitol.

Jessie K. Zeigler House, 509 Shelby Street.

Unquestionably the most outstanding early twentieth century dwelling in South Frankfort is the Jesse K. Zeigler house at 509 Shelby Street. This home, the only one in Kentucky designed by the distinguished architect Frank Lloyd Wright, was constructed in late 1910 for the Reverend Zeigler while he was pastor of First Presbyterian Church. The minister and the architect met aboard ship while enroute to Italy earlier the same year. Zeigler apparently

Juniper Hill, Gothic Music Room

Juniper Hill, Louisville Road. The large bay windows to the right define the music room addition.

George Franklin Berry

became fascinated with Wright's ideas and asked him to design his new home. Wright obliged the young pastor, prepared a set of sketches, and sent them back to his office in Oak Park, Illinois, where his staff completed the detailed plans. The finished house, distinguished by a low hipped roof, wide overhangs, and banks of windows, is a textbook example of the Prairie style which Wright had advanced as an ideal form of suburban housing.

Although most of the new housing within the city was constructed in South Frankfort, some new development was attempted beyond the city limits. In 1900 George F. Berry, vice president of W. A. Gaines & Company, purchased a tract on the north side of Louisville Road overlooking Frankfort. Naming it Juniper Hill for the profusion of juniper trees which grew on the site, he commissioned architect Hill Dodd to design an imposing, three-story Classical mansion. The home's most outstanding feature, added in 1912, was its Gothic Revival music room. Born into a musical family, Berry loved classical music and aspired to play the organ. Determined to pursue his dream, he engaged Sidney Durst of the Cincinnati Conservatory as his teacher. Under Durst's tutelage, he mastered the magnificent, four keyboard organ which occupied the music room. Within a short time, Juniper Hill was a center of Kentucky's music world, as Berry hosted lavish midnight dinner parties which attracted music lovers from throughout the Commonwealth.

Far more important in their long-term contribution to Frankfort's development, however, were three residential subdivisions platted near the edge of the city. In 1907 five prominent business and political figures—J. Morgan Chinn, C. W. Hay, E. M. Wallace, Polk Laffoon, and David D. Smith—organized the Frankfort Realty Company. Their intent was to develop the old Sayre-Rodman estate, which lay immediately southwest of the new capitol site between Louisville Road and the Kentucky River. To prepare the tract for development, Frankfort Realty engaged the services of the Bowman Realty Company, a West Virginia firm which specialized in the development of modern suburban subdivisions.

In September 1909, after months of preparations, the developers launched a high-powered campaign to sell lots in Capitol Heights. To generate interest, they published a slick booklet which praised the natural attributes of the site, extolled the economic, moral, and aesthetic virtues of life in Frankfort, and announced the details of a public auction of lots scheduled for September 24 and 25. To attract a good crowd, the developers promised free transportation to the site, free balloon ascensions, a band concert, daytime fireworks displays, and a free burgoo dinner. To sweeten the attraction, they also offered chances on three lots, which would be "given away absolutely free 'with no strings to them.'" For those who were truly interested in buying, the developers offered a variety of "liberal options" for settling their purchase. Despite all the hoopla, the initial development effort failed, and a dozen years later, Capitol Heights was still an unfulfilled dream.

Despite its short-term failure, the Capitol Heights situation did not appreciably affect growth elsewhere. In June 1911 the Adcock Realty Company laid out Normal Heights Addition. Situated immediately to the east of the State Normal School between East Main Street and the Frankfort & Cincinnati Railroad, the subdivision catered to college personnel and other middle class blacks. This was hardly the case, however, with Bellview Addition. Located astride Myrtle Avenue on the south side of East Main, about three-quarters of a mile east of Normal Heights, Bellview was platted in 1916 by Charles and Myrtle Bell. Laid out on a tract which the Bells had purchased two years earlier from W. A. Glanton, the subdivision's deed restrictions included racially restrictive covenants which prohibited the sale of lots to any person of African ancestry. Such measures, regularly employed by developers to maintain racially homogeneous neighborhoods, remained in force until 1948, when the United States Supreme Court outlawed their enforcement by the courts.

Franklin County's stagnant population growth no doubt impeded realization of the Commercial Club's dream that the community would accomplish major economic strides. Problems such as the capital removal issue, World War I, and prohibition affected the economy as well as the population. However, where the 1880s and 1890s experienced a major boom and bust cycle, the economic picture for the years between 1900 and 1920 is much more ambiguous. Generally speaking, these decades appear to have been a time of stabilization and consolidation, characterized by the elimination of marginal enterprises, a reallocation of resources to more profitable outlets, and, in some areas, a degree of expansion. However, this quest for stability was punctuated by occasional crises, and it often encountered contradictory growth trends.

Nowhere was this ambiguity more apparent than in agriculture, which remained the dominant sector of Franklin County's economic base. The number of farms in the county increased from 1,668 in 1900 to 1,880 in 1920. At the same time, however, total farmland declined from 129,042 to 126,667 acres, resulting in a reduction in the average size of local farms from 77.4 to 67.4 acres. On the other hand, the value of all farm property more than trebled, increasing from less than $4.5 million in 1900 to more than $14.6 million twenty years later. Since the 1920 census figures actually record 1919 values, this increase undoubtedly reflects, at least in part, the general inflation of land values that accompanied the expansion of cultivation during World War I.

The most stable element of Franklin County's farm economy was the livestock industry. This was hardly a coincidence. Except for a brief recession before World War I, the early twentieth century was a time of major expansion in Kentucky's livestock market. Annual cattle and calf receipts at Louisville's Bourbon Stock Yards nearly doubled between 1900 and 1919, and Kentucky emerged as one of the country's leading producers of stocker and feeder cattle. It also was during this period that the Commonwealth became the nation's leading producer of spring lambs, as many people in eastern cities considered Kentucky's Bluegrass, milk-fed spring lambs to be a delicacy. The hog market was the only segment of the state's livestock industry to experience a long-term decline.

Franklin County farmers took advantage of strong prices and heavy demand to produce and sell every head they could. This resulted in a remarkable stability in livestock inventories. The number of cattle recorded on local farms slipped from 8,880 in 1900 to 7,558 in 1910, and then rose to 8,282 head in 1920. The stability of the equine herd was even more notable, rising from 4,234 horses in 1900 to 4,240 in 1910 before declining to 3,913 head a decade later. At first glance, sheep inventories appear to have been highly unstable, soaring from 8,940 head in 1900 to 15,198 in 1910 and then plummeting to 7,847 in the 1920 count. However, both the 1900 and 1920 figures exclude spring lambs. When 6,977 of those wooly delicacies are deleted from the 1910 figure, it drops to 8,221 head, which is entirely consistent with counts for 1900 and 1920. Only the swine inventories, which dipped from 9,128 head in 1900 to 8,982 in 1910 and then dropped to 7,847 animals in 1920, experienced a steady decline during the first two decades of the century. However, this pattern is consistent with the Commonwealth as a whole, as the center of American hog production moved steadily westward during the early part of the century.

The story was much different in crop farming, where production of many commodities fluctuated wildly over the two decades. This was particularly the case with corn production, which soared from 378,540 bushels in 1900 to 512,012 a decade later. But in August 1917 the federal government imposed wartime prohibition to stop the diversion of corn and other grains from food preparation to liquor production. Franklin County's distilleries and breweries shut down the following month. The war barely had ended when passage of the Eighteenth Amendment and the institution of national prohibition in 1919 kept them closed for nearly fourteen years. Since the distilleries purchased a major portion of the local corn crop, the impact of prohibition was instantaneous. By 1920 local corn production had plunged to less than 308,000 bushels.

Although dramatic in scale, these fluctuations in corn production were

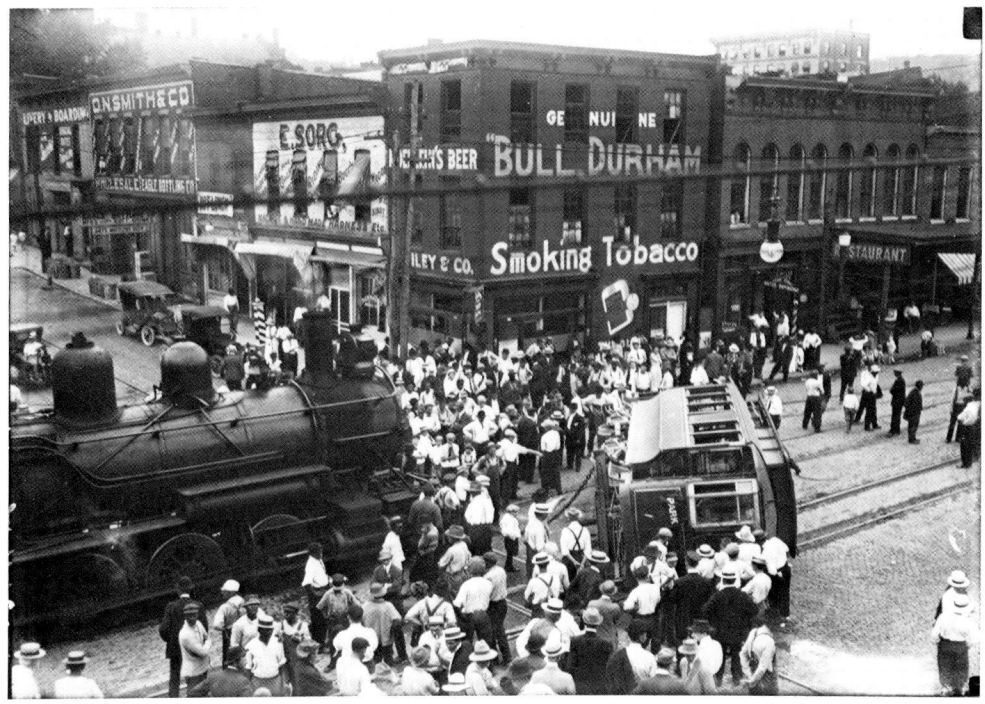

Kentucky Traction & Terminal street car accident showing the southwest corner of Broadway and Ann Street. The railroad engine is chained to the streetcar in an attempt to upright it.

hardly unique. Production of oats dropped from 38,950 bushels in 1900 to 21,985 bushels a decade later and then rose to 30,984 bushels in 1920. Perhaps mirroring the brief recovery in corn, the wheat harvest plummeted from 131,420 bushels in 1900 to 31,346 bushels in 1910 before recovering mildly to 69,786 bushels in 1920. Starting from an already tiny base, rye production slipped from 5,640 bushels in 1900 to 3,598 bushels in 1910 and then jumped to 5,672 bushels ten years later. The only cereal grain to show a steady, long-term increase was barley. From a mere 280 bushels at the beginning of the century, production rose to 4,115 bushels in 1910 and reached 9,858 bushels the following decade.

Production of other crops fluctuated just as much as cereal grains. The Irish potato harvest for 1900 was 13,537 bushels. It rose to 46,746 in 1910 and then plunged to 8,602 bushels a decade later. The apple crop remained stable during the first decade of the century, rising only slightly from 35,069 bushels in 1900 to 35,692 bushels in 1910. However, the bottom fell out of the county's entire orchard crop industry the following decade, and the 1920 apple harvest was only 4,257 bushels. Sorghum production, having peaked in 1880, remained at a modest level, increasing from 1,356 gallons in 1900 to 4,238 gallons in 1910 and then dropping back to 1,329 gallons in 1920. The period also witnessed the death knell of the Franklin County hemp market as production dropped from 105,280 pounds in 1900 to a mere 5,000 pounds ten years later. Production of the once mighty cash crop was so minuscule in 1920 that the federal census did not even record it.

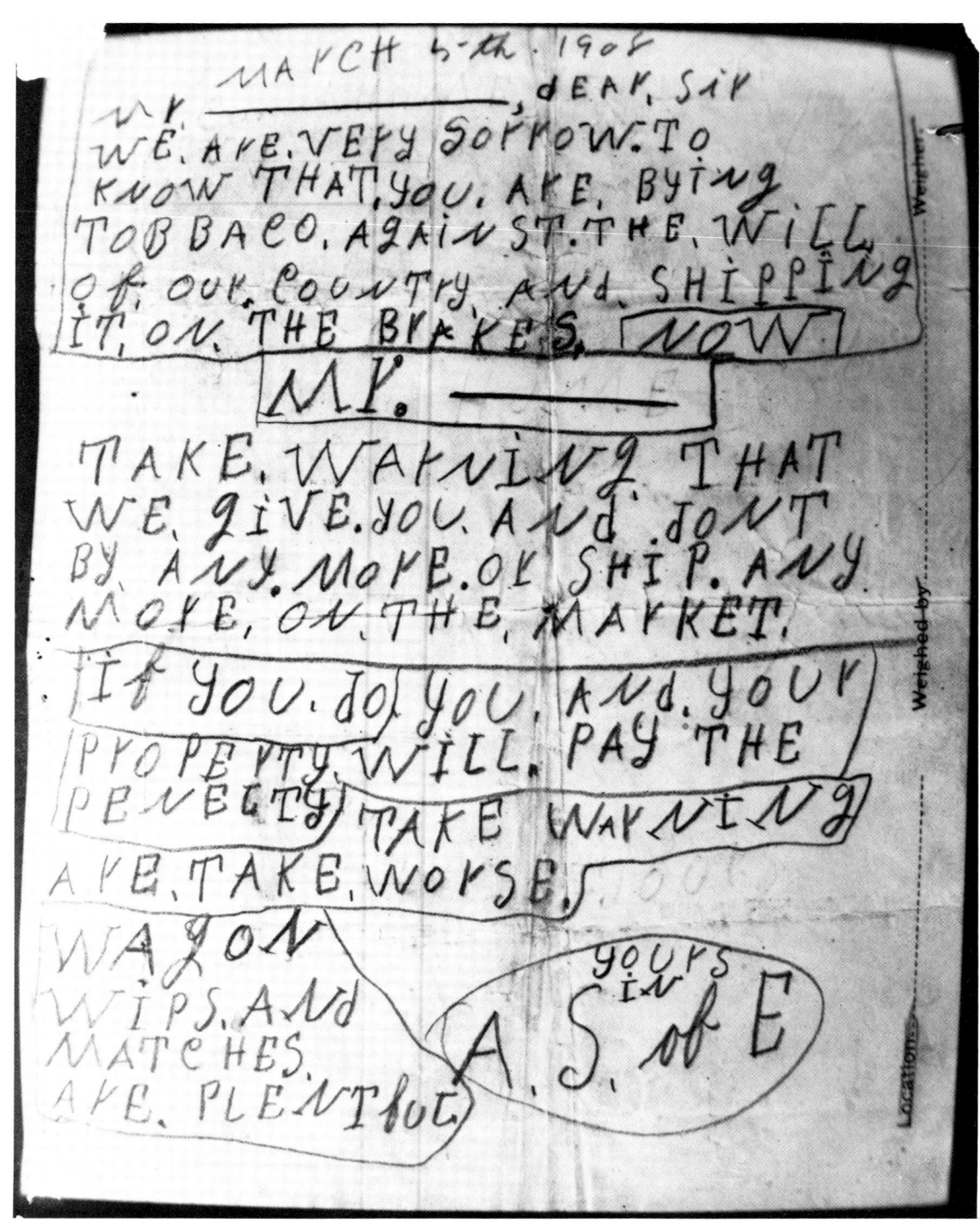

Night Rider letter, written to Edward Hume on March 5th, 1908. This letter was used as evidence in a court case.

So widespread were these production fluctuations that only two crops demonstrated steady, long-term growth. Reflecting perhaps the growing importance of the livestock industry, production of hay and related forage crops increased from 4,091 tons in 1900 to 8,681 tons in 1910 and to 9,599 tons in 1920. Equally dramatic was the growth of the tobacco harvest, which grew from about 2.75 million pounds in 1900 to nearly 4.25 million pounds in 1910 and passed the 5 million pound mark in 1920.

Despite often sharp fluctuations in production, crop values increased substantially. Specific data for 1900 are not available. However, the figures for 1910 and 1920 show that crop income, buoyed by strong prices, increased dramatically. The market value of all crops increased from $1.1 million to more than $2.5 million. Cereal grains followed the pattern, growing from $362,562 to $752,500. The value of hay and forage rose nearly fivefold, from $94,988 to $462,436, while the figures for vegetables grew from $116,271 to $124,679. The only area to suffer a reversal was fruits and nuts, which dropped from $41,069 to $20,445. With some exceptions, these figures suggest that Franklin County farmers were doing a reasonably effective job of adjusting their production to meet the demands of the marketplace.

In the case of tobacco, however, the rising income and production figures stemmed largely from a radical and sometimes violent restructuring of the marketplace itself. As the twentieth century began, the American industry was locked in the grip of James B. Duke's American Tobacco Company. With control of approximately 90 percent of the nation's growing cigarette production, along with substantial majorities of its cigar, snuff, pipe, and chewing tobacco sales, Duke's monopoly had managed by 1904 to depress leaf prices to a rock bottom level. No longer able to endure the monopoly's repressive strategy, tobacco farmers began to fight back, often violently.

Within the Commonwealth the struggle against the trust began in the "Black Patch" region of western Kentucky. Under the leadership of figures like Dr. David A. Amoss and Felix Grundy Ewing, angry farmers organized their own marketing association and attempted to withhold tobacco from the market until they could obtain a reasonable price. Independent farmers who tried to sell directly to the trust often faced intimidation by hooded "night riders," who burned houses and barns, destroyed tobacco beds, and flogged and murdered recalcitrants who defied the association. By 1908 the Black Patch War had become a full-scale guerrilla action, climaxed by major raids against trust warehouses and factories in Princeton, Russellville, and Hopkinsville.

While most of the violence occurred in the Black Patch, the white burley farmers of northern and central Kentucky also were victims of the trust. By 1907 they began to take action, forming the Burley Tobacco Society. Within a short time it had enrolled some 35,000 members. At a mass meeting at Shelbyville in the fall of 1907 the organization announced its intention to "cut out" the 1908 crop. During the months that followed, night riding burley farmers burned and dynamited trust facilities throughout the Bluegrass. Losses amounted to one million pounds of tobacco and an additional $500,000 in damages to the trust's factories and warehouses. In Franklin County, night riders allegedly killed N. B. Hazelett, a farmer who lived near the Shelby County line. The defendants in the case never came to trial.

As the violence spread and local officials proved unwilling or unable to take action against the farmers' flagrant lawlessness, public reaction against the night riders mounted. Governor Augustus Willson, elected in 1907 on a law and order platform, called out the militia after the raids in Hopkinsville and Russellville. Newspaper editors throughout the state, including some in the center of the storm, denounced the violence. And slowly but surely, victims of the violence began to fight back, bringing federal damage suits against those who had intimidated them. About the same time, legal action was initiated against the trust which would eliminate the cause of the violence. In May 1911 the United States Supreme Court upheld the 1908 decision of a federal appeals court in New York that the American Tobacco Company violated the Sherman Antitrust Act of 1890. The Supreme Court's action forced the breakup of the monopoly and restored competition to the tobacco market.

The economic impact of the Black Patch War and the Supreme Court decision was quickly apparent in Franklin County. The resumption of competition resulted in higher prices and improved income to the farmer. From a monopoly-era low of 1 to 3 cents a pound in 1904, burley prices rose to 9 to 12 cents in 1911. Eight years later burley fetched the magnificent price of 34 cents a pound. Higher prices and rising demand also meant increased volume for local warehouses. In 1909 the T. C. Geary Company sold about 2 million pounds of leaf. The following year the Farmers' Tobacco Warehouse Company built a large warehouse on Second Street, and the two firms sold about 8.5 million pounds. The market dipped in 1911, but in 1912 the Burley Tobacco Company built a new warehouse on Holmes Street; and estimates were that its business, combined with that of the Geary and Farmers' Tobacco warehouses, amounted to more than 10 million pounds. During this period most of the world's major tobacco companies stationed representatives in Frankfort, and cigarettes and other tobacco products containing Franklin County burley were shipped to nearly every section of the United States.

The early twentieth century also was a period of expansion and consolidation for Franklin County's commercial sector. By 1908, with the destructive effects of the Depression of 1893 now a fading memory, the city of Frankfort alone boasted more than 160 retail businesses. With fifty-seven grocery stores and meat markets scattered across the city, few residents had to walk more than a few blocks to purchase their daily necessities. Residents and travelers seeking to quench a powerful thirst could select from among twenty-six saloons, while those who wished to dine out had nine restaurants from which to choose.

Farmer's Tobacco Warehouse, Second Street.

John Mucci's Restaurant, interior in 1914.

The bustling central business district offered an increasingly wide array of goods and services. The discriminating shopper could purchase furs at C. Kagin and Bro. on St. Clair at the bridge, fine men's furnishings at John H. Cassell's store on Main Street, furniture from R. Rogers & Sons on St. Clair, and diamonds from M. A. Selbert's jewelry store, also on St. Clair. For those who desired to compare prices, downtown Frankfort provided nine clothing and shoe shops, six bakeries and confectioneries, seven drug stores, nine dry goods and notions businesses, and three hardware stores.

The central business district also attracted a growing number of professional and business service enterprises. By 1908 the city boasted forty-one practicing attorneys, twenty-six physicians and surgeons, four dentists, fourteen insurance agencies, and six real estate firms. Nearly all had offices downtown. The proliferation of such services created a growing demand for office space. Many were located in the recently completed McClure Building, Frankfort's first skyscraper, located at the northwest corner of St. Clair and Main streets. Built by the McClure Realty Company, the seven-story, steel frame structure exhibited a simple Chicago-style form with an Italianate bracketed cornice. The ground floor was occupied by R. K. McClure & Sons Dry Goods. In 1912 McClure Realty Company sold the building to the newly organized United American Insurance Company, which renamed it the United American Building. As one of the city's most prestigious addresses, the United American Building housed the offices of the Taylor Distilleries, the Frankfort Women's Club, and numerous prominent physicians, dentists, and lawyers, as well as the insurance company.

The McClure Building, northwest corner of Main and St. Clair Streets.

Western Union Telegraph Company. Staff and couriers are shown posing outside their office at the Capital Hotel.

The Capital Hotel. Interior of lobby in 1912.

The Capital Hotel after the fire.

New Capital Hotel. Now home of the State National Bank.

Another popular business address was the Capital Hotel. In addition to providing temporary quarters for visitors, the hotel served as offices for three insurance companies, a half-dozen physicians, and the Western Union Telegraph Company. These tenants were forced to find new quarters after a fire gutted the massive old hostelry on the afternoon of April 5, 1917. The blaze began in the basement, and soon flames and smoke enveloped the entire structure. Because the legislature was meeting in special session, nearly every room was occupied. A West Virginia newspaperman died from suffocation, while Lieutenant Governor James O. Black, his wife, and their daughter barely escaped. Property damage was estimated at $100,000.

During the immediate aftermath of the fire, nearly everyone who was able pitched in to assist the visitors whose accommodations and personal baggage had been destroyed. Governor and Mrs. Augustus O. Stanley opened the Executive Mansion to refugees, and numerous boarding houses, businesses, and other organizations provided temporary shelter to the city's homeless visitors. But such makeshift quarters were insufficient for the long run. Unfortunately, it proved much more difficult to replace the Capital Hotel than it had to construct it the first time. The problem was one of raising private construction capital to finance the replacement of a structure which originally had been built with public money but which was now under private ownership. While political and civic officials pondered ways to raise the money, complaints by newspapers and the general public over Frankfort's inability to house visitors on business in the capital increased steadily.

In September 1919, nearly thirty months after the fire, newspapers announced the incorporation of the New Capital Hotel Company and revealed its plans to erect a modern, four-story, $350,000 structure on the site of the old hotel. Among the major investors in the enterprise were the Weitzel family, the old hotel's owners, who agreed to purchase a majority of the new company's common stock and to operate the rebuilt hotel. Unfortunately, the remaining stock failed to sell, and nearly two years later the Capital Hotel remained a burned out shell. Such dilatory movement prompted one local resident to complain, "We boast of the glory and the chivalry, the hospitality and the generosity of our fair State and yet we must blush with shame when the hotel facilities of our capital city are referred to." This situation was a "source of humiliation to every Kentuckian," he added, "especially when visitors from Maine to California come to our capital and find this condition." The humiliation would continue until 1923 when the new Capital Hotel finally opened its doors.

Expansion and consolidation were particularly notable in the banking industry. In May 1905 the Capital Trust Company, with capital stock of $75,000, began operations at temporary headquarters in the Hume Building. A short time later, the bank moved into new offices at the southeast corner of Main and St. Clair. The officers were T. L. Edelen, president; William H. Posey, vice president and general manager; J. M. Craig, secretary-treasurer; and Susan J. McHenry, assistant secretary-treasurer. In addition to Edelen and Posey, the directors included such influential figures as manufacturer Charles E. Hoge, former Governor J. C. W. Beckham, attorney Frank Chinn, merchant Henry Ringold, manufacturing executive H. H. Roberts, insurance executive George L. Payne, and merchant William G. Simpson.

Joining the competition in the spring of 1909 was the Peoples State Bank. Organized with a capital stock of $50,000, the bank opened for business at 208 West Main Street. Three years later it moved into the McClure Building. Elected president of the new bank was O. H. Skiles. Serving as vice president and cashier respectively were G. F. Speer and J. M. Halmhuber. All three were directors, along with R. A. Frazier, W. V. Crossfield, Hyel Davies, and J. P. Hulette.

With the formation of Peoples State, the capital now had six banks. But this situation did not last very long. In September 1914 Farmers Bank and Deposit Bank consolidated under the name of Farmers Deposit Bank of Frankfort. The merged institution had a capital stock of $175,000 and a cash surplus of $35,000, making it for a time the city's largest bank. Elected president was John C. Noel, grandson of the venerable Baptist preacher and educator Silas M. Noel. The younger Noel had served since 1900 as president of Farmers Bank of Frankfort. Assuming the position of first vice president was J. Buford Hendrick, former president of Deposit Bank. A. W. Macklin was elected second vice president, while John A. Brislan became cashier. Elected to the honorary position of cashier emeritus was A. W. Overton, whose service at Farmers Bank stretched back more than thirty years. Ironically, when Brislan died before Overton, the latter reassumed his old post, which he held until his death in 1920. His successor was W. P. (Pat) Sullivan, who later served thirteen years as president of the bank.

Important though it was, most of Frankfort's commercial development

John C. Noel

Mary Hume Shaw, the only woman to serve as Franklin County Judge Executive. Miss Shaw was appointed by Judge Boone Hamilton to serve during his absence from the state.

during the early twentieth century represented the expansion of existing lines of business. There was, however, one major new area of commercial expansion. Its stimulus was the advent of the automobile. Howell Scott is said to have purchased the city's first auto in 1901. Dr. W. E. Baxter bought one some time later, and a local newspaper reported in 1909 that Dr. H. S. Keller had acquired a Reo Runabout in Louisville and that the vehicle "came through this morning in three hours and fifteen minutes." Based upon a road distance of about sixty miles between Louisville and Frankfort, this would amount to a speed of between eighteen and nineteen miles per hour. A few years later, Governor James B. McCreary, who served between 1911 and 1915, was traveling the state in a handsome new touring car.

In economic terms, the appearance of the automobile resulted in the establishment of new businesses to sell and service these strange vehicles. As late as 1908 only one business listed in the city directory was identified with the automobile. By 1917 the situation had changed considerably. The Frankfort Buick Company, organized the previous year, and the Frankfort Motor Car Company were selling cars. The latter firm, located at 109-111 West Main and headed by L. B. Goodman, sold Ford cars and trucks. Once on the streets, these primitive machines had a voracious appetite for repairs, fuel, tires, and parts. Among the garages and other businesses that sprang up to service the automobile were Service Motor Company, at 315-317 West Second Street; O'Dell and Clark's garage, at 206 West Second; J. E. Manford's auto supplies, at 127 West Main; M. M. Allan Motors Company, 106 West Main; Central

LOUISVILLE AND NASHVILLE RAILWAY DEPOT ON BROADWAY

Garage, 118 West Broadway; and Nicol Garage, 320-322 Ann Street. In addition, long established businesses such as the Capital Foundry, Machine and Novelty Company, at 139-143 Holmes Street, and J. R. Sower's Hardware Company, at 217 St. Clair, added auto supplies and services to their other product lines.

While the automobile's presence on local streets grew steadily, more traditional transportation modes remained essential to the movement of goods and people. In touting the community's economic advantages, local promoters stressed the fact that Frankfort was now served by three railroad companies—the Louisville & Nashville, the Chesapeake & Ohio, and the Frankfort & Cincinnati. In 1908 the L & N completed construction of its new depot, a handsome Classical structure located on the south side of Broadway between Ann and High streets. For the large number of citizens who did not yet own any form of personal transportation, the Frankfort & Versailles Traction Company not only provided the local streetcar system but operated an interurban line which ran hourly between Frankfort and Lexington by way of Versailles. And at several points rural Franklin Countians still depended upon ferry boats to get them across the Kentucky River. Nevertheless, the diversification of the transportation network not only bolstered the economy, but it also helped stimulate future expansion of the population.

Frankfort Buick Company, 319 West Second Street.

The tendency toward economic expansion and consolidation was most pronounced in the area of manufacturing. Unfortunately, the precise dimensions of these trends are difficult to measure because of a lack of consistent, comparable data. The census provided statistics for the city of Frankfort alone in 1900 and 1910 and for the county alone in 1920. Nevertheless, certain definite trends are apparent. Despite the formation of several new industrial concerns, which further diversified the county's manufacturing base, the total number of firms dwindled significantly between 1900 and 1920. At the same time, however, the surviving firms experienced substantial growth, both in scale and in value of production.

The magnitude of these trends is immediately apparent for Frankfort during the first decade of the century. In 1900 the city boasted sixty-six individual establishments. A decade later the number had dropped to only thirty-one. During the same period, however, the total capital investment in manufacturing increased from less than $1.6 million to more than $2.4 million, while the value of their production increased from just over $2 million to nearly $3.1 million. In the process, the work force grew from 456 persons to 701, including hourly workers, clerks, and other salaried personnel. A decade later, Franklin County as a whole had only forty-four industrial plants. However, their products were valued at nearly $5.2 million, including more than $2 million in value added by manufacturing. These establishments employed a blue collar work force of 593 employees with an annual payroll of $408,953.

A critical factor of the community's industrial growth during this period was the establishment of several new companies. The Frankfort Modes Glass Works, established about 1907 and located on Owenton Pike in Thorn Hill, specialized in the production of flint and amber bottles. The company grew quickly under the leadership of president George B. Harper and by 1909 was one of Frankfort's largest firms, with 350 employees and a weekly payroll of more than $4,000. No doubt much of the company's production was consumed by local breweries and distilleries, as well as two new soft drink companies—Coleman & McKeever, at 322 St. Clair Street, and the Eagle Bottling Company, at 324 Ann Street. However, the bottle works also had customers in Louisville, Cincinnati, and throughout the South.

O. N. Smith & Co. Building, 324–326 Ann St.

Another firm organized during the first decade of the century was the Frankfort Canning Company, Inc. Situated on the Frankfort & Cincinnati Railroad, this concern provided a significant market for local fruit and vegetable growers, who might realize a profit of $75 to $125 per acre, depending on the crop. One of the company's more noted products was the "Ky. Capital" brand of tomatoes, which, according to a newspaper of the time, "gained a remarkable reputation for high grade goods."

While new plants such as the glass works and the canning factory represented a diversification of the community's manufacturing base, most of Franklin County's industrial expansion resulted from the growth of existing companies or the entry of new competitors into well-established fields of enterprise. Among the city's most rapidly growing concerns was the Hoge-Montgomery Company. Originally organized in 1889 as the Frankfort Shoe Manufacturing Company, the plant was located near the Kentucky Penitentiary and had an initial capacity of about seven hundred pairs of women's and children's shoes daily. In 1905, under the management of Charles E. Hoge, president, and James F. Montgomery, vice president and general manager, the firm was reorganized as the Hoge-Montgomery Company. With the assistance of secretary H. H. Roberts, treasurer S. French Hoge, and sales manager

Charles F. Strassner, the company expanded steadily, turning out some 7,200 pairs daily by 1912.

The Hoge-Montgomery Company operated daily except for Sunday and legal holidays, and it owned the most modern machinery in the industry. But the key to its success was the widespread use of prison labor. Under a contract with the Commonwealth, the company paid the state treasury an annual fee of about $250,000 to employ convicts. A portion of the fee was set aside for the prisoners' families, but the majority of the revenue went into the state's operating budget. The labor force did not consist entirely of prisoners, however. In 1912 the shoe company employed approximately 300 free workers, including a large number of women and girls. L. F. Johnson described their working conditions as "pleasant and light . . . at good wages." Johnson's "good wage" averaged about ten dollars per week. To sell its wares, the firm employed a sales force of thirty-five men, who peddled "Frankfort Shoes" in every state of the Union.

Hoge-Montgomery Company, 600–608 High St. Originally the Frankfort Shoe Manufacturing Company, this building was located at the northwest corner of Mero and High Streets across from the twin castillated towers of the penitentiary.

Franklin County remained one of Kentucky's major lumbering and woodworking centers into the twentieth century. As late as 1908 the capital still boasted six saw and planing mills and numerous related businesses, such as chair and furniture manufacturers and building materials suppliers. The leading newcomer to the industry was the Capital Lumber & Manufacturing Company, located on the Kentucky River at the foot of Capital Avenue. Blessed with some of the industry's most advanced sawing and planing equipment, the company produced tens of thousands of board feet of building lumber along with a variety of finished goods, such as boxes, roofing material, window sashes and blinds, door frames, and tobacco hogsheads.

A closely related concern was Ford & Johnson, Inc. Owners of a saw mill located at Fourth and Fowler streets in South Frankfort, the firm also operated a varnish manufacturing plant at 535 Ann Street and a chair factory at Broadway and High Streets. With such breadth of resources and experience in the industry already in place, a Louisville newspaper's remark that "a furniture manufacturing company would find no place of better location for business" is hardly surprising.

The lumber industry remained an important constituent of Franklin County's industrial base through World War I. Indeed, war orders placed an additional demand on Frankfort's saw mills. It was a totally different story, however, for the county's distilleries. As the century began distilling was still the county's leading industry, and it remained so until the war. In 1908 no fewer than four distilling firms—W. A. Gaines and Company, Labrot & Graham, Geo. T. Stagg Company, and E. H. Taylor, Jr. & Sons—had offices in the city. Outside the capital, on the Kentucky River bank opposite W. A. Gaines's Hermitage Distillery, the Kentucky Distillers & Warehouse Company operated the Spring Hill Distillery, formerly the property of John Cochran. About three and one-half miles to the east, near the Frankfort & Cincinnati Railroad's Elkhorn Station, the Frankfort Distillery, owned by Baker Bros., pro-

FRANKFORT DISTILLERIES

E. H. Taylor, Jr. Company and George T. Stagg Company Building.

The Baker Brothers Distillery.

George T. Stagg in his office about 1913.

The Hermitage Distillery, 1911. Note the absence of the Executive Mansion.

duced its famed Swastika whiskey. Located about a mile west of the capital was the Old Judge Distillery, operated by the S. C. Herbst Importing Company.

Regardless of the grade, all Franklin County whiskies were produced according to the specifications of the federal Pure Food and Drug Act and bottled-in-bond under the supervision of the United States Treasury Department. Altogether, the county's liquor warehouses had an estimated capacity in 1912 of nearly 600,000 barrels. Some individual warehouses held from 10,000 to 40,000 barrels. Daily capacity during the bottling season was about 36,000 bottles or about 3,000 cases. After taking into account in the wages of the industry's large labor force and the price of grain purchases from local farmers, one knowledgeable observer figured that distilling accounted for approximately 85 percent of all municipal, county, and state taxes paid by Franklin Countians.

But cognizant businessman and politicians recognized that the future of Franklin County's basic industry was precarious. In Kentucky, as in the rest of the nation, prohibition forces were gaining strength rapidly. In 1874 the General Assembly had passed a local option law which allowed citizens to petition for a referendum on the prohibition of the sale of liquor in any district of the county. By 1915, under the leadership of the Women's Christian Temperance Union, a total of 106 counties had voted themselves dry, and Frankfort was one of only twenty-three towns in the Commonwealth which still granted saloon licenses. But the WCTU and its allies were not satisfied. They wanted complete, statewide prohibition.

The wets temporarily stalled the prohibitionists' momentum when Augustus O. Stanley defeated the dry candidate, former Secretary of State Henry V. McChesney, in the 1915 Democratic gubernatorial primary. Prohibition had little impact in either the Republican primary or the general election, as Democrats closed ranks behind Stanley and overwhelmed his close personal friend and Republican opponent, Edwin P. Morrow. On the strength of Stanley's victory, the wets defeated early prohibitionist efforts to push a statewide prohibition amendment to the state constitution through the state senate. But the drys refused to quit. As their persistent efforts continued to divert public attention from more critical issues, many legislators began to support prohibition in order to remove it from the arena of debate. Adding to the drys' momentum was the institution of wartime prohibition in 1917, which shut down all of the state's distilleries, except for a couple licensed for medicinal production.

The triumph of prohibitionism acquired an aura of inevitability in December 1917, when the United States Congress passed the Eighteenth Amendment. In the wake of Congressional action, the wet legislators gave up their efforts to block a similar state constitutional amendment. The death knell for Kentucky's distilleries and breweries came in 1920 when the voters approved both state and national prohibition.[46] John Barleycorn's long struggle to blunt the forces of temperance had come to an end, or so it seemed.

The closing of the distilleries and the accompanying loss of income and jobs placed major new burdens upon a corps of business and civic leaders who had been working with increasing effectiveness to promote the county's economic growth. The Commercial Club, which remained active until at least 1912, continued to spearhead development during the early years of the century. By 1908, however, it had been eclipsed by the Frankfort Business Men's Club. Headed by George B. Harper, president of the Frankfort Modes Glass Company, the club included some of the city's most influential commercial, industrial, and professional leaders. Alonzo B. Hammond, a local lumberman, served as vice president. Merchant John H. Cassell and insurance executive George L. Payne held the positions of secretary and treasurer respectively. Among the directors were hardware merchant John R. Sower, dry goods merchants James Heeney and R. K. McClure, shoe manufacturer Charles E. Hoge, banker W. H. Posey, and General Daniel W. Lindsey, the aging but venerated attorney.

The Business Men's Club coordinated the city's economic growth campaign until 1915. Focusing particularly upon industrial development, the club endorsed the city council's tax abatement program, which promised a five-year tax exemption to all new factories or industries established in the city. In addition, the club itself pledged to make a "liberal contribution" towards the purchase of any new factory site in the Frankfort area and to purchase a large block of stock in any "substantial enterprise" locating in the city. Observing that "this spirit pervades the entire business community," the editors of Frankfort's 1912 city directory predicted that "with the energy and sound business principles employed, many manufacturing plants should be added to those already here."

In 1915 the Business Men's Club gave way to the Frankfort Chamber of Commerce. The chamber moved vigorously during its first five years to improve the community's commercial and industrial climate. One of its highest priorities was better transportation. Recognizing the long-term potential of the automobile, the chamber lobbied successfully to have three major interstate highways—the National Midland Trail, from Washington, D.C. to San Francisco; the Jackson Highway, between New Orleans and Niagara Falls; and the Boone Way, which crossed five states—routed through the capital. Within the state the chamber cooperated with similar groups in other cities and towns in efforts to develop a network of good roads throughout the Commonwealth. In cooperation with city officials, the chamber helped to develop local traffic regulations and to create parking space. The organization also was instrumental in the establishment of twice-daily, round-trip bus service between Frankfort and Lawrenceburg. Finally, it promoted plans to improve commercial navigation on the Kentucky River.

Capitalizing on the city's scenic beauty and historic buildings, the chamber aggressively promoted Frankfort as a tourist mecca and convention center. Sensitive to the importance of agriculture to the city's economic health, the chamber worked closely with the county agent to form the Franklin County Development League. Composed of 500 farmers, this organization set out systematically to improve the future of agriculture in the county.

All of these efforts supported the chamber's ultimate objective, which was to improve the environment for enterprise in Franklin County. In 1917, using the slogan "A Good Location For Any Vocation," the chamber launched an aggressive industrial development campaign, which exploited virtually every resource and advantage at the community's disposal. The economic growth recorded between 1910 and 1920 is at least partial testimony to these efforts, but the onset of prohibition and the closing of the distilleries presented a challenge of a far greater magnitude than any other which the community had faced during the first two decades of the century.

One of Frankfort's most significant advantages, the chamber believed, was its position as the state capital. For an enterprise which desired a location near the seat of power, Frankfort was the ideal location. For most people, however, such physical attractions as the old capitol, the new capitol, the Frankfort Cemetery, and a rich mixture of historic sites and scenic views made the city even more inviting. But Frankfort had to struggle once again to preserve its coveted status. This time, however, the city at the bend of the Kentucky River came out of the fight even more secure than before.

The final round of debate over the "Capital Question" began in 1890 on the eve of the Constitutional Convention of 1890. As in the past, the major protagonists in the debate were proponents of Louisville and Lexington, both of which yearned for the prestige and potential economic impact that might result from being the seat of government. Supporters of the Falls City argued that its size and commercial prominence justified its selection as capital. In like manner, Lexingtonians claimed that their city's larger size and better position as a railroad center made it superior to Frankfort as Kentucky's capital of the future.

But Frankfort partisans refused to hear such malarky. In September 1890 Judges William H. Sneed and William Lindsay laid out the capital city's position in documents addressed directly to the constitutional convention delegates, who were now in session in Frankfort. The following year they joined a group of prominent Frankfort citizens in laying out their positions to the public at large. Sneed and Lindsay made several pointed arguments. First, they asserted, the proponents of removal had shown no evidence that the citizens of Kentucky wanted to change the seat of government. Neither had they demonstrated that the city was unhealthy nor that it lacked the hotel accommodations and other public facilities necessary to support the work of government. In addition, the judges raised a serious legal issue, suggesting that removing the capital would constitute a breach of faith between the Commonwealth and those early citizens, such as Andrew Holmes, who had committed their personal resources to the establishment of the capital in Frankfort. Since those resources could not be used for any other purpose,

Kentucky State Capitol Building. The original elevation submitted by architect Frank M. Andrews of Dayton, Ohio. Inscribed "Broadway Elevation," it was originally intended to replace the old Capitol.

removal might cause all donated properties as well as the buildings on them to revert to the heirs of the contributors. This could result in expensive litigation.

As a practical matter, Sneed and Lindsay noted that continual agitation on the question, or even its submission to popular vote, was a waste of time. On the issue of capital removal, current law required an affirmative two-third's vote by both houses of the legislature. Given prevailing urban and regional rivalries, obtaining such majorities would be highly improbable, if not impossible. Another major drawback of removal was economic. Regardless of the donations that might be received from a new host city, the establishment of a new political seat would be terribly expensive. Initial land purchase and construction costs alone were estimated at from $3 million to $4 million. At Frankfort, much of the physical structure needed for the capital was already in place and had been built at a much lower cost.

Aside from the general disadvantages of removing the capital to any new city, the jurists argued that Frankfort possessed certain inherent advantages which more than justified its continued role as the capital. Frankfort already possessed many "public buildings commensurate with the wealth, dignity and grandeur of the Commonwealth." When it came to future buildings, such as a new capitol, the city was blessed with beautiful sites "that none of her ambitious rivals can equal." Moreover, Frankfort's costs of living and administering government were reasonable, and local society was "as intelligent, refined and hospitable as any to be found within the . . . state." The city's location on two major rail trunk lines, the L & N and the C & O, made it accessible to all parts of the state. The general health of the community was excellent, and its modest population, as opposed to that of Louisville and Lexington, prevented the host city from governing the state—although precisely that charge had been leveled against Frankfort before the Civil War. Finally, the fact that Frankfort Cemetery held the remains of Kentucky's great political and military heroes was of considerable symbolic importance.

Sneed and Lindsay's arguments carried the day, and the constitutional convention refused to tamper with the location of the capital. But the city's leadership remembered the jurists' exposition. In 1904, when the issue of building a new capitol surfaced, they polished off the judges' major points and published them in a booklet which outlined the history of the "Capitol Question." Every member of the General Assembly received a copy, as did many newspapers and prominent citizens across the state. Again, Frankfort triumphed. In January 1904, when a Franklin County legislator introduced a measure to appropriate $1 million for the erection of a new statehouse in Frankfort, the bill passed almost unanimously in both houses. The only problem was an amendment which required that the new structure be erected on the site of the old capitol. Despite this hitch, the issue of capital removal finally was settled.

In the wake of the 1904 act, the legislature constituted the state's Sinking Fund Commissioners as a State Capitol Building Commission and authorized it to proceed with plans for a new capitol. In April the commissioners selected C. M. Fleenor of Bowling Green to supervise construction. Two months later they commissioned Frank Mills Andrews to design the new statehouse. As specified by the legislature, the structure was to sit on the old capitol grounds. But when Andrews' design came in, it was clear that the old site was too small to accommodate the structure as he had conceived it. In 1905 Governor J. C. W. Beckham called a special session of the legislature, which repealed the restrictive clause and appropriated an additional $40,000 to acquire a new site. A short time later the commissioners purchased a large tract in South Frankfort about six blocks south of the Kentucky River. The site consisted primarily of the old "Hunt Place," several vacant lots and residences purchased from attorneys Frank Chinn and John W. Rodman, banker John C. Noel, and Mrs. Mary L. Johnson, Mrs. Jane Buttimer, and Sally Handy.

Hunt House. Formerly located on the site of the new Capitol, it was demolished to make way for the new structure.

Site clearance began in May 1905, and construction started three months later. Governor Beckham laid the cornerstone during ceremonies on June 16, 1906, before an estimated crowd of more than 20,000. Because of construction delays, the new capitol was not completed as planned in 1907. A change of administration in January 1908 resulted in the complete replacement of the Capitol Building Commission, which in turn threatened to cause additional delays. But the new commission retained Fleenor and Andrews, and construction progressed without further interruption. By December 1909 all appropriate departments of state government had moved into their new offices. The General Assembly convened in the new edifice for the first time in January 1910. The capitol was dedicated on June 2, 1910. The main speaker was United

KENTUCKY STATE CAPITOL SHOWING VARIOUS PHASES OF CONSTRUCTION.

States Senator and former Governor William O. Bradley. Visiting dignitaries included the governors of twenty-two other states.

The structure was built primarily of Vermont granite and Bedford limestone, at a cost of $1.8 million. The chief supplier of materials was the J. B. Blanton Company, headed by J. Bacon Blanton, whose grandfather, Harrison Blanton, had furnished materials for the old capitol in 1827. Closely resembling the United States Capitol at Washington, the new edifice measures two inches short of 403 feet in length, from east to west, and 180 feet through the central pavilion from north to south. The first floor of the imposing French Renaissance structure is composed of huge, rusticated blocks of granite. The second and third floors are supported by seventy monolithic Ionic columns, while the dome rests on twelve pairs of Ionic columns. The magnificent front pediment was conceived and executed by sculptor Charles H. Niehaus of New York City, with the assistance of Austrian sculptor Peter Rossak. The pediment was financed through a supplementary appropriation from the legislature in 1906. The appropriation also included funds to finish the corridors, nave, and other interior spaces in Georgia marble and Vermont granite instead of Bedford limestone, as originally planned.

Ground-breaking ceremony for the new Capitol, May 30, 1905. Governor J. C. W. Beckham is holding the shovel in the center. To his immediate right are C. M. Fleenor (rear), H. V. McChesney, and to the left, S. W. Hager.

The cornice line of the great marble nave rests on thirty-six monolithic columns, thus providing light and ventilation for the second and third floors. The two lunettes in the nave, executed by Gilbert White, cost the state an additional $7,000. Each lunette depicts events associated with Kentucky's early history. The one in the east wing shows Daniel Boone and his companions as they first cast their eyes on "the beautiful level of Kentucky" in 1769. The lunette in the west wing is White's conception of the Treaty of Watuga in 1775, in which Colonel Richard Henderson's Transylvania Company purchased Kentucky from the Indians.

In addition to vastly increasing the space available for conducting state government, the grand new capitol provided another tourist attraction for the city. However, it also left the governor relatively isolated from the capitol, in the aging mansion at the southwest corner of High and Clinton streets. Compounding his isolation was the fact that the recent southward movement of the population had left the state penitentiary, located diagonally across the intersection, as his most conspicuous, if less than inviting, neighbor. Also, a fire in February 1899 had destroyed the roof and caused other structural damages to the mansion, raising some concern over its long-term usefulness. Given the governor's distance from the new capitol and the somewhat precarious condition of his residence, a movement to build a new governor's mansion was all but inevitable.

The first step came in 1912, during the administration of Governor James B. McCreary, when the General Assembly appropriated $75,000 to build a new house for the chief executive. A short time later the Capitol Building Commission purchased the property of attorney L. F. Johnson which adjoined the eastern border of the capitol grounds, overlooking the Kentucky River. The

Kentucky State Capitol, the East Wing under construction (left) and finished (right), showing Daniel Boone lunetta in distance.

price was $9,500. Commissioned to design the new mansion were architects C. C. and E. A. Weber of Fort Thomas, Kentucky. Their original plans included all of the necessary office and residential space for an executive mansion. But when the commission submitted the drawings to Governor McCreary, he noted the absence of a ballroom. Insisting that a ballroom would be necessary for official entertainment, he demanded that one be added.

Ground was broken in late July 1912. The mansion was erected on a foundation of brick, stone, and concrete. Its walls are of brick, covered with Bowling Green limestone. The main entrance of the Beaux Arts structure is protected by a handsome portico, which is supported by four pairs of Ionic columns. The contractor was the Capital Lumber & Manufacturing Company, which completed the project at a cost of approximately $62,000. Governor McCreary occupied the executive mansion shortly before the end of his term. Before leaving office he held many elegant parties, several of which were open to the public.

The new capitol and executive mansion were major additions to Frankfort's landscape. But for most Franklin Countians the politics which most affected their lives were played out in the courthouse and city hall. One of the more distressing events of the period was an investigation of county finances in 1909. For a considerable period, rumors had been circulating about graft in county government. When they failed to subside, an official inquiry by a panel of citizens was ordered. Chairing the committee was General Daniel W. Lindsey, the distinguished attorney. Other members included County Judge R. C. Hieatt, businessman George B. Harper, Sidney Bedford, and the Rev. C. R. Hudson, pastor of First Christian Church. The committee engaged an expert accountant to examine the county's books. On September 29, 1909, the investigator submitted his report. It showed that over $7,500 had been paid into the county treasury because of the investigation, but that an additional sum of more than $4,275 was still due from county officials who had withheld

General Daniel W. Lindsey

Some of the workmen who built the mansion.

The Executive Mansion in its original context. Note the tobacco field behind the garage.

funds. On a more positive note, the Franklin County Fiscal Court expended $46,000 to remodel, enlarge, and beautify the courthouse in 1910.

Within the city the emphasis was on expanding services and refining operations of a governmental structure which had been radically altered during the last decade of the previous century. In the area of public health, the city council passed an ordinance in 1901 which regulated the dispensation of narcotics and other dangerous drugs by pharmacists. In 1909 the city spent more than $12,500 on street and sidewalk improvements and street cleaning. Two years later the figure exceeded $13,700. In addition, the city spent $3,070 to improve the sewers in 1911. The following year, under the authority of its franchise with the city, the Frankfort Water Company initiated construction of its $75,000 water filtration plant, located atop Louisville Hill, a short distance to the west of the new capitol. Completed in 1914, the new plant had a daily capacity of six million gallons.

Also in 1912 the city council passed an ordinance setting forth purchasing regulations for the city. A year later, picking up the reform spirit which pervaded many other American cities, the body enacted a comprehensive set of building and housing regulations. The measures required building permits for the construction, alteration, repair, or enlargement of any building which cost in excess of $1,000. The ordinance also established sanitary regulations for dwellings and provided for a structure of fines in cases where offending conditions were not promptly abated. Finally, under the leadership of Chief George Conway, who served from 1906 to 1942, the Frankfort Fire Department became a more disciplined, uniformed, and mechanized body. As early as 1914 the department owned a combination chemical and hose motor car. But most of its apparatus was still horse-drawn. That changed three years later, however, when the department discontinued the use of horses and purchased a gasoline-driven hose wagon and chemical truck built by the American LaFrance Engine Company.

As it had for more than a century, local political leadership remained primarily in the hands of the business and professional class. There were some exceptions to this rule, however. John H. Triplett, a bartender, represented the third ward on the city council during 1908-1909. Blacksmith Lee Shelton represented the first ward on the council during 1910-1911, while another blacksmith, Isaac (Ike) O'Dell served from the same ward in 1916-1917. Serving with O'Dell was Curtis Farley, a shipping clerk at Hoge-Montgomery Company.

While the election of such figures suggests the growing political influence of the working class, the fact remains that the council was dominated throughout the early twentieth century by persons such as shoe manufacturer Zach J. Montgomery, lumber dealers Thomas E. Kenney, William Congleton, William S. Rosson, and Edwin E. Elliott, clothier William G. Simpson, druggists W. McKee Hardie and Thomas Averill, merchants Joseph Rupert, John R. Sower, George C. Shaw, and Ferd Jacobs, and automobile dealer Joseph Serverance. Moreover, such persons managed to attain greater longevity on the council. Along with Rosson and Simpson, for example, journalist James L. Newman, Capital Hotel proprietor Edward B. Weitzel, and bookkeeper Egbert Stephens served on the council for a minimum of six years each between 1908 and 1917.

James H. Polsgrove

The city council also was an excellent training ground for the mayor's chair. James S. Darnell, mayor from 1902 to 1905, served on the council during the closing years of the nineteenth century. Between 1914 and 1921, former councilmen Joseph Rupert and William S. Rosson served successive terms as the city's chief executive. However, Franklin County's most prominent politician of the era did not serve on the council before becoming mayor. James H. Polsgrove, who succeeded Dr. Edgar E. Hume in 1910, ascended to the mayorship after the first phase of a distinguished career in county government. An astute attorney, Polsgrove began his life of public service in 1894, when he was elected county attorney. Reelected four years later, he held the post until 1902, when he was elected Franklin County Judge. Elected again in 1904, he continued in office until 1908, when he relinquished the seat to R. C. Hieatt, the former county sheriff. After a brief respite, Polsgrove was elected mayor in 1910. It was during his term that the city witnessed major advances in street construction and maintenance, building and housing regulation, water filtration, and fire department operations. After leaving office in 1914, Polsgrove completed the first codification of city ordinances and resolutions in twenty-three years. He returned to the county judge's office during the mid-1920s and remained there into the early years of the Great Depresssion.

Judge R. C. Hieatt

Frankfort and Franklin County were anything but stagnant when it came to the development of cultural, intellectual, and social institutions. Many of the organizations established during the closing decades of the nineteenth century began to flourish during the twentieth. At the same time, others sprang up to perform a variety of new functions. In the field of education, opportunities to attend school expanded for county as well as city children. By the end of 1912 the Frankfort school system operated seven classroom buildings. Along with the recently rebuilt Second Street School, which encompassed the high school, and Clinton Street School, for black children, the system included a new, six-room building adjoining the Second Street School; a four-room primary school on Wilkinson Street; and other buildings in Bellepoint, on Holmes Street, and on Murray Street in South Frankfort.

Second Street School, 1912.

Even more notable, perhaps, was the emergence of a rural school system for children outside the city of Frankfort. Small public schools had been scattered hither and yon around the county for decades. It was not until about 1909, however, that the system began to reach a majority of the school-age children in Franklin County. By 1912 the county had been aligned into four educational divisions which coincided with the rural magisterial districts. The Forks of Elkhorn division contained nine schools; the Peak's Mill and Bald Knob divisions each boasted fourteen; and the Bridgeport division had eleven.

Included in the system were five county high schools. One offered a four-year course, while the remaining four conducted two-year programs. These high schools enrolled a total of seventy-five students. At first these figures seem rather meager. But in view of the fact that some students had to travel up to seven miles to school, such enrollment is quite remarkable. Indeed, L. F. Johnson, a prominent lawyer and state legislator, observed that "no part of the school system is more popular than . . . the high school." Even more important was the growth of the system as a whole. To Johnson this signified that "the farmers of the county are interested in good schools as never before. They are beginning to realize that the money expended in the education of their children is not a cost, but a splendid investment."

The most significant event in the newspaper business was the evolution of the *State Journal*. On January 1, 1900, the Kentucky Publishing Company, headed by the Rev. Lew G. Wallace, initiated publication of the *Kentucky State Democrat*. The editor of this afternoon daily was John M. Meloan. Six days later Wallace and Meloan published the first issue of the *Kentucky State Journal*, the *Democrat*'s morning companion. Both papers ceased publication within six months. But in June 1900, J. W. Marksbury and W. W. Longmoor reestablished the *Journal*, operating out of offices on Main Street across from the Capital Hotel. The publishers incorporated in May 1901 as the Kentucky Journal Company and changed the paper's name to the *Kentucky Journal*. It appeared as a weekly from June to December 1901, when it resumed publication as a daily. Marksbury and Ben Watt served as editors until 1905, when they were succeeded by William P. Walton, who held the editor's chair until 1910. At that time former Governor J. C. W. Beckham and James L. Newman acquired the company.

Meanwhile, in October 1908, Graham Vreeland established the *Frankfort News*. Published by the Frankfort Printing Company and edited by A. R.

Dunlap, this evening daily remained in circulation until February 1911, when it merged with the *Kentucky Journal*. The merged paper was known as the *Frankfort News-Journal*. Its publisher was the Frankfort News-Journal Company, whose officers were Hubert Vreeland, president; James L. Newman, vice president; and A. R. Dunlap, secretary-treasurer. Dunlap also edited the new paper, which appeared as a morning and evening daily. The *News-Journal* lasted under that name until June 1912, when it became the *State Journal*. From new offices at 321 Main Street, Graham Vreeland presided both as editor of the *State Journal* and as president of the newly organized State Journal Company from 1912 until his death in July 1920. His successor was James L. Newman, who had been associated with the paper and its predecessors since 1910. Under the leadership of Vreeland and Newman, who remained at the helm until 1938, the *State Journal* emerged not only as Franklin County's most powerful newspaper but as one of the most politically influential papers in the Commonwealth.

Along with its predecessors, the *State Journal* eclipsed many rivals in its rise to prominence. One of the first casualties was John B. Dryden and Llewellyn B. Marshall's the *Daily Call*, which suspended operations in late 1906, a few months after Dryden's death in August of that year. The *State Journal*'s historical link with the demise of George A. Lewis's *Frankfort Roundabout* is more direct. The *Roundabout* remained in publication until February 1908, when it was succeeded by the *Frankfort Weekly News and Roundabout*. Its publisher was Hubert Vreeland's Frankfort Printing Company, and its editor was A. R. Dunlap. The *Weekly News* folded in April 1909, but not before earning an opportunity to claim a niche as a predecessor of the *State Journal*.

An important adjunct to local intellectual life was the Frankfort Public Library, organized in 1906 by the Frankfort Women's Club. Originally located in the McClure Building, the library was open one day each week, and patrons paid an annual user fee of one dollar. As patronage grew the availability of services increased. By 1910 the library was open on Wednesdays and Saturdays, and in 1913 it became free to the public. Increased patronage and a growing collection created a need for more space, and by 1914 the library had relocated in the old state capitol, which it shared with the Kentucky Historical Society. Three years later the collection numbered about 4,000 volumes, and the library had about 1,800 patrons. Also in 1917, in an effort to give the library a permanent location, a committee of the city council and several civic leaders initiated a drive to reorganize it as a Carnegie library. Regrettably, the effort failed, and the Frankfort Public Library moved at least twice more before settling at its present site in the old Post Office Building.

The early twentieth century also witnessed the establishment of several important social and health agencies. By 1910 local Episcopalians had organized the Episcopal Orphanage, located at 311 Washington Street. The Franklin County Court had established an alms house on Louisville Road about four miles west of Frankfort and an eruptive hospital on Owenton Pike just outside

William Jennings Bryan addressed this large crowd on April 25, 1911 as part of a lecture series sponsored by the YMCA. Seated on the platform are (from left to right) Bryan, J.C.W. Beckham, Judge Polsgrove and Governor Augustus E. Willson.

Detail of Bryan's address.

the city limits. Another important health institution was Winnie Scott Hospital, established in 1903 to treat Franklin County's black population. Originally known as the Women's Improvement Club Hospital and located at 228 East Second Street, the institution's name was changed later to honor an early chairman of the hospital's board of directors. This large, rambling frame structure, surrounded by closely set residential dwellings, served the city's black population and provided a place where black physicians could practice until the desegregation of King's Daughters Hospital in 1959.

Perhaps no other element of local society witnessed more vigorous growth than organizational life. Between 1900 and 1920 voluntary societies not only increased in numbers, but they also expanded in type and function, embracing professional, business, and labor associations as well as a variety of social, fraternal, and benevolent purposes. Already a popular facet of the social scene, benevolent and fraternal organizations continued to attract a large membership. By 1908 Franklin County claimed nearly forty chapters of almost every conceivable fraternal lodge. The Masons and Odd Fellows remained the most popular organizations, but the Red Men, Eagles, and Knights of Columbus formed lodges during the first decade of the century. Founded in April 1901, Blackfoot Tribe No. 67 of the Independent Order of Red Men was instrumen-

People's Pharmacy, 429 Washington St. This building principally served as the home of Capitol City Lodge 1597, Household of Ruth 170, Frankfort's black Masonic order. The building was constructed in 1908.

The Elk Home, 309–311 Elks Place.

Judge James H. Hazelrigg

tal in organizing a free street fair and fall carnival in October 1902. Also in 1902, the three-year-old Elks Club laid the cornerstone of its new lodge hall, located downtown at 309 Lewis Street.

Closely related to the fraternal organizations were the various veterans and patriotic societies which commemorated the nation's past wars. Black Union veterans from the Civil War belonged to the George W. Monroe Post of the Grand Army of the Republic, while rebel veterans adhered to the Thomas B. Monroe Camp of the United Confederate Veterans. Younger citizens who revered the memory of the Lost Cause joined the Fayette Hewitt Camp of Sons of Confederate Veterans or the Joseph H. Lewis Chapter of United Daughters of the Confederacy. Some members of the latter organization no doubt belonged as well to the Susannah Hunt Shelby Chapter of the Daughters of the American Revolution. Many Franklin Countians with German roots belonged to the German Benevolent Society or the Ladies German-American Society.

Reflecting perhaps the reformist spirit of the day, the early twentieth century also spawned numerous charitable and community improvement organizations. Associated Charities attempted to oversee the funding and program activities of local social agencies to insure that their resources and services were distributed efficiently in a businesslike manner. The Citizens' Improvement Association, organized in 1909, spearheaded a variety of public service endeavors. Between 1909 and 1916 they promoted public playgrounds and kindergartens and conducted sewing classes, a sign removal campaign, and a program to clean up the river bank. The organization's first president was Judge James H. Hazelrigg. Other officers included Judge B. G. Williams, first vice president; Miss Lilian Lindsey, second vice president; Charles F. Strassner, third vice president; Miss Rebecca Averill, secretary; and Frank Heeney, treasurer. A very popular group, the Citizens' Improvement Associa-

Leo L. Oberwarth's original 1910 perspective of YMCA Building, 104 Bridge St.

tion had about ninety dues-paying members by 1912. One of its strategies was to initiate activities and then to turn them over to other organizations for long-term implementation. By 1916 most of its programs already had been spun off, and in May 1917 the newly organized chapter of the National Red Cross took over its remaining functions. Other organizations representing specific concerns ranged from the Franklin County Humane Society, which fought cruelty to animals, to the Kentucky Equal Rights Association, organized during World War I and devoted to voting rights for women.

The major organizations committed to the interests of young people were the Young Men's Christian Association and the Boy Scouts of America. Organized in 1895, the YMCA's major accomplishment during this period was the construction of a permanent headquarters. In early 1910 the association launched a campaign to raise $300,000 to erect the structure at 104 Bridge Street, just north of the St. Clair Street Bridge. Completed two years later at a total cost of $60,000, the YMCA Building was designed by Leo L. Oberwarth, Frankfort's leading architect. Born in Brooklyn, New York, in 1872 and educated in Germany, Oberwarth moved with his family to Frankfort at the age of sixteen. After serving as a draftsman for two other firms, he opened his own office in 1893. During the early twentieth century his commissions included the Elks Club building in 1902, the expansion of King's Daughters Hospital in 1904, and improvements to the Franklin County Courthouse in 1906.

While its new building was the YMCA's most conspicuous achievement, it also played a significant role in making Frankfort a pioneer in the Boy Scout movement. In 1908 Stanley Harris, the association's professional director, met

Judge Benjamin G. Williams

BOY SCOUTS OF AMERICA, TROOP 1

Fourth Row: Stanley A. Harris (Scoutmaster), Lee Wigginton, Ernest Marshall, John Wigginton, Shipman Wasson, Farrell Brady, Hinds Walcutt, Andrew Hill, Blakey, Herndon Evans, Lorenzo Martin, Sam Sneed, Walter Brown, Max Jacobs, Buzz Gaines.

Third Row: Leslie Marshall, Bo Gayle, Marvin Murphy, Charles Sutterlin, Stanley Stagg, Zack Montgomery, Allen W. Hughes, Ben Williams, Amy Henry.

Second Row: Julian "Teedle" Oberwarth, Robert "Sonkey" Polsgrove, Gus Smith, Victor Gretter, Tom Kenney, Ed Rogers, Marshall Adams, Rowland Gooch, William Eales, Ven Rogers, Leo Oberwarth, Ralph Gaines, William Scruggs.

First Row: "Scummy" Wingate, Jeff Adams, Harry Lee Pattie, Herman Jacobs, Lambert Suppinger, Tipton "Tip" Hubbard, Edgar Bacon, Hardin Shaw, Richard Ferguson, Lawrence Tobin, Lindsey Barnes.

weekly with a group of adolescent boys for activities such as hiking, camping, and rowing. One fall day one of the boys brought a magazine to the meeting which contained an article on Lord Robert S. S. Baden-Powell's British Boy Scouts. His young charges asked Harris if he would write Baden-Powell's office to see if a Scout unit could be organized in Frankfort. Harris favored their request, and on January 9, 1909, he received a letter from Lord Baden-Powell formally chartering Troop 1 of Frankfort as a unit of the British organization. Sponsored by a group of citizens and based at the YMCA, Troop 1 became part of the new Boy Scouts of America in February 1910. Stanley Harris was the first Scoutmaster. Troop 1 remained the city's sole troop until 1917, when two more units were formed. All three met at the YMCA, but each was under separate sponsorship—Troop 1 by First Baptist Church, Troop 2 by First Christian Church, and Troop 3 by Church of the Good Shepherd. So it remained until 1926, when officials of the Bluegrass Council in Lexington determined that the troop at the Christian Church had the closest direct connection with the original Troop 1. Accordingly, the numbers were reversed, with the unit at First Christian becoming Troop 1. Thus is based its claim as one of the oldest Boy Scout troops in the United States.

As the capital, Frankfort became the headquarters for numerous agricultural, business, and professional associations whose economic interests might be affected by actions of state government. As early as 1910 the city hosted such trade organizations as the Franklin County Board of Control of the Burley Tobacco Society, the Franklin County Medical Society, and the Retail Grocers Association. Two years later the Kentucky Pharmaceutical Association and the Kentucky Board of Fire Underwriters had established offices in the city, and by 1914 they had been joined by the Kentucky River Saw Mill Association.

No doubt many members of these organizations did some of their socializing at the country club. Organized in 1903 and located on the Frankfort-Lexington Pike, about four miles from the city, the club was established by the city's social and economic elite "for the encouragement of athletic exercises and sports and the establishment and maintenance of places for reading-rooms and social meetings." Members had access to a variety of club house facilities, and many deals undoubtedly were cut on the club's nine-hole golf course.

As business and professional men organized to advance their economic and political well-being, so too did skilled tradespeople. Challenged on one side by changing industrial technology and on the other by employers who tried to keep wages as low as possible, workers in Franklin County began to join trade unions. Local printers joined the International Typographical Union, which for a brief period in 1911 published a journal called the *Frankfort Labor Advocate*. At one point, the paper had some 4,000 subscribers. By 1914 the typographers had been joined by the American Federation of Musicians, Local 568. During the next three years two more unions were formed—Local 14 of the Bricklayers Union and Local 440 of the Moving Picture Operators' Union.

A major stimulus of organizational development was American entry into World War I, as patriotic Franklin Countians from all walks of life threw themselves into the war effort. When the armed forces issued their calls for troops, so many Franklin Countians enlisted that only four men were drafted. By the end of the war scores of local men had served, and thirty made the supreme sacrifice. On the home front the war was directly responsible for the organization of the local chapter of the National Red Cross in May 1917. Spearheading the chapter's organization were Mrs. George Baker and Mrs. Eugene Ray. Farmer and businessman W. Pruett Graham was the first chairman and Governor A. O. Stanley served as honorary chairman. A month after its formation the Franklin County chapter launched an aggressive membership drive, seeking 1,000 members to participate in activities to support American troops who soon would be fighting in Europe. In July the chapter established its headquarters in the McClure Building. During the months that followed Red Cross members prepared refreshments for soldiers passing through the capital on troop trains bound for embarkation points on the East Coast and rolled thousands of feet of bandages for treating doughboys wounded in action.

Another organization that played a leading role in the war effort was the Franklin County Council on National Defense. Also chaired by W. Pruett Graham, the council sought to mobilize the community's economic resources in support of war production. During the summer of 1917, for example, it conducted a survey of local farmers to determine their labor needs for the fall harvest. The council likewise played a major role in two highly successful Liberty Bond drives, both of which oversubscribed their goals. When the federal government needed space for a depot for the manufacture of military shirts, the council helped to secure the old state capitol for this purpose.

Churches also became involved in the war effort. The Rev. Roger T. Nooe, pastor of First Christian Church, took a six-months leave of absence to serve with the YMCA in France. The Reverend Nooe's congregation opened an annex on Lewis Street near the church where it conducted a wide range of wartime community activities. Until the appearance of the Spanish influenza forced its closing in the fall of 1918, the annex was the scene of a steady stream of activities—entertainment for soldiers, Liberty Bond and War Stamp drive meetings, and interfaith patriotic prayer meetings. Similarly, Father John F. O'Dwyer, pastor of the Church of the Good Shepherd, carried on a substantial schedule of war service activities along with his regular pastoral duties. Soon after the declaration of war he was a featured speaker, along with Judge Hazelrigg, at a huge downtown patriotic rally designed to spur enlistments. Father O'Dwyer also had the sad distinction of conducting the funeral of Franklin County's first war casualty, Eugene Mitchell, a convert to Catholicism who died in an accident on a battleship at sea.

Reverend Roger T. Nooe

World War I generated the strongest outpouring of patriotic sentiment in Franklin County since the outbreak of the Civil War. But as the war came to an end in November 1918, the country's business and civic leaders became increasingly conscious of the difficult tasks which lay before them. Construction of the new capitol and the expansion of the county's industrial base had given them cause for optimism. But it would take more than mere boosterism to fill the gap created by the shutdown of the distilleries and to reverse three decades of stagnation and decline in the population. The decade ahead would require a good deal of energy and imagination, as well as a modicum of luck, to translate the sense of common purpose created by the war into a new era of growth and progress.

RAILROAD BRIDGE AT BROADWAY, JUST AFTER COMPLETION WITH CONSTRUCTION CREW.

10

The Capital in the New Era

MANY AMERICANS REMEMBER or imagine the years that immediately followed World War I as the "Roaring Twenties." The period is personified by the raccoon-coated college man who imbibed bootleg gin from a hip flask and danced the "Charleston" or "Black Bottom" with a bobbed-haired flapper in a back-street speakeasy or country roadhouse. While there is an element of truth to this image of the 1920s as a carefree "Jazz Age," it is generally shallow and misleading. The twenties were, in fact, a period of tremendous economic and social change. The 1920 census documented the nation's statistical transformation from an agrarian to an urban society. The convergence of a host of technological innovations created powerful new economic giants, including the radio, motion picture, and automobile industries. The latter triggered quantum growth in the steel, rubber, glass, and petroleum industries, and contributed to major changes in residential design, personal mobility, and youthful dating patterns. The nation's business and political leaders optimistically labeled the postwar years as a "New Era" in which rapid economic growth and technological progress would put an end to poverty and guarantee prosperity for all.

Unfortunately, this New Era also had its dark side. As the forces of change appeared to undermine traditional manners and morals, citizens from all walks of life began to strike out in fear against those people and ideas which seemed to threaten their own conception of the American way of life. The result was a wave of antidemocratic sentiment which manifested itself in the resurgence of the Ku Klux Klan, strict immigration restrictions, strident religious fundamentalism, and the repression of political dissent. In the arena of national politics, such incidents as the Teapot Dome Scandal and the hijinks of President Warren G. Harding and his "Ohio Gang" brought discredit to the highest levels of American government.

The people of Frankfort and Franklin County experienced both the banes and blessings of the New Era. Despite the closing of the distilleries and the problem of declining population, local decision makers looked upon the post-

Water-skiing on the Kentucky, c. 1920.

Old Taylor Distillery. Just prior to prohibition E.H. Taylor, Jr., entertained numerous dignitaries at the distillery.

war decade with a pronounced optimism and a willingness to confront the community's challenges head on. Writing in mid-1921, one sympathetic observer found Frankfort imbued with a "civic spirit . . . growing by leaps and bounds." The capital city had "stepped out of its ultra conservatism, out of its time worn and deterring political battle ground atmosphere, its shroud of self complacency and self sufficiency, into line with the other progressive and modern cities of Kentucky." Indicative of this growing civic spirit was Frankfort's increasing willingness to "cater to industrial development" and "to hold out a welcome hand to those who may be honestly and sincerely seeking a good place in which to work, conduct a business, and to live as a residential city."

These observations proved to be more than superficial rhetoric. There was hardly any way that Franklin County could make up the loss of its largest industry in the space of a decade. However, through aggressive promotion of the community's economic assets, local business and civic leaders attracted several large industries which made up a substantial portion of the deficit. In addition, the country witnessed significant advances in such areas as retail trade, distribution, banking, construction, and tourism.

Like the rest of the nation, however, Franklin Countians also experienced some of the pains of the 1920s. Unable to quench their alcoholic thirsts legally, some folks resorted to bootlegging and moonshining. A few citizens, shaken by the enormous changes going on about them, joined a rejuvenated Ku Klux Klan or supported legislative efforts to prohibit the teaching of evolution and related scientific theories in the public schools. But this county, which so recently had endured a long wave of violence, proved remarkably immune to the worst passions of the day. Indeed, the greatest source of anguish among local residents was not Klan violence or evolution but the loss of income suffered by many farmers as American agriculture entered a long depression following World War I. The anguish deepened when the stock market crash of October 1929 plunged Franklin County and the nation into the worst depression in American history.

One of the most important facets of Franklin County's development during the 1920s was a new surge of population growth following three decades of net outmigration. From a forty-year low of 19,357 inhabitants in 1920, the county's population grew to 21,064 in 1930, an 8.8 percent increase. The reversal proved strongest in Frankfort. As early as 1921, enumerators for the Caron Directory Company detected a new wave of urban growth in the capital. While the counters typically overestimated the magnitude of the growth trend, their recognition that it had begun was correct. After dropping back to 9,805 persons in 1920, the city's population surged to a new high of 11,626, an 18.6 percent increase, in 1930.

Growth was apparent throughout the city. The strongest increase occurred in the Second Ward, the area east of St. Clair and north of the Kentucky River, where the population ballooned from 4,017 persons in 1920 to 5,292 a decade later. While this reversed an earlier downward trend in the Second Ward, the First Ward's uninterrupted growth continued, moving from 3,041 in 1920 to 3,438 in 1930. New development in South Frankfort was particularly strong along Capitol Avenue (formerly Main Street) and in the once moribund Capitol Heights subdivision southwest of the capitol. Although not nearly so blessed with vacant land, even the Third Ward saw its population grow from 2,747 in 1920 to 2,896 in 1930.

W. G. Chapman Residence, 413 Wapping St.

The dynamic element in this decade of renewed urban growth appears to have been a steady increase in the number of state employees moving into the city. The size of state government had remained relatively static during the stormy years of the late nineteenth and early twentieth centuries. However, as the demands upon government expanded during the twenties, so did the number of personnel required to implement these new functions. According to one observer, this "increased population of State employees" constituted "one of the charms of Frankfort. These people are the best the state and country affords, and they come to the Capital City bringing with them new ideas and new civic spirit." This growing population also placed new pressures on the city's housing stock and created a demand for new construction. By mid-1924, Caron's Directory Company noted, "every house and apartment is occupied and a large number of residences are under construction or being planned. One concern is receiving bids for the construction of 22 bungalows, and others are preparing contracts for additional ones." Total construction for the year amounted to forty buildings, mostly residential dwellings.

Cornelius E. Collins Residence, 505 Murray St.

While the growing corps of state employees, who were almost exclusively white, accounted for a major portion of the capital's new residents, its black population continued to decline. In 1920 the city had 2,246 black citizens, who

E. H. Taylor, Jr.'s cattle at Thistleton. Charlie Marshall, overseer (middle).

constituted 22.9 percent of Frankfort's population. A decade later, the number had dropped to 2,205, only 19 percent of the city's residents. As they had for decades, most of the city's black residents continued to live in Craw, in South Frankfort east of Logan Street, and in the vicinity of the State Normal and Industrial Institute.

Population growth also resumed beyond the city limits. However, this rural growth was anything but evenly distributed. The heaviest increases occurred in the fertile Forks of Elkhorn district, where the population jumped from 2,568 in 1920 to 3,870 in 1930, an increase of 50.7 percent. Growth was especially pronounced in crossroads settlements such as Forks of Elkhorn, Switzer, and Jett. With their country stores, post offices, and other small businesses, such communities offered a semblance of town life mixed with the charms of country living for a population which was becoming increasingly nonagrarian. The picture was much the same in the southwestern part of the county, where the population of the Bridgeport district grew at a considerably lower rate, from 2,236 residents in 1920 to 2,431 a decade later. While agriculture remained the base of the district's economy, a substantial portion of the new population settled near hamlets such as Bridgeport, Farmdale, Choateville, and Benson.

It was a much different story, however, in the Peak's Mill and Bald Knob districts. With their steep, rugged hills and poor soils, both areas proved increasingly incapable of supporting the small-farm agriculture which had characterized the northern half of the county for generations. As more and more farm families abandoned the soil, the population of these two districts continued to slide. The tendency was especially apparent in Peak's Mill, whose population dropped from 2,555 in 1920 to 1,298 in 1930 for a loss of nearly half its inhabitants in the space of a decade. The new settlement which did occur was concentrated in villages such as Peak's Mill, Swallowfield, and Elmville. About the only difference between the experiences of Bald Knob and Peak's Mill was the extent of the population loss. Having already experienced severe losses for more than twenty years, Bald Knob began the decade as Franklin County's smallest rural magisterial district with a mere 2,193 inhabitants. During the 1920s, however, the rate of decline moderated. As new settlement in the vicinity of Polsgrove Landing, Harvieland, Flag Fork, and Bailey's Mill partially offset the effects of outmigration, the district ended the decade with 1,839 residents, a net loss of only 354 persons. As a result, Bald Knob yielded to Peak's Mill its dubious distinction as the county's smallest rural district.

Unfortunately, the growth in Forks of Elkhorn and Bridgeport failed to balance the losses in Bald Knob and Peak's Mill. Consequently, Franklin County's rural population declined for the fourth consecutive decade, from 9,552 persons in 1920 to 9,438 in 1930. On the other hand, a net loss of only 114 residents suggested that the rate of decline was slowing and perhaps on the verge of being reversed. Indeed, the rural white population increased for the first time in forty years. It was the net loss of 193 black residents which ultimately accounted for the overall decline of the country population.

Perhaps during no other period was Franklin County's economy so muddled as during the 1920s. Taking advantage of a decade of industrial and commercial prosperity, Frankfort's business leadership struggled mightily and with considerable success to fill the gap created by the closing of the distilleries. But it was a much different story in farming where the combined forces of prohibition and postwar depression dealt a double blow to the county's agrarian economy.

Agriculture had been a mainstay in Franklin County's economy since the late eighteenth century. Local farmers prided themselves on the high quality of their white burley tobacco. Publicists extolled the virtues of the pure bred Hereford cattle raised by former mayor and distillery magnate Colonel Edmund H. Taylor, Jr., and they described his stock farm, Woodford Belle, as "the mecca for cattle raisers from all parts of the United States." Eliciting similar praise were the Duroc Jersey hogs raised by the McKee brothers on their local farm. "These hogs sell for many thousand dollars each," one commentator noted, "and they have been shipped to every section of this country." And of course, Franklin County's fabled thoroughbred racehorses were famous throughout the racing world.

But most farmers were neither Colonel Taylors nor the McKee brothers. As the 1920s began, the typical farmer cultivated a small crop of tobacco, grew a few acres of corn or wheat, and perhaps grazed a few head of livestock on sixty-five or seventy-five acres of land. The chances are good that he had borrowed heavily to buy more land and equipment to expand production during World War I. Now that the war was over, he still had to pay back his loan, but the demand for his production was declining and so were prices. For many local farmers, this proved a formula for disaster.

The first half of the decade was particularly rough. In 1920 there were 1,880 working farms in Franklin County. Five years later, the number had fallen to 1,580. Hit especially hard were the smallest farmers. Of the net total of 300 who suspended operations, 251 cultivated fewer than fifty acres. Most of the remainder farmed under 100 acres. To a limited degree, the plight of the small farmer redounded to the benefit of the larger operator. Between 1920 and 1925 the number of farms between 100 and 400 acres in size increased from 398 to 417, and the size of the average spread rose from 67.4 acres to 71.8 acres. But the primary effect of the decline in the number of small farms was to take land out of cultivation as the county's total farm land dropped from 126,667 acres in 1920 to 113,423 in 1925.

Another indicator of the farmers' deteriorating economic situation was the declining value of farm property. During the first half of the decade, the value of all agricultural land and buildings declined by 34.8 percent from just under $13 million in 1920 to less than $8.5 million five years later. Similarly, the value of farm machinery dropped by 38 percent, from $505,410 to $313,364 during the same period.

Conditions improved slightly during the second half of the decade, but most farmers remained far from prosperous. The number of farms increased to 1,598, a net gain of eighteen over 1925. A handful of the new farmers operated fewer than twenty acres. But most of the growth occurred among those farming between 50 and 500 acres. At the same time, the average size of all farms rose to 77.1 acres; the value of land and buildings passed $8.8 million; and the value of machinery and implements increased to $331,381. But even as these minuscule improvements were being recorded, Franklin County farmers were finding themselves engulfed by the trauma of the Great Depression.

The effects of the agricultural depression of the 1920s are even more apparent in falling livestock and crop production figures. As in other livestock producing counties, Franklin farmers were forced by falling prices, declining peacetime demand, and shifting markets to reduce the size of their inventories. Again, the first half of the decade was especially devastating. In 1920 census takers counted 8,282 beef and dairy cattle on local farms. Five years later the figure had dropped to 6,466. The situation for hogs was even more severe. As Kentucky farmers found it increasingly difficult to compete with large Western producers, Franklin County farmers slashed their herds from 7,847 head of swine in 1920 to 4,479 at mid-decade. Already smaller than those for other species, horse inventories dropped from 3,913 head to 2,968 head during the same period.

By 1926 the postwar depression appeared to have bottomed out. As demand increased during the latter part of the decade, farmers expanded production

KENTUCKY STATE PENITENTIARY, 1921

in anticipation of better sales. The market improved steadily through 1928 and into 1929 before the Great Depression again suffocated demand. Unfortunately, a substantial number of farmers found themselves with excessive inventories. By 1930 Franklin County's cattle herd had grown to 9,441 animals, exceeding the 1920 figure by nearly 14 percent. Sheep production was even higher. In 1920 the local flock stood at 7,847 head. A decade later it stood at 13,257 mature animals plus 11,135 slaughter lambs. Swine producers also benefited from the temporary recovery and by 1930 had increased their inventory to 6,014 head. Only the horse breeders resisted the temptation to increase production. By 1930 the county's equine population had declined to 2,869 animals. Providing further evidence, however, that a recovery in inventories did not necessarily indicate the return of prosperity, the market value of all livestock of Franklin County farms dropped from $1.15 million in 1920 to just over $1.08 million a decade later, despite a substantial increase in the total number of animals.

For many grain farmers the problems created by the depression were compounded by prohibition. Hit particularly hard by the long dry spell were corn growers, who saw their harvest drop from an already disappointing 307,830 bushels in 1920 to 216,473 bushels in 1930. Similarly affected by the closing of the local breweries, the county's barley production fell from 9,858 to 5,596 bushels during the same period. Harvests of other cereal grains followed the same course, with oats declining from 30,984 to 2,670 bushels, wheat from 69,786 to 12,132 bushels, and rye from 5,672 to 2,144 bushels.

There were some exceptions to this downward trend. Apparently as a result of the brief recovery in the livestock industry, hay and forage production rose from 9,599 tons in 1920 to 12,244 tons a decade later. The potato harvests improved as well, from 8,602 bushels to 14,750 bushels for Irish potatoes and from 913 to 977 bushels for sweet potatoes. But most other crops, including sorghum, fruits, nuts, and vegetables, continued to decline. Indicative of the downward price spiral, the total value of all crops produced in Franklin County dropped from more than $2.5 millon in 1920 to just over $1.4 million a decade later. Cereal grains lost more than two-thirds of their value, dropping from $752,569 to $238,272. Despite a substantial increase in production, the value of hay and forage crops fell by nearly 55 percent, from $462,436 to $209,085 during the decade.

No single crop suffered more severely from the depression of the twenties than the county's chief crop. As the decade began, local tobacco farmers seemed to have every reason for optimism. Prices and production had risen steadily since the partition of the tobacco trust and in 1919 had culminated in a harvest of nearly 5.1 million pounds of leaf worth more than $1 million. But a combination of bad weather and a new round of problems in the market place soon made the banner year of 1919 just a fleeting memory. The rainy planting season of 1920 resulted in a large crop of poor quality. As a consequence, prices dropped from the highs of 34 cents a pound in 1919 to an average of 13.4 cents. The following year was worse yet. Although prices rose to about 22.2 cents a pound, the white burley crop was so small that even the price increase could not make up the difference. Compounding the farmers' problems was the failure of Kentucky's tobacco manufacturers to take advantage of the skyrocketing cigarette industry. By 1921 the white burley region was again on the verge of a new outbreak of violence.

Primary responsibility for preventing a new wave of lawlessness was Judge Robert Worth Bingham, owner and publisher of the Louisville *Courier-Journal* and the *Louisville Times*. Sensitive to the plight of the burley growers, Bingham organized a study committee and charged it with making recommendations to solve the growers' marketing problems. Members of the committee included New York financier Bernard Baruch, *Louisville Times* editor Arthur Krock, Congressman J. C. Cantrill, and several of Kentucky's leading tobacco men. The product of their work was the Burley Tobacco Growers Cooperative Association, a pooling and marketing agency which enabled its members to exert greater control over the sale of their crops and to assure a higher price for their leaf than it could fetch at public auction. In order to insure its effectiveness, the association required its members to pledge that they would sell all their burley exclusively through the association for the next five years.

At first the burley cooperative worked quite effectively. Franklin Countians

White Burley Tobacco and harvested hemp growing side by side in Franklin County.

were strongly represented among the 57,000 farmers who immediately committed to sell $50 million worth of tobacco through the association. To purchase warehouses and other facilities and to provide cash advances to farmers until their crops could be sold, Judge Bingham pledged $1 million; and James B. Brown, president of Louisville's National Bank of Kentucky, promised $500,000. Even more importantly, Brown arranged for the United States War Finance Corporation, of which he was a director, to advance $10 million for the same purposes. There was not much that the association could do to improve the price of the disastrous 1921 crop. However, as production soared in 1922 and 1923, the agency proved its ability to maintain reasonably strong and stable prices.

Regretably, as prices remained high, more and more farmers concluded that they could do even better on their own and began ignoring their pledges to sell exclusively through the association. In 1925 more leaf was sold at public auction than through the organization. When a bumper crop the following year depressed association and auction prices alike, large numbers of farmers failed to renew their commitments. Lacking the membership necessary to control market volume, the association folded, again leaving burley growers at the mercy of the auction. For tobacco planters in Franklin County, who produced barely over 3.7 million pounds of leaf in 1929, the combination of declining production and low prices was disastrous.

The collapse of the Burley Tobacco Growers Cooperative Association and

Willard Rouse Jillson, State Geologist and noted historian, poses overlooking the Hermitage Distillery.

the new era of low prices which ensued no doubt affirmed the belief of many local economic leaders that Franklin County's agricultural base should be diversified. In 1926 State Geologist Willard Rouse Jillson noted that "livestock are raised advantageously" and quoted approvingly the view of another authority that the county "is pre-eminently a grazing county and at least three-fourths of the land should be kept in permanent pasture." County Agent R. M. Heath likewise criticized the county's overdependence on tobacco. "I believe that our farmers should raise less tobacco and go more extensively into the production of sheep and dairy products," he noted, "always raising enough feed for the livestock which they keep." To further broaden the agricultural base, he urged the expansion of fruit production, "at least until the local market has been supplied." The city of Frankfort alone, Heath predicted, "will use $40,000 to $50,000 annually in fruit products which could be readily grown at a profit in a territory adjacent to Frankfort."

In an effort to educate farmers about the benefits of diversification and to improve the general quality of local livestock production, Heath initiated a series of training programs for farmers in the Bald Knob, Peak's Mill, Fox Gap, Switzer, Bridgeport, and Choateville communities. These sessions emphasized "the use of pure bred sires, better management, better housing, [and] care and feeding." Recognizing that young people were more open than their parents to modern, scientific agricultural techniques, Heath also established Junior Agricultural Clubs in Forks of Elkhorn, Peak's Mill, Switzer, and Bridgeport. By early 1927 these clubs had approximately 300 members.

Partly as a result of Heath's educational efforts, Franklin County's entry finished second only to Garrard County's in the 1926 Louisville Fat Cattle Show at Bourbon Stock Yards. But the plea for diversification fell largely on deaf ears. Those brief improvements in livestock production statistics recorded in 1930 were little more than a normal response to a temporary change in demand. The value of fruit and nut production in 1929 was only $9,603, less than half the $20,445 fetched by the meager harvest of 1919. About the only apparent increase in production occurred in table vegetables, exclusive of potatoes, which saw an expansion in land planted from 132 acres in 1919 to 202 acres a decade later. With a sale value of $24,152, this hardly constituted a major stride toward diversification.

If depression and failure to diversify were major problems for agriculture, then expansion and diversification were the fundamental hallmarks of commerce during the 1920s, especially in Frankfort. This was particularly the case in retail trade. By 1930 there were 238 retail businesses in Franklin County, 174 of them in the capital. Most were old, well-established enterprises. The majority of new stores, such as H. P. Mason's Capital Drug Company, opened at 207 West Main in 1926, following traditional lines of business. But a few of the new enterprises represented important innovations in local merchandising. By 1921 the F. W. Woolworth Company had established the city's first chain-owned 5 and 10 cents store at 312 St. Clair Street. Two years later, the

John Robinson's Circus unloading for Frankfort performance in the 1920's.

J. C. Penney Company opened Frankfort's first department store at 202-204 West Main Street. By the mid-1930s, under the management of B. E. Antwerp, Penney's employed eleven persons and attracted customers from all over the county.

Precisely because Frankfort was the commercial center of the county, retail trade outside the city was much less diversified. Of the sixty-four retail enterprises located outside the city in 1930, forty-eight were grocery and general stores. Most of these were situated in county hamlets such as Forks of Elkhorn, Bridgeport, Switzer, Jett, Peak's Mill, and Polsgrove Landing where they served as a source of food supplies and other necessities for farmers and other rural dwellers.

Crutcher and Simpson Store, Main St., interior.

A major force in diversifying both urban and rural commerce was the automobile. As Tin Lizzies proliferated during the 1920s, so did sales and service businesses. At the beginning of the decade there were some twenty establishments which catered to or directly depended upon the horseless carriage. In addition to established dealers such as the Frankfort Buick Company and the Frankfort Motor Car Company, the Nicol Garage sold Chevrolets, Oldsmobiles, and Reos and the Service Motor Company dealt in Buick automobiles, Federal trucks, and Samson trucks and tractors. Both companies, along with J. M. Perkins & Company, Collins Hardware, Bellepoint Motor Company, U. S. Motor Service Station, and the L. H. Fuqua Tire Company, sold such items as accessories, tires, and gasoline. Garages and repair shops included Frank Mazey's radiator service at 210 West Second Street; the Capital Garage at 317-319 West Broadway; Duval's Garage at 121 Bridge Street; and W. S. Brammell's Garage at 206 West Second Street. A resident who occasionally

Frankfort Buick,
319 West Second St.

needed automobile transportation but who did not own a car could select from among five taxicab companies.

Several of these businesses were still in operation at the end of the decade when there were twenty-seven auto-related enterprises in Frankfort and an additional thirteen in rural sections of the county. Frankfort now had no fewer than eight motor vehicle dealerships, which sold both new and used cars. Providing gas, repairs, and other services to city drivers were eight filling stations and eight garages. None of Franklin County's rural communities was large enough to support a car dealer. However, rural motorists did patronize ten service stations and three garages. These businesses had a powerful direct impact on the local economy, with total sales in 1929 estimated at more than $1.3 million. The automobile and the businesses which it spawned also had the indirect impact of displacing many enterprises which had depended on live horsepower. In 1891, before the advent of the automobile, Frankfort had eight blacksmith shops and six livery, feed, and sale stables. By 1921 all the livery stables were out of business, and only four blacksmiths remained in operation. Eight years later two more blacksmiths were out of business.

A major consequence of the increased personal mobility created by the automobile was a substantial rise in recreational and business travel. This in turn generated a demand for more facilities to accommodate overnight travelers. In Frankfort it stimulated still further pressure for the replacement of the crumbling shell at the northeast corner of Main and Ann streets which once had been the Capital Hotel. In June 1921, after nearly four years of ineffectual activity, the project began to move forward. The event which cleared the way was the dissolution in 1920 of the Capital Hotel Company, dominated by the Weitzel family, which already had failed to raise the capital necessary to finance a new hotel. When the Weitzels gave up, several of the city's civic leaders launched a public stock subscription drive to raise the money. By early 1921 they had raised half of the $250,000 subscription which they considered necessary to construct the new hostelry. Confident that they could sell the remaining stock, they incorporated the New Capital Hotel Company in June 1921. Indicative of the project's broad base of community support, the new company had 156 stockholders at the time its articles of incorporation were filed. Most of the shareholders owned from three to ten shares. Only eight men owned fifty or more shares—distiller Edmund H. Taylor, Jr., financier S. French Hoge, Judge Edward C. O'Rear, shoe manufacturers Charles F. Strassner and H. H. Roberts, building materials supplier J. Bacon Blanton, Dr. John P. Stewart, and Dr. John Patterson.

In the fall of 1921 the hotel company announced that a new, eighty-room establishment would be erected on the site of its predecessor. The designers of the massive colonial structure were Frank Packard, a prominent Columbus, Ohio, architect, and Frankfort architect Leo L. Oberwarth. Packard, who spent several weeks studying the environment of the site before he started making drawings, died just a month before the hotel's grand opening. Ground breaking ceremonies were conducted in 1922, and the new Capital Hotel opened in November 1923 with three days of celebration, including a stockholders banquet and a Thanksgiving dinner-dance. Although completed at a cost of $450,000, the new house had twenty more rooms than originally announced, as well as a huge lobby, ballroom, and roof garden.

The basic function of the Capital Hotel was to support the city's role as state capital. But even before construction began, perceptive observers recognized that the new inn, combined with Frankfort's historical and political character, scenic beauty, and accessibility by major highway routes, gave the city strong potential as a convention center and tourist destination. As early as 1921 the city directory reported that "Frankfort enjoys the distinction of being visited by more people annually than any other city in Kentucky." Perhaps assuming that the city's physical and aesthetic attributes were sufficient to attract visitors, local civic leaders exerted very little extra energy during the first half of the decade to promote tourism. In spite of this relaxed approach, the city regularly attracted substantial visitor business. In 1926, for example, the capital hosted eleven conventions, including such organizations as the Kentucky Sportsman's Convention, the State Business and Professional Women, Eastern Star, and the Regional Conference on State Parks.

The Southern Hotel, 216 West Second Street, just after completion.

By the beginning of 1927 community leaders began to realize that an aggressive promotion campaign might bring in even more convention business. And not without good reason. The completion of the seventy-room Southern Hotel, at 216 West Second, in December 1926 considerably increased the number of rooms available to the traveling public. Moreover, the fact that the city began the year with a half-dozen conventions—many of them repeat business—already booked, suggested that Frankfort was developing a substantial reputation as a reliable, experienced convention city. Thus, in early March the Frankfort Chamber of Commerce announced that J. Frank Dutton had been appointed chairman of its permanent convention bureau. Proclaiming the bureau's belief that "Frankfort is the real convention city of Kentucky," Dutton asserted that the agency "holds itself in constant readiness to give any services which might be requested of it by every important organization in the city which through its own resources and energies, has already secured a convention." Furthermore, he added, the bureau was "ready for suggestions from every source in its own active program to secure future conventions." Fifteen months later Dutton reported a "conservative estimate" that conventions had brought at least $235,000 in new money to the city during the previous two-year period. These figures, he concluded, clearly proved "that Frankfort is an ideal convention city and that we can enrich and advertise our community by a more determined effort to obtain conventions."

Among the major beneficiaries of Franklin County's accelerated commercial activity during the 1920s were Frankfort's banks. After the flurry of new starts and consolidations that characterized the first two decades of the century, the capital's five banks concentrated on expanding their capital assets. Between 1921 and 1928 the National Branch Bank of Kentucky, which had passed Farmers Deposit Bank as the city's largest financial institution, increased its capital stock, surplus, and undivided profits from $275,000 to $365,000. Farmers Deposit Bank, meanwhile, grew rather slowly, increasing its combined assets from $265,000 to just $275,000 during the same period. As a result of such laggard growth, Farmers Deposit Bank found itself competing on an even basis in 1928 with State National Bank of Frankfort. Seven years earlier, State National had combined assets of only $200,000.

The most aggressive financial institution during the decade was Peoples State Bank. In 1921 it was the city's smallest bank, with combined capital and surplus of $58,000. By 1928 these assets had more than tripled, reaching $189,000. In the process, it overtook the Capital Trust Company, which began the decade with capital stock and surplus of $75,000 each. Capital Trust's surplus increased to $100,000 over the next seven years, but this was not sufficient to keep up with Peoples Bank. As a result, Capital Trust Company ranked as the smallest bank in 1928. Taken together, Frankfort's banks increased their capital and surplus from $948,000 to nearly $1.3 million between 1921 and 1928.

The expansion of the local banking sector increased the capital available to all avenues of business. But it was especially critical to the community's efforts to fill the gap in the manufacturing base created by the closing of the distilleries and breweries. More than six decades after the fact, the prohibition era is shrouded in a veil of myth and folklore, dominated by images of violent, big-city gangsters and ignorant, backwoods moonshiners attempting to quench the nation's thirst with illegal beer and booze while trying to avoid the enforcement agent. But for Franklin and other Kentucky counties where the manufacture of alcoholic beverages had been a foundation of economic life for more than a century, the effects of prohibition were extremely painful. Prohibition meant not only the closing of major businesses and heavy unemployment, but a loss in local tax revenues. In Franklin County, for example, the scale of the loss is suggested by the fact that in 1915 government at all levels collected taxes on 63,999 barrels of bourbon withdrawn from storage at nine local distilleries. Nine years later, the four companies which still had liquor in storage paid taxes on a mere 8,865 barrels withdrawn for medicinal and other legal purposes.

For practical businessmen and politicians, quiet distilleries and empty liquor warehouses translated into silent cash registers, strained treasuries, and deteriorating roads and services. It was hardly a matter of altruism, therefore, when the Frankfort Chamber of Commerce combined forces with city and county governments to generate new economic development. Working primarily through the chamber's industrial bureau, they struggled valiantly throughout the decade to attract new plants and payrolls. City directories, brochures, and other promotional publications stressed Frankfort's rich natural resources; excellent transportation connections and utilities systems; low industrial tax rates; and abundant supply of reliable, unorganized, American-born labor. In 1920 the chamber spearheaded a bond issue which raised the money necessary to lay a mile of sanitary sewer between the state reformatory and the Kentucky River below the city. This made it possible to drain a large expanse of bottom land for use as industrial sites.

From a superficial, statistical perspective the results of these efforts appear to have been mixed. While the nation as a whole experienced a decade of industrial expansion, the number of manufacturing establishments in Franklin County declined from forty-four in 1919 to twenty-seven a decade later. Similarly, the value of all industrial production declined from about $5.2 million to approximately $4.6 million during the same period. But these figures are misleading by themselves. In the first place, well over half of the net loss is accounted for by the closing of the distilleries and other businesses directly affected by prohibition. The remainder succumbed primarily to the rigors of business life, including the continuing trend toward industrial consolidation which forced many smaller, less competitive concerns to close their doors. On the other hand, the community's industrial promotion efforts landed several major new industries, some of which set up operations in facilities abandoned because of prohibition. As a result of these new enterprises and the expansion of existing ones, total average employment in manufacturing increased from 593 in 1919 to 1,509 a decade later. However, while these figures indicate that employment increased by 154 percent, total wages grew by only 116 percent, from $408,953 to $883,930, during the same period. In short, industrial development created a host of new jobs, but at lower wages than during the war years.

Partly as a consequence of the industrial development campaign, Frankfort and Franklin County spawned approximately a dozen new industries during the 1920s. These enterprises not only pumped new capital and jobs into the community, but several also contributed to the further diversification of its

Ruth Hanly, left, and Rebecca Gooch, right, founders of Rebecca-Ruth Candy, with their friend Stella Funeaux horseback riding in 1916.

economic base. One of the first new industries was Rebecca-Ruth Candy, Inc. This enterprise was conceived in 1919 by Ruth Hanley and Rebecca Gooch, two young teachers who decided to turn their Christmastime tradition of making gift candy into a business. They set up shop in 1920 in an old Frankfort Hotel barroom which had been closed by prohibition. Despite a series of family and business crises, the business flourished. By the mid-1930s Rebecca-Ruth candies had become famous, especially after the invention of the unique Bourbon Candy Colonels in 1938.

Established about the same time as Rebecca-Ruth Candy, Inc. was the H & B Milk Company. Located at the foot of Holmes Street, the dairy's modern plant processed about 34,000 gallons of milk each month and shipped milk, cheese, and cultured buttermilk to markets as distant as Ashland and Hazard, Kentucky, and parts of Ohio and West Virginia, in addition to serving the local vicinity. Another industry which catered to area farmers was the Fincel & Company slaughter house. Operated by Norman Fincel and situated on Owenton Pike at the Cedar Cove Ravine, this modern establishment could slaughter and pack hogs, sheep, and cattle at a rate of 16,000 pounds per week.

Although prohibition devastated the beer and liquor industries, it provided an additional stimulus to soft drink bottling. In March 1927, Herbert G. Smith, N. B. Smith, and Elmer G. Hulett invested $10,000 to establish the Capital Bottling Works at 408 Ann Street. One of their chief competitors was the Anheuser-Busch Brewing Company, which joined the Eagle Bottling Company in its soft drink works located in the old Moerlein Brewing Company plant at 324 Ann Street. While the soft drink companies offered an alter-

Moerlein's Lager Beer, distributed by the Eagle Bottling Company, located in the O. N. Smith Building at 324 Ann Street. Railroad platform and the north side of Broadway are in the background.

native means of quenching the community's thirst, other firms moved into and converted vacant distilleries to new uses. In 1925, Eli H. Brown, Jr., Charles Irion, and E. E. Bowman incorporated the Brown-Irion Furniture Company. Capitalized at $100,000, the company remodeled the old Hermitage Distillery at the foot of East Third Street and began manufacturing fine upholstered living room furniture. By 1927 the firm was one of the largest employers in the county and was shipping furniture as far as the Atlantic Coast, Florida, and Texas. Shortly after establishing their new furniture company, Brown and Irion adapted part of their facilities as the general offices of their Fibercraft Chair Company, which had its primary production operations in Louisville.

Brown and Irion's decision to locate their enterprises in Frankfort reflected the city's long-established prominence in the furniture industry. This also was the case when J. M. Perkins, Adolph Wells, and R. E. Mills incorporated the Kentucky Table Company in September 1929. Still other industries reflected the advent of new technologies. During the early part of the decade, responding to the growing presence of the automobile, Alonzo A. Wallace, owner of the Frankfort Carriage Works at 206 Louisville Road, converted that operation to the manufacture of automobile bodies. A. A. Wallace & Sons Automobile Body Manufacturing Company remained in business well into the 1930s. Likewise, growing cities, industrial plants, and transportation systems required modern sewerage and drainage networks. In early 1928, Fred L. Conner, president of the Shearman Concrete Pipe Company in Knoxville, Tennessee, chose Frankfort as the location of a new pipe factory. In April he joined with local businessmen J. Bacon Blanton, W. D. Nicol, and Silas Wilson to incorporate the Kentucky Shearman Concrete Pipe Company, with Blanton as chairman of the board. Selected as the plant site was a twelve-acre tract near Holmes Street across the Frankfort & Cincinnati Railroad from the Blanton Stone Company. Ground was broken in May, and by March 1929 the new plant was turning out concrete sewer pipe which ranged in size from four to ninety-six inches in diameter.

Not all of the community's economic development efforts were successful. In October 1928, after months of negotiation and with a barrage of fanfare, Governor Flem Sampson announced that Franklin County had been chosen as the site of the $2.5 million Kentucky Cement Corporation. According to company president F. B. Drew, of McAlester, Oklahoma, the plant was to be located at the abandoned Baker Bros. Distillery at Forks of Elkhorn, with corporate headquarters in Frankfort. The deal which landed the commitment was worked out by the Kentucky Progress Commission, a state economic development agency, in cooperation with the Frankfort Chamber of Commerce, which obtained options on the distillery and transferred them to Drew. The executive attributed the site selection to Frankfort's excellent rail and water connections with key markets and the availability of raw materials necessary for "a high grade super-cement." Drew estimated that the plant would create about 400 jobs when complete.

But it was not to be. After the completion of engineering drawings, construction was scheduled to commence in November 1929. Unfortunately, the stock market crash dried up the capital necessary to build the plant, and the dream of this major manufacturing facility became a memory.

Though the acquisition of new manufacturing plants was the primary thrust of local economic development efforts, transportation improvements also had high priority. Receiving particular emphasis were bridges, streets, and roads. The year 1921 saw the complete reconstruction of the St. Clair Street Bridge. Seven years later the L & N Railroad initiated construction of a new, $600,000 railroad bridge across the Kentucky River at Broadway. After its completion in 1929, Chamber of Commerce Secretary H. A. Gretter praised the span as "a thing of which every citizen is extremely proud. The bridge is of the latest type and of the finest materials and it will stand in the years to come as an achievement of 1929 that was unsurpassed."

The growing presence of the automobile and other forms of motor transportation necessitated the comprehensive improvement of county roads and city streets. Unfortunately, the decline in local tax revenues which resulted from prohibition hindered progress for several years. During the middle of the decade, as local revenues started to increase, the chamber of commerce and other citizen groups began to agitate for the reconstruction of all county roads. Work commenced in mid-1927 on the reconstruction of Bald Knob

Road and Owenton Pike. By the end of 1928, almost every mile of county road had been rebuilt or regraded. The following year Lawrenceburg Pike was resurfaced and dangerous conditions on the Louisville Pike Hill, Bald Knob Hill, and Devil's Hollow Hill leading into Frankfort were eliminated by the installation of guard rails. Meanwhile, city government undertook an extensive street resurfacing program, repaving most of the streets with asphalt and regrading the macadam streets in Bellepoint and other less traveled parts of the city.

Along with street and road improvements came expanded bus service. In 1921 the Frankfort and Lawrenceburg Bus Line provided the only intercity highway coach service terminating at the capital. Six years later it operated three round trips daily between the terminal cities. In addition, the Lexington-based Barnes Brothers and Consolidated Coach Corporation lines conducted hourly service between Lexington and Louisville by way of Frankfort, and other lines provided regular service to Owenton and Georgetown.

Given the long tradition of political dominance by the business and professional elite, the close cooperation between the public and private sectors in Franklin County's economic development campaign during the 1920s is hardly surprising. In fact, the prevailing political ideology, espoused by Republicans such as Herbert Hoover and Democrats like New York Governor Alfred E. Smith, fostered close cooperation between business and government at all levels. What is remarkable is the record of accomplishment produced by the partnership, especially in view of the economic conditions which existed at the beginning of prohibition.

C. T. Coleman

Suggestive of this continued business and professional domination of local politics are the men who occupied the mayor's chair during the 1920s. William S. Rossen, who held office at the beginning of the decade, was a lumber dealer. His successor, David D. Smith, who served from 1922 to 1925, was a prominent insurance executive. Following him in 1926 was Dr. Clarence T. Coleman, who held office until 1930 and was elected to three more nonconsecutive terms.

An important development in city politics was the emergence of women as public officeholders. In 1923, three years after ratification of the nineteenth amendment gave women the right to vote, three prominent women were elected to the city council. Elected from the first ward was Eleanor Offutt, wife of insurance executive Henry Offutt. Her colleague from the second ward was Maria T. Fish, who was married to Dr. Carlos A. Fish, a local physician. Joining them from the third ward was Anne C. Vreeland, widow of publisher Graham Vreeland. None of these women was reelected in 1925. However, Agnes Gaines won a seat representing the second ward and was reelected two years later. In view of the prominent role which women played in benevolent activity, it is hardly surprising that Mrs. Gaines served on the council's charity committee. But she also occupied seats on the police and gas and lights committees as well as the hall committee. In addition, Ethel Wilson

Kentucky suffragist group watches as Governor Morrow signs suffragist amendment in January, 1920.

served in the appointive position of city treasurer for most of the decade. Her appointment, along with the election of four women to the city council, symbolized the new role of women in American politics.

A symbolic event of an entirely different nature occurred on the early morning of February 23, 1929, when fire swept through the upper stories of the old State Executive Building immediately adjacent to the old state capitol. The alarm was sounded about 1:05 o'clock by police officer David Reagan. Within twenty-five minutes the second and third floors had been completely gutted and flames were shooting through the roof. With aid from the state reformatory fire department and some twenty-one inmates, the Frankfort Fire Department struggled valiantly to control the blaze. Except for preventing the inferno from engulfing the old capitol, however, their exertions were fruitless. Total damages amounted to at least $200,000, including the destruction of valuable records and drawings owned by the State Highway Commission and the State Geological Department, which had their headquarters in the building. Only the highway commission auditor's books and a collection of recent highway and bridge drawings, stored in four newly purchased, fireproof safes, survived the blaze.

While the highway commission and geological department settled into temporary headquarters scattered throughout the core of the city, the State Sinking Fund Commission began contemplating the highway commission's future location. At first it appeared that the offices might be reassembled in Lexington, which made a strong bid for the agency. But within just three days after the fire, the sinking fund commission authorized the expenditure of $25,000 for the construction of a one-story brick building on a vacant lot adjacent to a local state garage. The new structure would serve as temporary offices until adequate permanent quarters could be secured. It was clear, however, that the highway commission would remain in the capital, a decision hailed by the *State Journal* as "a victory for Frankfort of good sense over pure commercialism." Instrumental in influencing the sinking fund commission's decision was chamber of commerce President Edmund W. Taylor, who, after more than a decade of involvement in local industrial development efforts, recognized that state government was still Frankfort's most important business and chief reason for existence.

Not surprisingly, one of the first public announcements that the highway agency would remain in the capital came at a regular meeting of the Frankfort Rotary Club. Organized in the early 1920s, the Rotary Club gave local business and professional men an opportunity to assemble for weekly rounds of food, fun, and fellowship, as well as to organize occasional community service programs. More importantly, like brother clubs around the world, it nurtured the image of the businessman as a builder, a doer, a dreamer who was forever seeking new and imaginative ways to employ his boundless energy for the benefit of his community. But this service ethic was hardly the monopoly of the Rotarians. By mid-decade it was equally apparent in the Lions Club and Kiwanis Club. Nor was it possessed solely by men. The Women's Club of Frankfort had espoused a similar ethic for years. During the 1920s the Kentucky Federation of Women's Clubs established its headquarters in the capital, while the Frankfort Business and Professional Women's Club attracted its membership from the growing numbers of women working outside the home.

Service clubs were among the many additions to Franklin County's expanding organizational, social, and cultural life during the 1920s. World War I veterans established the Frankfort Post of the American Legion. In 1923 several prominent black citizens, including Dr. E. E. Underwood, organized the Citizens Mutual Savings Association, a mutual benefit group, whose purposes were to encourage thrift, instill the habit of saving, promote industry, and establish unity and prestige among its members. Representing the particular interests of retail businessmen was the Retail Merchants Association. Reflecting a considerably different economic position were the carpenter's and shoemaker's unions, which worked to improve the wages and working conditions of their members.

Franklin Countians took pride in their recreational opportunities. The Kentucky River, Elkhorn Creek, and other streams, frequently stocked with black bass and other game species by the State Game and Fish Commission, provided excellent fishing. The river also was favored by boaters and swimmers. One of the county's most popular acquatic playgrounds was the Mayflower Hotel and Cabins, situated near Swallowfield at the junction of the Kentucky River and Elkhorn Creek. For those who preferred their recreation on dry land, there were the Frankfort Gun Club, which offered trap shooting, and the Frankfort Tennis Club, whose courts testified to the sport's growing pop-

Mayflower Hotel near Swallowfield at the junction of the Kentucky River and Elkhorn Creek.

ularity during the 1920s. Meanwhile, the Frankfort Baseball Club played its games at Glenwood Park in Thorn Hill. Another popular sports facility was Sower Athletic Field, which hosted many of Frankfort High School's sports events. Built at a cost of $12,000, it was located on the north side of Benson Avenue west of Kentucky Avenue in Bellepoint. Finally, the Hoge-Montgomery Company, employing a tactic used by many companies to keep their workers happy, established an employee athletic field and clubhouse near the plant between downtown and Thorn Hill.

The technological innovations perfected during the 1920s substantially broadened cultural and entertainment choices. Perhaps nothing changed home entertainment more radically than the radio. Beginning with the primitive crystal and headphone sets of 1920, the broadcasting industry brought everything from "Barney Google" and Rudy Vallee to Beethoven and Graham McNamee into the American living room. As L. C. (Church) Hughes, who grew up in Woodlake, recalled more than a half-century later, "Our family was the first to have a radio" back in 1920. "All the sets in those days only had headphones. We would take one head set and remove each earpiece, thereby making two listening devices." With "this little one-tube set" the Church family "used to pull in stations all over the U.S. . . ., getting as far west as Kansas City."

The 1920s also witnessed the flowering of motion pictures as a popular entertainment form. In Frankfort the Capital Theatre management installed projection equipment and alternated movies with legitimate stage plays and other productions before eventually switching entirely to motion pictures. The first house devoted exclusively to movies was the Grand Theatre at 310 St. Clair Street. Owned by William Pattie, the Grand had been operated as a legitimate stage for some years before World War I. During the 1920s, with assistance from Louis LeCompte, Pattie converted the house for use as a mo-

Dance Boat of Charles Armstrong being pushed by the *Helen M.*

tion picture theatre. Apparently the technical expert of the project, LeCompte built and installed the turntables, amplifier system, pick-up arms, and all of the wiring which extended from the projection room to the speakers behind the screen. According to Church Hughes, "It worked beautifully." For years thereafter, the Capital and the Grand were Frankfort's leading movie houses. On Saturday morning children flocked in to see matinees featuring western idols such as Tom Mix and Buck Jones. The older set, meanwhile, spent many an evening viewing the comedies of Charlie Chaplin and Buster Keaton, the romances of Douglas Fairbanks and Mary Pickford, and the steamy affairs of Gloria Swanson or Clara Bow, the "It Girl." Whatever the titles or the players, the movies brought a new cultural perspective to this capital on the Kentucky.

Dancing was another favorite pastime, especially among young adults. "We danced in Sower Hall on the third floor . . . , the Capital Hotel ballroom, the Hoge-Montgomery Clubhouse . . . and on the excursion boat *Summer Girl*," which plied the Kentucky River during the summer, Herbert G. Jackson recalled decades later. Most dances were conducted on an admission fee basis. But there were hop clubs in Frankfort and other nearby cities such as Paris, Georgetown, Versailles, Eminence, and Shelbyville which held their own dances and invited the other clubs. "Very few weeks went by when there wasn't a dance someplace," Jackson remembered, "and you almost always saw the same people at any place." These dances were nearly always formal, "and it made a pretty sight with the girls in long dresses and the boys in tuxedos."

The automobile played an important role in the popularity of dancing and other forms of youthful entertainment. As Jackson explained, "the big problem was finding a ride for you and your date to the out-of-town dances. Anyone who had a car always had all it would carry, many times with folks sitting

Maypole Dance, Holmes St. School in 1926.

on the others' laps." The automobile also enabled young people to take in the big bands. Every year Benny Goodman, Guy Lombardo, Cab Calloway, Count Basie, and other top band leaders took their organizations on national tours. Frequently scheduled were one-night stands at Iroquois Gardens and Fontaine Ferry in Louisville, Castle Farms and Coney Island in Cincinnati, and Joyland Park in Lexington. The audiences invariably included several carloads of enthusiastic dancers and jazz lovers from Franklin County.

Another favorite musical organization among capital residents was the Frankfort High School Band. In 1929 the chamber of commerce congratulated the local ensemble for being "one of the best high school bands in the South" and noted that it already was heavily booked for county fairs throughout Kentucky. Along with the athletic and debate teams, the band was just one of several extracurricular activities which made the school a subject of fierce pride among the local populace. Reinforcing that pride was the handsome new Frankfort High School building at Fourth and Shelby Streets, completed in 1925 at a cost of $125,000. The 1920s were in fact a decade of considerable progress in all areas of local education. In 1922, during the pastorage of Father Edward G. Klosterman, the Church of the Good Shepherd reopened its parish high school, which had been closed shortly after the church purchased it, along with the elementary school, from the Sisters of Charity of Nazareth in 1917.

Frankfort High School

In the realm of higher education, the former State Normal School, by now known as the Kentucky Normal and Industrial Institute, had become a major educational and economic force in Frankfort. In a 1927 address to the chamber of commerce, President G. P. Russell reported that his school had reached a capacity enrollment of 284 students and was pumping over a quarter of a million dollars into the local economy. Unfortunately, the school also was the victim of one of the decade's most tragic events when fire swept through the women's dormitory in early December 1926. At least two young women died and several more were injured jumping from upper-story windows to escape the flames.

Despite this tragedy, the pride of accomplishment evident in President Russell's report to the chamber suggested that the booster spirit had come to pervade all sectors of the community, even an institution whose very existence testified to the indignities of segregation and discrimination. Beneath the veneer of official optimism, however, the ravages of economic dry rot were beginning to take their toll in Franklin County. The continuing depression in agriculture eroded the purchasing power upon which small retail businesses depended for their livelihood. In late 1928 the proprietor of a leading Frankfort dry goods store wrote to his son, who was away at college, that "business has not shown any signs of improvement since Hoover has been elected." As the new year matured, his hope that business would pick up proved increasingly fleeting.

In the face of a growing number of trouble signs, however, the dizzying upward spiral of the stock market continued to give optimists reason for confidence. On October 30, 1929, the *State Journal* read: "Stock Sale Largest in Exchange History." During the following days the paper's front page regularly documented the market's ups and downs, and the editorial page featured occasional jibes at the behavior of brokers. But the falling stock prices apparently failed to strike any alarms at the editorial desk. On November 16, less than three weeks after the crash began, the editors admitted that "there is a 'mystery' in further slumps," but they reaffirmed their belief that "the condition of the country's business is all right and that the stock market will come back into shape."

At first such confidence appeared warranted. Little if anything seemed different as 1930 dawned. Indeed, officials at the chamber of commerce expected the new year to be even better than the one just ended. But the failure of the Kentucky Cement Corporation to make its appearance, the gradual deterioration of retail sales, and the accelerating decline of the national economy soon made it clear that rough times lay ahead.

HERMITAGE DISTILLERY, 1933.

11

A Generation of Crisis

NO OTHER GENERATION in Franklin County's history endured such a sustained period of hardship as that which lived from 1930 to 1945. Between the stock market crash and the surrender of Japan, Franklin Countians suffered a devastating drought, the severest depression in American history, the ravages of the 1937 flood, and the shortages and sorrows of World War II. In spite of the privations, the citizens persevered. By the end of the war Frankfort and Franklin County stood on the brink of the greatest period of growth and progress in their history.

Few residents could have anticipated, however, the magnitude of the crises ahead as the 1930s began. Still imbued with the optimism which pervaded the 1920s, most local businessmen considered the crash nothing more than a temporary and much needed corrective for an overheated market. Reinforcing their optimism were developments such as the announcement in late January 1930 by Harry A. Gretter, secretary of the Frankfort Chamber of Commerce, that the Franklin County Fiscal Court had agreed to assist the chamber in its efforts to obtain a municipal airport. Early in February, the chamber executive declared emphatically that "Frankfort has secured an airport." The facility was to be built on a seventy-acre tract located about four miles from the city on Versailles Pike near the Frankfort Country Club. By early September, however, the time scheduled for the airport to begin operations, Franklin County already was engulfed fully in its first major emergency.

The crisis began silently as the spring showers and thunderstorms which normally watered the fields, pastures, and tobacco patches failed to come. As spring turned to summer, crops started to wilt, and it was apparent that Franklin County and the rest of Kentucky were in the grip of a drought which stretched horizontally across the nation's midsection from Virginia and Maryland to Arkansas and Missouri. By early August the rain shortage had reached disastrous proportions. County Agent Robert M. Heath reported that only about 15 percent of the county's corn and hay crops had survived. Local livestock farmers would need an additional 5,000 tons of hay and from 20,000 to 25,000 bushels of corn and other grains from outside sources to make up the deficit, he added. Among the hardest hit farmers were those around Switzer, Peak's Mill, Polsgrove Landing, Elmville, Swallowfield, Bald Knob, Bailey's Mill, Bloomington, and Benson. Things were only slightly better in the extreme southern part of the county, where showers during the second week of August relieved some of the distress.

As the drought deepened in severity, all sections of the community mobilized to relieve the suffering. The Frankfort Lions Club joined with the chamber of commerce and the fiscal court in sending water trucks into the county to fill cisterns and to supply drinking and stock water for farmers. On August 15, at the request of the secretary of agriculture and the American National Red Cross, representatives from a broad range of community organizations met at the chamber of commerce office to discuss strategies for combating the emergency. After much debate, James B. O'Rear, an official of the Frankfort & Cincinnati Railroad, moved successfully that an advisory committee chaired by County Agent Heath and composed of one representative of each interested organization, be appointed to survey the situation and to formulate a relief plan. Meanwhile, Governor Flem Sampson established his own State Drought Relief Committee to coordinate the work of similar local committees across the Commonwealth. By the end of the month, Heath's committee had divided the county into twenty-four districts and had appointed teams to conduct a house-to-house canvass to gather information necessary for drought relief planning.

Within a week the survey teams had completed their work. Meanwhile, Harry Volz, chairman of the State Drought Relief Committee, had recommended that official county drought relief committees be established in each drought-stricken county. Hence, in early September County Judge James H. Polsgrove disbanded the advisory committee and replaced it with a broadly based Franklin County Drought Relief Committee. Selected to chair the eighteen-member body was Howard Black, a local farmer. Other members included chamber Secretary H. A. Gretter, County Agent Heath, Judge Polsgrove, and Frank Kavanaugh and Elizabeth Herman, both representing the Red Cross. Among other organizations and interests represented were the Lions Club, Rotary Club, American Legion, and the Frankfort & Cincinnati Railroad.

Over the next four months the drought relief committee effectively coordinated activities to reduce the suffering created by the water shortage. Working out of the chamber of commerce office in the Capital Hotel, the committee collected and reviewed applications for water and arranged for the delivery of tank car after tank car of the precious liquid to parched farm neighborhoods throughout the county. So effective were the committee's efforts that a month after its formation, Gretter and Heath traveled to Cynthiana to discuss with Harrison County farmers how they might organize a similar body. But in the final analysis, it was not the committee's work but the arrival of winter and spring rains that eventually ended the crisis.

The end of the drought did not appreciably improve conditions in rural Franklin County. Indeed, the dry spell compounded the agricultural depression of the 1920s. By 1931 local farmers were beginning to feel the brunt of a new depression, which would take them even lower into the economic doldrums. After a very modest increase during the second half of the previous decade, the number of farms dropped from 1,598 in 1930 to 1,512 in 1935. At the same time, 3,805 acres were removed from cultivation, which reduced total farmland from 123,245 to 119,440 acres. Especially hard hit were farmers who operated between ten and forty-nine acres. During the first half of the decade approximately 18 percent of all farmers cultivating between ten and nineteen acres, and 25 percent of those operating between twenty and forty-nine acres abandoned agriculture for other pursuits.

Neither were the depression's effects limited to those who gave up. Farmers who remained in business suffered severe losses in the value of land, buildings, and machinery. During the first five years of the decade, Franklin County farms lost a third of their value, declining from $8.8 million in 1930 to less than $6 million five years later. The value of the average farm fell from $5,534 to $3,947, while the value of farmland dropped from nearly $72 to less than $50 an acre.

The impact of the depression upon agricultural production during the first half of the decade was mixed. Cereal grain harvests actually increased between 1929 and 1934, with corn production advancing from 216,473 to 226,500 bushels, wheat from 12,132 to 35,433 bushels, and barley from 5,596 to 8,769 bushels. While these improvements appear quite remarkable in light of the depression, it must be remembered that by 1934 many of Kentucky's distilleries and breweries were back in operation, creating a renewed demand for all three grains. More clearly indicative of the condition of the rural economy during the depression are the production figures for commodities not heavily consumed in local alcoholic beverage industries. Production of oats fell from an already low 2,670 bushels in 1929 to 860 bushels five years later. Rye production dipped only slightly, from 2,144 to 2,100 bushels, but hay and forage production dropped from 12,244 to 10,113 tons, Irish potatoes from 14,750 to 6,800 bushels, and sweet potatoes from 977 to 491 bushels during the same period.

The greatest disaster occurred in tobacco. As late as 1930, after the collapse of the Burley Tobacco Growers Cooperative Association, Franklin County farmers still raised over 3.7 million pounds of leaf on 5,632 acres of land. But as the depression deepened and prices fell, more and more farmers halted production. By 1935, in their efforts to raise prices, they had removed nearly 46 percent of their land from cultivation. In the process the 1935 crop dropped to less than 2.5 million pounds.

Things were equally uncertain for livestock farmers. In response to falling prices and declining demand, farmers slashed production of all species. During 1934 the market began to stabilize and demand increased. As a result, farmers in many counties expanded their herds. But cautious Franklin County

Standard Oil Company, Second and Conway Streets. The station and house, used for apartments, were owned by Harry Gretter.

farmers appear to have resisted this trend. Horse breeders reduced their inventories from an already low figure of 2,869 head in 1930 to a minuscule 2,284 animals in 1935. Swine farmers cut their inventories from 6,014 to 3,586 head during the same period.

Kentucky farmers continued to supply a goodly number of spring lambs to the affluent Eastern and Great Lakes markets. But the spring lamb market could not consume the entire production of local sheep farms. Consequently, the county's sheep and lamb population fell from 24,392 head in 1930 to 16,259 head in 1935. Perhaps the most optimistic picture appeared in the cattle figures. Reflecting the realities of the market, cattle farmers cut their herds from 9,441 to 7,856 head during the first half of the decade. However, their inventory of cows and heifers two years old and over increased from 4,428 to 4,523, suggesting that farmers remained ready to increase production as soon as demand improved.

Farmers were not alone in facing the problem of sliding demand and prices. By mid-1930 local merchants and shopkeepers had begun to feel the crunch. As sales declined, many hard-pressed merchants found it necessary to lay off clerks and other personnel. Often the employees who survived had to take wage cuts. A few long-established businesses suffered bankruptcy, and some proprietors incorporated to protect their homes and other personal and family assets in case the weakening economy forced them into bankruptcy.

Despite the hardship, the vast majority of local enterprises survived. Nevertheless, some three dozen or more businesses closed their doors between 1928 and the inauguration of Franklin D. Roosevelt as president of the United States. Among the businesses which suffered most heavily were grocery stores. By mid-1932, twenty-one of the fifty-two grocers in business in 1928 had shut down. The depression also was a baneful experience for auto-related businesses. One of the major casualties was the Lehrman Motor Company, a car dealership located at 409 Ann Street. Nor were dealers the only sector of the auto market to suffer. Both Monroe's Auto Repair Service and Lewis Rent-A-Ford, which shared quarters at 103 East Main Street, closed their doors, as did the Main Street Garage at 111 East Main and M. G. Sullivan's Repair Service at 202 West Second.

For M. G. Sullivan the depression inflicted a double blow, as his building supply company at 152 East Clinton also went out of business. Three downtown men and boys' clothing stores closed—the Busy Bee Store at 211 West Broadway; Ferd Jacob's Store at 327 St. Clair Street; and Max Rosenstein's Sons Company at 321 St. Clair. Other commercial enterprises that went out of business included Hulette's Confectionery, 223 Grace Avenue, and the Kenney Furniture Company, at the southwest corner of Wilkinson and Clinton streets.

Merchants tried numerous measures to generate demand and bolster community confidence. In 1930, working through the chamber of commerce, they initiated a mammoth downtown Christmas lighting and window-showing program. In an effort to draw window shoppers into the stores, merchants were asked to illuminate their windows and brighten their displays "so that the popular feminine sport of window shopping, especially heavy during the Christmastime, will not be hindered by any lack of sufficient lighting at night." Monetary prizes went to the stores having the best lighting and the best window displays. The program commenced with a parade. Led by Santa Claus and the Frankfort High School band, the 1930 parade included 260 cars and floats. It began on Capitol Avenue in South Frankfort, proceeded across the St. Clair Street Bridge, and wound along St. Clair, Main, High, and Broadway streets before finally terminating at Main and Wilkinson streets. The event proved so successful in raising community spirits that it continued for several more years.

Although the Christmas lighting program had a salutary impact upon seasonal feelings, it evidently generated little sustained sales growth. In the fall of 1932, having concluded that a new approach was necessary, several prominent retailers created the Frankfort Merchants' Vigilance Board. Headed by an executive committee composed of David Davis, Murray Scott, and Fayette Crutcher, the board's expressed purpose was "to foster local prosperity" by encouraging area residents to "buy locally." The board made every effort to assure the potential customers that they could "buy locally and at the same prices, the type of goods, and articles which are offtimes [sic] bought in other communities than Frankfort."

The organization spent weeks planning its campaign. To guarantee that its claims were genuine, the board dispatched a "vigilance committee" to surrounding towns where they surveyed the prices and quality of merchandise available at similar, competing stores. Joining Davis and Scott on the vigilance committee were John B. Sower, Orville Harrod, Cecil Farmer, Horatio Mason, Paul Meagher, and Hugh Hudson. Once having determined the validity of its claims, the board launched its six-weeks "buy locally" campaign in mid-October.

Like the Christmas lighting program, the drive began with a gigantic parade. A half-hour before the parade began, a trumpet blast gave merchants the signal to unveil new window displays, while "gaily-decorated light streamers strung across the principal streets were illuminated to lend a holiday appearance and a spirit of optimism to the occasion." After the parade the crowd converged on the courthouse where Mayor T. E. Kenney, County Judge James H. Polsgrove, and chamber of commerce President Orville Harrod stressed the importance of patronizing local merchants. "The blessings of prosperity might as well start in Frankfort as in any other place," Judge Polsgrove remarked. During the weeks that followed, vigilance committees continued to visit stores in other communities and to compare their merchandise and prices with those in Frankfort. Serving as headquarters for the campaign was a large display booth located in front of the courthouse. Designed in the shape of an English cottage, the booth contained display rooms where merchants could show their wares to the public. Presentations changed every two days to increase public awareness of the range of goods available from local merchants.

Manufacturers, too, felt the impact of the depression. By 1932 such enterprises as the Frankfort Table Company, the Frankfort Baking Company, and the Standard Bakery had gone out of business. A short time later the Brown-Irion Furniture Company, A. A. Wallace & Sons auto body manufacturing company, and the Hoge-Montgomery Shoe Company had failed as well, throwing hundreds of employees out of work.

While merchants employed a variety of promotional techniques to stimulate sales, they joined with the city's industrial leadership to rebuild the community's manufacturing base. A major break came in the spring of 1931 when officials at the chamber of commerce learned that a small Indianapolis firm, the Union Underwear Company, was considering a relocation. Chamber President Orville Harrod immediately recruited a committee which traveled to the Indiana capital to talk with the company's owner, Jacob A. Goldfarb, about his capital, labor, and space needs for a new plant. The meeting went well, and a short time later Goldfarb visited Frankfort to inspect prospective plant sites. Favorably impressed with the community but unable to find a suitable existing facility, Goldfarb expressed his interest in moving to Frankfort if the city could raise the money necessary to build an adequate plant. The chamber accepted the challenge, and by early June it had obtained pledges of approximately $35,000 toward the estimated $50,000 needed to begin construction.

Convinced that Frankfort's business community was commited to the project, Goldfarb signed a contract in early July agreeing to move his company to the capital. A week after the contract signing six local businessmen—Orville R. Harrod, Thomas P. Rogers, J. M. Perkins, Bowman S. Gaines, W. J. Hulette, and Greene R. Lyons—incorporated the Frankfort Industrial Foundation. Harrod was elected president. Capitalized at $50,000, the foundation served as a holding company to raise the necessary capital, purchase land, and oversee construction for new industrial development in Franklin County. Demonstrating the broad-based community support for the Union Underwear project, sixty-four individuals and companies already had pledged anywhere from $100 to $2,500 in stock subscriptions in the Frankfort Industrial Foundation.

Selected as the plant site was a tract located just outside the city limits on Holmes Street near the railroad tracks. The foundation paid $800 for the land, and the seller immediately invested half the proceeds in foundation stock. Construction began in October 1931 and continued through the winter, despite problems with mud, snow, and cold. As the completion date neared, scores of Franklin County's more than five hundred unemployed citizens began filling out job applications for Union Underwear. The plant opened in March 1932 with twenty employees making union suits and men's shorts. Two years later, the company employed some three hundred workers at a total annual payroll of $350,000.

For the hundreds who obtained new jobs the Union Underwear plant was a godsend. But for several hundred other unemployed workers the nightmare of depression remained. Indeed, as the economic crisis deepened it cut across all sectors of local society. When their business and securities soured, numerous members of the community's elite found it necessary to reduce substantially their standard of living. Many laid off their servants. Others, especially widows, took in roomers, and a few converted their spacious homes into apartments in order to support themselves. Along with many middle and working class families, some of the more affluent families also found it necessary to double up in order to make ends meet. Nevertheless, most preserved their sense of dignity and maintained the demeanor which traditionally had befitted their station in the community.

But for hundreds of working class families whose breadwinners were unemployed, survival was fast becoming even more important than dignity. For the chronically poor, such as prisoner families in Craw, widows with young children, and families whose husband and father had deserted, the situation was even worse. Unfortunately, Frankfort's public resources for dealing with the social consequences of a depression of such magnitude were woefully limited and quickly exhausted. As a consequence, responsibility for alleviating the suffering fell upon the churches and other private organizations. Especially active in charitable work were the Salvation Army, Elks Club, YMCA, American Legion, and Hiram Lodge of Masons.

Most churches took care of their own members, often through discretionary funds controlled by the pastor. South Frankfort Presbyterian Church, for example, had a "Love Fund," which was supported by special offerings collected on communion Sundays. Churches also received frequent requests for food, clothing, shelter, and financial assistance from persons outside the parish. To insure that their congregations' limited resources were spent as effectively as possible, the Frankfort Ministerial Association entered into an arrangement with the Salvation Army, which agreed to serve as a clearing house for all church-sponsored relief. Under this agreement, any church which received an aid request checked immediately with the Salvation Army to determine if the person seeking assistance was in genuine need. If the army approved, the church extended the aid directly to those in need.

Certain occasions required extra cooperation. One was Christmas. In November 1930 many of the organizations engaged in charitable activity realized that unless they pooled their efforts, all could be overwhelmed with requests for Christmas food and toys for needy children. The challenge, according to the *State Journal*, was to provide "for the poor at Christmas so as to eliminate any duplication of charity acts and to insure that each family will be provided for, and no needy family . . . suffer because of certain families getting duplicated offerings." In a meeting chaired by chamber of commerce Secretary Harry A. Gretter, some fifteen organizations and churches agreed to sponsor a Community Christmas Tree.

The plan called for church members to turn in the names and addresses of families who might need food baskets or toys. A committee composed of representatives of the Salvation Army and the participating churches screened the names for degree of need. Meanwhile, the Women's Club received donations of clothing, gifts, or money, and the Charity Ball Club gave a dance in December to raise money for the program. A few days before Christmas the cooperating agencies met, reviewed the names of eligible applicants, and accepted the responsibility to provide food baskets for specific families. On Christmas Eve morning, at a beautifully decorated Christmas tree in front of the Capitol Theatre, Santa Claus presented gifts, fruit, candy, and theatre tickets to approximately nine hundred children. That afternoon Christmas food baskets were gathered at the State Armory on High Street and delivered to some 250 eligible families by Boy Scouts. Like the merchants' Christmas illumination, the Community Christmas Tree program gained strong public favor and remained a popular event through the worst years of the depression.

The Community Christmas Tree and the charity work of churches, clubs, and benevolent associations represented a valiant effort on the part of Franklin Countians to take care of their own. By mid-1932, however, it was becoming increasingly clear to President Herbert Hoover and the Congress that local industrial development, charitable, and relief measures were inadequate to combat the worst effects of the depression. In late July Congress passed and President Hoover signed the Relief and Construction Act, which empowered the recently created Reconstruction Finance Corporation to make loans to state and local governments for public works projects of a self-liquidating character.

Funds provided under the legislation began trickling into local communities in early January 1933. Franklin County's allotment was $5,000, which was administered by a County Relief Committee chaired by Judge Polsgrove and whose other members included Mayor Kenney, County Agent Heath, former Secretary of State Emma Guy Cromwell, and chamber President Harrod. Supervising daily operations was the committee's social worker, Mrs. Bowman S. Gaines. With such a small allocation, individual benefits were anything but generous. Program regulations allowed unemployed men selected for the work relief program to be paid $1.50 a day for no more than three days of work each week. Workers were to be paid in script, which could be exchanged for food and clothing, or in some cases, medicine and fuel. Despite the pitiful wages and stringent restrictions, approximately 230 desperate men had applied for work by mid-January. On January 17, nineteen men started to work on various public projects around the county. The same day Mrs. Gaines announced that fifty-six additional applicants had been approved and would be working by the end of the week.

The Franklin County Relief Committee remained a part of the local depression-fighting apparatus after the inauguration of President Franklin Roosevelt. During the spring and summer of 1933 the committee worked through County Agent Heath to develop a community garden program. The core of the project was a large garden at Bellepoint, located on land secured by the Frankfort Ministerial Association. By the end of June, 132 families with 660 persons had gardens in the community plot. In addition, the project assisted individual families to locate and prepare their own garden patches. Viewed by community leaders as a means of promoting self-sufficiency and, ultimately, of replacing the relief system, the garden project produced several thousands of dollars worth of greens, radishes, lettuce, onions, beets, beans, and other vegetables. Production at the Bellepoint Community Garden alone amounted to nearly $4,377, which, said the *State Journal*, "should represent the savings of a like sum in city and county charity work this winter."

An important outgrowth of the Community Garden Project was the Franklin County Homemaking program. In September 1933, Mrs. Mary Mason Scott, Miss Marietta Jackson, and Mrs. Albert Pommering realized that many gardeners would produce surpluses that should be preserved. They took their concern to the Frankfort Altrusa Club. After consulting with the University of Kentucky College of Agriculture, the club hired Ritchie Stevenson of Elizabethtown as home demonstration agent. Beginning in the fall and continuing through the spring of 1934, Miss Stevenson conducted canning demonstrations for 4-H girls and adult homemakers in communities throughout the county. These demonstration meetings stimulated an interest in creating neighborhood homemakers clubs. In May clubs were organized in Peak's Mill, Fox Gap, Flat Creek, Woodlake, and Swallowfield. Two more clubs were started before the end of the year, and some two dozen had been formed by the end of 1945. The homemakers clubs conducted classes on subjects ranging

First Barrel of Old Taylor after prohibition.

from canning to hat-blocking, studied the history of Franklin County, and, in June 1936, established a Saturday morning curb market in Frankfort where members could sell produce, baked goods, handicrafts, and seasonal meats.

Meanwhile, the advent of the New Deal broadened the scope of the Franklin County Relief Committee's responsibilities. During the fall and winter of 1933-34, the committee reviewed and approved hundreds of applications for public works jobs created by funds provided by the Federal Emergency Relief Administration and its subsidiary agency, the Civil Works Administration. It also evaluated road improvements and other proposed work projects before they were submitted to the Kentucky Emergency Relief Administration for its approval.

As the New Deal gathered momentum it brought an array of new programs intended to create jobs, stimulate economic growth, and relieve human suffering. Some of these left permanent, if not always conspicuous, imprints on the local landscape. In 1935 the Public Works Administration (PWA) provided $125,000 for construction of a new dormitory at the Kentucky State Industrial College. Two years later work was completed on the new Second Street School. This neoclassical structure, designed by the firm of L. L. Oberwarth & Son and built by Howell & Goin masonry contractors, was financed with $209,000 from PWA. The Works Progress Administration (WPA) sponsored a variety of projects ranging from drainage, street, and sidewalk construction to the grading and sodding of Sower Athletic Field. New Deal-funded street improvements became especially critical after January 1934 when court-appointed receivers permitted the strike-plagued and financially troubled Kentucky Traction & Terminal Company of Lexington to suspend its streetcar operations at the capital.

For Franklin County's economy, however, the most important consequence of the New Deal was the repeal of prohibition. On November 26, 1933, a special convention assembled in the Kentucky House of Representatives chamber to ratify the Twenty-first Amendment to the Constitution. Less than a month later, enough states had approved the amendment to end the nation's "Noble Experiment." Even before the end of prohibition, potential investors began inquiring into the availability of Franklin County's abandoned distilleries. As early as July 1933 negotiations were underway for the purchase of the old Hermitage Distillery. Two months later Eli Brown and Charles Irion, owners of the recently defunct Brown-Irion Furniture Company, sold the facility to the Allied Brewing and Distilling Company, Inc., of Brooklyn, New York, for $200,000. The new owners, however, intended to use the old plant as a cooperage rather than as a distillery.

Several new distillery firms were incorporated in Franklin County during the months that followed repeal. Some failed to get beyond paper. By 1935, however, five distilleries had reopened or begun new operations. The George T. Stagg Company resumed production at the old O. F. C. Distillery at Leestown. Also reestablished were W. A. Gaines & Company's Old Crow Distillery, one of Stagg's traditional competitors, and the Old Taylor Distillery, located near the Old Crow facility on Glenn's Creek Pike. However, both now were owned by the New York-based National Distillers Products Corporation. The Kennebec Distilling Company, incorporated in early 1935 by John W. Perkins and Dr. Willard Rouse Jillson, both of Frankfort, and Lexingtonian William T. Fowler, was located on Benson Valley Pike northwest of Frankfort. The K. Taylor Distillers Company, Inc. occupied the former Frankfort Distillery at Forks of Elkhorn. In 1941 National Distillers bought the latter company and it became the Old Grand Dad Distillery.

Old Taylor Distillery. Barbecue at the Spring House in the 1930's.

Partially as a result of the New Deal, Franklin County began to experience a substantial recovery by mid-1935. Signs of economic revival appeared as early as the previous Christmas, when local stores experienced their best year since 1929. As the *State Journal* noted, "Stores were packed and jammed each . . . day and night as the Yule season neared and stores were kept open after the supper hour. Money appeared as if by magic and the realization suddenly dawned that a new era of confidence and prosperity was at hand." Confidence mounted early in the new year when tobacco farmers, now receiving higher prices as a result of the production quotas established under the Tobacco Control Act of 1934, started making purchases which they had postponed during the lean years. The farmers' new willingness to spend extended the holiday mercantile boom and encouraged many merchants to expand the size and variety of their merchandise inventories and to remodel and redecorate their stores in hope of attracting new customers.

Meanwhile, the reopening of the distilleries triggered a resurgence in the industrial economy. By early 1935 the Stagg Distillery alone employed 700 workers and stood as the county's largest employer. Ranking second with 600 workers was the Union Underwear Company. These two firms accounted for a weekly payroll of $18,000. The other four distilleries, still in a process of construction and remodeling, already employed approximately a hundred persons, with more expected on the employment rolls in the near future. Several smaller companies reported increases of 500 to 900 percent in the size of their work forces. A major consequence of this industrial recovery was a considerable decrease in the length of the county's relief and unemployment lists.

As winter turned to spring, the combined effects of renewed optimism, economic recovery, and federally insured loans stimulated a new wave of residential and commercial construction. By May 1935 virtually every building tradesman in Frankfort was on the job. Building lots once considered less than choice were bringing good prices. The lumber and building materials business was booming. And the lumber mills were approaching full employment. The construction boom pervaded every part of the city. Bellepoint experienced a housing explosion "unparalleled in that section of Frankfort in the past five years." Capitol Heights, which became a "popular suburban division" during the 1920s witnessed a "mushroom-like growth" as homes sprang up almost overnight and building lots fetched "fantastic prices." Several large residences and duplexes were constructed in South Frankfort, which experienced the city's heaviest construction activity. But Thorn Hill and Arlington Heights were not far behind. Development was particularly heavy along Park Avenue, which was "filling up rapidly with residences on both sides of the street" extending "as far as the garment factory."

Accompanying the community's economic recovery was the further expansion and consolidation of its banking structure. In 1932, at the depth of the depression, Frankfort's five banks had a combined capital and surplus of less than $1.25 million—a drop from $1.3 million four years earlier. The National Branch Bank of Kentucky, headed by H. F. Lindsey, was still the county's largest bank with capital stock, surplus, and undivided profits of $365,000. Ranking well back were Farmers Deposit Bank of Frankfort and State National Bank with assets of about $300,000 each. Capital Trust Company and Peoples State Bank stood fourth and fifth respectively with assets of $175,000 and $100,000.

While more than five thousand American banks failed during the depression, all of Frankfort's survived. As recovery set in, however, the disparity in their strength soon became apparent. The most aggressive institution was Farmers Deposit Bank. By the fall of 1936 it had greatly expanded its capital and other assets. At the stockholders' meeting in late October, the bank went one step further, approving a resolution submitted by President Leslie W. Morris to consolidate with the smaller Capital Trust Company. When the merger was completed, the new Farmers Bank & Capital Trust Company had a capital stock of $700,000 and resources of about $10 million. Farmers Bank moved again in February 1939, this time purchasing the assets of Peoples State Bank. As a result of these consolidations, Farmers Bank & Capital Trust Com-

R. S. Scott Hardware, 311 West Main Street. Local merchant R. S. Scott expressed the frustration of the era by the "Hanging of Mr. Depression" in 1932.

pany was by far the largest financial institution in Franklin County by the end of the depression decade.

Another important development on Frankfort's financial scene was the creation of First Federal Savings and Loan Association. Coming in the wake of the Home Owners Loan Act of 1933, it was organized in September 1934 as the Greater Frankfort Building and Loan Association. It had an initial capital stock of $200,000, and its organizers were Joseph C. Jones, J. B. Brislan, Lambert N. Suppinger, Carl A. Kagin, former Mayor T. E. Kenney, R. S. Scott, H. K. Rogers, W. P. B. Wachtel, and Clayton Fincel. Like its older competitor, the Capital Building and Loan Association, the new association's purpose was to provide a safe, profitable investment instrument which would enable local citizens to save the money necessary to purchase homes. In April 1938, under new provisions of the Home Owners Loan Act, Greater Frankfort reincorporated as First Federal Savings and Loan Association. Under both names, however, with mortgage guarantees and loan insurance programs available through the HOLC and FHA, the association played a major role in channeling capital into the city's construction boom during the second half of the decade.

Although prosperity had begun to reappear by mid-1935, few Franklin Countians were ready to abandon the New Deal and return to the predepression, business-as-usual style of operation. Indeed, the second half of the decade witnessed several major public improvements, most of which were at least partially financed with New Deal monies. One of the first such projects was a long-sought second bridge across the Kentucky River. As early as June 1933

NEW CAPITOL AVENUE BRIDGE IS PROMINENT IN THIS RIVER VIEW OF THE 1930's.

Governor Ruby Laffoon recommended that a span be constructed, possibly at Capitol Avenue. A bridge at this location, he observed, would provide a direct approach from North Frankfort to the capitol, as well as create a strikingly beautiful vista. However, the governor cautioned, the availability of federal funds for the project would depend upon the Commonwealth's ability to match the government money. Given the state's tight budget, the likelihood of its providing the match was limited. Five months later, as the Civil Works Administration prepared to distribute grants to the states, Mayor Kenney, County Judge James H. Polsgrove, Mayor-elect Clarence T. Coleman, and several local business leaders traveled to Louisville to make the city's case for a bridge construction grant.

As Governor Laffoon had anticipated, the application proved futile. But political and civic leaders in the capital remained undaunted. When the General Assembly convened in 1934, bridge advocates persuaded the legislature to authorize construction of a memorial bridge on the site of the existing St. Clair Street span. On August 31, 1935, Laffoon signed an executive order which directed the State Highway Commission to proceed with "all necessary surveys, plans and specifications for the construction of the bridge." At the same time he announced that the commission had submitted an application to the state director of the PWA requesting a grant for 45 percent of the project's $400,000 total cost. A few days later the overjoyed residents of Frankfort expressed their appreciation in a "Governor's Night" celebration which featured a huge parade and a succession of ceremonial tributes.

But Governor Laffoon's bridge plans changed suddenly in mid-November when Modjeski, Masters and Case, Inc., the project's Philadelphia-based engineering consultants, reported that the St. Clair Street location was inadequate for a span with the specifications demanded in the 1934 legislation. As alternatives the engineers advanced two proposals. The first would place the bridge between Shelby Street and Main Street opposite the Capital Hotel. The second choice would situate the span between Shelby Street and Capitol Avenue, where south-bound traffic would empty in either direction onto Second Street. The consultants considered a site directly opposite Capitol Avenue unsatisfactory because of the steep grades of the Main Street approaches. However, the report also indicated that neither location would cost significantly more than the St. Clair Street site. Three days after receiving the engineers' report, Governor Laffoon issued a second executive order authorizing construction at the Shelby Street site. A week later, over the opposition of Shelby Street residents, the chamber of commerce endorsed Laffoon's decision and urged governmental bodies at all levels to move expeditiously to bring the memorial bridge to fruition.

Everything went smoothly at first. In early December the State Highway Commission signed construction contracts which totaled over $226,000. Progress was sidetracked temporarily, however, when Albert B. Chandler succeeded Laffoon as governor the same month. Chandler, though he favored the bridge, disagreed with his predecessor as to its appropriate location. In the spring of 1936 he ordered the allocation of $150,000 from state road funds to the project, which was to be matched by a federal grant. But he also insisted that the span be located on the St. Clair Street site. Like Laffoon, Chandler soon recognized that the St. Clair location was unsuitable. On the other hand, the new chief executive appreciated the Capitol Avenue approach which Modjeski, Masters & Case had disparaged the previous year.

Chandler's persuasive and executive powers triumphed. On June 4, 1938, after five years of political wrangling, Chandler's daughter Mimi snipped a white ribbon and officially opened the War Mothers Memorial Bridge to traffic. The dedication of the modern concrete structure highlighted a day of festivities, including a typically gigantic capital parade and speeches by a host of local and state politicians. In his own remarks Governor Chandler dedicated the bridge to the "Glory of God and the young men who went out with high hopes to fight in battles to protect the lives, liberty, and happiness of the people of Kentucky, and to the memory of the war mothers and their sacrifices."

Before concluding his speech Chandler announced that "in a few days . . . work will be started on Capitol avenue so that it will match the Capitol building and conform with the beauty of the new bridge." Executed in accordance with bids opened a week earlier, the Capitol Avenue project resulted in the construction of ten-foot grass medians which separated traffic traveling in opposite directions between the capitol and the memorial bridge. The $53,698 project, conducted by the Louis des Cognet Company of Lexington, also included reconstruction of curbs and gutters as well as the construction of new sewers.

Although the dedication of the memorial bridge was the highlight of the day, it was not the final event. When the dedication ceremonies ended, the crowd moved north from the speakers' stand at Capitol between Second and Third streets to the site of the old state penitentiary, most of which already had been demolished. There Chandler turned the first spade of ground for construction of a new, long-needed State Office Building. Despite the fanfare, the ceremonial ground breaking marked nothing more than a false start. Plans for the ten-story structure, drawn by the University of Kentucky College of Engineering, had been made public in December 1937. But even after the ground breaking, months of financial and legal work remained to be done before construction could begin. Finally, in November 1938 the State Real Estate Board authorized the highway department to receive construction bids for the new edifice. Bids were opened in mid-January 1939, with the award going to the Skilton Construction Company of Louisville. Skilton's low bid was $450,583. However, $216,000 already had been expended on foundation work, most of the materials having come in the form of brick and stone from the old penitentiary. Since the legislature had appropriated only $500,000 for the building, Governor Chandler found it necessary to shift money from emergency funds by executive order. Nevertheless, construction on the main structure began in late January. After more than a year of work, most of the Commonwealth's nonelective executive departments moved into their new quarters in early 1941.

Another of the New Deal's long-term contributions was the city's slum clearance and public housing program. The anticipated source of financing was the Public Works Administration's Housing Division, which operated a loan and grant program for such purposes. In January 1937, under the authority of slum clearance legislation recently enacted by the General Assembly, the city council approved creation of the Frankfort Municipal Housing Commission. Later in the month Mayor Clarence T. Coleman appointed businessmen J. W. Brooker, J. M. Perkins, J. Bacon Blanton, and Fred Sutterlin as members of the commission. The mayor assumed the ex-officio position of chairman. Under Coleman's leadership the commission prepared and submitted an application for approximately $190,000 in slum clearance funds from the PWA.

The State Office Building

Two months later the city council approved an application for federal aid for the construction of a low-rent housing project. The application was part of a plan under which the demolition and clearance of a section of Craw in the vicinity of Wilkinson and Broadway would be coupled with construction of a public housing project further to the north near Commissioner Blanton's estate. This site was selected because the water levels of the 1937 flood indicated that it was safe from inundation. By the same token, PWA regulations prohibited the construction of federally sponsored housing in flood plains such as Craw, which was to be made into a park.

As with many other federal programs, progress on public housing was slow. One impediment was a comprehensive reorganization of the nation's public housing bureaucracy, which resulted from passage of the National Housing Act in September 1937. This legislation abolished the PWA Housing Division and replaced it with the United States Housing Authority. In February 1938 the city finally received notification from the USHA that $450,000 had been allotted for a low-rent housing project and that one-tenth of the cost would have to be provided from local sources. One distillery pledged $20,000 toward the local match.

On September 1, USHA officials announced approval of a grant to the city for the construction of 100 units of public housing. Eighty-five apartments were to be reserved for white families, while the remaining fifteen would house blacks. The following August, USHA approved bids of approximately $258,313 for the construction of the project, which now had been designated Leestown Terrace. Receiving the general contract was the George H. Rommell Company, Inc., of Louisville. Construction began a few weeks later, and work was completed in December 1940.

Although New Deal projects such as the War Mothers Memorial Bridge, the State Office Building, and Leestown Terrace remain as physical reminders of the depression, the era was not without cause for celebration. Oblivious to

At left, Sesquicentennial Queen Miss Patricia O'Rear with Governor A.B. Chandler. At right, the Court of Honor with Miss O'Rear and some of her attendants.

Mrs. Jouett Taylor Cannon

the city's economic situation, the inexorable movement of time dictated that Frankfort commemorate its sesquincentennial in October 1936. Planning for the celebration began in midsummer under the directior of a committee headed by Mayor Coleman. Working closely with the committee were Mrs. Jouett Taylor Cannon, secretary of the Kentucky Historical Society, and Mrs. Eleanor Hume Offutt, who chaired the celebration's women's committee. President Orville R. Harrod pledged the full support of the chamber of commerce, and the *State Journal* prepared a special sesquicentennial edition which featured highlights of the city's history, biographical tributes to numerous political and business figures, and sketches of many local businesses.

The Frankfort Sesquicentennial Celebration, which began on Sunday, October 4, and continued for two more days, was one of the most festive occasions ever witnessed by residents of a city where parades and other celebrations were a frequent occurrence. Sunday's festivities began with regular morning worship services in which pastors shaped their sermons around some historical subject. Registration also began for thousands of visitors for whom the sesquicentennial was a homecoming event. That evening scores gathered on the old capitol lawn for a joint worship.

On Monday Governor A. B. Chandler crowned Miss Patricia O'Rear, a University of Kentucky senior, as sesquicentennial queen. After the coronation, the governor's children joined local youngsters for a parade led by the Frankfort High School band. Afternoon events included power boat races on the Kentucky River. The highlight of the day was the first of two performances of a historical pageant which depicted key events in the city's development. The presentation featured 500 men, women, and children. The climax of the day was a gigantic fireworks display. The closing day opened with a grand parade along streets lined with 25,000 viewers. More than twenty floats lent color to the event. Enthusiasm was so intense that a sudden downpour which drenched Governor and Mrs. Chandler and Mayor and Mrs. Coleman, who were riding in an open car, failed to disperse the crowd. The day concluded with a repetition of the historical pageant.

The mood of celebration barely had subsided when Frankfort suffered the worst flood in its history. On Wednesday, January 6, 1937, rain began falling up and down the Ohio River. Intermittent downpours, sometimes exceeding three inches, continued for more than two weeks. At first flood-hardened Frankfort residents took little notice of the gradually rising waters. The situation did not even merit front page coverage until January 19, when the *State Journal* reported "All Ky. Streams at Flood Stage and Still Rising." Early that morning the Kentucky River crested at 33.9 feet, and a few residents had to be evacuated from Craw and Bellepoint. It appeared at the moment, however, that the worst might be over. As the weather turned colder the rain stopped, and during the evening of the nineteenth the river began to recede. By the next morning it had dropped to 31.4 feet.

But the decline in the water level was indeed only momentary. As the rains resumed and flood plains on the upper Ohio approached capacity, the Kentucky and other tributaries began to rise again. On the morning of the twenty-second the river reached a record crest of 45 feet, exceeding the old mark of 42.8 feet set in 1883. The *State Journal* noted the event in a double banner headline: "Unprecedented Flood in Height and Suddenness Sweeps Frankfort." Four days later the flood reached its highest point at 47.2 feet.

The sudden increase in the water level created a full-scale emergency. By the twenty-second the rampaging waters had stopped transportation, driven more than two thousand people from their homes, and inflicted thousands of dollars worth of property damage. Schools were closed; waters backing through the sewers flooded business houses and restaurants along Broadway and St. Clair streets; and one woman died from exhaustion while being taken to safety in a taxicab. On January 23 the Frankfort Water Company cut off service to conserve water in case of fire. Twenty-four hours later, the city had been virtually bisected as water covered the approaches of the St. Clair Street Bridge. Four-fifths of the city now lay under water, and 1,500 residents of the Bellepoint area were inaccessible except by boat. On January 25 the state reformatory was evacuated in an operation personally supervised by Governor Chandler.

Hundreds of people from all walks of life pitched in to fight the flood and to relieve the suffering of its victims. On January 22 local officials organized a general committee, chaired by County Judge L. Boone Hamilton, to work with the Red Cross in coordinating relief efforts. Mayor Coleman took charge of the food and housing committee, while more than a dozen local physicians joined a medical subcommittee. The next day state troopers were assigned to assist in floor relief, and on the twenty-fourth National Guardsmen arrived to patrol the capitol. Meanwhile, trucks loaded with clothing, milk, bedding,

VIEWS OF THE 1937 FLOOD

Top: St. Clair Street, *Middle:* St. Clair from Broadway, *Bottom:* Ann & Broadway

fresh water, typhoid vaccine, and other supplies began arriving from Lexington. First Methodist Church began filling up with clothing and other supplies which poured in from surrounding communities, and First Christian Church established a feeding center for refugees in its community annex. Boy Scouts seemed to be almost everywhere running errands and carrying messages.

As the rains came to an end, the flood waters receded quickly after reaching their peak on the twenty-fifth. By midnight the following day the level had dropped to 41.7 feet, and downtown businesses, now drained of three feet of water, reopened on the twenty-eighth. But weeks of hard work lay ahead as the city set about the tasks of assessing damages and readying homes and businesses for reoccupancy. To expedite the process, Judge Hamilton appointed city and magisterial district committees to survey the damages and develop cost estimates needed to justify requests for federal disaster assistance. Within a few days it was determined that 1,500 homes had been damaged. More than 600 of these were unfit for rehabitation. In late February Isaac Kennedy, the city assessor, estimated damage in the city at nearly $700,000, not counting state property.

Meanwhile, the work of reconstruction moved ahead. Transportation returned to normal on the twenty-eighth and water and gas services had been restored by the beginning of February. WPA workers, using city and county trucks, performed yeoman service in cleaning the city of mud, filth, and debris. The Red Cross registered a constant stream of flood victims to ascertain their needs, while the city health officer checked homes before approving them for reoccupancy. By early February most refugee camps stood deserted and the community resumed a semblance of normality.

But the trauma was not soon forgotten. Chastened by their lack of preparation, the Red Cross and other community leaders now combined forces to perfect a permanent group to deal with floods, tornados, fires, and any other disasters that might hit Franklin County in the future. Officially named the American National Red Cross Disaster Preparedness Relief Committee, the 119-member unit formed itself into nine subcommittees dealing with survey, rescue, medical aid, shelter, food, clothing, transportation, registration, and fund raising. Headed by retired Navy Lieutenant Commander S. I. M. Major III, the committee proved its mettle during a minor flood in early 1939 which necessitated the evacuation of 240 homes.

Despite its destructive force, the 1937 flood failed to blunt either the resurgent population growth which began during the 1920s or the economic recovery which commenced in early 1935. Population trends were particularly significant. While many American communities lost population during the depression decade, Franklin County, with a particularly anomolous exception, experienced widespread population growth. For the county as a whole the number of inhabitants grew from 21,064 in 1930 to 23,308 in 1940, an increase of 2,244 persons, or 10.7 percent. These figures obscure several significant dimensions. The white population advanced from 18,429 to 21,140 persons, an increase of 2,711, or 14.7 percent. This more than offset a 17.5 percent decrease in the black population, which dropped from 2,627 to 2,168 persons.

Perhaps the most important aspect of these numbers, and one which accounts for the major portion of the lost Negro population, is a slight decrease in Frankfort's population. Despite the substantial increase in the number of county residents, the capital's population slipped from 11,626 in 1930 to 11,492 a decade later. Given the city's history of stable population growth—the slight drop during the World War I decade notwithstanding—this phenomenon seems peculiar. Upon closer examination, however, the cause is clear: the abandonment of the state reformatory in 1937 abruptly deprived the city of 2,273 resident inmates. In addition, many prisoner families who occupied homes in Craw undoubtedly left the city when the inmates were transferred to LaGrange. What is remarkable, therefore, is the fact that Frankfort almost made up this loss through natural increase and attraction of new residents. To the extent that the gap was closed, the racial balance favored whites. Indeed, Frankfort's white population increased from 9,413 to 9,812 during the decade, while the number of black inhabitants fell from 2,205 to 1,680. Since a substantial number of the reformatory inmates were black men whose transfer was not made up by new inmigration, the penitentiary's closing alone accounts for a major portion of the county's lost black residents.

Much of the community's new settlement occurred in South Frankfort and Bellepoint and in suburban neighborhoods such as Capitol Heights and Thorn Hill. But urbanization also took the form of new subdivisions developed on raw land. Within the city, Coleman Springs Addition, located between the capitol and Louisville Road north of Capitol Heights, was platted in July 1937. The following May, George D. Kittridge and C. A. Coleman platted Montrose Park Addition on a tract between East Main and the Frankfort & Cincinnati Railroad less than a quarter-mile west of the Kentucky State Industrial College.

Meanwhile, several more subdivisions sprang up outside the city. Crestwood Subdivision was laid out on the north side of East Main opposite Bellview in September 1935. The following April, J. R. Butler initiated development of Norwood Subdivision on a large tract near the southeast corner of East Main and Versailles Pike. Six months later the Moore-Riner Realty Company of Shelbyville platted the A. L. Glass estate, located on the northeast side of Buttimer Hill, in preparation for its sale at public auction. In April 1937, William H. Pickett initiated the first of two small subdivisions on the north side of East Main Street immediately west of and adjacent to Crestwood Subdivision. A brief recession blunted development for about a year. But activity resumed in September 1938 when the owners of a large tract roughly bounded by Versailles Pike, Stevenson Drive, Lincoln Drive, Capitol View Subdivision, Dewey Drive, and Bender Drive platted Franklin Heights. The same month, the Austin Moore Realty Company laid out the Hoge-Montgomery Subdivision on a parcel which lay astride Holmes Street be-

"The Little White House," 121 E. Campbell. Residence of Col. Noel Gaines in 1933.

tween the old Owenton Road and the Frankfort & Cincinnati Railroad east of Meagher Avenue.

A major source of the demand for this new housing was the rapid expansion in government employment generated by the New Deal. By 1940 nearly nine hundred persons, who constituted almost one-fourth of Franklin County's nonagricultural labor force, were employed in government at some level. Some worked in the state and local offices of federal agencies such as the Social Security Administration, Civilian Conservation Corps, Department of Agriculture, Farm Security Administration, Forest Service, Public Roads Administration, and Works Progress Administration. Even more jobs were created in state agencies which had to be expanded or created to administer many of the federally financed programs. By 1940 no fewer than a dozen federal organizations had offices in the capital, and the number of state departments and bureaus had increased to at least thirty-nine, many of which had multiple subdivisions. A substantial number of the appointed officeholders were middle class professional and clerical persons who expected housing commensurate with their status and traditional standard of living. Frankfort's real estate agents, land developers, and home builders were more than willing to accommodate their needs.

Although essentially urban in character, the housing boom accounted for a major portion of the population growth registered in the county's rural magisterial districts. As a result of new suburban growth, Peak's Mill nearly tripled its population and emerged in 1940 as the largest of the four rural districts with 3,427 residents. In the process it pushed Forks of Elkhorn, the only district which actually lost population, into second place with 3,133 inhabitants. At the same time, the population of Bald Knob grew from 1,769 in 1930 to 2,203 in 1940, while Bridgeport's population increased from 2,431 to 3,053. By 1940, moreover, only one-third of Forks of Elkhorn's population and barely 44 percent of Peak's Mill's inhabitants remained on the farm. For all practical purposes, 1940 marked Franklin County's emergence as an urban county, with the majority of residents living in an urban rather than a rural setting.

In addition to stimulating Frankfort's physical expansion, the influx of government workers and the consequent housing boom helped to sustain Franklin County's economic recovery between 1935 and 1940. Regardless of the stimulus, however, all sectors of the economy experienced a substantial degree of recovery. Out in the country the number of farms continued to decline. With New Deal programs such as the Agricultural Adjustment Acts and Soil Conservation and Domestic Allotment Act pushing smaller, less efficient farmers out of business, the total number of farms dropped from 1,512 in 1935 to 1,363 in 1940. At the same time, however, total land available for cultivation increased from 119,440 to 124,188 acres. As operators who farmed more than 100 acres purchased this newly available land, the size of the average farm increased from 79 acres in 1935 to just over 91 acres five years later. In the process local farms regained a major portion of their lost value as the worth

Frankfort Ice & Coal Company, 516–522 W. Main St., in 1932.

of all farmland and buildings, which had stood at $8.8 million in 1930, bounced back from less than $6 million in 1935 to nearly $8.6 million in 1940. The value of machinery and implements showed an even greater improvement, rising from $331,381 in 1930 to $483,944 a decade later.

Yet the recovery was anything but even, as local farmers continued to specialize instead of diversify. Livestock production demonstrated remarkable long-term strength, with 1940 inventories for horses and cattle roughly approximating those of 1930, while hog and sheep populations showed substantial growth over the previous decade. Crop production, however, appears to have been linked even more closely to the fortunes of the liquor, livestock, and tobacco industries. Corn production grew from 226,500 bushels in 1934 to 251,497 bushels in 1939, while barley harvests increased from 8,769 to 16,598 bushels. Similarly, hay and forage production expanded from 10,113 tons in 1934 to 13,846 tons five years later, exceeding in the process the 12,244 ton mark of 1929. On the strength of the new federal allotment program, tobacco output soared from about 2.5 million pounds in 1934 to nearly 4.5 million pounds by the end of the decade. On the other hand, wheat production dropped from 35,433 to 16,809 bushels; and oats, rye, sorghum, and potatoes became virtually insignificant in the county's agricultural sphere.

While agriculture became more and more specialized, commercial businesses offered an ever-widening array of goods and services. As a result of the purchasing power created by hundreds of new government, distillery, and underwear company employees, the number of retail businesses in Franklin County increased from 238 in 1929 to 257 a decade later. Total retail sales in 1939 exceeded $6.8 million. Almost all of the retail growth occurred in Frankfort, where the number of establishments expanded from 174 to 205 during the same period.

By 1940 local residents could shop in a variety of new downtown stores. The Sears, Roebuck & Company store opened at 209 St. Clair Street in 1934. Within a short time it employed twenty people and served as a key mercantile center for residents of adjacent counties as well as for those living in Franklin County. Among the store's eventual neighbors on the block were the Frankfort Music Shop, at 221 St. Clair, and Urdang Bros. furniture store, at 215 St. Clair. Urdang Bros.' competitors included two other new establishments, the Frankfort Furniture Company, at 108 Bridge Street, and M. Simons' Furniture Store, 215 West Broadway. Joining the competition in the pharmaceutical business during the late 1930s were the Frankfort Drug Company, situated at 238 West Main Street, and the Gayle Drug Store, opened by George M. Gayle at 325 Ann Street. In addition, the city boasted a strong and lucrative service sector, which employed 137 persons in fifty-eight establishments ranging from beauty and barber shops to funeral homes. These businesses counted receipts of $356,000 in 1939.

Frankfort Drug Company, 238 West Main, 1934.

While a healthy proliferation in the number of business establishments characterized the commercial recovery, precisely the opposite was true for the community's industrial base. Despite their best efforts, the city's business and civic leaders proved unable to stave off the inexorable process of consolidation which had been eroding the breadth of its industrial foundation for several decades. By the end of 1939 Franklin County had only seventeen manufacturing plants of any significance. With the notable exception of the relatively new Union Underwear Company, most of these produced such traditional local products as whiskey, lumber, quarry materials, hemp twine, and furniture. In addition, production of shoes resumed for a brief time after the Barrett Shoe Company took over the assets of the Hoge-Montgomery Shoe Company, Inc., and moved the equipment to 514-516 Barrett Avenue. The firms which survived the shakeout employed only 1,249 workers, compared to 1,509 similarly employed a decade earlier. However, combined industrial wages increased from $883,930 to $915,000, and the value of production grew from about $4.65 million to nearly $6.7 million during the same period. These figures suggest that the positions of both employers and employees whose concerns survived the depression were on a much sounder footing than they had been a decade earlier.

The recovery which characterized the second half of the 1930s gave Franklin Countians every reason to believe that the 1940s would bring a new age of sustained growth. Reinforcing this view was the completion during 1941 of two road projects which had important economic development ramifications. The opening of a long-planned Thorn Hill and Leestown Road in March 1941 provided a direct connection between two neighborhoods located less than a mile apart but which had been separated historically by the lack of a road. Completed with aid from WPA, the new road created a direct route to the Stagg Distillery for many Thorn Hill residents who previously had to drive some five miles to reach their jobs. Local officials, such as Judge Hamilton and Mayor David D. Smith, considered the new thoroughfare "one of the most important road developments in the county in many years."

Eight months after the Thorn Hill and Leestown Road opened, work was completed on the reconstruction of U.S. Highway 60 between Shelbyville and Frankfort. The $1.5 million project entailed not only an extensive rerouting, but also the straightening and leveling of substantial portions of the once hilly, winding highway. Except for short, unfinished stretches between Lexington and Frankfort and in Boyd County near Ashland, the reopening provided access to and from the capital on a two-lane, concrete surface which stretched 537 miles across the Commonwealth, from Catlettsburg on the Big Sandy River to Wickliffe on the Mississippi.

By the time the new roads were completed, however, Franklin Countians were becoming increasingly preoccupied by affairs in other parts of the world. For several years the *State Journal* and other newspapers had been chronicling the aggressive expansion of Nazi Germany across Europe and of the Japanese empire throughout East Asia. As the Roosevelt administration intensified its commitment to the British war, effort local citizens became steadily more engrossed in national defense preparations. In September 1940 Congress passed the Selective Training and Service Act, which created the first peacetime draft in American history. A month later Edwin K. Suppinger, William H. Pickett, Owen Caplinger, and J. M. Perkins were appointed to the Franklin County Draft Board.

As the prospect of direct American participation in the war deepened, governments at all levels began to wrestle with the possibility of having to defend the United States against direct enemy attack. In the spring of 1941 President Roosevelt established the Office of Civilian Defense and appointed New York City Mayor Fiorello LaGuardia to direct a nationwide civil preparedness program. But County Judge L. Boone Hamilton had anticipated the need for such efforts and in mid-January had appointed the Franklin County Home Defense Commission. Some prominent residents thought the judge was being an alarmist. But when businessman Fred Sutterlin told him "we ought to get ready for the worst," Hamilton forged ahead. By the time LaGuardia assumed office the commission already had surveyed possible air raid shelters within the city; identified and inspected caves which could serve as overflow shelters; designed a pontoon bridge capable of holding ten-ton trucks in case of the destruction of the local bridges; organized first aid and emergency medical services; recruited volunteers for special police, fire, and guard duties; and established mechanisms to coordinate state, county, and city defense efforts. During the months that followed, the commission stockpiled whisky barrels to support the pontoon bridge, stationed aircraft lookouts atop the hills around the city, and organized a women's auxiliary to coordinate first aid and related activities.

Preparedness measures intensified following the Japanese attack on Pearl Harbor on December 7, 1941. At 3:30 p.m. on December 15, only eight days

Judge L. Boone Hamilton

after the attack, traffic on streets packed with Christmas shoppers came to a standstill when an old steamboat whistle screamed an air raid alarm. Although planned for fifteen minutes, the drill lasted a mere five minutes; but the response was overwhelmingly favorable. Intended primarily to determine pedestrian reaction, the drill also halted vehicular movement as motorists immediately pulled into the nearest parking space or stopped their cars at the edge of the business district. Less than two weeks later plans were well under way for the organization of the Women's Defense Corps, a uniformed unit which was "to be trained and disciplined as thoroughly as soldiers in shooting and other work essential to the defense of the capital."

While it eventually became apparent that neither women nor anyone else would have to use weapons to defend the capital, women performed important supportive roles throughout the war. In 1942, Robert Brawner, Jr., organized the Women's Voluntary Auxiliary Corps. Fifteen young women, decked out in blue jackets and skirts similar to the uniform of the WAVES, met regularly for two-hour drills in the yard of Second Street School. More importantly, they assisted the Red Cross in rolling bandages, took first aid courses, aided in blackout drills, served as aircraft spotters atop the State Office Building, and entertained patients at the Veterans Administration Hospitals in Lexington and Danville. Perhaps the auxiliary's most significant contribution came in 1943 when it joined with Mrs. Robert Brawner and the Odd Fellows Lodge to establish the Frankfort USO. The USO opened at the Odd Fellows Hall in February, and the auxiliary performed maintenance chores, planned and conducted outings, and helped in a variety of other ways to entertain servicemen passing through the city.

During 1942 the homefront war effort began to stress mobilization of material resources necessary to arm, feed, and supply the troops on the battlefield. On December 27, 1941, the administration had instituted tire rationing. Within a short time Fred J. Sutterlin, chairman, Thomas P. Rogers, and Robert L. Vaughn had been appointed as the Franklin County Tire Rationing Board. Before 1942 was over, Franklin Countians, like other Americans, were carefully husbanding ration coupons for sugar, coffee, gasoline, and fuel oil. The following year, a variety of food products was added to the rationed list. In March 1944, Frankfort became the state headquarters for Food for Victory, Inc., a nonprofit organization formed to encourage the production and conservation of food and to conduct a statewide victory garden campaign.

Along with rationing came a series of salvage drives to collect every possible scrap of iron, steel, tin, aluminum, and rubber, as well as such mundane products as kitchen grease. In July 1942 Governor Keen Johnson appointed Judge Edward C. O'Rear, a distinguished Frankfort attorney, to chair the Commonwealth's Salvage-for-Victory campaign. Before long local residents were vigorously collecting everything from old aluminum pie pans to surplus railroad tracks for the scrap drive. Some of the city's distinguished residences and public buildings were even stripped of their fine decorative ironwork.

Kentucky State Penitentiary. Solitary cell under demolition.

Two local contributions were particularly notable. In early September state officials turned over to the War Department two old cannons which had decorated the lawn of the National Guard Armory. One was a German gun captured during World War I. The other dated to the War of 1812. The following month, State Engineer Ralph C. Wyatt announced that the solitary cell block of the old state penitentiary, one of the few sections of the facility that remained standing, would be stripped of its ninety-six massive iron doors and six sets of outside locking bars. Soon attacked by workmen armed with acetylene torches, the structure which prisoners once had called "the hole" yielded approximately forty tons of prime wrought iron.

While most of the scrap collected in Franklin County was shipped to reprocessing sites in other parts of the country, local industry did its share to make the United States the great "Arsenal of Democracy." The Union Underwear Company won special recognition from the government for producing more than 50 million pairs of shorts for the armed forces. Local distilleries, like others in the Commonwealth, provided large quantities of industrial alcohol for the manufacture of synthetic rubber and other war goods. In September 1943 the War Production Board approved the construction of a $553,000 protein recovery plant by the Schenley Distillers Corporation at the George T. Stagg Distillery in Frankfort. The purpose of the new plant was to produce dried grain food for military use.

Perhaps the most unusual war producer was the firm of George W. Gayle & Son. Established in 1855 and located in a tiny shop behind 514 Logan Street, the company had earned its reputation making custom, hand-crafted fishing reels which sold for $100 to $300 each. But the firm also developed a small, machine-made reel that retailed for fifty cents. In the early 1930s, however, Japanese manufacturers duplicated the Gayle reel—down to the "George W. Gayle & Son" label on the reel and bolt—and sold it to American retailers at a price well below Gayle's. It was not without special enthusiasm, therefore, that in May 1943 owner Clarence Gayle accepted his first government war contract. The company's assignment was to make part of the firing mechanism for floating bombs, which were manufactured by the F. H. Lawson Company in Cincinnati. A short time later Gayle began making components for the Clinton Engineering Works, a major contractor in the development of the atomic bomb at Oak Ridge, Tennessee. Because of strict secrecy requirements Gayle had no idea what his company was helping to produce. The work was so sensitive that drawings had to be returned to the contractor upon completion of each part of each job. By the end of the war, however, Gayle had turned out about 30,000 parts of some twenty different items.

In the final analysis, though, the war had to be won on far-flung battlefields and oceans by young men—and women—who answered their nation's call to the colors. Hundreds of Franklin Countians responded, and most came back. But a total of eighty-one were killed in action, died of wounds, or succumbed to illness, accident, or other noncombat causes. Over half of the victims were in the Army, with the remainder divided among the other services, primarily the Navy and Marines.

With the surrender of the Japanese in September 1945, Franklin Countians looked forward to the prospects and challenges of peace. Factories which had been geared to war production returned to their traditional product lines. Returning G. I.s and their families attempted to resume their normal civilian lifestyles. And local government struggled to refurbish and expand public facilities which had been allowed to deteriorate because of shortages of money, materials, and labor during four long years of war-imposed stringencies. The challenges of peace were even larger than anyone might have imagined. Compounding the difficulties was the lack of a well-established business organization to mobilize private support for public improvements. A major local war casualty was the Frankfort Chamber of Commerce, which was forced to disband when too many businesses found it impossible to pay their dues. In May 1945 nine local business operators attempted to fill the gap by incorporating the Frankfort Board of Trade. Its stated purpose was to promote "the economic, civic, and social welfare of the people of Frankfort, Kentucky, and vicinity by any appropriate means and methods." The new organization struggled for three years before giving away to a new Frankfort Chamber of Commerce. In the meantime, however, Frankfort and Franklin County were engulfed in the greatest wave of urban growth in their history.

CAPITAL PLAZA UNDER CONSTRUCTION IN 1971.

12

The Urban Explosion

DESPITE THE VARIOUS physical improvements and economic changes which had occurred since the beginning of the century, the discharged servicemen who returned to Frankfort and Franklin County after World War II found a community which remained in many important respects much as it had been in 1900. While many businesses had changed ownership, the appearance of the central business district had been altered only slightly. Frankfort's population, which stood at less than 9,500 in 1900, had risen by barely 2,000 residents during the intervening forty-five years. Most inhabitants remained concentrated in the city's historic core, between the new State Capitol and Fort Hill, where the visual images of dozens of aging homes and public buildings, and the memories and stories of old political intrigues mingled with the pungent odor of sour mash to evoke the nostalgic sense of eras gone by.

But for Frankfort and Franklin County, as for other American communities, the quarter-century that followed World War II brought a host of social, economic, political, and technological changes. These forces unleashed a wave of urban development which dramatically transformed the landscape and significantly increased the complexity of life in Kentucky's capital. By 1970 Frankfort was as different from the city of 1940 as the capital of 1940 was from that of 1840.

An immediate factor in this urban explosion was the spectacular population growth which followed the war. On the eve of the conflict Franklin County's population stood at 23,308 persons. Thirty years later it had reached 34,481, an overall increase of nearly 48 percent. The population boom began slowly during the second half of the war decade and gathered momentum over the next twenty years. In 1950 the county's population reached 25,933, an increase of 11.3 percent over the previous census. Ten years later the figure had grown by 13.5 percent to 29,421. During the 1960s the county added more than 5,000 new residents and increased its population by 17.2 percent.

The growth rate was even more pronounced in Frankfort, whose population increased by 85.8 percent from 11,492 inhabitants in 1940 to 21,356 three decades later. But the city's growth was also more erratic than the county's. During the 1940s the capital's population remained fairly static, increasing a mere 3.7 percent to 11,916 in 1950. The seams burst during the 1950s, however, when the population increased by 54.1 percent to 18,365 in 1960. Such growth proved impossible to sustain. Nevertheless, the population reached 21,356 ten years later, a healthy 16.3 percent increase.

Frankfort's dramatic yet erratic growth rate reflected the interaction of rapid residential development on the city's fringes and the timing of the city government's annexation program. Between 1945 and 1970 local land developers platted no fewer than ninety new residential subdivisions on the city's outskirts. Nine tracts were laid out during the 1940s, all but one of which were executed after the war. As the demand for housing climbed, twenty-eight new tracts were platted during the 1950s and an additional fifty-four were recorded during the 1960s.

Development during the immediate postwar years was scattered within two distinct corridors, one which roughly followed Louisville Road to the south and southwest of the city and a second along East Main Street and Versailles Road to the east and southeast. Some of the earliest development in the Louisville Road corridor appeared in Tanglewood, an upper middle class subdivision situated behind the capitol adjacent to Capitol Heights and overlooking the Kentucky River. Originally platted in the spring of 1941 by a family group headed by real estate magnate E. H. Taylor Hay, Tanglewood's development was retarded somewhat by wartime materials shortages. But the subdivision filled up quickly after the war, and by early 1950 Frankfort attorney Clifford Smith was ready to move forward with a small addition to the original tract. Meanwhile, horse breeder George A. Collins already had begun subdividing a large section of Thistleton Farms, which he had purchased during the 1920s from the estate of the late Colonel Edmund H. Taylor, Jr., as Cloverdale Subdivision. Platted in 1946, Cloverdale's initial tract was located at the southern end of Collins Lane just north of Sleepy Hollow Branch. Three years later Harold K. Hines, manager of the Frankfort Electric and Water Plant Board, and an associate, George McDonald, recorded the plat for Haukeegan Park, located on the north side of Louisville Road west of the present Capital City Airport.

The first postwar subdivision platted in the East Main-Versailles Road corridor was Franklin Acres, situated at the southern terminus of Lyons Drive and recorded by lumber dealer Greene R. Lyons in April 1946. Three months later an addition to the Crestwood Subdivision was laid out on a large parcel immediately to the north of the original tract bounded by the Frankfort & Cincinnati Railroad and U.S. 60. The following year the Carter-Morris Realty Company, headed by Charles Morris, platted Grandview Heights; Roy Lewis, of Lewis & Dudley Realty Company, and L. T. West recorded Rolling Acres; and Lewis laid out Country Club Heights.

As the population boom accelerated during the 1950s, so did the conversion of rural land to residential purposes. Development in the Louisville Road corridor continued with the initiation of Cavelawn Subdivision, located at Old Soldier Lane and Louisville Road opposite Lawrenceburg Road, by Harold K. Hines in September 1951. Six years later Standard Oil agent William D. Yount, Benson Valley Milling Company executive Charles E. Watson, and former mayor Robert C. Yount undertook development of Willowcrest. Their development was situated on the south side of Louisville Road just outside the present city limits opposite the State Game Farm. About three-quarters of a mile to the west on the north side of Louisville Road, J. A. Jennings laid out Broadview Manor in June 1959. Meanwhile, Warner U. Hines, son of Harold K. Hines, and Jack McDonald, owners of Hines & McDonald Real Estate Company, took over and expanded the Cloverdale development in June 1957.

One of the most prominent developers of the postwar period was Ward J. Oates, a local real estate dealer who also served at one time as State Highway Commissioner. In 1954, along with distillery executive C. Orville Schupp, Oates began transforming the Blanton family estate, located on the east side of Wilkinson Boulevard between Fort Hill and Thorn Hill, into Blanton Acres. The entire project, which included both single family dwellings and apartments, took more than a dozen years to complete. Meanwhile, in mid-1959 Oates's Juniper Hills Development Corporation began work on Juniper Hills, a subdivision located on the west side of Parkside Drive just north of the Capital City Airport.

The heaviest development during the 1950s occurred in the expanding East Main-Versailles Road corridor. The largest single project was Indian Hills, initiated in 1950 by the real estate firm of James C. Pickett and Franklin Goins. The first section was platted on the north side of Main Street east of Wilkinson Boulevard. Over the next fifteen years Pickett and Goins were joined at various times by such partners and investors as Warner U. Hines, former Governor A. B. Chandler, former Lieutenant Governor Harry Lee Waterfield, John M. Arnold, and real estate dealer Glenn Purdy. By 1965 the streets of Indian Hills wound from Georgetown Road northward to Schenkel Lane and eastward between Shenkel Lane and the Frankfort & Cincinnati Railroad to Stedmantown Road. Before its completion the project consisted of twelve primary sections and at least fifty individual plats for revisions, restrictions, and amendments.

While Pickett, Goins, and their associates pushed forward with Indian Hills, other developers proceeded with subdivisions of their own. In September 1953, Charles W. Black began converting his farm into The Woodlands, a subdivision which winds along Westover and Eastover drives south of East Main Street. A month later, the Brighton Engineering Company, owned by powerful highway builder William H. May, laid out Bon Air Hills on the east side of Versailles Road just outside the present city boundary. In December 1954 confectioner Earl Harrod platted the first section of Winding Way, a development which stretched from East Main to Myrtle Avenue by 1958. Finally, in October 1955 Wilburn Anderson recorded Cardinal Hills. Situated on a large tract between Versailles Road and Franklin Acres, Cardinal Hills extended the city's suburban fringe to the vicinity of the present East-West Connector.

As the 1960s dawned, extensive home construction was still underway—and would continue for some years thereafter—in such emerging neighborhoods as Indian Hills, Blanton Acres, Juniper Hills, Cloverdale, Willowcrest, and The Woodlands. But this development was not sufficient to quench the demand for new homes in a growing city. Throughout the decade local developers and homebuilders stayed busy at turning land which once had grown cattle, horses, and tobacco into instant residential neighborhoods. In November 1961, Warner Hines and Jack McDonald, along with Paul Sullivan, vice president of Farmers Bank, obtained approval from the city planning commission to start work on Westgate, situated in the triangle created by the junction of the Louisville and Lawrenceburg roads. Development in the triangle continued in 1966, when McDonald and Glenn D. Purdy, joined two years later by Oates, Hines, and Sullivan, initiated the adjacent Meadows Subdivision. Construction in the neighborhood continued well into the 1970s.

The most extensive project initiated during the decade in the Louisville Road corridor was Thistleton Heights. This development began in mid-1960 when Thistleton, Inc., paid George A. Collins $600,000 for a large tract of the former Edmund H. Taylor, Jr., estate. The members of the corporation were Charles B. McEachin, president; J. W. Davis, Jr., vice-president; and Robert T. Mayes, secretary-treasurer. McEachin and Davis were prominent Lexington developers, while Mayes was a major stockholder in a Lexington vending machine company. The first section of Thistleton Heights was recorded in November 1960. Nineteen more sections followed during the next eight years.

Directly to the west of Frankfort new subdivisions included Parkview Estates, platted in March 1965 by Dr. Harry Cowherd, a local physician. Located high above the city at Hill Drive and Brown Ferry Road, the subdivision grew slowly and is still undergoing construction. Further to the east, on Devil's Hollow Road between Buttimer Hill and Choateville, Charles and Geraldine Weaver platted Sunny Hills in August 1963. Five years later they added an adjoining tract called Sunny Hills Manor.

Seven new subdivisions were initiated on Frankfort's east side during the 1960s, in addition to subsequent sections of earlier projects such as Indian Hills. In May 1962 Frankfort attorney Louis Cox, acting as trustee for the owners, moved ahead with Cherokee Subdivision, located south of East Main Street at Missouri and Cold Spring avenues adjacent to the L&N Railroad. Fourteen months later the College Park Development Corporation won approval from the city planning commission to begin work on College Park. This subdivision, located at the southern end of Cold Harbor Drive near the

Kentucky State College athletic field, drew a major portion of its residents from among the city's black middle class.

The year 1964 was particularly active for developers in East Frankfort. In April the Caudill Realty Company, headed by Dr. C. M. Caudill, a local dentist with a passion for land development and real estate, began work on the initial section of Tierra Linda. Located on the west side of Versailles Road south of Cardinal Hills, Tierra Linda proved to be the most extensive subdivision project begun in East Frankfort during the 1960s. About the same time, Inverness Estates, Inc., headed by Attorney E. Gaines Davis, Jr., platted Inverness Estates on a tract just to the southwest of Tierra Linda. Before the year was out, Franklin Goins had initiated work on Capital View Subdivision, which bordered Franklin Acres on the west. The following year real estate dealer Louis Stivers, president of EDCO, Inc., moved forward with Hickory Hills Addition, situated on a tract between Winding Way and Cherokee Subdivisions. Finally, in April 1969, Melvin Carter platted the initial section of Colony Subdivision, which adjoins the west side of Shenkel Lane between Wilkinson Boulevard and the Frankfort & Cincinnati Railroad.

The rapid growth of Frankfort's suburban fringes inevitably created the demand for a variety of urban services, ranging from water and sewer systems to waste disposal and fire and police protection. The only government with the capacity to provide such services was the city of Frankfort. Before the city would extend these services, however, it required that the suburban districts be annexed. Thus the 1950s and 1960s witnessed the steady expansion of Frankfort's municipal boundary. Some residents opposed the new taxes that annexation entailed. But in many cases annexation occurred at the request of the developers, who recognized that without appropriate services homeseekers and contractors would be reluctant to buy their building lots.

The postwar expansion of the capital's boundaries began in 1950 with the annexation of Capitol Heights and Tanglewood. Three years later, in one of the largest expansion measures in its history, Frankfort annexed Berry Hill on the west and a large eastern swath which stretched from Wilkinson Boulevard on the north, along the Versailles Road south of the Frankfort & Cincinnati Railroad, to the vicinity of Cardinal Hills. Included in the addition were such neighborhoods as Thorn Hill, Crestwood, Fairview Heights, Bellview, Rolling Acres, Franklin Acres, and Grandview Heights. In 1957 the city annexed a portion of land on Georgetown Road which soon became the site of Franklin County High School and the Elkhorn Middle School. Two years later, a series of ordinances resulted in the annexation of a substantial area south of Kentucky State College, a large section of Indian Hills between East Main Street and Schenkel Lane, and the entire Capital City Airport.

Expansion accelerated during the 1960s, when the city commission enacted seventeen separate annexation ordinances. Thistleton Heights became part of the city in 1961. Between 1963 and 1966 the remainder of Indian Hills joined Frankfort along with Tierra Linda and portions of Westgate and the Meadows. Five separate actions in 1969 resulted in the annexation of the Colony and Collins Lane School as well as portions of the Meadows and The Woodlands. After two decades of expansion, Frankfort had at least tripled in area between 1940 and 1970.

The causes of Franklin County's urban explosion were numerous. The postwar baby boom sent hundreds of middle and lower middle class families into the home-ownership market for the first time. Unable to find adequate housing in the older sections of Frankfort, they formed a significant pool of demand for suburban home builders. The deep-seated desire of these homeseekers to attain the American dream of owning their own homes was enhanced by the mortgage insurance programs of the Federal Housing Administration and the Veterans Administration, which enabled banks, savings and loan associations, and other lenders to write loans for many people who previously could not have qualified financially for them. Reinforcing the mortgage insurance programs were federal income tax provisions which still allow deductions for interest and property taxes, thus providing a hidden subsidy for home ownership.

A critical force in urban development was the rapid growth of state government and the consequent expansion in state employment. Already an important factor in the local economy, government employment at all levels still accounted for fewer than 900 members of Franklin County's resident labor force in 1940. By 1950 more than 2,300 Franklin Countians worked in government, including 853 Frankfort residents. Twenty years later the number of government workers living in the county, excluding those at the local level, exceeded 4,700. Of these, nearly 3,400 lived in the capital. This steady accretion in the number of state employees generated a continuing demand for new middle class housing.

Another significant factor in urbanization was a series of major capital improvements, particularly in transportation and utilities, which enabled formerly agrarian land to support urban uses. Between 1950 and 1970, despite the obstacles created by Franklin County's hilly and rocky terrain, the Frankfort Electric and Water Board and the city of Frankfort struggled to keep up with the needs of the city's fringe communities for water, electricity, and sewers. The water board installed a series of eight-, ten-, and twelve-inch mains along such major arteries as the Louisville, Lawrenceburg, Georgetown, and Versailles roads, thereby providing primary service for the proliferating subdivisions. The construction of two new electrical substations during the early 1960s supplied the city's electricity needs for more than a decade. In 1955 the city constructed a new sewage treatment plant on the Kentucky River behind the Bellepoint neighborhood. During the next fifteen years the construction of major outfall lines by the city, combined with the installation of residential sewer lines by subdivision developers, had extended the sanitary sewage disposal system throughout the entire city. By mid-1970 the only subdivision which lacked service was the recently annexed Cardinal Hills, and plans were in progress to rectify that situation.

While the expansion of the utilities systems made it possible for the fringe areas to support urban activity, several major transportation improvements provided the circulatory system which made these neighborhoods accessible to suburbanites. Beginning in the mid-1950s major portions of such key thoroughfares as Louisville Road, East Main Street, Georgetown Road, and Versailles Road were widened from two to four lanes. Construction in 1959-1960 of the Green Hill-Thorn Hill By-pass, which linked U.S. 60 with Wilkinson Boulevard, created a direct connection between North Frankfort and East Frankfort and provided immediate access from the East Frankfort neighborhoods to industrial plants in the Thorn Hill area. One negative side effect of these improvements was to create a terribly awkward bottleneck at the hilltop junction of East Main, Georgetown Road, Versailles Road, and the by-pass. In efforts to prevent the situation from causing chronic traffic jams, state highway officials experimented with a succession of signalization adjustments to speed the flow of traffic through the intersection.

The coming of Interstate 64 in the early 1960s played an indirect role in the urbanization process. Because of its distance from the city, the expressway did not open any new territory for immediate development. However, it did create major new access points to the city and redirected through traffic away from overburdened city streets. The first new access point, which highway planners called the "western gateway," resulted when the State Highway Commission rerouted State Highway 35 (U.S. 127) from Lawrenceburg so that it would interchange with I-64 and then join Louisville Road along the right-of-way of the old Harrodsburg Road. This new route, in addition to providing access from the expressway, created a new entry point which spurred the development of such neighborhoods as Cloverdale, Thistleton Heights, Westgate, and the Meadows. Across town, the junction of Versailles Road and I-64 constituted an "eastern gateway" which improved access to the entire East Frankfort corridor.

In addition to making the city more accessible, I-64 and related transportation improvements undergirded another major force in the urban development process—the suburbanization of industry. Despite the rapid growth of state government, manufacturing remained an important and growing element of Franklin County's economic base. But some companies which had been located for years near the center of town moved to suburban sites where they were joined by plants built by firms new to the community. These new factories created a magnet for further residential development as employees sought to minimize their journeys to work by establishing their homes in neighborhoods close to their jobs.

Industry's exodus to the suburbs began during the early 1960s, when the General Shoe Company, later Genesco, Inc., moved from 514 Barrett Avenue near downtown to Myrtle Avenue in East Frankfort. Firms that moved in later years chose even more distant locations. During the mid-1960s, George W. Gayle & Sons transferred from their old shop on Logan Street to 517 Parkside Drive near Capital City Airport. About the same time, Ken-Wel, Inc., which began producing electronic parts at 112 Logan Street in 1954, moved its operations to Industrial Park Road, located on the edge of an emerging industrial area east of the community of Jett. In 1968 Union Underwear Company joined the suburban migration, relocating about a mile to the northwest of Ken-Wel on U.S. 421 in the same industrial complex.

Meanwhile, several new firms joined Franklin County's industrial scene, nearly all of which chose suburban locations. In the fall of 1956 the Sessions Engineering Company began work on what would become a $2 million, 76,000 square-foot manufacturing plant for an unidentified client. The plant was constructed on part of a thirty-acre tract located on the east side of Stedmanton Road just north of Georgetown Road near Forks of Elkhorn. In September 1957, as construction drew to an end, the Frankfort Chamber of Commerce announced that the plant was being erected for the Central Screw Company, a Chicago firm which manufactured approximately 3,500 types of screws, nuts, and specialty fasteners. Six years after Central Screw began operations, Trigometer, Inc., a manufacturer of electronic and emissions components, set up shop on U.S. 127 north of I-64.

While companies like Central Screw and Trigometer, Inc. chose independent plant sites, other new firms were attracted by the amenities offered by the industrial complex east of Jett. Actually composed of several separate sites, including two on the south side of U.S. 421 owned by the L & N Railroad and a third between the L & N tracks and I-64 east of Versailles Road owned by the Franklin County Industrial Foundation, this industrial park setting offered excellent transportation connections by highway and rail as well as immediate water, gas, sewer, and electrical services. One of the earliest firms attracted to the park was the Frank Taylor Company. Noted as a manufacturer of baby strollers and other children's equipment, Taylor completed a 200,000 square foot plant on a twenty-five acre tract between U.S. 421 and the L & N tracks in 1964. Three years later, Bendix-Westinghouse Automotive Air Brake Company opened a large factory for the fabrication of air brake components at the southeast corner of U.S. 421 and Industrial Park Road.

The consequences of urbanization were as varied as the causes. Indeed, one very important result was the decline of Frankfort's industrial tax base. For more than a century the vast proportion of Franklin County's industrial enterprises had been located within the city. But with the relocation of companies like Ken-Wel and Union Underwear and the arrival of new firms such as Bendix and Central Screw, the balance shifted away from the city. By 1970 nearly every manufacturer in the county which employed 100 or more people was located outside the city of Frankfort.

Another consequence of urbanization was a substantial homogenization of the city's domestic architecture. The compact, prewar city possessed a rich blend of residential styles, the product of more than a century of changing aesthetic tastes. After World War II, however, such factors as heavy demand, rising costs of labor and craftsmanship, and changes in building technology, including standardization and mass production of building materials, triumphed over aesthetics as the primary influences in the design of American homes. Thus most new construction exhibited a high degree of uniformity, with a minimum of ornamentation and other artistic elements. Within any given neighborhood or subdivision, differences in appearance tended to reflect cosmetic variations among standard patterns rather than unique artistic expressions.

These tendencies followed two primary stylistic directions, the historical revival and the contractor modern. The former, which imitated the characteristic motifs of such historic forms as the Colonial, Georgian, Federal, and Tudor, is prevalent in upper middle class subdivisions such as Capitol Heights, Tanglewood, the Colony, and some sections of Thistleton Heights. The contractor modern embraces a range of contemporary expressions such as the ranch, bilevel, and split level. Most are constructed of brick, but other materials include wood, stone, and artificial sidings such as asbestos, aluminum, and vinyl. Large contractor modern dwellings are mingled with historical revival houses in several affluent neighborhoods, while similar structures of a less imposing scale prevail in middle and working class neighborhoods such as Cloverdale, Westgate, the Meadows, Blanton Acres, and Indian Hills. In short, in Frankfort as elsewhere in urban America, rising incomes, mass production of building materials, and liberal financing techniques enabled far more families than ever before to own their homes, but at the cost of aesthetic originality.

As the suburban movement of the population accelerated, retailers and other commercial businesses quickly followed. By 1960 major arteries on either side of Frankfort were gradually becoming lined with service stations, restaurants, branch banks, grocery stores, laundromats, and other businesses that catered to suburban consumers. Many of these businesses collected in commercial strips, particularly along East Main Street, where they sought to attract shoppers arriving by car or truck rather than on foot. But as the strip developments proliferated, the jumble of signs and traffic congestion which resulted became a source of concern to political and civic leaders plotting the community's future. At the advice of professional urban planners, they began to encourage the construction of strategically located shopping centers where several businesses under the same roof could share common parking space.

The first major suburban complex of this type was the Eastwood Shopping Center, located on a fifteen-acre site at Versailles Road and Lyons Drive. Developed by Dr. Charles M. Caudill and his wife, Dr. Louise Caudill, the center had 70,000 square feet of commercial space under roof when it opened in the spring of 1963. Two more centers opened before the end of the decade—the East Frankfort, or Winn Dixie, shopping center on East Main at Myrtle Avenue, and Frankfort Plaza, on Louisville Road opposite Juniper Hill Park in West Frankfort. Frankfort Plaza was situated near another of the decade's major suburban projects, the Holiday Inn motel. Completed in late 1962, the inn was constructed by Charles B. McEachin, J. W. Davis, Jr., and Robert T. Mayes as the initial segment of their Thistleton Farm development. With a price tag of approximately $900,000, the eighty-four-unit motel immediately became the capital's most popular home for travelers.

Accompanying the suburbanization of retail commerce was the steady transformation of downtown Frankfort from a primary retail district into a service center. At the end of World War II the central business district was still the unrivaled center of retailing in Franklin County. Many stores bore names that extended back to the late nineteenth century. During the 1950s and early 1960s, however, some of the old businesses began to close their doors. A few, such as Kagin Bros. and Lutkemeier's Dry Goods Store, suspended operations after the death or retirement of proprietors who lacked relatives interested in continuing the enterprises. Others gave way to suburban competition or to the decision by their operators to move to a suburban location. By 1970 such local firms as Rosenstein Bros., formerly at 231 West Broadway, had given way to an army goods store; the Starr Clothing Company had been replaced at 210 West Broadway by a radio and television repair service; and the Guidi Fruit Company had abandoned its operation at 212 West Broadway. At the same time, chain stores such as Sears-Roebuck, J. C. Penney, and Kroger found more lucrative locations on the city's outskirts.

One of the most dramatic early indications of the downtown's changing character was the closing of the stately Capital Hotel in May 1962, shortly before completion of the new Holiday Inn. The immediate expectation was that the old hostelry, whose roots dated back to the historic Weisiger House of 1797, would be replaced by a new downtown motel-convention center and riverfront marina. Since the federal government had almost simultaneously approved nearly $450,000 for planning, surveying, and land acquisition costs for such a project, civic and business leaders had every reason to believe that the future of downtown was bright. It was not a matter of abandoning the downtown in face of adversity but of repositioning it to compete more effectively. As *State Journal* editor S. C. Van Curon noted, "This new structure would have a magnetic appeal to the downtown area, charming tourists, persons who come here on business, a center for civic clubs and private gatherings [sic], and be a trump card for Frankfort to draw conventions."

But when the premature demolition of the two fire-damaged buildings slated for inclusion in the project caused the city to lose its federal grant, the vacant Capital Hotel became available for other purposes. In late 1963, State National Bank leased and renovated the ground floor and moved its headquarters into the old hotel. The new bank featured an innovative drive-in window which used closed-circuit television to enable the customer to communicate with the teller while conducting a transaction. By this time, however, it would have taken much more than a unique drive-in window and its historic new headquarters for State National to overtake its only remaining rival, Farmers Bank & Capital Trust Company. Resuming its aggressive prewar acquisition program, Farmers Bank bought the venerable National Branch Bank of Kentucky in June 1948. By 1964, partly as a result of its position as a major state depository, Farmers Bank's assets of $56.6 million and its deposits of $53.4 million were more than seven times the respective figures for its competitor.

Commerce and industry were not the only activities affected by the urbanization process. All manner of public and private services had to be expanded, shifted, or created to meet the needs and demands of a new generation of suburbanites. One of the first services to feel the impact of the population shift was education. As late as the 1950-1951 school year a majority of the nearly 2,600 school children in Frankfort and its immediate environs were enrolled in the Frankfort Independent School District. At that time the city system served all school-age children living in Frankfort while the Franklin County School District educated those who resided outside the city. However, the proportion and number of youngsters attending the city schools had been declining steadily since 1940, while enrollments were increasing in the county schools located near the city.

As the suburban migration gathered momentum, the burden of climbing enrollments fell increasingly upon the essentially rural Franklin County system. Contributing to the problem was the fact that Kentucky law made it nearly impossible for the Frankfort district to expand its attendance area as the city's boundary grew through annexation. By 1958 overcrowding was approaching crisis proportions. The situation was particularly severe at the Bridgeport, Elkhorn, and Thorn Hill schools, which attracted most of the new enrollment generated by the growing capital city. Elkhorn School, located at the northeast corner of U.S. 60 and East Main Street, carried an extra burden because it served as a high school as well as an elementary school.

The first step in alleviating the county system's enrollment problems came in 1958 with the completion of the new Franklin County High School. Located on the north side of Georgetown Road near the eastern edge of Frankfort, the modern new facility consolidated all of the system's secondary programs into a single building with a capacity of more than 1,200 students. But substantial overcrowding remained at the elementary schools where the total enrollment for 1958-1959 exceeded permanent capacity by nearly 200 pupils. Portable classrooms had to be installed by the Bridgeport, Thorn Hill, and Elkhorn schools to accommodate the excess enrollments. Construction of the new Elkhorn Elementary School, at 928 East Main, and Collins Lane Elementary School, between Thistleton Heights and Cloverdale, in 1967 greatly reduced the burden. By 1970, however, plans were on the drawing board for a new junior high school, which would be located near Franklin County High School.

Closely related to the problem of schools was that of parks and recreation. In 1951 a nationally known urban planning firm noted with some dismay that "Frankfort has the dubious distinction of being one of the very few cities in

Franklin County High School, Georgetown Road.

the United States possessing no public parks." The deficiency was especially apparent "because of the unsurpassed opportunities for recreational areas occasioned by the diverse topography. There are many wooded and rugged areas unsuitable for private development but extremely attractive as park sites." But recreation was another story. The city recreation department, staffed by a director and seven other employees, offered a "well rounded program" of "supervised play activities both to children and adults" throughout the community. Centered primarily at the city schools, recreational facilities consisted largely of traditional playground apparatus, ball diamonds, volleyball courts, and a small wading pool and gymnasium at Second Street School.

But even recreation had its deficiencies. The playground space at most schools was severely limited. The county schools lacked any type of organized recreational program. Most distressing was the absence of a public swimming pool and tennis courts. By late 1951 community leaders had concluded that the lack of adequate parks and recreation facilities could no longer be tolerated. It not only hindered the attraction of new industry, but it weakened the city's image among the professional and technical persons whose skills were increasingly in demand by state government.

After developing a clear picture of what was needed, city officials moved quickly to create an excellent parks and recreation system. In 1953 the city of Frankfort paid $185,000 for the 165-acre George Berry estate, situated just outside the city on Louisville Road. Using revenues from a $500,000 bond issue, the Municipal Park and Recreation Board transformed Berry Hill into the Juniper Hill Community Center. Immediate improvements included the construction of a club house, ball field, tennis courts, and picnic facilities. In July 1956, Juniper Hill became the site of Franklin County's first public swimming pool. Constructed at a cost of $210,000, the complex included wading and junior pools for young children and a diving well and swimming pool which met Olympic and Amateur Athletic Union specifications. By the time the pool opened, local golfers were playing the front nine holes of the park's new eighteen-hole golf course. The back nine opened later in the year.

Juniper Hill Community Center was a justifiable source of pride. Coupled with a playground system which by 1959 included facilities of the county schools, it served as the backbone of a well-developed program of active recreation. But public areas where one could relax, enjoy a quiet picnic, or just absorb the sights and sounds of nature were in short supply. During the early 1960s, the historic consciousness which resulted from the Civil War centennial, combined with its popularity as a hiking area for Boy Scouts and other groups, spurred a flurry of interest in developing Fort Hill as a park. But interest soon waned. A major step toward obviating the need for park space came in 1970 with completion of the East Frankfort Park, located between Myrtle Avenue and Bonnycastle Drive east of College Park Subdivision and the L & N Railroad. Despite this improvement, there remained a shortage of small neighborhood parks and playlots as the continual expansion of the city boundaries outstripped the Parks and Recreation Board's ability to provide new services.

No other institution was more successful in adapting to the suburban migration than the church. In 1951 there were seventeen houses of worship, representing a broad range of Christian persuasions, in the city of Frankfort. Three years later, after the sweeping annexation of East Frankfort and Thorn Hill, the number had increased to thirty-one. By 1970 there were forty churches scattered throughout the entire city. The Baptists represented by far the most predominant affiliation, with eleven congregations.

First Christian Church, 316 Ann St.

The effects of urbanization extended well beyond creating a demand for new schools, parks, recreation facilities, and churches. Indeed, the urban explosion challenged local and state officials as never before to wrestle with the problems of controlling the direction and timing of urban growth, providing for the orderly extension of services, and revitalizing those older parts of the city most directly affected by the centrifugal movement of population, commerce, and industry. Community leaders responded to these challenges with a host of new strategies, most of which already had become commonplace in other American cities.

One of the first and most fundamental of these strategies was urban land use planning. The roots of city planning in the capital extend back to the early 1930s when the Frankfort Garden Club and other civic groups made a concerted but futile effort to halt blasting and related operations at a privately owned quarry on Buttimer Hill and at a city-owned quarry on Fort Hill. Despite favorable local sentiment and support from other Kentuckians who believed that all citizens of the Commonwealth had a stake in preserving the beauty of the capital city, the decade-long campaign to stop the blasting failed. Nevertheless, the struggle dramatized for many the need for land use regulations and other planning mechanisms which would protect the community's scenic attractions and conserve real estate values. Toward these ends the 1938 session of the General Assembly enacted legislation creating the State Capital Planning and Zoning Commission and vesting it with the power "to establish and carry out an orderly and comprehensive plan of development for the Capital of Kentucky and its environs." The commission's area of jurisdiction encompassed all of Franklin County within a one-mile radius of the county courthouse. Chaired by Governor Albert B. Chandler, the commission's other members included Mayor David D. Smith, State Parks Director Bailey P. Wootton, State Highway Commissioner Robert Humphrey, and State Highway Engineer Thomas Cutler.

Not to be outdone, the city initiated its own planning process. In November 1939 the city council passed two planning ordinances. The first created a City Zoning Commission, and the second declared a two-year emergency period during which permission of the city council was required before any new construction could begin. Appointed by Mayor Smith to the new commission were Harold W. Hines, banker W. P. Sullivan, lawyer Dyke Hazelrigg, businessman J. M. Perkins, and City Attorney Guy H. Briggs, who served as the commission's administrative officer. Mayor Smith was an ex-officio member. Soon after its appointment the commission drafted, and the council ordained, a city zoning ordinance. In early 1940, however, after the city attempted to use the new ordinance to prevent the establishment of a flower shop at Second Street and Capitol Avenue, the State Court of Appeals declared the zoning ordinance invalid. With the coming of World War II local and state governments turned their energies to war mobilization activities. The planning measures remained on the books, but without operating budgets the planning and zoning agencies ceased to function.

Frankfort was nearly five years into its postwar building boom before problems such as traffic congestion, inadequate classroom space, haphazard subdivision development, and insufficient parking again raised the need for comprehensive city planning. In January 1950 the General Assembly amended the 1938 statute to create a new seven-member Capital Planning and Zoning Commission. Designated by law to serve on the new commission were Governor Earle C. Clements, chairman; Mayor Clarence T. Coleman, vice chairman; John A. Keck, state highway commissioner; D. H. Bray, state highway engineer; and Mrs. Lucy L. Smith, state parks director. Appointed by Governor Clements to represent the citizens of Frankfort were real estate dealer and coal yard operator Ward J. Oates and hardware store proprietor Frank Sower.

Once in office the new planning commission moved quickly to confront the problems of an expanding capital city. Their most important action was to retain the St. Louis planning firm of Harland Bartholomew & Associates to prepare a workable comprehensive city plan. Bartholomew's planners spent more than a year analyzing the city's population growth and economic base and making detailed recommendations pertaining to land use, zoning, transportation, housing, schools and recreation, and long-range public works requirements. As a foundation for long-term regulatory and enforcement activity, Bartholomew developed zoning and subdivision regulations and minimum housing standards.

Bartholomew's planning documents served the community well for nearly a decade. By the late 1950s, however, the combined forces of rapid urban growth, soaring state employment, and annexation had rendered them obsolete. In 1958 the Kentucky Department of Economic Development, in cooperation with the planning commission and other state and local officials, engaged the Atlanta consulting firm of Hammer and Company Associates to develop a new set of planning documents. Building on the foundation laid by Bartholomew, Hammer analyzed the conditions and needs of individual neighborhoods, formulated major thoroughfare and community facilities plans, developed a long-range capital improvements program, and outlined a plan for preserving and revitalizing the downtown. Apparent throughout the Hammer documents were a recognition of and an emphasis on the special needs of Frankfort as the seat of government.

With a few unanticipated exceptions, Hammer's projections for the distribution of residential, commercial, and industrial activity proved remarkably accurate. The firm's recommendations for downtown revitalization eventually would be implemented through the city's urban renewal program, and its comprehensive land use plan remained in effect until 1970. At that time the land use plan was superseded by a new one developed by Planning and Research Associates, a Lexington company. The new plan, which encompassed all of Franklin County, followed the abolition of the Capital Planning and Zoning Commission and its replacement during the mid-1960s by the joint Frankfort-Franklin County Planning Commission.

While the accomplishment of Hammer's recommendations for the revitalization of the downtown ultimately depended upon urban renewal, the advent of the federally supported urban redevelopment strategy in the capital had at best a limited relationship to the situation downtown. After the failure of the proposed convention hotel-riverfront marina project, downtown urban renewal had to wait until the 1970s. The notion that Frankfort should undertake a major renewal program first arose in January 1955, when Farnham Dudgeon, president of the chamber of commerce and local printing company executive, proposed that the city seek federal monies to revitalize the Craw neighborhood. Dudgeon's idea encountered a mixture of skepticism and enthusiasm. More than three years of political wrangling and preliminary planning followed before the city commission, in April 1958, authorized the Municipal Slum Clearance and Urban Redevelopment Agency to pursue an urban renewal contract with the federal government. Three months later, city and federal officials signed contracts totaling $1.57 million for land acquisition and clearance in Craw.

Designated the North Frankfort Urban Renewal Area, the fifty-two acre target district was the subject of conflicting emotions and images. To most civic leaders and city officials it was an unmitigated slum, a collection of "rickety, leaky and insanitary houses, cottages, hovels and shacks which more or less kept the rain off the city's most badly housed . . . community." Proponents of the project viewed Craw as a "hotbed of vice and corruption" populated by a "rough class of people, who didn't mind killing or being killed." To much of the city's white middle class the area was symbolized by such hangouts as the Blue Moon, the Tiptoe Inn, and the Peach Tree Inn, where prostitution and gambling were rampant. Long-time politicians paid homage to the "King of Craw," the neighborhood boss who controlled bootlegging and gambling and whose legendary ability to turn out the vote could swing an election to his chosen candidate.

Residents of Craw were no less aware of the neighborhood's seamy side. They lived with it every day. But most of the citizens were peaceful, law-abiding people who managed to develop a sense of community and even a fondness for the place. No doubt it was a community forged at least partially out of the realization of a common predicament, where poor blacks and whites made a virtue of necessity. As one former resident recalled, "the people in Craw formed a bond of togetherness that has not been equalled before or since.... We lived together, played together, fought with one another, cried together and all other things that make people close." Strengthening the bond was a shared perception that Craw was exploited by "city fathers [who] needed a place to get rid of what they said was a bunch of disgraceful elements.... With all these people out of their hair, high society would not be disturbed." In the final analysis, though, togetherness based on common grievance was not sufficient to prevent the neighborhood's destruction when it faced the combined resources of local, state, and national governments and a civic leadership determined to eliminate a center of blight which appeared to retard economic growth.

If anything threatened to derail the project it was the incredibly slow progress toward the formulation of a financially feasible development plan. By early 1965 approximately 70 percent of the structures in the target area had been cleared, including the Mayo-Underwood School, formerly the Clinton Street School for black children. But the various designs presented to the Frankfort Urban Renewal Agency since 1958 had proved woefully inadequate. The primary difficulty was the project area's historic flooding problem. Federal regulations demanded that any urban renewal project subject to flooding be protected by a flood control system constructed under the supervision of the Army Corps of Engineers. That agency required in turn an assurance that this protected area could generate additional development sufficient to justify the investment of tax dollars.

Their inability to develop a plan which met the Corps of Engineers' specifications finally convinced city officials that larger resources than those available from the city were necessary to secure federal participation. To hardly anyone's surprise, that source proved to be the Commonwealth of Kentucky. Negotiations leading to state participation began on Memorial Day 1964, when a small cadre of Frankfort leaders, including Farnham Dudgeon, now Urban Renewal Commission chairman, *State Journal* publisher Albert E. Dix, banker Paul Sullivan, and County Attorney William Young, met to discuss the situation with Governor Edward T. Breathitt. "They drove me down ...[to the project site] and painted the picture of what this would mean for Frankfort and for Kentucky," Breathitt later recalled. "Frankly, I'd like to claim credit for it, but the idea [was] generated in Frankfort.... They came with the idea and we worked with them on how to make it work."

Once committed to the project, Governor Breathitt instructed Finance Commissioner Felix Joyner to draw up a plan for the state's financial and managerial participation in what soon became known as the Capital Plaza complex. In 1966 the governor authorized a state-sponsored bond issue. He also took part in the selection of the internationally renowned architect Edward Durrell Stone, whose works included the Standard Oil Building in Chicago and the General Motors Building in New York, to design the complex.

An initial $45.5 million revenue bond issue was conducted in September 1967, and construction began shortly thereafter.

Built in several phases and originally scheduled for completion in 1970, Capital Plaza was completed in 1972 at a cost of more than $49 million. The first critical element, a levee to protect the plaza from flood waters, was finished by the Corps of Engineers in 1969. Two years later work was completed on Fountain Place, a pedestrian plaza and parking complex which included 636 parking spaces, a cafeteria, and 40,300 square feet of commercial space. Completed about the same time were a new sports and convention center and a privately financed YMCA building. The convention center, which seats more than 8,000 people, became the home of the Kentucky State University Thoroughbreds basketball team as well as serving as a magnet for conventions. It was designed by Lee Potter Smith & Associates. The YMCA building, located at the northeast corner of Broadway and Wilkinson streets, was designed by the Frankfort architectural and engineering firm of Gray and Coblin.

Another element of the project was a new federal office building. Designed by the Louisville firm of Luckett and Farley and located on the north side of Broadway between the new YMCA and the old capitol, the structure replaced the historic home of John Marshall Harlan, associate justice of the United States Supreme Court from 1877 to 1911, and the house in which Colonel Solomon P. Sharp was assassinated by Jereboam O. Beauchamp in 1825. Although its completion was delayed by a controversy over the demolition of the Harlan and Sharp houses and a brief moratorium on federal construction, the building was fully occupied by 1973. The Federal Building subsequently was dedicated to the late Sixth District Congressman John C. Watts.

The centerpiece of the Capital Plaza was its twenty-eight story state office tower. The new structure consolidated the offices of state agencies scattered among public and private buildings throughout the city and created a dramatically new work environment for hundreds of state employees. Standing in stark contrast to the surrounding hills and the slums it replaced, the tower and plaza also generated considerable pointed comment. To some residents who remembered the squalor of Craw, architect Stone's modernistic shaft was a dramatic improvement. To a Louisville architectural critic, on the other hand, it was a "chillingly frightening," "neo-Fascist, formalistic exercise" that was totally out of place in Frankfort's "delicate urbanscape." All could agree, however, with a retired police officer's observation that "there's simply no comparison" between the Capital Plaza complex and the now eradicated Crawfish Bottom.

One of the less fortunate consequences of the project was the displacement of scores of people from their homes without adequate provision for their relocation. The situation was particularly acute for blacks, who constituted nearly half of the population displaced by the redevelopment program. Compounding their problems were the city's segregated housing market and a

Robert C. Yount

John Gerard

limited supply of low rent public housing, which until 1965 was segregated as well. No doubt some black families found housing in Sutterlin Terrace, a public housing complex completed near Kentucky State College in 1963. Although officially nonsegregated, the project was informally intended for Negroes. By early 1965, however, Urban Redevelopment Commission Chairman Farnham Dudgeon was complaining that "we don't have the housing to take care of the people relocated by the demolition. And we can't buy the remaining 92 structures [in Craw] until homes are found to house those people." Completion in 1967 of Riverview Homes, a public housing complex at the base of Fort Hill between the Capital Plaza site and Leestown Terrace, provided the additional units needed for the renewal project to go forward. But by this time most Craw residents already had made their own housing arrangements. In some cases their "new" quarters were even less satisfactory than those they had left behind.

Frankfort's rapid growth after World War II also produced major innovations at city hall. By 1956 the capital's population growth warranted its elevation to the status of a second-class city. This reinforced the view of many civic leaders that the city's administrative affairs should be placed on a more professional, businesslike footing. Under the reformers' proposal, the part-time mayor would continue to serve as the city's chief executive. But the board of city councilmen would be replaced by four elected city commissioners, and a professional city manager would be hired to oversee the community's day-to-day business affairs. In late July 1956 the Frankfort League of Women Voters, one of the organizations spearheading the drive, began circulating petitions to put the question on the fall ballot. The campaign proved successful, and in November the voters approved the manager-commission form of government by the overwhelming vote of 2,742 to 962.

Frankfort's elevation to second-class status also created a political and legal crisis in the mayor's office. The crux of the issue was a conflict between a provision of the Kentucky Constitution which required that mayors be elected to four-year terms and a statute which dictated that mayors of second-class cities be elected during the same year that governors are elected. Under the terms of the question approved in 1956 a new mayor and commission were to be elected in November of 1957, but the length of the new mayor's term was not specified. Elected to replace retiring incumbent Robert C. Yount was John Gerard, a businessman and former city councilman. Gerard took office in January 1958 expecting to serve four years. In an effort to secure his position, he asked the State Court of Appeals to review the matter. In late October 1959, just days before the quadrennial gubernatorial election, the court ruled by a four to two vote that Gerard was entitled to a four-year term.

But another mayoral aspirant was not so sure. Convinced that Gerard was merely serving an interim term until Frankfort could join the gubernatorial cycle, Paul Judd, owner of an office supply store and former city councilman, filed for the mayor's race in the 1959 election. Gerard, equally certain that his position was secure, declined to run. Judd was elected on November 3 and immediately petitioned the high court for a rehearing. Meanwhile, two of the judges who had ruled in Gerard's favor had been replaced. In mid-December the reconstituted court ruled for Judd. One of the new justices, Squire N. Williams, declined to participate in the decision involving his fellow Frankfortians. But the other novice justice, John Palmore of Henderson, joined Chief Justice Morris C. Montgomery, who reversed his previous position, and Judges Brady Stewart and John Moorman, the earlier minority, in upholding Judd's election. "That's the court's decision and it's amen for me," Gerard responded upon hearing of the court's action. "I've done my best ever since I've been here." Gerard nevertheless petitioned for a rehearing. But Judd, who took office on January 4, 1960, prevailed, as the court of appeals turned down Gerard's petition the following month.

Although he served only two years, Mayor Gerard's tenure was not without its accomplishments. After taking office in 1958, Gerard and the new city commission hired Russell Marshall as Frankfort's first city manager. On December 23, 1959, less than two weeks before leaving office, Gerard presided at the dedication of the new Municipal Building, located on the south side of Second Street between Conway Street and Thomas Place opposite Bridge Street. Constructed at a cost of $450,000, the structure provided space for the city's administrative offices, police and fire departments, court chamber, and the Municipal Electric and Water Plant Board. The main speaker at the dedication ceremonies was the recently inaugurated Governor Bert T. Combs. The new Municipal Building meant the abandonment of the old city hall at 290 Main Street, adjoining the Capital Theatre, which had housed city offices since late 1883.

The need for a new city hall was created in part by the expansion of municipal services in response to the capital's physical growth. In July 1950, for example, the Frankfort Fire Department consisted of a single fire station manned by a chief, an assistant chief, and nine full-time firefighters. Their equipment included two pumpers, one of which was more than twenty years old, and a hose truck which had been around for nearly three decades. By 1964 the department included the new downtown station adjoining the Municipal Building and an East Frankfort fire house located at 601 East Main Street. The downtown station housed three modern pumpers, including one with a seventy-five foot aerial ladder, and a half-ton rescue truck. Apparatus at the East Frankfort station consisted of two pumpers. The stations were staffed by a total of thirty-eight professional fire fighters, including the chief, two assistant chiefs, three lieutenants, and a full-time fire inspector. A key factor in the department's expansion and modernization was financial support from state government, which in 1958 provided funds to construct the East Frankfort station. In turn the city agreed to staff and equip the fire house and to provide protection for state offices and other property.

The Frankfort Police Department grew at a similar pace. In 1950 the force

Paul Judd

Old City Hall, 290 Main Street, as it appeared in 1956, just prior to its abandonment when city offices were relocated in the Municipal Building.

Municipal Building, 315 W. Second Street

Capitol Annex

consisted of fourteen officers, including the chief, assistant chief, four sergeants, and four corporals. To patrol the city the department owned only two cruisers and two motorcycles, all of which were radio-equipped. Fourteen years later, after the city had more than tripled in area and nearly doubled in population, the force had increased to thirty officers. Reporting to the chief were two assistant chiefs whose subordinates included two captains, three lieutenants, and six sergeants. While the department had only four police cars, it now had two patrol ambulances and three three-wheeled motorcycles to aid in the growing problem of traffic control. Operating on the same radio frequency as the city department was the county sheriff, who with his six deputies patrolled the balance of Franklin County.

State government experienced an even greater need than the city for new office space. More than fifteen years before Governor Edward T. Breathitt yielded to the blandishments of local civic leaders and committed the Commonwealth to support the Capital Plaza, officials faced the unanticipated difficulty of housing the mushrooming state bureaucracy. In 1941 most observers believed that the new State Office Building, recently erected on the old penitentiary site, would meet the state's office space demands for years to come. By 1948, however, burgeoning administrative agencies were again overflowing. Thus in September Governor Earle C. Clements announced that his administration intended to erect a new office building in Frankfort.

In early February the State Building Commission reported that planning was under way for a $4 million, four-story office structure. The new building was to be situated directly behind the state capitol on the abandoned site of a proposed judicial building. The latter had been initiated in 1946 during the administration of Republican Governor Simeon Willis and canceled by Clements soon after he took office in late 1947. It was appropriate, therefore, that the gaping hole adjacent to the statehouse be filled by the proposed new Capitol Annex. Construction bids totalling more than $4.1 million were awarded in June 1950. The following month the State Court of Appeals upheld the issuance of $3.9 million in revenue bonds to partially finance the project.

A virtual replica of the capitol, but without the dome, the Capitol Annex was completed at a cost of $6 million and dedicated on October 8, 1952. The main speaker at the ceremonies was now-United States Senator Earle Clements. His successor in Frankfort, Governor Lawrence Wetherby, marked the occasion by smashing a bottle of ginger ale against the structure's Indiana limestone facade. By this time the Capitol Annex had been occupied by the state treasurer, the Division of Engineering, the departments of economic security, revenue, finance, and conservation, and the Agricultural and Industrial Development Board.

While construction of the Capitol Annex alleviated the Commonwealth's office space needs for several years, the surplus hardly was adequate to absorb a major department previously headquartered outside Frankfort. But in 1958 the General Assembly ordered the transfer of the State Health Department from Louisville to Frankfort. The move involved the relocation of about 460 employees and an annual payroll of about $1.5 million. An agency of this size, with its associated needs for laboratory and clinical space, required its own building. Thus, in August 1958 Governor A. B. Chandler broke ground for a new State Health Department building adjacent to the grounds of the old Kentucky Training Home, formerly the Feeble-Minded Institute. Constructed in conjunction with the $2.5 million project was a $120,000 City-County Health Department building on the same site.

Undoubtedly the most unusual construction project instigated by the Commonwealth was the Kentucky Floral Clock, constructed on the front lawn of the Capitol Annex in the spring of 1961. Governor Bert T. Combs conceived the project as a means of making the capitol grounds more attractive to tourists. The project quickly captured the attention of the Garden Clubs of Kentucky, Inc., which joined the Commonwealth in financing the clock.

Designed by the Frankfort architectural firm of Oberwarth & Livingston, the clock consists of a cylindrical clock house fifteen feet in diameter. It supports a planter which measures thirty-four feet in diameter, on a slope of twenty-six degrees. The planter rises to a height of twenty feet above a ground-level reflecting pool, which is fifty-six feet in diameter. The planter projects ten feet on all sides of the clock house and creates the illusion that it is floating in air. The exposed surfaces of the planter are covered with Kentucky River pebbles, and the walls of the clock house and reflecting pool are planted with over 13,000 alternanthera and santolina of different colors. The plants serve as a background for the hands of the clock and the quarry chip inserts which spell Kentucky and provide the design which designates the hours. A 1,100 pound map of Kentucky surrounds the clock shaft. Dedicated in early May 1961, the floral clock was completed at a cost of approximately $57,000.

A state-supported improvement of a much different sort was the Capital City Airport. Since the early 1930s Frankfort-area business and political travelers had depended primarily upon several small, private airports for their flying needs. During the immediate postwar period, most local aviation centered at the Silver Lake Airport, located near Georgetown Road between Frankfort and Forks of Elkhorn. The state paid the airport $250 per month hangar rent to store the two planes owned by the Commonwealth. As the 1950s dawned, the increasing costs and complexity of commercial and general aviation were forcing a growing number of small airports to suspend operations. By the fall of 1951 business at Silver Lake, except for the state's hangar rent, consisted almost totally of crop spraying. And the growing season was coming to an end. On October 1 Silver Lake Airport closed.

Its demise was no surprise to anyone. As early as 1945 the State Aeronautics Commission had hired Louisville architect Stratton O. Hammon to conduct a preliminary survey to determine the best site for a state-owned airport. But as William Tanner, state deputy aeronautics commissioner, noted when Silver Lake closed, "The last thing we want to do is to get the State in the airport business." As a practical matter, the Commonwealth could not entirely avoid being in the airport business. But it made every effort to spread the cost of a new facility as broadly as possible among other levels of government. Less than two weeks after Silver Lake's shutdown, Aeronautics Commissioner Charles H. Gartrell began negotiating with city and county governments, seeking their financial participation in a new airfield. Among other things, he promised that the federal and state governments would put up three-fourths of the airport's cost and that the state would maintain and operate it.

By the spring of 1952 planning was well along for a $320,000 facility with a 3,500-foot runway. At the same time, condemnation proceedings were progressing against a 367-acre tract on the north side of U.S. 60 two miles west of Frankfort. After some additional modifications in the plan, construction began in 1954. In late June 1955, Governor Wetherby dedicated the newly opened Capital City Airport. Completed at a cost of approximately $657,000, the initial phase included a 2,800-foot runway, taxiway, and hangar. Plans for the immediate future included construction of a 1,200-foot extension of the runway and the installation of lights.

Nor were anticipated improvements limited to those planned by the state. Governor Wetherby announced in his dedication speech that the federal government had committed to transfer the United States Property and Finance Office from Louisville's Bowman Field to the Frankfort airport. The relocation of this agency, which managed the equipment used by the Frankfort-based Kentucky National Guard, necessitated an investment by the Department of Defense of more than $1 million in physical improvements. It also involved the addition of seventy-five technical employees and an annual payroll of nearly $295,000 to Franklin County's economy. A short time later, the Kentucky State Police moved its Frankfort headquarters and the State Police Academy to the new airport.

Along with new schools, parks, and recreational facilities, the Capital City Airport, as an adjunct of local economic development, was just one more public improvement which helped to expand the quality of life in Frankfort and Franklin County. For while the quarter century that followed World War II was a period of rapid growth and change, it was likewise a time of cultural and social enrichment for people in all walks of life. Less than a year after the war ended Franklin Countians began turning their radios to broadcasts by station WFKY, owned and operated by the Frankfort Broadcasting Company, Inc. The firm was organized in 1945 by a dozen local business and civic leaders who believed that Kentucky's capital needed its own radio voice. After receiving approval of its application from the Federal Communications Commission in late November, the station went on the air in March 1946.

Station WFKY drew much of its news and entertainment programming from the Mutual Broadcasting Company. But its programs also demonstrated a strong local emphasis. Area singers, instrumentalists, and dancers had frequent opportunities to perform. A Saturday night barn dance program attracted country artists from miles around. News and public affairs programs reflected the importance of state government, with as many as a dozen state officials going on the air each week to discuss the concerns of their agencies. Local citizens had an opportunity to express their views and to talk back to government in regular man-on-the street interviews. As Louisville *Courier-Journal* radio editor Bill Ladd observed, WFKY's operators strove "mightily, to tell Frankfort what Frankfort is doing."

While WFKY built a strong audience in Franklin County and nearby Shelby, Anderson, Scott, Woodford, Owen, Henry, and Spencer counties, the chief communications innovation of the postwar era was not far behind. But television did not come into Frankfort homes by the airwaves. Because the hills surrounding the city blocked reception, it proved necessary to use cable to bring the new medium to capital residents. The idea of cable service was conceived in early 1951 by a group of local television dealers. They proposed to the Frankfort Electric and Water Plant Board that a transmission tower be erected on a tract of city reservoir property west of the capitol, where the television reception was good. From there the poles owned by the light and water board and Southern Bell Telephone & Telegraph Company would be used to bring coaxial cable from a master aerial to the homes of individual subscribers.

The Electric and Water Plant Board reacted favorably to the concept but insisted that because the company was city owned, only a nonprofit corporation could use its poles. This led to the organization of Community Services,

Inc., a not-for-profit corporation formed expressly to provide cable television to capital residents. The president of the firm was future Mayor John Gerard. Under an arrangement concluded in August 1952, Community Services, Inc. agreed to install and operate cable service for a basic installation charge and a reasonable monthly usage fee. Any profit which the company realized would be donated to charity. At the same time, the local utility company consented to have the tower built on reservoir property and, along with Southern Bell, to allow use of their poles for the cable. Within a few months, television was accessible by cable to virtually every household in Frankfort.

Although television quickly became a popular entertainment form, Frankfort remained a community of readers. In 1953 the Frankfort Public Library, still maintained by the Frankfort Women's Club, housed approximately 12,000 books. A dozen years later the number had increased to about 32,000. Meanwhile, the Franklin County Homemakers Clubs, in cooperation with the State Department of Libraries, initiated a countywide bookmobile in 1955. By 1965 its collection stood at about 10,000 volumes. With a combined total of approximately 42,000 books, the library and bookmobile collections provided an adequate core for a proposed Frankfort-Franklin County Public Library.

Serious planning for such a facility began as early as mid-1961, when a study committee appointed by the Franklin County Community Council reported that local library services were inadequate. The Frankfort Women's Club, for whom management of the collection at its offices at Washington and Wapping streets was becoming increasingly burdensome, could not have agreed more. The first active attempt to develop a new library came in the spring of 1962, when city, county, and state officials discussed building a $500,000 structure in the North Frankfort Urban Renewal Area which would house a city-county library and the State Library Department. But this plan was just one of many which got sidetracked in the tediously slow process of developing a feasible urban renewal package.

Library advocates still were marking time when the United States General Services Administration came to the rescue. In April 1964 construction ended on a new Post Office building at High and Mero streets near the State Office Building. The old post office at St. Clair and Wapping streets continued to house the federal court and related agencies, but planning for a new Federal Building already was under way, and the life of the handsome Victorian structure appeared threatened. A major unresolved issue was the site of the new government building. Some city officials and civic leaders wanted to demolish the old edifice and erect the new one on the same site. But other political figures, including Congressman John C. Watts, balked.

The matter was resolved temporarily in mid-January 1965, when Mayor James W. (Pete) Flynn negotiated an agreement with GSA officials in Washington, D.C., which enabled a recently organized city-county library board to lease the partially vacant post office building as temporary quarters for the

J. W. Flynn

new Paul Sawyier Public Library. Under this agreement the holdings at the Women's Club and the county bookmobile were transferred to the post office building and merged into a single collection. The affairs of the new library were directed by a library board chaired by William Davies. The remaining members included Kenneth Vance, architect Granville Coblin, Dr. Joseph Liebman, and Mrs. Lloyd Robinson. The board chose Miss Emily Peel, former Franklin County High School librarian, for the same post at the new library. Selected as her assistant was Mrs. Albert Shram, who had been librarian at the women's club.

What began as a temporary solution became permanent in 1975. After completion of the new Federal Building near the old state capitol, the GSA transferred the deed for the old post office to the library board. In late 1975, after ten years in its "temporary" quarters, the library was moved to 31-32 Fountain Place, where it remained for about eight months while the post office building was completely renovated. On August 15, 1976 the old structure was rededicated as the permanent home of the Paul Sawyier Public Library.

For many of Franklin County's business, professional, and political figures one of the most important cultural and social developments of the period was the new Frankfort Country Club. Before the depression the old country club, which dated back to the early part of the century, had been a popular center for social activity and entertainment for the city's elite. But the economic crisis of the 1930s made it difficult for many members to pay their dues. Consequently, by the end of World War II Frankfort was one of the few state capitals in America without a country club. As the end of the 1940s approached, several of the community's movers and shakers, led by Frankfort Electric and Water Plant Board executive Harold K. Hines, launched a movement to establish a new club. After purchasing a tract of the old S. French Hoge estate on Versailles Road, then about two miles from Frankfort, they erected a $250,000 brick club house.

Dedicated in May 1949, the plush facility included lockers and a caddy house in the basement and a spacious entry way, paneled bar, ladies' lounge, private dining room, and "lush main room" which opened onto a long veranda on the first floor. From the window of the main room one could gaze out upon a nine-hole golf course, two tennis courts, a swimming pool, and, in the distance, rolling bluegrass farmland enclosed by clean white fences. Under the leadership of president Louis Cox, a prominent Frankfort attorney and state senator, the club opened with 300 local and 50 out-of-town members.

No doubt a frequent topic of conversation at the country club was the problem of rearing children. With soaring birth rates and burgeoning school enrollments reshaping the landscape of Frankfort and other American cities, the joys and frustrations of family life were a pervasive concern for millions of Americans. One of the more troublesome issues in many communities involved reckless driving by teenagers behind the wheels of "hopped up" cars.

Judge John D. Darnell

Franklin County attracted national attention for its approach to the teenage driving problem in the 1950s. The innovation came in a rather fortuitous manner in 1955 when two youthful speed demons, after having their licenses suspended for two months for driving seventy miles per hour in a thirty-five-mile zone, complained to juvenile court Judge John D. Darnell that teenage traffic violators should be tried before jurors their own age. Smarting from what they considered excessive punishment, the errant drivers seemed convinced that other teens would be more sympathetic than the adult judge.

Perhaps to the young men's surprise, Judge Darnell liked their suggestion. The results were amazing. In December 1955 the initial group of eleven juvenile offenders appeared before a panel of teenage jurors. The number of teens brought to court declined steadily over the next six months, dropping to two each in June and July 1956. Judge Darnell hesitated to offer a sweeping explanation for the decline in juvenile traffic offenses. But the general consensus outside the courtroom, according to the *Saturday Evening Post*, was that the high school jurors "turned out, in the main, to be considerably tougher than the kindly, even indulgent juvenile court judge had been." By the fall of 1956 Judge Darnell was being deluged by inquiries from judges, traffic enforcement officials, and juvenile delinquency workers across the nation.

For Franklin County's black citizens, by far the most important improvements in the quality of life involved the desegregation of schools, public accommodations, and other facets of life in which racial separation had been the rule, either by custom or law, since the end of Reconstruction. As in many other communities, the civil rights struggle in Frankfort and Franklin County centered for many years on the desegregation of the public schools. The primary stimulus behind the movement was the United States Supreme Court's 1954 decision in *Brown v. Board of Education of Topeka*, which reversed the 1896 doctrine of "separate but equal" and declared that segregated schools were "inherently unequal."

For residents of Frankfort the *Brown* decision held a unique historical irony. The court's sole dissenter in the 1896 *Plessy v. Ferguson* case, which approved segregation, was Justice John Marshall Harlan, a former capital resident who had served as a Franklin County judge and later as governor of Kentucky. In his dissent from the *Plessy* decision, Justice Harlan declared that "our Constitution is color-blind." Compounding the irony was the fact that fifty-nine years later, a second John Marshall Harlan, appointed to the court by President Dwight D. Eisenhower after the first *Brown* decision, helped to vindicate his grandfather's position when he participated in the second *Brown* decision, which ordered that segregated schools be desegregated "with all deliberate speed."

At the time of the *Brown* decisions Franklin County had two segregated school systems. Most Negro children living in the city attended the Mayo-Underwood School, which still offered both elementary and secondary curricula. The Franklin County system operated no schools for black youth. Rather, the board of education paid tuition for black children in grades one through eight to attend the Rosenwald School, an educational laboratory center operated by Kentucky State College. Once the county pupils had graduated from Rosenwald they were transferred at county expense to Mayo-Underwood for high school. Rosenwald also attracted a few pupils from the city of Frankfort. Both Mayo-Underwood and Rosenwald ranked well below the other county schools in the quality of facilities and the quantity of resources devoted to the education of each child.

The struggle to desegregate the city schools began in November 1955 when the Frankfort Board of Education proposed to transfer black high school students from Mayo-Underwood to Frankfort High School the following September. The board took no action toward integrating the elementary schools. On the evening of September 5, 1956, two days before integration was to commence, two crosses were set ablaze on the lawn of Frankfort High School. Police attributed the incident to teenage pranksters rather than to die-hard opponents of racial mixing. Two days later the high school was desegregated as scheduled and without further significant incident.

Despite the peaceful desegregation of Frankfort High School, the board of education delayed action on the elementary schools for seven years. In mid-1962, after considerable pressure from the Frankfort chapter of the National Association for the Advancement of Colored People, the board agreed to begin desegregating the lower grades. However, when twenty-four Negro children and their parents appeared at the Murray Street and Second Street schools in early September to be enrolled, all but four were turned away. The children who remained were admitted to the first grade at Murray Street. When parents and NAACP officials protested, school officials replied that the board's policy was to integrate one grade each year, with the possibility of speeding the process if everything progressed smoothly in 1962.

But eight years already had passed since the initial *Brown* decision, and black citizens were determined to wait no longer. While the parents whose children had been denied admission at previously all white schools kept them at home, the school board rejected a plea by a delegation of black citizens to speed up the desegregation process. In mid-September, after school officials threatened legal action against parents who were boycotting the schools, the pupils reluctantly returned to Mayo-Underwood. In response to the continuing indignity of segregation, black parents carried out an earlier threat to file suit in federal court to force complete and immediate desegregation of the elementary schools. In early July 1963, after a long legal fight, Judge H. Church Ford of the United States District Court in Lexington approved a plan for the immediate integration of Frankfort's elementary schools and the closing of Mayo-Underwood School. Two months later the capital's elementary schools opened on schedule on an integrated basis.

Hampered in part by overcrowding, the Franklin County system moved even more slowly in integrating its small black student body into the public schools. But Judge Ford's decision on the Frankfort case finally forced the school board to cease paying tuition and transportation costs for black children to attend Rosenwald. Moreover, the closing of Mayo-Underwood made it impossible to send black teenagers there for high school classes. Consequently, about sixty Negro youths enrolled at Elkhorn School that fall. About eighty children still attended Rosenwald in 1964, but not at county expense.

The campaign for equal education had its counterparts in other aspects of life. Generating particular heat was the demand by blacks for desegregation of local theaters, restaurants, retail stores, and other places of public accommodation. The Frankfort campaign for open accommodations commenced in the late fall of 1961, when professors and students at Kentucky State College began picketing, boycotting, and staging sit-ins at downtown businesses which refused to seat or otherwise discriminated against blacks. Such direct tactics were accompanied by periodic efforts to negotiate a solution fair to all concerned. Shortly before Christmas 1961, in an effort to demonstrate their sincerity, leaders of the demonstrations announced in the *State Journal* that they were willing "as continuing proof of our cooperation and fairness [to] . . . accept opening of local eating facilities to all on a trial basis of 30 to 60 days."

While this initial round of demonstrations was unsuccessful, the movement won an important public relations victory. In early January 1962 the Frankfort Ministerial Association, the long-established public voice of the city's pastors, formally requested that the city's restaurants and business houses be integrated. Urging the community to recognize the inevitability of integration, the ministers recommended that "all facilities and business establishments in Frankfort be made available to all people." Perhaps in a pastoral rebuke to those who accused blacks for seeking too much too fast, the association commended the black citizens of Frankfort and the students of KSC for their patience in waiting for local civil rights leaders "to bring about an end to segregation in eating establishments."

As the weather turned colder and the issue remained unresolved, demonstrations broke off for the winter. But direct action resumed in the beginning of April 1962. About fifty Negroes picketed a local drive-in restaurant, while all downtown eating establishments became the targets of peaceful demonstrations. The first arrests associated with civil rights activity came on April 4, when four young blacks were charged with breach of peace during a sit-in at the lunch counter of a downtown drug store. Such demonstrations and periodic arrests continued into 1963, when Governor Bert Combs finally issued an executive order ending segregation in private businesses catering to the public. By the end of the year, blacks were being served in many downtown restaurants. But the right to desegregated service was not secured until the following July with passage of the federal Civil Rights Act of 1964.

Frequently obscured by the rapid social, economic, and demographic growth which engulfed Frankfort during the postwar years was the impact which these forces of change had upon the rest of the county. One significant consequence was a serious erosion of the rural population base in several sections of the county as some country folk moved to the city and others had the city come to them through annexation. The population of Bald Knob dropped from 2,203 in 1940 to 1,829 in 1970. Forks of Elkhorn's population fell from 3,133 to 2,623, and Peak's Mill's declined from 3,427 to 2,311 persons during the same period. Only Bridgeport, where the intersection of State Highway 151 with U.S. 60 and I-64 created a strong suburban growth node, experienced a long-term population increase. By more than doubling in population, from 3,052 persons in 1940 to 6,362 in 1970, Bridgeport grew strongly enough to guarantee that the county still would experience a net increase in rural population between 1940 and 1970.

Unfortunately, much of the new residential development in rural Franklin County occurred in a very haphazard fashion. In the absence of subdivision and zoning regulations, a good deal of scattered residential construction on large lots occurred along major rural arteries such as Owenton Pike and Lewis Ferry, Harvieland, Bald Knob, Peak's Mill, and Benson roads. Much of this unregulated growth was not only aesthetically unattractive but also quite costly when it came to providing services such as water, sewers, law enforcement, and fire protection. Numerous small subdivisions platted beyond the reach of Frankfort's subdivision regulations were developed with streets which failed to meet even the most minimal construction standards. Moreover, such uncontrolled development, especially in the fertile southern and southeastern sections of the county, had the effect of depriving future Franklin County farmers of some of the area's best agricultural land.

Although urbanization and scattered residential development contributed to the loss of nearly 14,000 acres of crop and grazing land between 1940 and 1970, agriculture remained an important element in Franklin County's economy. However, the well-established trend of a declining number of farmers operating fewer farms of growing acreage not only continued but accelerated during the postwar years. The number of working farms in the county dropped by one-third, from 1,363 in 1940 to just 905 three decades later. On the other hand, the size of the average farm increased from barely 91 acres to approximately 122 acres during the same period. Furthermore, virtually all the farmers who went out of business operated less than 500 acres, while the number of farms in excess of 500 acres increased from eight in 1940 to twenty-two in 1970.

This increase in the scale of farming was not necessarily matched by long-range growth in productivity and prices. Prices did improve rather dramatically during the immediate postwar years, as the value of livestock production jumped from $1.3 million in 1945 to more than $2 million five years later. Similarly, the value of the local burley crop rose from less than $827,000 in 1939 to nearly $2.3 million in 1949. Over the next two decades, however, growth was rather stagnant, with livestock values dropping below $2 million in 1969, while the tobacco harvest fetched only about $2.8 million. Neither did the county's agricultural economic base experience appreciable diversification. In 1969 only the tobacco and cattle industries realized sales in excess of $1 million. Sales of sheep, lambs, and wool amounted to about $345,000, and dairy products brought approximately $236,000. The picture was even more dismal in grains and forage crops, where sales figures dropped substantially below those of 1939. Meanwhile, poultry sales barely managed to reach $26,000, and total sales for vegetables, fruits and nuts, and other field crops amounted to just $10,000 in 1969. Any number of circumstances, of course, might account for this situation, but it also seems reasonably clear that the unrelenting expansion of the city contributed significantly to the erosion of the county's agricultural base.

The modest decline in agricultural activity and the steady increase in the size of farms, combined with the proliferation of nonfarm housing along the country roads, had a pronounced impact upon Franklin County's rural landscape. As a growing number of farmers quit the land, some of their aging farmsteads began to deteriorate. By 1970 distinct pockets of blight had begun to appear throughout the county.

The heaviest deterioration occurred in the Bald Knob district where in 1970 over 67 percent of the housing units were valued at less than $10,000 each, and nearly 27 percent of all homes were classified by the planning commission as either deteriorating or dilapidated. The deterioration was especially apparent along sections of Harp Pike and Harvieland, Flat Creek, and Goose Creek roads. Deterioration was minimal in the Bridgeport district as a whole; but sizable concentrations of blight could be found in the Benson Valley west of Frankfort, where nearly all the houses were dilapidated, and in Choateville, where approximately one-quarter of the homes were in a similar state of disrepair. In the Peak's Mill district small groups of dilapidated houses could be found in Swallowfield and Elmville and along Peak's Mill Road between Indian Gap Road and Elmville. As the wealthiest of the county's rural districts, Forks of Elkhorn had the lowest proportion of poor housing. Nevertheless, small pockets of dilapidation were apparent in the Switzer vicinity and along a stretch of Glenn's Creek Road about a mile south of Frankfort.

But if the price were right these scattered clusters of deteriorated houses did not prevent those desiring country homes from building on nearby lots. Thus by 1970 it was not uncommon to see new contractor modern houses sitting cheek by jowl with aging and often dilapidated farm houses. Truly the same forces of change which had shaped Frankfort's expansion during the quarter century that followed World War II also had begun to transform the countryside.

13

A Heritage Rediscovered

AS THE 1970S DAWNED, residents of Frankfort and Franklin County found themselves still engulfed in the throes of an urban explosion which had dramatically transformed the landscape since 1945. By 1980, despite the end of the baby boom, they had experienced one of the heaviest decades of growth in the community's history. Likewise, local population and economic growth continued to follow directions similar to those which had been established during the previous twenty-five years.

Certainly most observers considered such growth a positive development. By mid-decade, however, a few discerning civic leaders were beginning to realize a need to improve the quality of growth and to reduce urban sprawl. Accompanying this stress on the quality of growth was an increasingly pervasive awareness of the richness of the community's past. This historic sensitivity generated numerous efforts to identify and preserve those elements of the built environment which symbolize the city's heritage and to revitalize them for functions appropriate to today's society and economy. Thus as Kentucky's capital enters its third century, its people can look to the future with a sense of confidence built upon a tangible foundation of two hundred years of individual and collective achievement.

Propelling Franklin County's growth during the 1970s was a 21.3 percent increase in the population, from 34,481 inhabitants in 1970 to 41,830 in 1980. Frankfort experienced an almost identical growth rate, as its population jumped from 21,356 to 25,973, a 21.6 percent increase, during the same period. By 1980 more than 62 percent of the county's residents lived in the capital city. Frankfort ranked as the commonwealth's sixth largest city and Franklin as its seventeenth most populous county.

During the early 1970s much of the city's growth centered in large subdivision projects whose development had begun during the middle and late 1960s. On the west, additional sections were added to the Meadows, Westgate, and Cloverdale subdivisions. To the northeast three more sections of the Colony subdivision began their development between 1971 and 1974. Several miles to the south, on a parcel between and slightly to the north of Inverness Estates and Tierra Linda, real estate broker Walter Malmer commenced the development of Tierra Linda III.

In the meantime, developers started moving forward with plans for the first of nearly a dozen totally new subdivisions which would be platted between 1970 and 1985. In 1972 James C. Bishop received approval from the planning commission to proceed with work on his Park Hills Development, located on the northern third of a large, triangular tract bounded by Schenkel Lane, Wilkinson Boulevard, and the Frankfort & Cincinnati Railroad. Four years later, a development firm headed by Bobby Matthews, Jr., began laying out the remainder of the tract as the Landings subdivision. The same year, A. L. (Dick) Barbour, a prominent automobile dealer, initiated development of Ridgeview Estates on a large tract north of Wilkinson Boulevard and Schenkel Lane adjacent to Indian Hills. Joining Barbour in 1977 was attorney Michael Judy. Together they had platted ten sections of the development by 1983.

On the city's western fringe a new wave of development began in August 1976 when real estate brokers Glenn Purdy and Warner Hines initiated Westwood Park on a long tract which extended from Cardwell Lane to Old Harrodsburg Road south of the Meadows. The following month, Walter Malmer, David C. Collins, and Russell W. Rice, Jr. platted the first of three sections of River Bend subdivision. Joined in 1979 by attorney and politician William Curlin, who replaced Rice, the group transformed the hills from Buttimer Hill to Devil's Hollow Road into an affluent residential neighborhood. In April 1979 Woodlin Properties, a firm composed of clothier Fayette Crutcher, Jr., dentist John D. Sutterlin, Woodford County attorney and businessman Leonard K. Nave, and drug store heiress Louise H. Ward, platted the first section of Cedars subdivision, situated on the east side of King's Daughters Drive south of Bondurant Drive. With the beginning of phase two of Cedars in January 1984, the city's residential area extended all the way to I-64.

The residential development of the 1970s triggered a major wave of annexation. Between 1971 and 1980 Frankfort added nearly 4,370 acres of territory and hundreds of new residents. During the first half of the decade the city concentrated its expansion efforts on the western fringe. In 1971 it annexed a recent section of the Meadows and two small parcels on U.S. 60 adjacent to Capital City Airport and the Kentucky State Police headquarters. Added the following year were the remaining portion of Cloverdale adjacent to Collins Lane Elementary School, Buttimer Hill, a parcel north of Juniper Hill subdivision, and several large, irregular pieces of commercial and future institutional property along Lawrenceburg and King's Daughters Drive between I-64 and Juniper Hill Municipal Park. Included was the eastern half of Westwood Park. In 1973 the city absorbed a 23.4-acre tract west of Juniper Hills. Two years later Frankfort added the remaining elements of the Meadows subdivision near U.S. 60. But east Frankfort was not wholly ignored. In 1973 the city annexed the remainder of the Colony, all of Park Hills, and the projected sites of the Landings and Ridgeview Estates subdivisions.

While some annexation occurred on both east and west during the second half of the decade, the heaviest activity was along the capital's southern edge. In the spring of 1976 the city took in Brighton Park Mall on Versailles Road opposite Sunset Drive. Later that year, the city limits were extended to embrace Parkview Estates, situated between Devil's Hollow Road and Juniper Hill Park. In May 1978 Frankfort annexed the entire River Bend complex and the remaining portion of Westwood Park. But the largest single annexation in the city's history occurred in late November when it added a 2,061-acre swath which extended along the southern fringe between the Kentucky River on the west and Hanley Lane on the east. The new addition was bisected by the new East-West Connector and included the Inverness Estates subdivision. A second major addition came the following year when Frankfort annexed a 915-acre tract bounded roughly by Cloverdale on the north, Cedar Run on the east, I-64 on the south, and Old Harrodsburg and Lawrenceburg roads on the west. The capital reached its present limits in 1980 with the annexation of three undeveloped parcels along Wilkinson Avenue and the Kentucky River in order to rationalize the northern boundary between Ridgeview Estates and Benson Creek.

While the combination of residential development and annexation fueled a major increase in the capital's population during the 1970s, the urbanizing tendency was not confined to the changing city limits. Between 1970 and 1977 no fewer than forty-nine separate subdivision developments were initiated in Franklin County outside the present boundary of Frankfort. A fourth of them were small tracts which amounted to no more than ten lots, but an even larger proportion included more than a hundred lots. Most were concentrated in the southern and central portions of the county, but Webb Acres, with thirty-four lots, was platted at Flag Fork in the county's northwest corner.

The heaviest development outside the city occurred in a corridor which stretches in a northeasterly direction from Versailles Road to Forks of Elkhorn. Its development began in 1970 when Community Development, Inc., headed by businessman Owen Caplinger, platted Country Lane Estates on a large tract adjoining Versailles Road at U.S. 421. Adjacent to Country Lane Estates is Two Creeks, a complex of large, upper middle class homes which stretches to the South Fork of Elkhorn Creek. William H. May's Brighton Engineering Company initiated Two Creeks in July 1972. Four more subdivisions, platted along U.S. 460 in the vicinity of Forks of Elkhorn between 1970 and 1975, contributed to a belt of urban development consisting of no less than 1,000 lots, including a 132-space mobile home park.

Several nearby communities experienced lesser degrees of residential development between 1970 and 1977. Four subdivisions with more than 700 lots were platted in the Evergreen vicinity. Nearly 300 lots were laid out in four subdivisions in the Farmdale neighborhood. Over 160 lots in four subdivisions were recorded in nearby Bridgeport. And some 240 lots in seven small subdivisions were staked out along Owenton Road between the northern edge of Frankfort and Elkhorn Creek.

Frankfort's continuing growth likewise resulted in the expansion or relocation of numerous public services and community facilities. The pressures of urbanization were especially severe for the Franklin County public school system, which built four new schools between 1970 and 1980. Hearn Elementary School, located near Sunset Drive west of Versailles Road, opened in 1973. Completed the same year was Bondurant Middle School, situated in southwest Frankfort near I-64. Constructed two years later was Elkhorn Middle School, which adjoins Franklin County High School on Georgetown Road. By 1979 expanding teenage enrollment necessitated construction of Western Hills High School at Bondurant Drive and Doctors Drive near the middle school. When Western Hills opened the following year, the county school system was divided into two high school attendance districts, with Franklin County High serving the area east of the Kentucky River and Western Hills the area west of the river.

Urbanization also had a major impact upon the older schools, both city and county. As a result of rapid growth in Frankfort's western fringe, enrollment at the county's Bridgeport Elementary School, erected in 1940, shot up 25 percent between 1973 and 1977. On the other hand, declining population in the city's core resulted in the closing of the Murray Street, Holmes Street, Bellepoint, and Wilkinson Street schools. By 1977 Frankfort High School and Second Street Elementary School were the only educational facilities still operated by the Frankfort Board of Education. Also in 1977 Kentucky State University, racially integrated since the mid-1960s, closed the aging Rosenwald School, which had become an expensive relic of the days of segregated education. Raised to its present status in 1973, KSU also experienced major expansions in both facilities and enrollment during the 1970s. Contributing to this growth was the large number of state employees and other area residents who took advantage of the University's wide range of degree programs, including a master of public affairs, to improve their professional skills.

Some major institutions responded to the suburban trend by relocating their operations in new, larger quarters on the city's fringes. Perhaps the most conspicuous locational change involved King's Daughters' Memorial Hospital. By early 1972 its aging facility on Hanna Place in South Frankfort was overcrowded and in severe financial straits. After intense community discussion of the hospital situation, the sponsoring Silent Workers Circle decided in the fall of 1972 to sell the hospital to Hospital Corporation of America, the nation's largest owner and operator of hospitals. Shortly after completing the purchase, the Nashville, Tennessee firm began construction of a new, technologically advanced facility on a large tract near I-64 west of Lawrenceburg Road. Designed by Graham & Smith Architects and built by the Joe M. Rogers Construction Company, both of Nashville, the $7 million facility housed 130 beds in 128,500 square feet of floor space. The new hospital was opened in July 1974 and has since been expanded to 190 beds. Seven years after the new hospital opened, the Silent Workers Circle converted the old facility into an apartment complex for the elderly.

King's Daughters Hospital, King's Daughters Road.

Another institution which moved into new suburban quarters was the Kentucky Department of Libraries and Archives. Formerly located in the old Berry Hill mansion near Juniper Hill Municipal Park, the department moved into its Brutalistic concrete headquarters on Coffee Tree Road in October 1982. Authorized four years earlier during the administration of Governor Julian Carroll, the structure was designed by the architectural firm of Peck, Flannery, Gream, and Warren, Inc. The Library and Archives Building was one of the first major projects which followed completion of the East-West Connector (State Road 676) between U.S. 127 and Versailles Road in December 1970. In addition to opening for development hundreds of acres of hillside land on Frankfort's southern edge, this four lane highway improved access to the state capitol and Kentucky State University.

Kentucky State Library and Archives, Coffee Tree Road.

Situated immediately to the southwest of the Department of Libraries and Archives on the Kentucky River is another major public improvement of the period. In 1970 consulting engineers reported to the Frankfort Electric and Water Plant Board that the existing water treatment plant, completed in 1914, was no longer adequate to meet the community's water needs. Heeding the engineers' warning, the board let contracts in the summer of 1972 for construction of a new treatment plant with a daily capacity of 18 million gallons. Financed through a $5.5 million revenue bond issue, the new facility was dedicated in late September 1975, following delays which cost the contractor $250 a day in penalties for ten months. The ultimate construction cost was $7.5 million. As the plant neared completion, Marshall Tinder, general manager of the plant board, estimated that it would supply local industrial, commercial, and residential water needs for at least sixty years.

Commerce and industry, like public services, continued to follow their customers and employees to the suburbs. This was especially the case with retail stores and personal services businesses, which sought locations on well-traveled arteries where they could attract both transient and local traffic. Commercial development was especially heavy along Versailles Road in east Frankfort and Louisville and Lawrenceburg roads in west Frankfort. By the early 1980s both roads were lined on either side with dozens of fast food restaurants, drive-in banks, service stations, and numerous other retail and service establishments. Scores of other businesses, from department stores and specialty shops to theaters and automobile service shops, concentrated in no fewer than eight community and regional shopping centers erected in the city during the 1970s.

During the early 1970s a couple of shopping centers were built in other locations. Fort Boone Plaza, which opened in 1973, was constructed at Wilkinson Avenue and Reilly Road. Completed about the same time was Rolling Acres Shopping Center, at 125 Rolling Acres Drive near East Main Street. By mid-decade, however, the focus of community development clearly had shifted to the Louisville-Lawrenceburg road and Versailles Road corridors. By 1975 Shoppers Village at 310-320 Versailles Road and Pine Hill Plaza at 1121 Louisville Road were open for business. Within two years construction had been completed on Brighton Park Mall on Versailles Road, Century Plaza at Lawrenceburg Road and Springhill Drive, and Franklin Square at Lawrenceburg Road and the East-West Connector. By far the largest and most strategically located of Frankfort's new commercial facilities, Franklin Square ranks as the community's only regional shopping center, drawing heavy patronage from Shelby, Anderson, Woodford, and Scott counties as well as local shoppers.

Franklin County experienced very little new industrial development during the 1970s. However, that which did occur took place in the suburban industrial park near Jett. In 1971 the General Electric Company erected a plant at U.S. 60 and I-64 for the manufacture of plastic components and materials. Three years later Southern Mouldings opened a metal stamping plant on Chenault Road near Industrial Road. By 1978 the two firms employed approximately 335 workers. However, the new jobs created by General Electric and Southern Mouldings were almost entirely offset by the closing in 1977 of the Genesco Shoe Company, which was forced out of business by foreign competition. Still, industrial employment in 1978 stood at nearly 3,500 workers. Over 3,300 of these jobs were in plants outside the city limits, with Union Underwear Company, Inc. and National Distillers Products Company ranking as the county's two largest employers. Standing a distant third with 350 employees was Schenley Distillers, Inc., which occupied the old Stagg distillery at Leestown. The distillery still employed 325 workers when the Ancient Age Distilling Company purchased it from Schenley in 1983.

Frankfort's expansion also continued to have a substantial impact upon local agriculture. Because of the increasing instability of American agriculture between 1970 and 1985, it is difficult to distinguish precisely the effects of urbanization from those directly attributable to prevailing agricultural conditions. One clear trend was a significant increase in "gentleman farming." Even as the total amount of farm acreage continued its long-term decline, residents with a variety of occupations purchased farms of fifty acres or less. Thus, as total acreage declined while the number of farms increased, the size of the average farm began to decline, dropping from 128 acres in 1964 to 116 acres in 1982.

After a period of stagnation during the 1950s and 1960s, many Franklin County farmers found the 1970s a time of relative prosperity. Tobacco sales soared from less than $3 million in 1969 to more than $10 million in 1982. Likewise, sales of livestock, after dropping from about $1.9 million in 1969 to less than $1.7 million in 1974, topped $4.3 million in 1982. Grain sales also showed substantial improvement. On the other hand, sales of hay and silage and dairy products, after improving significantly between 1974 and 1978, dropped sharply between 1978 and 1982. By early 1985, with the federal tobacco price support program in serious jeopardy, many Franklin County farmers were facing the future with a deep sense of uncertainty.

State government remained the core of Franklin County's

economic base and the chief source of jobs during the 1970s and early 1980s. During the mid-1970s the Commonwealth employed an estimated 5,500 Franklin Countians and an additional 2,500 to 3,000 commuters from the surrounding counties, especially Anderson, Fayette, Henry, Owen, Scott, Spencer, and Woodford. By 1980 the number of state workers employed in Franklin County may have exceeded 13,000.

But as early as 1977 some of the city's business and political leaders were voicing concern over Frankfort's image as a "company town" whose economy was excessively dominated by state government. They fully recognized the historic importance of the state as a source of economic prosperity and stability. In 1976 state workers paid the city treasury nearly $1 million in occupational taxes and pumped additional millions into the community through their transactions with local financial institutions, apartment and real estate developers, utility companies, automobile dealers, service stations, physicians, attorneys, restaurants, appliance dealers, clothing stores, and a host of other businesses. On the other hand, some community leaders sensed that "Frankfort's special association with state government," and the city's "access to high level state officials and the state treasury" tended to "make local government lazy, less aggressive and complacent in tackling its own problems and solving them."

James Burch

Reinforcing the civic leaders' apprehensions was a feeling that Frankfort was failing to "get our share of state attention," as a local banker complained. As the state capital, he suggested, "Frankfort should be a model for the whole state of Kentucky." Furthermore, he added, state personnel possessed the technical and professional knowledge necessary for the city to realize such a dream. The problem was a "lack of coordination between the state and local governments." Too many talented state employees had become permanent residents of Frankfort without becoming part of the community. The challenge, as Mayor James Burch observed, was "to get that talent to identify with Frankfort and to be a part of Frankfort."

The concerns of these community leaders were vindicated in 1980, when newly elected Governor John Y. Brown, Jr., facing a severe revenue shortage, initiated extensive layoffs in an effort to slash state expenditures. An estimated 5,000 state workers lost their jobs. About one-third of those dismissed worked in Franklin County. The effects of the cutbacks reverberated throughout the local economy. Consumer spending and city revenues dropped off and the local unemployment rate increased by more than 1 percent.

Many angry Frankfortians charged that Brown had "acted without Frankfort's best interests in mind." The extent of local bitterness was suggested in November 1981, when Franklin County voters rejected a proposed gubernatorial and sheriff's succession amendment to the Kentucky Constitution by a vote of six to one while the rest of the state defeated it by two to one. But some considered Brown's actions a healthy demonstration of Frankfort's excessive dependence upon state government. Mayor John R. Sower, for ex ample, warmly endorsed the governor's recommendation that the community undertake an aggressive program to promote tourism and industrial development and to diversify the local economy. Patricia Badgett, executive director of the chamber of commerce, agreed that "we do need to do more for ourselves." Farmers Bank & Capital Trust Company expressed its concurrence by hiring two former employees of the state commerce cabinet to seek business and industrial prospects for Frankfort.

The governor's challenge to diversify was more than hollow rhetoric. Accompanying it was a commitment for state assistance in obtaining a developer and putting together financing for a long-sought hotel for the Capital Plaza. Plans for a new downtown hotel, which was considered essential for the expansion of Frankfort's convention and tourism business, had cropped up frequently since the new Capital Hotel closed in 1962. The most recent proposal, for an $11 million convention hotel in the Capital Plaza had fizzled in 1977 when the Julian Carroll administration failed to obtain approval of a $3.5 million bond issue to help finance the project.

Capital Plaza Hotel, northeast corner of Wilkinson and Clinton Streets.

It took more than a year after Governor Brown endorsed the project to recruit a developer and to assemble a financing package. But in December 1982 Lexington developer and financier Wallace Wilkinson, with the aid of a $7 million state industrial revenue bond, began construction of the 189-room Capital Plaza Hotel at the northeast corner of Wilkinson Avenue and Clinton Street. When financing arrangements were finished, City Manager Paul Royster estimated that the completed hotel would generate "five to 10 million dollars . . . in tourist-related commerce" every year. Architecturally consistent with the rest of Capital Plaza, the new hotel opened in early 1984. Its facilities include two dining rooms, a variety of seminar and meeting rooms, complete banquet and catering services, and the Assembly Ballroom, which accommodates up to 700 persons.

In addition to energizing the city's convention and tourism program, the Capital Plaza Hotel also was a boon to the revitalization of the central business district, which had not seen the construction of a major new building since the completion of the Farmers Bank & Capital Trust Company building in 1971. The movement to pump new life into downtown Frankfort involved the convergence of two essentially antagonistic strategies—urban renewal and historic preservation. Proposals to revitalize the downtown date back to 1959, when Phillip Hammer & Associates of Atlanta recommended measures to reduce congestion, improve traffic circulation, expand parking, and eliminate or upgrade structurally obsolete buildings. Two years later a group of local businessmen calling themselves the Frankfort Committee proposed the construction of a downtown motel and convention center and an underground garage with 300 parking spaces. The committee recommended a riverfront location at the southwest corner of Main and Ann streets. The central idea was to stimulate downtown business growth by channeling tourists and conventioneers directly into the downtown. Although it won preliminary approval for urban renewal funding, the project had to be scrapped when the premature demolition of some buildings in the renewal area made the entire enterprise ineligible for federal funding.

Despite this failure, the dream of downtown revitalization remained alive. In 1963 the Capital City Planning Commission, with the support of city and county governments and the chamber of commerce, undertook an extensive new study of downtown Frankfort's problems and needs. The commission developed a plan to improve the central business district's accessibility, to preserve its compactness, to upgrade circulation, and to create a more attractive appearance to visitors and shoppers. The commission's report included several specific recommendations, including widening of Wilkinson and Dailey avenues from Thorn Hill By-pass to Broadway (completed in 1974), a series of one-way street pairs to improve traffic circulation and reduce congestion, and development of about 1,000 additional parking spaces. But the plan's key proposal was to close St. Clair Street from Main to Broadway to vehicular traffic and to convert it into a pedestrian mall.

Deeply involved at the time in the North Frankfort urban renewal project, the Urban Renewal Commission was not inclined in 1963 to embark upon a brand new enterprise downtown. But the idea of a mall proved a durable one. As the Capital Plaza neared completion in the early 1970s, the mall proposal began to attract new attention. By early 1973 a groundswell of support had developed. But a critical figure who remained unconvinced was Maurice H. Scott, a retired interior decorator and furniture store operator, who served as chairman of the Urban Renewal and Community Development Agency. Scott changed his mind, however, after he and several other members of the Frankfort Downtown Merchants Association had an opportunity to visit Dubuque, Iowa, and to talk with some of that city's merchants about their mall.

Now an enthusiastic supporter of the mall concept, Scott returned to the capital and pushed forward with the proposal. After several months of design work and financial planning, construction contracts were let in the fall of 1973. By the end of the year roar of jackhammers tearing into the asphalt could be heard up and down St. Clair Street. Completed in September 1974 at a cost of approximately $280,000, the new mall featured red brick pavement and two ranks of sixteen-foot linden trees encased in stone planters. In 1975 it was supplemented by construction of a 200-car parking garage on the west side of St. Clair. As designed by the architectural firm of Burris and Thompson, the garage was erected behind a brick facade which blends with the rest of the streetscape.

The St. Clair Mall quickly generated a new sense of hope for the future of the downtown. Even before construction ended, numerous merchants began to experience some increase in sales. Several shopowners spruced up their storefronts and removed unsightly overhanging signs. But it soon became apparent that the mall had both aesthetic and economic limitations. Fourteen months after it opened, architectural consultant Lockwood Martling characterized the mall as unimaginative "rows of trees [that] are too formal and regimented looking, giving the impression [that] they are marching down the street."

More importantly, the mall alone proved insufficient to reverse the downtown's competitive decline relative to the suburban shopping centers. After an initial flurry of new business starts, the loss of such stores as the J. C. Penney Company made it clear that removing the cars from a single block would not revive the entire downtown business area. To a growing number of observers, a solution was required which recognized and took advantage of downtown Frankfort's historic architectural fabric.

The notion that Frankfort's architectural heritage should be preserved was hardly a new one. As far back as June 1964 Governor Edward T. Breathitt, by executive order, had created the Capital City Heritage Commission and charged it with overseeing the preservation and development of the Corner in Celebrities neighborhood. The immediate occasion for creation of the commission was a controversy over the threatened destruction of the ancient Vest-Lindsey home at the southwest corner of Washington and Wapping streets by two Louisville developers who planned to replace it with a three-story office building. Governor Breathitt finally intervened in the case, persuaded the developers not to exercise their option on the property, and enabled them to find another location for their building. Soon thereafter the Capital City Heritage Commission, under the executive directorship of Mrs. Ida Willis, wife of former Governor Simeon Willis, established its headquarters in the Vest-Lindsey house. In 1966 the General Assembly enacted legislation which transformed the commission into a statewide body, the Kentucky Heritage Commission.

Although frequently maligned as a collection of dilettantes who lacked an appreciation for economic reality, the preservation movement gathered momentum during the late 1960s and early 1970s. A major impetus behind preservation's popularity was growing public concern over the loss of such historic landmarks as the Solomon Sharp and John Marshall Harlan houses on Madison Street to the new Federal Building, and the destruction of the Terraces, the Greek Revival home of nineteenth century businessman Philip Swigert located on the south side of Wapping Street between Washington Street and the Sawyier Library, for a municipal parking lot. In 1969 a group of preservation advocates formed Historic Frankfort, Inc. The new organization devoted its efforts not only to the preservation of the community's distinguished old residences but to the practical reuse of its commercial buildings as well. In December 1970 the City-County Planning Commission designated the Corner in Celebrities area and a portion of Capitol Avenue in South Frankfort as a historic district warranting special protection. Three months later the National Park Service accepted the Kentucky Heritage Commission's recommendation that the Corner in Celebrities district and nineteen individual structures in Frankfort and Franklin County be listed on the National Register of Historic Places. Among the latter were the old state capitol, the Kentucky State Arsenal, the old governor's mansion, and the Rev. Jesse Zeigler (Frank Lloyd Wright) house. An additional thirty-three structures, including several in the Corner in Celebrities and Statehouse neighborhoods, were individually identified as having state significance and designated as Kentucky landmarks.

During the late 1970s the preservation movement turned much of its attention to the growing number of vacant downtown commercial buildings. The preservationists' focus on downtown, including the St. Clair Mall, was no mere exercise in civic and aesthetic altruism. The federal Tax Reform Act of 1976 provided major incentives for the careful renovation and reuse of certified, income-producing historic properties. Three years later the Kentucky Heritage Commission successfully nominated the central business district to the National Register of Historic Places, making downtown structures eligible for Tax Reform Act benefits. Armed with these and other economic incentives, numerous preservationists became investors, and even more investors discovered the values of preservation.

One of the first Frankfort residents to join the preservationist ranks as an investor was building contractor William Crumbaugh, a former teacher and Franklin County High School baseball coach, who in 1980 purchased the Murray Building, located on the mall. He renovated the second and third floors into four apartments and leased the ground floor to neighboring Judd's Office Products for its furniture division. (Judd's had moved to the mall from its former location at 202 West Main a year earlier.) Crumbaugh purchased and renovated several more buildings over the next three years, including 231 West Broadway, which became The Tin Ceiling, an Appalachian arts and crafts gallery; the V. Kaltenbrun Building, also on the mall; and the former Guidi Building, at the northeast corner of Broadway and Lewis streets, which became the site of Kentucky Quilt Corner, Crumbaugh's offices, and five apartments. Crumbaugh also renovated buildings at 235 and 239 West Broadway, owned by local attorney and preservation advocate John Gray.

Meanwhile, a KSU English professor, Dr. Richard Taylor, and his wife Elizabeth purchased 233 West Broadway and opened Poor Richard's Books in August 1981. About the same time, Frankfort architect Milton Thompson and partners Charles Wiechers and Donald Dunstall purchased the Fitzgerald Building (formerly the W. A. Gaines & Co. building) at 229 West Main. With the aid of a $1 million city industrial revenue bond, DTW Partnership converted the century-old distillery office and warehouse building into offices which today house the Kentucky Department of Labor. By the beginning of 1985 more than a dozen downtown renovation projects had been completed or were in progress.

While historic preservation became a pivotal economic tool in the revitalization of the central business district, preservation activities were confined neither to downtown nor to the city of Frankfort. In 1976 the Kentucky Her-

At left, Poor Richard's Books at 233 Broadway shortly after its move to this location. Above the bookstore the warehouse of Gnomon Press is evident. At right, Debra Gray supervises painting of 235 Broadway.

itage Commission undertook an extensive survey of historically and architecturally significant structures throughout Franklin County. As a result of this inventory, 110 structures were documented as having potential significance. Within the city the historic neighborhood surrounding the old state capitol was added to the National Register of Historic Places as the Old Statehouse Historic District in June 1980. Twenty-six months later South Frankfort received similar recognition. With the approval of the South Frankfort district nearly everything that remains of Frankfort's historic core was listed on the National Register.

While preservationists dedicated themselves to saving Frankfort and Franklin County's architectural heritage from the wrecking ball and neglect, the community remained vulnerable to the destructive forces of nature. So it was on Wednesday, April 3, 1974. The morning dawned much as any other early spring day in central Kentucky. The air was cool and damp, but the weather forecast was for a warm day with a possibility of rain. But as Franklin Countians prepared to face their daily rounds, forces were building up hundreds of miles away which would, within a few hours, shatter the peace and tear a path of death and destruction across southern Franklin County.

For nearly forty-eight hours a massive storm system had been building over the Great Plains and the Rocky Mountains. Early Wednesday morning the storm center began moving eastward, picking up warm, moist Gulf air as it traveled toward the Mississippi and Ohio valleys. Soon severe thunderstorm warnings were issued for northern Alabama and Georgia, part of Missouri, and all of Tennessee, Kentucky, Indiana, and Ohio. To make matters worse, the Jet Stream was moving rapidly over the Ohio Valley, pulling pressure from the path of the colliding storm systems and, according to Louisville journalist John Ed Pearce, "acting as a suction valve to speed the storm even more swiftly on its way." Conditions were growing ideal for a severe tornado.

The U.S. Weather Service in Louisville had begun tracking the storm before dawn. The first tornado warning was issued at 10:28 A.M. Subsequent warnings were broadcast at 1:19 and 2:34 P.M. Shortly after the third warning, the system began thrusting off a series of deadly tornados which soon extended from Alabama to the Canadian border. The first sighting in the Louisville region occurred about 2:45 near Palmyra, Indiana. Over the next two hours the storm traveled 120 miles, destroyed hundreds of homes and businesses, and left several people dead before dying out as a rainstorm over Cincinnati.

Meanwhile, the weather service detected another funnel cloud near Irvington in Breckinridge County, Kentucky. A warning was broadcast immediately, but within moments the tornado smashed more than sixty houses, several businesses, and scores of trees in the vicinity of Irvington, Hardinsburg, and Midway. At 4:10 P.M. the twister slammed into the small Meade County town of Brandenburg, killing 30 of the town's 1,700 residents and flattening the business district and the adjoining residential area. As the Brandenburg tornado crossed the Ohio River into southern Indiana, another storm struck

Louisville near Standiford Field. It cut a swath across the city's east end, killing two residents and destroying or severely damaging more than 1,800 homes and scores of business properties.

The twister that hit Franklin County was born about four o'clock near the Butler-Grayson county line, approximately 100 miles to the southwest of Frankfort. After inflicting minor damage in Grayson County, it reached its full fury, cutting a path of terror across Hardin, Nelson, Spencer, and Anderson counties. About six o'clock it roared into southern Franklin County. Traveling parallel to I-64, it slammed into the Evergreen Road community and skirted the southwest corner of Frankfort before striking Inverness Estates, Tierra Linda, and the Jett community. Fifteen minutes after its arrival the twister roared into Scott County. But in less than fifteen minutes it had killed four people, injured more than one hundred, and destroyed or damaged an estimated 200 homes.

The tornado also caused considerable damage to several local commercial and industrial facilities in the Versailles Road area. When he arrived on the scene a few minutes later, Robert B. Mitchell found his Jettown Plaza shopping center a "mass of twisted metal." Company officials estimated damage to the Union Underwear plant at $2 million. The Taylor Tot and Bendix-Westinghouse plants also sustained severe damage. On the western edge of the city the storm damaged the Franklin Square Shopping Center and the Trigometer plant on U.S. 127.

While only the southern edge of the county and the southeast and southwest corners of the city felt the wind's destructive power, the tornado's impact extended much more broadly, as electric power was knocked out throughout the county. Local officials imposed an 8:00 P.M. curfew which continued through Friday. At 10:00 P.M. Governor Wendell Ford, who had watched the tornado from the Executive Mansion, declared a state of emergency. National Guardsmen patrolled the streets and highways, and radio WFKY stayed on the air all night relaying messages for persons needing to communicate with relatives.

Although a stunning blow, the tornado did not break the community's spirit. Within a day thousands of volunteers were busily at work clearing the damage, while the Red Cross assisted the disaster victims in obtaining temporary shelter, food, and clothing. Likewise, management and employees worked overtime to repair the wrecked plants in the industrial park. Less than two months after the tornado, every damaged plant was back in full operation.

As residents of a river city, Frankfortians were somewhat more accustomed to floods than to tornadoes. But no one was prepared for the deluge of December 1978. It rained hard for several days during the first week of December, but not with such sustained intensity that an emergency situation seemed imminent. As late as December 7 the rain had drawn barely any attention from the newspaper. By the eighth it was clear that a flood was on the way, but its

Capital Avenue underwater during 1978 flood.

Frankfort today.

projected crest of 35 feet the following day was well below the record 47.6 foot mark during the 1937 flood. But the forecast proved tragically incorrect, catching city and weather service officials and Frankfort residents totally unprepared. "The crisis came on so suddenly," the *State Journal* noted, "that City Hall had not even received the usual calls over water problems until the river started backing up into the South Frankfort sewers."

On December 9 the crest reached 43.75 feet. The streets of Bellepoint were inundated, and heavy flooding downtown and in South Frankfort forced 125 families to leave their homes or to move to upper floors. The high water forced the Municipal Sewage Treatment Plant to close, requiring that raw sewage be pumped directly into the river. In the face of the crisis, Governor Julian Carroll declared a state of emergency and imposed a 5:00 P.M. curfew. To enforce his order and to aid in crisis management, he immediately called on the National Guard, which already was assembled in the capital for monthly drills.

The emergency reached its zenith on Sunday, December 10, as the flood crested at 48.5 feet, breaking the 1937 record by nearly a foot. Hundreds of homes and approximately one thousand residents had to be evacuated. Most evacuees found shelter with friends or relatives, but a few were housed by the Salvation Army, Red Cross, or the Days Inn motel. The Convention and Sports Center filled with furniture salvaged by fleeing victims of the rising waters. Meanwhile, the Frankfort Electric and Water Plant Board found it necessary to shut off the water to conserve the supply; the Singing Bridge was closed to traffic; and the flooded city schools closed until after the Christmas holidays. Most surprising, perhaps, was the flooding of the Leestown Terrace public housing complex, whose location at the base of Fort Hill had been selected because it had remained above the 1937 flood level.

Even before Sunday ended, the water slowly started to recede. On Monday evening water service was restored, and the city began struggling to a semblance of normal. But the costs of the flood were enormous. Nearly 1,300 homes and ninety-five businesses were destroyed or damaged, and private and public property damage in the Kentucky River basin exceeded $14.5 million. The immediate concern of residents and city officials alike during the weeks that followed was to clean up the debris and to repair the damage. But an even greater long-term preoccupation was to protect the city, especially South Frankfort, against future floods.

Lessons learned from the 1978 deluge enabled city government to conduct a reasonably efficient evacuation from parts of South Frankfort, Bellepoint, and Taylor Avenue when a moderately severe flood struck in the spring of 1984. Reinforcing the city's evacuation plans was a new pumping system designed to prevent the sewers from backing up during a flood. But one measure proposed by the city—a floodwall down the center of Second Street—remains a source of controversy. The city commission has endorsed the project, but because of intense opposition from many residents of Second Street and the cross streets near the river, along with a lukewarm evaluation by the Army Corps of Engineers, the floodwall's future remains uncertain.

The problem of flood control is just one of many challenges facing the capital on the Kentucky River as it prepares to enter its third century. It is impossible, of course, to predict with any degree of certainty the course of the community's development or the issues which will dominate public attention during the decades to come. For the foreseeable future, though, Frankfort and Franklin County are confronted with the challenge of expanding and diversifying their economic base. Fortunately, those charged with this responsibility will have several advantages in their favor. Paradoxically, their greatest advantage is Frankfort's position as state capital, which remains a primary source of economic stability. More importantly, in a time when small business is the most rapidly growing segment of the American economy, Frankfort boasts a wide array of such enterprises. Today most of them depend heavily upon state government for their survival. However, many of these companies, if effectively nurtured, constitute a potential foundation for future economic growth. The task is to enable them to broaden their own markets and to reduce their dependence upon state orders and contracts.

Frankfort as it appeared approximately 100 years ago.

Similarly the community's rich historical and architectural heritage, combined with its scenic beauty and role as capital, offers opportunities for the tourist business which still are largely untapped. Frankfort's strategic location between Louisville and Lexington is advantageous for tourism and industrial development alike. From the standpoint of the travel industry, the capital is in a position to draw visitors bound for either or both of the Commonwealth's two largest cities. From an industrial development perspective, Frankfort's location at the center of a well-established, multi-county labor market assures future employers an adequate pool of highly motivated workers in a region virtually unaffected by serious labor-management conflicts. Finally, Franklin County offers an ample supply of land suitable for industrial development, including all major utilities and transportation connections by interstate highway, river, rail, and air.

In addressing the challenges of economic growth and diversification, however, community leaders must overcome some serious obstacles. A critical need is for a comprehensive economic development plan. Such a document should assess in detail the community's attributes, identify the types of enterprises most appropriate to those attributes, outline strategies to obtain or promote the development of those enterprises, and assign responsibilities, with clear goals and objectives, for accomplishing those strategies. An essential task in implementing any growth plan will be to improve intergovernmental coordination and cooperation at all levels and to forge a strong working partnership between the public and private sectors. The historic evidence is clear that Frankfort has experienced its greatest economic advances when

View of Frankfort, circa 1956.

government and private enterprise worked in harmony. In a period of economic change, such cooperation is even more imperative.

The community's long-term economic growth is likewise contingent upon the achievement of several improvements in local services. Among the more obvious problems which must be addressed are the inadequacy of local solid waste disposal facilities and the condition of the Franklin County Jail. An even more fundamental challenge is to strengthen the local educational system. In the future an individual's ability to make a living and to achieve self-fulfillment will rest largely upon his or her ability to adjust readily to economic and technological change. This will require an educational system which teaches young people how to learn and think while it transmits specific academic knowledge and vocational skills. Because economic development will depend heavily upon the intellectual attributes of the work force, it behooves educators and business leaders alike to build a strong cooperative relationship intended to assure educational excellence at all levels.

A resource which should not be overlooked in this respect is Kentucky State University. One of the community's largest single employers, it likely will continue to perform its traditional role as a center of undergraduate education. But in the economy of tomorrow, which will require most people to change employment and to learn new skills again and again, KSU's more recent function as a provider of graduate, professional, and continuing education will be even more crucial. Moreover, the university's faculty and professional staff constitute an invaluable reservoir of talent in efforts to attract new business, to improve the vitality of existing enterprises, and to strengthen the operations of local government and other community institutions. KSU is an asset whose potential has only begun to be realized.

Like the shifting channels of the river that gave it life, the Capital on the Kentucky will confront myriad, undreamed of problems during the century ahead. Few of these problems will be resolved easily or permanently. In a world where change is one of the few constants, Frankfort's growth and progress will require leaders endowed with vision, courage, and imagination, tempered with prudence and compassion. But this review of two centuries of history reveals that at critical points in the capital's development, leaders with precisely these qualities have stepped forward to build a capitol, save a railroad, found a bank, or secure a factory site. If the past is any indicator of the future, the city's ability to generate such dedicated leadership will remain as constant as the majestic pallisades which have guarded the Kentucky River since time immemorial.

Photographic Credits

1. Prelude to Settlement

Page 7: The Filson Club; p. 8: Adapted from *The Woods-McAfee Memorial* (1905) by William B. Scott, Jr.; p. 11: The Filson Club; p. 12: (*above*) Longacre and Herring, *National Portrait Gallery of Distinguished Americans* (1834–39), vol. 4, (*below*) Cresswell, *Journal of Nicholas Cresswell* (1924); p. 13: Colonial Williamsburg Foundation; p. 15: Kentucky Historical Society (hereinafter cited as KHS); p. 16: Jillson, "First Landowners of Frankfort, Kentucky," *Register* 43 (1945).

2. The Settlement of Frankfort

Page 20: Whitley, *Kentucky Ante-Bellum Portraiture* (1956); p. 22: KHS; p. 24: Masonic Temple, Hiram Lodge #4; p. 25: Collins, *History of Kentucky* (1874); p. 26: (*above*) Jillson, *Early Frankfort and Franklin County* (1936), (*below*) The Filson Club; p. 27: Coleman Collection, Transylvania University; p. 31: Jillson, *Early Frankfort*.

3. Statehood to Capital

Page 35: KHS; p. 38: The Filson Club; p. 39: The Filson Club; p. 40: Library of Congress; p. 42: (*above*) William Talbot, (*below*) Mrs. Alice Hume; p. 43: Special Collections, University of Kentucky; p. 44: KHS; p. 45: Masonic Temple, Hiram Lodge #4; p. 48: The Filson Club; p. 51: Jillson, *Early Frankfort*; p. 53: (*above*) Sneed, *Report on the History of the Kentucky Penitentiary* (1860), (*below*) The Filson Club; p. 56: J.B. Speed Art Museum; p. 57: J.B. Speed Art Museum; p. 58: (*above*) J.B. Speed Art Museum, (*below*) The Filson Club; p. 59: (*above*) The Filson Club, (*below*) Jillson, *Early Frankfort*; p. 60: Corcoran Gallery of Art; p. 63: Mrs. Pinky M. Richardson; p. 64: KHS; p. 66: KHS; p. 68: Masonic Temple, Hiram Lodge #4; p. 69: KHS.

4. Building Up, Reaching Out

Page 72: Collins, *History*; p. 73: The Filson Club; p. 74: KHS; p. 75: (*above*) Mrs. Joseph Murphy, (*below*) Mrs. Hugh Hudson, Jr.; p. 76: (*above*) Jillson, *Literary Haunts and Personalities of Old Frankfort* (1941), (*below*) Farmington; p. 77: (*above*) Mrs. George Gilpin, (*below*) Miss Alice Blanton; p. 78: Mrs. Nash Cox Shayon; p. 80: KHS; p. 82: KHS; p. 83: Sneed, *Kentucky Penitentiary*; p. 84: KHS; p. 85: Coleman Collection, Transylvania University; p. 86: *Democratic Review* (1845); p. 87: Kendall, *Autobiography of Amos Kendall* (1872); p. 88: KHS; p. 90: KHS; p. 91: Mrs. N.M. Berry; p. 93: Harold Jeffers; p. 95: KHS; p. 96: Levin, *Lawyers and Lawmakers of Kentucky* (1897); p. 97: KHS; p. 101: KHS; p. 103: KHS; p. 107: Cincinnati Historical Society; p. 108: Masonic Temple, Hiram Lodge #4; p. 109: (*above*) KHS, (*below*) Jillson, *Early Frankfort*; p. 110: First Christian Church; p. 111: Walter Weitzel III; p. 112: Jillson, *Newspapers and Periodicals of Frankfort* (1945); p. 113: J.B. Speed Art Museum.

5. Transition & Turmoil

Page 118: Walter Weitzel III; p. 119: (*above*) Walter Weitzel III, (*below*) Masonic Temple, Hiram Lodge #4; p. 120: Mrs. Hugh Hudson, Jr.; p. 121: KHS; p. 123: Special Collections, University of Kentucky; p. 124: (*above*) Averill, *History of First Presbyterian Church* (1901), (*below*) *Kentucky State Gazetteer* (1859); p. 125: Colonial Dames of America; p. 127: Frankfort *Roundabout*, Feb. 15, 1890 (hereinafter cited as *Roundabout*); p. 128: KHS; p. 129: KHS; p. 131: Mason Parker Collection; p. 132: Mrs. Carolyn Crittenden; p. 133: Mason Parker Collection; p. 134: Photographic Archives, University of Louisville; p. 135: KHS; p. 136: KHS; p. 137: Photographic Archives, University of Louisville; p. 138: KHS; p. 139: Jillson, *Early Frankfort*; p. 140: (*above*) First Christian Church, (*middle*) KHS, (*below*) KHS; p. 141: KHS; p. 142: KHS; p. 143: KHS; p. 144: (*above*) Mr. and Mrs. V.O. Barnard, (*below*) KHS; p. 145: KHS; p. 146: KHS; p. 148: E.H. Taylor Hay; p. 149: William B. Scott, Jr.; p. 150: KHS; p. 152: KHS.

6. The Agony of War

Page 154: Armstrong, *Biographical Encyclopaedia of Kentucky* (1878); p. 155: KHS; p. 156: J.B. Speed Art Museum; p. 157: (*above*) E.H. Taylor Hay, (*middle*) Elliott, *Queens of American Society*, (*below*) KHS; p. 159: Library of Congress; p. 160: Library of Congress; p. 161: (*above*) Library of Congress, (*below*) Masonic Temple, Hiram Lodge #4; p. 163: Sneed, *Kentucky Penitentiary*; p. 166: Library of Congress; p. 167: Library of Congress; p. 168: Library of Congress; p. 170: Walter Weitzel III.

7. The Violent Years

Page 180: (*above, left*) *Roundabout*, (*above, right*) KHS, (*below, left*) Walter Weitzel III, (*below, right*) *Roundabout*; p. 185: *Roundabout*; p. 186: (*above, left*) Walter Weitzel III, (*bottom, right*) Mason Parker Collection, all others KHS; p. 188: (*above*) Mrs. Agnes M. Gordon, (*below*) *The Headlight* (1898); p. 189: Walter Weitzel III; p. 190: Mrs. V.O. Barnard; p. 191: KHS; p. 192: Walter Weitzel III; p. 193: Jillson, *Literary Haunts*; p. 194: Mason Parker Collection; p. 195: (*above*) *Roundabout*, (*below*) KHS; p. 196: (*above, left*) National Distillers Products Company, all others KHS; p. 197: KHS; p. 199: Jim Sames; p. 200: KHS; p. 202: Collins, *History*; p. 203: Special Collections, University of Kentucky; p. 205: Mason Parker Collection; p. 207: *Roundabout*; p. 208: (*above*) *Roundabout*; (*below*) First Christian Church; p. 209: KHS; p. 210: (*above*) KHS; (*below*) Jillson, *Literary Haunts*; p. 211: KHS.

8. Expansion & Turbulence

Page 214: KHS; p. 215: (*above, left*) Mrs. N.M. Berry, (*above right*) Walter Weitzel III; p. 219: Mrs. Carolyn Crittenden; p. 220: KHS; p. 221: Mason Parker Collection; p. 223: John Gray; p. 224: KHS; p. 226: (*above*) Mrs. Pinky M. Richardson, (*below*) John Gray; p. 227: (*above*) Mrs. N.M. Berry, (*below*) *Roundabout*; p. 228: (*above*) *Roundabout*, (*below*) Mrs. Mary Rob Kagin; p. 229: KHS; p. 230: KHS; p. 231: (*above*) Library of Congress, (*below*) KHS; p. 232: Mason Parker Collection; p. 233: (*below*) Mrs. N.M. Berry, others KHS; p. 234: (*above*) City of Frankfort, (*below*) John Gray; p. 235: KHS; p. 236: KHS; p. 237: (*left*) Wendell McChord, (*right*) Historic Frankfort; p. 238: Levin, *Lawyers and Lawmakers*; p. 239: Louisville *Courier-Journal and Times*; p. 240: (*above*) City of Frankfort, (*below*) Franklin County Judge's Office; p. 241: (*above*) Franklin County Judge's Office, (*below*) City of Frankfort; p. 242: *American Architect and Building News*; p. 244: (*above*) *Roundabout*, (*below*) Mrs. Wilena Cinnamond; p. 245: *Roundabout*; p. 246: KHS; p. 247: *Roundabout*; p. 249: Mason Parker Collection; p. 251: Mrs. N.M. Berry; p. 252: Armstrong, *Biographical Encyclopaedia*; p. 253: KHS; p. 255: KHS.

9. A New Century Dawns

Page 258: KHS; p. 259: (*above*) Mrs. Bettie Ireys, (*left*) William B. Scott, Jr.; p. 260: (*above*) KHS, (*below*) Mrs. Bosworth Todd; p. 263: KHS; p. 264: KHS; p. 266: KHS; p. 267: KHS;

p. 268: (*above*) KHS, (*middle*) Mason Parker Collection, (*below*) State National Bank; p. 269: John C. Noel; p. 270: John Gray; p. 271: (*above*) Wendell McChord, (*below*) KHS; p. 272: KHS; p. 273: KHS; p. 274: (*left*) Mason Parker Collection, (*right*) KHS; p. 278: Cincinnati Historical Society; p. 279: Dr. Amanda Lange; p. 280: KHS; p. 281: KHS; p. 282: (*above*) KHS, (*below*) Franklin County Judge's Office; p. 283: (*left*) KHS, (*right*) Photographic Archives, University of Louisville; p. 284: Franklin County Judge's Office; p. 285: KHS; p. 287: (*left*) KHS, (*right*) Mason Parker Collection; p. 288: (*above*) KHS, (*below*) *The Greenbag* (1900); p. 289: (*above*) KHS, (*below*) Mrs. E.H. Taylor Hay; p. 290: Mrs. Carolyn Crittenden; p. 291: KHS; p. 292: First Christian Church.

10. *The Capital in the New Era*

Page 294: Mrs. Pinky M. Richardson; p. 296: (*above*) Harold Jeffers, (*below*) KHS; p. 297: KHS; p. 298: KHS; p. 301: Photographic Archives, University of Louisville; p. 303: KHS; p. 304: KHS; p. 305: (*above*) Harold Jeffers, (*below*) KHS; p. 306: KHS; p. 307: KHS; p. 310: John Booe; p. 311: KHS; p. 313: City of Frankfort; p. 314: KHS; p. 316: Edward Strohmeier; p. 317: KHS; p. 318: KHS.

11. *A Generation of Crisis*

Page 320: National Distillers Products Company; p. 324: KHS; p. 330: National Distillers Products Company; p. 331: National Distillers Products Company; p. 333: KHS; p. 334: Ky. Dept. of Tourism; p. 337: Ky. Dept. of Tourism; p. 338: (*above*) Mrs. V.O. Barnard, (*below*) KHS; p. 340: Mrs. N.M. Berry; p. 342: KHS; p. 344: KHS; p. 345: KHS; p. 346: Franklin County Judge's Office; p. 348: Coleman Collection, Transylvania University.

12. *The Urban Explosion*

Page 350: Louisville *Courier-Journal* and *Times*; p. 361: Ky. Dept. of Tourism; p. 363: First Christian Church; p. 368: City of Frankfort; p. 369: (*above*) City of Frankfort, (*middle*) Louisville *Courier-Journal* and *Times*, (*below*) William B. Scott, Jr.; p. 370: Ky. Dept. of Tourism; p. 374: Franklin County Judge's Office; p. 376: Franklin County Judge's Office.

13. *A Heritage Rediscovered*

Page 384: William B. Scott, Jr.; p. 385: Miss Holly I. Schaper; p. 387: City of Frankfort; p. 388: William B. Scott, Jr.; p. 391: John Gray; p. 393: Frankfort *State Journal*; p. 394: Louisville *Courier-Journal* and *Times*; p. 396: *The Headlight* (1898); p. 397: Dr. Bernard E. Burch, Jr.

Index

Abolition Intelligencer and Missionary Messenger 113
Acton, W. D. 160
Adair, John 94, 111
Adams, Daniel Weisiger 160
Adams, George 94
Adams, James R. 143
Adams, John Quincy 133
Adams, Samuel 10
Adams, William W. 160
Adcock Realty Company 261
Alanant-O-Wamiowee (Buffalo Trace) 5, 6, 9, 10
Allan, M. M. Motor Company 270
Allen, George H. 198
Allen, John 39, 68
Allen, Julia 141
Allen, Marshall J. 198
Allen, Robert D. 141
Allen, Robert T. P. 140, 141
Alley, James 177
American Colonization Society 150
American Federation of Musicians 291
American Legion 315, 322, 327
American Republic 60
American Tobacco Company 265, 266
Amoss, David A. 265
Ancient Age Distilling Company 386
Anderson, Robert 157, 158
Anderson, Wilburn, 354
Andrewartha, John 202
Andrews, Frank Mills 279
Angraves, John 187
Anheuser-Busch Brewing Company 310
Antwerp, B. E. 305
Apperson, Richard 45, 54

Argus of Western America 59, 60, 76, 113, 143
Armstrong, John 102
Arnold's Ferry 49
Arnold's Spring Distillery 198
Arnold's Station 28, 29, 31
Arnold, James 27, 28, 49
Arnold, John 17, 45
Arnold, John M. 353
Arnold, Stephen 28, 29, 55
Arrowhead 79
Asbury, Francis 109
Assembly Ball Club 144, 145
Associated Charities 288
Averill, Rebecca 288
Averill, Thomas 284
Averill, William H. 188, 190
Ayers, E. W. 224

Bacon, E. F. 187
Bacon, Albert G. 161
Bacon, Charles P. 99
Bacon, John M. 162
Bacon, William W. 162
Badgett, Patricia 388
Bailey's Mill 182, 187, 299, 322
Bailey, A. A. 187
Bailey, Abraham 78, 79
Bailey, Bettie M. 246
Bailey, Shelah 79
Baker, Mrs. George 292
Baker, R. Philip 102
Bald Knob 155, 182, 222, 285, 298, 299, 304, 322, 343, 379, 380
Baltzel, George 57
Bank of Kentucky 58, 89, 94, 95, 97, 124
Bank of Louisville 104
Bank of the Commonwealth 95–97
Barbee, Samuel P. 145

Barbour, A. L. (Dick) 382
Barker, M. I. 187
Barkley, George 185
Barnes Brothers Bus Lines 315
Barnes, Trolius 60
Barr, Mervin 8
Barrett Shoe Company 345
Barrett's Bookstore 211
Barstow, Ellen 110
Baruch, Bernard 302
Baxter, W. E. 270
Beauchamp, Ann Cook 96
Beauchamp, Jereboam 96, 367
Beaumont, William H. 59, 60
Beaverson, Jacob 137
Beckham, J. C. W. 255, 269, 279, 285
Bedford, Sidney 282
Beeches, The 78
Bell, Charles 261
Bell, Clement 79, 113
Bell, John 154, 155
Bell, Myrtle 261
Bellepoint 74, 76, 181, 182, 194, 199, 214, 215, 219, 250, 285, 339, 342, 395
Bellepoint Community Garden 329
Bellepoint Motor Company 305
Bellepoint School 384
Bellsgrove 79, 113
Bendix-Westinghouse Automotive Air Brake Company 358, 393
Benson 222, 298, 322
Benson, Richard 76
Berberich, Valentine 119
Berry Hill 355, 385
Berry, Elijah C. 60
Berry, George F. 122, 217, 230, 260
Berry, Hiram 122, 197, 217

402

Bethel Baptist Church 58
Bibb, Charles S. 76
Bibb, George M. 111
Bibb, John 119
Bingham, Robert Worth 302, 303
Birch, Frank S. 198
Bird, Charles M. 45
Birney, James G. 113, 150
Bishop, James C. 382
Bishop, Silas N. 176
Black Patch War 265, 266
Black, Charles W. 353
Black, Howard 322
Black, James D. 268
Black, Stephen 224
Blackburn, Churchill J. 125
Blackburn, Luke P. 125
Blaine, John L. 97
Blair, Francis Preston 76, 77, 86, 113
Blair, James 54, 58, 76
Blakemore, J. N. 198
Blanton Stone Company 312
Blanton, Alexander M. 125
Blanton, J. Bacon 281, 307, 312, 337
Blanton, Harrison 77, 81, 89, 92, 175, 281
Bledsoe, Lewis 29
Bledsoe, Moses C. 105
Bledsoe, Moses G. 60
Bledsoe, Moses O. 113
Bloomington 322
Blue Grass Bugle 247
Boggs, Alexander 91
Bondurant Middle School 384
Boone, Daniel 7, 9, 134, 136
Boone, Nathan 9
Boone, Rebecca 134, 136
Boone, William 136
Bourbon Stock Yards 89, 262
Bourbon, Prince Louis Philippe 26
Bowen, J. H. 224
Bowman Realty Company 260
Bowman, E. E. 311
Boy Scouts of America 289, 291, 328, 341, 362
Boyer, Alfred Z. 74
Boyle, Jeremiah T. 170
Boyle, John 95
Braddock, Edward 7
Bradford, Benjamin J. 59
Bradford, James M. 59
Bradford, John 17, 59
Bradley, William O. 254, 281
Bradshaw, H. P. 202
Bragg, Braxton 161, 162, 164, 166
Bramlette, Thomas 167, 170, 171
Brammell, W. S. 305

Brawner, Alexander G. 181
Brawner, Robert, Jr. 347
Bray, D. H. 364
Breathitt, Edward T. 366, 370, 390
Breckinridge, John C. 146, 154, 155, 166
Breckinridge, Robert 155
Breckinridge, Robert 36, 58
Breckinridge, Robert J. 150, 151, 152, 171
Breckinridge, William C. P. 178, 250
Breckinridge, William L. 150, 151
Bricklayers Union 292
Bridgeport 78, 79, 122, 155, 171, 182, 222, 250, 258, 285, 298, 299, 304, 305, 343, 379, 380
Bridgeport Elementary School 384
Bridgeport Female Institute 205
Bridgeport Lattice School 205
Briggs, Guy H. 364
Brighton Engineering Company 353, 383
Brighton Park Mall 383, 386
Brislan, J. B. 333
Brislan, Jerry 211, 217, 224
Brislan, John A. 269
Brodhead, Lucas 76
Brooker, J. W. 337
Brooks, Thomas L. 247
Browder, S. P. 206
Brown, Eli H., Jr. 387, 388
Brown-Irion Furniture Company 311, 326, 331
Brown, James 58
Brown, James B. 303
Brown, John 36, 37, 42, 51, 59, 69, 73, 74, 80
Brown, John Mason 175, 205, 211, 250
Brown, John Y., Jr. 387, 388
Brown, John Young 254
Brown, Margareta 58, 59
Brown, Mason 92, 104, 111, 125, 134, 145
Brown, Orlando 74, 92, 111, 113, 126, 134, 143, 145, 150
Brown, Preston 73
Brown, Samuel R. 55
Bryan, Edward P. 217, 219, 229
Bryant, William 18
Buchanan, James 155
Buckley, Claude 209
Buckley, John T. 219, 221
Buckner, Simon B. 159, 164, 252
Buell, Don Carlos 162
Buford, Mary 177, 178
Buford, Napoleon B. 102, 199
Buford, Thomas 177, 178

Bugle Publishing Company 247
Buhr Hotel 189, 210, 230, 250
Buhr, George 189
Bullitt, Alexander Scott 53
Bullitt, Joshua T. 170
Bullitt, Thomas 10, 11
Bullock, John O. 144
Bullock, Joseph J. 137
Bullock, Rice 36
Burbridge, Stephen 166, 169, 170, 171, 174
Burch, James 387
Burckhardt, Henry 233
Burley Tobacco Growers Cooperative Association 302, 303, 323
Burley Tobacco Society 265, 291
Burnley, George B. 160
Burns, James (Paddy) 123
Burr Conspiracy 60, 67
Burr, Aaron 19, 20, 26, 60, 67
Bush, W. P. B. 211
Busy Bee Store 325
Butler, J. R. 342
Butler, Mann 87, 110
Buttimer Hill 342, 354, 382
Buttimer, Jane 279

Cabb, Stuart M. 209
Caldwell, Adam 57
Callendar, W. L. 143
Cameron, Simon 157
Cammack, John P. 93
Campbell, Alexander 110
Campbell, Daniel 14
Campbell, Duncan 193
Campbell, George 17
Campbell, John 17
Cann, M. Stuart 209, 247
Cannon, Mrs. Jouett Taylor 338
Cantrill, J. C. 302
Capital Bottling Works 310
Capital Building and Loan Association 333
Capital City Airport 352, 353, 355, 357, 372, 373, 382
Capital City Heritage Commission 390
Capital City Orchestra 246
Capital City Planning Commission 389
Capital Drug Company 304
Capital Foundry, Machine and Novelty Company 271
Capital Garage 305
Capital Gas & Electric Light Company 217
Capital Gazette 209
Capital Hotel (New) 307, 322, 335, 360, 388
Capital Hotel (Old) 123, 124, 144, 145, 158, 178, 188, 189, 255,

Capital Hotel (Old) *cont'd.*
    268, 269, 306
Capital Lumber & Manufacturing Company 273, 282
Capital Planning and Zoning Commission 364, 365
Capital Plaza 366–368, 370, 388
Capital Plaza Hotel 388
Capital Printing Company 247
Capital Railway Company 219–221
Capital Steam Laundry 233
Capital, The 247
Capital Theatre 316, 317, 328
Capital Trust Company 269, 308, 332
Capitol Annex 371
Capitol Heights 261, 297, 332, 342, 352, 355
Caplinger, Owen 346, 383
Cardwell's Ferry 49
Cardwell, John 49, 211
Carlisle Distillery 197, 251
Carneal, Thomas 56, 119
Carpenter, D. W. 175
Carr, F. C. 195
Carroll, Julian 385, 388, 394
Carter's Seminary 112
Carter-Morris Realty Co. 352
Cassell, John H. 276
Cassell, Samuel D. 227
Catholic Knights of America 248
Caudill Realty Company 355
Caudill, Charles M. 355, 359
Caudill, Louise 359
Cedar Cove Spring 51, 66, 104, 112, 142, 217
Cedar Creek Saw and Flouring Mill 195
Cedar Creek Turnpike Road Company 199
Cedar Run Distillery 198
Central Garage 270, 271
Central Screw 358
Century Plaza 386
Chambers, Frank 145, 146
Champion Saw Mill 195
Chandler, Albert B. 335, 336, 338, 339, 353, 363, 371
Chandler, Mrs. Albert B. 339
Charity Ball Club 328
Chesapeake & Ohio Railroad 271
Chinn, Frank 269, 279
Chinn, Jack 254
Chinn, J. Morgan 260
Chinn, William J. 190, 203, 223
Choateville 298, 304, 354, 380
Church of St. Pius 110
Church of the Good Shepherd 124, 139, 174, 291, 292, 318

Church, A. J. 160
Cincinnati Southern Railroad 236
Citizen's Bank of Frankfort 229
Citizens Mutual Savings Association 315
Citizens' Improvement Association 288
Civil Rights Act of 1964 378
Clark, George Rogers 12, 13, 36
Clark, James 95
Clarke, Charles J. 231
Clay, Henry 26, 52, 58, 67, 68, 88, 89, 143, 150, 201
Clay, Henry, Jr. 146
Clay, Porter 109
Clements, Earle C. 364, 370, 371
Clinton Street School (Mayo-Underwood School) 245, 285, 366, 376–378
Clinton, George 23
Cobb, Oscar 230
Coblin, Granville 375
Coburn, John 53
Cochran Distillery 49
Cochran, John 198, 273
Coharn, G. W. 187
Coleman & McKeever Company 272
Coleman Springs Addition 342
Coleman's Spring 31
Coleman, C. A. 342
Coleman, Clarence T. 313, 335, 337–339, 364
Coleman, Edward Spillsbee 66
Coleman, Mrs. Clarence T. 339
Coleman, Sallie E. 206
Coleman, Winston 176
College Park Development Corporation 354
Collins Hardware 305
Collins Lane Elementary School 361, 382
Collins, W. L. 219, 229
Collins, Cornelius 188
Collins, David C. 382
Collins, George A. 352, 354
Collins, Michael 188
Combs, Bert T. 369, 371, 378
Combs, Leslie 103
Commentator 113
Commercial Club of Frankfort 234, 261, 276
Commonwealth 113, 143, 144, 155, 208
Community Services, Inc. 373, 374
Condict, Lewis 41
Congleton, T. J. & Brothers Lumber Yard and Saw Mill 219
Congleton, William 284

Conner, W. J. 247
Conner, Fred L. 311–312
Consolidated Coach Corporation 313
Constitutional Advocate 113
Conway, George 283
Conway's Mill 32
Cook, C. N. 137
Cook, Hosea 29–30
Cook, Jesse 29–30
Cook's Station 29–32
Coppersmith, William L. 228, 234
Corinthian Baptist Church 208
Corner in Celebrities 73, 119, 179, 390, 391
Cowan, A. M. 150
Cowherd, Harry 354
Cox, Austin P. 125, 134, 142
Cox, Louis 354, 375
Craddock, George W. 143, 175
Craig, J. M. 269
Craig, Benjamin 40
Craig, Jeremiah 40
Craig, John 21
Craig, Elijah 49, 55, 56
Craig, Lewis 26
Cramer, Zadoc 114
Crawfish Bottom 179, 251, 298, 327, 337, 339, 342, 365–367
Cresap, Michael 12
Cresswell, Nicholas 12
Crittenden Compromise 156–157
Crittenden, George B. 159–160
Crittenden, Henry 94
Crittenden, John J. 42, 80, 95–96, 111, 156, 158–160
Crittenden, Richard 177
Crittenden, Thomas L. 136, 159–160
Crockett, D. S. 160
Crockett, Anthony 45, 108
Crockett, Joseph 21
Cromwell, Emma Guy 329
Crossfield, W. V. 269
Crow, James C. 198
Crumbaugh, William 391
Crutcher, D. C. 188, 219
Crutcher, Fayette 282, 325
Crutcher Building 231
Cullum, Fanny V. 206
Cumberland Telephone Company 216
Cuming, Fortescue 41, 42, 46, 47
Curlin, William 382
Curtis, George M. 178
Cutler, Thomas 363

Daily Call 247, 286
Dandridge, W. F. 229

Darby, Patrick H. 96, 113
Darnell, James S. 220, 227, 241, 284
Darnell, John D. 376
Darnold, Aaron 17
Daughters of the American Revolution 288
Davidson, James 81, 87, 150
Davies, Hyel 269
Davies, William 375
Daviess, Joseph Hamilton 60, 61, 67
Davis, David 325
Davis, E. Gaines 355
Davis, Isadore 188
Davis, J. W., Jr. 354, 360
Davis, Moses A. 246
Days Inn Motel 395
Deering, Ben 209
Dehoney, W. S. 240
Delaney, Joseph 39
Demint, Gerard 30
Deposit Bank of Frankfort 189, 269
Desha, Joseph 95, 108
Devil's Hollow 18, 46, 165
Dix, Albert E. 366
Dodd, J. W. 210
Dodd, Hill 260
Dotson, Abe 175
Douglas, Stephen A. 154, 155
Douglass, James 10, 11
Downey, James 32, 33
Downey, Joe 250
Downey, Mary 32, 33
Downtown Merchants Association 389
Drake, Cornelius 189
Drane, George C. 205, 211
Dryden, John B. 247, 286
Dudgeon, Farnham 365, 366, 368
Dudley Institute 205
Dudley, Ambrose W. 137, 145, 189
Dudley, Isham T. 160
Dudley, Jeptha 70, 105
Dudley, Peter 68, 69, 80, 99, 105, 211
Dudley, Thomas U. 205
Dumont, Ebenezer 166
Dunlap, A. R. 285, 286
Dunmore, Benjamin 115
Dunn, William 29, 30
Dunstall, Donald 391
Dutton, J. Frank 307, 308
Duvall Building 192, 231
Duvall, Benjamin 160, 189

Eagle Bottling Company 272, 310
Eagles Lodge 287
East Frankfort Park 362
East Frankfort Shopping Center 359
Edwards, H. 79
Edelen, T. L. 269
Edmiston, Robert 14
Edwards, John 39
Egbert, Clarence 247
Egbert, Frank 253
Elk Hill 78
Elkhorn Elementary School 361
Elkhorn Middle School 384
Elks Club 288, 327
Elliott, E. H. 234
Elliott, Edwin E. 284
Elliott, John Milton 177, 178
Elmville 182, 187, 222, 299, 322, 380
Episcopal Orphanage 286
Epperson, Daniel 75
Estis, J. A. 222
Estop, Frank A. 162
Evans, Evan 80, 87
Evans, Humphrey 81
Ewing, Baker 45, 65
Ewing, Felix Grundy 265
Excelsior Collegiate Institute 205

Fall, Philip S. 110, 137, 140
Farley, Curtis 284
Farmdale 171, 177, 242, 298, 383
Farmer, Cecil 326
Farmer, Thomas 189
Farmer, B. & Son 187
Farmers Bank and Capital Trust Company (Farmers Bank of Kentucky, Farmers Bank of Frankfort, Farmers Deposit Bank) 124, 241, 269, 308, 332, 360, 361, 388
Farmer's Tobacco Warehouse Company 266
Faux, William 71
Federal Building 390
Feeble-Minded Institute (Institute for the Education and Training of Feeble-Minded Children) 207, 215, 350, 371
Female Eclectic Institute 110
Fibercraft Chair Company 311
Field's Female Academy 111, 112
Field, Emmet 256
Fields, Henry 52
Fillmore, Millard 147
Fincel, Clayton 333
Fincel, Norman 310
Finley, John 67
Finnell, John W. 143, 193
Finnell, Lewis 162
Fireside Journal 209
First Baptist Church 109, 110, 208, 291
First Baptist Church (Black) 115, 208
First Christian Church 110, 137, 192, 208, 282, 292, 341
First Federal Savings and Loan Association 333
First Methodist Church 139, 341
First Presbyterian Church 87, 109, 151, 259
Fish Trap Island 50, 51
Fish, Carlos A. 313
Fish, Maria T. 313
Fitzgerald Building 391
Flag Fork 182, 299
Flaget, Benedict 110
Flat Creek 329
Fleenor, C. M. 279
Flood of 1937 321, 339, 341
Flood of 1978 393, 394
Floyd, John 11
Flynn, James W. (Pete) 374
Ford & Johnson, Inc. 273
Ford, H. Church 377
Ford, Laura C. 210
Ford, Wendell 393
Forks of Elkhorn 78, 79, 113, 122, 155, 182, 187, 222, 224, 237, 238, 242, 257, 258, 285, 298, 299, 304, 305, 331, 343, 379, 383
Forks of Elkhorn Baptist Church 26, 58, 109, 110
Forrest, Nathan Bedford 161
Forrester, W. S. 247
Fort Boone 167, 169
Fort Boone Plaza 385
Fort Hill 134, 167, 169, 179, 204, 251, 368, 395
Foster, Thomas P. 209
Fountain Place 367, 375
Fowler, William T. 331
Fowler, John, Jr. 21
Fox Gap 304, 329
Fox, Morris 79
Frank, Stephen 18, 19
Frankfort & Cincinnati Railroad 238, 271, 312, 322
Frankfort & Lawrenceburg Bus Line 313
Frankfort & Lawrenceburg Turnpike Road Company 127
Frankfort & Lee's Branch Turnpike Road Company 127
Frankfort & Lexington Turnpike Road Company 99
Frankfort & Suburban Railway Company 221
Frankfort & Versailles Traction Company 271
Frankfort-Franklin County Public Library 374

Frankfort Altrusa Club 329
Frankfort Baking Company 326
Frankfort Bank 94
Frankfort Baseball Club 316
Frankfort Bellepoint & Leestown Street Railway Company 219
Frankfort Board of Education 377, 384
Frankfort Board of Trade 349
Frankfort Bridge Company 47, 49, 128
Frankfort Broadcasting Company (WFKY) 373, 393
Frankfort Buick Company 270, 305
Frankfort Building & Loan Association 190
Frankfort Business and Professional Women's Club 315
Frankfort Business Men's Club 276
Frankfort Canning Company 272
Frankfort Carriage Works 311
Frankfort Cemetery 136, 146, 147, 215, 279
Frankfort Cemetery Company 134
Frankfort Centennial Association 249
Frankfort Chamber of Commerce 276, 307, 309, 312, 321, 349, 358
Frankfort Committee 388
Frankfort Cotton Company 126
Frankfort Country Club 321, 375
Frankfort Daily Dispatch 209, 247
Frankfort Distillery 233, 273
Frankfort Drug Company 345
Frankfort Electric and Water Plant Board 356, 369, 373, 385, 395
Frankfort Fire and Marine Insurance Company 190
Frankfort Fire Company 105, 106
Frankfort Fire Department 52, 283, 314, 369
Frankfort Furniture Company 345
Frankfort Gun Club 315
Frankfort Heating Company 217
Frankfort Herald 247
Frankfort High School 245, 316, 318, 325, 338, 377, 384
Frankfort Ice Company 233
Frankfort Independent School District 361
Frankfort Industrial Foundation 327
Frankfort Kiwanis Club 315
Frankfort Labor Advocate 291
Frankfort League of Women Voters 368
Frankfort Ledger 247
Frankfort, Lexington & Versailles Turnpike Company 100
Frankfort Library Company 61, 112
Frankfort Lions Club 315, 322
Frankfort Lyceum 112, 210, 211, 246
Frankfort Merchants' Vigilance Board 325
Frankfort Mining, Reducing and Manufacturing Company 233
Frankfort Ministerial Association 328, 329, 378
Frankfort Modes Glass Works 272
Frankfort Motor Car Company 270, 305
Frankfort Municipal Housing Commission 337
Frankfort Music Shop 345
Frankfort News 285
Frankfort News-Journal 286
Frankfort Police Department 369, 370
Frankfort Post Office and Federal Building 243
Frankfort Printing Company 285
Frankfort Public Library 286, 374
Frankfort Realty Company 260
Frankfort Resolutions 94
Frankfort Rotary Club 315, 322
Frankfort Roundabout 209, 246, 286
Frankfort Safety Vault and Trust Company 229
Frankfort Sesquicentennial Celebration 338
Frankfort State Bank 229
Frankfort Table Company 326
Frankfort Tennis Club 315
Frankfort Tin Ware Manufactory 93
Frankfort Urban Renewal Agency 366
Frankfort Warehouse 89
Frankfort Water Company 51, 218, 283, 339
Frankfort Women's Club 248, 267, 315, 328, 374
Frankfort Zoning Commission 363
Frankfort, Paris & Big Sandy Railroad Company 200, 201
Frankfort-Franklin County Planning Commission 365, 390
Frankfort & Clifton Turnpike Road Company 127
Franklin County Community Council 374
Franklin County Council on National Defense 292
Franklin County Courthouse 46, 72, 86
Franklin County Development League 277
Franklin County Drought Relief Committee 322
Franklin County High School 361, 384
Franklin County Home Defense Commission 346
Franklin County Homemakers Clubs 329, 374
Franklin County Humane Society 289
Franklin County Industrial Foundation 358
Franklin County Jail 204, 397
Franklin County Medical Society 291
Franklin County Natural Gas-Light and Heating Company 217
Franklin County Relief Committee 329, 330
Franklin County Tire Rationing Board 347
Franklin Exchange 92
Franklin Female Seminary 112
Franklin Mining & Smelting Company 93
Franklin Paper Mill 93
Franklin Square Shopping Center 386, 393
Franklin, Agnes L. 206
Franklin, Massie 106
Frayne, Richard F. 162
Frazier, R. A. 269
Fuqua, L. H. Tire Company 305

Gaines, Agnes 313
Gaines, Bowman S. 327
Gaines, D. J. 222
Gaines, J. T. 160, 206
Gaines, Mrs. Bowman S. 329
Gaines, William A. 190, 197, 200, 243
Gaines, W. A. and Company 197, 198, 215, 231, 273, 331
Gano, Isaac E. 43, 57, 61
Garden Clubs of Kentucky 371
Garrard, James 42, 74

Garrard, Daniel, Jr. 162
Garrett, Freeman 175
Gartrell, Charles H. 372
Gas Works 133, 134
Gay, John R. 175
Gayle, Clarence 348
Gayle Drug Store 345
Gayle, George M. 345
Gayle, George W. & Sons 348, 357
Geary, T. C. Company 266
General Electric Company 386
General Shoe Company 357, 386
Georgetown and Frankfort Turnpike Road Company 99
Gerard, John 368, 369, 374
Gerard, William 60
German Benevolent Society 248, 288
Gist, Christopher 6, 7
Glanton, Daniel 217
Glanton, W. A. 261
Glen Willis 77, 219
Glenn's Creek Ferry 49
Glenwood Park 316
Glover, John 54, 83
Goebel, William 213, 254–255
Goins, Franklin 353, 355
Goins, Samuel 108
Goins, Sanford 75
Goldfarb, Jacob A. 326
Gooch, Rebecca 310
Good Samaritans 248
Goodman, John 74
Goodman, L. B. 270
Gordon, Thomas 178
Gore, Henry 60
Gore, Joseph 27
Gouldman, Saunder's/Bryants Mill 78
Gouldman, Thomas H. 78
Grace Methodist Episcopal Church 208
Graham, A. Jud 167
Graham, J. R. 208
Graham, Robert 171
Graham, W. Pruett 292
Grand Army of the Republic 288
Grand Theatre 316, 317
Grand United Order of Odd Fellows 248
Grant, Ulysses S. 158, 167
Gray & Coblin Architects 367
Gray, John 391
Gray, M. P. 234
Gray, William K. 162
Green, John 49, 55
Green, Thomas M. 143, 144, 147, 149
Greenup, Christopher 47, 50, 59, 76

Gretter, Harry A. 312, 321, 322, 328
Grundy, Felix 58
Guardian of Freedom 59
Guidi Building 391
Guidi Fruit Company 360
Gullion, Robert 31
Guthrie, James 177, 178
Gwin, George W. 87, 120, 188, 203

H & B Milk Company 310
Hallem, Theodore 178
Halmhuber, J. M. 269
Haly, Denis L. 205, 230
Haly, John 124, 125, 139, 203, 230
Haly, Mahoney & Company 202
Hamilton, Alexander 19, 56
Hamilton, Archibald 17
Hamilton, Boone L. 339, 341, 345–346
Hamilton, Robert 30
Hamilton's Station 30, 31
Hammond, Alonzo B. 276
Hampton, John 92
Handy, Sally 279
Hanley, Ruth 310
Hanna, John H. 66, 75, 92, 94, 99, 100, 104, 123, 124, 126, 133, 139, 144, 145
Hannan, George L. 188
Harbinger, The 113
Hardie, W. McKee 234, 241, 284
Hardin, Martin D. 58, 59
Harding, William 83
Harlan, George 115
Harlan, James 123–125, 150
Harlan, James M. 123, 124, 125, 376
Harlan, John Marshall 367, 376
Harlan, Richard D. 145
Harper, George B. 272, 282
Harris, J. C. 102
Harris, Samuel 142
Harris, Sol 250
Harris, Stanley 289, 291
Harrison, Benjamin 15
Harrison, William H. 69, 76, 83, 143
Harrod, Earl 353
Harrod, Hugh 171
Harrod, James 76
Harrod, Orville 326, 327, 329, 338
Harvie, John 80, 99
Harvie, Lewis E. 149
Harvieland 299
Hatchett, James G. 243, 250
Hawes, Richard J. 164
Hawkins, Martin 50, 51

Hawkins, Ruben 146
Hawkins, Strother J. 91
Hawkins, William 177
Hay, C. W. 260
Hay, E. H. Taylor 352
Hayden, William 40
Haydon, William 15
Haydon's Station 26
Hazelett, N. B. 266
Hazelrigg, James H. 255, 288, 292
Hazelrigg, Dyke 363
Hazelrigg, James H. 288, 292
Head, Edmund 123
Hearn Elementary School 384
Heath, Robert M. 304, 321, 322, 329
Heeny, Frank 227, 288
Heeny, James 226, 241, 276
Heffner, John B. 190
Henderson, H. A. M. 210
Henderson, Richard 34
Hendrick, J. Buford 269
Henry, Patrick 17, 21, 76
Hensley, Benjamin 75, 87
Hensley, Clark & Company 229
Hepponstall, Abraham 11
Herman, Elizabeth 322
Herman, Leopold 190
Hermitage Distillery 181, 197, 198, 251, 273, 331
Herndon, John C. 125
Herndon, William C. 241
Herndon, William T. 120
Herrensmith, Margaret 123
Hewitt, Fayette 219, 229
Hewitt, John M. 125, 211
Hickman, Benjamin 105, 110
Hickman, Paschal 68, 69
Hickman, William 26, 68
Hieatt, R. C. 282, 284
Hines, Harold K. 352, 353, 375
Hines, Warner U. 353, 354, 382
Hines and McDonald Real Estate Company 353
Historic Frankfort, Inc. 390
Hite, Isaac 10, 11
Hodges, Albert G. 113, 123, 134, 143, 150, 155, 208
Hoge, Charles E. 227, 229, 269, 272, 276
Hoge, French S. 227, 228, 272, 307
Hoge-Montgomery Clubhouse 317
Hoge-Montgomery Company 272, 273, 316, 326, 345
Holbert, Jack 81
Holder, Thomas H. 177
Holiday Inn 359, 360
Holman, Jacob H. 113
Holman, William 109

407

Holmes, Andrew 25, 39–41
Holmes, Charles 177
Holmes Street School 384
Holton, John A. 211
Home Construction Company 238
Home Telephone Company 216
Hoover, Herbert 328
Hopkins G. W. 187
Hord, Lysander 125, 189
Horton, Elijah 171
Hudson, C. R. 282
Hudson, Hugh 326
Hudson, William P. 227
Hughes, L. C. (Church) 316, 317
Hughes, G. C. 187
Hughes and Chiles Drug Store 217
Hulett, Elmer G. 310
Hulette, J. P. 269
Hulette, L. D. 187
Hulette, W. J. 327
Hulette's Confectionary 325
Hume, Edgar E. 234, 284
Hume Building 229, 269
Humphrey, Robert 363
Humphries, T. F. 227
Humphries, Mary 75
Hunley, Benjamin 115
Hunt, Thomas 171
Hunter, James G. 45
Hunter, John 54
Hunter, William 58, 59, 60, 69, 94, 114
Hyde, H. J. 241

Independent Order of Odd Fellows 248, 287, 347
Independent Order of Red Men 287
Innes, Harry 27, 36, 40, 53, 56, 59, 67
Innes's Station 30–32
Institute for Boys 140
Instone, John 23, 63, 114
International Typographical Union 291
Irion, Charles 311

Jackson, Andrew 60, 76, 102, 108, 141
Jackson, Herbert G. 317
Jackson, James S. 163
Jackson, John H. 245
Jackson, Marietta 329
Jackson, Mary E. 246
Jacob, Ferd 284, 325
Jacob, Richard Taylor 165, 171
James, A. J. 203
James, Daniel 40
Jeffers, B. B. 241

Jefferson, Thomas 11, 23, 36, 67
Jefferson County Courthouse 81
J.E.M. Flour Mill 233
Jenkins, John 79
Jennings, J. A. 353
Jett, Thomas 78
Jett, Virginia 248
Jett, William L. 189
Jett 78, 79, 242, 298, 305, 358
Jett's Enterprise 247–248
Jetttown Plaza 393
Jilson, Robert B., Jr. 241
Jillson, Robert K. 188
Jillson, Willard R. 9, 14, 304, 331
Johnson, Edward P. 97, 100
Johnson, Henry 176, 177
Johnson, Hugh 52
Johnson, J. H. 143
Johnson, John T. 110
Johnson, Keen 347
Johnson, L. Frank 174, 235, 249, 281
Johnson, Mary E. 49
Johnson, Mary L. 279
Johnson, Mollie F. 206
Johnson, Polk 247
Johnson, Richard Mentor 58, 136, 143, 146
Johnson, Robert 21, 59
Johnson, Samuel D. 227
Johnston, J. Stoddard 200, 208–211, 249
Jones, C. M. 187
Jones, Joseph C. 333
Joshua, 182, 187, 242
Joyner, Felix 366
Judd, Paul 368, 369
Judd's Office Products 391
Julian, Alexander 189
Julian, Ira 240
Juniper Hill 260
Juniper Hill Community Center 362
Juniper Hill Park 359, 382–383

Kagin, Carl 228, 229
Kagin, Carl A. 333
Kagin, C. T. Bros. (Kagin Bros., Inc.) 229, 267, 360
Kagin, Edwin 228, 229
Kagin, Elizabeth Burgin 228
Kagin, G. E. 229
Kagin, Urban 228
Kaltenbrun, Vincent A. 192
Kaltenbrun, Vincent A., Jr. 234
Kaltenbrun Building 192, 391
Kavannaugh, Frank 322
Keck, John A. 364
Keenon, Edward 167
Keenon, John G. 162

Keenon, Uberto 167
Keenon's Bindery 142
Keller, H. S. 270
Ken-Wel, Inc. 357, 358
Kendall, Amos 59, 60, 76, 78, 86, 91, 93, 113
Kennebec Distilling Co. 331
Kennedy, Isaac 341
Kennedy, Thomas 39
Kenney, Thomas E. 284, 326, 329, 333, 335
Kentucky Abolition Society 150
Kentucky Academy 140
Kentucky Anti-Slavery Society 150
Kentucky Board of Fire Underwriters 291
Kentucky Cement Corporation 312, 319
Kentucky Colonization Society 150, 151, 152
Kentucky Department of Economic Development 364
Kentucky Department for Libraries and Archives 385
Kentucky Distillers and Warehouse Company 273
Kentucky Emergency Relief Administration 330
Kentucky Equal Rights Association 289
Kentucky Federation of Women's Clubs 315
Kentucky Floral Clock 371
Kentucky Furniture Company 325
Kentucky Heritage Commission 390–392
Kentucky Historical Society 112, 286, 338
Kentucky Investment and Building Company 229
Kentucky Journal 59, 247, 286
Kentucky Medical Society 125
Kentucky Midland Railroad 237
Kentucky Military Institute 140, 141, 243
Kentucky Pharmaceutical Association 291
Kentucky Progress Commission 312
Kentucky Public Service Company 217
Kentucky Publishing Company 285
Kentucky River Company 50
Kentucky River Mills 193, 194, 232, 233
Kentucky River Navigation Company 199
Kentucky River Saw Mill Association 291

Kentucky Shearman Concrete Pipe Company 312
Kentucky Seminary 60, 80, 86, 110, 111
Kentucky State Democrat 285
Kentucky State Journal 247, 285
Kentucky State Register 209
Kentucky State University (State Normal School for Colored Persons, Kentucky Normal and Industrial Institute, Kentucky State College) 215, 245, 246, 261, 318, 330, 355, 367, 368, 377, 378, 384, 385, 397, 398
Kentucky Table Company 311
Kentucky Telegraphe 59
Kentucky Telephone Exchange 216
Kentucky Traction & Terminal Company 330
Kentucky Yeoman 74, 143, 144, 155, 201, 208, 209, 246, 247
Kersey, Hick 177
King's Daughters Hospital 243, 244, 287, 289, 384
King, Robert H. 161
Kinney, W. R. 178
Kittridge, George D. 342
Klosterman, Edward G. 318
Knights and Ladies of Honor 248
Knights of Columbus 287
Knights of Friendship 248
Knights of Pythias 248
Knott, Richard M. 122, 124
Krock, Arthur 302
Ku Klux Klan 175, 176, 177, 295, 296

Labrot & Graham Distillery 273
Ladies German-American Society 288
Lafayette, Marquis de 26, 108
Lafferty, Thornton 171
Laffoon, Polk 260
Laffoon, Ruby 335
Lancaster, James M. 124, 139
Lane, Edward W. 247
Launitz, Robert E. 136
Lawson, S. P. 208
LeCompte, Charles B. 187
LeCompte, Louis 316
Ledgerwood, James 39
Ledgerwood's Bend 39
Lee, Hancock 12–15, 28, 39, 45, 77
Lee, Henry 39
Lee, Jerry 176, 253
Lee Potter Smith & Associates 367
Lee, Robert E. 173

Lee, Willis 14
Lee, Willis Atwell 45, 77
Leestown 12, 13, 18, 19, 28, 39, 74, 77, 89, 193, 219–221, 331
Leestown Terrace 337, 368, 395
Lehrman Motor Company 325
Leonard, Richard 176
Letcher, Robert P. 42, 74, 125, 129, 136
Lewis & Dudley Realty Company 352
Lewis, Anthony 11
Lewis, George A. 209, 211, 214, 246, 248, 253, 286
Lewis, Mary 123
Lewis Rent-a-Ford 325
Lewis, Samuel 89, 94
Lewis, W. H. 224
Lewis, W. J. 224
Lewis, William 68
Lewis, Zachary 171
Lexington & Frankfort Railroad Company 103, 129, 131, 132
Lexington, Frankfort & Louisville Railroad 132, 133
Lexington and Frankfort Turnpike Company 99
Lexington and Louisville Transportation Line 129
Lexington & Ohio Railroad Company 103, 130–132
Liberty Hall 42, 59
Liebman, Joseph 375
Lillard, Eph 254
Lillard, Jerry 178
Lillard, Thomas 45
Lincoln, Abraham 154–156, 173
Lindsay, William 229, 237, 238, 250, 277–279
Lindsey, Daniel Weisiger 161, 163, 167, 189, 200, 211, 217, 243, 249, 276, 282
Lindsey, H. F. 332
Lindsey, John B. 189, 230
Lindsey, Lilian 288
Lindsey, Thomas N. 125, 163, 165, 211
Littell, William 58, 60
Logan, Benjamin 35, 36, 65
Logan, John 43, 45
London, Catherine 52
Long, Henry C. 145
Long, John 171
Longmoor, Woodford W. 247, 285
Loofburrow, Thomas V. 47, 59, 87
Loomis, Arthur 231
Loomis, Warham P. 91
Louisville & Frankfort Railroad 132

Louisville & Nashville Railroad 47, 198, 236, 254, 271, 312, 358
Love, Elizabeth 58, 59
Love, Thomas 25, 54
Love's Tavern 25, 61, 67, 92
Lower Benson Presbyterian Church 58
Loyal Company 6, 14–15
Luscher, Sigmund 211, 233
Lutkemeier, William C. 233, 241
Lutkemeier's Dry Goods 360
Lyne, Edmund 17, 76
Lyons, Greene R. 327, 352
Lyons, Fannie A. 123

MacAdam, John Loudon 99
Macklin, A. W. 224, 269
Macklin, A. W. and Co. 126
Macklin, George B. 119, 190
Macklin, George W. 215
Macklin, Jim 174, 175
Madison, George 59, 61, 74
Madison, James 23, 36
Magoffin, Beriah 157
Mahoney, Thomas 161
Main Street Garage 325
Major Hall 210, 211, 230, 243, 246, 250
Major, James 79
Major, John 17, 26
Major, Patrick U. 125, 175, 189
Major, Samuel I. M., Sr. 76, 87
Major, Samuel I. M., Jr. 74, 143, 144, 145, 155, 189, 190, 203, 208, 211, 217, 219, 243, 246, 247
Major, Samuel I. M., III 341
Major's Station 26
Mallory, Uriel 17
Malmer, Walter 382
Manford, J. E. 270
Mangan, Lewis 227, 241
Mansion House 61, 92, 123, 216, 242, 243
Manson, Mahlon D. 162
Marksbury, J. W. 285
Marrs, Henry 206
Marshall, Humphrey, Sr. 15, 17, 21, 24, 36, 58, 60, 77, 113
Marshall, Humphrey, Jr. 161
Marshall, J. J. 92
Marshall, John (Chief Justice) 67, 68
Marshall, John J. 58, 85, 99
Marshall, Llewellyn B. 215, 286
Marshall, Russell 369
Marshall, Thomas 17, 21, 56
Marshall, Thomas F. 152
Marshall, William, Jr. 17
Mason, George 15
Mason, H. P. 229, 304
Mason-Hoge Building 231

Mason, Horatio 326
Masonic Lodge 231, 248, 287, 327
Masters, Howard 250
Mastin, Lewis 29
Mathews, Bobby, Jr. 382
Mathews, Shaler 103
May, William H. 353, 383
Mayes, Robert T. 354, 360
Mayflower Hotel and Cabins 315
Mayhall, Thomas J. 177
Mayo, William H. 245, 247
McAfee, George 10
McAfee, James, Jr. 10
McAfee, Robert 10, 11, 15
McAfee, Robert B. 58
McBrayer, William 15
McChesney, Henry V. 275
McChesney, S. 143
McClear, James 57
McClelland's Station 26
McClure Building 267, 269, 286
McClure, R. K. and Brother 209
McClure Realty Company 267
McClure, Richard K. 188, 234, 276
McClure, William M. 188
McCook, Alexander McDowell 166
McCord, W. S. 187
McCoun, James, Jr. 10
McCracken, Cyrus 17
McCreary, James B. 270, 281, 282
McCurdy, Allen F. 87, 105
McDaniel, Charles 175
McDonald, George 352
McDonald, J. N. 247
McDonald, Jack 353, 354
McDonald, Patrick 217, 219, 221, 229, 235, 247, 253, 254
McDowell, H. C. 224
McDowell, Samuel 35
McEachin, Charles B. 354, 360
McGee, John D. 93
McGrain, Thomas 93
McHenry, Susan J. 269
McKee, George R. 193
McKee, James H. 145
McKee, Robert 55
McKee, William R. 129, 130, 131, 146
McKendrick, J. S. 229
McManama, O. D. 178
McNeil, Archibald 54
McRery, Russell W. 193
Meagher, John 214, 219, 220
Meagher, Paul 326
Meek, Benjamin F. 93, 190, 211
Meek, Jonathon B. 93

Melcher, John C. 93
Meloan, John M. 247, 285
Metcalf, Thomas 42
Metropolitan Hall 210
Milam, Benjamin C. 93, 145, 146, 234, 241
Milam, John 74
Miles, Benjamin 95
Miles, Charles 91, 114
Miles, J. E. 194
Miles, James I. 83
Miles, James N. 241
Miller, Anderson 83
Miller, Andrew 54
Mills, Elizabeth 142
Mills, Fay B. 244
Mills, James 52
Mills, John M. 205
Mills, R. E. 311
Miro, Don Esteban Rodriguez 23, 24
Mitchell, Eugene 292
Mitchell, R. H. C. 208
Mitchell, Robert B. 393
Mitchell's Spring 18
Modjeski, Masters and Case, Inc. 335, 336
Moerlein Brewing Company 310
Monroe, Andrew 125
Monroe's Auto Repair Service 325
Monroe, Ben J. 160
Monroe, George B. 167
Monroe, George W. 162
Monroe, James 125
Monroe, James 145
Monroe, James (President) 36
Monroe, Thomas B. 149, 160
Montgomery, James F. 272
Montgomery, Morris C. 369
Montgomery, Richard 23
Montgomery, Zach J. 284
Montrose Park Addition 342
Moore, John 104
Moore, Lewis 57
Moore-Riner Realty Company 342
Moore, William T. 137
Moorman, John 369
Morehead, Charles S. 76, 85, 92, 97, 125, 147
Morris, Leslie W. 332
Morrison College 81
Morrow, Edwin P. 275
Morgan, Louis 240
Morgan, John Hunt 160, 166, 167, 169
Morse, Jedidiah 28
Morton, Jennie Chinn 210, 250
Moving Picture Operators' Union 292

Mullanphy, John 57
Municipal Building 369
Municipal Slum Clearance & Urban Redevelopment Agency 365
Murphy, D. A. 243
Murray Building 391
Murray, James (Lord Dunmore) 9, 10, 11
Murray Street School 384
Murray, William 65

Nash, L. B. 140
National Association for the Advancement of Colored People 377
National Branch Bank of Kentucky 308, 332, 361
National Distillers Products Company 386
Nave, Leonard K. 382
Navigator, The 114
New Capital Hotel Company 268
Newman, James L. 284–286
Newman, William 176
Nicol Garage 271, 305
Nicol, W. D. 312
Niehaus, Charles H. 281
Noel, John C. 269, 279
Noel, Lawson 171
Noel, Samuel M. 87
Noel, Silas M. 109
Nolan, Mrs. Martin 253
Nolan, Philip 26
Nooe, Roger T. 292
North Fork Baptist Church 58, 78
Norton, John N. 139
Nourse, James 12

Oates, Ward J. 353, 354, 364
Oberwarth & Livingston Architects 371
Oberwarth, L. L. & Son 330
Oberwarth, Leo L. 289, 307
O'Conner, Mose 247
Odd Fellows Building 247
Odd Fellows Hall 192, 250
O'Dell and Clark's Garage 270
O'Dell, Isaac 284
O'Donnell, Harry B. 227
O'Dwyer, John F. 292
O.F.C. Distillery 197, 251, 331
Offutt, Eleanor 313, 338
Offutt, Henry 313
Ogden, George W. 71, 72
O'Hara, Kean 61, 100, 111
O'Hara, Theodore 143
Ohio Company 6, 14, 15, 34
Old Crow Distillery 198, 331
Old Grand Dad Distillery 331

Old Guard 152
Old Judge Distillery 275
Old Statehouse Historic District 392
Old Taylor Distillery 197, 331
Oliver, J. W. 187
Order of the Star Spangled Banner 147
O'Rear, Edward C. 307, 347
O'Rear, James B. 322
O'Rear, Patricia 338
Overton, A. W. 269
Owen, William 92
Owens, Abraham 39
Owings, John C. 17
Owsley, William 73, 92, 95, 143

Packard, Frank 307
Page, James R. 161
Page, Thomas M. 161
Page, Thomas S. 81, 104, 125, 150
Palladium 59, 60, 61
Palmer, John M. 171, 174
Palmore, John 369
Parker, Addison S. 97
Parker, George W. 195, 222
Parker, John T. 222
Parker, Wyatt 222
Parrent, Richard H. 161
Parrish, James H. 208
Patriot, The 113
Patterson, Charles 78
Patterson, Elizabeth 78
Patterson, John 307
Pattie, William 316
Paul Sawyier Public Library 375, 390
Paxton, Thomas 17, 109
Payne, William 54, 55
Payne, George L. 230, 234, 269, 276
Peak, John J. 78
Peak's Mill 78, 122, 155, 171, 182, 187, 222, 242, 258, 285, 298, 299, 304, 305, 322, 329, 343, 380
Pearce, John Ed 392
Peel, Emily 375
Pemberton, Bennett 40, 45, 50
Pemberton, John C. 161
Pence, Tom 250
Penney, J. C. Company 305
Peoples State Bank 269, 308, 332
Perkins, J. M. 311, 320, 337, 364
Perkins, J. M. and Company 305
Perkins, John W. 331, 346
Perry, J. W. 178
Perryville, Battle of 166
Pettit, F. D. 92
Phelps, Samuel 91

Philanthropist, The 113
Phillips, William J. 105
Pickett, James C. 353
Pickett, William H. 342, 346
Pillow, Gideon 158
Pine Hill Plaza 385
Pleasants, George W. 59
Polk, Charles 177
Polk, Leonidas 158
Polsgrove, Ambrose 253
Polsgrove, James H. 284, 322, 326, 329, 335
Polsgrove Landing 182, 187, 242, 299, 305, 322
Polymnian Society 210, 211
Pommering, Mrs. Albert 329
Poor Richard's Books 391
Pope, H. C. 143
Pope, John 47
Porter, William 57
Posey, W. Horace 219
Posey, William H. 269, 276
Prentice, George D. 201
Prentiss, James 94
Preston, William 11, 15
Price, Hannah 92
Price, Mary Helen 142
Price, Richard 61
Price, W. T. 125
Proclamation of 1763 7, 9
Procter, John R. 193
Pruett, John W. 211–212, 219, 229
Pryor, Moses Tandy 167
Purdy, Glenn 353, 354, 382
Purviance, William 140

Randolph, Edmund 36
Ray, Mrs. Eugene 292
Reading, W. T. 212
Reagan, David 314
Rebecca-Ruth Candy, Inc. 310
Red Cross 289, 292, 322, 339, 341, 393, 395
Reid, T. Augustus 246
Rennick, Mary 112
Retail Grocers Association 291
Retail Merchants Association 315
Reynolds, F. 91
Reynolds, Hunt 216
Reynolds, J. 91
Rice, David 62
Rice, Russell W., Jr. 382
Richardson, Nathaniel 54
Richardson, Turner 45
Richmond, Ezra 97
Ries, John 233
Ringold Building 192
Ringold, Henry 234, 269
River Raisin, Battle of 68, 69
Riverview Homes 368

Robb, Frederick 79
Robb, J. C. 160
Roberts, Benjamin 21
Roberts, H. H. 269, 272, 307
Roberts, James 43
Roberts, John J. 161, 165
Roberts, Joseph W. 162
Robertson, William D. 145
Robinson, Edgar W. 143
Robinson, George W. 120
Robinson, James S. 163
Robinson, Mrs. Lloyd 375
Robinson, Stuart 124, 137, 150, 151
Rodman, G. R. 195
Rodman, G. R. and Company 230
Rodman, John 178, 189
Rodman, John W. 189, 279
Rodman, Julia W. 210
Rodman, Thomas 208
Rodman, William B. 189
Rogers, H. K. 333
Rogers, Isaiah 124
Rogers, R. and Sons 267
Rogers, Thomas P. 327, 347
Rolling Acres Shopping Center 385
Roosevelt, Franklin 324
Rosecrans, William S. 159
Rosenstein Brothers 360
Rosenstein's Sons Company 325
Rosenwald School 377, 378, 384
Rossale, Peter 281
Rosson, William S. 284, 313
Rowan, John 58
Royal Flour Mill 233
Royal Temples of Temperance 248
Royster, Paul 388
Runyon, Mary Train 119, 140, 205
Rupert, Joseph 284
Russell, G. P. 319
Russell, Gervas E. 59, 91, 113
Russell, J. B. 59

Saffell, James 190, 198
Saffell, James M. 198
Saffell's Distillery 232, 251
Saffell's Valley Mill 243
Salender, George 233, 241
Salvation Army 248, 327, 328, 395
Sampson, Flem 312, 322
Samuel, Churchill 97
Samuel, E. L. 234
Samuel, Giles 40
Samuel, Larkin 75
Sanders, Nathaniel 40
Sanford, James 187
Sawyier, N. J. 193

411

Sawyier, Pamelia 193
Sawyier, Paul 205
Sayre, Burwell B. 75, 140
Sayre, S. C. 249
Scarce, Stephen 253
Schenley Distillers Corporation 348, 386
Schields, Robert G. 177
Schraff, Joseph 233
Schupp, Orville C. 353
Scott, Charles 39
Scott, Howell 270
Scott, James Andrew 217, 219
Scott, Joel 27, 81, 83, 96
Scott, John L. 249
Scott, John R. 189
Scott, John S. 163, 166
Scott, Mary Mason 329
Scott, Maurice H. 389
Scott, Murray 325
Scott, Preston B. 160
Scott, R. S. 333
Sears, Roebuck and Company 345
Sebastian, Benjamin 36
Second Street School 205–206, 245, 285, 330, 347, 362, 384
Selbert, John 188
Selbert, M. A. Jewelry 188, 267
Selbert, Mary A. 188
Selbert, Philip 188
Select Seminary 111
Service Motor Company 270
Settle, Evan E. 178
Serverance, Joseph 284
Shaler, Nathaniel S. 193
Shannon, James 80, 85
Shannon, Samuel 58
Sharp, Leander J. 97
Sharp, Solomon P. 74, 76, 96, 97, 367
Shaw, George C. 226, 241, 284
Sheets, Henry J. 161
Shelby, Isaac 39, 45, 53, 65
Shelton, Lee 284
Sheridan, Philip 166
Sherman, William T. 170
Shoppers Village 385
Short, Peyton 24, 55
Shram, Mrs. Albert 375
Shryock, Gideon 74, 80, 81, 85
Sill, Joshua 164, 166
Silver Lake Airport 372
Simons' Furniture Store 345
Simpson, William G. 269, 284
Skelton, D. E. 208
Skiles, D. H. 269
Smith, David D. 260, 313, 346, 363, 364
Smith, Edmund Kirby 161, 162, 164, 166
Smith, Green Clay 211

Smith, Herbert G. 310
Smith, Howard D., Jr. 177
Smith, John 45
Smith, Lucy L. 364
Smith, N. B. 310
Smith, Benjamin B. 110, 139
Smith, Eli 87, 109
Smith, James 41
Sneed, Achilles 51, 60, 74, 87
Sneed, J. L. 195
Sneed, Russell 247
Sneed, William C. 143
Sneed, William H. 162, 241, 249, 277–279
Sons of Confederate Veterans 288
South Benson Baptist Church 58
South, Eudora Lindsay 205, 250
South Frankfort 74–76, 87, 108, 116, 120, 181, 342
South Frankfort Presbyterian Church 248, 327
South, Martin V. 177
South, James K. Polk 205
South, Samuel 87
Southern Bell Telephone and Telegraph Company 216
Southern Gas Company 216, 217
Southern Hotel 307
Southern Mouldings 386
Sower Athletic Field 316, 330
Sower, Frank 364
Sower, John 387
Sower, John B. 326
Sower, John R. 271, 276, 284
Sower, Peter C. 233, 234, 250
Spanish Conspiracy 24
Speer, G. F. 269
Spencer, David J. 193
Spencer, John T. 222
Spirit of '76 113
Spring Hill Distillery 198, 273
Sprole, Charles 42
St. Clair, Arthur 23
St. Clair Mall 389, 391
St. Clair Street Bridge 128, 234, 235, 251, 253, 289, 312, 325, 335, 339
St. John African Methodist Episcopal Church 115
St. Joseph's Catholic Society 248
Stagg, George T. Company 273, 331, 345, 348
Stancliffe, Charles 202
Standard Bakery 326
Stanley, Augustus O. 268, 275, 292
Stanton, Edwin 171

Stanton, Henry T. 208–210, 217, 250
Stapp, W. W. 143
Starks, John P. 219, 229
Starling, William 76, 83
Starr Clothing Company 360
State Arsenal 81, 83
State Capital and Zoning Commission 363
State Capitol (first) 41
State Capitol (new) 279, 281, 351
State Capitol (old) 80, 83
State Capitol (second) 71, 72, 79, 80
State Capitol Building Commission 279
State Journal 285, 286, 315, 346
State National Bank 229, 308, 332
State Office Building 336, 337, 370
State Penitentiary 53, 54, 83, 85, 281, 336, 339, 348
Stealey, M. R. 134
Stedman, Ebenezer H. 78, 93
Stedman, John 171
Stedman, Samuel 93
Stedmantown 78, 171, 182
Steele, William 65
Stephens, Egbert 284
Stephens, Walker 177
Stevenson, John W. 190
Stevenson, Ritchie 329
Stevenson, Thomas B. 142, 143, 145
Stewart, Brady 369
Stewart, Daniel 56
Stewart Home Training School 243, 244
Stewart, John (explorer) 9
Stewart, John D. 244
Stewart, John P. 244, 307
Stewart, John Q. A. 243, 244
Stivers, Louis 355
Stone, Edward Durrell 366
Stout, Amos 105
Stout, John B. 205
Strassner, Charles F. 273, 288, 307
Street, Joseph M. 59
Strickland, William 80, 81
Strother, James 11
Stuart, Mrs. J. H. 244
Stumm, C. C. 208
Sullivan, M. G. 325
Sullivan, Paul 354, 366
Sullivan, W. P. (Pat) 269, 363
Sunday Leader 247
Suppinger, Edwin K. 346
Suppinger, Lambert 233, 333
Sutterlin, Fred J. 233, 248, 337, 346, 347

Sutterlin, John D. 382
Sutterlin Terrace 368
Swallowfield 299, 315, 322, 329, 380
Swigert, Jacob and Company 230
Swigert, Jacob, Jr. 162
Swigert, Jacob, Sr. 73, 74, 97, 100, 123, 126, 134, 139, 142, 145, 150
Swigert, Philip 75, 87, 100, 104, 123, 124, 125, 126, 129, 130, 133, 134, 136, 137, 144, 145, 189, 190, 200, 211
Switzer 78, 122, 182, 187, 242, 298, 304, 305, 322, 380
Switzer, John 78
Symmes, William W. 206

Talbott, Isham 58
Tanner, William 113, 143, 372
Tate, James William 252
Taylor, Charles E. 216
Taylor Distilleries 267
Taylor, E. H. Jr., and Sons 273
Taylor, Edmund 13
Taylor, Edmund H., Jr. 73, 176, 190, 195, 197, 200, 203, 211, 216, 229, 230, 240, 250, 299, 307
Taylor, Edmund H., Sr. 81, 92, 97, 104, 123, 134, 137, 144, 145
Taylor, Edmund W. 315
Taylor, Elizabeth 391
Taylor, Frank Company (Taylor Tot Company) 358, 393
Taylor, Hancock 10, 11
Taylor, K. Distillers Company, Inc. 331
Taylor, Richard 53, 55, 69, 72, 85, 92, 99
Taylor, Richard 391
Taylor, Samuel 54
Taylor, Thomas Hart 161
Taylor, William S. 254, 255
Taylor, Zachary (President) 137, 145, 146, 159
Taylor, Zachary 11, 15, 108
Tecumseh 69
Temple, John B. 125, 143, 150, 203
Theobald, Thomas S. 85, 97, 142
Thomas, George H. 159
Thomas, Landon A. 119, 125
Thomas, W. D. 246
Thompson, Milton 391
Thompson, Phil 178
Thompson, R. P. 229
Thompson, Robert A. 160
Thompson, W. G. 176
Thorn Hill 51, 214, 221, 272, 332, 342, 353, 355, 363
Throckmorton, Richard 51, 104
Thurston, Buckner 45
Tin Ceiling, The 391
Tinder, Marshall 385
Tobacco Control Act of 1934 331
Tobin, Richard 240
Todd, Harry Innes 130, 190, 211
Todd, James M. 126
Todd, James W. 243
Todd, John R. 228
Todd, Monarcha Fenwick 76
Todd, Robert 30, 31, 39
Todd, Samuel 76
Todd, Thomas 35, 42, 43, 50, 58, 60, 61, 65, 75
Todd, William M. 120, 122
Toler, Henry 109
Tollgate Wars 253, 254
Tomlin, Nicholas 18
Toombs, W. K. 229
Tornado of 1974 392
Trabue, Stephen F. J. 189, 233
Transylvania Company 34
Trigg, William 47, 51, 61, 63
Trigometer, Inc. 358, 393
Triplett, John 175
Triplett, John H. 284
Trumbo, Henry 123
Trumbo, L. A. 248
Tubman, Emily 208
Tunstall, Thomas 47, 57
Turnbull, William 102
Turner, John 54
Turner, T. M. 205
Tyler, John 143, 156
Tymann's Public Seminary 112

U.S. Motor Service Station 305
Underwood, Edward E. 247, 315
Union Baptist Church 58
Union Underwear Company 326, 327, 332, 345, 358, 386, 393
United Brothers of Friendship 248
United Confederate Veterans 288
United Daughters of the Confederacy 288
Upper Benson Presbyterian Church 58, 109
Urban Renewal and Community Development Agency 389
Urdang Brothers 345

Van Curon, S. C. 360
Van Duerson, S. A. 91
Van Winkle, W. H. 246
Vance, Kenneth 375
Vaughn, Robert L. 347
Vaughn, Walker 79
Vest, John J. 104
Violette, James A. 187
Vodges, F. W. 202
Volz, Harry 322
Voorhies, Peter G. 68
Vreeland, Anne C. 313
Vreeland, Graham 285, 286, 313
Vreeland, Hubert 286

Wachtel, W. P. B. 333
Walker, Leroy P. 157
Walker, Thomas 6, 7
Wallace, A. A. and Sons 326
Wallace, Alonzo A. 311
Wallace, Caleb 21, 53
Wallace, L. G. 247
Wallace, Lew G. 285
Wallace, Samuel 99
Waller, William 42, 73
Walton, Mun 298
Walton, William P. 285
War Mothers Memorial Bridge 336, 337
Ward, David 102
Ward, John 115, 123
Ward, Louise H. 382
Ware, H. B. 249
Ware, William 45
Waring, John U. 96
Washington, George 19, 23, 56
Washington Globe 77
Washington, Henry 176, 177
Waterfield, Harry Lee 353
Watson, Charles E. 353
Watson, E. H. 125
Watson, George H. 214
Watson, John 190
Watt, Ben 285
Watts, John C. 367, 374
Weaver, Charles 354
Weaver, Geraldine 354
Weber, C. C. 282
Weber, E. A. 282
Weekly News 286
Weisiger, Daniel 43, 47, 54, 59, 61, 63, 69, 80, 87, 100
Weisiger's Tavern 61, 92, 96
Weitzel, Charles J. 227
Weitzel, Edward B. 284
Weitzel Family 286, 306
Weitzel, Lewis 190
Weitzel, Louis 119, 233
Welby, Adlard 71
Wells, Adolph 311
West, John 93
West, L. T. 352
Western Argus, 241, 247
Western Hills High School 384
Western World 59, 60, 67
Wetherby, Lawrence 371, 372

Wheatland 79
White, Ambrose 30
White, Gilbert 281
White, James 31
Whiteside, E. 208
Whitesides, Nevil P. 206
Whitestone, Henry 124
Wiechers, Charles 391
Wigginton, S. D. 222
Wigginton, Town of 222
Wilkinson, James 19, 20, 21, 23, 24, 25, 26, 28, 33, 35, 36, 37, 39, 50, 55, 67, 68
Wilkinson, Ann Biddle 20, 25
Wilkinson Street School 384
Wilkinson, Wallace 388
Wilkinson's Ferry 65
Williams, B. G. 288
Williams, Evan 56
Williams, John 15
Williams, Mace 241
Williams, Henderson 115
Williams, Squire N. 369
Williams, U. V. 234
Williams, W. L. 233
Williams, Willson E. 18
Williamson, Jerry 253
Willis, Ida 390
Willis, Simeon 371
Willson, Augustus 266
Willson, John 175
Willson, O. S. 125
Wilson, Ethel 313
Wilson, Isaac 125
Wilson, Robert Burns 205, 210
Wilson, Samuel 28
Wilson, Silas 312
Winchester, James 68
Wingate, Henry 85, 87, 134, 142
Wingate, Isaac 224
Winnie Scott Hospital 287
Winter, James 176
Witherspoon, James F. 217
Women's Christian Temperance Union 275
Women's Defense Corps 347
Women's Voluntary Auxiliary Corps 347
Wood, John 59
Wood, John D. 247
Woodlake 182, 316, 329
Woods, John 105
Woolworth, F. W. Company 304
Wootton, Bailey P. 363
Wright, Frank Lloyd 259, 260
Wright, William 177
Wyatt, Ralph C. 348

Young Men's Christian Association 248, 289, 291, 327, 367
Young, John C. 151
Young, Lambert 174, 175
Young, William 366
Young, William D. 112
Yount, Robert C. 353, 368
Yount, William D. 353

Zeigler, Jesse K. 259, 391
Zollicoffer, Felix 159